SECURITY STUDIES

Security Studies is the most comprehensive textbook available on security studies.

It gives students a detailed overview of the major theoretical approaches, key themes and most significant issues within security studies.

- Part 1 explores the main theoretical approaches currently used within the field from realism to international political sociology
- Part 2 explains the central concepts underpinning contemporary debates from the security dilemma to terrorism
- Part 3 presents an overview of the institutional security architecture currently influencing world politics using international, regional and global levels of analysis
- Part 4 examines some of the key contemporary challenges to global security from the arms trade to energy security
- Part 5 discusses the future of security

Security Studies provides a valuable new teaching tool for undergraduates and MA students by collecting these related strands of the field together into a single coherent textbook.

Paul D. Williams is Associate Professor of International Security at the University of Warwick, UK, and currently Visiting Associate Professor in the Elliott School of International Affairs at the George Washington University, USA.

Contributors: Deborah D. Avant, Sita Bali, Alex J. Bellamy, Didier Bigo, Pinar Bilgin, Ken Booth, Stuart Croft, Simon Dalby, John S. Duffield, Colin Elman, Louise Fawcett, Lawrence Freedman, Fen Osler Hampson, William D. Hartung, Adam Jones, Danielle Zach Kalbacher, Stuart J. Kaufman, Michael T. Klare, Peter Lawler, Matt McDonald, Colin McInnes, Cynthia Michota, Sara Ann Miller, Cornelia Navari, John T. Picarelli, Paul R. Pillar, Michael Pugh, Srinath Raghavan, Paul Rogers, Waheguru Pal Singh Sidhu, Joanna Spear, Caroline Thomas, Thomas G. Weiss, Nicholas J. Wheeler, Sandra Whitworth, Paul D. Williams and Frank C. Zagare.

SECURITY STUDIES:
AN INTRODUCTION

Edited by Paul D. Williams

Routledge
Taylor & Francis Group

LONDON AND NEW YORK

First published 2008
by Routledge
2 Park Square, Milton Park, Abingdon, Oxon, OX14 4RN

Simultaneously published in the USA and Canada
by Routledge
270 Madison Avenue, New York, NY 10016

Routledge is an imprint of the Taylor & Francis Group, an informa business

© 2008 Editorial selection and matter, Paul D. Williams; individual
chapters the contributors

Typeset in Garamond by
Keystroke, 28 High Street, Tettenhall, Wolverhampton
Printed and bound in Great Britain by
MPG Books Ltd, Bodmin

British Library Cataloguing in Publication Data
A catalogue record for this book is available from the British Library

Library of Congress Cataloging in Publication Data
Security studies: an introduction/edited by Paul D. Williams.
    p. cm.
    Includes bibliographical references and index.
  1. Security, International. 2. International relations. I. Williams, Paul, 1975–
JZ5588.S4297 2008
355'.033—dc22   2007048272

ISBN 10: 0–415–42561–1 (hbk)
ISBN 10: 0–415–42562–X (pbk)
ISBN 10: 0–203–92660–9 (ebk)

ISBN 13: 978–0–415–42561–2 (hbk)
ISBN 13: 978–0–415–42562–9 (pbk)
ISBN 13: 978–0–203–92660–4 (ebk)

Contents

Boxes, figures and tables

Boxes

Figures

Tables

CONTRIBUTORS

Deborah D. Avant is Professor of Political Science and Director of International Studies at the University of California – Irvine, USA.

Sita Bali is Senior Lecturer in International Relations at Staffordshire University, UK.

Alex J. Bellamy is Professor of International Relations at the University of Queensland, Australia.

Didier Bigo is Professor of International Relations (maitre de conférences des universités), at Sciences-Po Paris, France, researcher at CERI/FNSP, and is currently Visiting Professor at the Department of War Studies, King's College London, UK.

Pinar Bilgin is Assistant Professor of International Relations at Bilkent University, Ankara, Turkey.

Ken Booth is E.H. Carr Professor of International Politics at the University of Wales, Aberystwyth, UK.

Stuart Croft is Professor of International Relations at the University of Warwick, UK, and currently Director of the UK Economic and Social Research Council's New Security Challenges Programme.

Simon Dalby is Professor of Geography and Political Economy at Carleton University in Ottawa, Canada.

John S. Duffield is Professor of Political Science at Georgia State University in Atlanta, USA.

Colin Elman is Associate Professor of Political Science at Arizona State University, USA, and Executive Director of the Consortium for Qualitative Research Methods.

Louise Fawcett is Fellow and Lecturer in Politics at St Catherine's College, Oxford University, UK.

Lawrence Freedman is Professor of War Studies and Vice Principal (Research) at King's College London, UK. He was awarded the KCMG in 2003.

Fen Osler Hampson is Director of The Norman Paterson School of International Affairs, Carleton University, Ottawa, Canada.

William D. Hartung is Director of the Arms and Security Initiative at the New America Foundation, Washington DC, USA.

Adam Jones is Associate Professor of Political Science at the University of British Columbia, Canada.

Danielle Zach Kalbacher is a Ph.D. student in the Department of Political Science at The CUNY Graduate Center, USA.

Stuart J. Kaufman is Professor of Political Science and International Relations at the University of Delaware, USA.

Michael T. Klare is the Five College Professor of Peace and World Security Studies (a joint appointment at Amherst College, Hampshire College, Mount Holyoke College, Smith College, and the University of Massachusetts at Amherst), and Director of the Five College Program in Peace and World Security Studies (PAWSS).

Peter Lawler is Senior Lecturer in International Relations at the University of Manchester, UK, and a Faculty Member of the International MA programme in Peace and Development Studies at Universitat Jaume I, Castellón, Spain.

Matt McDonald is Assistant Professor in International Security at the University of Warwick, UK.

Colin McInnes is Professor and Head of the Department of International Politics at the University of Wales, Aberystwyth, UK, and is Director of the Centre for Health and International Relations (CHAIR) in that Department.

Cynthia Michota is a Ph.D. student in political science at Georgia State University, specializing in International Relations, Comparative Politics, and Conflict and Security Studies.

Sara Ann Miller is a graduate student in political science at Georgia State University, concentrating on International Relations and Comparative Politics.

Cornelia Navari is formerly Senior Lecturer and Honorary Senior Research Fellow at the University of Birmingham, UK, and is now Visiting Lecturer in International Affairs at the University of Buckingham.

John T. Picarelli is Research Lecturer, School of International Service, and Program Director, Center for the Study of Transnational Crime and Corruption (TraCCC) at American University, Washington DC, USA.

Paul R. Pillar is Visiting Professor and Core Faculty Member of the Security Studies Program at Georgetown University, USA.

Michael Pugh is Professor of Peace and Conflict Studies at the University of Bradford, UK.

Srinath Raghavan is Lecturer in the Defence Studies Department, King's College London, UK.

Paul Rogers is Professor of Peace Studies at the University of Bradford, UK.

Waheguru Pal Singh Sidhu is Faculty Member at the Geneva Centre for Security Policy (GCSP), Switzerland.

Joanna Spear is Director of the Security Policy Studies Program in the Elliott School of International Affairs at the George Washington University, USA.

Caroline Thomas is Deputy Vice Chancellor and Professor at the University of Southampton, UK.

Thomas G. Weiss is Presidential Professor of Political Science at the Graduate Center of The City University of New York, USA, and Director of the Ralph Bunche Institute for International Studies, where he is also co-director of the United Nations Intellectual History Project and Chair of the Academic Council on the UN System.

Nicholas J. Wheeler is Professor of International Politics at the University of Wales, Aberystwyth, UK.

Sandra Whitworth is Professor of Political Science and Women's Studies at York University in Toronto, Canada.

Paul D. Williams is Associate Professor of International Security at the University of Warwick, UK, and currently Visiting Associate Professor in the Elliott School of International Affairs at the George Washington University, USA.

Frank C. Zagare is UB Distinguished Professor of Political Science at the University at Buffalo, SUNY, USA.

ACKNOWLEDGEMENTS

For their permission to reproduce material within this book, thanks go to the United Nations, specifically the Department of Public Information and the Cartographic Section, and the editors of the *Journal of Peace Research*.

Abbreviations

ABM	Anti-Ballistic Missile Treaty
ACC	Arab Cooperation Council
AECA	Arms Export Control Act (US)
AMIS	African Union Mission in Sudan
AMU	Arab Maghreb Union
ANWR	Arctic National Wildlife Refuge
ANZUS	The Australia, New Zealand, US Security Treaty
APEC	Asia–Pacific Economic Cooperation
ARF	ASEAN Regional Forum
ASEAN	Association of Southeast Asian Nations
AU	African Union
AWACS	Airborne Warning and Control System
BATF	Bureau of Alcohol, Tobacco and Firearms (US)
BMD	Ballistic Missile Defence (US)
BTUs	British thermal units
BWC	Biological and Toxin Weapons Convention
CACO	Central Asian Cooperation Organization
CARICOM	Caribbean Community
CAT	Conventional Arms Transfer
CCS	Carbon capture and sequestration
CEMAC	Economic and Monetary Community of Central Africa
CENTO	Central Treaty Organization
CFSP	Common Foreign and Security Policy (EU)
CIA	Central Intelligence Agency (US)
CICS	Centre for International Cooperation and Security (Bradford, UK)
CIS	Commonwealth of Independent States
CND	Campaign for Nuclear Disarmament
COW	Correlates of War Project
CPA	Coalition Provisional Authority (Iraq)
CSCE	Conference on Security and Cooperation in Europe
CSIS	Center for Strategic and International Studies (US)
CSTO	Collective Security Treaty Organization
CTBT	Comprehensive Test Ban Treaty
CTBTO	Prep Com for the Nuclear-Test-Ban-Treaty Organization
CTC	UN Counter-Terrorism Committee
CWC	Chemical Weapons Convention
DDR	Disarmament, Demobilization and Reintegration
DOD	US Department of Defense
DoE	Department of Energy (US)
DPA	UN Department of Political Affairs
DPKO	UN Department of Peacekeeping Operations

DPRK	Democratic People's Republic of Korea
DRC	Democratic Republic of the Congo
EC	European Community
ECO	Economic Cooperation Organization
ECOSOC	UN Economic and Social Council
ECOWAS	Economic Community of West African States
END	European Nuclear Disarmament
EO	Executive Outcomes (PSC)
ESDP	European Security and Defence Policy (EU)
EU	European Union
EUFOR RD	EU Force in the DRC
EUFOR	EU Force (Bosnia)
FATF	Financial Action Task Force
FMCT	Fissile Material Cutoff Treaty
G-77	Group of 77
G-8	Group of 8
GCC	Gulf Cooperation Council
GDP	Gross domestic product
GOARN	Global Outbreak Alert and Response Network
GWOT	Global War on Terror
H5N1	Avian influenza virus, subtype H5N1
IAEA	International Atomic Energy Agency
ICC	International Criminal Court
ICISS	International Commission on Intervention and State Sovereignty
ICJ	International Court of Justice
ICO	Islamic Conference Organization
ICTY	International Criminal Tribunal for the Former Yugoslavia
IDPs	Internally displaced persons
IED	Improvised explosive device
IFOR	Implementation Force (Bosnia)
IGAD	Intergovernmental Authority on Development
IGADD	Inter-Governmental Authority on Drought and Development
IMF	International Monetary Fund
INF	Intermediate Range Nuclear Forces Treaty
INGOs	International non-governmental organizations
Interpol	International Criminal Police Organization
IOM	International Organization for Migration
IPS	International Political Sociology, academic subfield of
IR	International Relations, academic discipline of
IRA/PIRA	Provisional Irish Republican Army
JNA	Yugoslav National Army
KLA	Kosovo Liberation Army
LAS	League of Arab States

LDCs	Least Developed Countries
LTTE	Liberation Tigers of Tamil Eelam (Sri Lanka)
MDGs	Millennium Development Goals
MERCOSUR	The Southern Common Market
MLATs	Mutual legal assistance treaties
MONUC	UN Mission in the Democratic Republic of the Congo
MRTA	Tupac Amaru Revolutionary Movement (Peru)
MTCR	Missile Technology Control Regime
NAFTA	North American Free Trade Agreement
NAM	The Non-aligned Movement
NATO	North Atlantic Treaty Organization
NEPDG	National Energy Policy Development Group (US)
NGOs	Non-governmental organizations
NNSA	National Nuclear Security Administration (US)
NPT	Treaty on the Non-proliferation of Nuclear Weapons
NSG	Nuclear Suppliers Group
NWFZs	Nuclear Weapon Free Zones
OAS	Organization of American States
OAU	Organization of African Unity
OECD	Organization for Economic Cooperation and Development
OECS	Organization of Eastern Caribbean States
OPCW	Organization for the Prohibition of Chemical Weapons
OPEC	Organization of Petroleum Exporting Countries
OSCE	Organization of Security and Cooperation in Europe
P-5	Permanent Five members of the UN Security Council
PIF	Pacific Islands Forum
PMC	Private military company
PMF	Privatized military firm
PRI	Institutional Revolutionary Party (Mexico)
PRIO	International Peace Research Institute of Oslo (Norway)
PSCs	Private security companies
PSI	Proliferation Security Initiative
PTBT	Partial Test Ban Treaty
R2P	Responsibility to protect
RAWA	Revolutionary Association of the Women of Afghanistan
RMA	Revolution in Military Affairs
RRW	Reliable replacement warhead
RUF	Revolutionary United Front (Sierra Leone)
SAARC	South Asian Association for Regional Cooperation
SACEUR	Supreme Allied Commander Europe (NATO)
SADC	Southern African Development Community
SADCC	Southern African Development Coordination Conference
SALT	Strategic Arms Limitation Talks
SALW	Small arms and light weapons

SANG	Saudi National Guard
SARS	Severe Acute Respiratory Syndrome
SAS	Special Air Services (UK)
SCO	Shanghai Cooperation Organization
SEANWFZ	Southeast Asia Nuclear Weapons Free Zone
SEATO	Southeast Asia Treaty Organization
SFOR	Stabilization Force (Bosnia)
SIPRI	Stockholm International Peace Research Institute (Sweden)
SORT	Strategic Offensive Reductions Treaty
SPF	South Pacific Forum
START	Strategic Arms Reduction Treaty
TB	Tuberculosis
UfP	'Uniting for Peace' resolution (UN General Assembly)
UN	United Nations
UNAIDS	The Joint UN Programme on HIV/AIDS
UNAMSIL	UN Assistance Mission for Sierra Leone
UNDP	UN Development Programme
UNGA	UN General Assembly
UNHCR	UN High Commission for Refugees
UNICEF	UN Children's Fund
UNIFIL	UN Interim Force in Lebanon
UNITA	The National Union for the Total Independence of Angola
UNMIK	UN Mission in Kosovo
UNMIS	UN Mission in Sudan
UNMOVIC	UN Monitoring, Verification and Inspections Commission (Iraq)
UNODC	UN Office for Drugs and Crime
UNOMIL	UN Observer Mission in Liberia
UNPROFOR	UN Protection Force (former Yugoslavia)
UNSC	UN Security Council
UNSCOM	UN Special Commission (Iraq)
UNSCR	UN Security Council Resolution
UCDP	Uppsala Conflict Data Program
WEU	Western European Union
WFP	World Food Programme
WHO	World Health Organization
WMD	Weapons of mass destruction
WTO	World Trade Organization

CHAPTER 1

Security Studies

An Introduction[1]

Paul D. Williams

Security matters. It is impossible to make sense of world politics without reference to it. Every day, people somewhere in the world are killed, starved, tortured, raped, impoverished, imprisoned, displaced, or denied education in the name of security. The concept saturates contemporary societies all around the world: it litters the speeches of politicians and pundits; newspaper columns and radio waves are full of it; and images of security and insecurity flash across our television screens and the internet almost constantly. All this makes security a fascinating, often deadly, but always important topic.

But what does this word mean and how should it be studied? For some analysts, security is like beauty: a subjective and elastic term, meaning exactly what the subject in question says it means; neither more nor less. In the more technical language of social science, security is often referred to as an 'essentially contested concept' (see Gallie 1956), one for which, by definition, there can be no consensus as to its meaning. While in one sense this is certainly true – security undoubtedly means different things to different people – at an abstract level, most scholars within International Relations (IR) work with a definition of security that involves the alleviation of threats to cherished values.

Defined in this way, security is unavoidably political; that is, it plays a vital role in deciding who gets what, when, and how in world politics (Lasswell 1936). Security studies can thus never be solely an intellectual pursuit because it is stimulated in large part by the impulse to achieve security for 'real people in real places' (see Booth 2007). This involves interpreting the past (specifically how different groups thought about and practised security), understanding the present, and trying to influence the future. As such, the concept of security has been compared to a trump-card in the struggle over the allocation of resources.

1

Think, for example, of the often huge discrepancies in the size of budgets that governments around the world devote to ministries engaged in 'security' as opposed to, say, 'development' or 'health' or 'education'. An extreme example of prioritizing regime security would be the case of Zaire during President Mobutu Sese Seko's rule (1965–1997). For much of this period the only thing that the Zairean state provided its people with was an ill-disciplined and predatory military. In contrast, Mobutu's government spent almost nothing on public health and education services. Security is therefore 'a powerful political tool in claiming attention for priority items in the competition for government attention. It also helps establish a consciousness of the importance of the issues so labelled in the minds of the population at large' (Buzan 1991: 370). Consequently, it matters a great deal who gets to decide what security means, what issues make it on to security agendas, how those issues should be dealt with, and, crucially, what happens when different visions of security collide. This is the stuff of security studies and the subject matter of this book.

Before moving to the substantive chapters in this volume, this introductory chapter does three things. First, it provides a brief overview of how the field of security studies has developed. Second, it discusses four central questions which help delineate the contours of the field as it exists today. Finally, it explains what follows in the rest of this book.

What is security studies? A very short overview

As you will see throughout this book, there are many different ways to think about security; and hence security studies. Rather than adopt and defend one of these positions, the aim of this textbook is to provide you with an overview of the different perspectives, concepts, institutions and challenges that exercise the contemporary field of security studies. Consequently, not everyone agrees that all of the issues discussed in this book should be classified as part of security studies. The approach adopted here, however, is not to place rigid boundaries around the field. Instead, security studies is understood as an area of inquiry focused around a set of basic but fundamental questions; the answers to which have changed, and will continue to change over time.

Not surprisingly, security has been studied and fought over for as long as there have been human societies. As any study of the word's etymology will show, security has meant very different things to people depending on their time and place in human history (Rothschild 1995). But as the subject of professional academic inquiry security studies is usually thought of as a relatively recent and largely Anglo-American invention that came to prominence after the Second World War (see Booth 1997, McSweeney 1999: Part 1). In this version – and it is just one, albeit popular version – of the field's history, security studies is understood as one of the most important subfields of academic IR, the other areas usually being defined as international history, international theory, international law, international political economy and area studies. Although it was given different labels in different places (National

Security Studies was preferred in the USA while Strategic Studies was a common epithet in the UK), there was general agreement that IR was the subfield's rightful disciplinary home.

According to some analysts, the field enjoyed its 'golden age' during the 1950s and 1960s when civilian strategists enjoyed relatively close connections with Western governments and their foreign and security policies (see Garnett 1970). 'During this golden age,' as Lawrence Freedman (1998: 51) noted, 'Western governments found that they could rely on academic institutions for conceptual innovation, hard research, practical proposals, and, eventually, willing recruits for the bureaucracy. Standards were set for relevance and influence that would prove difficult to sustain.' In particular, security analysts busied themselves devising theories of nuclear deterrence (and nuclear war-fighting), developing systems analysis related to the structure of armed forces and resource allocation, and refining the tools of crisis management.

Particularly as it appeared during the Cold War, the dominant approach within security studies may be crudely summarized as advocating political realism and being preoccupied with the four Ss of states, strategy, science and the status quo. It was focused on *states* inasmuch as they were considered (somewhat tautologically) to be both the most important agents and referents of security in international politics. It was about *strategy* inasmuch as the core intellectual and practical concerns revolved around devising the best means of employing the threat and use of military force. It aspired to be *scientific* inasmuch as to count as authentic, objective knowledge, as opposed to mere opinion, analysts were expected to adopt methods that aped the natural, harder sciences such as physics and chemistry. Only by approaching the study of security in a scientific manner could analysts hope to build a reliable bank of knowledge about international politics on which to base specific policies. Finally, traditional security studies reflected an implicit and conservative concern to preserve the *status quo* inasmuch as the great powers and the majority of academics who worked within them understood security policies as preventing radical and revolutionary change within international society.

Although dissenting voices had always been present they did not make a great deal of intellectual or practical headway during the Cold War. Arguably the most prominent among them came from scholars engaged in peace research and those who focused on the security predicament of peoples and states in the so-called 'third world' (for more detail see Thomas 1987, Barash 1999). However, a key development within the academic mainstream of security studies occurred in 1983 with the publication of Barry Buzan's book *People, States and Fear* (see also Ullman 1983). This book fundamentally undermined at least two of the four Ss of traditional security studies. In particular, Buzan argued persuasively that security was not just about states but related to all human collectivities; nor could it be confined to an 'inherently inadequate' focus on military force. Instead, Buzan developed a framework in which he argued that the security of human collectivities (not just states) was affected by factors in five major sectors, each of which had its own focal point and way of ordering priorities. The five sectors were:

- *Military*: concerned with the interplay between the armed offensive and defensive capabilities of states and states' perceptions of each other's intentions. Buzan's preference was that the study of military security should be seen as one subset of security studies and referred to as strategic studies in order to avoid unnecessary confusion (see Buzan 1987).

- *Political*: focused on the organizational stability of states, systems of government and the ideologies that give them their legitimacy.

- *Economic*: revolved around access to the resources, finance and markets necessary to sustain acceptable levels of welfare and state power.

- *Societal*: centred on the sustainability and evolution of traditional patterns of language, culture, and religious and national identity and custom.

- *Environmental*: concerned with the maintenance of the local and the planetary biosphere as the essential support system on which all other human enterprises depend.

Of course, there were limitations to Buzan's framework, not least the lack of attention paid to the gendered dimensions of security and the philosophical foundations of the field, particularly its dominant epistemology. As a consequence, Buzan's book did far less to disrupt the traditional focus on scientific methods or concerns to preserve the international status quo. Nevertheless, the considerably revised and expanded second edition of *People, States and Fear*, published in 1991, provided a timely way of thinking about security after the Cold War that effectively challenged the field's preoccupation with military force and rightly attempted to place such issues within their political, social, economic and environmental context.

Despite such changes, from today's vantage point, there are several problems with continuing to think of security studies as a subfield of IR – even a vastly broadened one. First of all, it is clear that inter-state relations are just one, albeit an important, aspect of the security dynamics that characterize contemporary world politics. States are not the only important actors, nor are they the only important referent objects for security. Second, there are some good intellectual reasons why security studies can no longer afford to live in IR's disciplinary shadow. Not least is the fact that IR remains an enterprise dominated by Anglo-American men where the orthodoxy remains wedded to the tradition of political realism (see Hoffman 1977, Smith 2000). More specifically, and not surprisingly given its origins, traditional security studies stands accused of being written largely by Westerners and for Western governments (Barkawi and Laffey 2006). What this means is that the questions, issues and ways of thinking traditionally considered most important within the field were neither neutral nor natural but were, as Robert Cox famously put it, always 'for someone and for some purpose' (Cox 1981).

In addition, studying the traditional canons of IR may not be the best preparation for a student whose primary interest is understanding security dynamics in contemporary world politics. Today's security problems require analysis and solutions that IR cannot provide alone. Students should therefore look for insights in a wide variety of disciplines, and not only those within the humanities or social sciences. For example, analysing issues related to weapons of mass destruction (WMD) requires a degree of scientific and technical knowledge, understanding the causes of terrorism will involve a psychological dimension, assessing health risks requires some access to medical expertise, understanding environmental degradation involves engaging with biology and environmental history, while combating transnational crime will necessarily involve a close relationship with criminology. We therefore need to think very carefully about who the real 'security' experts are in world politics and where we might find them.

In sum, while security studies has its professional roots in the discipline of IR, today's world poses challenges that will require students to engage with topics and sources of knowledge traditionally considered well beyond the IR pale. As a consequence, it is unhelpful to think of security studies as just a subfield of IR. Instead, this book begins from the assumption that security studies is better understood as an area of inquiry revolving around a set of core questions.

Defining a field of inquiry: four fundamental questions

If we think about security studies as a field of inquiry, arguably four basic yet fundamental questions stand out as forming its intellectual core:

- What is security?

- Whose security are we talking about?

- What counts as a security issue?

- How can security be achieved?

Let us briefly examine what is entailed by posing each of these questions.

What is security?

Asking what security means raises issues about the philosophy of knowledge, especially those concerning epistemology (how do we know things?), ontology (what phenomena do we think make up the social world?) and method (how we should study the social world). If we accept the notion that security is an essentially contested concept then, by definition, such debates cannot be definitively resolved in the abstract. Instead some positions will become dominant and be enforced through the application of power.

With this in mind, security is most commonly associated with the alleviation of threats to cherished values; especially those which, if left unchecked, threaten the survival of a particular referent object in the near future. To be clear, although security and survival are often related, they are not synonymous.

Whereas survival is an existential condition, security involves the ability to pursue cherished political and social ambitions. Security is therefore best understood as what Ken Booth (2007) has called, 'survival-plus,' 'the "plus" being some freedom from life-determining threats, and therefore some life choices'.

Put in rather stark terms, it is possible to identify two prevalent philosophies of security, each emerging from fundamentally different starting points. The first philosophy sees security as being virtually synonymous with the accumulation of power. From this perspective, security is understood as a commodity (i.e. to be secure, actors must possess certain things such as property, money, weapons, armies and so on). In particular, power is thought to be the route to security: the more power (especially military power) actors can accumulate, the more secure they will be.

The second philosophy challenges the idea that security flows from power. Instead, it sees security as being based on emancipation; that is, a concern with justice and the provision of human rights. From this perspective, security is understood as a relationship between different actors rather than a commodity. These relationships may be understood in either negative terms (i.e. security is about the absence of something threatening) or positive terms (i.e. involving phenomena that are enabling and make things possible). This distinction is commonly reflected in the ideas of 'freedom from' and 'freedom to'. Understood in a relational sense, security involves gaining a degree of confidence about our relationships that comes through sharing certain commitments, which, in turn, provides a degree of reassurance and predictability. This view argues that it is not particular commodities (such as nuclear weapons) that are the crucial factor in understanding the security–insecurity equation but rather the relationship between the actors concerned. Thus while US decision-makers think Iran's possession of nuclear weapons would be a source of considerable insecurity, they do not feel the same way about the nuclear arsenals held by India or Pakistan. Consequently, in the second philosophy, true or stable security does not come from the ability to exercise power over others. Rather, it comes from cooperating to achieve security without depriving others of it. During the Cold War, such an approach was evident in Olaf Palme's call for 'common security', particularly his suggestion that protagonists 'must achieve security not against the adversary but together with him'. 'International security', Palme argued, 'must rest on a commitment to joint survival rather than on the threat of mutual destruction' (Palme 1982: ix). In practical terms, this means promoting emancipatory politics that take seriously issues about justice and human rights.

As the chapters in this book make clear, different perspectives and particular security policies subscribe to these philosophies to varying degrees. In practice, the differences are often stark with advocates of the former philosophy prioritizing military strength while supporters of the latter emphasize the importance of promoting human rights.

Whose security?

Asking whose security we are talking about is the next important and unavoidable step in the analytical process. Without a referent object there can be no threats and no discussion of security because the concept is meaningless without something to secure. As a result, we need to be clear about the referent objects of our analysis. In the long sweep of human history, the central focus of security has been people (Rothschild 1995). As noted above, however, within academic IR, security was fused with 'the state'. Even more specifically, it was fused with a particular conception of 'the national interest' as set out in the US National Security Act of 1947. This helped promote the rather confusing idea that security in international politics was synonymous with studying (and promoting) 'national security'. In fact, it is more accurate to say that what was being studied (and protected) was 'state security', not least because many states were often hostile to particular nationalities contained within their borders.

There are many plausible answers to the question 'Whose security should we be talking about?' Not surprisingly, therefore, debates continue to rage over who or what should constitute the ultimate referent object for security studies. For many decades, the dominant answer was that when thinking about security in international politics, states were the most important referents. Particularly after the end of the Cold War, this position has come under increasing challenge. In contrast, some analysts argued for priority to be given to human beings since without reference to individual humans, security makes no sense (e.g. Booth 1991a, McSweeney 1999). The problem, of course, is which humans to prioritize. This position has underpinned a large (and rapidly expanding) literature devoted to 'human security'. According to one popular definition, 'Human security is not a concern with weapons. It is a concern with human dignity. In the last analysis, it is a child who did not die, a disease that did not spread, an ethnic tension that did not explode, a dissident who was not silenced, a human spirit that was not crushed' (Haq 1995: 116). A third approach has focused on the concept of 'society' as the most important referent object for security studies because humans do not always view group identities and collectivities in purely instrumental terms. Rather, to be fully human is to be part of specific social groups (Shaw 1994). Another perspective approached the question as a level of analysis problem; that is, it offered an analytical framework for thinking about possible referent objects from the lowest level (the individual) through various sources of collective identities (including bureaucracies, states, regions, civilizations), right up to the level of the international system. In this schema, the task of the analyst was to focus on the unavoidable relationships and tensions between the different levels of analysis (Buzan 1991, 1995).

In recent decades, a fifth approach has gained increasing prominence, calling for greater attention to be paid to planet Earth rather than this or that group of human beings who happen to live on it. This perspective argues that at a basic level, security policies must make ecological sense. In particular, they must recognize that humans are part of nature and dependent on ecosystems and the environment (Hughes 2006). After all, as Buzan (1991) put it, the environment is the essential support system on which all other human enterprises depend. Without an inhabitable environment, discussions of all other referents are moot.

What is a security issue?

Once an analyst has decided on the meaning of security and whose security they are focusing upon, it is important to ask what counts as a security issue for that particular referent. This involves analysing the processes through which threat agendas are constructed. In other words, who decides which of a referent object's cherished values are threatened, and by what or whom?

In one sense, every thinking individual on the planet operates with a unique set of security priorities shaped, in part, by factors such as their sex, gender, age, religious beliefs, class, race, nationality as well as where they are from, where they want to go, and what they want to see happen in the future. In spite of our individual concerns and anxieties, most of life's insecurities are shared by other individuals and groups. This means that when studying security it is important to pay attention to how representatives of particular groups and organizations construct threat agendas. It is also important to recognize that not all groups, and hence not all threat agendas, are of equal political significance. Clearly, what the US National Security Council considers a threat will have more significant and immediate political consequences for world politics than, say, the threat agendas constructed by Ghana's National Security Council, or, for instance, the concerns of HIV/AIDS sufferers living in one of Africa's many slums. The huge inequalities of power and influence that exist across individuals and groups in contemporary world politics raise significant methodological issues for students of security. Should we focus on the agendas of the powerful or the powerless or both? And where should an analyst's priorities lie if these agendas conflict with one another, as they almost always do?

One recent illustration of the politics of constructing threat agendas was the UN Secretary-General's High-level Panel on Threats, Challenges and Change (2004), comprising sixteen eminent international civil servants and former diplomats. After much debate, the Panel's report, *A More Secure World*, identified six clusters of threats exercising the world's governments: economic and social threats, including poverty, infectious disease and environmental degradation; inter-state conflict; internal conflict, including civil war, genocide and other large-scale atrocities; nuclear, radiological, chemical and biological weapons; terrorism; and transnational organized crime (UN High-level Panel 2004: 2). It quickly became apparent, however, that there was no consensus as to which of these clusters should receive priority: some, mainly developed Western states, considered threats from terrorism and WMD to be most pressing, while many states in the developing world thought that most resources should be devoted to tackling armed conflict and economic and social threats.

Arguments about what should count as a security issue also animate the academic field of security studies. One perspective argues that security analysts should focus their efforts on matters related to armed conflict and the threat and use of military force (e.g. Walt 1991b, Brown 2007). From this point of view, not only is armed conflict in the nuclear age one of the most pressing challenges facing humanity but the potentially endless broadening of the field's focus will dilute the concept of security's coherence, thereby fundamentally limiting its explanatory power and analytical utility.

On the other hand, there are those who argue that if security is supposed to be about alleviating the most serious and immediate threats that prevent people from pursuing their cherished values, then for many of the planet's inhabitants, lack of effective systems of healthcare are at least as important as the threat of armed conflict (e.g. Thomas 1987, 2000). After all, the biggest three killers in the developing world are maternal death around childbirth, and paediatric respiratory and intestinal infections leading to death from pulmonary failure or uncontrolled diarrhoea. To combat these killers, the world's governments have been urged to focus on building local capacities to achieve two basic but fundamental goals: increased maternal survival and increased overall life expectancy (Garrett 2007). In a world in which a girl born in Japan in 2004 has a life expectancy of 86 years compared to 34 years for a girl born during the same year but in Zimbabwe, such issues are increasingly viewed as a legitimate part of the global security equation. Security analysts have traditionally focused on the challenges posed by war and the careers and needs of soldiers, who now number over 53 million globally (IISS 2005: 358). Perhaps in the future they should pay more attention to the challenges posed by sickness and the careers and needs of healthcare workers, which according to one estimate, the world needs at least four million more of (Garrett 2007: 15).

How can security be achieved?

In the final analysis, studying security is important because it may help people – as individuals and groups – to achieve it. Asking how security might be achieved implies not only that we know what security means and what it looks like in different parts of the world, but also that there are particular actors which, through their conscious efforts, can shape the future in desired ways. In this sense, how we think about security and what we think a secure environment would entail will unavoidably shape the security policies we advocate. Most analysts reject the idea of total or absolute security as a chimera: all human life involves insecurities and risks of one sort or another. The practical issue is thus: What level of threat are actors willing to tolerate before taking remedial action? As the US government's response to the 9/11 attacks demonstrates, tolerance levels can vary significantly in light of events and as circumstances change.

In contemporary world politics, the agents of security can come in many shapes and sizes. IR students are usually most familiar with the actions of states and the debates about how they formulate and implement their security policies. Similarly, the actions of international organizations have long been a staple of security studies courses. Less attention has been devoted to analysing a wide range of non-state actors and the roles they can play as agents of both security and insecurity (but see Ekins 1992, Keck and Sikkink 1998, Evangelista 1999). Important examples might include social movements, humanitarian and development groups, private security contractors, insurgents, and criminal organizations. In addition, some individuals have the capacity to help provide security for particular referents in certain contexts. Sometimes this is because of the military power they may wield. On other occasions, however, their power may stem from their ability to disseminate a persuasive message; think, for example, of how Archbishop Desmond Tutu's ideas about reconciliation helped South Africans deal with apartheid's powerful legacies.

In sum, the world is full of actors engaged in the politics of security provision, whether or not they articulate their agendas in such terms. Understanding the environments in which these actors operate and how analysts should respond when their agendas conflict is a central theme of this book.

How to use this book

No textbook, even one as long as this, can be completely comprehensive in its coverage, not least because the field's focus will alter as political priorities and conceptions change. But, hopefully, the chapters that follow add up to more than just a snapshot of the field. They are intended to provide students with a clear yet sophisticated introduction to some of the enduring theories, concepts, institutions and challenges that animate security studies.

As we have seen, all security policies rest on assumptions, concepts and theories whether or not their proponents recognize it or make these assumptions explicit. Consequently, Part 1 of this book examines eight major theoretical approaches that lie beneath contemporary security policies. Although significant cracks have appeared in political realism's hegemonic hold over academic security studies, its various strands retain their powerful influence within most of the world's governments. As a result, some of the theoretical approaches examined in this book are reflected in the current security policies of powerful actors to a greater degree than others. But theories not only reflect political practices, they also help construct them. Like tinted lenses that illuminate certain features at the expense of others, each theoretical approach offers a different perspective on what security studies is, and should be, about. Whether these perspectives are mutually exclusive or whether some or all of them can be combined in some form of eclectic synthesis remains the subject of ongoing debate but is not discussed in great detail in this book. Instead, each chapter sets out what security studies looks like from the perspective concerned. Of course, students should decide their preferences for themselves but in making such judgements one should carefully assess what a particular theory has to say about the core questions identified above.

While this plurality of theoretical perspectives has inevitably encouraged debates about the terms in which security studies is discussed, some concepts have proved a more durable part of the lexicon than others. The chapters in

Part 2 therefore analyse ten concepts that appear at the centre of contemporary debates about security. Some of them, including war, coercion and the security dilemma, formed the traditional core of the field, while others, such as poverty, environmental change and health, are more recent, but important, arrivals.

Parts 1 and 2 of the book thus provide students with an introduction to the theoretical menu for choice in security studies and the central conceptual vocabulary used to debate the issues. Parts 3 and 4 of the book build on this foundation to explore the institutional framework and practical challenges currently exercising security analysts.

Part 3 surveys the current institutional architecture of world politics as it relates to security studies. It does so through three chapters which examine relevant institutions at the international, regional and global levels. For almost all of the theoretical perspectives analysed in Part 1, and as suggested by most of the conceptual discussions in Part 2, institutions can play significant roles in security policies, although the extent and nature of those roles remain hotly contested. Where there is greater consensus is that the significance of institutions (such as alliances, regional organizations or the United Nations) should be judged in large part on how well they help humanity cope with a variety of contemporary security challenges. The chapters in Part 4 therefore reflect upon ten key challenges related to armaments (nuclear and conventional), terrorism, insurgency, mass killing and armed conflict, privatization, population movements, organized crime and energy provision. As the authors make clear, overcoming these challenges will be far from easy and will require changes of attitude as well as behaviour.

As long as it is, reading this book alone is not enough. In particular, I would encourage you to combine this book with some area studies and also to look for insights in disciplines other than IR. Hopefully, you will relate what you read in this book to real places that interest you, and reflect upon which arguments resonate most with developments in specific parts of the world. Security studies without area studies encourages ethnocentric ways of thinking and is likely to exacerbate exactly the kinds of tensions that most people are trying to avoid. If we do not take the time to study areas of the world other than our own and understand why others may see us in very different ways than we see ourselves, negative political consequences and insecurity will undoubtedly follow.

Finally, as Stuart Croft's concluding chapter makes clear, security studies has not been entirely confined to IR; nor should it be. The next generation of security analysts should thus continue to resist one of the negative consequences of the professionalization of academia, namely the erection of rigid boundaries between disciplines. While a degree of specialization has its uses, it can degenerate into academic hair-splitting that loses sight of the bigger historical picture and the important links between different forms of human activity. Future students of security should thus happily dismantle disciplinary boundaries wherever they stifle innovative and critical thinking. In our current era, security is simply too important and too complex to be left to one group of specialists. This may make for longer and more complicated reading lists but it might just help produce more sophisticated analysis of the fundamental issues that lie at the heart of this fascinating and important subject.

Note

1 Thanks go to Alex Bellamy, Stuart Croft and Matt McDonald for their helpful comments on earlier drafts of this chapter.

PART 1
THEORETICAL APPROACHES

- REALISM

- LIBERALISM

- GAME THEORY

- CONSTRUCTIVISM

- PEACE STUDIES

- CRITICAL THEORY

- FEMINIST PERSPECTIVES

- INTERNATIONAL POLITICAL SOCIOLOGY

CONTENTS

Realism

Colin Elman

▌ Abstract

This chapter reviews six different strands of the realist research tradition, and contrasts their approach to security studies: classical realism, neo-realism, rise and fall, neoclassical, offensive structural, and defensive structural realism. Although sharing a pessimistic outlook about the continuity of inter group strife, each of these research programmes is rooted in different assumptions and provides different explanations for the causes and consequences of conflict.

▌ Introduction

Looking back over the development of the security studies field, there is little doubt that the realist tradition has exercised an enormous influence. Even its harshest critics would acknowledge that realist theories, with their focus on power, fear and anarchy, have provided centrally important explanations for conflict and war. Even when disputed, these accounts have often set scholars' baseline expectations. Proponents of other approaches often frame their value by claiming superiority over realist alternatives, especially their traction over deviant or puzzling cases for realism.

This chapter (which is an amended version of Elman (2007), and draws and expands upon Elman (1996a, 1996b, 2001, 2003, 2004, 2005a, and especially 2005b)) discusses several different realist approaches to security studies. Although there are significant differences among variants of realism, they largely share the view that the character of relations among states has not altered. Where there is change, it tends to occur in repetitive patterns. State behaviour is driven by leaders' flawed human nature, or by the pre-emptive unpleasantness mandated by an anarchic international system. Selfish human appetites for power, or the need to accumulate the wherewithal to be secure in a self-help world, explain the seemingly endless succession of wars and conquest. Accordingly, most realists take a pessimistic and prudential view of international relations (Elman 2001), though for an unusually optimistic realist approach see Glaser (1994/95, 1997).

In describing and appraising the realist tradition, it is customary to take a metatheoretic approach which differentiates it from other approaches, and which separates realist theories into distinct sub-groups (see Elman and Elman 2002, 2003). Accordingly, accounts of twentieth-century realism typically distinguish political realist, liberal and other traditions, as well as describe different iterations of realist theory. As noted in Figure 2.1, this chapter distinguishes between six different variants of realism – classical realism, neorealism, and four flavours of contemporary realism: rise and fall, neoclassical, offensive structural, and defensive structural realism. While this ordering is not intended to suggest a strict temporal or intellectual succession, classical realism is usually held to be the first of the twentieth-century realist research programmes.

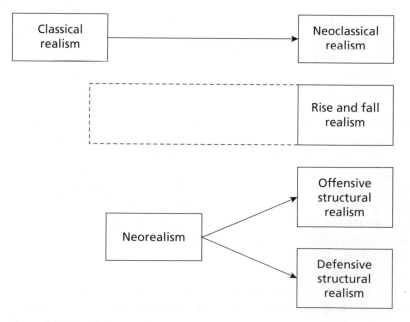

Figure 2.1 Six realist research programmes

Realism's proponents argue that realist thinking extends well before the twentieth century, and often suggest that current theories are the incarnations of an extended intellectual tradition (e.g. Walt 2002: 198, Donnelly 2000). Hence scholars make the – often disputed – claim that realist themes may be found in important antiquarian works from Greece, Rome, India and China (e.g. Smith, M.J. 1986, Haslam 2002: 14; see Garst (1989) for a contrasting view). Since this chapter begins with twentieth-century classical realism we need not dwell on this controversy. It should be noted, however, that while realism's interpretation of particular episodes has been disputed, even its critics (e.g. Wendt 2000) acknowledge that humankind has, in most times and in most places, lived down to realism's very low expectations.

Classical realism

Twentieth-century classical realism is generally dated from 1939, and the publication of Edward Hallett Carr's *The Twenty Years' Crisis*. Classical realists are usually characterized as responding to then-dominant liberal approaches to international politics (e.g. Donnelly 1995: 179) although scholars (e.g. Kahler 1997: 24) disagree on how widespread liberalism was during the interwar years. In addition to Carr, work by Frederick Shuman (1933), Harold Nicolson (1939), Reinhold Niebuhr (1940), Georg Schwarzenberger (1941), Martin Wight (1946), Hans Morgenthau (1948), George F. Kennan (1951) and Herbert Butterfield (1953) formed part of the realist canon. It was, however, Hans Morgenthau's *Politics Among Nations: The Struggle for Power and Peace* which became the undisputed standard bearer for political realism, going through six editions between 1948 and 1985.

According to classical realism, because the desire for more power is rooted in the flawed nature of humanity, states are continuously engaged in a struggle to increase their capabilities. The absence of the international equivalent of a state's government is a permissive condition that gives human appetites free reign. In short, classical realism explains conflictual behaviour by human failings. Wars are explained, for example, by particular aggressive statesmen, or by domestic political systems that give greedy parochial groups the opportunity to pursue self-serving expansionist foreign policies. For classical realists international politics may be characterized as evil: bad things happen because the people making foreign policy are sometimes bad (Spirtas 1996: 387–400).

Although not employing the formal mathematical modelling found in contemporary rational choice theory (see Chapter 4, this volume), classical realism nevertheless posits that state behaviour may be understood as having rational microfoundations. As Morgenthau notes:

> we put ourselves in the position of a statesman who must meet a certain problem of foreign policy under certain circumstances and we ask ourselves

> what the rational alternatives are from which a statesman may choose who must meet this problem under these circumstances (presuming always that he acts in a rational manner), and which of these rational alternatives this particular statesman is likely to choose. It is the testing of this rational hypothesis against the actual facts and their consequences that gives theoretical meaning to the facts of international politics.
>
> (Morgenthau 1985: 5)

State strategies are understood as having been decided rationally, after taking costs and benefits of different possible courses of action into account.

Neorealism: Waltz's *Theory of International Politics*

Kenneth Waltz's *Theory of International Politics* replaced Morgenthau's *Politics Among Nations* as the standard bearer for realists. In *Theory of International Politics*, Waltz (1979: 77) argues that systems are composed of a structure and their interacting units. Political structures are best conceptualized as having three elements: an ordering principle (anarchic or hierarchical), the character of the units (functionally alike or differentiated), and the distribution of capabilities (Waltz 1979: 88–99). Waltz argues that two elements of the structure of the international system are constants: the lack of an overarching authority means that its ordering principle is anarchy, and the principle of self-help means that all of the units remain functionally alike. Accordingly, the only structural variable is the distribution of capabilities, with the main distinction falling between multipolar and bipolar systems.

One difference between classical realism and neorealism is their contrasting views on the source and content of states' preferences. Contra classical realism, neorealism excludes the internal make-up of different states. As Rasler and Thompson (2001: 47) note, Morgenthau's (1948) seminal statement of classical realism relied on the assumption that leaders of states are motivated by their lust for power. Waltz's (1979: 91) theory, by contrast, omits leaders' motivations and state characteristics as causal variables for international outcomes, except for the minimal assumption that states seek to survive.

In addition, whereas classical realism suggested that state strategies are selected rationally, Waltz is agnostic about which of several microfoundations explain state behaviour, several of which are mentioned in the volume. States' behaviour can be a product of the competition among them, either because they calculate how to act to their best advantage, or because those that do not exhibit such behaviour are selected out of the system. Alternatively, states' behaviour can be a product of socialization: states can decide to follow norms because they calculate it is to their advantage, or because the norms become internalized.

Since the theory provides such a minimal account of preferences and microfoundations, it makes only indeterminate behavioural predictions, and Waltz is correspondingly reluctant to make foreign policy predictions (Waltz 1996; see also Elman 1996a, 1996b, Fearon 1998, Wivel 2005). Waltz nevertheless suggests that systemic processes will consistently produce convergent international outcomes. Waltz notes that international politics is characterized by a disheartening consistency; the same depressingly familiar things happen over and over again. This repetitiveness endures despite considerable differences in internal domestic political arrangements, both through time (contrast, for example, seventeenth- and nineteenth-century England) and space (contrast, for example, the United States and Germany in the 1930s). Waltz's purpose is to explain why similarly structured international systems all seem to be characterized by similar outcomes, even though their units (i.e. member states) have different domestic political arrangements and particular parochial histories. Waltz concludes that it must be something peculiar to, and pervasive in, international politics that accounts for these commonalities. He therefore excludes as 'reductionist' all but the thinnest of assumptions about the units that make up the system – they must, at a minimum, seek their own survival.

By focusing only minor attention on unit-level variables, Waltz aims to separate out the persistent effects of the international system. Jervis (1997: 7) observes that: 'We are dealing with a system when (a) a set of units or elements is interconnected so that changes in some elements or their relations produce changes in other parts of the system; and (b) the entire system exhibits properties and behaviors that are different from those parts.' Because systems are generative, the international political system is characterized by complex nonlinear relationships and unintended consequences. Outcomes are influenced by something more than simply the aggregation of individual states' behaviour, with a tendency towards unintended and ironic outcomes. As a result, there is a gap between what states want and what states get. Consequently, unlike classical realists, neorealists see international politics as tragic, rather than as being driven by the aggressive behaviour of revisionist states (Spirtas 1996: 387–400). The international political outcomes Waltz predicts include that multipolar systems will be less stable than bipolar systems; that interdependence will be lower in bipolarity than multipolarity; and that regardless of unit behaviour, hegemony by any single state is unlikely or even impossible.

Waltz's *Theory of International Politics* proved to be a remarkably influential volume, spinning off new debates and giving new impetus to existing disagreements. For example, the book began a debate over whether relative gains concerns impede cooperation among states (e.g. Grieco 1988, Snidal 1991a, 1991b, Powell 1991, Baldwin 1993, Grieco *et al.* 1993, Rousseau 2002), and added momentum to the extant question of whether bipolar or multipolar international systems are more war prone (e.g. Deutsch and Singer 1964, Wayman 1984, Sabrosky 1985, Hopf 1991, Mansfield 1993).

Partly because of its popularity, and partly because of its own 'take-no-prisoners' criticism of competing theories, Waltz's *Theory of International*

Politics became a prominent target. As time went by, detractors (for example, the contributors to Robert Keohane's (1986) edited volume *Neorealism and its Critics*) chipped away at the book's dominance. Non-realist work, in particular neoliberal institutionalism and investigations of the democratic peace, became more popular (see Keohane and Martin (2003) and Ray (2003) for summaries). Realism's decline in the 1990s was amplified by international events. The closing years of the twentieth century seemed to provide strong support for alternative approaches. The Soviet Union's voluntary retrenchment and subsequent demise; the continuation of Western European integration in the absence of American–Soviet competition; the wave of democratization and economic liberalization throughout the former Soviet Union, Eastern Europe and the developing world; and the improbability of war between the great powers all made realism seem outdated (Jervis 2002). It appeared that liberal or constructivist theories could better appreciate and explain the changes taking place in the international arena. Not surprisingly, the post-9/11 arena seems much more challenging, and it comes as no revelation that political realism is regarded as being better suited to address threats to national security. It is, however, ironic that its renaissance is at least partly owed to transnational terrorist networks motivated by religious extremism–actors and appetites that both lie well outside realism's traditional ambit.

Excluding neorealism, there are at least four contemporary strands of political realism: rise and fall realism, neoclassical realism, defensive structural realism, and offensive structural realism. All four take the view that international relations are characterized by an endless and inescapable succession of wars and conquest. The four groupings can be differentiated by the fundamental constitutive and heuristic assumptions that their respective theories share. Briefly, the approaches differ on the sources of state preferences – the mix of human desire for power and/or the need to accumulate the wherewithal to be secure in a self-help world – while agreeing that rational calculation is the microfoundation that translates those preferences into behaviour.

Defensive structural realism

Defensive structural realism developed, but is distinct, from neorealism (Walt 2002, Glaser 2003). Defensive structural realism shares neorealism's minimal assumptions about state motivations. Like neorealism, defensive structural realism suggests that states seek security in an anarchic international system – the main threat to their well-being comes from other states (Walt 2002, Glaser 2003). There are three main differences between neorealism and defensive structural realism. First, whereas neorealism allows for multiple microfoundations to explain state behaviour, defensive structural realism relies solely on rational choice. Second, defensive structural realism adds the offence–defence balance as a variable (see Van Evera 1999: 10). This is a composite variable combining a variety of different factors that make conquest harder or easier (for outstanding reviews of the offence–defence literature see Lynn-Jones

1995, 2001). Defensive structural realists argue that prevailing technologies or geographical circumstances often favour defence, seized resources do not cumulate easily with those already possessed by the metropole, dominoes do not fall, and power is difficult to project at a distance (see, respectively, Christensen and Snyder 1990, Liberman 1993, Jervis and Snyder 1991, Mearsheimer 2001). Accordingly, in a world in which conquest is hard it may not take too much balancing to offset revisionist behaviour. Third, combining rationality and an offence–defence balance that favours defence, defensive structural realists predict that states should support the status quo. Expansion is rarely structurally mandated, and balancing is the appropriate response to threatening concentrations of power (see, for example, Walt 1987, 1988, 1991a, 1992a, 1992b, 1996). Rationalism and an offence–defence balance that favours defence means that states balance, and balances result.

Perhaps the best-known variant of defensive structural realism is Stephen Walt's 'balance of threat' theory (Walt 1987, 1988, 1991a, 1992a, 1992b, 1996, 2000. See also Snyder 1991, Glaser 1994/95, 1997, Van Evera 1999). According to Walt (1987: x), 'in anarchy, states form alliances to protect themselves. Their conduct is determined by the threats they perceive and the power of others is merely one element in their calculations'. Walt (2000: 200–201) suggests that states estimate threats posed by other states by their relative power, proximity, intentions, and the offence–defence balance. The resulting dyadic balancing explains the absence of hegemony in the system:

> Together, these four factors explain why potential hegemons like Napoleonic France, Wilhelmine Germany, and Nazi Germany eventually faced overwhelming coalitions: each of these states was a great power lying in close proximity to others, and each combined large offensive capabilities with extremely aggressive aims.
>
> (Walt 2000: 201)

Because balancing is pervasive, Walt (1987: 27) concludes that revisionist and aggressive behaviour is self-defeating, and 'status quo states can take a relatively sanguine view of threats. . . . In a balancing world, policies that convey restraint and benevolence are best.'

One difficult problem for defensive structural realism is that the research programme is better suited to investigating structurally constrained responses to revisionism, rather than where that expansionist behaviour comes from. To explain how conflict arises in the first place, defensive structural realists must appeal to either domestic-level factors (which are outside of their theory), or argue that extreme security dilemma dynamics make states behave as if they were revisionists. John Herz (1950: 157) was an early exponent of the concept of the security dilemma, arguing that defensive actions and capabilities are often misinterpreted as being aggressive (see also Butterfield 1951: 19–20).

Steps taken by states seeking to preserve the status quo are ambiguous, and are often indistinguishable from preparations for taking the offence. 'Threatened' states respond, leading to a spiralling of mutual aggression that all would have preferred to avoid. This is international relations as tragedy, not evil: bad things happen because states are placed in difficult situations.

Defensive structural realism has some difficulty in relying on security dilemma dynamics to explain war (see also Chapter 10, this volume). It is not easy to see how, in the absence of pervasive domestic-level pathologies, revisionist behaviour can be innocently initiated in a world characterized by status quo states, defence–dominance and balancing (see Schweller 1996, Kydd 2005). Because increments in capabilities can be easily countered, defensive structural realism suggests that a state's attempt to make itself more secure by increasing its power is ultimately futile. This is consistent with Arnold Wolfers' (1962: 158–159) reading of the security dilemma, that states threatened by new, potentially offensive capabilities respond with measures of their own, leaving the first state in as precarious a position, if not worse off, than before. Hence, defensive realists suggest that states should seek an 'appropriate' amount of power, not all that there is. If states do seek hegemony, it is due to domestically generated preferences; seeking superior power is not a rational response to external systemic pressures.

Offensive structural realism

Offensive structural realists disagree with the defensive structural realist prescription that states look for only an 'appropriate' amount of power. The flagship statement, John Mearsheimer's (2001) *The Tragedy of Great Power Politics*, argues that states face an uncertain international environment in which any state might use its power to harm another. Under such circumstances, relative capabilities are of overriding importance, and security requires acquiring as much power compared to other states as possible (see also Labs 1997). The stopping power of water means that the most a state can hope for is to be a regional hegemon, and for there to be no other regional hegemons elsewhere in the world.

Mearsheimer's (2001: 30–31) theory makes five assumptions: the international system is anarchic; great powers inherently possess some offensive military capability, and accordingly can damage each other; states can never be certain about other states' intentions; survival is the primary goal of great powers; and great powers are rational actors. From these assumptions, Mearsheimer (2001: 32–36) deduces that great powers fear each other; that they can rely only on themselves for their security; and that the best strategy for states to ensure their survival is the maximization of relative power.

In contrast to defensive structural realists, who suggest that states look for only an 'appropriate' amount of power (e.g. Glaser 1994/95, 1997, Van Evera 1999), Mearsheimer argues that security requires acquiring as much power relative to other states as possible. Mearsheimer (2001: 417, n. 27) explicitly rejects Glaser's (1997), and thus Wolfers' (1962) reading of the security dilemma, and argues that increasing capabilities can improve a state's security without triggering a countervailing response. Careful timing by revisionists, buckpassing by potential targets, and information asymmetries all allow the would-be hegemon to succeed. Power maximization is not necessarily self-defeating, and hence states can rationally aim for regional hegemony.

Although states will take any increment of power that they can get away with, Mearsheimer (2001: 37) does not predict that states are 'mindless aggressors so bent on gaining power that they charge headlong into losing wars or pursue Pyrrhic victories'. States are sophisticated relative power maximizers that try 'to figure out when to raise and when to fold' (2001: 40). Expanding against weakness or indecision, pulling back when faced by strength and determination, a sophisticated power maximizer reaches regional hegemony by using a combination of brains and brawn.

Mearsheimer (2001: 140–155) argues that ultimate safety comes only from being the most powerful state in the system. However, the 'stopping power of water' makes such global hegemony all but impossible, except through attaining an implausible nuclear superiority. The second best, and much more likely, objective is to achieve regional hegemony, the dominance of the area in which the great power is located. Finally, even in the absence of either type of hegemony, states try to maximize both their wealth and their military capabilities for fighting land battles. In order to gain resources, states resort to war, blackmail, baiting states into making war on each other while standing aside, and engaging competitors in long and costly conflicts. When acting to forestall other states' expansion, a great power can either try to inveigle a third party into coping with the threat (i.e. buck-pass), or balance against the threat themselves (2001: 156–162). While buckpassing is often preferred as the lower cost strategy, balancing becomes more likely, *ceteris paribus*, the more proximate the menacing state, and the greater its relative capabilities.

In addition to moving Mearsheimer's focus to the regional level, the introduction of the stopping power of water also leads to his making different predictions of state behaviour depending on where it is located. While the theory applies to great powers in general (2001: 5, 403, n. 5), Mearsheimer distinguishes between different kinds: continental and island great powers, and regional hegemons. A continental great power will seek regional hegemony but, when it is unable to achieve this dominance, such a state will still maximize its relative power to the extent possible. An insular state, 'the only great power on a large body of land that is surrounded on all sides by water' (2001: 126), will balance against the rising states rather than try to be a regional hegemon itself. Accordingly, states such as the United Kingdom act as offshore balancers, intervening only when a continental power is near to achieving primacy (2001: 126–128, 261–264). The third kind of great power in Mearsheimer's theory is a regional hegemon such as the USA. A regional hegemon is a status quo state that will seek to defend the current favourable distribution of capabilities (2001: 42).

Mearsheimer's (2001: 337) theory provides a structural explanation of great power war, suggesting that 'the main causes . . . are located in the architecture of the international system. What matters most is the number of great powers and how much power each controls.' Great power wars are least likely in bipolarity, where the system only contains two great powers, because there are fewer potential conflict dyads; imbalances of power are much less likely; and miscalculations leading to failures of deterrence are less common. While multipolarity is, in general, more war prone than bipolarity, some multipolar power configurations are more dangerous than others. Great power wars are most likely when multipolar systems are unbalanced; that is, when there is a marked difference in capabilities between the first and second states in the system, such that the most powerful possesses the means to bid for hegemony. Mearsheimer hypothesizes that the three possible system architectures range from unbalanced multipolarity's war proneness to bipolarity's peacefulness, with balanced multipolarity falling somewhere in between (2001: 337–346).

Rise and fall realism

Rise and fall realism sees the rules and practices of the international system as being determined by the wishes of the leading (i.e. most powerful) state. Since considerable benefit accrues to the leader, other great powers seek this pole position. Rise and fall realism explains how states first rise to, and then fall from, this leading position, and the consequences of that trajectory for state foreign policies. In particular, the approach is concerned with the onset of great power wars which often mark the transition from one leader to the next. The microfoundation which explains this behaviour is rational choice. Given a narrowing of the gap between the first and second ranked states, the leader will calculate the need for preventive action. Failing that, the challenger will opt for a war to displace the current leader.

Perhaps the best and best-known work in the rise and fall tradition is Robert Gilpin's (1981) *War and Change in World Politics*. Gilpin (1981: 7) suggests that 'the fundamental nature of international relations has not changed over the millennia. International relations continue to be a recurring struggle for wealth and power among independent actors in a state of anarchy.' Domestic and international developments lead to states growing at different rates, and as states rise and fall relative to one another, conflict ensues. States choose to engage in conflict because they calculate that the benefits of doing so exceed its costs. In particular, because the international system is created by and for the leading power in the system, changes in power lead to conflict over system leadership. Gilpin suggests that these dynamics have, *mutatis mutandis*, always applied to relations among states, and hence his framework is applicable to a wide swathe of human history (see also Gilpin 1988).

A.F.K. Organski's (1968) power transition theory also argues that differential rates of growth cause wars over system leadership (see also Organski and Kugler 1980, Kugler and Organski 1989, Kugler and Lemke 2000).

However, because he argues that it is the timing of industrialization that causes states to rise and fall *vis-à-vis* one another, his theory applies to a much narrower time frame than Giplin's, bracketed by the first and last great power to industrialize. Organski argues that states go through three stages: potential power, where an agrarian state has yet to industrialize; transitional growth in power, where a state modernizes both politically and economically, and enjoys a substantial increase in growth rates; and finally power maturity, where a state is industrialized. Because states go through the second stage at different times, it follows that their relative power position changes. When states that are dissatisfied with the current status quo gain on the system leader, war is likely to ensue. Consequently, peace is most likely when current system leaders enjoy a substantial lead over other states. According to DiCicco and Levy (1999: 680), 'three generations of scholars have self-consciously identified with this research program and continue to refine the theory and test it empirically'. These have partly been aimed at testing Organski's original insight, and partly at extending the theory's domain (see also DiCicco and Levy 1999, 2003, Doran and Parsons 1980, Doran 1989, 2000). For example, Douglas Lemke (1995, 1996) applies power transition theory to dyads other than those involving states directly contesting for system leadership. Woosang Kim (1991, 1992, 1996, 2002) amends power transition theory to allow alliances, and not just internal growth rates, to be counted.

The most prominent recent incarnation of rise and fall realism is Dale Copeland's (2001) dynamic differentials theory, which suggests that major wars are typically initiated by dominant military powers which fear significant decline. Copeland's theory also incorporates structural realist arguments, however, since he sees the main virtue of power as ensuring survival, rather than allowing the arrangement of international affairs to suit the dominant state's interests.

Neoclassical realism

In part responding to what were perceived as the anti-reductionist excesses of neorealism (e.g. Snyder 1991: 19), neoclassical realism suggests that what states do depends in large part on domestically derived preferences (see Rose 1998, Schweller 2003). For example, Schweller (1993: 76–77, 84, 1994: 92–99) insists that realism is best served by acknowledging and including different state motivations. As Rasler and Thompson (2001: 47) note, neoclassical realists stress a wider range of revisionist motives than classical realism's earlier reliance on human nature: 'things happen in world politics because some actors – thanks to domestic structure and institutions, ideology, and ambitions – practice disruptive and predatory strategies.' One prominent version of neoclassical realism is Randall Schweller's (1993, 1994, 1996, 1998) 'balance of interests' theory, which develops a typology based on whether states are primarily motivated by, and the extent of, their fear and greed. Thus, states rationally decide on foreign policies depending on a combination of power and interests (see also Snyder 1991, Wohlforth 1993, Christensen 1996, Zakaria 1998).

In addition to emphasizing the distinction between status quo and revisionist states, neoclassical realists also focus on the domestic 'transmission belt' connecting resource endowments and power (Schweller 2006: 6). Neoclassical realists agree that material capabilities and the distribution of power are the starting points for an analysis of international outcomes. They insist, however, that state characteristics and leaders' views of how power should be used intervene between structural constraints and behaviour. Accordingly, they also investigate domestic political features, such as the abilities of foreign policy-makers to extract resources for the pursuit of foreign policy goals. For example, Schweller argues that:

> states assess and adapt to changes in their external environment partly as a result of their peculiar domestic structures and political situations. More specifically, complex domestic political processes act as transmission belts that channel, mediate, and (re)direct policy outputs in response to external forces (primarily changes in relative power). Hence states often react differently to similar systemic pressures and opportunities, and their responses may be less motivated by systemic level factors than domestic ones.
>
> (Schweller 2006: 6)

While most political realist theories predict that states will balance against threatening competitors, either by building their own arms or by making alliances, Schweller argues that a review of the historical record demonstrates that, contra this prediction, states often 'underbalance'. That is, they balance inefficiently in response to dangerous and unappeasable aggressors, when effective balancing was needed to deter or defeat those threats. Schweller (2006) locates his explanation for underbalancing at the domestic level of analysis: the more fragmented and diverse a state's various elite and societal groups, the less we can expect it to respond appropriately to external strategic pressures. Schweller formalizes this insight into a four-variable model comprising elite consensus, elite cohesion, social cohesion and regime vulnerability.

Conclusion

This chapter has reviewed six variants of realism: classical realism, neorealism, rise and fall realism, neoclassical realism, defensive structural realism and offensive structural realism. As the discussion has shown, realism is a multifaceted and durable tradition of inquiry in security studies, with an extraordinary facility for adaptation. The development of the realist tradition within these separate components has at least three significant ramifications.

First, while the research programmes have some common characteristics with each other, none make wholly overlapping arguments or predictions. Although it is possible to support some general remarks about the realist tradition (for example, the observations about realism's continuity and pessimism in the introduction to this chapter) one should otherwise be leery of statements that begin: 'Realism says . . .' or 'Realism predicts . . .'. Different realist theories say and predict different things. They will also have very different implications when considered as the basis for prescriptive policy. For example, the best offensive structural realism has to offer the world is an armed and watchful peace anchored in mutual deterrence, punctuated by wars triggered by structurally driven revisionism when a state calculates it can gain at another's advantage. The best defensive structural realism has to offer is a community of status quo states which have successfully managed to signal their peaceful intentions and/or refrained from obtaining ambiguously offensive capabilities.

Second, realism's capacity for change opens the tradition to some criticisms. For example, realists have recently been scolded for making self-serving adjustments to their theories to avoid contradiction by empirical anomalies. John Vasquez (1997) argues that balance-of-power theory, as described and defended by Kenneth Waltz (1979), Stephen Walt (1987), Thomas Christensen and Jack Snyder (1990), Randall Schweller (1994) and Colin Elman and Miriam Fendius Elman (1995), is degenerative when judged by Imre Lakatos' (1970) criteria. Vasquez suggests that balance-of-power theory is empirically inaccurate, but that succeeding versions of the theory have become progressively looser to allow it to accommodate disconfirming evidence. A related critique was launched by Jeffrey Legro and Andrew Moravcsik (1999), who argue that recent realists subsume arguments that are more usually associated with competing liberal or constructivist approaches. The result, they argue, is that realist theories have become less determinate, coherent and distinctive. These critiques have provoked vigorous and ongoing responses from realist scholars (see e.g. Feaver *et al.* 2000, Vasquez and Elman 2003).

Finally, despite its internal divisions and external critics, the realist tradition continues to be a central contributor to security studies. Now fully recovered from the excessive optimism of the immediate post-Cold War milieu, the tradition is likely to provide a substantial share of our explanations and understandings of the causes of conflict and war.

Further reading

Robert Gilpin, *War and Change in World Politics* (New York: Cambridge University Press, 1981). A leading work in the 'rise and fall' realist tradition, which investigates the consequences of unequal growth rates for great power politics.

John J. Mearsheimer, *The Tragedy of Great Power Politics* (New York: W.W. Norton, 2001). The flagship statement of offensive structural realism suggests that states pursue sophisticated power maximization to achieve security.

Hans Morgenthau, *Politics Among Nations: The Struggle for Power and Peace* (6th edn) (New York: McGraw-Hill, 1985). The most important classical realist text, and one of the two most influential realist books written since the Second World War, this volume suggests that unchanging human nature is the root cause of conflict.

Randall L. Schweller, *Deadly Imbalances: Tripolarity and Hitler's Strategy of World Conquest* (New York: Columbia University Press, 1998). A ground-breaking neoclassical realist volume which argues for the importance of greedy (and not just security-seeking) states in the international system.

Stephen M. Walt, *The Origins of Alliances* (Ithaca, NY: Cornell University Press, 1987). An important contribution to the defensive structural realist research programme, which argues that threat (and not just aggregate capabilities) determines how states respond to one another.

Kenneth N. Waltz, *Theory of International Politics* (Reading, MA: Addison Wesley, 1979). The seminal neorealist work, and the second of the two most important realist volumes, this book has shifted the realist research tradition away from the individual and towards the international system.

Contents

Liberalism

Cornelia Navari

▌ Abstract

This chapter provides-an overview of the debates about security within liberal thought. The first section outlines traditional/Kantian liberalism. The second section introduces liberal economic thought regarding peace and war and the ideas of *douce commerce*. The third section describes the democratic peace thesis, and reviews the major discussions on the idea that liberal states do not fight wars with other liberal states. The final section outlines the major arguments in neoliberal institutionalism. It concludes by highlighting the main differences between realist approaches to security and liberal approaches.

▌ Introduction

True internationalism and world peace will come through individual freedom, the free market, and the peaceful and voluntary associations of civil society.

(Richard M. Ebeling 2000)

The liberal tradition in thinking about security dates as far back as the philosopher Immanuel Kant, who emphasized the importance of 'republican' constitutions in producing peace. His pamphlet *Perpetual Peace* contains a peace plan, and may fairly be called the first liberal tract on the subject. But liberal security has been elaborated by different schools within a developing tradition of liberal thought. Andrew Moravcsik (2001) has distinguished between ideational, commercial and republican liberalism following Michael Doyle (1998) who distinguished international, commercial and ideological liberalism, each with rather different implications for security planning; and Zacher and Matthews (1995) have identified four different tendencies in liberal security thought. Each is reflecting upon a family of loosely knit concepts, containing in some cases rather opposed approaches. Kant believed that trade was likely to engender conflict, while later 'commercial' liberals saw in trade a beneficial and beneficent development. Republican liberals argue that peace is rooted in the liberalism of the liberal state – the internal approach – while neoliberal institutionalists emphasize the role of international institutions, which could ameliorate conflict from without.

This chapter provides an overview of the debates about security within liberal thought. The first section outlines traditional/Kantian liberalism. The second section introduces liberal economic thought regarding peace and war and the ideas of *douce commerce*. The third section describes the democratic peace thesis, and reviews the major discussions on the idea that liberal states do not fight wars with other liberal states. The final section outlines the major arguments in neoliberal institutionalism. It concludes by highlighting the main differences between realist approaches to security and liberal approaches.

Traditional or Kantian liberalism

Immanuel Kant was an enlightenment philosopher (some would say the greatest enlightenment philosopher), often noted for his approach to ethics. (Kant argued that moral behaviour resulted from moral choices and that these were guided by an inner sense of duty – when individuals behaved according to duty, they were being moral.) But he was not only an ethicist; he philosophized the 'good state' as well as its international relations. According to Kant, the only justifiable form of government was *republican government*, a condition of constitutional rule where even monarchs ruled according to the law. Moreover, the test of good laws was their 'universalizability' – the test of universal applicability. The only laws that deserved the name of 'law' were those one could wish everyone (including oneself) obeyed. Such laws became 'categorical imperatives'; they were directly binding, and monarchs as well as ordinary citizens were subject to them.

Kant argued that republican states were 'peace producers'; that is, they were more inclined to peaceful behaviour than other sorts of states. He attributed this to habits of consultation; a citizenry which had to be consulted before going to war would be unlikely to endorse war easily. He also attributed it to the legal foundations of the republican state because he believed a state built on law was less likely to endorse lawless behaviour in international relations.

But being republican was not sufficient to ensure world peace. According to Kant – and it was the critical argument of *Perpetual Peace* – the situation of international relations, its lawless condition, unstable power balances and especially the ever-present possibility of war endangered the republican state and made it difficult for liberal political orders to maintain their republican or liberal condition. Hence, he argued, it was the duty of the republican state to strive towards law-regulated international relations; they could not merely be liberal in themselves.

A critical part of Kant's argument, which initiated the debate between liberals and 'realists', was his critique of the concept of the 'balance of power': he refuted the argument, becoming prevalent in his day, that the balance of power was a peacekeeper. The idea of conscious balancing was fallacious, he argued, since 'It is the desire of every state, or of its ruler, to arrive at a condition of perpetual peace by conquering the whole world, if that were possible' (Kant (1991b), a view shared by some leading realists e.g. Mearsheimer (2001)). As to the automatic operations of such a balance, he held Rousseau's view that such tendencies did indeed exist. Rousseau (1917) argued that states were naturally pushed into watching one another and adjusting their power accordingly, usually through alliances. However, this practice resulted merely in 'ceaseless agitation' and not in peace.

Kant's peace programme consisted of two parts (Kant 1991a). There were the 'preliminary articles' – the initial conditions that had to be established before even republican states could make much contribution to a more peaceful international environment. These included the abolition of standing armies, non-interference in the affairs of other states, the outlawing of espionage, incitement to treason and assassination as instruments of diplomacy, and an end to imperial ventures. These had to be abolished by a majority of states, non-liberal as well as liberal, to end the condition Hobbes had described as 'the war of all against all'. There were then the three definitive articles; these went further and provided the actual foundations for peace:

1 The civil constitution of every state should be republican.
2 The law of nations shall be founded on a federation of free states.
3 The law of world citizenship shall be limited to conditions of universal hospitality.

Spreading republican constitutions meant, in effect, generalizing the striving for peace, since according to Kant, striving for peace was part of the natural orientation of the republican state. The 'federation of free states' would provide for a type of collective security system; and the provision of 'universal hospitality' would, in Michael Howard's formulation, 'gradually create a sense of cosmopolitan community' (2000: 31). Kant distinguished between the end of war and the establishment of positive peace, and his plan made peace 'more than a merely pious aspiration'. Accordingly, he may properly be regarded as 'the inventor of peace' (Howard 2000: 31).

During the nineteenth century, liberals tended to emphasize only Kant's views that liberalism inclined to peace. Through most of the nineteenth century, the liberal approach to peace consisted of critiques of the ancient regime, and promised that peace would automatically follow the overthrow of autocracy and the establishment of constitutional regimes. According to Raymond Aron (1978), nineteenth-century liberals had no peace plan. With the outbreak of the First World War, however, the emphasis changed. Then, the dangers that Kant had foreseen for liberalism in a dangerous international environment were rediscovered; and liberal thinkers turned from internal reform towards emphasizing arbitration, the development of international law and an international court, to protect liberalism from without. When the League of Nations failed, moreover, some would go so far as to recommend either the abolition of, or severe restrictions upon, state sovereignty.

Douce commerce

According to Moravcsik, 'commercial liberalism' focuses on 'incentives created by opportunities for trans-border economic transactions' (2001: 14). This contemporary formulation attempts to make specific the causal mechanisms behind the inclination of economically liberal states to prefer peace to conflict. According to Moravcsik, 'trade is generally a less costly means of accumulating wealth than war, sanctions or other coercive means' (2001: 50). But it is not the only theory – other commercial liberals stress the structure of a liberal economy, not merely the preferences of individual economic actors.

The origins of modern commercial liberalism lie in the nineteenth-century theory of *douce commerce* ('beneficent commerce') – the developing liberal critique of mercantilism, the aggressive economic policies recommended to, and to a degree practised by, the autocrats of the ancient regime. Mercantilist doctrine advised doing all to increase the amount of bullion held by a country, in an environment where bullion was believed to be a fixed quantum. The effect of generalizing mercantilism was made explicit by Voltaire in 1764: 'It is clear that a country cannot gain unless another loses and it cannot prevail without making others miserable.' The economic *philosophes* (called physiocrats) such as François Quesnay and Victor de Mirabeau identified a structural proclivity in mercantilism towards trade wars and territorial conquests. If your own nation was to be wealthy, it could only be so by making others poorer. Tariff walls were needed to protect the prosperity of domestic producers from the 'attacks' of foreign competitors. Subsidies were required for export producers so that they could 'seize' the wealth of others in foreign markets. Resources in foreign lands had to be militarily 'captured' to keep them out of the hands of commercial rivals in opposing nation-states who would use them to defeat 'our' nation-state.

The explicit association between non-mercantilist, open trading orders and peace was, however, not French but a British development. It first appeared in Adam Smith's *Wealth of Nations*, where he argued that 'the hidden hand' besides increasing wealth also promoted a lessening of economic hostilities. But even earlier, Smith's Scottish colleague and friend David Hume had demonstrated that an international division of labour and trade benefited all participants, and David Ricardo had formulated the theory of comparative advantage. According to Ricardo, wealth accrued in the degree to which states concentrated production in areas where they had 'comparative advantage' and traded for other products. Ricardo's theory underpinned the notion of a benevolent division of labour as well as the idea that trade was non-hostile competition.

The nineteenth-century 'commercial liberals' developed these ideas into doctrine. Liberal trade doctrine held that trade among states, like trade among individuals, was mutually beneficial. All men would gain through participation in a global division of labour – a way of life in which they offered to each other the various products in the production of which they specialized. Market competition was not conflict, they argued, but rather peaceful cooperation: each producer helped to improve the quality of life for all through the production and sale of superior and less expensive products than the ones offered by his market rivals. The market was civil society and peace; economic policy in the hands of governments was conflict and war.

Commercial liberalism also took on a sociological aspect. James Mill described the British Empire as outdoor relief for the upper classes. Joseph Schumpeter argued that conquest and imperialism had economically favoured the old aristocratic elites, and that the social changes which accompanied capitalism made modern states inherently peaceful, since they led to the decline of the aristocratic class.

The only formal non-liberal nineteenth-century riposte to the commercial liberals (that is, the only argument one could credit with some respect) was the mid-nineteenth-century idea of protecting infant industries. The German nationalist Jahn argued that because of the time lag between developed and developing countries, there was an argument for initial protection for 'infant' industry, but even then only until it could compete in an open market. In the twentieth century, under the press of the Great Depression, liberals would also argue that there was some justification for protecting economies from storms in the world economy, but again temporary measures only. (The liberal tendency came to be to improve international regimes so that storms could be avoided or ridden out without closures.) There also developed a more refined critique of the argument that everyone benefited through trade. This made it clear that the wealth accruing through opening up economic exchange did not automatically benefit everyone in society; this depended on social policies which, among other things, deliberately fostered the skills which would allow individuals to participate in market economies.

During the twentieth century, the initial successes of Nazism, government-directed labour programmes and the much vaunted 'Soviet model' led the commercial liberals to focus on government involvement in the economy and on protectionist ideologies. Indeed, twentieth-century commercial liberals spoke less of economy than of ideology, particularly attacking ideas of economic closure and planning that derived from 'scientific socialism' and especially economic nationalism. The most famous of these is Friedrich Hayek's *Road to Serfdom*, but it had many echoes, especially in Central Europe. During the 1930s, the German economist Wilhelm Röpke declared that the 'genuinely liberal principle' required 'the widest possible separation of the two spheres of government and economy'. He recommended the greatest possible 'depoliticization' of the economic sphere. In 1936, the Swiss economist and political scientist William Rappard (the Rappard Chateau which houses the World Trade Organization in Geneva is named after him) in a lecture entitled 'The Common Menace of Economic and Military Armaments' identified 'economic armaments' with all of the legislative and administrative devices governments use to politically influence imports and exports as well as the allocation of commodities. Rappard argued that a new world order of peace and prosperity would only come about when governments exited from control of the economy. In similar fashion, in 1952, the free-market economist Michael A. Heilperin delivered a lecture entitled 'An Economist's Views on International Organization'. He told his audience,

> It is an elementary, but often forgotten, knowledge that policies of national governments have always been the principal obstacle to economic relations between people living in various countries, and that whenever these relations were free from government restrictions, equilibrium and balanced growth would follow by virtue of the spontaneous and anonymous mechanism of the market.
>
> (cited in Ebeling 2000)

Attacks on ideology came to include some liberal ideas, particularly the idea that peace could come through the abolition of sovereignty, a favourite liberal idea of the late 1930s and 1940s. According to the Austrian economist Ludwig von Mises:

> [Classical] liberalism did not and does not build its hopes upon abolition of the sovereignty of the various national governments, a venture which would result in endless wars. It aims at a general recognition of the idea of economic freedom. If all peoples become liberal and conceive that economic freedom best serves their own interests, national sovereignty will no longer engender conflict and war. What is needed to make peace durable is neither international treaties and covenants nor international tribunals and organizations like the defunct League of Nations or its successor, the United Nations. If the principle of the market economy is universally accepted, such makeshifts are unnecessary; if it is not accepted, they are futile. Durable peace can only be the outgrowth of a change in ideologies.
>
> (Mises 1949: 686)

The notion that economic openness produces a more peaceful international posture has become the subject of close empirical examination. In 1997, Oneal and Russett (1997) declared that the 'the classical liberals were right' in their study of the record in the post-war period. Similarly, Mansfield and Pollins (2001) have summarized a large body of empirical work that, for the most part, supports the thesis. There are various exceptions and qualifications which are seen to limit the circumstances under which economic interdependence results in conflict reduction. Stephen Van Evera (1994) has argued that the more diversified and complex the existing transnational commercial ties and production structures the less cost-effective coercion is likely to be. By extension, the less diverse the production structure of a country and the more it is characterized by monopolies, the more fragile will be the inclination to peace.

Moving beyond economic interdependence to the issue of economic freedom within states, Erik Gartzke (2005) has found empirical evidence that economic freedom (as measured by the Fraser Institute Economic Freedom Index) is about 50 times more effective than democracy in reducing violent conflict. Gartzke's conclusions are crucial for the direction of liberal reforms, since they imply that it is less important what sort of political regime a country has as its degree of economic freedom.

The policy prescriptions enjoined by the commercial liberals – often called 'economic disarmament' – focus on limiting the power of governments to impose trade restraints, primarily through international regulation. Foreign exchanges were to be open; tariffs were to be reduced to the minimum and quotas and other quantitative restrictions positively forbidden. Governments were to pledge themselves to open tariff borders, to abolish quotas and to allow currencies to move in line with market forces. These policy prescriptions were immensely influential in the architecture of the newly established international economic organizations, set up at the end of the Second World War.

Recently, the literature on globalization has suggested that globalization, in its aspect as unfettered free trade on a global scale, is a peace producer. Graham Allison has opined that 'global networks, particularly in economics, create demands by powerful players for predictability in interactions and thus for rules of the game that become, in effect, elements of international law' (Allison 2000: 83). Thomas Friedman's *The Lexus and the Olive Tree* declares that 'When a country reaches the level of economic development, when it has a middleclass big enough to support a McDonald's network, it becomes a McDonald's country. And people in McDonald's countries don't like to fight wars anymore, they prefer to wait in line for burgers' (Friedman 2000: 14).

But it is not obvious that globalization has firmly entrenched economic liberalism. Commenting on America's foreign economic policy of the 1980s, Professor Richard Ebeling, of the Future of Freedom Foundation, has observed the emergence of traditional mercantilist methods:

> If some of America's Asian trading partners 'capture' a large share of the American consumer market, the government responds with a tariff-wall 'defense.' If American agriculture cannot earn the profits it considers 'fair,' the U.S. government takes the 'offensive' by 'attacking' other lands through export price-subsidies. If other nations will not comply with the wishes of the Washington social engineers in some international dispute, the American government influences and persuades them with government-to-government financial loans, grants and subsidized credits – all at American taxpayers' expense, of course.
>
> (Ebeling 1991)

The reputed peace effects of globalization are also countered in the literature by some reputed war effects. These include increased vulnerability to threats from the failure of the complex systems globalization relies upon, as well as from non-state actors whose access to weapons and potential for disruption increases in a globalized world. Advances in technology may also have made states more vulnerable to coercive threats than would have been possible earlier (on some of the implications of globalization for security, see Navari 2006). Liberal unease with globalization is well represented in a recent collection of essays (Held 2007), where Michael Doyle, among other noted liberals, outlines the problem of democratic accountability in a globalized political system.

The democratic peace thesis

The 'democratic peace' thesis is the argument that liberal states do not fight wars against other liberal states. It was first enunciated in a keynote article by Michael Doyle in the journal *Philosophy and Public Affairs* (Doyle 1983). Doyle argued that there was a difference in liberal practice towards other liberal societies and liberal practice towards non-liberal societies. Among liberal societies, liberalism had produced a cooperative foundation such that 'constitutionally liberal states have yet to engage in war with one another'. Doyle based his findings on David Singer's Correlates of War Project (COW) at Michigan University and the COW's list of wars since 1816 (see Small and Singer 1982). Using the list, Doyle observed that almost no liberal states had fought wars against other liberal states, and that in the two instances in which it seemed that liberal states had fought against other arguably liberal states, liberalism had only recently been established. Doyle sourced the tendency in Kant's 'three preconditions'; namely republican constitutions, collective security arrangements and civic hospitality, in which Doyle included free trade.

The specific causes of the 'liberal peace' have become the subject of robust research and discussion. The two major contending theories focus on liberal institutions and liberal ideology respectively. Liberal institutions include the broad franchise of liberal states and the need to ensure broad popular support; the division of powers in democratic states which produces checks and balances; and the electoral cycle, which makes liberal leadership cautious and prone to avoid risk (Russett 1996). But liberal institutions would tend to inhibit all wars, whereas liberal states have fought robust wars against non-liberal states. The other contender, which can explain the difference, is liberal ideology or 'culture'. According to the liberal culture argument, liberal states tend to trust other liberal states and to expect to resolve conflict through discussion and compromise. But, equally, they distrust non-liberal states. The major argument for liberal ideology has been put forward by John M. Owen who suggests that, 'Ideologically, liberals trust those states they consider fellow liberal democracies and see no reason to fight them. They view those states they consider illiberal with suspicion, and sometimes believe that the national interest requires war with them' (1996: 153).

Since Doyle first produced his findings, the theory has developed two variants: one maintains that democracies are more peaceful than non-democracies; that is, that they are more pacific *generally* (see Russett 1993). This is sometimes referred to as the *monadic* variant. The other maintains that liberal states are not necessarily more peaceful than non-liberal states, but that they eschew the use of force in relation to other democracies; that is, the use of force depends on the recipient's form of government. In the later variant, sometimes called the *dyadic* variant, a few have argued that democracies may be even more robust in the use of force than non-democracies, due partially to the ideological nature of democratic wars and partially to the fact that liberal democracies are generally strong states with a large wealth base (see Barkawi and Laffey 2001).

From the security point of view, the recommendations of democratic peace theory are clear – in the final analysis, security depends on encouraging liberal institutions; and a security policy must have as its long-term aim the spread of liberalism. In the short term, it must protect liberalism, including liberal tendencies in non-liberal states. Doyle himself argues that where liberalism has been deficient 'is in preserving its [liberalism's] basic preconditions under changing international circumstances' (1983: 229). The route to peace is to encourage democratic systems, the universal respect for human rights and the development of civil society.

But such a conclusion depends on an untroubled and robust correlation between the democratic nature of a state and a peaceful inclination, at least towards other liberal states, and it is not entirely clear that such a direct correlation exists. Chris Brown (1992) has pointed out that liberal states have, during the period that many states became liberal, faced determined enmity from non-liberal states. The fact that liberal states have faced enemies of liberalism distorts the historical record; we do not know how they may have diverged in the absence of such an enmity. It may also be that in a world of diverse states in situations of conflict, that is, in an anarchical society, liberal states make more reliable allies – that they do not fight one another because they ally with one another. (This is called the liberal alliance thesis and is compatible with Realist approaches.) There is also the not insignificant fact that the majority of liberal states are locked into economic integration via the European Union (a fact that may support the *douce commerce* variant). Finally, the democratic transition phenomenon may be a statistical aberration. David Spiro (1996), for instance, has argued that historically there have not been many liberal states, and that most states do not fight wars against one another anyway. The fact that liberal states have not fought wars against one another may not be statistically significant.

As to whether liberal states are more intrinsically peaceful than other states, this is perhaps even more contentious. Kant, for his part, seemed to support the monadic theory; he claimed not only that republics would be at peace with each other, but that republican government is more pacific than other forms of government. But the empirical work is indeterminate since it has so far concentrated on traditional state-to-state wars and has ignored interventions – intervention could also be considered an intrinsically hostile act involving the use of force outside of one's borders. Recent 'liberal' attempts to bring other states to liberal democracy (in Iraq, for example) have raised fears that, far from being a recipe for peace, liberal foreign policy may have its own tendencies towards war. This 'dark side of liberalism' has occupied much of the recent research, which has turned to the conditions which may lead liberal states to fight wars (see Geis *et al.* 2006).

Despite some hesitations from the academy, the theory that democracies do not fight wars against other democracies has been immensely influential in public policy. For example, it underpinned President Clinton's *A National Security Strategy for a New Century* (United States 1998); it was also extensively used to support the neoconservative case for war in Iraq and has guided post-war reconstruction in insisting on a broadly inclusive post-war government in Iraq and an early move to self-government with elections. The democratic transition thesis has also come to dominate the peace-building programme of the UN. Michael Barnett (2006) has been critical of what he calls the 'civil society' model for post-war reconstruction, since it places emphasis on mobilizing social forces in often unstable and divided societies, when more attention should be placed on building state capacity and strengthening governmental powers (see also Paris 1997).

The association between war, democracy and rights, prevalent in the immediate aftermath of the Second World War, has also been revived. Founded upon the principles of territorial integrity and state sovereignty, the UN has recently begun to shift towards an emphasis on the rights of human beings as being at least as important as the rights of states in the international realm. In a discussion on the relevance of the Security Council, UN Secretary-General Kofi Annan clearly indicated that 'the last right of states cannot and must not be the right to enslave, persecute or torture their own citizens'. In fact, rather than rally around sovereignty as its sole governing idea, the Security Council should 'unite behind the principle that massive and systematic violations of human rights conducted against an entire people cannot be allowed to stand' (Annan 1999a: 514).

Neoliberal institutionalism

Neoliberal institutionalism concentrates on the role of international institutions in mitigating conflict. Robert Keohane (1984) and Robert Axelrod (1984), who have played a central role in defining this field, point to the ability of institutions such as the UN to redefine state roles and act as arbitrators in state disputes. Although institutions cannot absolve anarchy, they can change the character of the international environment by influencing state preferences and state behaviour. International institutions do this through a variety of methods that either create strong incentives for cooperation like favourable trade status, or through powerful disincentives like trade sanctions.

'Under what conditions will cooperation emerge in a world of egoists without central authority?' This question was posed by Robert Axelrod (1984) in his central contribution to the theory, where he identified several crucial factors. The first was the practice of tit-for-tat. He argued that when agents returned good for good, this initiated a potential spiral of cooperative behaviour. If this practice were repeated, egoistic agents would gradually learn to trust one another, particularly when their interests coincided. This situation was formally modelled as a reiterated prisoner's dilemma situation (see Chapter 4, this volume). It implied that if states repeatedly found themselves in a situation in which they feared that their self-restraint would be taken advantage of, they would not defect but would, instead, devise reinsurance devices that would allow cooperation to ensue. Reinsurance devices produce institutions. He also theorized the 'shadow of the future'; arguing that once cooperation was institutionalized, states would hesitate to abandon it, for fear of what lay ahead. Axelrod went further by advising participants and reformers to increase the likelihood of mutual cooperation by enlarging the shadow of the future, by making interactions more durable and/or more frequent – for example, by breaking issues under negotiation into smaller pieces – and by changing the payoffs faced by the players.

Central to neoliberal institutionalism is the notion of transaction costs. These include 'the costliness of information, the costs of measuring the valuable attributes of what is being exchanged and the costs of protecting rights and policing and enforcing agreements' (North 1990: 27). Thus institutions are desirable, despite the constraints they impose on states, because they reduce transaction costs associated with rule-making, negotiating, implementing, enforcing, information gathering and conflict resolution. They are also durable. Existing regimes persist even after the conditions that facilitated their creation have disappeared 'because they are difficult to create or reconstruct' (Keohane 1984: 12–14, 50). This is the logic that lies at the core of neoliberal institutionalism: cooperation in situations modelled by an iterated prisoner's dilemma can be achieved in highly institutionalized settings, because institutions can serve as means of providing information, reducing transaction costs, and altering the payoffs associated with cooperation. In consequence, many neoliberal institutionalists argue that international actors should promote institutionalization as a means of promoting the collective interest in international stability.

Constructivist institutionalism, on the other hand, conceptualizes institutions as a collection of norms, rules and routines, rather than a formal structure (see Chapter 5, this volume). In contrast to rational choice theories like Axelrod's, institutions do not simply change the preferences of actors, but can also shape their identity (Barnett and Finnemore 1999). Constructivism focuses on the central role of ideology, rules and norms that institutions diffuse to constitute agents. Against a 'logic of instrumentality' or 'logic of consequences' of rational choice institutionalism, constructivism posits a 'logic of appropriateness', arguing that individuals' actions are guided by social expectations rather than utility maximization calculations. Institutional routines are followed even when there is no obvious self-interest involved (see March and Olsen 1989, Finnemore and Sikkink 1998).

There is, however, no single model of the most desirable sort of institution. On the contrary, the notion of transaction costs points to very different sorts of institutions for different cooperation problems. For example, the Strategic Arms Limitation Talks (SALT II) during the 1970s between the USA and Soviet Union required a set of specialists to determine what might be meant by a 'technical advance', while avoiding the dangers of misreading technical information required a telephone hotline between the major nuclear antagonists. Neoliberal institutionalism has spawned a voluminous institutional design literature that points to the variation in international institutions and outlines the different institutional arrangements necessary to address different types of cooperation problems (see e.g. Koremos *et al.* 2004, Mitchell 2006).

In this approach, unlike other liberal approaches, states are central. They are the agents who design institutions to advance their joint interests. Interests are first defined outside the institutional context (in the formal language 'individual preferences are exogenous'; they are defined outside of institutional contexts), and then institutions are designed by state actors to facilitate the achievement of their joint interests (Keohane 1989, Jupille and Caporaso 1999). Thus, institutions emerge and survive because they serve to maximize the exogenously determined interests and preferences of their members, especially those founding members who designed the institution.

But state-centredness has also led to a central ambiguity in the approach: what if the state is no longer able to cope with the pressures of interdependence? This has led to a radical liberal school exemplified by David Held (1995) and Seyom Brown (1996). In this version, the state is no longer able to cope with international crises such as degradation of the environment, mass migration, starvation and disease. In such a situation, Brown (1996) recommends that we substitute world interests for the state interests envisioned by more conservative neoliberals. These world interests would include survival of the human species, reduction in world violence, provision of conditions for healthy subsistence to all people, preservation of cultural diversity and preservation of the world's ecology. But the approach is rather vague about who should build these new 'world interest' organizations.

Neoliberal institutionalism contrasts with realism in several crucial areas. Both agree that powerful states influence the formation and shape of international institutions, but for different reasons. According to liberals, states create institutions to maximize shared interests; for realists, however, it is to realize and maintain domination. According to the leading American realist John Mearsheimer, 'The most powerful states in the system create and shape institutions so that they can maintain their share of world power, or even increase it' (1994/95: 13). Realism also focuses on the extent to which powerful states dominate institutions; they argue that latecomers or less powerful members will have less control over institutional decisions and outcomes, benefit less from their creation and will have less commitment to maintaining the institution (Gruber 2000). This is quite apart from the general critique that realists make of institutional approaches. 'Realists maintain that institutions are basically a reflection of the distribution of power in the world. They are based on the self-interested calculations of the great powers, and they have no independent effect on state behavior' (Mearsheimer 1994/95: 7). Neoliberal institutionalists argue, on the contrary, that the 'shadow of the future' – the possibility to attain gains in the future – provides a strong incentive for all states to cooperate and create institutions that benefit all parties.

An equally harsh realist critique of neoliberal institutionalism is Grieco (1993) with his concept of relative gains. Grieco argues that relative gains, what a state in a competitive situation might gain from cooperation relative to what his opponent might gain, are more important than 'absolute gains' – the overall calculus of gains versus loses. This is so, he argues, because power is a relational concept; power can only be measured in relation to another's power; that is, by comparison with another power-seeker. It matters not if the other gains and I lose, but if the other gains more than I do. He maintains that the calculus of relative gains often sabotages hoped-for cooperative ventures, if the cooperative venture threatens to change the balance of power (for discussion of the relevance of the absolute vs. relative gains argument to neoliberal institutionalism, see also Powell 1991, Snidal 1991b).

The question is: How suitable is neoliberal insitutionalism with regard to security issues? Jervis has observed that the realm of security has special characteristics that at the same time make regime creation more difficult and increase its need: 'Security regimes, with their call for mutual restraint and limitations on unilateral actions, rarely seem attractive to decision-makers' under the security dilemma (Jervis 1982: 360). Basic to the neoliberal institutionalists is the idea of common interests that states could achieve together. But what if antagonists do not share common interests? According to Jervis (1999: 54), 'states will establish an institution if and only if they seek the goals that the institution will help them reach'. It does not seem, superficially, that institutions could do much to increase security.

The notion that security might lie outside the scope of neoliberal cooperation has led neoliberal institutionalists to focus on cooperation in low politics such as economy, society and environment and pay much less attention to military security cooperation. But the persistence and expansion of NATO after the end of the Cold War created a theoretical puzzle for realists and an opportunity for neoliberal institutionalism to move into high politics. Wallander and Keohane (1999), for instance, explicitly regard NATO as a security institution and try to theorize the conception of 'security institution'. First, due to transaction costs and uncertainty, it is easier to maintain than to create new institutions, which is a basic assumption argued by Keohane (1984) in *After Hegemony*. Second, the duration of an institution mainly relies on the function and extent of institutionalization and organization. Third, and most importantly, the conditions and objects for a security institution's persistence are not as narrow as those of alliances. An alliance is for dealing with common threats while an institution is for coping with risks, including regional uncertainty. David A. Lake distinguishes hierarchic institutions from anarchic ones. He argues that the former are effective in taking actions but can be evanescent while the latter, lacking dominant authorities, are less effective but more adaptable to a changing environment and can last (Lake 2001: 136). In short, Lake, Keohane and Wallender argue that NATO persisted because it was not a simple alliance; rather it was becoming a security institution.

The distinction drawn by Wallander and Keohane (1999) between an alliance and a security institution has led to a significant new typology. Dittgen and Peters (2001) have contrasted two ideal-type security systems – the alliance-type system and the community of law-type system – which provide models for the construction of the respective security systems (see Table 3.1). The first is rooted in a realist perspective; the second in a liberal perspective. The key difference is the response to the threat. In a liberal community of law,

Table 3.1 Realist and liberal security systems

Theoretical base		Realist (alliance)	Liberal (community of law)
Structure of the international system		Material; static; anarchic; self-help system	Social; dynamic; governance without government
Conceptions of security	*Basic principles*	Accumulation of power	Integration
	Strategies	Military deterrence; control of allies	Democratization; conflict resolution; rule of Law
Institutional features	*Functional scope*	Military realm only	Multiple issue areas
	Criterion for membership	Strategic relevance	Democratic system of rule
	Internal power structure	Reflects distribution of power; most likely hegemonic	Symmetrical; high degree of interdependence
	Decision-making	Will of dominant powers prevails	Democratically legitimized
Relation of system to its environment		Dissociated; perception of threat	Serves as an attractive model; open for association

potential disturbances are not dealt with by mobilizing superior power but rather are diffused through integration, by reinsurance and by conflict resolution. Threats are circumvented by common membership in a security institution.

Conclusion

In liberal International Relations theory, the state is not an actor but an institution 'constantly subject to capture and recapture, even construction and reconstruction' by coalitions of social actors (Moravcsik 2001: 5). The theory has distinct variants which supply different motivations for action and which have different implications for security theory. In ideational liberalism, the underlying motive is social identity and conflict will ensue if borders do not accord with social identity. Conflict will also ensue across social identities. In commercial liberalism, the underlying motivation is economic benefit, which does not necessarily lead to cooperation, but which identifies under what sorts of circumstances the economy can be a peace-producer. In republican liberalism, the crucial factor is state form and states can be integrated into long-term peace arrangements which at the same time encourage democratization and internal state reform. The contribution of liberalism to security theory is dense, specified and progressive.

Further reading

David Baldwin (ed.), *Neorealism and Neoliberalism: The Contemporary Debate* (New York: Columbia University Press, 1993). This collects the major articles in the debate between realists and liberals, which still constitutes, arguably, the major axis of theory in contemporary International Relations.

Michael E. Brown, Sean Lynn-Jones and Steven Miller (eds), *Debating the Democratic Peace* (Cambridge, MA: MIT Press, 1996). This contains all the classic writings on the democratic peace and the major criticisms.

Michael Howard, *War and the Liberal Conscience* (Cambridge: Cambridge University Press, 1978). This presents what has become the classic account of real liberals in their encounters with war.

Robert O. Keohane, *After Hegemony: Cooperation and Discord in the World Political Economy* (Princeton, NJ: Princeton University Press, 1984). This lays out the first systematic statement of neoliberal institutionalism.

Andrew Moravcsik, *Liberal International Relations Theory: A Social Scientific Assessment* (Cambridge, MA: Harvard University Press, 2001). This sets out what the various liberal theories explain, their limits, and how to operationalize them.

Game Theory

Frank C. Zagare

▐ Abstract

This chapter describes the basic assumptions, and illustrates the major concepts, of game theory using examples drawn from the security studies literature. For instance, an arms race game is used to illustrate the strategic form of a game, the meaning of an equilibrium outcome, and the definition of a dominant strategy. Backwards induction and the definition of subgame perfection are explained in the context of an explication of an extensive-form game that features threats. A short review of the many applications of game theory in international politics is provided. Finally, the chapter concludes with a discussion of the usefulness of game theory in generating insights about deterrence.

▐ Introduction

Game theory is the science of interactive decision-making. It was created in one fell swoop with the publication of John Von Neumann and Oskar Morgenstern's *Theory of Games and Economic Behavior* (1944) by Princeton University Press. Widely hailed when it was published, the book became an instant classic. Its impact was enormous. Almost immediately, game theory began to penetrate economics – as one might well expect. But soon afterwards, applications, extensions and modifications of the framework presented by Von Neumann and Morgenstern began to appear in other fields, including sociology, psychology, anthropology and, through political science, International Relations and security studies.

In retrospect, the ready home that game theory found in the field of security studies is not very surprising. Much of the gestalt of game theory may easily be discerned in the corpus of diplomatic history and in the work of the most prominent theorists of international politics.[1] And its key concepts have obvious real-world analogues in the international arena.

Primitive concepts

The basic concept is that of a game itself. A *game* may be thought of as any situation in which an outcome depends on the choices of two or more decision-makers. The term is somewhat unfortunate. Games are sometimes thought of as lighthearted diversions. But in game theory the term is not so restricted. For instance, most if not all interstate conflicts qualify as very serious games.

In game theory, decision-makers are called *players*. Players may be individuals or groups of individuals who in some sense operate as a coherent unit. Presidents, prime ministers, kings and queens, dictators, foreign secretaries and so on can therefore sometimes be considered as players in a game. But so can the states in whose name they make foreign policy decisions. It is even possible to consider a coalition of two or more states as a player. For example, in their analysis of the July crisis of 1914, Snyder and Diesing (1977) use elementary game theory to examine the interaction between 'Russia–France' and 'Austria–Germany'.

The decisions that players make eventually lead to an *outcome*. In game theory, an outcome can be just about anything. Thus, the empirical content associated with an outcome will vary with the game being analysed. Sometimes, generic terms such as 'compromise' or 'conflict' are used to portray outcomes. At other times, the descriptors are much more specific. Snyder and Diesing use the label 'Control of Serbia' by Austria–Germany to partially describe one potential outcome of the July crisis.

Reflecting perhaps the intensity of the Cold War period in the USA in the early 1950s, almost all of the early applications of game theory in the field of security studies analysed interstate conflicts as *zero-sum games*. A zero-sum game is any game in which the interests of the players are diametrically opposed. Examples of this genre include an analysis of two World War II battles by A.G. Haywood (1954) and a study of military strategy by McDonald and Tukey (1949).

By contrast, a non-zero-sum game is an interactive situation in which the players have mixed motives; that is, in addition to conflicting interests, they may also have some interests in common. Two states locked in an economic conflict, for instance, obviously have an interest in securing the best possible terms of trade. At the same time, they both may also want to avoid the costs associated with a trade war. It is clear that in such instances, the interests of the two states are not diametrically opposed.

The use of non-zero-sum games became the standard form of analysis in international politics towards the end of the 1950s, due in no small part to the scholarship of Thomas Schelling (1960, 1966) whose works are seminal. When Schelling's book *The Strategy of Conflict* was republished in 1980 by Harvard University Press he remarked in a new Preface that the idea that conflict and common interest were not mutually exclusive, so obvious to him, was among the book's most important contributions. In 2005, Schelling was awarded the Nobel Prize in economics for his work on game theory and interstate conflict. The award was well deserved.

Most studies also make use of the tools and concepts of non-cooperative game theory. A *non-cooperative game* is any game in which the players are unable to irrevocably commit themselves to a particular course of action. By contrast, binding agreements are possible in a *cooperative game*. Since it is commonly understood that the international system lacks an overarching authority that can enforce commitments or agreements, it should come as no surprise that non-cooperative game theory holds a particular attraction for theorists of interstate conflict.

Strategic-form games and Nash equilibria

Game theorists have developed a number of distinct ways to represent a game's structure. Initially, the *strategic-form* (sometimes called the *normal-* or the *matrix-* form) was the device of choice. In the strategic-form, players select *strategies* simultaneously, before the actual play of the game. A strategy is defined as a complete contingency plan that specifies a player's choice at every situation that might arise in a game. Figure 4.1 depicts a typical arms race game between two states, State A and State B, in strategic-form.[2] Although the generic name for this game is Prisoners' Dilemma, it is referred to here as the Arms Race game.[3]

In this representation, each state has two strategies: to *cooperate* (C) by not arming, and to *defect* from cooperation (D) by arming. If neither arm, the outcome is a compromise: a military balance is maintained, but at little cost. If both arm, both lose, as an arms race takes place, the balance is maintained, but this time at considerable cost. Finally, if one state arms and the other does not, the state that arms gains a strategic advantage, and the state that chooses not to arm is put at a military disadvantage.

Each cell of the matrix contains an ordered pair of numbers below the names of the outcomes. The numbers represent the payoff which the row (State A) and the column player (State B) receives, respectively, when that outcome obtains in a game. Payoffs are measured by a *utility* scale. Sometimes, as in this chapter, only *ordinal utilities* are, or need be, assumed. Ordinal utilities convey information about a player's relative ranking of the outcomes. In many studies of interstate conflict, however, *cardinal utilities* are assumed. A cardinal scale indicates both rank and intensity of preference.

State B

		Not arm (C)	Arm (D)
State A	Not arm (C)	*Tacit arms control* (3,3)	*B gains advantage* (1,4)
	Arm (D)	*A gains advantage* (4,1)	*Arms race* (2,2)*

Key: (x,y) = payoff to State A, payoff to State B
   * = Nash equilibrium

Figure 4.1 Arms Race game (Prisoners' Dilemma)

In this example, the outcomes are ranked from best (i.e. '4') to worst (i.e. '1'). Thus, the ordered pair (4,1) beneath the outcome *A gains advantage* signifies that this outcome is best for State A and worst for State B. Similarly, the outcome *Tacit arms control* is next best for both players.

In game theory the players are assumed to be instrumentally *rational*. Rational players are those who maximize their utility. Utility, though, is a subjective concept. It indicates the worth of an outcome *to a particular player*. Since different players may evaluate the same outcome differently, the rationality assumption is simply another way of saying that the players are purposeful, that they are pursuing goals (or interests) that they themselves define.

Rationality, however, does not require that the players are necessarily intelligent in setting their goals. It may sometimes be the case that the players are woefully misinformed about the world and, as a consequence, have totally unreasonable objectives. Still, as long as they are purposeful and act to bring about their goals, they may be said to be instrumentally rational.[4]

Rationality also does not imply that the players will do well and obtain their stated objective, as is easily demonstrated by identifying the *solution* to the Arms Race game. A solution to any strategic-form game consists of the identification of (1) the best, or optimal, strategy for each player, and (2) the likely outcome of the game. The Arms Race game has a straightforward solution.

Notice first that each player (State) in the Arms Race game has a *strictly dominant strategy*; that is, a strategy that is always best regardless of the strategy selected by the other player. For instance, if State B chooses not to arm, State A will bring about its next-best outcome (3) if it also chooses not to arm, but will receive its best outcome (4) if it chooses to arm. Thus, when State B chooses (C), State A does better by choosing (D). Similarly, if State B chooses to arm, State A will bring about its worst outcome (1) if it chooses not to arm, but will receive its next-worst outcome (2) if it chooses to arm. Again, when State B chooses (D), State A does better by choosing (D). Regardless of what strategy State B selects, therefore, State A should choose (D) and arm. By symmetry, State B should also choose to defect by arming. And, when both players choose their unconditionally best strategy, the outcome is an arms race – which is next worst for both players.

The strategy pair (D,D) associated with the outcome labelled *Arms Race* has a very important property that qualifies it to be part of the solution to the game of Figure 4.1. It is called a *Nash equilibrium* – named after John Nash, the subject of the film *A Beautiful Mind* and a co-recipient of the Nobel Prize in economics in 1994 which, not coincidentally, was the fiftieth anniversary of the publication of Von Neumann and Morgenstern's monumental opus. If a strategy pair is a Nash equilibrium, neither player has an incentive to switch to another strategy, provided that the other player does not also switch to another strategy.

To illustrate, observe that if both States A and B choose to arm (D), State A's payoff will be its second best (2). But if it then decides to not arm (C), its payoff is its worst (1). In consequence, State A has no incentive to switch strategies if both states choose to arm. The same is true of State B. The strategy pair (D,D), therefore, is said to be stable or in equilibrium.

There is no other strategy pair with this property in the Arms Race game, as is easily demonstrated. For instance, consider the strategy pair (C,C) associated with the outcome *Tacit arms control*. This outcome is second-best for both players. Nonetheless, both players have an incentive to switch, uni-laterally, to another strategy in order to bring about a better outcome. State B, for instance, can bring about its best outcome (4) by simply switching to its (D) strategy. Thus, the payoff pair (C,C) is not a Nash equilibrium. The same is true for the remaining two strategy pairs in this game, (C,D) and (D,C).

For reasons that will be more fully explained below, strategy pairs that form a Nash equilibrium provide a *minimum* definition of rational choice in a game. By contrast, strategy pairs that are not in equilibrium are simply inconsistent with rational choice and purposeful action. This is why only Nash equilibria can be part of a game's solution.

But notice that *both* players do worse when they are rational and select (D) than when *both* make an irrational choice and select (C). In other words, two rational players do worse in this game than two irrational players! Paradoxically, however, it is also true that *each* player always does best by choosing (D), all of which raises a very important question for the two states in our game. Can they, if they are rational, avoid an arms race and, if so, under what conditions? More generally, can two or more states ruthlessly pursuing their own interests find a way to cooperate in an anarchic international system?

Space considerations preclude an answer, game-theoretic or otherwise, to this question here. Suffice it to say that it is an issue that lies at the heart of the ongoing debate between realists and liberals about the very nature of international politics. That the (Prisoners' Dilemma) game in Figure 4.1 both highlights and neatly encapsulates such a core problem must be counted among game theory's many contributions to the field of security studies.[5]

Even though rational players do not fare well in this game, the game itself has a well-defined solution that helps to explain, *inter alia*, why great states sometimes engage in senseless and costly arms competitions that leave them no more secure than they would have been if they had chosen not to arm. The solution is well defined because there is only one outcome in the game that is consistent with rational contingent decision-making by all of the players, the unique Nash equilibrium (D,D).

Not all games, however, have a solution that is so clear-cut. Consider, for example, the two-person game in Figure 4.2 that was originally analysed by John Harsanyi (1977), another 1994 Nobel Prize laureate in economics. As before, the two players, States A and B, have two strategies: either to cooperate (C) or to defect (D) from cooperation. State A's strategies are listed as the rows of the matrix, while B's strategies are given by the columns. Since each player has two strategies, there are $2 \times 2 = 4$ possible strategy combinations and four possible outcomes. The payoffs to State A and State B, respectively, are again represented by an ordered pair in each cell of the matrix.

Of these four strategy combinations, two are Nash equilibria, as indicated by the asterisks (*). Strategy pair (D,D) is in equilibrium since either player would do worse by switching, unilaterally, to its other strategy. Specifically, were State A to switch from its (D) strategy to its (C) strategy, which would induce Outcome CD, State A's payoff would go from '2' – A's best – to '1' – its next

		State B	
		Cooperate (C)	Defect (D)
State A	Cooperate (C)	*Outcome CC* (1,3)*	*Outcome CD* (1,3)
	Defect (D)	*Outcome DC* (0,0)	*Outcome DD* (2,2)*

Key: (x,y) = payoff to State A, payoff to State B
    * = Nash equilibrium

Figure 4.2 Strategic-form game with two Nash equilibria (Harsanyi's game)

best. And if State B were to switch to its (C) strategy, B's payoff would go from '2' – its next best – to '0' – its worst. Thus, neither player benefits by switching unilaterally to another strategy, so (D,D) is a Nash equilibrium. For similar reasons, strategy pair (C,C) is also a Nash equilibrium; neither player benefits by switching, unilaterally, to its (D) strategy. By contrast, neither of the remaining two strategy pairs is stable in the sense of Nash because at least one player would gain by changing to another strategy.

The existence of two or more Nash equilibria in a strategic-form game can confound analysis. When only one Nash equilibrium exists in a game, it is easy to specify a game's solution. But when two or more equilibria exist, it is clearly more difficult to identify the likely outcome of a game or the best strategy of the players – unless there are criteria that allow discrimination among equilibria and the elimination of some stable strategy pairs from the solution set.

Of course, the possible existence of multiple Nash equilibria in a strategic-form game would not be problematic if all equilibria were *equivalent* – that is, if all extant equilibria have exactly the same consequences for the players – and *interchangeable* – in the sense that every possible combination of equilibrium strategies are also in equilibrium.

John Nash (1951) proved long ago that when multiple equilibria exist in a zero-sum game, all equilibrium pairs are both equivalent and interchangeable. But this is clearly not the case in the non-zero-sum game in Figure 4.2. The two equilibria are not equivalent simply because the player's payoffs are different under each equilibrium. For instance, State A's best outcome is associated with the strategy pair (D,D); its next-best outcome with the strategy pair (C,C). The two equilibria are also not interchangeable. Although the strategy pairs (C,C) and (D,D) are in equilibrium, the pairs (C,D) and (D,C) are not. This means that the players cannot use the strategies associated with the two Nash equilibria interchangeably.

Although the two Nash equilibria in the game in Figure 4.2 are neither equivalent nor interchangeable, there is one way in which they can be distinguished. Notice that State B's defection (D) strategy *weakly dominates* its cooperation (C) strategy; that is, it provides State B with a payoff that is at least as good, and sometimes better, than its other strategy, no matter what strategy State A selects.[6] Thus, there is a good reason to expect that State B will choose (D).

Notice also that, if State B defects, State A does better by also defecting. Given that State B defects, State A will receive its highest payoff (2) by defecting, but only its second highest payoff (1) by cooperating. Since the strategy pair (D,D) is associated with State B's unconditionally best (or *dominant*) strategy, and State A's best response to B's unconditionally best strategy, one may very well argue that it, and not strategy pair (C,C), is the equilibrium that best qualifies as the solution to Harsanyi's game.

However, before this conclusion is accepted, there is one significant objection that must be considered: the fact that strategy pair (D,D) favours State A at the expense of State B. State B's payoff is clearly better under (C,C) than it is under (D,D), while it is the other way around for State A. Is there nothing that State B can do to induce the more preferred payoff associated with the equilibrium (C,C)?

One might argue that State B could do better in this game by threatening to choose (C) if State A selects (D), thereby inducing State A to choose (C) and bringing about State B's most preferred outcome. But this line of argument is deficient. To understand why, we next explore an alternative representation of Harsanyi's game, the *extensive-form*.

Extensive-form games, backwards induction and subgame perfect equilibria

Figure 4.2 represents Harsanyi's game in strategic-form; Figure 4.3 represents it in extensive-form. There are a number of important differences between the two forms of representation. In the strategic-form, players select strategies which, it will be recalled, are a complete plan of action specifying what a player will do at every decision point in a game. As well, the players are assumed to make their choice simultaneously or, in what amounts to the same thing, without information about what strategy the other player has selected.

By contrast, in the extensive-form, the players make *moves* sequentially; that is, they select from among the collection of *choices* available at any one time. In the extensive-form, moves are represented by *nodes* on a game tree. The *branches* of the tree at any one node summarize the choices available to a player at a particular point in a game. The payoffs to the players are given by an ordered pair at each terminal node. In an extensive-form game of *perfect*

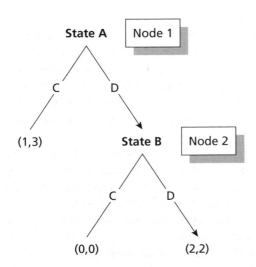

Key: (x,y) = payoff to State A, payoff to State B
———→ = rational choice

Figure 4.3 Extensive-form representation of Harsanyi's game

information, the players know where they are in the game tree whenever there is an opportunity to make a choice. Harsanyi's game is an example of a game of perfect information. In a game with *imperfect information*, the players may not always know what prior choices have been made.

To solve any extensive-form game, a procedure known as *backwards induction* must be used. As its name suggests, backwards induction involves working backwards up the game tree to determine, first, what a rational player would do at the last node of the tree, what the player with the previous move would do given that the player with the last move is rational, and so on until the first node of the tree is reached. We will now use this procedure to analyse the extensive-form representation of Harsanyi's game. More specifically, we now seek to establish why State B cannot rationally threaten to select (C) at node 2 in order to induce State A's cooperation at node 1, thereby bringing about State B's highest ranked outcome (1,3).

To this end, we begin by considering the calculus of State A at the first node of the tree. At node 1 State A can either select (C) and induce its second-best outcome, or select (D), which might result either in State A's best or its worst outcome. Clearly, State A should (rationally) choose (C) if it expects State B to also select (C), since the choice of (D) would then result in State A's worst outcome. Conversely, State A should select (D) if it expects State B to select (D), since this induces State A's best outcome. The question is: What should State A expect State B to do? Before we can answer this question, we must first consider State B's choice at the last node of the tree.

If State A assumes that State B is rational, then State A should expect State B to select (D) if and when State B makes its choice at node 2. The reason is straightforward: State B's worst outcome is associated with its choice of (C), its next-best outcome with its choice of (D). To expect State B to carry out the threat to choose (C) if A chooses (D), then, is to assume that State B is irrational. It follows that for State B to expect State A to select (C) is to assume that State B harbours irrational expectations about State A. To put this in a slightly different way, State B's threat is not credible; that is, it is not rational to carry out. Since it is not credible, State A may safely ignore it.

Notice what the application of backwards induction to Harsanyi's game reveals: State B's rational choice at node 2 is (D). In consequence, State A should also choose (D) at node 1. Significantly, the strategy pair (D,D) associated with these choices is in equilibrium in the same sense that the two Nash equilibria are in the strategic-form game of Figure 4.2: neither player has an incentive to switch to another strategy provided the other player does not also switch. But, also significantly, the second Nash equilibrium (C,C) is nowhere to be found. Because it was based on an incredible threat, it was eliminated by the backwards induction procedure.

The unique equilibrium pair (D,D) that emerges from an analysis of the extensive-form game of Figure 4.3 is called a *subgame perfect equilibrium*.[7] The concept of subgame perfection was developed by Reinhard Selten (1975), the third and final recipient of the 1994 Nobel Prize in economics.[8] Selten's perfectness criterion constitutes an extremely useful and important refinement of Nash's equilibrium concept. It is a refinement because it eliminates less than perfect Nash equilibria from the set of candidates eligible for consideration as a game's solution. As well, Selten's idea of subgame perfection helps us to understand more deeply the meaning of rational choice as it applies to individuals, to groups, or even to great states involved in a conflictual relationship.

It is important to know that all subgame perfect equilibria are also Nash equilibria, but not the other way around. As demonstrated above, those Nash equilibria, such as the strategy pair (C,C) in the game in Figure 4.2, which are based on threats that lack credibility, are simply not perfect. As Harsanyi (1977: 332) puts it, these less than perfect equilibria should be considered deficient because they involve both 'irrational behavior and irrational expectations by the players about each other's behavior'.

Applications of game theory in security studies

Speaking more pragmatically, the refinement of Nash's equilibrium concept represented by the idea of a subgame perfect equilibrium and related solution concepts – such as *Bayesian Nash equilibria* and *Perfect Bayesian equilibria* – permits analysts to develop more nuanced explanations and more potent predictions of interstate conflict behaviour when applying game theory to the field of security studies.[9] It is to a brief enumeration of some of these applications, and a specific illustration of one particular application, that we turn next.

As noted earlier, applications, extensions, modifications and illustrations of game-theoretic models began to appear in the security studies literature shortly after the publication of *Theory of Games and Economic Behavior* (1944). Since then, the literature has grown exponentially and its influence on the field of security studies has been significant.[10] As Walt has observed:

> Rational choice models have been an accepted part of the academic study of politics since the 1950s, but their popularity has grown significantly in recent years. Elite academic departments are now expected to include game theorists and other formal modelers in order to be regarded as 'up to date,' graduate students increasingly view the use of formal rational choice models as a prerequisite for professional advancement, and research employing rational choice methods is becoming more widespread throughout the discipline.
>
> (Walt 1999: 5)

Walt (1999: 7) goes on to express the fear that game-theoretic and related rational choice models are becoming so pervasive, and that their influence has been so strong, that other approaches are on the cusp of marginalization.

Although Martin (1999: 74) unquestionably demonstrates, empirically, that Walt's fear is 'unfounded', there is little doubt that game-theoretic studies are now part and parcel of the security studies literature.

Among the subject areas of security studies that have been heavily influenced by game-theoretic reasoning are the onset (Bueno de Mesquita and Lalman 1992) and escalation (Carlson 1995) of interstate conflict and war, the consequences of alliances (Smith 1995) and alignment patterns (Zagare and Kilgour 2003), the effectiveness of missile defence systems (Powell 2003, Quackenbush 2006), the impact of domestic politics on interstate conflict (Fearon 1994), the dynamics of arms races and the functioning of arms control (Brams and Kilgour 1988), the spread of terrorism (Bueno de Mesquita 2005), the dangers of nuclear proliferation (Kraig 1999), the implications of democratization for coercive diplomacy (Shultz 2001), the characteristics of crisis bargaining (Banks 1990), and the operation of balance of power politics (Niou *et al.* 1989), to name but a few.[11] In addition, as noted above, game-theoretic models have played a central role in the debate between realists and liberals about the relative importance of absolute and relative gains and about the possibility of significant great power cooperation (see note 5).

It is clear, however, that there has been no area of security studies in which game theory has been more influential than in the study of deterrence. Accordingly, I now turn to a brief discussion of this subject and attempt to illustrate, with a simple example, how game theory can help not only to clarify core concepts, but also to shed light on the conditions that lead to successful deterrence.

Although it may be somewhat of a stretch to say that Schelling was the inventor of classical deterrence theory, as does Zakaria (2001), his work is a good place to start (for an overview see Zagare 1996). Like all classical deterrence theorists, Schelling's work is characterized by two core assumptions: (1) that states (or their decision-makers) are rational; and (2) that, especially in the nuclear age, war or conflict is the worst possible outcome of any deterrence encounter. It is not difficult to demonstrate that these two assumptions are incompatible with the conclusion of most deterrence theorists that bilateral nuclear relationships, such as that between the USA and the Soviet Union during the Cold War, are inordinately stable.

To see this, consider now the Rudimentary asymmetric deterrence game as given in Figure 4.4. In this, perhaps, the simplest deterrence game one can imagine, State A begins play at node 1 by deciding whether to *concede* (C) and accept the status quo, or to *demand* (D) its alteration. If State A chooses (C), the game ends and the outcome is the *Status Quo*. But if State A defects, State B must decide at node 2 whether to *concede* (C) the issue – in which case the outcome is *A wins* – or *deny* (D) the demand and precipitate *Conflict*. Notice that the endpoints of this simple deterrence game list outcomes rather than player payoffs. I list outcomes and not payoffs in this example in order to use the same game-form to analyse the strategic implications of more than one payoff configuration.

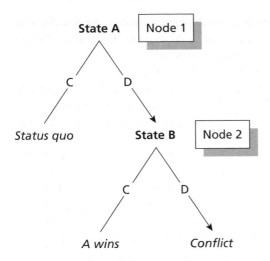

Figure 4.4 The rudimentary asymmetric deterrence game

Next we determine what rational players would do in this game – given the assumption that *Conflict* is the worst outcome for both players – by applying backwards induction to the game tree. Since the application of this procedure requires one to work backwards up the game tree, we begin by considering State B's move at decision node 2.

At node 2, State B is faced with a choice between choosing (C), which brings about outcome *A wins*, and choosing (D), which brings about *Conflict*. But if *Conflict* is assumed to be the *worst* possible outcome, State B, if it is rational, can *only* choose to concede since, by assumption, *A wins* is the more preferred outcome.

Given that State B will rationally choose to concede at node 2, what should State A do at node 1? State A can concede, in which case the outcome will be the *Status Quo*, or it can defect, in which case the outcome will be *A wins* – because a rational State B will choose to concede at node 2. If State A has an incentive to upset the *Status Quo*, that is, if it needs to be deterred because it prefers *A wins* to the *Status Quo*, it will rationally choose (D). Thus, given the core assumptions of classical deterrence theory, the *Status Quo* is unstable and deterrence rationally fails.

To put this in a slightly different way, one can reasonably assume that states are rational, and one can also reasonably assume that war is the worst imaginable outcome for all the players, but one cannot make both these assumptions at the same time and logically conclude, as classical deterrence theorists do, that deterrence will succeed.

Logically inconsistent theories are clearly problematic. Since *any* conclusion can be derived from them, inconsistent theories can explain *any* empirical observation. Inconsistent theories, therefore, are non-falsifiable and of little practical use. When used properly, formal structures, like game theory, can help in the identification of flawed theory.

If the core assumptions of classical deterrence theory are inconsistent with the possibility of deterrence success, what assumptions are consistent? It is easy to demonstrate that in the rudimentary asymmetric deterrence game the *Status Quo* may remain stable, and deterrence may succeed, but only if State B's threat is credible in the sense of Selten; that is, if it is rational to carry out.

To understand this, assume now that State B prefers *Conflict* to *A wins*. (Note that this assumption implies that *Conflict* is not the worst possible outcome for State B.) With this assumption, State B's rational choice at node 2 changes. Given its preference, its rational choice at node 2 is now to choose (D) and deny State A's demand for a change in the *Status Quo*.

However, State B's rational choice is not the only rational choice that changes with this new assumption. The rational choice of State A is also different. Applying backwards induction to State A's decision at node 1 now reveals a choice between *Status Quo* and *Conflict*. This means that the *Status Quo* will persist, and deterrence will succeed, *as long as State A's preference is for peace over war*. On the other hand, it will fail whenever this latter preference is reversed, even when State B's node 2 threat is credible.

At this juncture, two final observations can be made. The first is about the relationship between credible threats and deterrence success. Apparently, credibility is not, as Freedman (1989: 96) claims, the 'magic ingredient' of deterrence. As demonstrated above, a credible threat is not sufficient to ensure deterrence success. Deterrence may rationally fail even when all deterrent threats are rational to execute.

Still, in order to explain even the possibility of deterrence success in this simple example, a core assumption of classical deterrence theory had to be modified. But any analysis that proceeds from a different set of assumptions will constitute an entirely different theory. This is no small matter. As illustrated in the films *Sliding Doors* and *Run Lola Run*, and as demonstrated in Zagare (2004) and Zagare and Kilgour (2000), small differences in initial assumptions can have important theoretical consequences and significant policy differences. It is one of the strengths of game theory that its formal structure facilitates the identification of inconsistent assumptions, highlights the implications of initial assumptions, and increases the probability of logical argumentation.

Coda

This chapter provides a gentle introduction to the key concepts and assumptions of game theory as it applies to the field of security studies. The examples used to illustrate many of these terms were meant to be suggestive, and not definitive. In the space of such a short chapter, this is the best that could be done. And although an attempt has been made to point the reader to relevant applications of the theory, this effort, too, can only be thought of as being cursory. The securities studies literature that draws on, or has been influenced by, game-theoretic reasoning is vast. Nonetheless, the reader should now possess the conceptual tools that are a prerequisite for further exploration of this increasingly important body of literature.

Notes

1 For the connections between realism and game theory, see Jervis 1988.
2 For obvious reasons, such a game is called a two-person game. Games with three or more players are referred to as *n-person games*. The latter are not discussed in this brief chapter.
3 Space considerations preclude a discussion of the story that gives this game its more common name. It is told, however, in most game theory textbooks, including Zagare 1984.
4 For an extended discussion of the rationality assumption see Zagare 1990.
5 A good place to start when exploring this and related issues is Oye 1986. Baldwin (1993) contains a useful collection of articles, many of which are seminal. Axelrod (1984), who provides one prominent game-theoretic perspective, should also be consulted. See also Chapter 10, this volume.
6 By contrast, a *strictly dominant strategy* always provides a player with a strictly higher payoff than any other strategy, no matter what strategies other players select. Both players in the Arms Race game in Figure 4.1 possess strictly dominant strategies. For a further discussion of this and related concepts, see Zagare 1984.
7 A *subgame* is that part of an extensive-form game that can be considered a game unto itself. For a more detailed definition, with pertinent examples, see Morrow 1994: ch. 2.
8 Recall that John Nash and John Harsanyi were the other two.
9 Nash and subgame perfect equilibria are the accepted measures of rational behaviour in games of *complete* information, in which each player is fully informed about the preferences of its opponent. In games of *incomplete* information in which at least one player is uncertain about the other's preferences, rational choices are associated with *Bayesian Nash equilibria* (in strategic-form games) and with *perfect Bayesian equilibria* (in extensive-form games). See Gibbons (1992) for a helpful discussion.
10 An insightful review of the accomplishments and the limitations of the approach may be found in Bueno de Mesquita (2002). See Brams (2002) for an example of the theory in action.
11 This listing is meant to be suggestive. It is by no means exhaustive. Useful reviews include O'Neill (1994a, 1994b) and Snidal (2002).

Further reading

Michael Brown, Owen R. Coté Jr., Sean M. Lynn-Jones and Steven E. Miller (eds), *Rational Choice and Security Studies* (Cambridge, MA: MIT Press,

1999). Contains a spirited debate about the contributions of game-theoretic and related approaches to the security studies literature.

Sylvia Nasar, *A Beautiful Mind* (New York: Simon & Schuster, 1998). A very readable biography of John Nash, one of the central figures of game theory.

Thomas C. Schelling, *Arms and Influence* (New Haven, CT: Yale University Press, 1966). One of the earliest and certainly one of the most influential works to draw on game theory in the analysis of interstate conflict.

Duncan Snidal, 'Rational choice and International Relations' in Walter Carlsnaes, Thomas Risse and Beth A. Simmons (eds), *Handbook of International Relations* (Thousand Oaks, CA: Sage, 2002). A fair and balanced assessment of the strengths and weaknesses of the rational choice approach.

Frank C. Zagare and D. Marc Kilgour, *Perfect Deterrence* (Cambridge: Cambridge University Press, 2000). Uses simple and advanced game-theoretic models to develop a general theory of interstate conflict initiation, limitation, escalation and resolution.

Constructivism

Matt McDonald

Abstract

Constructivism has become an increasingly prominent theoretical approach to International Relations since its emergence in the 1980s. Focusing on the role of ideational factors and the social construction of world politics, it is perhaps best described as a broader social theory which then informs how we might approach the study of security. The exception in this case is the Copenhagen School, which develops a framework for approaching the construction of security based on 'speech acts' that designate particular issues or actors as existential threats. This chapter begins by drawing out some of the shared assumptions of constructivist approaches to the study of security. It then outlines the Copenhagen School framework in more depth, exploring the nature of its contribution to our understanding of security.

Introduction: constructivism and security

Constructivism has become an increasingly prominent theoretical approach to International Relations since its emergence in the 1980s. Drawing on a combination of sociological approaches and critical theory, constructivists argue that the world is constituted socially through intersubjective interaction; that agents and structures are mutually constituted; and that ideational factors such as norms, identity and ideas generally are central to the constitution and dynamics of world politics. It is less a theory of International Relations or security, however, than a broader social theory which then informs how we might approach the study of security. The exception in this case is the Copenhagen School, which develops a framework for approaching the construction of security based on 'speech acts' that designate particular issues or actors as existential threats. This chapter begins by drawing out some of the shared assumptions of constructivist approaches to the study of security. It then outlines the Copenhagen School framework in more depth, exploring the nature of its contribution to our understanding of security.

Constructivism: central tenets and shared assumptions

Constructivism, a term first elaborated by Nicholas Onuf in his groundbreaking book *World of Our Making* in 1989, is a broad theoretical approach to the study of International Relations that has been applied to a range of issues, from political economy (Blyth 2002) to international organization (Ruggie 1999: 41–130, Barnett and Finnemore 2004) and security (Katzenstein 1996b, Weldes *et al.* 1999). Despite attention to security issues, however, the extent to which constructivists have developed a theory of international security is limited. This distinguishes constructivists from critical theorists (with their conception of security defined as a commitment to emancipation) and realists (whose theory of world politics as a whole is to a significant degree a theory of security and power politics). From the realist perspective, one prominent (if misguided) perception is that constructivism has generally eschewed a focus on the power politics of security and focused instead on the development of benign norms for managing interstate competition and institutionalizing broader forms of political community (see Mearsheimer 1994/95).

Such a perception indicates the commitment of realists to a narrow conception of security, defined in terms of states, militaries and the use or threat of force. But it is also little more than a caricature of constructivism in International Relations. Constructivists would argue that their approach actually enables a more sophisticated and complete understanding of dynamics traditionally associated with realist approaches to security, from that of the nature of power generally (Barnett and Duvall 2005) to the security dilemma and the balance of power (Hopf 1998). And as Friedrich Kratochwil (1993) and Alexander Wendt (1992) have argued, constructivist approaches are able to come to terms with periods of structural change enabled by strategic actors in world politics; most prominently the end of the Cold War. This places such approaches in a particularly strong position relative to structuralist theories such as neorealism that assume sets of interests held by all actors created by the nature of the international system itself.

Security as social construction: identity and norms

Arguably the central shared assumption of constructivist approaches to security is that security is a social construction. As Karin Fierke (2007: 56) has argued, 'to construct something is an act which brings into being a subject or object that otherwise would not exist'. This does not necessarily mean that there is no such thing as 'security' or that security is devoid of meaning. Security may be understood, for example, as the preservation of a group's core values. But such a broad definition of security tells us little about who the group itself is; what its core values are; where threats to those values may come from; and how the preservation or advancement of these values might be achieved (McDonald 2002). For constructivists, answers to these questions are different in different contexts and develop through social interaction between actors. And it is the answers to these questions – articulated and negotiated in a particular social and historical context through social interaction – that bring security into being.

Constructivists are therefore united in their commitment to avoiding universal and abstract analytical definitions of security, but the form this commitment takes is different for different authors. At its most obvious, Ted Hopf (1998) points to the impossibility of making universal and abstract claims about the source of threat in world politics. For Hopf (1998), state political leaders designate other states as 'friend' or 'enemy' – and approach them as such – on the basis of conceptions of identity.

The invasion of Iraq in 2003, for example, highlights the way in which the meaning of security is constructed and mediated through different understandings of identity. Why, in this context, was the possibility that Saddam Hussein *might* be developing nuclear weapons in 2002 to 2003 deemed far more of a threat for the United Kingdom and the United States than the existing nuclear arsenals of states such as Russia, China, France, Pakistan, India or Israel, indeed enough to warrant military intervention and regime change? A constructivist analysis would emphasize the importance of a range of social, cultural and historical factors that encourage particular forms of meaning to be given to different actors and their intentions. In this context, these might include historical experiences of conflict with the Saddam Hussein regime in the first Gulf War or Iraq's radically different political system than that of the USA and the UK. Some working within the constructivist tradition would go so far as to suggest that the 'threat' posed by Iraq was itself brought into being (i.e. constructed) through *representations* of the Iraqi regime as a dangerous or threatening 'other'. Such an approach might focus on how political leaders in the USA and UK denounced Hussein's regime as a rogue or pariah state, operating outside the bounds of legitimate statehood in international society. These different approaches to the security–identity relationship are elaborated in Box 5.1.

Acknowledging the relevance of identity to security in constructivist approaches leads to a more fundamental shared assumption for constructivists: that non-material or ideational factors in general are central to the construction and practices of security in world politics. Aside from identity (perceptions of

BOX 5.1 CONSTRUCTIVISMS AND IDENTITY

While all constructivists share a belief in the centrality of identity to the construction of security, different strands of constructivism see the relationship between identity and security quite differently. In fact debates over 'identity' are a useful site for exploring the difference between 'conventional' and 'critical' constructivist frameworks (Hopf 1998: 181–185). *Conventional constructivism* is closer to traditional theories of International Relations such as realism and liberalism in suggesting the possibility of depicting a world external to the analyst – a world 'out there' to be discovered and described objectively. *Critical constructivism*, on the other hand, points to the importance of forms of representation in constituting the 'real' world.

For *conventional constructivists*, the central concern in outlining the relationship between security and identity is to point to how national identity (and associated historical experience or cultural context) helps determine the content of a state's interests and therefore the way it will 'act' in global politics. Here, identity is something to be discovered or unearthed through analysis. This view is consistent with a commitment to a positivist epistemology: a belief that analysts can potentially hold a mirror to a world 'out there'. Within this framework, identities are defined as relatively stable or sedimented, enabling the analyst to explore 'why' states act the way they do in ways that suggest a causal relationship between identity and interests. The work of Peter Katzenstein (1996a) and Alexander Wendt (1999) is emblematic of this approach: both have suggested the possibility of working within the epistemological and methodological frameworks of traditional International Relations theory, and both ultimately position constructivism as an ideational supplement to materialist approaches within the discipline.

For *critical constructivists*, the central concern in exploring the relationship between security and identity is to outline how narratives of national identity (and representations of history, for example) become dominant in a particular context. These, in turn, help set the limits for legitimate or feasible political action. Here, identity is inherently unstable, contingent and a site of constant competition. Representations of security and threat can be central in this regard, serving to define who 'we' are and the 'other/s' from whom 'we' need protection. The study of identity, then, becomes the study of different representations that compete with others to provide realistic accounts of who a particular group is and how that group should act. For critical constructivists, analysts attempting to define a nation-state's 'national identity' risk engaging in this power–political struggle by privileging some narratives of identity and marginalizing others. Such a position is consistent with a post-positivist epistemology, in which it becomes impossible for the analyst to stand outside the world s/he is attempting to define or describe. The concern here is less with 'why' states act the way they do than 'how possible' questions: 'how meanings are produced and attached to various social subjects/objects, thus constituting particular interpretive dispositions which create certain possibilities and preclude others' (Doty 1993: 298). Key theorists working in this strand of constructivism include Jutta Weldes (1996), Roxanne Lynn Doty (1993), Karin Fierke (1998) and Michael Barnett (1999), whose work we will look at more closely later.

who we are) the most prominent ideational dimension of world politics addressed by constructivists is the role of norms. Norms may be defined as shared expectations about appropriate or legitimate behaviour by actors with a particular identity. Most commonly, this is applied to dominant ideas about what constitutes appropriate behaviour for the key members of international society: states. Such a research programme builds on English School approaches to International Relations (Reus-Smit 2002). Constructivists have devoted a significant amount of time and research activity to exploring how international norms evolve and come to provide limits to acceptable state behaviour in general (Finnemore 1996), and regarding issues as disparate as colonialism (Crawford 2003) and the use of nuclear weapons (Tannenwald 2007).

In the example of the intervention in Iraq in 2003, a focus solely on the material capabilities of different actors clearly provides an incomplete and potentially misleading account of how dominant understandings and practices of security in world politics emerge. Instead, constructivists would point to the role of both identity and norms in conditioning perceptions of the Saddam Hussein regime as a threat to global or regional security. For constructivists, expectations of appropriate behaviour mattered in the construction of threat in this case. This may be seen in the relatively consistent definition of Iraq as a pariah state, and in the invocation of Saddam Hussein's specific violations of rules and norms regarding the use of chemical and biological weapons. Constructivists are able to highlight the ways in which perceptions of threat are linked (for example) to both the politics of identity and perceptions of the legitimacy of particular actors according to sets of shared norms.

The example of the Iraq war above suggests that security is socially constructed in the sense that 'threats' are brought into being rather than meeting an abstract set of criteria about what counts as a security issue. But it is also possible to argue, as some constructivists have, that security is constructed in the sense that different actors behave according to different discourses – 'frameworks of meaning' – of security. Roxanne Lynn Doty (1998/99) gives the example of the US government's approach to the Haitian coup crisis of the 1990s in suggesting that the determinant of how the US dealt with refugees from Haiti had less to do with their designation as 'threats' than the understanding of security with which the US government was operating. She suggests that from 1991 to 1994, different discourses of security captured the way the US government approached Haitian refugees. These different discourses – from a realist national security discourse to a human security one

– had radically different implications for the way refugees themselves were treated. In this analysis, it is less a case of security having meaning through the designation of threat than the designation of threat occurring because of the adoption of a particular perspective on security. This suggests that conceptions of who we are and what we value encourage particular ways of thinking about where threats to those values might come from, what form they might take and how they might be dealt with.

One particularly useful way of conceptualizing a constructivist approach to security is to think of security itself as a 'thick signifier' (Huysmans 1998). This involves moving away from ascribing a specific meaning to security (as 'emancipation' or 'the territorial preservation of the state', for example), and instead focusing on what particular political function security plays in social life. For Huysmans (1998: 228), a definition of security 'articulates particular understandings of our relations to nature, other human beings and the self. "Security" refers to a wider framework of meaning . . . within which we organize particular forms of life.' In other words, different articulations of security suggest different definitions of political community and that community's core values.

Negotiation and contestation

For constructivists, then, security is a context-specific social construction. Instead of developing abstract definitions of security, constructivists work from the premise that we would do better to focus on how security is given meaning within these contexts and analyse the implications this has for political practice. In exploring how security is given meaning, constructivists have emphasized that security is a site of negotiation (between political leaders and domestic audiences in particular) and contestation (between different actors elaborating different visions of 'our' values and how 'we' should act).

The idea of security as a site of negotiation between actors claiming to speak for a particular group and members of the group is a prominent feature of constructivist approaches to security. In realist approaches, security is enacted at the level of policy elites with negotiation between policy elites and the public having little or no role. In post-structural approaches, meanwhile, a state's general public is a relatively passive target of elite policy discourses that bind the individual to the nation-state (Campbell 1992). Constructivist approaches contest these positions and point to the importance of public support for or acquiescence to elite discourses. They would further suggest that they are in a relatively strong position to account for instances where members of the public within states, for example, are able to effect change in foreign or security policy discourse and practices. Such change might occur through the work of various non-state actors in altering the normative context in which policy elites operate (Keck and Sikkink 1998).

Constructivists, particularly 'critical constructivists', have attempted to make sense of the relationship between political leaders and domestic audiences in a range of ways, emphasizing the role of representation. Roxanne Lynn Doty

(1993: 303) suggests that 'even speeches and press conference statements produced for specific purposes, in order to be taken seriously, must make sense and fit with what the general public takes as "reality"'. Karin Fierke (1998) points to the role of 'language games' in suggesting that representations of security policy must be located in particular frameworks of communication to make sense, frameworks that change across different social contexts. Jutta Weldes (1996), meanwhile, develops Althusser's concepts of articulation and interpellation to suggest that representations of security can become acceptable if they are able to 'hail' individuals into particular subject positions. A prominent question here in security terms might be whether – in elite representations of the key beliefs and values of a nation-state – individuals recognize themselves as members of such a community. A further example of security as a site of negotiation is illustrated briefly in Box 5.2.

If public support or acquiescence – however defined – is important to the construction of security and enabling for political action, it follows that security itself becomes a site of contestation. This contest takes place between actors searching to put forward their own visions of society and templates for action. Some constructivists (particularly of a critical variety) would agree with post-structuralists' claim that representations of security and threat are potentially

BOX 5.2 BARNETT AND RABIN'S APPROACH TO THE OSLO PEACE ACCORDS

Michael Barnett (1999) attempts to make sense of the relationship between political elites, public audiences and security policy in his analysis of Israeli Prime Minister Yitzhak Rabin's embrace of the Oslo Peace Accord Process with Palestine in the early 1990s. Barnett begins by suggesting that Rabin's proposed withdrawal from the occupied territories would previously have been seen as an abdication of national responsibility and security. He goes on to argue that Rabin was able to position such a withdrawal as a legitimate and even desirable policy option. He did this, Barnett suggests, through locating this policy within particular narratives of Israeli identity and particular historical representations. In the process, not only did Rabin strategically draw on available cultural resources to enable such a policy to resonate with domestic constituents, but he was also effective in marginalizing alternative stories of national identity and history. Rabin, Barnett suggests, was able to emphasize an emergent liberal democratic strand or narrative of national identity while marginalizing the traditionally powerful Jewish–Zionist narrative, thus enabling a more conciliatory approach to Palestinians. This account not only provides insights into how constructivists have understood 'security' as a site of contestation and negotiation, it also provides insights into the relationship between security policy and national identity from a critical constructivist perspective. Here, *representations* of identity and history become central.

performative; that is, they enable or constrain certain types of action. This raises the central question of where dominant security discourses come from. For Weldes *et al.* (1999: 16), definitions of security and threat are contestable and contested, and 'considerable ideological labour' is required to ensure that particular security discourses become and remain dominant. Political elites are central figures in this process, but a range of other actors engage in the construction of security. Stuart Croft (2006), for example, has pointed to the role of the media and popular culture in both reproducing and contesting the security narratives of the US government in the context of the 'war on terror'. For critical constructivists, competition over how to define security and threats to it are played out in a range of different contexts, all potentially with important political implications.

Agents, structures and change

If the above account of security as a site of negotiation and contestation positions world politics generally as a social realm, nowhere is this conception more apparent in constructivist thought than in the view of the relationship between agents and structures and associated possibilities for structural change. For constructivsts, agents and structures are mutually constituted. This view is most neatly captured in Alexander Wendt's seminal 1992 article, 'Anarchy is What States Make of it'. Here, Wendt engages with Kenneth Waltz's neorealist theory of International Relations, which holds that state interests and actions are determined by the structure of the international system itself and its central feature: anarchy. For Waltz, the absence of a higher authority than states in the international system means that states can only rely on themselves for their own survival, requiring a kind of paranoid vigilance and constant preparation for conflict.

For Wendt, there is nothing inevitable about anarchy conditioning state interests and action in the way Waltz suggests. Drawing on the sociologist Anthony Giddens' conception of 'structuration', Wendt suggests that agents (in this case states) can influence the content and effects of a particular structure (in this case anarchy) through the way they act. This meaning is not (and cannot be) a simple reflection of an external material reality, but is developed through intersubjective interaction in the international system. To the extent that anarchy seems to encourage self-help, an overwhelming concern with survival and a view of conflict as an inevitable feature of world politics, it is one of several particular *cultures* of anarchy, rather than a timeless reality. Through their practices, states can either maintain this culture of anarchy or disrupt it, in turn either validating or questioning the normative basis of the international system itself.

This belief in the mutual constitution of agents and structures, and indeed in the socially constructed nature of world politics generally, leads constructivists to conclude that change is always possible. Some care is required here. Constructivists believe that shared understandings about appropriate and legitimate behaviour can become particularly sedimented and even hegemonic.

Indeed, a range of constructivist analyses point to the ways in which particular expectations of appropriate behaviour can become so powerful as to effectively limit the range possibilities for political action globally. This is particularly applicable to norms surrounding trade and the organization of political economy, in which opting out of the international economic framework or acting according to different sets of principles carries penalties for those 'deviants'.

Nevertheless, the belief that structures are socially constructed necessarily suggests the possibility of these structures becoming other than they are. An important example here is the end of the Cold War, which was enabled by actors such as Mikhail Gorbachev 'acting as if' an alternative normative structure was in place and subsequently changing the nature of the structure itself (Fierke 1998). Other constructivists have focused on the possibility for the security dilemma to be ameliorated in different contexts. This is apparent in literature exploring the possibilities for the emergence and development of 'security communities', namely groups of actors (usually states) for whom the use of force in resolving disputes between each other has become unthinkable over time (Adler and Barnett 1998). Here, European security cooperation since 1945 is taken as emblematic of the possibility of building alternative security futures through the development and institutionalization of shared norms. This focus is similarly based on the recognition that the security dilemma and the assumption of mutual distrust upon which it is based is not an inevitable feature of world politics produced by anarchy. Rather, it should be viewed as a social construction that is specific to particular historical moments and particular forms of identity politics.

In summary, constructivists share a belief that security is a social construction, meaning different things in different contexts. Security is also seen as a site of negotiation and contestation, in which actors compete to define the identity and values of a particular group in such a way as to provide a foundation for political action. Identity and norms are seen as central to the study of security, together providing the limits for feasible and legitimate political action. Finally, agents and structures are mutually constituted and, because the world is one of our own making, even structural change is always possible even if difficult. There are not unimportant distinctions between critical and conventional constructivist approaches over conceptual and empirical issues including epistemology and identity, but the core shared commitment to the idea of security as a social construction allows a discussion of a 'constructivist approach to security'.

While constructivists agree that security is a social construction, however, attempts to point more explicitly to how security works and how we might study its construction are more controversial. Most constructivists have avoided this question, but the Copenhagen School has attempted to develop a more coherent theory for the study of security, and is therefore worth exploring in depth.

The Copenhagen School

As noted earlier, the work of the so-called Copenhagen School constitutes the most concerted attempt to develop a theory or framework for the study of security in the constructivist tradition. The Copenhagen School was a label given to the collective research agenda of various academics at the (now defunct) Copenhagen Peace Research Institute in Denmark, centred around the work of Barry Buzan and Ole Wæver. From the early 1990s, various combinations of authors developed a series of observations and arguments about the operation of security in Europe. This collaborative work culminated in the 1998 text, *Security: A New Framework for Analysis*, co-authored by Barry Buzan, Ole Wæver and Jaap de Wilde. The 'School' itself and its central concepts developed over time, less initially as a specific project for the study of security than as a series of interventions on different concepts and cases.

To the extent that a core theme animates the Copenhagen School, it is a primary concern with how security 'works' in world politics. Their approach developed in the context of post-Cold War calls to broaden definitions of security that sought to include a range of pressing and hitherto neglected concerns such as environmental change, poverty and human rights on state security agendas. The Copenhagen School simultaneously contributed to these calls for broadening the concept and attempted to place analytical limits on it. Its adherents have not attempted to develop a framework for how security should be defined or how key actors should approach external security dynamics or crises. Rather, the Copenhagen School has focused on how security itself is given meaning through intersubjective processes and (to a lesser extent) what political effects these security constructions have. Ole Wæver (2004) has suggested that the central concepts are 'sectors', 'regional security complexes' and 'securitization'. Building on the work of Barry Buzan (1991), sectors are defined as arenas entailing particular types of security interaction (Buzan *et al.* 1998: 7–8). Including military, political, economic, societal and environmental fields, for the Copenhagen School these sectors encourage different forms of relationships between relevant actors to develop and generally encourage different definitions of referent object (the 'whom' in 'security for whom?').

Regional security complexes, again developing from Buzan (1991: 186–229) but receiving its fullest treatment in Buzan and Wæver's *Regions and Powers* (2003), are defined as sets of units whose security processes and dynamics 'are so interlinked that their security problems cannot reasonably be analysed or resolved apart from one another' (Buzan *et al.* 1998: 201, Buzan and Wæver 2003: 44). These security complexes are defined in terms of mutually exclusive geographic regions, with *Regions and Powers* focusing on security interaction and dynamics in Europe, the Americas, Asia, the Middle East and Africa. The suggestion here is that the regional level of analysis is becoming increasingly important for global security dynamics but has been poorly theorized.

While these are all important ideas for the approach at an organizational level, the central contribution of the Copenhagen School is the concept of 'securitization'. Indeed, 'sectors' and 'regional security complexes' are significant for the broader framework primarily as either sites for securitization practices or as dynamics conditioning the success or failure of such practices in particular geographical areas.

Securitization, first outlined in depth by Wæver in 1995, refers to the discursive construction of threat. More specifically, securitization may be defined as a process in which an actor declares a particular issue, dynamic or actor to be an 'existential threat' to a particular referent object. If accepted as such by a relevant audience, this enables the suspension of normal politics and the use of emergency measures in responding to that perceived crisis. Security, in this sense, is a site of negotiation between speakers and audiences, albeit one conditioned significantly by the extent to which the speaker enjoys a position of authority within a particular group. Ultimately, Wæver (1995: 57) suggests that successful securitization tends to involve the articulation of threat 'only from a specific place, in an institutional voice, by elites'.

The articulations of threat themselves come in the form of 'speech acts'. Borrowing from the language theory of Austin, speech acts are conceived as forms of representation that do not simply depict a preference or view of an external reality. A parallel illustration here would be that of a marriage, in which saying 'I do' at a particular moment and context *creates* the marriage itself, bringing it into being. For Wæver (1995: 55), by using the language of security and threat 'a state-representative moves a particular development into a specific area, and thereby claims a special right to use whatever means are necessary to block it'. This is one (albeit prominent) example of conceptual development in the Copenhagen School: from originally positioning the speech act itself as securitization, by 1998 these 'speech acts' were defined as securitizing moves, with an 'issue securitized only if and when the audience accepts it as such' (Buzan *et al.* 1998: 25). This acceptance is itself conditioned by the existence of a series of 'facilitating conditions', including the form of the speech act; the position of the securitizing actor; and the 'conditions historically associated with that threat' (Wæver 2000: 252–253, Buzan *et al.* 1998: 31–33).

As its advocates suggest, there is nothing about the securitization framework that prevents it from being applied to groups other than states, but this is certainly the context in which it has been most frequently employed. Here, political leaders can, from a position of authority, claim to be speaking on behalf of the state or the nation, command public attention and enact emergency measures (such as the deployment of troops). This is less a normative choice for the Copenhagen School – a belief in where the study of security *should* be focused – than an analytical one based on the commitment to the idea that 'at the heart of the (security) concept we still find something to do with defence and the state' (Wæver 1995: 47).

Aside from privileging the state in their framework, a further area of bias is arguably that towards the 'West'. For the Copenhagen School, security is defined in opposition to a conception of 'politicization' or 'normal politics' that

---

BOX 5.3 THE COPENHAGEN SCHOOL'S KEY TERMS

▋ *Facilitating conditions*: particular contexts (including the form of the speech act; position of the speaker; and historical conditions associated with threat) that enable the acceptance of a particular securitizing move by the relevant audience.

▋ *Securitizing move*: an actor's attempt to construct an issue or actor as an existential threat to a particular group through a security 'speech act'.

▋ *Securitization*: the process whereby a securitizing actor defines a particular issue or actor as an 'existential threat' to a particular referent object and this move is accepted by a relevant audience.

▋ *Desecuritization*: the process whereby particular issues or actors are removed from the security realm and (re-)enter the realm of 'normal politics'.

▋ *Regional security complex*: a set of units in a particular geographical area whose security processes and dynamics are interlinked to the extent that their security problems need to be understood or addressed in conjunction with each other.

▋ *Security sectors*: fields of activity or arenas (military, societal, political, economic and environmental) that entail particular forms of security interactions and particular definitions of referent objects.

---

is defined by the rule of law, open political deliberation, and is ultimately suggestive of a Western liberal democratic state. Prominent applications of the framework, then, include the ways in which Western political leaders have characterized a particular issue as an existential threat both to the sovereignty of the state and the national identity and cohesion of the nation.

It is when it is applied to the depiction and treatment of immigrants by liberal democratic states that the framework is arguably at its explanatory best: illustrating the ways in which the linguistic depictions of threat serve to give meaning and content to security and enable emergency responses. It also points to the ways in which an issue such as immigration – viewed in traditional security studies as largely irrelevant to security – may be addressed politically in very similar ways to traditional security 'threats'. Closing off borders and even deploying troops – actions seen as the preserve of 'real' security – have been among the responses to immigrants and asylum-seekers in Europe and Australia, for example, particularly in the post-September 11 context (Huysmans 2006, McDonald 2005).

In developing a relatively elegant and tight theoretical framework for security, a number of questions are left unanswered in the Copenhagen School framework. How do we know when an issue has been successfully securitized? Which audience needs to be convinced of the legitimacy of a securitizing move? Can forms of representation other than speech (images, for example) act as such securitizing moves? How significant is the room to move of actors in positioning different actors or issues as threats? For its central theorists, the answers to these questions should depend on the case being explored. For others, there are costs associated with the relatively narrow framework the Copenhagen School has developed (McDonald 2008). Lene Hansen (2000), for example, suggests that the Copenhagen School's ultimate focus on 'dominant voices' contributes to further silencing those already marginalized from security debates. It could also be suggested that the Copenhagen School's expressed preference for *desecuritization* – the removal of issues from the realm of security – is a product of a narrow view of the logic of security that has important normative implications.

One of the key 'moves' of the securitization framework is to suggest that while the content of security is malleable (anything can potentially be viewed as a threat) the logic of security is timeless and universal. In other words, the effects of securitization – the suspension of the normal rules of the game and enabling of emergency measures – will be substantively the same. These effects are generally viewed in a negative light, with 'securitization' implying a form of 'panic politics' (Buzan *et al.* 1998: 34) opposite to politicization. For the Copenhagen School, issues that have moved into the realm of security are dealt with in urgency and secrecy, with few actors able to contribute to political debate about how that issue should be addressed. This form of politics, associated with the work of political theorist Carl Schmitt, is clearly inconsistent with an openly deliberative liberal democratic politics. This explains Wæver's (1995: 56–57) expressed normative preference for desecuritization: the removal of issues from the security agenda.

Two important implications of this point are worth drawing out here. The first is that it suggests a logic of security – associated with secrecy, urgency and 'panic politics' – that is actually quite 'unconstructivist' in the sense that it is positioned as relatively fixed and inevitable. This is taken up by emancipatory critical security theorists who suggest that security can operate according to a different logic: that progressive ends can be achieved *through* security rather than outside it. Roxanne Lynn Doty advances this argument in her analysis of the US government's approach to Haitian refugees, as does Pinar Bilgin in Chapter 7 of this volume. The second key point is that the general preference expressed for desecuritization suggests normative concerns at the heart of a project that has been depicted at other times as an exclusively explanatory one. Along with the stated desire of some critical constructivist scholars of destabilizing dominant (statist) security practices (e.g. Weldes *et al.* 1999), this suggests that constructivists can and do advance normative concerns in their analyses of security. Such a position stands in contrast to the conclusions of conventional constructivists, who would suggest that employing a constructivist approach entails leaving normative concerns to more radical theories (e.g. Farrell 2002). This, in turn, raises important questions about the position of constructivist thought in security studies, given ongoing debate about whether constructivists would be best advised to pursue dialogue and cooperation with critical theorists (Price and Reus-Smit 1998) or with mainstream scholars such as realists and liberals (Wendt 1999, Farrell 2002).

Conclusion

Within International Relations, constructivism is often more readily associated with the development of norms for global governance and the role of ideational factors in world politics generally than with the militarized power politics that characterizes most accounts of security in global politics. Yet constructivists would argue – rightly – that the tools of their analysis enable a far more sophisticated understanding of 'traditional security' dynamics than traditional security approaches. Can we really understand the security dilemma or a state's perceptions of threat without some attention to the role of standards of legitimacy or the politics of identity, for example? And of course, security is – and has always been – far more than the protection of the territorial integrity or sovereignty of the state. Constructivists, with their shared emphasis on the social construction of security, are in a particularly strong position to give us a deeper insight into how security 'works' in world politics, and how politically important conceptions of security and threat actually come into being in different contexts.

Further reading

Barry Buzan, Ole Wæver and Jaap de Wilde, *Security: A New Framework for Analysis* (Boulder, CO: Lynne Rienner, 1998). The key statement to date on the Copenhagen School approach to security.

Karin Fierke, *Critical Approaches to International Security* (Oxford: Polity Press, 2007). An excellent introduction to what it means to think of security as a social construction.

Ted Hopf, 'The promise of constructivism in International Relations theory', *International Security*, 23(1) (1998): 171–200. An excellent overview of the constructivist contribution to the study of International Relations.

Peter Katzenstein (ed.), *The Culture of National Security: Norms and Identity in World Politics* (New York: Columbia University Press, 1996). One of the key texts outlining a (largely conventional) constructivist approach to security and applying it to various cases.

Jutta Weldes *et al.* (eds), *Constructing of Insecurity* (Minneapolis: University of Minnesota Press, 1999). A key text in outlining a critical constructivist approach to security and applying this to various cases.

Alexander Wendt, 'Anarchy is what states make of it: the social construction of power politics', *International Organization*, 46(2) (1992): 391–425. A seminal article pointing to the mutual constitution of structures and agents.

Contents

Peace Studies

Peter Lawler

▍ Abstract

The origins of peace studies lie in the 1950s when scholars on both sides of the Atlantic endeavoured to establish the fields of conflict research and peace research. Initially, the focus was on developing systematic, interdisciplinary studies of conflict and war within the confines of a positivist understanding of social science. This commitment coexisted somewhat uncomfortably with the normative leanings of those early pioneers. Using the work of peace studies' most famous and prolific contributor, Johan Galtung, as the key reference point, this chapter surveys the evolution of contemporary peace studies out of early peace and conflict research, a process which involved both the redefinition of violence and peace, the constant expansion of peace studies' purview, and ultimately a decisive shift away from the foundational commitment to positivism. Given the developments in cognate fields of enquiry, the chapter suggests that the defining feature of peace studies is a normative commitment to non-violence. The chapter concludes by offering two views of contemporary peace studies: a celebratory reading and a more critical view that speculates as to whether the widening of peace studies concerns has come at a price, not least the capacity to address contemporary forms of armed conflict.

Introduction: What is peace studies?

The central concerns of peace studies – the reduction and eventual eradication of war and the control and resolution of violent conflict by peaceful means – do not self-evidently mark it out as a distinct field. Such concerns have also threaded through the discipline of International Relations (IR) from its inception immediately after the First World War. Indeed, most histories of IR start off by identifying its 'idealist' origins in the wake of the carnage on the battlefields of France, Belgium, the Dardanelles and elsewhere. Although the supposedly naive aspirations of IR's Liberal founders were supplanted by a more hard-headed Realism after the Second World War, even a realist-dominated IR discipline could plausibly claim war and peace at the heart of its concerns.

Peace studies' other key focus – the definition of peace itself – is arguably a better basis for distinguishing it from other cognate fields, not least because it highlights peace studies' overt, and often controversial, normative content. Certainly, in its earlier days, and in spite of considerable efforts by its key figures to present their work as an example of social *science*, it was the normative commitment to promote peace that principally marked it out from IR as well as such fields as strategic studies. These largely took war and other forms of violent conflict to be perennial, if tragic, features of an anarchical international system of sovereign states. In contrast, peace studies has always presented war as a problem in need of eradication. At the very least, someone who chose to identify themselves as working within 'peace research' or 'peace and conflict research' (the preferred labels of peace studies' key founding figures in the 1950s) was signalling a normative standpoint of sorts. In spite of the efforts of the early pioneers to mask their normative leanings beneath a commitment to otherwise orthodox social scientific methods, this was enough to ensure a sceptical or even hostile reception within cognate fields. With the more recent development of post-positivist, critical approaches in IR as well as the emergence of critical security studies, however, such overt normativity alone is no longer a particularly distinguishing or, indeed, controversial feature (see Chapter 7, this volume).

Peace studies has also been marked from the outset by the interdisciplinary origins of its key figures. It has provided a site for researchers initially trained in the natural sciences, economics, psychology, anthropology, education and sociology, more so in fact than the obvious disciplinary starting points of political science and IR, to come together in the pursuit of peace. To this day, it remains an interdisciplinary field of enquiry, although, again, this has become a decreasingly distinctive feature due to the growth of interdisciplinary approaches and outlooks in the social sciences more generally. The multi-disciplinary origins of the founders of peace research helped arguably to stymie their original goal of establishing a methodologically distinctive and theoretically robust field of social scientific enquiry. This was not least due to widely varying conceptual assumptions and methodological commitments, disputes about the ultimate origins of violence and war (whether it stems from intrapersonal, interpersonal, intercommunal or international politics, for example), as well as disagreements about what the condition of peace actually entails. Does peace merely refer to the absence, perhaps permanently, of war, what in peace studies is now referred to as 'negative peace'? If peace does refer to something more than this, what peace studies calls 'positive peace', what is it and would we agree on when it could be said to have arrived? Today an intellectual or practical concern with the problem of peace clearly overlaps with explorations of such things as conflict resolution (at all social levels), global exploitation, human rights, international social justice, environmental security, alternative world orders and so on. These are evidently issue areas of concern to a wide range of scholars working under a variety of disciplinary labels. Peace studies is perhaps now best understood, then, as a site or intellectual space for the bringing together of scholars who, by and large, openly declare a commitment to non-violence, or – to borrow from the title of a book by peace research's most famous figure – the realization of 'peace by peaceful means' (Galtung 1996). This commitment also highlights the historical and, again, at times controversial connections between peace studies as an academic field and the activism of peace movements.

It is important to note from the outset that peace studies does not aim to eliminate all conflict. Just as the medical sciences acknowledge the useful, indeed essential functions of some bacteria, so too do peace researchers recognize the social functions of conflict. Again, it is violence that is key. As the editors of a leading peace studies textbook see it:

> Peace and conflict studies does, where possible, seek to develop new avenues for cooperation, as well as to reduce significantly (and eventually to eliminate) violence, especially organized and increasingly destructive state-sanctioned violence. It is this violence, by any definition the polar opposite of peace, that has so blemished history and that – with the advent of nuclear weapons, biochemical weapons and other weapons of global destruction – now threatens the future of all life on this planet. And it is the horrors of such violence, as well as the glorious and perhaps even realistic hope of peace (both negative and positive) that makes peace and conflict studies especially frustrating, fascinating, and essential.
>
> (Barash and Webel 2002: 26)

Peace studies: a brief history

The field of peace studies is a relatively recent creation, but thinking about peace has a much longer history. The prevalence of violent conflict and war in human history has spawned innumerable reflections on war's causes as well as on the possibility (or impossibility) of 'perpetual peace' (the title of a famous and influential essay by the philosopher Immanuel Kant). All of the great religious traditions offer reflections on war and peace, although few absolutely prohibit recourse to war. As Pascal, the seventeenth-century philosopher, mathematician and devout Catholic, famously observed: 'Men never do evil so completely and cheerfully as when they do it from religious conviction.' What religious thought does offer is an enormous and often highly ambiguous body of reflection on the moral constraints surrounding war. The Christian tradition has been particularly influential here. Initially pacifist, since the fourth century it has been a key source for the contemporary laws of war which attempt to set down the moral limitations of either going to war (jus ad bellum) or fighting in war (jus in bello). As Barash (2000: 202) notes, however, 'there is a powerful and persistent tradition of explicit pacifism and antiwar activism within Christianity, as within most of the world's traditions'. Although peace studies is not characterized by a particular emphasis on religious imperatives to pursue peace, many of its modern founders were undoubtedly impelled by private religious commitments and organized religions remain a key source of funding.

The secular view that war is an inhibitor of human progress and thus irrational emerges out of the Enlightenment, most notably in the reflections of philosophers such as Rousseau and Kant. It was Kant who argued that universal justice and perpetual peace were categorical imperatives that humanity was compelled to pursue by virtue of its rational nature. In so doing, Kant's name became synonymous with an 'idealist' or 'utopian' tradition of thinking about global reform, founded upon a conception of universal reason and human perfectibility coupled with a more pragmatic pursuit of the domestication of international politics through the institutionalization of interaction between states and the development of international law (see Chapter 3, this volume). As noted above, it is widely held that such thinking underscored the foundation of the modern IR discipline as well as concrete, and largely unsuccessful, efforts in the early twentieth century to eradicate the scourge of war. Key indices of the apparent impotence of early global reformism included the 1928 Kellogg–Briand Pact that sought to outlaw war and, of course, the League of Nations. The failure of the League's system of collective security in the 1930s to halt Nazi Germany's expansion, the Italian invasion of Abyssinia or Japan's invasion of China contributed to a widespread intellectual denigration of global reformism and undoubtedly contributed to the coming to dominance of Realism in the post-1945 era. Prominent scholars such as E.H. Carr in the UK and Hans Morgenthau in the USA railed against what they saw as the naivety of early inter-war IR scholarship, focusing particularly on the failure to adequately conceptualize the role of power in international politics.

Of course, in many respects the widespread presentation of thinking about war, peace and the international system within a simplistic dualism of Realism versus idealism resulted in the caricaturing of protagonists on both sides of the equation which has persisted until relatively recently (on this see Osiander 1998, Rosenthal 1991). In fact, so-called idealism and reformism never disappeared (witness, for example, the emergence of the UN system and the rapid institutionalization of world politics alongside the rise of Realism), just as many Realists expressed a real despair at humankind's apparent incapacity to escape the limited confines of an always potentially violent anarchic system of sovereign states. Nonetheless, the early founders of peace research in the 1950s had to battle against a widespread scepticism in intellectual and policy circles premised on the view that it was symptomatic of a return to a now discredited inter-war idealism, or was little more than an intellectual protest movement tainted by its connections with an emerging public campaign in some Western states against the spread of nuclear weapons. They did this largely through adherence to the dominant trends within the social sciences more generally, notably the emergence of positivist empiricism and the trappings of objectivity.

Peace research as science

Peace research emerged during the 1950s in both the USA and Europe, in the latter case principally in the UK and the Scandinavian states. On both sides of the Atlantic it was marked initially by an emphasis on the possibility of systematic and rigorous research into peace, underscored by a belief in the redemptive and universal power of scientific knowledge. The early focus was less on peace itself and more on the systematic analysis of war. The difficult relationship between the commitment to science and a normative concern with the problem of war was personified in the British academic Lewis Richardson who, alongside the US scholar Quincy Wright, pioneered the large-scale quantitative study of war. A Quaker and a mathematician, Richardson argued that 'science ought to be subordinate to morals' while simultaneously insisting that science itself required moral neutrality in the name of objectivity (Eckhardt 1981a). Wright was an international law specialist who in 1942 published the first edition of his monumental *A Study of War*, the product of a 15-year interdisciplinary research project. In it Wright surveyed the history and causes of war from primitive conflict onwards and in subsequent editions the study went on to look at the advent of nuclear weapons. Wright used anthropological data and scaling techniques to hypothesize a definitive relationship between aggression and levels of civilization (Eckhardt 1981b).

The then less prominent work of the US psychologist Theo Lentz arguably most clearly foreshadowed the foundational model of a self-consciously labelled peace research. Lentz saw positivist scientific method as sound but subject to abuse. Through a process of 'democratization' and expansion he thought science could divorce itself from prejudice and transcend social and political barriers. Inspired by the adage that 'war is made in the minds of men', Lentz argued in his *Towards a Science of Peace* for extensive research into human character and attitudes which, in contrast to what he saw as the earnest amateurism of peace movements, would be thoroughly professional. He expressed a paradoxical 'faith' in science's capacity to assist in the release of a human potentiality to harmonize diverse purposes and achieve universal betterment (Lentz 1955). Of course the belief in the possibility of putting science and positivist social science to work in the cause of peace was a minority position in the 1950s. A lot of scientific research was servicing a weapons industry undergoing rapid technological advancement due to the strategic rivalries of the Cold War. Nonetheless, the invention of nuclear weaponry did stimulate the founding of the *Bulletin of Atomic Scientists* by former Manhattan Project physicists in 1945 and the establishment of the Pugwash Conferences on Science and World Affairs in 1957. This was in response to the 1955 Russell–Einstein Manifesto, named after its two key signatories, Bertrand Russell and Albert Einstein (who signed just eight days before his death), which called upon scientists to alert the public to the danger of weapons of mass destruction and for world leaders to seek the peaceful resolution of conflicts.

Much, perhaps most, of the social science at the time was more focused on systematically categorizing, explaining and indeed shoring up conventional social and political practices and policies. In this context the development of an explicitly normative branch of social science was improbable. What did ensue, notably in the USA, was the establishment of 'conflict research' as an intellectual orientation that led to the establishment of the *Journal of Conflict Research* in 1957 and the Center for Research on Conflict Resolution at the University of Michigan in 1959. Both of these developments reflected some of the normative sentiments of Huxley and Lentz and were certainly inter-disciplinary in structure. The founders of the Michigan Center all shared an enthusiasm for the application of new social scientific techniques (culled from the fields of economics, social psychology and sociology) to the study of large-scale social conflict. Their research output fell into a limited range of categories: psychological studies of the origins, management and resolution of conflict; game-theoretic analyses of the dynamics of conflict; and statistical analyses of arms races and the correlates of war.

Although the field of conflict research was very much a precursor of contemporary peace studies, a noticeable absence was reference to the word *peace* in their endeavours. There was undoubtedly a political dimension to this; conflict research quickly acquired respectability and its boundaries soon blurred with developments in other disciplines, notably IR. Nonetheless, even conflict research had an oppositional political dimension to it insofar as its output was from its inception designed to counteract that of well-established institutes of strategic studies and the pessimism and perceived moral silence of mainstream realist IR. There is an irony to be detected in the attempts of some scientifically minded philosophers to eschew the uncertainties of philosophy and political theory yet at the same time embrace, however hesitantly, a need to provide an ethically driven counterpoint to the political and philosophical assumptions that underpinned orthodox thinking about international relations and the provision of national security in particular. This ambiguity about the tensions between moral and political commitment to the cause of peace and the conduct of scientistic social and political research arguably dogged the early years of peace research, not only in the USA but also in Europe where a more overtly named peace research community was also emerging.

The first appearance of peace research as a disciplinary label was in Norway. In 1959 the International Peace Research Institute of Oslo (PRIO) was established, initially as part of Oslo University, and this was followed five years later by the founding of the Stockholm International Peace Research Institute (SIPRI) in Sweden. The setting up of PRIO (and, in a related development, the first Chair in Peace and Conflict research) was not an easy task. The driving force behind it was Johan Galtung, who as a young, US-trained, Norwegian sociologist and Gandhi-inspired conscientious objector embodied the tensions between the commitments to applied research on peace and positivist methodology (Lawler 1995). He overcame considerable official political reluctance – particularly over the inclusion of the seemingly unscientific word 'peace' – to garner the financial support of the Norwegian government. Galtung was later to admit that the mantle of science proved very useful in the quest for legitimacy and, of course, funding (interview with author; Galtung 1975a: 17–18). The fact that Norway and Sweden were social-democratic welfare states beginning to develop distinctly internationalist dimensions to their foreign policies no doubt also helps explain why they were the first states in the world to support the establishment of institutionalized peace research. In 1964 the Scandinavian peace research community came of age and to greater prominence moreover with the founding of the *Journal of Peace Research* under Galtung's editorship.

From peace research to peace studies

Galtung's influence on the subsequent development of peace research, initially in Europe but eventually almost everywhere it emerged, cannot be overstated. It was Galtung who set its tone and helped distinguish it from conflict studies. He introduced much of its distinctive lexicon, some of which – notably the concepts of positive and negative peace as well as structural violence and cultural violence – was to flow well beyond its boundaries. Under Galtung's aegis, the purview of peace research expanded dramatically and rapidly. Although the first decade of his work and that of peace research more generally was to retain a commitment – honoured perhaps more in the breach than in the observance – to the dictates of positivistic social science, his later work helped establish the breadth of peace studies as it is today. It is perhaps because the foundational project of establishing a field of peace research, with its own distinctive research methodology that would accord with the (then) mainstream views of what constituted social scientific research, failed to consolidate that peace studies now more openly exhibits its normative leanings and promotes itself as a broad church. Positivistic peace research has not disappeared. However, it constitutes only part of what is now a wide-ranging field of enquiry that cannot be defined by any particular methodology or disciplinary orientation alone. As Galtung himself was to write nearly 40 years after the establishment of PRIO:

> peace and violence have to be seen in their totality, at all levels of organisation of life (and not only human life). . . . Moreover, as the purpose of the whole exercise is to promote peace, not only peace studies, a non-positivistic epistemology is indispensable, with explicit values and therapies, rather than stopping once the diagnosis has been pronounced.
>
> (Galtung 1996: vii)

The problem for contemporary peace studies remains that of clearly marking itself off from other fields of scholarly enquiry, notably IR and critical security studies, which have also undergone considerable expansions of their purview as well as extensive methodological diversification. Many scholars working in such fields today would, to all intents and purposes, share the normative orientation and research interests of those who choose to overtly locate themselves in peace studies. Perhaps then the distinctiveness of peace studies today boils down to rejection of any role for violence of any kind in the pursuit of a better or preferred world, as suggested by Galtung's formulation of 'peace by peaceful means' as the departure point (see Box 6.1). If so, this would suggest that, ultimately, a commitment to pacifism constitutes the defining hallmark of peace studies today. As we shall see, however, defining violence has not been without its controversies.

Key concepts

In reflection of his own background as a physician's son, Galtung's earlier work frequently drew upon an analogy between peace research and medicine, a theme he would return to throughout his subsequent work and which still permeates much of peace studies today. For Galtung, medicine offered an attractive

---

BOX 6.1 JOHN GALTUNG'S CONCEPTION OF THE 'POINT OF DEPARTURE' FOR PEACE STUDIES: 'PEACE BY PEACEFUL MEANS'

To start with, two compatible definitions of peace:

▌ *Peace is the absence/reduction of violence of all kinds.*
▌ *Peace is nonviolent and creative conflict transformation.*

For both definitions the following holds:

▌ *Peace work is work to reduce violence by peaceful means.*
▌ *Peace studies is the study of the conditions of peace work.*

(Galtung 1996: 9)

benchmark. It was a relatively young science, multidisciplinary in orientation and focused on restoring bodily health. Medicine's professional ethics, encapsulated in the Hippocratic oath, also appealed to him. To be professional was 'to stand in a contractual relationship to the rest of society' and, in medicine's case, professional ethics obliged the physician to always try and save life regardless of whose life was in question. Although aware that the analogy between the bodily health of individuals and the health of the international body politic was imperfect, Galtung nonetheless depicted medicine and peace research as both in the business of ensuring survival. The early depiction of the peace researcher was as an 'oriented' scientist who, drawing upon an expanding methodological and empirical toolbox, would help to put a professional peace research 'at the disposal of the development of international order' (Galtung 1975b: 170–172; see also Galtung 1975c). Writing in 1967, Galtung (1975b: 172) acknowledged that this vision was perhaps utopian but speculated nonetheless that perhaps in 15 to 20 years peace research institutions would be flourishing 'as a matter of course, as a matter of survival'.

Of course in drawing an analogy between health and peace, Galtung was presenting the value of peace in a commonsensical form that seemingly put it above politics. Indeed, a key theme throughout his early depictions of the young 'science' of peace was an attempt to lift it out of the overly abstracted realm of philosophy or the biases and prejudices of politics, hallmarks of what he pejoratively termed 'traditional peace thinking'. In the case of IR, for example, peace was treated in an unscientific and value-laden way, largely 'for ritualistic and expressive purposes' and not with the intent of clarifying or realizing a clearly defined end state. For Galtung, orthodox IR scholarship relied too heavily on dictums – such as 'if you want peace prepare for war' – which had acquired the status of apodictic truth. It was also excessively and, in his view, unjustifiably state-centric and relied on insufficiently tested assumptions about such things as the centrality of the 'balance of power'. In addition, 'traditional peace thinking' was replete with biases; it was predominantly the product of the upper social echelons of developed Western states. Galtung's ideal-type peace researcher, on the other hand, would adopt a resolutely global and more sociological focus. Thus: the peace researcher's 'field of identification' was to be 'world problems in a world perspective'; the object domain was to be the global social system; and the research focus was to be '*human* survival', a conception of the peace researcher which retains considerable currency in the field today. How then might peace research escape the partisanship and looseness of traditional scholarship? For Galtung the answer lay in a combination of multidisciplinarity, political autonomy, a commitment to the scientific pillar of intersubjective agreement and a Hippocratic-like professional commitment to look beyond personal preferences and biases.

Positive and negative peace

Galtung's idealized picture of the peace researcher was not to survive unscathed, not least because the scientism underpinning it was vulnerable to the swathe of anti-positivist criticism that at the same time was building within the social sciences more widely. Nonetheless, the notions that peace research was to be global in focus, take a broadly sociological view, and try to rise above a range of social and political prejudices arguably still remain key features of peace studies. The fleshing out of those early commitments also required a redefinition of peace. It was in the editorial of the first edition of the *Journal of Peace Research* that Galtung introduced his famous dual definition of peace (Galtung 1964: 1–4). There peace was defined as having two aspects: *negative* peace, being the absence of war and actual physical violence; and *positive* peace, initially described as 'the integration of human society'. This dualism was premised upon the identification of two global empirical tendencies that undermined the widespread image of an anarchical world order condemned to a perpetual condition of anticipating war.

The first was that 'man identifies'; humans display a capacity for mutual empathy and solidarity. Echoing a theme that was to become a hallmark of Liberal scholarship in IR under the guise of the concept of interdependence (Keohane and Nye 1977), Galtung argued that individuals 'see (themselves) as a member of groups where a norm of reciprocity is valid and cooperation a dominant mode of interaction. . . . In the real world integration is a fact'. Although Galtung acknowledged that outside of spheres of 'amity and mutual aid' it could be said that 'enmity and mutual destruction may rule', the implication was clearly that there was an identifiable and demonstrable human capacity to identify with others that was universalizable. Galtung eschewed reference to states, preferring the less rigid and more flexible categories of groups and spheres. The task confronting the peace researcher was, therefore, how to extend community and achieve consonance between an innate human sociability and global social structure.

The second empirical observation, also familiar to Liberal IR scholars, was that no matter how bellicose relations between human communities are, 'man rarely uses all of his means of destruction against all enemies all of the time'. There were 'limitations and rules . . . elements of a game in the fight'. Again, the clear implication was that there is an evident capacity to constrain the resort to violence and this was amenable to extension. Galtung went on to propose that if we imagined the extrapolation of these two demonstrable human capacities, then a vision of the elimination of violence and the dissolution of the distinction between the domestic and international social realms appears on the horizon. The extrapolation of the capacity to limit recourse to violence would only produce the condition of negative peace, whereas the extrapolation of the human capacity to cooperate would realize a condition of positive peace. In combination, however, they would produce a 'general and complete peace'. The distinctiveness of peace research lay, then, in its commitment to simultaneously research and promote both negative and positive peace. It can now be seen how Galtung was then presenting peace research as a form of functionalist sociology. Violence arises from the relations between sub-systemic groups, but humanity also displayed a capacity to cooperate and integrate. Cast in this light, the value of peace, like that of health, was not seen to be in need of defence. 'If this is a value,' Galtung claimed, 'it is amongst the most con-sensual ones.' If peace could acquire an objective and hardly disputable quality, then, by extension, so too could the depiction of the peace researcher as a kind of technician-physician dedicated to the preservation *and* improvement of the health of the global body politic.

The term 'positive peace' remains one of Galtung's most enduring legacies, but quite what belonged under the category rapidly became a matter of dispute. As the peace research community evolved, it also diversified, and within a few years Galtung's foundational dual definition of peace came under critical scrutiny. Galtung never fleshed out his original conception of positive peace very much and he soon became embroiled within a heated schism in peace research. This was very much a product of the times. For all of Galtung's appeals to the principles of scientific research and the role model of the physician, peace research was bound to attract critical attention not only from a sceptical orthodoxy but also from more radical intellectual quarters. The latter were in turn the product of the late 1960s when not only the social scientific research community but also Western society more widely was undergoing a wave of radical upheaval. This led ultimately to the introduction by Galtung of another concept that also remains as a hallmark of contemporary peace studies: the concept of structural violence.

Structural violence

Four years after the publication of the first issue of the *Journal of Peace Research* the peace research community became embroiled in an internal conflict that was played out, in part, within the journal itself. At a series of conferences held in 1968 and 1969 a group of young European peace researchers questioned the broad direction the field was taking. Reflecting widespread concern about the war then raging in Vietnam, they mounted a challenge to the depiction of peace research as a science that aspired to be above politics and to a balanced or 'symmetric' analysis of actual conflicts. The schism largely but not entirely reflected a division between peace and conflict research as it was evolving in the USA and the European or 'Galtungian' wing. At the heart of the dispute was the question of whether peace research should more openly embrace a more critical standpoint and abandon the quest for symmetrical analysis in favour of an openly asymmetrical approach that would explicitly adopt an overtly political stance (key examples of the radical critique include Schmid (1968) and Dencik (1970)). Being very much the architect of the European approach to peace research, which though differing from its US counterpart in the emphasis on positive peace otherwise largely shared its positivism, Galtung was initially a target of criticism. At the same time he was revising his own conception of the field. The critics were mostly young Marxists and at its high point the debate became very heated, with many US peace researchers choosing to disassociate themselves from what they saw as an increasingly unscientific trend in European peace research. Many older European peace researchers recognized the legitimacy of some of the questions raised but also deeply resented the aggressive manner in which they were put (Boulding 1970). As one was to put it, for the radical critics 'pacifism has been replaced by Marxism, conflict-resolution by class-struggle, peace by revolution and if necessary bloody revolution', an assessment the leading radical described as 'essentially correct' (Goldmann and Dencik cited in Lawler 1995: 72). Although the radical critics saw Galtung's original conception of positive peace as largely vapid, Galtung managed to stay relatively aloof from the debate. This was not least because in 1969 he published an article entitled 'Violence, Peace and Peace Research' in the *Journal of Peace Research* (Galtung 1969). Here he proposed a reconstruction of the conceptual fundamentals of peace research that clearly moved it closer to the emergent radical position, while maintaining a pacifist taboo on violence.

Galtung's revision did not directly address the question of the relationship between peace research and policy-making – the core focus of the radical critics – but it did take up the demand that peace research should focus more on the social origins of conflict and address the question of 'invisible' or 'latent' conflict that, the radicals claimed, arose out of economic, social and political inequalities. The implications of Galtung's revisions were highly significant. Above all, they signalled a considerable expansion of peace research's purview and began in effect the transition from peace research (understood here in the sense of a commitment to a quasi-objectivist scientism) to a more openly normative peace studies. Henceforth peace research would embrace not merely the analysis of visible, large-scale violent conflicts and wars but would also now look at inequality and injustice, understood as breeding grounds for future violent conflicts. Although continuing to espouse non-violence as a *sine qua non* for anything worthy of the name peace research, Galtung also accepted that pacifism could not provide an excuse for failing to tackle the issue of social conflict. Equally, he recognized that peace research should not descend into a kind of behaviouralism in which conflict resolution was largely seen in terms of attitudinal or behavioural modification, something that was prominent in US peace and conflict studies. Although not a Marxist, Galtung shared with the radicals the view that peace research had to address the *structural* determinants of conflict.

Galtung's revised depiction of peace research commenced with a revised understanding of violence. Retaining the maxim that 'peace is the absence of violence', Galtung (1969: 168) went on to propose that 'Violence is present when human beings are being influenced so that their actual somatic and mental realisations are below their potential realisations'. An important quali-fication is that 'potential' was to be understood as a contingent category connected to 'the given level of insights and resources'. Therefore a failure to realize potential is only indicative of violence if it is knowingly avoidable. Thus the research focus of peace research needed to extend beyond the realm of direct or manifest violence into anything that inhibits individual human develop-ment. In other words, peace research had to begin to analyse 'structural violence' in which 'the violence is built into the structure and shows up as unequal power and consequently as unequal life chances' (Galtung 1969: 171).

One clear consequence of the redefining of violence was the need to revise also the definition of positive peace. Galtung now equated it with 'social justice'. Although this formulation moved Galtung much closer to peace research's Marxist critics, Galtung argued that both Liberal and Marxist political systems produced structural violence: the former through economic inequality and the latter through the unequal distribution of political power. This refusal to firmly come down on the side of Marxism (or, indeed, to firmly locate himself within any of the main schools of political and social thought), in spite of the fact that much of his subsequent work on global inequality – in particular his 'Structural Theory of Imperialism' (Galtung 1971), introduced two years later – clearly drew from it, was to remain a hallmark not only of Galtung's work but also of peace studies more generally. Thus he subsequently preferred to equate positive peace with the less economistic notion of 'human fulfilment'.

Cultural violence

In Galtung's subsequent work he began to explore the idea of alternative world orders, a theme that was also emerging on the reformist and more critical wing of IR. Through his involvement in the World Order Models Project, Galtung developed his interest in the multifaceted nature of violence and his criticism of dominant models of global social development. Bringing together human needs theory, a lifelong interest in Gandhi and a growing ecological sensibility, Galtung's *The True Worlds* (Galtung 1980) signalled a much more open drawing of the connections between peace research and peace activism and a depiction of peace studies as embracing a multifaceted approach to addressing the multiple crises of a global modernity. As with all of his work, the normative foundations of this rapidly expanding purview remained radically underexplored even if they were much more visible (Lawler 1995: 135–190). A key theme in Galtung's work from that point on was the need for peace studies to escape the confines of Western modernist thinking and orthodox political and economic solutions to the various crises that underpinned the emergence of violence in its myriad forms. In 1990, Galtung introduced the term 'cultural violence', thus beginning the connection of peace studies with what remains one of the most difficult and controversial areas of research today: the politics of identity (Galtung 1990).

For Galtung, the West (or the Occident in Galtung's language) is understood as a civilization underpinned by a social cosmology. Indeed, social cosmology is to a civilization as 'the psychological construct of a personality' is to a human being (Galtung 1981: 147; see also Galtung 1996: 211–222). Seen thus, the West is a kind of metanarrative that permeates all aspects of social life to cement together a cacophony of voices resulting in the dominance of a single narrative of intellectual and social practice. Somewhat controversially, Galtung's Occident includes Islam because as with the other two major religions of the West it is seen to promote the notion of people in a subordinate relationship to a singular God. Galtung's Occident is exclusionary, virulently hierarchical and proselytizing, and, perhaps not surprisingly, seen as a poor source of peace thinking. Above all it is a key but by no means the only practitioner of cultural violence.

The meaning of cultural violence is grasped through its relationship to the other two categories of violence. Thus, it refers to 'those aspects of culture, the symbolic sphere of our existence . . . that can be used to justify or legitimate direct or structural violence'. In comparison to other forms of violence, cultural violence is an 'invariant' or a 'permanence'; it flows steadily through time providing a 'substratum from which the other two can derive their nutrients' (Galtung 1990: 291, 294; see also Galtung 1996: 210). A violent culture 'preaches, teaches, admonishes, eggs on and dulls us into seeing exploitation and/or repression as normal or natural, or into not seeing them (particularly exploitation) at all' (Galtung 1990: 295). Galtung posits a causal flow from cultural violence via structural violence through to direct violence, while also suggesting that violence can emerge from any of the three corners of the violence triangle.

Of course, in the spirit of the foundational emphasis on negative and positive peace, peace studies is not confined to the analysis of violence but also to the realization of peace. The antithesis of cultural violence is, according to Galtung (1990: 291, 301–303), 'cultural peace', a condition brought about by 'aspects of a culture that serve to justify and legitimise direct peace and structural peace'. As Galtung admits however, this sets peace research a rather gargantuan task. In addition to the issue of how one goes about identifying, analysing and changing extant cultures or social cosmologies, there is the question of how to construct a preferred, peaceful cultural form. In both cases the question of values haunts analysis as well as prescription. In this respect Galtung's work and peace studies generally confront a problem that is at the forefront of contemporary debates in social and political theory as well as IR.

As I have argued at length elsewhere (Lawler 1995), Galtung's own work has been marked throughout by a positivistic preoccupation with classification and the development of taxonomies (of peace, violence, forms of exploitation and so on). His analysis of cultures and cosmologies is no exception in this regard. However, his rather idiosyncratic taxonomy (his inclusion of Islam within the 'Occident' being a case in point) runs the risk of setting definitive boundaries around features of social life that are highly resistant to definitive classification. Thus, as was the case with Huntington's controversial 'Clash of Civilisations' thesis (Huntington 1996), his depictions of specific cultures as inherently more violent or peaceable than others could be accused of simplifying, essentializing, and even caricaturing highly complex fluid aspects of collective identity. On a more positive note, the identification of deep cultural dimensions to the problematics of violence and peace has pushed peace studies much more towards notions of promoting ongoing, open-ended dialogue between cultures, epistemologies and civilizations. As Galtung (1988: 78) himself observes, 'dialogue is not neutral, not above or below politics, it *is* politics'. The foundational enthusiasm for defining violence and peace and the possibility of a science of peace has given way then to a much looser and more diverse enterprise which spans a still growing number of subfields of social and political enquiry and which is not confined to a singular epistemological approach or level of analysis.

The future of peace studies?

The brief tour through some key features of Galtung's work was not intended to suggest that peace studies is reducible to his work alone. Equally, it would be wrong to suggest that all of the peace studies community have followed Galtung's path. Many have followed him up to different stages in the development of his work only to then take a different direction. Nonetheless, given that he is easily peace studies' most prolific writer who has been prominent throughout the five decades of its existence, Galtung's work tells us a lot about the field's evolution. Within contemporary peace studies one can now find work which still focuses on some of its earliest concerns, such as arms control, analysis of the causes of wars, critical studies of contemporary wars (including the so-called 'war on terror'), and conflict mediation and resolution; in short the pursuit of negative peace. Much of this output overlaps very strongly with a range of cognate fields such as IR and critical security studies (see Chapter 7, this volume). Since the rupture in the 1960s, the relationship between violence, exploitation and development has become a central concern, producing today a considerable overlap between peace studies and development studies. In addition, there is a huge volume of work on the much more difficult area of building positive peace. Here is to be found work on such issues as human rights, environmental security and ecological well-being, gender and violence, peace education, and explorations of non-Western thinking such as Gandhian conceptions of non-violence and the various branches of Buddhism as the basis for constructing a culture of non-violence (for illustrations of the current agenda of peace studies see Galtung 1996, Jeong 1999, Barash and Webel 2002). It is this area of writing that can arguably be more fully described as unique to peace studies.

Two views may be taken on the state of contemporary peace studies. Positively one might celebrate its diversity and ever-expanding range, in spite of the fact that peace studies cannot be said to represent in and of itself a distinctive philosophical or theoretical viewpoint. It could be understood as a very large exercise in collation, of ideas, analyses, proposals and prescriptions that straddle the boundaries between formal social scientific research, normative enquiry and political activism, and which is loosely connected by an imprecise normative orientation that may be derived from a number of sources. Peace studies may be conceived of as a site or a space in which critical cognitive intent is brought to bear in myriad ways upon the problem of violence and the prospects for its eventual eradication. Peace studies is on the curricula of hundreds of universities, predominantly in the USA but also in most corners of the globe. There are also public and private research institutes dedicated to the analysis of peace and conflict throughout the world (a directory may be found at http://ipra.terracuranda.org), along with the half a dozen or so dedicated journals, some of these being as old as the field itself.

A more critical view might wonder if the constant expansion of the purview of peace studies has meant that it has acquired the qualities of an intellectual black hole wherein something vital – a praxeological edge or purpose – has been lost, not least because the ostensible subject domains of violence and peace remain so essentially contested. On this view, a case might be made for a restoration of focus, a re-narrowing of its subject domain towards the continuing problem of direct violence at all levels of social life. A sobering fact remains that if peace studies is to be judged by the relative prevalence of direct violence during its half-century life span then it would be hard to declare it a success. This is not to suggest that peace studies should abandon its traditions of interdisciplinariness, epistemological diversity, or its historical relationship with peace activism. However, the changing nature of warfare and the growing salience of the issue of armed humanitarian intervention in the post-Cold War era present a raft of new challenges to peace studies (see Chapters 11, 13, 14, 27, 28, this volume). More controversially, it opens up the possibility that if peace studies is to offer viable, less violent alternatives to the currently dominant modalities of intervening in the various wars and complex political emergencies that are hallmarks of the current era, then its historical association with an absolute prohibition on the resort to violence in the name of peace may warrant critical review (Lawler 2002). In the absence of such a prohibition of course, the maintenance of a distinctive quality to peace studies would in itself become a real challenge.

Further reading

David P. Barash and Charles P. Webel, *Peace and Conflict Studies* (Thousand Oaks, CA: Sage, 2002). One of the more comprehensive textbooks available that gives a good sense of the range of issues now falling under the label of peace studies.

Johan Galtung, *Peace by Peaceful Means: Peace, Conflict, Development and Civilisation* (London: Sage and PRIO, 1996). Perhaps one of the easiest entry points into Galtung's voluminous work, as it distils much of his earlier and more recent work into a single volume.

Ho-Won Jeong (ed.), *The New Agenda for Peace Research* (Aldershot: Ashgate, 1999). Offers an insight into some of the more recent conceptual and policy-oriented developments in peace research.

Peter Lawler, *A Question of Values: Johan Galtung's Peace Research* (Boulder, CO: Rienner, 1995). This remains the only comprehensive, critical overview of Galtung's work in English. The focus is predominately theoretical and conceptual.

Ghanshyam Pardesi (ed.), *Contemporary Peace Research* (Brighton: Harvester Press, 1982). A collection of some of the key contributions to peace research, focusing on the debate between some of the founding figures and their Marxist critics.

Various authors, 'The future of peace studies', *Peace Review*, 14(1) (2002). This issue of one of the leading US peace studies journals is devoted to a series of short essays on the current state and future of peace studies.

Critical Theory

Pinar Bilgin

▮ Abstract

This chapter introduces students to critical security studies; that is, an approach that takes Gramscian and Frankfurt School critical theory as its guiding framework. It is also known as the 'Welsh School' or 'emancipatory realism'. The chapter begins by tracing the origins of critical security studies. It then explores the key concepts of approaches to security that have been inspired by critical theory by using empirical illustrations from regions such as the Middle East and Southern Africa, and issues such as nuclear weapons, 'state failure' and post-9/11 prospects for emancipation in the Muslim world.

▮ Introduction: the need for a critical perspective

Although the origins of critical security studies as a distinct school of thought go back to the early 1990s, the ideas and struggles it feeds upon have been around for much longer. Citizens, social groups and movements, intellectuals and activists have long called for thinking beyond the Cold War categories that have restricted our ways of 'thinking' about and 'doing' security. Examples include the Non-Aligned Movement whose underlying principle reminded the world that there existed insecurities other than the United States–Soviet Union standoff; the calls for a New International Economic Order in the 1970s which underscored that the North–South tension was of no less significance for world politics than that of the East–West; contributors to the World Order Models Project who during the 1960s and 1970s outlined visions of alternative and sustainable world orders; the 'Alternative Defence' school that helped transform security relations across 'Europe' during the 1980s through informing various social movements including the US-based 'Freeze', UK-based CND (Campaign for Nuclear Disarmament) and END (European Nuclear Disarmament); the disciples of Mahatma Gandhi who have sought non-violent ways of doing security and contributed to academic peace research; women's movements that have pointed to the 'arms vs. butter' dilemma as a cause of disproportionate suffering for women; feminist scholars who have underlined the relationship between the personal, the political and the international; and students of North/South and 'Third World' security who turned on its head the prevalent assumption that the inside/domestic realm was one of security whereas the outside/foreign realm was one of insecurity by pointing to the ways in which 'national security projects' imported from (and supported by) the 'West' have had a mixed record in the rest of the world.

In the years of euphoria that followed the end of the Cold War, the contributions of these groups were more or less forgotten not only by those who claimed 'victory' on the part of the Ronald Reagan administration in the USA (to the neglect of a variety of other factors and actors that helped to bring the Cold War to an end) and returned to business as usual (with an admixture of constructivism in some cases), but also by the more theoretically oriented students of critical security studies who have pursued the task of rethinking security on mostly metatheoretical grounds, thereby failing to challenge existing ways of 'thinking' about and 'doing' security. The September 11, 2001 attacks and other al-Qa'ida-linked bombings that shook various parts of the world were tantamount to a wake-up call in more ways than one. For students of security studies who were sceptical of the contributions of critical perspectives, 9/11 served as a reminder that prevalent approaches to security are far from being able to account for let alone address the world's current insecurities. For students of critical security studies, 9/11 underscored the need to engage directly with issues related to war and peace, hard and soft power, state and non-state actors in world politics. It is in this context that the call for rethinking security (in theory and in practice) has gained new urgency.

Rethinking security

While scarcely a day passes without some mention of 'security', what it means is often far from clear. This is not because of a lack of effort, but because security is a 'derivative concept'; one's understanding of what 'security' is (or should be) derives from one's political outlook and philosophical worldview (Booth 1997: 104–119). Failure to recognize this point and practices shaped by ostensibly universal conceptions of security have rendered the world less secure.

BOX 7.1 SECURITY AS A DERIVATIVE CONCEPT: THE CASE OF ISRAEL

One may observe the 'derivative' character of security by analysing the views of different groups within the same political community. In the state of Israel, for example, those who have remained sceptical of the virtues of making peace with the Arabs in general and the Palestinians in particular have insisted on an agreement that would deliver 'peace with security', which often meant holding on to the territories acquired in the 1967 War in order to gain 'strategic depth'. When, during a brief period in the early 1990s the Israelis and the Palestinians seemed to be on the same 'peace' track, members of the 'Peace Now' movement celebrated by putting up banners that read 'Peace is my security' (Sharoni 1996: 116). This latter view rested on the belief that positive relations with the Palestinians 'inside' and the Arabs 'outside' Israel would provide the kind of 'security' for Israelis that the search for 'strategic depth' had thus far failed to deliver. The point being that it is possible to find within the same political community struggles informed by different conceptions of security (see Booth 1979).

Differences in understanding security and defining threats partly derive from but cannot be reduced to the psychological process of mis/perception. While applying cognitive psychology to decision-making (Jervis 1976) went some way towards explaining differences between, say, India and Pakistan's definitions of threat and conceptions of 'security', understanding their respective 'national security projects' also requires an analysis of political processes within the two states (Pasha 1996, Abraham 1998). After all, it is politics that helps shape historical memory, through the prism of which emerge the psychological processes that produce our interpretations of current events. As such, it is not mis/perception alone that produces different conceptions of security; rather, it is different conceptions of security which derive from one's political outlook that allow different perceptions of threat to emerge. The process is political through and through.

Understanding security as a derivative concept, thereby recognizing its culture-bound character, does not render the search for security any more difficult. This is because security is also an 'instrumental value . . . that frees people(s) to some degree to do other than deal with threats to their human being' (Booth 2005a: 22). While no single universal definition of security may be possible, working definitions are nevertheless needed to inform our practices. Notwithstanding their differences, all philosophical worldviews agree on the human need for security, since 'it frees possessors to a greater or lesser extent from life-determining constraints and so allows different life possibilities to be explored' (Booth 2005a: 22). Recognizing security as an 'instrumental value' also guards against the tendency to treat it as an end-point rather than as a process through which human beings find 'anchorages . . . as [they] contemplate navigating the next stage of history' (Booth 1995: 119). This, in turn, opens up the possibility for people with different political outlooks to negotiate with each other and to work towards finding ways of coexistence without depriving the others of their life chances (Alker 2005: 203–207).

Since the early 1990s, attempts to rethink security have generated lively debates and insightful writings – an important milestone was a conference held at York University in Canada in December 1994 which brought together analysts working on the fringes of security studies. Those scholars were on the fringes at the time due to the defiant character of the questions they asked and the answers they sought. The brand of critical security studies introduced in this chapter is different from the understanding that shaped the York Conference and the book that followed (see Krause and Williams 1997), in that while locating its roots in the aforementioned ideas and historical struggles originating in different parts of the world it is firmly grounded in 'critical theory' as the guiding framework.

The precursor of this approach is Ken Booth who, in his seminal article 'Security and Emancipation' (Booth 1991a), called for a rethinking of security, defined it as 'emancipation' and coined the phrase 'critical security studies'. Together with Richard Wyn Jones (1999, 2005), Booth set up the first postgraduate-level course on critical security studies at the University of Wales, Aberystwyth in 1995, which eventually became the core course of a Master's degree in security studies. What distinguishes the 'Welsh School' or 'emancipatory realism' from other strands of critical security studies is the influence of the Gramscian and Frankfurt School tradition of 'critical theory' (see Bilgin *et al.* 1998).

Critical theory

It was Robert W. Cox who familiarized students of International Relations with the ideas of the Italian political theorist and activist Antonio Gramsci (1891–1937), most notably through his distinction between 'critical theory' and 'problem-solving theory'. The distinction between the two rests on the purpose for which theory is built. Whereas critical theory 'stands apart from the prevailing order and asks how that order came about', problem-solving theory is content with fixing glitches so as to make 'existing relationships and institutions work smoothly' (Cox 1981: 129). The labels used for the two strands of theorizing often confuse readers into thinking that 'critical theory' is not interested in solving problems but merely presents a critique and/or a utopia. This is a misnomer. 'Critical theory' does engage with present problems but without losing sight of the historical processes that have produced them, and proposes alternatives that are 'feasible transformations of the existing world' (Cox 1981: 130; see also Booth 1991b).

Another source of inspiration for critical scholars is the Frankfurt School theorist Max Horkheimer (1895–1973) who drew an important distinction between 'critical theory' and 'traditional theory' (Horkheimer 1982 [1937]).

> ## BOX 7.2 PROBLEM-SOLVING AND CRITICAL THEORY: THE CASE OF SOUTH AFRICA
>
> Between 1948 and 1994, South Africa was governed by the National Party's apartheid regime, which rested on assumptions of white supremacy. During this period, problem-solving accounts portrayed South Africa as an embattled 'bastion of Western civilization' (quoted in Booth and Vale 1995: 287) and represented South African security in terms of 'Western security' – a term that served to cloak the interests of the ruling whites. The recommended security strategy, in turn, was one of 'forward defence', designed to overpower potential threats at home and in the neighbouring region.
>
> Critical perspectives, in turn, recognized apartheid for what it is – just another idea reified into being through intersubjective understandings and coalescing practices. Viewed through the lens of critical approaches, security in South Africa was conditional upon a non-racial and freely elected government that would seek security not at the expense of, but together with, its people and its neighbours (Booth and Vale 1995). Whereas problem-solving accounts took the status quo as given and considered its maintenance as the only possible way of producing 'security', critical theory laid bare the ways in which beliefs about white supremacy had facilitated the establishment of the apartheid regime and warranted policies that maintained the status quo. It also proposed alternative policies which eventually contributed to apartheid's demise (see Ungar and Vale 1985/86).

According to Horkheimer, traditional theory is defined by its reification of ideas into institutions, which are then represented as immutable 'facts of life' that have to be lived with – all this while denying the role played by theory and the theorist. In contrast, critical theory rejects such rigid distinctions between subject and object, observer and observed, and lays bare the role played by theories and theorists throughout the process of reification. Pointing to the role played by certain actors in bringing about the existing order of things (i.e. denaturalizing the present which some analysts take as pre-given) opens up room for human agency to come up with solutions that go beyond mere 'problem-solving' within the parameters of the existing order (Wyn Jones 1999: 100–102).

In security studies, 'traditional' and 'critical' approaches differ most notably in their treatment of the state. Traditional security studies views the world from a state-centric (if not statist) perspective. In contrast, critical security scholars have argued that states are a means and not the ends of security policy, and hence they should be de-centred in scholarly studies as well as in policy practice (Booth 1991a). Proponents of traditional approaches to security, however, have brushed aside such concerns and continued to point to the centrality of the

BOX 7.3 STATISM AND STATE-CENTRISM

'Statism' is a normative position that treats the state as the ultimate referent object and agent of security, where all loyalty and decision-making power is assumed to be concentrated. Statism in security studies has taken many guises: while some elements of the literature are unabashedly statist, others deny their statism by identifying their stance as one of state-centrism. State-centrism, in contrast to statism, is a methodological choice that involves treating the state as the central actor in world politics and concentrating on its practices when studying international phenomena. Statism and state-centrism are thus not the same thing, although the distinction between the two may be difficult to sustain given the constitutive relationship between theory and practice. For instance, the Realist argument that since it is states that act to provide security, the security of states should be given analytical primacy is a clear case of confusing agents with referents. By way of this rather uncritical acceptance of the centrality of the state's agency, the potential of human agency is at best marginalized and at worst rendered invisible. Broadly speaking, state-centric perspectives do not simply reflect a state-dominated field, but also help constitute it. According primacy to states in our analyses does not simply reflect a 'reality' out there; it also helps reinforce statism in security studies by making it harder to move away from the state as the dominant referent and agent (Bilgin 2002).

roles states play in contemporary world politics. On closer inspection, however, this traditional (Realist) argument turns out to be rather unrealistic. As Wyn Jones (1999: 96) has pointed out,

Although no one can doubt the elegant simplicity of this position, crucial questions remain: Is the realist's statism analytically useful? Can the internal politics of the state be ignored, thus allowing analysts to concentrate their attentions on the determining influence of the international realm of necessity?

(Wyn Jones 1999: 96)

The failure of traditional accounts to capture the end of the Cold War – in terms of how and when it happened – attests to their limited analytical value. The roles played by ideas and transnational movements in helping to bring the Cold War to an end were not visible to those who looked through the state-centric lens of traditional security studies (Wyn Jones 1999: 94–102).

Although the end of the Cold War underscored the inadequacy of theoretical frameworks that fail to take into account transnational and intra-national factors, traditional approaches to security soon returned to business as usual. Even the 9/11 attacks, which reminded the world of the increasingly influential role non-state actors play in world politics, seem to have made only a minor impact on the traditional approach, which has included such actors in its analysis but failed to change the way it approaches actor–system dynamics. Part of the problem is that post-9/11 security studies treats non-state actors in a way that is reminiscent of how Realists treat states – that is, as unitary actors the behaviour of which can be understood without becoming curious about their internal dynamics and the transnational factors which help shape those dynamics.

Viewed as such, traditional security studies fails not only by the standards set by critical theory (in terms of serving emancipatory interests; see below) but

---

BOX 7.4 REALISM'S NOT-SO-REALISTIC APPROACH TO 'STATE FAILURE'

Viewed through the lens of traditional security studies, 'state failure' is a problem not because those states fail to provide security for their citizens, but because they fail to fulfil their responsibilities towards the 'international community' by allowing non-state actors to use their territories to stage attacks against 'Western' interests. From this perspective, it is not state security per se that is privileged, but the security of some ('Western') states. Identified as such, the problems caused by 'state failure' are addressed through intervention and regime-building often to the neglect of the interests of the citizens of those states. A more sophisticated understanding of 'state failure' would involve taking stock of the ways in which the 'standard' concepts, and practices shaped by those concepts have contributed to such 'failure' (Bilgin and Morton 2004).

A critical security studies perspective begins by asking the question 'Who has failed the "failed state"?' It then goes on to consider the possibility that the 'failure' may rest with 'standard' conceptions of the 'state' rather than with those individual states (Milliken and Krause 2002). It then identifies the socio-economic context which allows some states to 'fail' while others 'succeed'. Such contextual factors include (but are not limited to) the academic division of labour between 'economics' and 'politics' (to the impoverishment of both); remnants of 'orientalism' in international studies that condition and limit understandings of the 'non-West'; and the legacy of imperialism which finds new guises in the global economic order (Bilgin and Morton 2002). The difficulties faced in rebuilding Afghanistan's institutions attest to the need for a comprehensive understanding of the state (and sub-state actors) in the study of 'state failure' cognizant of inside–outside dynamics in the realms of 'security' as well as 'political economy'.

also by its own standards. Comparing outcomes with stated objectives is captured by the Hegelian concept of 'immanent critique' (also employed by Frankfurt School scholars; see Wyn Jones 2005: 220–229). This type of critique re-evaluates a position from its own standpoint (as opposed to one's own) and reveals its shortcomings inside out. The aim, however, is not only to deconstruct but also to reconstruct. As Stamnes has shown in her study of UN peace operations, whereas the deconstructive task involves uncovering 'unfulfilled potential for change inherent in an organization of, or arrangement within, society', the reconstructive task 'makes possible a choice between the various alternatives – it points out potentialities for *emancipatory change*' (Stamnes 2004: 164). The growing critical security studies literature is replete with examples of such critique (see below).

Theory/practice

What allows students of 'critical theory' to identify processes through which ideas are reified into institutions and then treated as 'reality' (as with 'apartheid' and 'state failure') is their rejection of an objectivist conception of the theory/practice relationship in favour of an understanding that views theory as constitutive of the very reality it seeks to explain. In Steve Smith's words:

> Theories do not simply explain or predict. They tell us what possibilities exist for human action and intervention; they define not merely our explanatory possibilities but also our ethical and political horizons.
>
> (Smith 1996: 13)

Theories help organize knowledge, which, in turn, informs, enables and privileges (or legitimizes) certain practices while inhibiting or marginalizing others. That said, not all theories get to shape practices. The reason why some theories may become self-constitutive (such as traditional security studies) but others do not (as with peace research) is rooted in the power–knowledge relationship. The competition between theories over shaping practices and therefore the future never takes place on equal terms. To conceive of theory as constitutive of 'reality' is not to suggest that once we get our theories right the rest will simply follow. What shape the future might take will depend on whose theories get to shape practices. For example, the reason why the lands to the southwest of Asia and north of sub-Saharan Africa were lumped together and labelled the 'Middle East' as opposed to something else is rooted in the dominance of British and US security discourses. The sources of their dominance could, in turn, be found in the material (military and economic) as well as representational power enjoyed by these states (Bilgin 2004).

Here I distinguish between the representational and material dimensions of power for analytical reasons in an attempt to stress that the workings of the power–knowledge relationship cannot be accounted for by adopting a narrow or purely material conception of power. Rather, one's conception of power should account for its representational dimension as well; that is, the power to shape ideas (on the Gramscian conception of hegemony see Cox 1983). One potential problem involved in trying to account for the representational dimension of power is that it cannot be observed in the same way as the material dimension can be; the latter is often utilized to keep issues outside security agendas, thereby averting conflict. In the absence of overt (or latent) conflict, no observable behaviour change takes place. However, the absence of an observable power relationship does not necessarily mean one does not exist (see Lukes 1986).

Neither material nor representational dimensions of power can be monopolized by one actor only. This is more so in the case of the latter. For, although it is true that it is a combination of ideas and material resources that has enabled some discourses to prevail, nevertheless, history is replete with examples of the ideas of the weak coming to the fore (by being taken up by those who are in power, or directly through revolutions). One example of this phenomenon is the 1989 revolutions in Eastern Europe and the role played by Pope Jean Paul II and the Catholic Church. Previously Stalin had famously ridiculed the lack of material power possessed by the Vatican when he quipped 'how many divisions has the Pope?' It was therefore somewhat ironic that Pope Jean Paul II would play a significant role in the 1989 revolutions that eventually culminated in the dissolution of the Soviet Union (Booth 2005b: 350).

Students of critical theory consider theory as a form of practice – but not the only form! They are equally attentive to other forms of practice, as may be seen in relation to nuclear strategy. Whereas traditional security studies views technology (including nuclear technology) in neutral terms – as a realm with an autonomous logic of its own – and considers the production and use of nuclear weapons as a process which overrides cultural particularity, critical approaches recognize its 'ambivalent nature' (Wyn Jones 1999: 134–139). Technology, writes Wyn Jones (1999: 139), 'opens up a range of options or choices for society, and the options chosen depend in part on the configuration of power relationships within that society and almost invariably serve to reinforce the position of the hegemonic group'. Revealing the ways in which both superpowers throughout the Cold War made decisions regarding nuclear procurement that reflected 'bureaucratic and political power struggles rather than any rational enemy threat' (Wyn Jones 1999: 140) or India's decision to acquire nuclear weapons as partly (but not wholly) in consequence of a post-colonial search for security through modernity (nuclear weapons constituting an aspect of being/becoming 'modern'; see Abraham 1998) allows analysts to rethink the 'fetishism of nuclear weapons' and to ponder their removal from world politics as a *realistic* possibility. The idea would be to replace a MAD (mutual assured destruction) world with a SANE (security after nuclear elimination) one (Booth 1999a, 1999b).

The 'Welsh School' of critical security studies

Ken Booth laid out the rationale for critical security studies as follows:

> Security is what we make of it. It is an epiphenomenon intersubjectively created. Different worldviews and discourses about politics deliver different views and discourses about security. New thinking about security is not simply a matter of broadening the subject matter (widening the agenda of issues beyond the merely military). It is possible – as Barry Buzan (1991) has shown above all – to expand 'international security studies' and still remain within an asserted neorealist framework and approach.
>
> (Booth 1997: 106)

The first analytical move made by the students of the 'Welsh School' of critical security studies is to deepen our understanding of security. This reveals the politics behind scholarly concepts and policy agendas, which allows analysts to de-centre states and consider other referent objects above and below the state level. The second move is to broaden our understanding of security in order to consider a range of insecurities faced by an array of referent objects. In this sense, students of critical security studies do not 'securitize' issues, but 'politicize security' (Booth 2005a). They do this to reveal the political and constitutive character of security thinking and to point to 'men's and women's experiences of threat' (Alker 2005: 195) so as to be able to de-centre the military and state-focused threats that dominate traditional security agendas. This stance is at odds with the Copenhagen School (Buzan *et al.* 1998) which calls for 'desecuritization' out of a fear that those issues that are labelled as 'security' concerns will be captured by state elites and addressed through the application of zero-sum military and/or police practices, which may not necessarily help address human insecurities. Critical scholars, while sympathetic to those concerns, prefer to hold on to 'security' as a concept for scholarly studies while scrutinizing its use in practice.

The divide between the two schools on this issue (whether to seek 'desecuritization' or to use 'security' for raising and addressing the concerns of referents other than the state/regime) is not one of 'objectivist' vs. 'constitutive' understandings of theory, since both approaches understand theorizing as 'a form of practice' (see Chapter 5, this volume). Whereas the Copenhagen School makes a case for 'desecuritization' (taking issues outside of the security agenda and addressing them through 'normal' political processes), the Welsh School re-theorizes security as a 'derivative concept' and calls for 'politicizing security'.

Welsh School scholars' preference for 'politicizing security' as opposed to 'desecuritization' rests on three main arguments. The first argument is *strategic*.

BOX 7.5 'POLITICIZING SECURITY': THE CASE OF THE MIDDLE EAST

'Standard' textbooks informed by traditional security studies invariably define security in the Middle East in terms of the uninterrupted flow of oil at a 'reasonable' price to 'Western' markets, the cessation of the Arab–Israeli conflict, and the prevention of the emergence of a regional hegemon. A distinguishing feature of this conception of regional security is its top-down character that views security in the Middle East from the perspective of extra-regional actors, and privileges the security of (some) states and military stability.

Critical approaches juxtapose non-regional actors' conception of regional security with that of many (but not all) regional states who voice other concerns shaped along the axis of Arab/non-Arab or Islamic/non-Islamic. Their agendas, in turn, often clash with that of non-state actors of various persuasions who call for more democratic accountability and political participation, respect for human rights and the expansion of women's rights, to name a few. Such concerns reveal the fact that although the 'standard' textbook perspective – that military instability in the Middle East threatens global security – is valid, it captures only one dimension of regional insecurity (Bilgin 2004, 2005). What is more, conceiving security in the Middle East solely in terms of military stability helps to gloss over the structurally based (economic, political, societal) security concerns. 'Politicizing security,' therefore, refers to rethinking security to uncover the 'political' character of 'defining' security and the 'drawing up' of security agendas, to open up space to include other issues identified by myriad actors, and to de-centre the statist concerns of some by highlighting human insecurities.

Desecuritization, they argue, would amount to leaving security as a tool with a high level of mobilization capacity in the hands of state elites who have not, so far, proven to be sensitive towards the security concerns of referents other than the state and/or regime. While the Copenhagen School makes a case for desecuritization for exactly this reason, the Welsh School turns that argument around and asks: 'Are existential threats to security simply to be abandoned to traditional, zero-sum, militarized forms of thought and action?' (Wyn Jones 1999: 109). Viewed as such, 'politicizing security' facilitates questioning of the state elite's uses of security and the merits of policies based on zero-sum, statist and militaristic understandings.

The second argument is *ethico-political*. The fact that security has traditionally been about the state and its concerns does not mean it has to remain that way. When defined by the state elite, the definition of 'security' could include anything and everything depending on their policy agenda. Depending on the historico-political context, security agendas of states may indeed translate into zero-sum, militarist, statist and, at times, dehumanizing practices. When defined by some others (as with environmental NGOs) security may be more likely to be conceived globally and practised locally with an eye on the future implications of current thinking and practices. While some are more able than others to voice their insecurities, there nevertheless remain opportunities to open up room for dialogue, debate and dissent. From this perspective, the role of the scholar is viewed, in Edward Said's terms, as one of amplifying the voices of those who otherwise go unheard (Said 1994; Enloe 1996).

The third argument is *analytical*. Ultimately, the question of whether it is 'desecuritization' or 'politicizing security' that would help address those concerns is one that 'must be answered empirically, historically, discursively' (Alker 2005: 198). Empirical evidence suggests that the framing of HIV/AIDS as a global security issue has been of immense help in addressing its pernicious effects in Africa (Elbe 2006). Representing migration to Western Europe in an alarmist language, in turn, while reflecting the concerns of some, has, at the same time, rendered 'constructive political and social engagement with the dangerous outsider(s) more difficult' (Huysmans 2006: 57).

Emancipation

In his 1991 article, Booth laid out the linkage between security and emancipation in the following way:

> Security means the absence of threats. Emancipation is the freeing of people (as individuals and groups) from those physical and human constraints which stop them carrying out what they would freely choose to do. War and the threat of war is one of those constraints, together with poverty, poor education, political oppression and so on. Security and emancipation are two sides of the same coin. Emancipation, not power or order, produces true security.
>
> (Booth 1991a: 319)

Understanding security and emancipation as 'two sides of the same coin' is not some utopian and/or imperialistic project, but rests on the ideas and struggles of individuals and social groups in different parts of the world. In Wyn Jones' (1999: 126) words, 'security in the sense of the absence of the threat of (involuntary) pain, fear, hunger, and poverty is an essential element in the struggle for emancipation'. Deepening and broadening our conception of security (in our scholarly studies) is only necessary to catch up with and lend a helping hand to already existing struggles in the world (practice).

While it is difficult to precisely describe emancipation in abstract, theoretical terms, it may be easier to define it in practical cases. Let us take the hard case of the 'Muslim world'. It is a hard case because it is considered by some to be antithetical to the very idea of emancipation (of women in particular). Al-Qa'ida has framed the 9/11 attacks in terms of its opposition to Western imperialism and interventionism. The 9/11 attacks were interpreted by some Westerners as the non-West's rejection of modernity. 'Al Qaeda does not simply oppose the United States because of its presence in the Middle East generally and its support for the West specifically,' wrote Steve Smith (2005: 43), '[Al-Qa'ida] opposes the United States, and regimes such as Saudi Arabia in the Middle East, because it sees them as pursuing modernization, which it deems as diametrically opposed to authentic Islamic identity.' While statements by prominent Al-Qa'ida leaders seemingly give credence to this view, it is worth emphasizing that such representations, when coupled with mainstream understandings of emancipation as a uniquely 'Western' idea and process, makes it very difficult to engage with the 'non-West' on this emancipatory ground. The problem is not only that some Islamic fundamentalists do not have a conception of women's emancipation, but also that some do: some Muslim clerics, for instance, have declared women's participation in suicide bombings in Israel/Palestine as emancipatory! Students of security should indeed question whether the desire for emancipation is universally valid. This should not, however, stop them interrogating claims that women undertaking acts of 'suicide bombing' could be considered as emancipatory for those taking part and helping secure the others who stay behind. Considering such intricate and politically and culturally sensitive issues would require students of security to rethink various dimensions of power (hard and soft, material and representational) including the power to define what is 'security' and 'emancipation' within a given cultural community – be it the 'West' or the 'Muslim world'.

In the face of the currently prevailing dichotomized representations and seemingly irreconcilable positions, the Welsh School's response has been critical engagement rather than despair. Alker, for example, has called for 'culturally sensitive concepts of emancipation' to 'be linked in a posthegemonic way to similarly culturally sensitive, concretely researchable conceptions of existential security' (2005: 208). Elements of such a project are already in the making. The universality of some notion of human rights is common to all cultures, notwithstanding the claims of those who have the power to define what is 'true knowledge' and what is not in the 'Muslim world'. After all, there is nothing that makes authoritarian regimes such as Saudi Arabia and al-Qa'ida more representative of Muslim traditions than those Muslims writing about 'non-violent' thought and action (see e.g. Satha-Anand 1990). As Booth reminds us,

> the debate about authenticity takes place at the level of texts and inter-
> pretation, but at base it is about the distribution of political/cultural power.
> Cultural authenticity . . . is not a fact, it is an interpretation; and what prevails
> at any period is not some absolute truth.
>
> (Booth 1995: 114)

One can make a case for defining security in terms of emancipation in, say, Saudi Arabia, purely on the grounds of Muslim women's calls for emancipation (see Mernissi 1989). The fact that these women have little power (in comparison to the Saudi regime or some Muslim clerics) does not make their call for emancipation less authentic. Nor does it render imperialistic the Welsh School's understanding of security as a 'vital precursor to the fuller development of human potential' (Wyn Jones 1999: 126) in the Muslim world and elsewhere.

Conclusion

Writing in 1998, the 'Welsh School' submitted their approach as the 'next stage' of security studies (Bilgin *et al.* 1998). The growing number of contributions to this approach attests to that potential. Examples include studies on security in Africa (Paul Williams 2007), Southern Africa (Booth and Vale 1995, 1997, Vale 2003) and Burundi (Stamnes and Wyn Jones 2000), South African foreign policy (Williams 2000), regional security in the Middle East (Bilgin 2002, 2004, 2005), human rights in Kosovo (Booth 2000), Canadian security discourse (Neufeld 2004) and peace operations (Stamnes 2004, Whitworth 2004), 'state failure' (Bilgin and Morton 2002, 2004), international political economy (Tooze 2005), women's emancipation in Central Asia (Kennedy-Pipe 2004) and rape in war (Kennedy-Pipe and Stanley 2000), identity and security in Northern Ireland and Western Europe (McSweeney 1999), the peace process and emancipation in Northern Ireland (Ruane and Todd 1996), human security (Linklater 2005), nuclear strategic thinking (Booth 1999a, 1999b, Wyn Jones 1999: 125–144) and nuclear proliferation in Latin America and South Asia (Davies 2004). In addition to a critical theory anchorage, what unites this body of work is taking seriously both the deconstructive and reconstructive aspects of critique in critical security studies.

Further reading

Pinar Bilgin, Ken Booth and Richard Wyn Jones, 'Security studies: the next stage?', *Naçao e Defesa*, 84(2) (1998): 129–157. A basic introduction to critical security studies.

Ken Booth (ed.), *Critical Security Studies and World Politics* (Boulder, CO: Lynne Rienner, 2005). An introduction to critical security studies structured around three key concepts: security, community and emancipation.

Ken Booth, *Theory of World Security* (Cambridge: Cambridge University Press, 2007). The most comprehensive elaboration of 'emancipatory realism'.

Keith Krause and Michael C. Williams (eds), *Critical Security Studies: Concepts and Cases* (London: UCL Press, 1997). A broad range of perspectives not necessarily grounded in 'critical theory'.

Richard Wyn Jones, *Security, Strategy and Critical Theory* (Boulder, CO: Lynne Rienner, 1999). This book lays out the foundations of a Frankfurt School critical theory approach to security studies.

CONTENTS

Feminist Perspectives

Sandra Whitworth

▌ Abstract

This chapter outlines a number of feminist perspectives and the kinds of questions they raise about international security. It also examines some of the empirical research conducted by feminists around questions of security, including work that focuses on the impacts of armed conflict on women, the ways in which women are actors during armed conflict, and the gendered associations of war-planning and foreign policy-making. The argument here is that, whichever feminist perspective one adopts, greater attention to gender enriches our understanding and expectations associated with international security.

▌ Introduction

When feminist scholars and activists first began to engage with both the academic and policy practitioners of global politics, the idea that feminist thought might contribute to thinking about international security was sometimes met with hostility or ridicule. What could feminist theory – which surely concerned only the activities of women – tell us about the workings of global politics, national militaries, nuclear deterrence, or the decision-making of Great Powers? That kind of reaction was very revealing, since it illustrated well part of the point that feminism sought to make. For most feminists, whatever their particular theoretical orientation within feminism, the workings of security have long been presented as though they are gender-neutral when in fact international security is infused with gendered assumptions and representations. The effects of presenting international security as though it is gender-neutral are numerous, and not least that it makes invisible the gender-differentiated understandings and impacts of security on women and men and the ways in which security is constituted in part through gender.

The early ridicule that greeted feminist interventions in global politics is now far more difficult to sustain. For one, more traditional theoretical orientations within International Relations (IR) have been critiqued for a variety of exclusions, as numerous chapters in this collection have highlighted. Within this context, raising issues of gender no longer seems out of step with the rest of the literature on global politics. Explicit attention to the gendered dimensions of security is now also more widespread within some of the more mainstream sites of global politics. The UN Security Council, for example, adopted Resolution 1325 in October 2000 on 'Women, Peace and Security' – a resolution which noted both that women and girls are affected by armed conflict in ways that differ from the impact on men and boys, and the importance of incorporating a 'gender perspective' into peace operations. This kind of acknowledgement underscores the feminist observation that gender permeates all aspects of international peace and security.

One question that continues to surface, however, is: *How* does gender permeate international security? Even sympathetic observers of feminist thought and global politics do not always find a simple or straightforward answer to this question. The reason for this is that there is no single or straightforward answer to be given, because the answer is in part dependent on the particular feminist perspective one adopts in exploring questions of security. As with the study of IR itself, feminists are not agreed on one theoretical perspective, rather feminist thinking approaches political questions using a variety of theoretical lenses. How to understand the gendered nature of questions of peace and security is thus dependent on the theoretical perspective one adopts. This chapter will outline some of those perspectives and illustrate the kinds of questions about international security that result from them. The argument here is that, whichever perspective one adopts, greater attention to gender enriches our understanding and expectations associated with international security.

Feminist approaches in international security

A theoretical lens, as V. Spike Peterson and Anne Sisson Runyan have written, 'focuses our attention in particular ways', helping to 'order' or make sense of the world around us (Peterson and Runyan 1999: 1). These lenses draw our attention to specific features of our world, ways of looking at the world and usually offer prescriptions for ways of acting in the world. In focusing our attention to certain areas or concerns, our attention is simultaneously drawn away from other areas or concerns – in order to simplify the world we are observing, some elements are emphasized over others. This has been true of the study of IR and international security which traditionally focused our attention towards states and away from 'people'. But it is true also within feminist thinking. Most feminists may share an interest in focusing attention on (gender-differentiated) people, but beyond this there is no single feminist lens or perspective which directs us to the single best way in which to study international peace and security. Each feminist perspective draws our attention to different ways of thinking about gender, different ways of conceptualizing the gendered nature of international security and different ways of responding to the problems of global politics. This does not mean there will not be overlap between these perspectives; and indeed, as theoretical perspectives are adapted and modified, they may incorporate the insights of one or another perspective. Nonetheless, it is useful to map out some of the basic differences between the most important approaches to feminist theory in order to understand their different emphases and insights.

Liberal feminists privilege notions of equality and have tended to focus on questions of women's representation within the public sphere (see Whitworth 2008). Feminists who work from this perspective collect empirical information about women's roles – are women present as decision-makers in areas of international security? If not, why not? Are they present in national militaries? When they are present, what is the impact of their presence, and if they are not present, what are the barriers to their participation? Many liberal feminists focus on the ways in which within governments and international institutions, women remain highly under-represented. Where women are present, they are still largely relegated to clerical and support work, and do not figure prominently in the middle and upper management levels of institutions. As of June 2006, for example, women in the United Nations comprise some 60 per cent of General Service employees, but less than 40 per cent in the Professional categories (and only 15 per cent of the highest professional category of Under Secretary General) (Office of the Special Advisor on Gender Issues and Advancement of Women 2006). For liberal feminists, the barriers to women's participation need to be identified so that they can be removed, in this way permitting those women who are interested in equal opportunity to take on the challenges of political and public life.

Radical feminists, by contrast, focus less on notions of equality and more on notions of difference. For radical feminists, women and men are essentially quite different from one another (and essentially quite similar *to* one another). Whether as a result of biology or socialization, radical feminists tend to agree that men as a group are less able to express emotion, are more aggressive and more competitive while women as a group are more nurturing, more holistic and less abstract. By this view, much of the way in which society is organized supports the power of men over women and their bodies – what is called patriarchy – and the privileging of masculine norms. This impacts upon both the ways in which the world actually operates, and on the ways in which we think about the world. Radical feminists differ from liberal feminists in that they view the political as existing everywhere – it includes, but is not limited to, the public spheres of life. Indeed, many of the most pernicious ways in which patriarchy impacts upon women's lives are effected through control of the 'private' – through domestic violence, control over women's reproductive freedoms and control of women's sexuality. On questions of representation, radical feminists might agree with liberals that women ought to be represented in positions of public power, but not for the equality rights reasons the liberals give, rather because women bring a different point of view to politics, one that is more focused on cooperation and peace.

Whereas liberal and radical feminists tend to focus on 'women' and 'men', some of their insights hint at an emphasis that is seen most clearly in some other approaches to feminist thought, those that examine prevailing assumptions around 'gender'. Focusing on gender attempts to distinguish between the biological and the social – between the facts of biological differences and the prevailing ideas and meanings associated with masculinity and femininity. It is these kinds of observations that have informed a variety of what are called 'post-positivist' approaches to feminist theory. *Feminist critical theory*, for example, examines prevailing assumptions about both women and men: what it is to be a man or a woman, what is appropriately feminine or masculine behaviour, the appropriate roles of women and men within society, within the workforce, the family and so on (Whitworth 1994: 24). Critical feminist theorists often argue that prevailing norms associated with masculinity, as much as with femininity, must be examined, and likewise that these norms can have an enormous impact on men, particularly marginalized men (Connell 1995, Hooper 2001). Critical feminists insist also that the assumptions that exist around women and men/masculinity and femininity take place not just at the level of discourse, but that gender depends also on the real, material, lived condition of women and men in particular times and places, which includes but is not limited to the lived conditions of race, class, sexuality, ethnicity and religion.

This draws on an insight made by *feminist postmodernists* who argue that any definition or standpoint will necessarily be partial and any attempt to posit a single or universal truth needs to be deconstructed (Steans 1998: 25). Deconstruction entails exploring, unravelling and rejecting the assumed naturalness of particular understandings and relationships, and examining the impact that otherwise 'taken-for-granted' assumptions and understandings have on our ability to act in the world. For feminist postmodernists, as Marysia Zalewski (2000: 26) explains, any truth claim is an assertion of power which silences or makes invisible possibilities that do not fit easily into prevailing discursive practices.

Postcolonial feminist theorists also draw on these insights and argue further that of the partial truths in circulation around gender, imperialism constitutes one of the crucial moments, or processes, through which modern identities in all of their guises become established. For postcolonial theorists, although some feminists acknowledge the interrelationships between race, class and gender there is nonetheless 'a discernible First World feminist voice' in IR which does not sufficiently foreground the 'erasures surrounding race and representation' (Chowdhry and Nair 2002: 10). Postcolonial feminist theory attempts to do precisely this, unpacking further the assumed universality of experience between women that earlier (and particularly liberal and radical) feminisms relied upon.

These latter approaches remind us that gender relations are informed by, and in turn sustain, relations of power. As Carol Cohn, Felicity Hill and Sara Ruddick write:

> Gender is not only about individual identity or what a society teaches us a man or woman, boy or girl should be like. Gender is also a way of structuring relations of power – whether that is within families where the man is often considered the head of the household, or in societies writ large, where men tend to be the ones in whose hands political, economic, religious and other forms of cultural power are concentrated. These two phenomena – individual identity and structures of power – are significantly related to each other. Hence it is the meanings and characteristics culturally associated with masculinity that make it appear 'natural' and just for men to have the power to govern their families and their societies.
>
> (Cohn *et al.* 2005: 1)

The manifestations of these relations of power will emerge in a variety of ways, and, in the case of questions of security, can inform how we understand what security means and how it (and insecurity) is experienced by women and by men. The next section will explore these issues.

Women, gender and security – the impacts of armed conflict

What have gendered analyses of security focused on and revealed? This too requires a multifaceted response. One common set of questions within security is to focus on war and armed conflict, what Peterson and Runyan (1998: 115) describe as 'direct violence'. Some of the work examining gender and armed conflict takes a largely liberal feminist position and documents the differential impact of armed conflict on women and girls as compared to men and boys. By itself this is a very large undertaking, as the impact of armed conflict on all people is enormously complex, and highlighting the ways in which its impact differs for women requires nuanced and detailed analyses. 'Gender-neutral' analyses of armed conflict regularly do not focus on people at all – conflict is conducted between states or armed groups, the specific impact on people's lives is a marginal concern and instead the focus of analysis is on territory and resources gained (or lost) and the outcome (in terms of winners and losers) of battles and wars.

Where some analysts do focus on people affected by war, the tendency has been to focus on the experiences of men – the central players in most war stories – whether it is as combatants, prisoners of war, generals, war planners, fighter pilots, infantrymen, war criminals and so on. Women are assumed to more rarely be combatants in armed conflict, and so they are assumed to be impacted only indirectly by war. Their lives may be disrupted during war, and they are sometimes injured or killed as a result of 'collateral' or indirect damage, but women's particular experiences were generally not thought to be worthy of specific or sustained study, or in any way important in determining how we might understand both 'security' and 'insecurity'.

Early feminist work in IR disrupted these assumptions. Cynthia Enloe (1983, 2000a), for example, has documented the varieties of ways that militaries require women's work, whether or not that work was ever formally acknowledged. As Enloe writes:

> thousands of women were soldiers' wives, cooks, provisioners, laundresses, and nurses. Sometimes they served in all of these roles simultaneously. When they weren't being reduced verbally or physically to the status of prostitutes, camp followers were performing tasks that any large military force needs but wants to keep ideologically peripheral to its combat function and often tries to avoid paying for directly.
>
> (Enloe 1983: 3)

But women do not merely take up the invisible jobs associated with supporting fighting forces; they are regularly and directly affected by the violence of armed conflict itself. This has always been true, but during the post-Cold War era it became increasingly apparent that in the new forms of conflict that began to emerge, women were targeted specifically, and in specifically gendered ways.

Studies by scholars, human rights organizations and international institutions began to focus on the impact of armed conflict on women. Much of this work focuses on the ways in which, most commonly, women and girls are subjected to heightened levels of sexual violence during wartime, including sexual torture, enforced prostitution, sexual slavery and mutilations and sexual trafficking (UN Secretary General Study 2002: 17, International Alert 1999, International Committee of the Red Cross 2001; see also articles in Kumar 2001, Moser and Clark 2001, Turshen and Twagiramariya 1998). In some conflicts acts of sexual violence have been so widespread, and so widely and clearly documented, that international protective measures have been developed which acknowledge the systematic use of sexual violence as a weapon of war. In both the International Criminal Tribunals for Yugoslavia and

Rwanda, as well as in the Rome Statute which formed the basis for the newly established International Criminal Court, there has been an acknowledgement that sexual violence in wartime constitutes a violation of the laws of war (UN Secretary General Study 2002: ch.3).

Although in very important ways the widespread use of sexual violence during armed conflict demands our collective attention, and a focus on sexual violence against women has received the most sustained empirical analysis from feminist researchers, exclusive focus on sexual violence during war obscures a number of important issues. One is that, as Judith Gardam and Michelle Jarvis (2001: 94) note, most formal acknowledgements of women's experiences during wartime, especially in the form of legal redress, tend to reproduce very stereotypical assumptions about women: they are visible, valued and deemed worthy of protection primarily in terms of the sexual and reproductive aspects of their lives. This means that other ways in which armed conflict impacts upon women may be ignored or not receive equally necessary legal recognition and protections.

These other impacts may include being targeted for acts of violence – women are not only sexually assaulted during wartime, they are also regularly killed and maimed. They may also be sexually and physically assaulted and exploited by those ostensibly sent to 'protect' them – peacekeepers, refugee and aid workers, guards and police. Women are also affected by the economic impact of armed conflict – they struggle with the loss of economic livelihoods and the inflation that normally accompanies conflict, making the cost of basic items or foodstuffs prohibitively high. In some cases local sources of food have been destroyed altogether, with the destruction of agricultural lands, market-places and the poisoning of water sources. The same is true of sources of shelter – when home communities become part of the battleground or combatants force civilians to flee, women and their families become internally displaced persons (IDPs) or, when they cross borders, part of the burgeoning number of global refugees. During conflict, women also struggle for continued access to health care or other social services such as educational facilities, after these have been destroyed or are simply unavailable to internally displaced people and refugees (Gardam and Jarvis 2001: ch.2, UN Secretary General Study 2002: ch.2, Giles and Hyndman 2004, Whitworth 2004).

Thus, focusing strictly on the sexual violence perpetrated against women and girls during armed conflict directs our attention away from the many other effects of armed conflict on their lives. Importantly however, it also draws our attention away from the sexual violence perpetrated against men and boys during armed conflict. Whereas women are presumed to be targets of sexual violence during wartime, the same assumption is not made of men. Yet, sexual violence – including rape, torture and sexual mutilation – is also used against men and boys during war and conflict, usually in an effort to attack their sense of manhood (UN Secretary General Study 2002: 16). Female prisoners of war often find they are disbelieved if they report they were not sexually abused or assaulted while held prisoner – this was true of US prisoners of war Melissa Rathbun-Nealy who was taken prisoner during the 1991 Gulf War and Jessica

Lynch who was taken prisoner a little more than a decade later during the US invasion of Iraq. By contrast, male prisoners are rarely even asked whether they were sexually assaulted, their captivity is assumed to be asexual where a woman's captivity is highly sexualized, in both cases irrespective of whether sexual violence actually takes place (see Nantais and Lee 1999: 183–186, Howard and Prividera 2004: 90–91).

The United States' own sexual torture techniques against Iraqi prisoners of war illustrate well the ways in which men can be targets of sexual violence, with an explicit intention to injure and humiliate. The interrogations involved smearing fake menstrual blood on prisoner's faces, forcing them to masturbate or simulate and/or perform oral and anal sex on one another, to disrobe in one another's presence, to touch one another, to touch women, and to be photographed in these and other positions (Highman and Stephens 2004). Prisoners were also made to walk on all fours with a leash around their necks, or to stand balanced precariously on boxes, or to pile on top of one another to form a pyramid of naked bodies. Most often, it was female soldiers who were photographed perpetrating these and other acts. Zillah Eisenstein (2004) has written of the ways in which the male targets of this violence were depicted as 'humiliated' precisely because they were treated like women. Male Iraqi prisoners were the targets of a violence aimed in one instance directly at themselves, but as Eisenstein and other feminist commentators have noted, in another instance they were also the subjects of a violence that sent a larger message about empire and imperialist masculinity. Manipulating racialized and gendered assumptions of appropriately masculine (and feminine) behaviour, the sexual torture at Abu Ghraib also illustrates the gendered dimensions of contemporary imperialism and empire building (Eisenstein 2004, Enloe 2007, Philipose 2007, Richter-Montpetit 2007, Sjoberg 2007).

Women, gender and security – action and activism

Feminist accounts of armed conflict do not focus only on the 'impacts' of war on women (and men); they also explore the ways in which women are actors in armed conflict. We have seen above that women and men can both be 'victims' of conflict and political violence. They can also both be active 'agents' in armed conflict. It is normally men who are depicted as the primary actors in war, most often serving as combatants in armed conflicts. But women also regularly take up arms and commit acts of violence in war. In some cases it is because they are forced to do so, but in others it is because they are committed to the goals of the conflict, and they choose to become combatants themselves. Women have also been documented as serving as messengers for combatants, as spies, and as providing assistance through smuggling weapons and providing intelligence (UN Secretary General Study 2002: 3 and 13, Turshen and Twagiramariya 1998, Jacobs et al. 2000, Mansaray 2000, Moser and Clark 2001).

The positioning of women and men as either combatants (men) or victims (women) has implications for both women and men (Whitworth 2004: 27). Because women are seldom viewed as having served as combatants, they may experience greater freedom in organizing informal peace campaigns. Much feminist analysis focuses on the varieties of peace campaigns that women are involved in, from peace marches to silent vigils, to working across combatant groups to establish communications. Some authors note the ways in which some women peace activists have used prevailing assumptions about their roles as 'mothers' to protect themselves against state and non-state authorities who would otherwise prohibit public criticisms of local and foreign policies concerning a conflict (Samuel 2001; see also Giles *et al.* 2003). However, at the same time that women have been documented as being actively involved in informal campaigns, they are usually ignored when formal peace processes begin, they are rarely invited to formal 'peace tables' and are normally excluded from disarmament, demobilization and reintegration (DDR) programmes which give former combatants access to educational, training and employment opportunities (UN Secretary General Study 2002: ch.4).

Men, on the other hand, are presumed to have held power and decision-making authority prior to the emergence of conflict and to have been combatants and instigators throughout the conflict itself. This assumption can make all men (and boys) targets of violence within a conflict, whether or not they are actually combatants or directly involved in the conflict. Some critics point out that the assumption of men as combatants – or at the very least 'able to take care of themselves' – has resulted in their exposure to greater dangers and levels of violence during armed conflict. In the former Yugoslavia, the protection of women and children was prioritized as the goal of UN peacekeeping forces, resulting in a massacre of unarmed Bosnian Muslim men and boys who were left largely unprotected (Carpenter 2005).

The assumption of men as combatants also sometimes makes their motivations suspect when they become involved in efforts to bring conflict to an end – they are often assumed to have alternative agendas. At the same time, however, it is men who are normally invited to the formal 'peace table' once it has been established, and they are the ones who primarily receive the benefits of DDR and other post-conflict activities (UN Secretary General Study 2002: ch.4). The assumption of men's 'activity' in conflict is what may impact upon their insecurity when conflict is ongoing, but it is also what ensures a 'place at the table' when the formal efforts to bring a conflict to an end are underway.

Women and men can thus both be 'active' in wars and armed conflicts in a variety of ways, either as perpetrators of violence or as participants in peace processes. However, the prevailing understandings and assumptions about women and men in conflict – whatever their actual experience – can significantly shape and limit those experiences in both profoundly positive and negative ways.

Women, gender and security – talking and making weapons and war

Although many feminist analyses of security focus on the impact on and involvement of women and men in war and armed conflict, as discussed in previous sections, these are not the only forms of scholarly intervention taken by feminists who explore questions of international security. Instead, many feminists focus on the ways in which gender is constructed through security (and insecurity) and on the ways in which security is constructed through gender. The previous sections have already pointed to some of these types of arguments – it is prevailing assumptions about women and men/masculinity and femininity that position men and women differently in conflict: as targets of violence, as targets of sexual violence, as actors and as victims. Other feminist scholars have examined the practices of national security think-tanks, of nuclear strategy, of foreign policy decisions and even of weapons of mass destruction, to uncover the way in which assumptions around gender impact upon, and are impacted by, these processes.

One of the most important early interventions in this area was the work of Carol Cohn (1987), who argued that the apparently gender-neutral and objective (or by contrast highly sexualized) language of defence strategists and planners was used as an 'ideological curtain' to obfuscate and naturalize the deployment and possible use of nuclear weapons (see also Cohn 1993, Taylor and Hardman 2004: 3). She showed how the language used by defence planners either drew attention away from the real implications of their plans and analyses (for example, by describing hundreds of thousands of civilian casualties in a nuclear confrontation with highly sanitized terms such as 'collateral damage'), or how sexualizing weapons and weapons systems made them appear more controllable by symbolically equating them with women's bodies (for example, through such terms as 'pat the bomb').

Cohn has also examined the ways in which the 'symbolic dimensions' of weapons or foreign policy decisions can impact upon decision-makers in ways clearly tied to their own sense of masculinity. As Cohn, Hill and Ruddick write:

> When India exploded five nuclear devices in May 1998, Hindu nationalist leader Balasaheb Thackeray explained 'we had to prove that we are not eunuchs.' An Indian newspaper cartoon depicted Prime Minister Atal Behari Vajpayee propping up his coalition government with a nuclear bomb. 'Made with Viagra' the caption read. Images such as these rely on the widespread metaphoric equation of political and military power with sexual potency and masculinity.
>
> (Cohn *et al.* 2005: 3)

When linked to notions of manliness in this way, the decision to choose nuclear weapons, as Cohn *et al.* point out, is characterized as 'natural'. A symbolic association with strength and potency, in other words, becomes a substitute for careful and rational analysis that would explore all costs and benefits associated with acquiring nuclear weapons.

These kinds of concerns are in keeping with questions asked by Cynthia Enloe (2000b: 1) of foreign policy more generally: 'Are any of the key actors motivated by a desire to appear "manly" in the eyes of their own principal allies or adversaries? What are the consequences?' These questions have been raised in assessing the US reaction to the events of 11 September 2001, where calls for an appropriately 'manly' response were made almost immediately after the attacks on New York and Washington DC (see Whitworth 2002). Former Defense Intelligence Agency officer Thomas Woodrow (2001) wrote within days of the attacks that 'To do less [than use tactical nuclear capabilities against the bin Laden camps in the desert of Afghanistan] would be rightly seen . . . as cowardice on the part of the United States'. Journalist Steve Dunleavy commented:

> 'This should be as simple as it is swift – kill the bastards. A gunshot between the eyes, blow them to smithereens, poison them if you have to. As for cities or countries that host these worms, bomb them into basketball courts.' Not to be outdone, George W. Bush sought to establish his credentials when he said of Osama bin Laden: 'Wanted Dead or Alive.'
>
> (Dunleavy 2001)

For feminists, this kind of masculinist frame can lead decision-makers down paths that could be avoided, and predisposes decision-makers to naturalize highly militarized and violent responses. In turn, it likely forecloses other policy options precisely because they are not deemed to be 'manly' enough. Some observers suggested that the US government could make an enormously profound statement after 11 September by 'bombarding Afghanistan with massive supplies of food instead of warheads. Such an approach would surely earn America's commander-in-chief the media label of wimp – and much worse. Obviously, it's the sort of risk that the president wouldn't dare to take' (Solomon 2001).

The expectation that the terrorist attack on the USA demanded a swift and manly response was simultaneously linked to a sudden concern for the 'plight' of Afghan women. Part of the justification for the intervention focused on the Taliban's treatment of women in Afghanistan. As Krista Hunt (2002: 117) argues, representation of Afghan women as passive is part and parcel of the way in which 'we' will dehumanize 'them', depicting the women of Afghanistan as uncivilized and in need of saving. As Hunt points out, the United State's and the West's sudden interest in the plight of Afghan women was, at best, suspicious. There had long been information available about the systematic abuse of women in Afghanistan – much of it raised by the Revolutionary

Association of the Women of Afghanistan (RAWA) – which until 11 September went largely ignored by Western governments and the international media. For Hunt, this means not only that women's bodies are being 'written' in a way which justifies particular forms of military response, but moreover, that the enormous impact upon women which will result from that military response will be rendered if not invisible, at least 'justified'.

This is not to suggest, however, that the situation of women in Afghanistan was *not* horrifying, and indeed a final set of questions which feminists raise about 11 September concerns the relationship between the deep misogyny inherent in fundamentalisms (*all* fundamentalisms) and the kinds of violence which erupt from them. The group Women Against Fundamentalisms (2007) write: 'Fundamentalism appears in different and changing forms in religions throughout the world, sometimes as a state project, sometimes in opposition to the state. But at the heart of all fundamentalist agendas is the control of women's minds and bodies.' How much does the violence which we saw on 11 September emerge from a complex of factors, one part of which is the offer to 'desperate, futureless men the psychological and practical satisfaction of instant superiority to half the human race' (Pollitt 2001)?

Conclusions

This chapter has outlined some of the kinds of interventions feminists make into questions of international security: those that focus on the differential impact of armed conflict on women and men, the impact upon women and men of naturalized assumptions about their behaviour and actions, and the ways in which assumptions around masculinity and femininity figure into conflict and decision-making. The argument here has been that the ways in which gender is implicated in questions of international security are multi-faceted, but in all of its variations, feminist analyses of security direct our attention to a much broader set of practices and concerns than more traditional perspectives which insist international security is a gender-neutral set of practices.

Further reading

Sanam Anderlini, *Women Building Peace; What They Do, Why it Matters* (Boulder, CO: Lynne Rienner, 2007). This book examines through a series of case studies the ways in which women contribute to peace and security processes and the ways in which women's experiences need to figure into peace-building efforts.

Wenona Giles and Jennifer Hyndman (eds), *Sites of Violence: Gender and Conflict Zones* (Berkeley, CA: University of California Press, 2004). This edited collection focuses on the gendered and racialized dimensions of contemporary armed conflict by exploring both comparatively and conceptually over half a dozen specific examples (including the former Yugoslavia, Sudan, Ghana, Guatemala, Sri Lanka, Iraqi Kurdistan and Afghanistan).

V. Spike Peterson and Anne Sisson Runyan, *Global Gender Issues* (2nd edn) (Boulder, CO: Westview Press, 1999). This book provides a general introduction to both theoretical approaches and empirical examples of issues in gender and International Relations, focusing explicitly on questions of security, economics, power and ecology.

Jill Steans, *Gender and International Relations: Issues, Debates and Future Directions* (Cambridge: Polity Press, 2006). This book provides an introduction to feminist contributions in International Relations, including overviews of feminist theories and specific chapters that examine feminist perspectives on war and peace and on feminist approaches to security.

Sandra Whitworth, *Men, Militarism and UN Peacekeeping: A Gendered Analysis* (Boulder, CO: Lynne Rienner, 2004). This book explores from a feminist perspective some of the issues that arise in UN peacekeeping missions, including charges of sexual harassment and assault, and also examines UN responses to these concerns through the strategy of gender mainstreaming.

CONTENTS

International Political Sociology

Didier Bigo

▊ Abstract

What security means and what security does are the two key questions posed by an international political sociology (IPS) of security. IPS is critical of a definition of security that is limited to survival or applied only to the international realm, as if such a realm clearly exists. IPS insists that only a constructivist stance can understand how both security and insecurity are the product of an (in)securitization process. This process involves both a 'speech act' calling for a politics of exception and a more general frame underpinning this moment of exception that is linked to the existence of different transnational networks of bureaucracies and private agents managing insecurity. These groups compete in order to frame what are and what are not considered to be the major threats to the world as well as which technologies should be used in the struggle against them. The (in)securitization process is then embedded in Weberian routines of rationalization, the use of technologies in everyday practices, and within the structures of a consumerist society.

Introduction

The International Political Sociology (IPS) of security emerged from the discussion surrounding European security studies in the 1990s and the moves that led to its structuration in what have been called the 'Aberystwyth', 'Copenhagen' and 'Paris' schools (Wæver 2004). These three 'schools' or locations of networks of researchers coming from all over the world and originally dealing with different subjects, human security and emancipation, the complex of security and securitization, internal security and professionals of management of (in)security, have certainly different backgrounds, especially at the epistemological level, and have explored different societal practice fields (from interstate power relations to migration, social exclusion and freedom of movement). Nevertheless, they share a common approach (or at least a common stance) for research on security, which is different from the current literature on security in International Relations (IR), which is still embedded in the debate between the primacy of norms, values and interests, and the positions of neorealist and neoliberal approaches.

These three approaches, and especially the so-called Copenhagen School, have been labelled by their opponents as constructivists, unrealists, and Europeans as a sign of inherent weakness. In addition, it is clear that many authors and dominant voices only engaged with the research of these scholars on the margins, as if they had no relevance for 'the world as it is', for 'problem-solving and policy-making', as if they were 'too' academic, because of their constructivist approach and because of their political and ethical considerations. This attitude, which had been substantially moderated following the end of the Cold War, reappeared after 11 September, which some scholars presented as a 'moment of truth'. Among some realists this 'moment of truth' was their vindication against their critics. The only 'serious' discussion in many US security journals of IR was the one between offensive and defensive realism (see Mearsheimer 2001, Mowle and Sacko 2007, Taliaferro 2001). Any critical view opposing the assertion that security is, first, the domain of international security and, second, that security is a key positive value has no echo in the 'international security' world of experts in the USA. It is thus no accident that the critical networks have been located and financed in Europe and include Canadian, Japanese, Palestinian and Brazilian voices. In order to give strength and recognition to these alternative voices, and to show that they were not isolated, a collective group of more than 20 scholars of different ages, gender and status worked together to produce a text in the form of a manifesto, the objective being to offer a different focus for the security agenda, and to change the way of writing IR, and especially security, by outlining an international political sociology dealing with security. The group's first article, entitled 'Critical Approaches to Security in Europe: A Networked Manifesto' was published in *Security Dialogue* (CASE 2007). The second is under preparation and will be published in the journal *International Political Sociology*. The group wants to pose new questions and stimulate dialogue about security beyond the boundaries of IR theory.

Building on this collective approach, I try to address what security means and what security does by discussing some points which are still often obscure for many students and which have been objects of contention inside the collective. The first point to question is the narrative of security studies as a 'branch' of IR and the refusal to accept that IR does not possess a monopoly on the meanings of security (see Chapter 33, this volume). The second is the analysis of what is at stake when a security claim is launched, and what are the effects of an '(in)securitization' move, i.e. the development of a constructivist approach beyond a theory of language, and rooted in sociology (see Chapter 5, this volume). The third is a question of analysing the actors and processes of (in)securitization in order to gain a better understanding of what security does for the actors who enunciate it, for the audience and for the third parties, who are often victims of the practices of violence, surveillance and punishment taken in the name of protection and security. In conclusion I propose some further lines of enquiries as well as some preliminary results coming from an EU research programme called 'Challenge: Liberty and Security in Europe', which deals with the effects of a regime of counterterrorism launched as a security practice after 11 September 2001 (Bigo *et al.* 2007a).

Security studies within IR: bordering and debordering what security means

IR theory has been set up by drawing a line (to be defended) between the realm of the internal and the realm of the international. By opposing the two universes, IR has separated itself from political sociology and political theory, and the disciplines have been constituted as mutually exclusive: the assertions at the roots of one discipline or its 'common sense' may be accepted only if they are not challenged and questioned by the assertions of the other discipline (Bigo and Walker 2007b, Walker 1993). For security, it has been a tremendous success. IR scholars have written about security ignoring completely works on the sociology of policing, of criminology, of historians concerning the feeling of insecurity, and they have borrowed only a little from the psychologists and sociology of decision to construct their theory of security. Their epistemic community considered that security was about 'serious' things: war, death, survival, and not everyday practices concerning crime, fear of crime, fear of poverty and illness. The definition of security studies has been mixed up with strategic studies. The other practices have been considered as 'beyond the scope' and downgraded to a 'law and order' question, irrelevant for security in IR. So, during more than three decades, each individual scholar who wanted to write about security as war and deterrence, but also about political violence and terrorism, felt obliged to start with the discussion set up by the realists and their definition of security as national security and mainly as defence. Some individuals gained in fame (think of Stephen Walt or John Mearsheimer) because they were always quoted, even if largely negatively, as a tribute paid to enter into the (magic) realist world of (international) security, and as an insurance that the article would not be rejected for being 'outside the scope of the journal'. Even writing 'critically', it was beyond the imagination not to address their 'realist' view in an article concerning security in IR theory.

This realist pre-eminence, inherited from the Cold War, faded a little bit with its end as it became clear that realist security analysts had failed to understand, let alone predict the Cold War's ending. But very soon after the end of bipolarity, the 'security' debate within IR was recentred around the same problematic following the emergence of a so-called 'neo neo' debate between those who insisted on studying interests and those who pleaded for the introduction of norms, values and ideas into a discussion about collective security, and their chicken-and-egg dialectic. Nevertheless, the conceptual shell of the concept of security was at risk. It was difficult in such a context where terrorism and organized crime were considered as going global and as new threats, more invisible but as dangerous as the old USSR threat, to completely dismiss the role of individuals and small groups in security issues, and then to look at what was going on 'inside' societies.

The development of environmental preoccupations has also challenged the core assumptions that collective security meant national security, and the notion of a human security both below and beyond the state emerged as another vision of security (see Chapters 16 and 18, this volume). But the 'central' discussion and the framing of the security debate continued to be seen as a subfield of IR, rather than a need to discuss with criminologists, sociologists and political scientists who had theorized political violence, forms of transnational mobilizations, and dynamics leading to a change of scales. Except for some authors, the individual-societal dimension and the sociological approaches have been dismissed; what was important was the move from the international to the global and the future of concepts such as the national interest, the role of the state and the structure of the interstate system. Security studies cannot get to grips with the corpus of knowledge already constituted in sociology, anthropology and cultural theory because it contradicts the field's initial definition of what security means. The 'solution' was the sudden conversion of some Kremlinologists to cultural anthropology, and missile specialists into sociology of religion and politics of mobilization, but with 'results' that have further enlarged the gap between the disciplines and have spoilt IR's reputation. There has been a mushrooming of easy narratives about global organized crime that were backed up by no field research but that repeated newspaper articles written in a foreign language (English) as primary sources, or at best repeated the discourse of local police authorities. They did not so much explain their object as reveal a lot about the writers and the desire to 'patrol' the boundaries of the IR discipline by refusing to discuss any other meaning for security than that of 'survival'.

Certainly this harsh account of one strain of IR cannot be taken for the full picture. Important books have been published within the realist framework on power politics and great powers. Many authors have tried to transform the security agenda of research. For example, Katzenstein's books on Germany and Japan have been seminal in introducing sociology into security studies

(Katzenstein 1996a, 1996b); Lapid and Kratochwil (1996) pleaded for the return of culture in IR, and Ashley and Walker (1991) had fundamentally questioned the security discourse of survival, and helped unpack the political dimension in the notion of security by insisting on the legitimating effects of the security label on massive practices of violence and coercion, perceived as the side effect of a necessary protection of a certain political community (see also Walker 1997). Alexander Wendt (1992, 1999) has also shown the limits of the traditional rationalist understanding of international anarchy and the intersubjective nature of 'threat' in international politics.

However, despite such 'openings', the concept of security has been 'locked' into the notion of 'survival' and the keys were (and remain) in the hands of the neorealists. Barry Buzan's (1983) work did much to suggest that security and strategic studies were not the same and that security was an essentially contested concept, but he retained the idea that security was conceived inside the 'international' domain (see also Buzan *et al.* 1998). With his notion of different sectors of security, Buzan was one of the first to discuss the legitimacy of the boundary of security studies as a subfield of IR as such, and then to their reduction to national security only. He pleaded for an enlargement of the concept of security, and was therefore heavily criticized by Stephen Walt (1991b). Following the approach by sectors, the national is one among many possibilities of applying security practices. The state has no monopoly and is not the only referent object possible for security. Other referent objects may be beyond the military, the political, the economic, the environmental and the societal. If the state merely controls the first two (and perhaps the third) and is the key agent, it is more complicated for the last two sectors. So, parallel to national security and the integrity of the state, we may have claims of security concerning identity and culture of a specific society or even local community, or specific religion. These claims are more mundane about threats. They are often less physical and come from speech, but they are important as they may create a change of regime if they are successful. It is therefore important to deepen the analysis of security, to look at the 'guts' of society. But of course, by doing so, the heterogeneity resurfaces and destroys the pretence of homogeneity of the state that has been so important in IR. For example, one of the consequences of the sector analysis which is not greatly emphasized by Buzan is the series of contradictions which may occur between sectors and the fact that the claims for security referring to different referent objects occur simultaneously and are supposed to prioritize those whose security is the most important. For example, national military security (survival of the integrity of the territory and the population) may be at stake if political security (i.e. the securing of the political regime) is prioritized. When the Argentinean generals attacked the Falkland Islands they hoped to rally a population to their cause and tried to fuse political and national security, undermining the latter. They cared less about the Falklands than about their regime.

The idea of societal security that differs from national or state security is even more challenging for the pre-eminence of loyalty to the collective security of the state. Are some groups entitled to claim that their secure national identity is at risk because of the politics of the state concerning the freedom of movement of persons? If we recognize large-scale collective identities that can function independently of the state, such as nations and religions with political parties claiming that they speak in the name of the nation or a religion, and if they construct migrants as a threat, are they defending the survival of their society? A long debate has followed this initial question, insisting on the contradiction between state and societal sectors of security (see Bigo 1998, Huysmans 1995, 1998, McSweeney 1999, Wæver 1994, Wæver *et al.* 1993). This has prompted inquiries into social activities that are not related to defence and IR, and introduced a sociological reasoning dealing with the basic questions of the role of language, structuration of practices, deconstruction of essentialism, and limits concerning the will to monitor and predict the future.

We will come back to that, but one final example of conflicting practices of security is the traditional relation of the individual and the state, so much discussed in political theory and so often absent from the IR debate, except in the work of the Aberystwyth School (Booth 1991a). Individual security is at stake when the state asks me to sacrifice my life for the defence of my community. Do I need to obey? Why is there such a hierarchy privileging collective security over individual security? Why is any defect a treason? A large part of the popular feeling against war is grounded in the suspicion that the state may lie when speaking of war as the only way to protect the community living inside the frontiers or of other political communities in need of help against genocide or against their own regime. The absence of military service and the professionalization of war-making have also contributed to the diminution of the ideas of sacrifice and loyalty to a collective beyond the self. A zero-death doctrine has emerged to alleviate the contradiction and to give to the military individual the hope that he is a technician and not a warrior. But war still produces death on both sides even if the sense of duty (and joy) of the sacrificial battles – with a large number of deaths on both sides – has disappeared. The asymmetry of forces has acted in favour of a relativization of the right of the strongest states to ask for individual sacrifices. The military establishment has still the nostalgia of the previous period when the state of war was simply the inversion of the state of peace and when dying for one's 'country' was the way to ensure security of the collective. They are uneasy with any claim for individual security, individual safety which challenges collective security and does not respect the summa division between time of peace and time of war; time of war being the exceptional moment where death is required in order to achieve security and survival. A peaceful society is not ready to sacrifice individual security and accept a time of war. The idea of human security as the collective of all the individuals living on Earth is even more challenging for national security than for individual security as it reverses the hierarchy of numbers. What if the collective security of a particular state endangers the collective security of all human beings nowadays or for the future? Whose security has to be 'sacrificed'? For Wyn Jones and Booth, the axis of security studies should be the emancipation of individuals. Booth has argued that emancipation should take precedence over concerns with power and order, as 'emancipation, not power or order, produces true security' (Booth 1999a, Wyn Jones 1999). While Buzan attempted to refine realism, traditional realists have blamed him for opening up a Pandora's Box of issues. In contrast, he has been applauded by most critical theorists despite the fact that he was careful to continue with the core assumptions of traditional IR.

Buzan *et al.* (1998: 21) argue, 'We are not following a rigid domestic/international distinction because many of our cases are not state-defined. But we are claiming that "international security" has a distinctive agenda. The answer to what makes something an international security issue can be found in the traditional military-political understanding of security. In this context, security is about survival.' And they add later, 'survival is about existential threat'. In their reasoning, the grammar of security moves from one referent object to another, but survival is the fixed meaning for all forms of international security as it is possible to distinguish what security is from what politics is only by analysing the dimension of existential threat (and not a simple threat or a feeling of unease). Security can be conceptualized as 'beyond politics' and a 'politics of exception' only if the existential threat is distinguished from the simple threat and feeling of unease, and if the existential threat is related to survival as the new boundary between the internal and the everyday politics on one side, and the international and the exceptional politics also called security on the other. In other words, the 'enlargement' of the meaning of security is possible but has limits, as it is necessary to maintain something as an essence of 'international' security in order to save the IR discipline from a possible invasion by the other disciplines. International security is a way of securing the existence of the international realm of the discipline of IR. In contrast, once we admit that security studies cannot be exclusively studied from an IR perspective then an international political sociology (IPS) of security is possible and necessary. This is why the CASE Collective and many other projects associating them with a more sociologically oriented 'Paris School' have been possible. But it still means that an IPS of security has to discuss in a more detailed manner what international means, and if it makes sense for the analysis of security to draw a line or a circle around the international. Discussion is open. It may be justified, but by other grounds than affirming the existence of an international realm secured by the IR discipline, which is in terms secured by the existence of the international (Bigo and Walker 2007a, 2007b).

It is impossible in such a short chapter to develop what security means in other disciplines and what practices are considered as security practices by historians, sociologists, political theorists or lawyers. They also have their own approach and assumptions. They are often blinded by the fact that they look too much to the security of the individual. But if we want to discuss the boundaries of the international and its relevance for security studies it may be interesting to investigate more what is shared and what is constructed as mutually exclusive. When lawyers insist that security means juridical and judicial guarantees for the individual and that security begins in trial by the certainty to have a fair trial, they have clearly a different view from the military asking detainees in Guantanamo Bay what they know in the name of security and for whom the imperative of security has to bypass the law (Guild 2003). For many disciplines to be secure, it is necessary to continue to live when death is around. In this sense, the term of survival is not exclusive to IR. Securing life is seen by some philosophers as the first form of freedom, and the first right of the individual. Security is freedom from . . . unwilling death, threat of death by an enemy, fear of death by unexpected accidents. However, for a large majority of authors beyond IR, security is radiating from life and expands to happiness. Security is not restricted to survival. Security is economic, social. This is the move that IR theorists do not recognize. Security may mean 'comfort', especially in a consumerist society. Security does not only mean avoiding an unwilling form of death, it has to do with management of life and its social and structural conditions. Security also describes a range of practices which are diverse but may be summarized by a mainstream position so as to protect and to reassure in order to stay alive, and if possible to have a good life. Security is then seen as a positive value. It is a good thing to be in security, and insecurity is a bad thing.

But as we will see, a critical view of security is not only critical of the IR narrative of survival, it needs also to be critical of this larger approach to security. A critical discussion certainly needs to remember that the knowledge of who needs to survive, to be protected and from what, also supposes knowing who is sacrificed in this operation. That is perhaps one of the limits of the understanding of security as survival or as protection and reassurance. Security is also and mainly about sacrifice. As we will see, the idea of conflicting practices of protection (and sacrifice of security and freedom of others by the same move) can be discussed either at the individual dimension or as a way to reframe and enlarge the traditional dilemma of security in IR where the efforts of State A to ensure its security are seen as a threat by State B that then justifies its own effort to build capacity for deterrence. Not only may security generate insecurity, but it assumes a choice and a sacrifice of one actor in favour of another one. Security cannot be global and for all. Security has winners and losers. The practices of securing some are simultaneously practices rendering others insecure. Security is never unlimited, contrary to the claims of politicians and academics seeing security as a public good for all. Security is about legitimacy and involves politics at the heart of its definition. Security meanings are then dependent on politics and on the legitimization strategies of dominant actors. The definition of what is security in relation to what is insecurity is a political struggle between the actors who have the capacity to declare with some authority whose security is important, whose security can be sacrificed, and why their own violence may be read as a form of protection when the violence of the others is seen as a form of aggression and sign of insecurity.

From security sectors to (in)securitization, a constructivist stance

The second move of the critique is then to abandon the pretence of a fixed normative value of security independently of the actors enunciating the claim and independently of the context (referent object, historical trajectory, involvement of practices of violence and coercion in the name of protection). Rather, it is important to take the notion of a politics of security seriously, not in the sense of a security debate in the political arena of the professionals of politics and their political spectacle, but in the sense of the recognition of the struggles for classification and assignment of content under a specific label, in this context security, as well as the analysis of the actors engaged in these struggles (Bigo 2002, Huysmans 2006). As Ole Wæver (1997) puts it, 'the central questions are: who can securitize what, and under what conditions?' It engages in a different way of thinking than the search for an essential definition bringing an internal coherence to any use of the term *security*, independently of the context and the actors engaged, i.e. survival or search for comfort. Here, the security terminology has no meaning per se, but it is socially and politically central in struggles for political decisions and justification of practices of surveillance, control and punishment as well as practices of protection, reassurance, worrying and surveillance.

From this perspective, security and insecurity are the results of a process of securitization, or more exactly of (in)securitization. If we use this terminology of (in)securitization, it is to show that the result of the process cannot be assessed from the will of an actor, even a dominant one. The actors never know the final results of the move they are making, as the result depends on the field effect of many actors engaged in the competitions for defining whose security is important, and of the acceptance of different audiences of their definition. It is also a critique of the normativity of many authors who jump from a definition of security (as positive) to a definition of insecurity (as negative), and then redefine security as its opposite (negative of the negative) as if it was possible to clearly oppose security to insecurity. In this move, insecurity is, for example, 'terror' or 'threat' or 'fear' or 'risk' or 'unease' depending on their disciplinary background . . . and security is the 'contrary': it is the struggle against, the freedom from. . . . But it is not sure at all that the rise of security practices, especially coercive ones, diminishes the insecurity practices. They are not communicating vessels.

For example, the arms race was the by-product of security measures, and, at a more mundane level, the rise in the number of policemen in a street may diminish the risk of aggression, but not the fear of the persons. On the contrary, they may be more aware that something goes wrong, or in fear of the police, even if they are guilty of nothing. Quite often, when an (in)securitization move is made, security and insecurity grow together, and it generates a self-sustaining dynamic if a large audience believe in it. The (in)securitization move may occur about approximately anything, but it has specific conditions of production and reception, and as such, this approach is grounded in a constructivist episteme.

From the discussion in the CASE Collective, and contrary to my previous works, it is clear that Ole Wæver was right to say that anything can be designated as a form of security (or insecurity). Even if the definitions given by the powerful actors freeze for a moment the legitimate meaning of security and whose security is important, the emergence of fears and worst case scenarios in many domains, namely health (avian flu H5N1 virus), communication (Y2K), can create new 'expert' competitions, far from the traditional bureaucracies working on military or police affairs. It also needs to be remembered that the fetishization of objects as objects of danger or of security is one of the key features of our late modern society.[1] Cities, drugs, planes, cars, mobile phones, databases, shopping malls, steak, salmon, milk are seen as securing our life or as useful objects for communication or just as a normal life activity (eating, drinking, sleeping) that can be transformed into a danger or/and the ultimate form of security against a danger. The only caveat on the 'anything' is related to the long-term repertory of action, enunciation and imagination of a specific culture. Actors are not free, they play into a repertory (Bayart 2005, Tilly 1978). This is particularly true in late modern society. Once destiny and fatalism have faded away and risk has been placed in the heart of reasoning, any choice may be insecure in the short or long term. So, as long as the political imagination of the actors can frame the world as a dangerous place within which enemies exist, any event may be seen as the result of a plot, and a paranoid rhetoric can take off, even if at the same time a danger can continue to be seen as destiny, fate, and not discussed at all, by lack of imagination. Furthermore, what is seen as an object of security today may be recognized tomorrow as a source of insecurity and distress (once again think about mobile phones and potential radiation damaging the brain, or side effects of drugs known 30 years later, or practices of undercover policing which have created more trouble and assassination than an agitated but peaceful movement may have done).

Thus, for an IPS of security the key questions are: Who is doing an (in)securitization move, under what conditions, towards whom, and with what consequences? Ole Wæver (1995: 54) and then Buzan et al. (1998), at the origins of the notion of securitization, have tried to explain that security is an outcome of a securitization process which is constructed socially and politically through the discursive practices of social agents. For them, the process of securitization is what is called a speech act in language theory. It is not interesting as a sign referring to something more real, it is the utterance itself that is the act: by saying it, something is done (e.g. betting, giving a promise, naming a ship) (Austin 1975: 98ff., Wæver 1995). A successful speech act is then a combination of language (the grammar of security) and society (the social and symbolic capital of the enunciator, the magic of the ministry he belongs to), an intrinsic feature of the speech, and the representativity of the spokesperson regarding the group that authorizes and recognizes it (Bourdieu and Thompson 1991). So the key question is: For whom does an issue become a security issue and in relation to whom? 'Security' is then dialogical. It is an intersubjective process. It supposes an enunciator of discourse where 'security' is a self-referential practice, because it is in this practice of speech act that the issue becomes a security issue, not necessarily because there is a real existential threat, but because the issue is presented by the authorities naming it as such a threat. However, as emphasized by Thierry Balzacq (2005), the enunciator of the discourse which takes the form of presenting something as an existential threat to a referent object is only performing a securitizing move, and the issue is only securitized if and when the audience accepts it. The audience may contest the securitization move and attack it as undemocratic, but, when the speech act is socially and politically successful, then labelling an issue a 'security issue' removes it from the realm of normal day-to-day politics, casting it as an 'existential threat' calling for and justifying 'extreme measures' (Williams 1998). Securitization is then combining the notion of speech act and the moment of the sovereign decision to name an enemy, another term for what Carl Schmitt referred to as a 'politics of exception'.

The modalities of the securitization process are related to emergency procedures beyond the normal realm of politics. Securitization may thus be seen, for Buzan and Waever, or for Williams, as a more extreme version of politicization where the move of securitization takes democratic politics beyond the established rules of the game. Securitization is at the edges of politics conceived as a debate (democratic or not). The securitization process changes the way everyday politics is conceived, and limits the time for discussion and debates which may be counterproductive if they paralyse action. It reframes the options for solution by moving the scope towards quick and coercive options, often police and military options, and by delegitimizing long-term solutions and negotiations. So in many cases, what is needed is a 'desecuritization' in order to come back to normal life and not to 'suspend' life into a time of exception. As they say, desecuritization would therefore bring issues back to the 'haggling of normal politics' (Buzan *et al.* 1998).

Is (in)securitization only a speech act enacting exception? The role of routines and technologies

For Buzan and Wæver the way to study a securitization process is then to study discourse and political constellations: When does an argument with this particular rhetorical/semiotic structure achieve sufficient effect that it makes an audience tolerate violations of normal rules which they would otherwise have insisted on? For the Paris School, the (in)securitization process has not only to do with a successful political speech act transforming the decision-making process and generating politics of exception often favouring coercive options (Bigo 1996, Bigo *et al.* 2007b, Ceyhan 1998, Huysmans 2006). It has to do with more mundane bureaucratic decisions of everyday politics, with Weberian routines of rationalization, of management of numbers instead of management of persons, of use of technologies, especially the ones which permit communication and surveillance at a distance through databases and speed of exchange of information.

Perhaps this argument is coming from the fact that, in Paris, contrary to Copenhagen (and Aberystwyth), the discussion began from a different angle, less oriented towards 'international' security, and more concerned with 'internal' security and its merging with 'external' security. Rooted in criminology, continental political sociology and political theory, the critique of the notion of security as peace and public order carried out by police forces was based on a more Foucauldian assessment of policing as a form of governmentality, and was less concerned with the notion of survival. Focused on an analysis of freedom of movement of persons inside the European Union (EU) and the destabilization of the notions of national sovereignty and frontiers as locus of controls, as well as the relation between liberty and security, the process of (in)securitization was described first as a move to govern populations in movement by following and tracing them. This process was mainly the routine work of public bureaucracies expanding beyond their national borders and working in networks. It was conducted by professionals of management of (in)security using high technologies of communication and surveillance in order to sort out, to filter who is entitled to freedom and who has to be placed under surveillance in the name of an assessment that he may be, in the future, a threat, an insecurity or just an inconvenience, an unwelcome or unwanted person (with no other reason to reject him than his supposed foreignness).

The sociological research about who was 'securing' the frontiers of Europe, and in the name of what, has shown that beyond the discourses of the professional of politics in their national arenas and their games involving claims of insecurity and necessity of exceptional politics, the leading factor was the existence of different transnational networks of 'professionals of (in)security' framing the priorities of the struggles against and framing what were the major threats, with strong competition about the definition of categories and their legal elements. The EU has certainly been a 'laboratory' for these transnational networks, providing them with a certain legitimacy, even if informally they go beyond the EU and are often transatlantic. European police liaison officers, customs officials, and border guards have developed competitive networks in the same social space located at the European level and beyond. This competition inside and between multiple fora has simultaneously created struggles for the prioritization of the major threats and a new common sense designating these major threats (terrorism, organized crime, illegal migration) as one global (or at least European) insecurity continuum mixing or articulating the threats between them, the local and the global, the internal and the international. And it is this simultaneous move of inner struggles, transformation of boundaries and closure inside a 'doxa' of the people which have the social capacities to claim with some success that they are professionals of management of threat or even unease.

New research concerning the involvement of private actors, the continuity of reasoning between terror, fear and unease management through risk assessment, has enlarged the number of actors who can, with some success, intervene in the struggle for the definition of what security is, by doing (in)securitization moves (for all these elements, see www.libertysecurity.org). The social and political construction of (in)security is then related to the political as such and to the enunciation of the discourses as elevating events into political problems, but they are not limited to politicians and political parties and their claims for exceptional measures in the political spectacle. They are more deeply rooted in society. So, along the lines of Murray Edelman and Pierre Bourdieu, it seems that Bigo, Huysmans, Wæver and many other members of the CASE Collective engaged in an International Political Sociology of security consider that the role of the speech act in the (in)securitization process is central, but it is important not to limit this (in)securitization process to the moment of exception as declared by the professional of politics. The professionals of management of (in)security (as terror, fear or unease), the many public and private agencies of risk management, the audience of a consumer society as such, are framing by their routines, the condition of possibilities of these claims and their acceptance. More importantly, some (in)securitization moves conducted by the bureaucracies or private agents are so embedded in these routines that they are never discussed and presented as exceptions, but on the contrary as the continuation of routines and logics of freedom. It is the case in everyday politics about migration. It is the case about health. It is also the case about terrorism in the UK now that the discourse of the war on terror has been abandoned. To give just one example at the EU level, the detention of foreigners at EU borders is presented in The Hague programme not as a security measure, not as a justice, law and order measure, but as an imperative for our freedom (Bigo 2006).

Conclusion

A very large number of actors may enter into competition to define (in)security and they will make different (in)securitization moves, but entering the field has a cost. It depends on the authority of the individual or institution that is making the claim with regard to a specific audience. It depends on the symbolic and social capital accumulated by the individual or by their role as spokesperson of an institution. In order to declare that something is secure or insecure, and to be believed, credentials are needed. Not everyone can perform a claim that an object, a situation or a person is a danger or is secure. It is specific to a certain kind of actor. Thus, security and insecurity are the results of an (in)securitization process achieved by a successful claim resulting from the struggles between actors in a field and which is very often different from what was expected by the actors in their strategies (including the most dominant ones). If desecuritization is just a way to come back to normal politics, it will not disturb the (in)securitization process whose roots are in the routines, even if the most obvious symptoms are playing with exception. Unmaking (in)security would then entail the disruption of the 'regime of truth' created by the professionals of (in)security about their categories, and by showing who is sacrificed and for what reasons. It will be a way to mock the will of power of an unlimited security and, by analysing the limits, the boundaries of security, resistance and freedom, it will be a way to reinvent the political on the shores as a struggle for democracy for the ones who have been sacrificed, who have been banned.

Note

1   I am grateful to Ian Loader for having suggested this line of enquiry about fetishization of objects as objects of (in)security.

Further reading

The new quarterly journal *International Political Sociology*, one of the five journals of the ISA, responds to the need for more productive collaboration among political sociologists, IR specialists and sociopolitical theorists. It is especially concerned with challenges arising from contemporary transformations of social, political and global orders given the statist forms of traditional sociologies and the marginalization of social processes in many approaches to IR: www.blackwellpublishing.com/journal.asp?ref= 1749–5679.

CASE Collective, 'Critical approaches to security in Europe: a networked manifesto', *Security Dialogue*, 37(4) (2007): 443–487. Presents the collective approach to security studies emerging from the convergence between the Aberystwyth, Copenhagen and Paris schools.

Didier Bigo and R.B.J. Walker, 'Political sociology and the problem of the international', *Millennium*, 35(3) (2007). Discusses the category of 'the international' and its limits as well as alternative ways to think about boundaries.

Didier Bigo, Laurent Bonelli, Emmanuel Guittet, Christian Olsson and Anastassia Tsoukala, *Illiberal Practices of Liberal Regimes: The (In)security Games* (London: Routledge, Challenge Series, 2007). Presents an international political sociology view of the transformation of police, intelligence and military practices after 11 September and the notion of the field of the professionals of (in)security.

Jef Huysmans, *The Politics of Insecurity: Fear, Migration and Asylum in the EU* (London: Routledge, 2006). Presents an international political sociology view of the migration question in Europe.

PART 2
KEY CONCEPTS

Uncertainty

Ken Booth and Nicholas J. Wheeler

▌ **Abstract**

The concept of the security dilemma engages with the existential uncertainty that lies in all human relations, and especially in the arena of international politics. The chapter argues that the security dilemma is a more fundamental concept for security studies than even war and strategy. After defining the meaning of the security dilemma, the chapter proceeds to explore its dynamics, giving illustrations from current and future dangers. It argues that if security studies is to live up to its name in the twenty-first century, uncertainty and the complex phenomenon of the security dilemma must be given a central place in the agenda.

▌ **Introduction**

The term 'security dilemma' describes a familiar predicament experienced by decision-makers in a world already overflowing with dilemmas. Despite its ubiquity, our claim is that the concept has been invariably misconceived by academic theorists, yet – properly understood – it should be regarded as the most fundamental concept of all in security studies, and as such should be at the centre of a reformed agenda of this field.[1] The security dilemma is a foundational concept because, above all, it engages with the *existential condition of uncertainty* that characterizes all human relations, not least those interactions on the biggest and most violent stage of all – international politics. That its significance has not been properly recognized has been the result of orthodox thinking failing to give due credit to the work and insights of its major early theorists (John H. Herz and Herbert Butterfield, and later Robert Jervis) and at the same time missing the opportunity (as a result of paradigm blinkers) to appreciate the extent of the theoretical and practical horizons it opens up. Our claim is that an understanding of the dynamics and potentialities involved in thinking about the security dilemma gets to the heart of the central questions of security studies more profoundly than do even the traditional canon of concepts such as 'war', 'strategy', 'conflict' and the rest.

The house of uncertainty

By describing uncertainty as the 'existential' condition of human relations we mean that it is not an occasional and passing phenomenon, but rather an everyday part of the existence of individuals and groups. It is uneven in its significance and how it is felt, but it is ultimately inescapable. Insecurity, however, cannot be simply correlated with uncertainty, since uncertainty is a house in which there are many rooms, and in some life is much less insecure than in others. It is preferable to live with the uncertainties of what Kenneth Boulding (1979) called 'stable peace' than with the insecurities of Stanley Hoffmann's (1965) condition of 'state of war'. When states practise coopera-tion, or when societies embed trust in security communities, significant degrees of security are attained, even within the house of uncertainty.

In the context of International Relations, the existential condition of uncertainty means that governments (their decision-makers, military planners, foreign policy analysts) can never be 100 per cent certain about the current and future motives and intentions of those able to harm them in a military sense. We call this situation one of *unresolvable uncertainty*, and see it at the core of the predicaments that make up the security dilemma.

The drivers of unresolvable uncertainty are multiple, but they can be reduced to material and psychological phenomena, and primarily the *ambiguous symbolism* of weapons and the psychological dynamic philosophers call the 'Other Minds Problem'. Together, these create the conditions for the concept first theorized by Herz (1951) and Butterfield (1951). Students of disarmament are familiar with the strategic meaning of the idea of the *ambiguous symbolism* of weapons, if not this actual label. The term refers to the difficulty (many would say the impossibility) of safely distinguishing between 'offensive' and 'defensive' weapons. As the old adage has it, whether you regard a gun as defensive or offensive depends on whether or not you have your finger on the trigger. This subjective interpretation, in principle, is the same in international politics, though in practice it is more complex. If, for example, it is argued that it is possible to distinguish between what is clearly offensive (a sword) from what is clearly defensive (a shield) with respect to individual weapons, strategists are

BOX 10.1 THE SECURITY DILEMMA DEFINED

The security dilemma is a *two-level strategic predicament* in relations between states and other actors, with each level consisting of two related lemmas (or propositions that can be assumed to be valid) which force decision-makers to choose between them. The first and basic level consists of a *dilemma of interpretation* about the motives, intentions and capabilities of others; the second and derivative level consists of a *dilemma of response* about the most rational way of responding.

First level: a dilemma of interpretation is the predicament facing decision-makers when they are confronted, on matters affecting security, with a choice between two significant and usually (but not always) undesirable alternatives about the military policies and political postures of other entities. This dilemma of interpretation is the result of the perceived need to make a decision in the existential condition of *unresolvable uncertainty*, about the motives, intentions and capabilities of others. Those responsible have to decide whether perceived military developments are for defensive or self-protection purposes only (to enhance security in an uncertain world) or whether they are for offensive purposes (to seek to change the status quo to their advantage).

Second level: a dilemma of response logically begins when the dilemma of interpretation has been settled. Decision-makers then need to determine how to react. Should they signal, by words and deeds, that they will react in kind, for deterrent purposes? Or should they seek to signal reassurance? If the dilemma of response is based on misplaced suspicion regarding the motives and intentions of other actors, and decision-makers react in a militarily con-frontational manner, then they risk creating a significant level of mutual hostility when none was originally intended by either party; if the response is based on misplaced trust, there is a risk they will be exposed to coercion by those with hostile intentions. When leaders resolve their dilemma of response in a manner that creates a spiral of mutual hostility, when neither wanted it, a situation has developed which we call the *security paradox*.

(Booth and Wheeler 2008: 4–5)

likely to reply, unanimously, that such distinctions are operationally meaningless when interpreted as a whole, because a shield can be a vital part of an offensive move when used in combination with a sword.

Such an understanding has informed Russian, Chinese and other strategic planners in their interpretation of various plans for US ballistic missile 'shields' over the years. In the early twenty-first century, the Administration of George W. Bush attempted to justify deploying missile defence systems with the argument that they would help protect the US homeland against limited missile attack from 'rogue states' in general, and crucially Iran and North Korea in particular. Washington's critics (in potential target countries and elsewhere) claimed to the contrary that the shield of missile defence can potentially be used in combination with the sword of US offensive nuclear missiles in a disarming strike against their enemies at some point in the future. The domestic critics of such a deployment in the USA for this reason see the move as destabilizing. 'What is not a weapon in the wrong hands?' is the question delegates at the World Disarmament Conference asked themselves in the early 1930s.

The closely related second dimension of unresolvable uncertainty is the 'Other Minds Problem'. This refers to the inability of the decision-makers of one state ever to get fully into the minds of their counterparts in other states, and so understand their motives and intentions, hopes and fears, and emotions and feelings. Obviously, some degree of understanding, sympathy, and (even) empathy is usually possible, but when it comes to matters of national security, the degree of confidence required by national security planners has to be very high, since the cost of getting it wrong is never trivial. A serious misjudgement could result in a waste of money and loss of prestige through the pursuit of bad policies; ultimately, defeat in war and foreign occupation might be the outcome.

The challenges posed by the 'Other Minds Problem' are evident from the numerous illustrations of misperception in international history. On many occasions, decision-makers and analysts have made more or less serious mistakes when trying to get into the minds of those with whom they have been dealing (Jervis (1976) is still the key work). These mistakes have ranged from misreading a signal in a diplomatic conference to misinterpreting intelligence information, and so failing to predict hostile military moves. We all know how difficult it can be sometimes to understand what is going on in the minds of those we know best; it is not surprising, therefore, that the decision-makers of one country sometimes (indeed often) fail to get inside the minds of those of others from a different cultural lifeworld, and so misinterpret their motives and intentions. What is more, the levels of difficulty in international politics are compounded by the fact that governments will normally go out of their way to keep secret a great deal of what they say and do, while on important strategic issues they may engage in methods of deliberate deception.

Together, the drivers of ambiguous symbolism and the 'Other Minds Problem' result in politics among nations being characterized by *the certainty of uncertainty*. This is why the security dilemma is the most fundamental of all concepts in security studies; it alone captures the existential condition of the future environment in which political groups frame their thinking.

The quintessential dilemma

The dilemmas caused by ambiguous symbolism and the 'Other Minds Problem' are as new as today's newspaper headlines ('Russia threatening new cold war over missile defence', declared the *Guardian* on 11 April 2007) and as old as international history. On the latter, it is fascinating to recall that in the first significant account of war in the West the security dilemma was thought to be the underlying cause. Writing in the fifth century BCE, the historian (and General) Thucydides argued that what led to war in ancient Greece between Athens and Sparta was the growth of Athenian power and the fear this had caused in Sparta (Thucydides 1972: 49). The leaders of both these major powers of the time faced a *dilemma of interpretation* and a *dilemma of response* regarding the other's military plans and political motives and intentions. This two-level predicament constituting the security dilemma links 26 centuries of politics among states and nations down to the present day, from the era of city-states and spears to today's era of globalization and intercontinental missile systems.

Those responsible for the security of a political community (be it a superpower in the Cold War or ethnic groups in the Balkan wars in the early 1990s) have to decide whether perceived military developments on the part of others are for defensive or self-protection purposes only (to enhance security in an uncertain world) or whether they are for offensive purposes (to seek to change the status quo to their advantage). Logically, the dilemma of response kicks in when the dilemma of interpretation has been settled (to the extent that it ever can be, because in practice, interpretation must be continuous if it is rational). Decision-makers must decide how they will react to what they perceive to be happening: should they signal by words and deeds that they wish to show reassurance, or should they seek to send deterrent signals because of anxiety about what they fear is developing (Jervis 1976: 58–113)? When those responsible for policy remain divided or unsure in the face of a dilemma of interpretation, then arriving at a decision on their dilemma of response – and turning it into diplomatic and military moves – becomes all the more difficult. In the mid-1930s, unsure about the motives and intentions of the new Nazi regime in Germany, the British government had to decide whether its response should be to try to confront rising German military power (and perhaps provoke German nationalism, already stoked by the 'humiliation' of the Treaty of Versailles) or to reassure Germany about its place in Europe by accepting its changing military status (and so risk allowing German rearmament to steal a march if an arms race developed).

When a dilemma of interpretation is settled in favour of the view that another state is a definite threat to one's own national security, there is no longer a security dilemma; the relationship is best understood as a *strategic challenge*. It may be, of course, that the interpretation is faulty, and the other state's defensive moves are misread as being aggressive. In such a situation, decision-makers who react in a militarily confrontational way risk creating a significant level of mutual hostility when none was initially intended by either party. The result is a round of security competition which makes everybody more insecure; this is best understood as a *security paradox*, a condition that many erroneously confuse with the security dilemma from which it derived.

It should be clear by now that what underlies the dynamics of the security dilemma is fear. Indeed, as traditionally understood, the international system may be conceived as a fear system. It is a competitive self-help system in which

BOX 10.2 THE SECURITY PARADOX

A security paradox is a situation in which two or more actors, seeking only to improve their own security, provoke through their words or actions an increase in mutual tension, resulting in less security all round.

(Booth and Wheeler 2008: 9)[2]

states fear being attacked, fear dropping in the prosperity league, fear leaving themselves open to attack, fear losing prestige, fear being oppressed by outsiders – and on and on. For many, fear makes the world go around.

For Herz, who first coined the term 'security dilemma', the issue at the base of social life was 'kill or perish' (Herz 1951: 3). For Butterfield, the other pioneer, the inability of one set of decision-makers to enter into the counter-fear of others was the 'irreducible dilemma' (1951: 20). In other words, for Herz fear created a structure of conflict between groups, while for Butterfield this fear derived from an inescapable inability of people(s) to understand how their own peaceful/benign motives and defensive/reactive intentions could be interpreted as threatening by others. The operating principle for those responsible for national security planning tends to be: 'You have nothing to fear from us, but we must be concerned that your motives, even if peaceful now, might not be in the future, and that your intentions – whether or not reactive now – give you the increased power to further your ambitions.' Clearly, the problems of mistrust are maximized when current predicaments are set against a historical record of a conflictual relationship.

Future uncertainty appears therefore to construct international politics as an inescapable insecurity trap. Even if, today, the government of State A considers the leadership group in State B to be peacefully inclined, can it afford to rely indefinitely on 'best-case' thinking in a situation where bad judgements of interpretation and response can have such negative consequences for one's own state (Copeland 2000, 2003, Mearsheimer 2001)? The conclusion drawn so often through history has been that those charged with responsibility for a state's or people's security must never rely on best-case forecasting when assessing potential threats to their well-being. Instead, the guiding principle must be very conservative. Barry Posen put it very baldly when he advised that states 'must assume the worst because the worst is possible' (Posen 1993: 28). The corollary of all this, in the language of US security dilemma theorists, is that defensively motivated states cannot 'signal type' (Glaser 1992, 1997, Kydd 1997a, 1997b, 2000, 2005, Mitzen 2006). That is, however peaceful State A believes itself to be, it can never transmit such intent with 100 per cent effectiveness to State B (and C, D) because others know that 'the worst is possible' in a world of future uncertainty.

If uncertainty and fear logically exist at the best of times in relations between states – when all the parties hold weapons only for self-protection, but cannot effectively signal this to others – then can there ever be any hope that humans can live together in a more peaceful world? In this understanding, the security dilemma depicts politics among nations as being a potential or actual war system *even* when all the units believe themselves as having peaceful/benign motives and defensive/reactive intentions. This is why it is the quintessential dilemma in international politics.

Butterfield, as a historian, claimed that it was only much later, when the guns had gone silent, that it became possible to reconstruct the past, and so to understand the motives and intentions of the key actors. But we now know that such a view belongs to an older and more confident era of historiography. Today we are more familiar with the idea of an endless debate among historians – adding further layers of uncertainty. If historians, with critical distance and abundant information, cannot make up their minds about the interpretations and responses of policy-makers in the past, students of security studies should show sympathy to the predicaments that had to be faced by those on whose shoulders rested great responsibilities, when operating with always limited information and often very compressed time in the face of terrible risks.

Three logics

The previous section concluded by recognizing the limited time and knowledge often faced by decision-makers in international politics. When this is the case, what tends to fill the gaps in their knowledge are their philosophical and theoretical understandings of how the world works. With this in mind, we identify below three a priori logics that have framed the way theorists and practitioners of international politics have thought about the security dilemma:

- *Fatalist logic* is the idea that security competition can never be escaped in international politics. Human nature and the condition of international anarchy determine that humans will live in an essentially conflictual world.

- *Mitigator logic* is the idea that security competition can be ameliorated or dampened down for a time, but never eliminated. Here, notions of regimes and societies are key, blunting the worst features of anarchy.

- *Transcender logic* is the idea that human society is self-constitutive, not determined. Humans have agency, as individuals and groups, and so human society can seek to become what it chooses to be, though inherited structural constraints will always be powerful. A global community of peace and trust is in principle possible if in practice it currently looks improbable.

From these three logical positions derive characteristic forms of international behaviour.

Fatalist voices say that the search for security is primordial, and because groups cannot trust each other in conditions of anarchy, relations between states are essentially competitive, sometimes violent, and always characterized by a degree of insecurity. The logic of interstate anarchy (there is no supreme authority above states) is to maximize power and especially military power. In such a worldview, rational behaviour consists of mistrusting all around, and taking what advantage one can whenever it is prudent to do so. Cooperation can take place, but only when it is in one's immediate interests to do so. States are conceived as 'rational egoists'. The ideal type of this worldview in contemporary International Relations theorizing is 'offensive realism'.

Mitigator logic accepts that the international system is technically anarchic, but does not believe that this must necessarily mean that anarchy is synonymous with chaos and violent conflict. A major strand of thought within mitigator logic has focused on the concept of 'security regimes'. The latter seek through mutual learning and institutionalization to bring a degree of predictable order into security relationships. An alternative strand of mitigator logic is that of the English School, though its exponents have strangely neglected comprehensive and constructive engagement with the theory and practice of security. English School thinking about 'society' has focused on the building of the institutions of international law, developing processes of moderate diplomacy, and experimenting with norms such as mutual military transparency. As a result, a society of states can exist with predictable order, and hence the amelioration of the security dilemma.

The view identified earlier with Butterfield that it is impossible to enter into another's counter-fear has been challenged by certain ideas within mitigator logic. In the 1980s 'common security' thinking in particular attempted to reduce the most dangerous features of the superpower confrontation. The key here was the idea of security not *against* others (the fatalist logic) but security *with* others (with the implication that the parties are able to understand to a reasonable degree the counter-fear of the other parties). In practice, this was most notably demonstrated by Mikhail Gorbachev, leader of the USSR after

---

BOX 10.3 JOHN MEARSHEIMER'S CONCEPTION OF OFFENSIVE REALISM

The sad fact is that international politics has always been a ruthless and dangerous business, and it is likely to remain that way. Although the intensity of their competition waxes and wanes, great powers fear each other and always compete with each other for power. . . . But great powers do not merely strive to be the strongest of all the great powers. . . . Their ultimate aim is to be the hegemon – that is, the only great power in the system. . . . Why do great powers behave this way? My answer is that the structure of the international system forces states which seek only to be secure nonetheless to act aggressively toward each other. . . . This situation, which no one consciously designed or intended, is genuinely tragic.

(Mearsheimer 2001: 2–3)

BOX 10.4 ROBERT JERVIS' DEFINITION OF A SECURITY REGIME

By a security regime I mean . . . those principles, rules, and norms that permit nations to be restrained in their behaviour in the belief that others will reciprocate. This concept implies not only norms and expectations that facilitate cooperation, but a form of cooperation that is more than the following of short-run self-interest.

(Jervis 1982: 357)

1985, who was able to begin to wind down the Cold War because he began to understand how the West felt threatened by Soviet forces and postures. As a result he sought to address the causes of such fears by offering to eliminate the most threatening parts of Soviet military deployments and foreign policy positions (Wiseman 2002: ch. 5). Here, Gorbachev showed his appreciation of how mutual mistrust and suspicion could result from security dilemma dynamics, and in seeking to dampen down these dynamics through his trust-building initiatives, he exercised what we call *security dilemma sensibility*.

What has characterized transcender logic has been the variety of viewpoints and theories it has sponsored, from the centralization of power globally necessitated in world government to the decentralization of traditional anarchist theory. Some strands have been reformist, others very revolutionary. What they all share is the belief that history rather than necessity has got us where we are, and that it is possible (if extremely difficult) to construct a radically different world order – including one in which dilemmas of interpretation and response are replaced by a successful politics of trust-building. One of the difficulties facing transcender logic as a whole is that the separate strands tend to reduce the problem of insecurity in world politics to one cause (capitalism, patriarchy, anarchy) and one related solution. One of the problems of the transcender logic, therefore, is that its various strands are themselves a major cause of disagreement.

BOX 10.5 SECURITY DILEMMA SENSIBILITY DEFINED

Security dilemma sensibility is an actor's intention and capacity to perceive the motives behind, and to show responsiveness towards, the potential complexity of the military intentions of others. In particular, it refers to the ability to understand the role that fear might play in their attitudes and behaviour, including, crucially, the role that one's own actions may play in provoking that fear.

(Booth and Wheeler 2008: 7)

Despite the generally limited success of much transcender thinking, all is not lost for those who hope for a more peaceful world. The most significant theory and practice within transcender logic – the one with most purchase in the real world – is the idea of 'security community'. Its political manifestation has been the project that developed in Western Europe from the late 1940s onwards, to bring peace, prosperity and security to the traditional cockpit of realist thinking and war. In this laboratory – now extending far across the continent – militarized security competition appears to have been *transcended* indefinitely, though some uncertainty can never be escaped – as in all human relations. In the security community of Europe there are interactions between states and societies at multiple levels; states have stopped targeting each other in a military sense; and war has become unthinkable (Deutsch 1957).

It is for each student of security studies to decide which of the three logics, and which strand within each, gives the best account of international politics, and which represents the most desirable and feasible guide for future policy-making. In our view, offensive realism may offer some short-term security (especially for the most powerful) but that ultimately its effect is to replicate the 'war system' (Falk and Kim 1980), and to do so with ever more dangerous weaponry. Security regimes, conceived and practised according to rational egoism,[3] will always contain 'the seeds of their own destruction' (Jervis 1982: 368), as they have in the past. A more sophisticated approach within mitigator thinking has been that of the English School, which for all its conceptual and practical lacunae has crucially focused on the potentialities for diplomats to construct lasting order in international society through developing shared interests and values that promote practices of common security. Within transcender logic we identify the idea of security communities as the most hopeful project for those who do not think that society must live fatalistically in a condition of war and the preparation for war.

The concept of the security dilemma has been much contested, and its empirical manifestations have been interpreted in a variety of not always positive ways; nonetheless, the practices of security communities have challenged in a fundamental manner some of the basic patterns of thought ('the

BOX 10.6 KARL DEUTSCH'S DEFINITION OF A SECURITY COMMUNITY

[A] group of people which has become 'integrated'. By *integration* we mean the attainment, within a territory, of a 'sense of community' and of institutions and practices strong enough and widespread enough to assure . . . dependable expectations of 'peaceful change' among its population. By *sense of community* we mean a belief . . . that common social problems must and can be resolved by processes of 'peaceful change'.

(Deutsch 1957: 5)

logic of anarchy') associated with the Westphalian era. In drawing special attention to the promise of security communities, we are not saying that their members have 'escaped' the security dilemma finally, since uncertainty is the existential condition as was argued above. What we do claim, however, is that the workings of such a security community have so shifted the conditions for politics that we can claim that the security dilemma has effectively been *transcended* because war has become practically unthinkable. In the case of the EU, the ambiguous symbolism of weapons has become irrelevant, because the members do not target each other, and the 'Other Minds Problem' has shifted from the life-and-death agenda of military competition to the normal politics of life under capitalism and liberal democracy. In the house of uncertainty, rooms marked 'security community' are promising places to live.

The security dilemma in the twenty-first century

We believe that the security dilemma should be at the heart of security studies not only because its significance pervades the 'very geometry' of human conflict, as Butterfield put it, but also because it speaks directly and urgently to some of the main challenges of our time. There are strong grounds for thinking that world politics has entered a period of unprecedented insecurity – a 'Great Reckoning', when human society locally and globally will increasingly come face-to-face with its most fundamental self-created difficulties (Booth 2007: ch. 9). The coming decades will see a potentially disastrous convergence of dangers unless sensible collective action is quickly taken to head them off. In a new era of uncertainty human society will be challenged by a novel combination of old and new security predicaments in relation to such issue areas as nuclear proliferation, terrorism, 'climate chaos', competition for non-renewable (especially traditional energy) resources, mass migration, great power rivalry, cultural/religious/civilizational clashes, and the growing gap between haves and have-nots. All these risks threaten to be exacerbated by the huge but uneven growth in the global population – a topic with which security studies and indeed International Relations in general has not yet begun to seriously engage. In most of these key risk areas,[4] as we discuss in the four major illustrations below, security dilemma dynamics threaten to heighten fear, provoke mistrust, and close down possibilities for building cooperation and trust.

First: the danger of a new Cold War with China. An immanent threat exists of Sino–US competition developing in dangerous ways. The crisis area of the Taiwan Straits continues to represent the functional equivalent of the Central Front in US–Soviet Cold War rivalry; that is, the symbolic and actual face-to-face line of confrontation. The Straits are an active theatre of security dilemma dynamics, being highly weaponized and the site of potentially uncontrollable military escalation. In the background, two related issues that have been fuelling mistrust between Beijing and Washington are missile defences and the weaponization of space. What worries strategic planners in Beijing is that

Washington might view Ballistic Missile Defence (BMD) as part of an offensive strategy of nuclear pre-emption designed to give the USA dominance over the process of escalation in any future crisis (Lieber and Press 2006: 52). Even if Chinese leaders are persuaded that a particular US administration does not harbour aggressive intent (a predicament recognized all too well by US offensive realists) what guarantees can they have that future US leaders will not seek to employ missile defences as part of an offensive strategy? At the same time, the White House has not been persuaded that China's motives and intentions are peaceful when it comes to outer space, a perception which Beijing did nothing to allay by its successful launch of an anti-satellite weapon in early 2007 (though the Chinese could easily justify this as a countervailing move in the light of US plans). Beijing has claimed that it wants to limit not accelerate the competition in space weapons, but the problem with such professions of peaceful intent is that the boundary between 'peaceful' and 'military' uses of technology is invariably blurred when it comes to outer space. Fatalist logic would argue that given the inability of the USA and China to 'signal type' in space, there is no alternative but for planners to assume the worst and treat all deployments as potentially offensive. While cautioning against the trap of applying offensive realist prescriptions to outer space, Bruce Blair and Chen Yali recognized that 'there is nothing China can do to convince American worst-case analysts that China could not possibly adapt its dual-use space capabilities for "possibly" posing military threats to the United States' (2006: 5). Consequently, under fatalist logic, there is no prospect of Sino–US cooperation in preventing space from becoming weaponized. Each set of decision-makers will feel compelled to seek security in space at the expense of the other, replicating key aspects of the dynamics that have historically driven security competition on Earth.

Second: the danger of new arms races. The post-Cold War peace dividend never materialized, and in a period of intensifying international tension it would not be a surprise to see the revival of competitive arms building. New arms races might be global (Russia versus United States) or regional (South versus North Korea), and they might be conventional (Pakistan versus India) or nuclear (Turkey versus Iran). In these cases, security dilemma dynamics work in well-understood ways, with future uncertainty about motives and intentions feeding existing mistrust, and resulting in a contagion of security paradoxes. Ostensible US worries about 'rogue states' (whatever their label) are used to justify missile defence deployment, which in turn provokes counters from Moscow, believing the moves really to be about placing the USA in a position of global dominance. The DPRK's fears about US intentions have led to a nuclear weapons programme that may have been intended for deterrent purposes but which intensifies existing anxieties in South Korea and Japan about the future motives of the regime in Pyongyang. Future Pakistani defensive moves in conventional forces in relation to its role in the so-called 'War on Terror' and in face of India's growing superpower potential might provoke Indian fears that such capabilities may be used to try to settle the Kashmir conflict, and so lead to a demand by Indian planners for more deterrent power at all levels. Finally, Iranian ambitions to develop a civilian nuclear capability have provoked regional as well as wider international fears about the possibility of weaponization, and if the latter fears grow – and certainly if Iran became a declared nuclear weapons state – then it would lead inexorably to similar developments on the part of Turkey and other neighbours.

Three: the danger of a world of many nuclear powers. The threat here is of the breakdown of the Nuclear Non-proliferation Treaty (NPT) regime, and with it the spread of nuclear weapons technology to an increasing number of states (see Chapter 24, this volume). Few believe that a world of many nuclear powers will be a safer world (Waltz (1981) is an important counter-thesis – see also the Sagan and Waltz (2003) debate), yet the diffusion of civilian nuclear facilities (accelerated by concerns about the growing depletion of fossil fuels and the search for clean energy) to an increasing number of states will make it easier than hitherto to make the move from being a state using nuclear technology for peaceful purposes (energy) to one using it for weapons. If, as a consequence of the resulting dilemmas of interpretation, states begin to hedge against the collapse of the NPT, the outcome will be a self-fulfilling prophecy of regime breakdown. This will multiply the range of nuclear risks including accidental war, 'loose nukes', nuclear entrepreneurship, acquisition by terror-ists, inadvertent nuclear war, crises resulting from non-nuclear weapon states rapidly moving towards nuclear status (especially in tense regional situations), and the problems of stability between nascent nuclear powers without sophisticated command-and-control arrangements.

Four: the danger of terrorism. The Bush Administration's declaration of a worldwide 'War on Terror' in the aftermath of 9/11 contributed to the globalization of the phenomenon of 'international terrorism', which had been perceived to be on the rise for some time. In many parts of the world, the use of terror tactics are ever more feared, though their actual occurrence (as yet) falls short of public perceptions of the danger. International terrorism feeds off local problems but has increasingly been synergistic with regional- and global-level confrontations between identity groups associated with cultural or religious markers. In this way, the terror threat has been globalized (see Chapter 12, this volume). It is also multi-level, with potential dangers ranging from individual attacks in cafés or public transport to 'dirty' bombs (see Barnaby 2004: 13, 37–39, 153, Martin 2006: 229, 279–282) and biological attacks (see Rees 2003: 47–57, Martin 2006: 282–285) aimed at mass casualties dis-rupting life on a huge scale. The apogee of the globalization of the security dilemma in this new age of uncertainty are those situations in which fellow citizens from different 'identity groups' may no longer be trusted to share the same values, and whom one may fear may be ready to use violence – including suicidal tactics – to further extremist causes. Moreover, in a world where nuclear materials are predicted to be more plentiful than previously, with significant proportions of it being unaccountable, the prospects for a nuclear-armed terrorist will grow (Barnaby 2004: 108–150). Looking beyond the early decades of the twenty-first century, some scientists and futurologists have warned of the dangers of genetic manipulation leading to terrifying diseases which could be used for political purposes by states or other entities.

It should be evident from these illustrations that the security dilemma – its vocabulary, dynamics and insights – speaks directly to some of the major issues of our time. Back in the 1950s, Herz had claimed that the security dilemma had reached its 'utmost poignancy' (1959: 241). There could be no doubt at that time about the relevance of the concept to the potential catastrophe of the Cold War spiralling out of control through failures to appreciate security dilemma dynamics. Nonetheless, we would claim that the global predicament has moved even beyond Herz's judgement in the late 1950s that bipolarity and the threat of nuclear annihilation had created conditions for the security dilemma's 'utmost' relevance (1959). We believe world politics have entered a new age of uncertainty. Its terrain is being shaped by manifold risk and danger, by mistrust and long-term fear, by the fragility of cooperation and unwillingness to trust, and by the expectation of a prolonged season of uncertainty. When Tony Blair introduced the British government's White Paper on the renewal of its Trident nuclear weapons system in December 2006 – in the view of many people well ahead of when he needed do it – he argued that the United Kingdom should continue as a nuclear weapons state for at least the next 50 years. He spoke for many governments around the world when he said, 'the one certain thing about our world today is uncertainty' (Blair 2006). This view, given authoritatively on the part of one of the most territorially secure states in the world, is a token of the power of the unresolvable uncertainty that characterizes the security dilemma.

Our general claim is that uncertainty in the twenty-first century is set to be intense and globalized, and multi-level and multi-directional, and that many of the key issue areas are likely to be subject to security dilemma dynamics, and hence amenable to analysis in terms of relevant frameworks of analysis (including the injunction to explore mitigator and transcender themes, such as security dilemma sensibility and security communities). Without doubt, the dynamics described by the concept continue to have impact in real sites of power and violence across the globe, and so the prospects for building world security would suffer if policy-makers and scholars conspire to marginalize the insights and prescriptions offered by security dilemma theorizing – as they did in the Cold War (Buzan 1991: 4). In the fast changing terrain of contemporary security and insecurity, the security dilemma deserves a special place for those wanting to understand our times and engage with them if human society in whole and in part is to have hope of developing in decent shape.

Towards a new agenda for security studies

Space allows only the briefest discussion of what a reformed agenda might look like, so we will confine ourselves to indicating some ways in which the concept of the security dilemma is central to answering some of the most basic questions of philosophy and social science: What is real? What can we know? How might we act? (Booth 2007).

What is real? In today's world, students of security studies are charged with analysing a wider set of referents and issue areas than was the case on the traditional agenda – namely states and military power/force. This certainly does not mean in our view that states and military force are irrelevant: far from it. We would oppose any approach to security studies that eschewed the military dimension of world politics, or the referent of sovereign states. However, we do believe that the traditional agenda should be approached through the perspective of what Robert Cox called 'critical' rather than orthodox or 'problem-solving' theorizing (Cox 1981). This means shifting the weight of the agenda from focusing on the problems *in* the status quo to the problems *of* the status quo (Booth 2005c). This means that insecurity should be understood first as the consequence of a wider range of threats (e.g. poverty, the environment, the global economy) than that of military violence, and second, contemplating a wider range of referents (e.g. individuals, regions, common humanity) than sovereign states. It took a decade or so before academic theorizing began to grasp the changes brought about by the advent of the atomic bombs and then hydrogen weapons and intercontinental delivery systems, and so began what has been called the 'golden age' of strategic studies. If security studies for the era of globalization is to produce its own golden age, then it is necessary to reorient its research into a deeper understanding of the role of uncertainty in world politics, and its potentialities. The security dilemma is fundamental to this, recognizing the existential reality of uncertainty in human affairs, but at the same time looking towards a realization that uncertainty is a house with many rooms.

What can we know? In the light of the changing context of world politics, security studies needs a much wider group of experts than those who dominated the mainstream during the Cold War and who still now set the agenda in a broadly business-as-usual direction. Security studies in the twenty-first century needs not only deterrence theorists but also those who understand economic development; not just conflict managers but confidence builders; and not just tinkerers with the status quo but global trust-builders. This is an argument for pluralism, to keep everybody honest, and for challenging the ethnocentrism in the Anglo-American orthodoxy. We believe that by focusing research on uncertainty, and its acute manifestation in the security dilemmas between political entities, there is an opportunity for issues to be addressed by a fruitful collaboration across a spectrum of theoretical perspectives – allowing each to bring its own special insights, as opposed to the dialogues of the deaf that currently take place. In other words, as the agenda of security studies is broadening and deepening under the pressure of real events, it is necessary to broaden and deepen the bases of knowledge accordingly, which in turn means inviting a wider range of areas of expertise to the academic conversation on security.

What might be done? It is evident that human societies will continue to want problem solvers in the status quo, though two warnings must be given. First, on matters of immediate policy relevance, academics can have only a limited impact, because bureaucracies have relative advantages in terms of information and access. And second, the status quo in the security field is overwhelmingly dominated by the agendas and perspectives of nations and states, and the tribal analyses and perspectives that tend to emerge are rarely best calculated to advance the interests of world security in an age threatened by global dangers. As the twenty-first century unfolds, the special role for academics lies in the opportunities they have for understanding the manifold dimensions of uncertainty in human relations and opening up pathways of thought and action regarding the global challenges that are moving from the horizon to centre-stage. These, overwhelmingly, derive from the problems *of* the status quo. If we are right, and the most important and interesting work relating to international and world security lies on the borderlands between, on the one hand certain strands of mitigator thinking (largely common security advocates and English School solidarists concerned with military confidence-building and post-national identity formation) and on the other, the reformist strand of transcender thinking (concerned with security community building and maintenance) then the implications for security studies are enormous.[5] Unless one espouses the fatalist outlook of offensive realism or the rational egoism of security regime theorists, a reformed agenda must seek to open up the potential for human agency to build cooperation and trust at all levels of political community. At the heart of this is the notion of security dilemma sensibility, which seeks to do what Butterfield thought impossible; namely to overcome the challenge of successfully signalling peaceful intent, and so transcend the dilemmas of interpretation and trust – and thus the likelihood of relations spiralling into armed competition, and the trap of the security paradox.

Security dilemma sensibility offers human society globally some hope of coming through the dangerous decades ahead in more positive shape than currently seems conceivable if governments and societies remain wedded to the global politics of business as usual. If security studies is to be other than an activity in which its exponents focus entirely on their own nation, then its students must accept that future uncertainty cannot be escaped through a mix of technology and rational egoism. Fatalism about global insecurity will be self-fulfilling. In contrast, a comprehensive understanding of the dynamics of the security dilemma and the requirements of the political conditions of trust offer at least a glimpse into the theory and practice of a radically different but still realistic world – a world characterized by the political, economic, social and philosophical uncertainties of human existence, but a world in which people are progressively emancipated from direct and structural violence. Relations characterized by mutual trust-building represent the mirror-image of those in which fatalist assumptions about world politics generate and exacerbate security dilemma dynamics. The theory and practice of trust-building must be a priority on the future agenda of academics if we are finally to see the emergence in the twenty-first century of a true security studies, as opposed to the 'insecurity studies' that has dominated International Relations since the Second World War.

Notes

1   The ideas in this chapter derive from Booth and Wheeler 2008.
2   For the phrase but not the definition we acknowledge Justin Morris.
3   Our use of the term 'rational egoism' follows that of Robert Jervis who defined it as a situation where actors place 'primary value on [their] own security . . . and [do] not care much about others' well-being as an end in itself' (1982: 364; see also Glaser 1997: 197).
4   The security dilemma is only relevant in situations where intentionality (and hence the 'Other Minds Problem') comes into play. This reduces its relevance in some of the key areas of insecurity now and in the future, such as the fear of pandemics or the consequences of climate change.
5   For 'solidarism' see Wheeler (2000) and for 'common security' see Wiseman (2002).

Further reading

Ken Booth and Nicholas J. Wheeler, *The Security Dilemma: Fear, Cooperation and Trust in World Politics* (Basingstoke: Palgrave, 2008). The most up-to-date and comprehensive exegesis of the concept, together with an extensive discussion of historical illustrations and its contemporary relevance.

Herbert Butterfield, *History and Human Relations* (London: Collins, 1951). Chapter 1 of this book, 'The Tragic Element of International Conflict', provides the first elucidation of the psychological dynamics driving the security dilemma, particularly the inability of decision-makers to realize that others do not necessarily see them as they see themselves.

John Herz, 'Idealist internationalism and the security dilemma', *World Politics*, 2(2) (1950): 157–180. The first article on the security dilemma.

John Herz, *Political Realism and Political Idealism: A Study in Theories and Realities* (Chicago, IL: Chicago University Press, 1951). This book locates the concept of the security dilemma in the context of realist and idealist theories of International Relations. The book is frequently interpreted as a classic realist text, but Herz opens up in the second half of the book the possibilities for 'mitigating' the security dilemma.

John Herz, *International Politics in the Atomic Age* (Columbia: Columbia University Press, 1959). This book develops Herz's position on the security dilemma, particularly his disagreements with Butterfield on the ubiquity of the security dilemma. However, the book is also important because it sets out his view that world conditions (the threat of nuclear annihilation) were creating the basis for a new universal politics of global survival.

Robert Jervis, *Perception and Misperception in International Politics* (Princeton, NJ: Princeton University Press, 1976). This book remains the most sophisticated and influential analysis of the psychological factors influencing security dilemma dynamics.

Robert Jervis, 'Cooperation under the security dilemma', *World Politics*, 40(1) (1978): 167–214. This article remains the seminal discussion of the role that offence–defence dynamics play in exacerbating or ameliorating security dilemma dynamics in international politics. It focuses on the inter-relationship between the material and psychological dimensions of the security dilemma.

War

Paul D. Williams

▌ Abstract

This chapter examines the concept of war and some of the major trends in armed conflict, especially in the period since 1945. Although the threat of major war between the great powers has receded with the end of the Cold War, many parts of the world are still suffering from ongoing armed conflicts or trying to overcome the legacies of old ones. Particularly in parts of the developing world, war remains a considerable source of insecurity. This chapter begins by outlining three different philosophies of war and examines how the concept has been defined within security studies. It then examines the major trends in armed conflicts since 1945 and asks who is doing the fighting and the dying in the world's contemporary war zones. The final section discusses whether the nature of warfare is changing by analysing recent debates about the idea of total war; the extent to which globalization has produced a novel form of armed conflict commonly referred to as 'new wars'; and the characteristics influencing how Western states have used military force in the contemporary period.

Introduction

Students of security cannot afford to ignore warfare: it has caused huge amounts of suffering but it has also prompted technological innovation and sometimes acted as a catalyst for social and political reforms. Sometimes it is considered a necessary part of maintaining what the United Nations (UN) Charter refers to as 'international peace and security'. Some people study wars in order to help their side win them; others draw an analogy with medical science's approach to disease and argue that one must study war in order to eradicate it. Whatever one's motivation, a concern with war has formed the traditional core of security studies; and some analysts think it should stay that way.

Although recent decades have seen wars decline in both their number and intensity, huge sums of money are still spent on waging them and developing weapons systems to win future ones. By late 2006, for instance, the US government was spending approximately $8 billion per month in Iraq alone (ISG 2006: 32), while the Stockholm International Peace Research Institute estimated that by 2005 worldwide military expenditure had reached $1,118 billion in current US dollars. Although the end of the Cold War has reduced the threat of major war between the great powers, many parts of the developing world in particular still suffer from the effect of (past and present) armed conflicts. This chapter examines some of the different ways of understanding war's place in world politics, some of the major trends that have been identified in armed conflicts since 1945, and the extent to which the nature of warfare has changed over time.

Three philosophies of war

In his introduction to the Penguin edition of Carl von Clausewitz's unfinished classic, *On War*, Anatol Rapoport (1968: 11) noted that although Clausewitz was often dubbed 'The Philosopher of War', there are in fact several philosophies of war and Clausewitz was simply the most important proponent of one of them. These different philosophies are important not only because they give different answers to the question 'What is war?' but also because humans are sentient beings and consequently what they think about an issue like warfare can have an important bearing on its nature. As Rapoport (1968: 12–13) suggested, 'We would be well advised to inquire into the way the acceptance or rejection of a particular philosophy of war is likely to influence the role of war in human affairs and so profoundly affect our lives.' In Rapoport's framework the three philosophies were labelled the *political*, the *eschatological* and the *cataclysmic*.

Clausewitz was arguably the most important proponent of the *political* philosophy of war, which famously defined warfare as 'an act of violence intended to compel our opponent to fulfil our will' (Clausewitz 1976: 75). This philosophy conceived of war as being rational, national and instrumental. By this Clausewitz meant that the decision to employ the military instrument by waging war ought to be made on the basis of a rational calculation taken by the political authority concerned in order to achieve some specified goal. In Clausewitz's schema political authority resided in sovereign states. During his lifetime (1780–1831), war was widely viewed as a legitimate instrument of state policy albeit one that should be used only with a clear purpose in mind. In practice, victory in such rational, national and instrumental wars usually went to those who were most accomplished in the arts of attrition and manoeuvre.

In contrast to this view, the *eschatological* philosophy revolves around 'the idea that history, or at least some portion of history, will culminate in a "final" war leading to the unfolding of some grand design – divine, natural, or human' (Rapoport 1968: 15). Rapoport suggested that this philosophy comes in two variants: messianic and global. In the messianic variant the agency destined to carry out the 'grand design' is presumed to exist already. Its 'mission' was likely to involve 'imposing a just peace on the world', thus 'eliminating war from future history'. Expressions of such a philosophy have included the crusaders' attempts to unite the known world under a single faith in the Middle Ages, the Nazi doctrine of the Master Race, or al-Qa'ida's vision of a global caliphate. In the global variant, the 'grand design' is presumed to arise from the chaos of the 'final war'. In Christian eschatology, for example, this would involve forces which will rally around Christ in the Second Coming. Alternatively, in communist eschatology the struggle for power was waged between classes rather than between states or religions. From this perspective the emergence of the 'world proletariat' was required to convert imperialist war into class war and, after defeating the bourgeoisie, to establish a world order in which wars will no longer occur.

Finally, the *cataclysmic* philosophy conceived of war 'as a catastrophe that befalls some portion of humanity or the entire human race' (Rapoport 1968: 16). In this view, war could be seen as a scourge of God or as an unfortunate by-product of the anarchic 'international system'. This philosophy also comes in two variants: ethnocentric and global. In the ethnocentric version, war is understood as something that is likely to befall us; specifically war is something that *others* threaten to do to us. The coming war is not seen as beneficial to us; all that can be done is to forestall the impending disaster or alleviate its worst effects. In the global variant, war is a cataclysm that affects humanity as a whole and not just this or that group of humans. No one is held responsible and no one will benefit from it. As a result, this philosophy focuses attention on the prevention of war; 'on uncovering the causes of war and on inventing institutionalized methods of conflict resolution' (Rapoport 1968: 40; see also Roberts 2005 and Chapter 6, this volume).

Based on these descriptions, Rapoport (1968: 16) suggested that 'in political philosophy war is compared to a game of strategy (like chess); in eschatological philosophy, to a mission or the dénouement of a drama; in cataclysmic philosophy, to a fire or epidemic'.

In historical terms, during the period from the Napoleonic era until the First World War, European politics provided just the right conditions to allow Clausewitz's political philosophy to flourish and become dominant. By the time Europe's major armies had become bogged down in the trench warfare of the First World War, however, it was clear that developments in military technology had rendered Clausewitzean methods of attrition incredibly costly to implement and the art of manoeuvre almost impossible. The industrialized slaughter of 'the Great War' thus ceased to serve the political aims of either side. The result was that the eschatological and cataclysmic philosophies gained increasing prominence.

A glance at the landscape of contemporary world politics reveals that in some important respects the political philosophy espoused by Clausewitz is under significant challenge. It is clearly alive and well in the military colleges of Western states but outside these corridors other philosophies are in the ascendancy. Indeed, as Box 11.1 illustrates, a debate continues to rage over the extent to which Clausewitzean thinking is still relevant to today's wars. From today's vantage point, several developments have eroded the appeal and power of the political philosophy of war.

First, the concept of the battlefield, so central to the way in which Clausewitz understood warfare, has dissolved. The 9/11 attacks, for instance, demonstrated that today's battlegrounds might be Western (or other) cities while the US-led 'War on Terror' – now rebranded as the 'long war' – conceives of the battlefield as literally spanning the entire globe. Even when Western states have been able to localize the theatre of war in places such as Serbia, Sierra Leone and Somalia, the need to use military force – often in the name of maintaining 'international peace and security' – usually highlighted the failure of those governments to achieve their stated objectives by other means. In the future, however, battles are unlikely to be confined to planet Earth as the US in particular will be forced to militarize space in an effort to protect the satellites upon which its communication and information systems depend (Hirst 2002). Back on planet Earth, rising levels of urbanization and the desire of anti-Western forces for concealment have contributed to more engagements being fought in urban areas including industrialized cities, shanty towns and even refugee/displacement camps (Hills 2004). Conducting military operations in urban areas poses many difficult challenges because they are far more interactive environments than jungles or deserts.

Second, as the speeches of both Osama bin Laden and US President George W. Bush make clear, the leadership cadres on both sides of the 'War on Terror' have often rejected political narratives of warfare. Instead, they have adopted eschatological philosophies in their respective rallying cries for a global jihad and a just war against evildoers.

A third problem for advocates of the political philosophy and one which Clausewitz obviously never encountered is war involving the 'exchange' of nuclear weapons. Far from furthering the political objectives of the participants this is more likely to resemble a mutual suicide pact between the states involved. As the technology to make nuclear weapons continues to diffuse and attempts

BOX 11.1 IS CLAUSEWITZ'S THINKING STILL RELEVANT?

Martin Van Creveld: 'contemporary "strategic" thought . . . is fundamentally flawed; and, in addition, is rooted in a "Clausewitzian" world-picture that is either obsolete or wrong. We are entering an era . . . of warfare between ethnic and religious groups. . . . In the future, war will not be waged by armies but by groups whom we today call terrorists, guerrillas, bandits, and robbers, but who will undoubtedly hit on more formal titles to describe themselves. Their organizations are likely to be constructed on charismatic lines rather than institutional ones, and to be motivated less by "professionalism" than by fanatical, ideologically-based loyalties. . . . If low-intensity conflict is indeed the wave of the future, then strategy in its classical sense will disappear' (Van Creveld 1991: ix, 197, 207).

General Sir Rupert Smith: In today's wars, fighting occurs among the civilian populace; it is 'war amongst the people'. The aim of using military force is 'to influence the intentions of the people.' Consequently, 'I do not agree with some who dismiss Clausewitz and his trinity as irrelevant: it is my experience in both national and international operations that without all three elements of the trinity – state, military and the people – it is not possible to conduct a successful military operation, especially not over time.' 'Clausewitz's trinity of state, army and people is a useful tool with which to analyse the actors' purpose and activities, despite their [often] not being states.' Even apparently formless non-state actors 'will also have some dependency and relationship with the people, there will be an armed force of some description and there will be some political direction to the use of force.' In this type of environment, however, there must be a shift in emphasis from destruction to communication. When communication to capture the will of the people is the objective, military operations must be conducted with an appreciation of how the mass media constructs its narratives and in such a way as to influence its interpretation of events. Furthermore, military force must be used within the appropriate legal frameworks: 'to operate tactically outside the law is to attack one's own strategic objective' (Smith, R. 2005: 277, 58, 303, 379).

to bolster the Nuclear Non-Proliferation Treaty continue to falter, the world may well be entering the most dangerous phase of nuclear confrontation since the second Cold War of the 1980s. In addition, the potential for nuclear weapons to fall into the hands of groups committed to carrying out 'terrorist spectaculars' without making specific demands is a worrying break from Clausewitzean tradition (see Chapter 24, this volume).

Finally, when confronted by 'revolutionary' wars which cry out for counter-revolutionary responses, Clausewitz's injunction to destroy the military forces of the adversary is problematic not just because such 'military forces' are often indistinguishable from the local populace but also because one can never be sure they have been eliminated 'unless one is ready to destroy a large portion of the population' (Rapoport 1968: 53; see also Chapter 26, this volume). The problem, as Rapoport noted, is that 'this usually conflicts with the political aim of the war' – to ensure the irrelevance of the revolutionary ideology in question – 'and hence also violates a fundamental Clausewitzean principle'.

As we have seen, different philosophies understand war in different ways. It is fair to say, however, that the political philosophy has been the most prominent in the traditionally Anglo-American-dominated field of security studies (on the ethnocentric tendencies of security studies see Booth 1979, Barkawi and Laffey 2006). All that can be said in general terms is that whatever approach to understanding warfare one chooses to adopt will have consequences, leading the analysis in certain directions and forsaking others. Within International Relations and security studies warfare has commonly been defined in ways that highlight its cultural, legal and political dimensions. These different approaches are illustrated in Box 11.2.

Trends in armed conflicts since 1945

Box 11.3 summarizes the central categories employed in one popular framework for distinguishing between different types and scales of armed conflicts. The remainder of this section provides a brief overview of the main trends in armed conflicts since 1945 as well as who does most of the fighting and dying in them.

From the data compiled by the Uppsala Conflict Data Program, four main trends can be identified in armed conflicts since 1945. First, as Figure 11.1 demonstrates, particularly from the mid-1970s there has been a significant decline in interstate armed conflict with internal conflicts accounting for the vast majority of organized violence. This trend has also encouraged the collection of new data about non-state conflicts. The early results reveal that a significant proportion of contemporary armed conflicts are now of the non-state variety (34 in 2002 but this number had reduced to 25 by 2005; see Mack 2007: 3).

A second major trend is that since reaching a peak of 52 state-based armed conflicts in 1991 to 1992, the number of these conflicts has dramatically declined, by some 40 per cent between 1992 and 2005 (Mack 2007: 1). Moreover, as Table 11.1 shows, the post-Cold War period has also seen a dramatic fall in the intensity of armed conflicts around the world. According to Andrew Mack (2007), the lower levels of armed conflict today as compared to the Cold War period may be explained with reference to four main factors. First, the end of colonialism removed a major source of political violence from world politics. In one sense, however, colonialism has not been completely eradicated inasmuch as many groups still waging state-formation conflicts see their struggle in terms of freeing themselves from imperial rule. The second key factor was the end of the Cold War. This encouraged the superpowers to stop fuelling 'proxy wars' in the developing world. The third, and for Mack the most

BOX 11.2 DEFINING WAR: CULTURAL, LEGAL AND POLITICAL APPROACHES

Cultural: Warfare looks different and conjures up different meanings depending on where and when in human history the analyst decides to look. As John Keegan (1994: 12) has suggested, war 'is always an expression of culture, often a determinant of cultural forms, in some societies the culture itself'. In this sense, war is best understood as a socially constructed category, but one with powerful material implications such as marriage, the market or society. This means that what 'we' choose to define as an act of war may not always coincide with how 'others' see things.

Legal: Another approach is to define war in juridical terms, for example, as 'the legal condition which equally permits two or more hostile groups to carry on a conflict by armed force' (Wright 1983: 7). From this perspective war is distinguished from peace because it is a state of legal contestation through military means. However, this does not mean that war is synonymous with the conduct of military engagements: parties can be legally in a state of war without overt violence occurring between them. The relationship between North and South Korea following the cessation of hostilities in 1953 would be one such instance. However, because the international legal framework is primarily defined by states, analysing war through solely legal lenses has limited applicability in cases of armed conflict where either the belligerents are not states or where the government of a particular state is loath to recognize the actions of its domestic opponents as constituting warfare rather than criminal activity.

Political: Arguably the most popular approach within security studies has been to define war, following Clausewitz, as a particular type of political activity involving violence. Hedley Bull, for instance, defines war as:

> organised violence carried on by political units against each other. Violence is not war unless it is carried out in the name of a political unit; what distinguishes killing in war from murder is its vicarious and official character, the symbolic responsibility of the unit whose agent is the killer. Equally, violence carried out in the name of a political unit is not war unless it is directed against another political unit; the violence employed by the state in the execution of criminals or the suppression of pirates does not qualify because it is directed against individuals.
>
> (Bull 1977: 178)

BOX 11.3 CLASSIFYING CONTEMPORARY ARMED CONFLICT

According to the Uppsala Conflict Data Program (UCDP) an armed conflict is defined as a contested incompatibility that concerns government or territory or both, where the use of armed force between two parties results in at least 25 battle-related deaths. The UCDP has developed a sophisticated framework for classifying the type and scale of armed conflicts (see www.ucdp.uu.se).

Types of armed conflict

1   *State-based armed conflicts* are those in which a government is one of the warring parties. There are several different types of state-based armed conflicts:
    - *Interstate armed conflict* occurs between two or more states.
    - *Intrastate armed conflict* occurs between the government of a state and internal opposition groups. These conflicts may be further subdivided into:
        - civil wars, which are fought for control of an existing government;
        - state-formation/secessionist conflicts, which are fought between a government and a territorially focused opposition group that is seeking to redraw the borders of the existing state.
    - *Internationalized intrastate armed conflict* occurs between the government of a state and internal opposition groups but with additional intervention from other states in the form of troops.
    - *Extrastate armed conflict* occurs between a state and a non-state group outside that state's territory.
2   *Non-state armed conflicts* are those where organized, collective armed violence occurs but where a recognized government is not one of the parties. Examples might include violent intercommunal conflicts or fighting between warlords and clans.

Scales of armed conflict

Minor armed conflicts involve at least 25 battle-related deaths per year and fewer than 1,000 battle-related deaths during the course of the conflict.

Intermediate armed conflicts involve at least 25 battle-related deaths per year and an accumulated total of at least 1,000 deaths, but fewer than 1,000 in any given year.

War is armed conflicts involving at least 1,000 battle-related deaths per year.

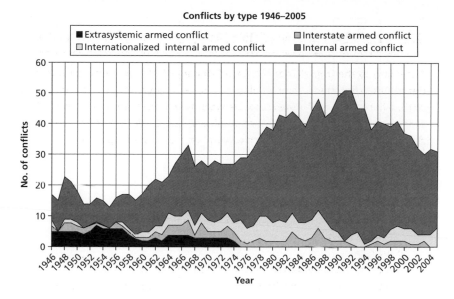

Conflicts by type 1946–2005

■ Extrasystemic armed conflict   □ Interstate armed conflict
□ Internationalized internal armed conflict   ■ Internal armed conflict

Figure 11.1 The number of state-based armed conflicts by type, 1946–2005

Source: www.pcr.uu.se/research/UCDP/graphs/type_year.pdf

important factor, was the increased level of international activism spearheaded by the UN that followed the end of the Cold War. This activism involved more serious efforts at preventive diplomacy, peacemaking, peace operations, and the increased number of 'Friends of the Secretary-General' and other mechanisms designed to support local efforts to foster peace (see Chapters 22 and 27, this volume). With greater engagement, international society has become better at ending wars. A final factor that provides some grounds for optimism about the future is the increasing popularity of global norms that proscribe the use of military force in human relationships.

A third significant trend in armed conflicts since 1945 is the decline in battle-deaths depicted in Figure 11.2. Whereas the average number of battle-deaths per conflict, per year was 38,000 in 1950, by 2005 it had fallen to just 700 – a 98 per cent decrease. Battle-death counts do not include either the intentional killing of civilians, or so-called 'indirect deaths' from war-exacerbated disease or malnutrition (see below). In relation to non-state armed conflicts a similar trend is emerging: between 2002 and 2005, the decline in battle-deaths in non-state conflicts was 71 per cent (Mack 2007: 7).

The final trend worth identifying here is the shifting regional spread of armed conflicts. In global historic terms, constraints imposed by geography and climate have meant that major wars have been confined to a relatively small portion of the earth's surface (Keegan 1994: 68–73). Since 1945, it is clear that at different times, different regions have experienced far more wars than others. As Figure 11.2 demonstrates, until the mid-1970s East and Southeast Asia suffered the most battle-deaths whereas during the latter stages of the Cold War most such casualties were spread between the Middle East, Asia and Africa.

Table 11.1 Intensity of armed conflicts, 1989–2006

Level of conflict	1989	1990	1991	1992	1993	1994	1995	1996	1997	1998	1999	2000	2001	2002	2003	2004	2005	2006
Minor	30	35	34	35	34	38	33	36	33	26	29	26	25	26	24	25	27	27
War	14	15	18	17	12	8	6	6	7	13	12	11	11	6	5	7	5	5
All conflicts	44	50	52	52	46	46	39	42	40	39	41	37	36	32	29	32	32	32
New conflicts	10	11	8	8	6	3	1	3	3	4	1	1	3	1	2	2	0	0

Source: Harbom and Wallensteen (2007: 624)

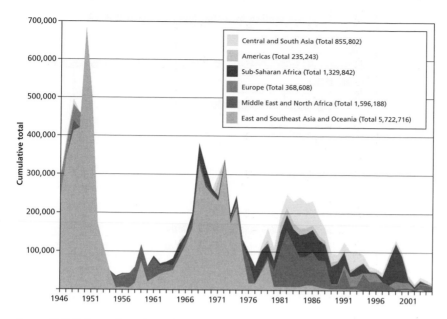

Figure 11.2 Estimated number of reported, codable deaths from state based armed
conflict, 1946–2005

Source: Mack (2007: 6)

Since the mid-1990s, however, sub-Saharan Africa has proved to be by far the
world's most conflict-prone region. Overall, in spite of the fact that most
African states did not become independent until the 1960s, as Figure 11.3
shows, between 1946 and 2005, Africa suffered 69 of the world's 187 armed
conflicts.

Who fights? Who dies?

As already noted, the belligerents in contemporary armed conflicts are not just
states; political units come in many shapes and sizes. The other main actors
engaged in warfare are international organizations and a variety of armed non-
state actors. Various international organizations have engaged in contemporary
armed conflicts for several reasons but primarily as a result of fielding peace
operations in zones of ongoing conflict. The UN, European Union, the North
Atlantic Treaty Organization, the Economic Community of West African
States, and the African Union among others have all fielded forces that have
engaged in combat (see Chapters 21 and 27, this volume). As far as armed non-
state actors are concerned, the most common participants in the world's
contemporary armed conflicts have been mercenaries, private military
companies, insurgents and a wide variety of paramilitaries, militias and self-
defence forces as well as the infamous suicide bombers. An additional recent
trend is the increasing number of child soldiers in contemporary armed
conflicts. They have been recruited by both states and most of the non-state

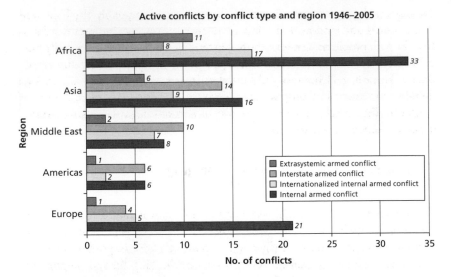

Active conflicts by conflict type and region 1946–2005

Figure 11.3 The number of state-based armed conflicts by region, 1946–2005

Source: www.pcr.uu.se/researcg/UCDP/graphs/type_reg.pdf

actors described above. Estimates suggest that there are about 300,000 child soldiers currently fighting or recently demobilized, and another 500,000 in armies currently at peace (Singer 2005).

With the reduction in the number of major engagements and the subsequent drop in the number of battle-deaths, it is not surprising that civilians account for a greater proportion of those killed in contemporary armed conflicts. One recent study suggested that between 30 and 60 per cent of violent deaths in today's armed conflicts are civilians (Human Security Centre 2005: 75). Ultimately, however, the difficulty of extracting reliable and systematic information from the world's war zones makes it impossible to know for sure how many civilians have been killed.

Part of the explanation for the rise in civilian deaths is that according to UCDP data there has been a 56 per cent increase in the number of campaigns of one-sided violence (i.e. massacres) against civilians since 1989. These have been perpetrated by both governments and non-state actors. Humanitarian aid workers have also found themselves more likely to become the targets of intentional violence. After decades of relative immunity, one study found that between 1997 and 2005 the number of humanitarian workers killed each year increased from 39 to 61, although the rate of violent assaults against aid workers had increased only marginally during the same period – from an average of 4.8 assaults per 10,000 workers between 1997 and 2001, to 5.8 between 2002 and 2005 (Stoddard *et al.* 2006).

The vast majority of fatalities in contemporary armed conflicts are so-called 'indirect deaths'. This refers to those people (mainly children, the elderly and women) who die from war-exacerbated disease and malnutrition, usually brought on and/or intensified by the process of displacement. Despite being the biggest single category of war deaths, this type is arguably the least well documented and understood. This is because measuring 'indirect deaths' is fraught with problems, not least those concerning methodology (especially how to measure and compare 'normal' as opposed to 'abnormal' mortality rates), data collection, and because publicized estimates are commonly inflated or deflated for reasons of propaganda. Nevertheless, there is a large degree of consensus that the changing demography of victims is linked to changes in the mode of contemporary warfare.

Is the nature of warfare changing?

Debates about whether and how the nature of warfare is changing are as old as the concept itself. In recent years, however, debates about three issues in particular have shaped how analysts have approached this important question. First, how useful is the concept of 'total war' for thinking about developments in warfare? Second, what is the relationship between war and globalization; specifically, has globalization given rise to a 'new' type of warfare? And, third, what changes can be identified in the way advanced industrialized democracies in the West are waging war today compared to earlier historical periods?

The idea of total war

Although the term 'total war' was coined by the German First Quartermaster General, Erich Ludendorff, in 1918, fear of such a prospect had dominated Western views of warfare since at least 1800. The fears were exemplified by the horrors of the First and Second World Wars which killed approximately 8.5 million and 55 million people respectively (see Bourne 2005, Overy 2005). Although few contemporary wars come close to matching the scale and intensity of these conflicts, the longevity of the idea of total war is evident in the continued use of the terminology of 'limited war' to refer, for instance, to the wars in Korea (1950–53), the Falklands/Malvinas (1982), and the Gulf (1991).

At its heart, the idea of total war revolved around the notions of escalation and participation (McInnes 2002). Fears of escalation derived from the concern that, once started, warfare was difficult if not impossible to control. This meant that wars were likely to increase in scale (both in terms of geographic spread and casualties) as well as intensity, thus eroding the various constraints on the conduct of war. Participation referred to the growing involvement of citizens in warfare, both as combatants willing to fight and die for their nation, and as workers willing to make important sacrifices to fuel the war effort at home. The image of national participation in the war effort was epitomized by the *levée en masse* decreed by France's revolutionary government in August 1793.

Although these trends are clearly apparent in modern history, total war is usually understood as an ideal type; that is, a set of circumstances which reality can approach but never reach. In practice, limits have always been placed or imposed on warfare. For example, some available weapons have not been deployed when they might have been, such as the US decision not to use nuclear weapons in the Korean War. Why some available weapons are not used is also a source of debate. For some analysts, the limited use of poison gas during the Second World War reflected the power that normative restraints have over the belligerents. Others argue that the non-use of poison gas is better explained by a pragmatic concern about its inconsistent and unpredictable effects. Another sense in which war is always less than total is that no belligerent has been able to commit the entirety of their resources to a war effort. Even during the Second World War, 'the major combatants mobilized between a half and two-thirds of their industrial work-force, and devoted up to three-quarters of their national product to waging war' (Overy 2005: 154). Nevertheless, some societies have come even closer to experiencing total war. For the North Vietnamese, for instance, war has often felt 'total'.

Given these practical limitations, why has the idea of total war occupied such an important place in the collective psyche of analysts and practitioners alike? One recent study has suggested that several tendencies encouraged the growing 'totality' of warfare between 1861 and 1945 (Chickering *et al.* 2005). These tendencies were arguably at their most intense from 1914 to 1945. First, technological and industrial advances during this period permitted the methods of warfare to become more destructive, thus facilitating the slaughter of people quickly and on a consistent basis. Second, governments were increasingly able to mobilize national resources (both through state institutions and the energies of private or semi-private actors) and harness them to the war effort. A third tendency was the expanding scope of war aims. In particular, as Imlay (2007: 554) has summarized, 'Limited goals such as territorial gains or economic advantage, were replaced by the determination to achieve outright victory, defined not simply as the defeat of an enemy's armed forces, but also more ambitiously as the replacement of its political regime, which often entailed a period of post-war occupation.' Fourth, the study noted war's increasingly global scope, as more and more states across the world's continents were drawn into conflicts originating in European politics.

Finally, these tendencies combined to blur the distinction between the civilian and military spheres; a key characteristic of 'total wars'. This had several effects, not least the fact that as ordinary citizens back home became more deeply involved in fuelling the war effort, it was not long before they became the targets of deliberate and large-scale violence. During the Second World War, for example, large-scale atrocities were committed by the Japanese military against Chinese civilians, on the Eastern Front in fighting between the Germans and Soviets, and with the atomic bombs and carpet bombing meted out upon Japanese cities. The temptation to target civilians was facilitated by advances in military technology which ultimately made possible the strategic bombing of cities such as Dresden, Coventry and Osaka during that war. As a result, the Second World War became the first conflict since Europe's Thirty Years' War where civilian deaths outnumbered military deaths (Imlay 2007: 556). In recent years Western states have attempted to re-solidify the distinction between civilian and military spheres (discussed below).

While the idea of total war has been a pervasive feature of the literature analysing warfare it is arguably a confusing and often unhelpful concept. Since real wars can never be 'total', debating how closely they approximate this ideal – which wars were more total than others? – makes little grammatical sense; something is total or it is not. Hence this mode of thinking can obscure more than it clarifies. Instead, a more useful approach to studying real wars is to analyse the varying degrees of 'intensity' of warfare across various indicators such as the efforts/resources expended and the costs/losses incurred during war (Imlay 2007: 566–567).

The 'new wars' debate

A second way of thinking about how warfare might be changing involves the argument that, especially since 1945, globalization has given rise to a distinctive form of violent conflict commonly labelled 'new wars' (Kaldor 1997, 1999, Munkler 2004, and see Box 11.4). According to Kaldor (1999), in new wars the traditional distinctions between war (violence between states or organized political groups for political motives), organized crime (violence by private associations, usually for financial gain), and large-scale violations of human rights (violence by states or private groups against individuals, mainly civilians) become increasingly blurred.

In Kaldor's framework, new wars are distinct from 'old wars' in terms of their goals, methods and systems of finance, all of which reflect the ongoing erosion of the state's monopoly of legitimate organized violence. The goals of combatants may be understood in the context of a struggle between cosmopolitan and exclusivist identity groups. The latter are understood to be seeking control of a particular territory by ethnically cleansing everybody of a different identity group or those people who espouse cosmopolitan political opinions (see also Chapter 14, this volume). In terms of methods, Kaldor suggests that new wars are fought through a novel 'mode of warfare' that draws on both guerrilla techniques and counter-insurgency. Yet this mode of warfare is distinctive inasmuch as decisive engagements are avoided and territory is controlled through political manipulation of a population by sowing 'fear and hatred' rather than winning 'hearts and minds'. It is thus not surprising that paramilitaries and groups of hired thugs are a common feature of these war zones as they can spread fear and hatred among the civilian population more effectively than professional armed forces (see Mueller 2000). This perspective may help explain the rise in one-sided massacres of civilians identified above. Bands of paramilitary forces are also useful because it can be difficult to trace back responsibility for their actions to political leaders. The final characteristic of Kaldor's new wars is that they are financed through a globalized war economy that is decentralized, increasingly transnational and in which the fighting units are often self-funding through plunder, the black market or external assistance (see also Duffield 2001b: ch. 6).

Wars that reflect these characteristics are often very difficult to bring to a decisive end. This is partly because some people can reap significant political and economic benefits from being at war. As David Keen (1998: 11–12) has noted, for some belligerents, 'Winning may not be desirable: the point of war may be precisely the legitimacy which it confers on actions that in peacetime would be punishable as crimes.' As a result, Kaldor suggests that the resolution of these new wars lies with the reconstruction of legitimate (that is, cosmopolitan) political communities that instil trust in public authorities, restore their control of organized violence, and re-establish the rule of law. In this context, the role of concerned outsiders should be to provide what she calls 'cosmopolitan law enforcement' in the form of robust peace operations involving a combination of military, police and civilian personnel.

Elements of Kaldor's arguments have been contested. First, many of the trends she identifies are not 'new' (see Shaw 2000, Kalyvas 2001, Berdal 2003, Newman 2004). Atrocities against civilians, for example, have been a feature of all wars and there is little evidence to suggest a temporal, qualitative shift in the use of atrocity across the twentieth century. A second set of criticisms has challenged Kaldor's view of globalization as a novel set of processes that has altered the nature of warfare after 1945. In contrast, Tarak Barkawi (2006) has argued that globalization is not the recent phenomenon that Kaldor suggests. Rather, globalization is a much older process that is essentially about circulation; that is, the processes through which people and places become interconnected. War, Barkawi observes, has been a historically pervasive and significant form of interconnection between societies and in this sense warfare has been a globalizing force for a long, long time (see Box 11.5). Understood in this manner, globalization is not a process separate from war which acts to change the nature of warfare in the way suggested by Kaldor. Instead, war has been intimately implicated in the globalization of world politics for thousands of years.

BOX 11.4 THE MAIN ELEMENTS OF THE 'NEW WARS' THESIS

- New wars are intrastate rather than interstate wars.
- New wars take place in the context of state failure and social transformation driven by globalization and liberal economic forces.
- In new wars, ethnic and religious differences are more important than political ideology.
- In new wars, civilian casualties and forced displacement are dramatically increasing. This is primarily because civilians are being deliberately targeted.
- In new wars, the breakdown of state authority blurs the distinction between public and private combatants.

(Newman 2004)

BOX 11.5 TARAK BARKAWI ON GLOBALIZATION AND WAR

'In and through war, people on both sides come to intensified awareness of one another, reconstruct images of self and other, initiate and react to each other's moves. To be at war is to be interconnected with the enemy. Such connections involve social processes and transformations that should be understood under the rubric of globalization. . . . From a war and society perspective, war can be seen as an occasion for interconnection, as a form of circulation between combatant parties. In and through war, societies are transformed, while at the same time societies shape the nature of war.'

'Militaries and war are also sites of cultural mixing and hybridity. Military travelling cultures expose soldiers to the foreign and lead them to reassess their ideas about home. Soldiers returning from abroad transmit new ideas and practice to their native lands. . . . [N]o matter how globalization is understood – as economic globalization, as transregional interconnectedness, or as consciousness of the global – war and the military play far more important roles than extant studies of globalization indicate. . . . [W]hat is needed is an assessment of the ways in which war is centrally implicated in the processes of globalization.'

(Barkawi 2006: xiii, 169–172)

The contemporary Western way of war

A third way of thinking about the changing patterns of warfare has focused on the ways in which Western states prefer to use military force. The point of departure for this debate is that although major war between Western states may well be becoming obsolete, the West is still willing and able to fight wars, and has been doing so regularly. This has led some analysts to argue that in the contemporary West, warfare has become akin to a spectator sport. The metaphor was first employed by Michael Mann, who argued that:

limited conventional wars involving client states aided by 'our' professional advisers and small expeditionary forces in 'our backyards,' do not mobilize nations as players but as *spectators* . . . wars like the Falklands and the Grenadan invasion are not qualitatively different from the Olympic Games. Because life-and-death are involved, the emotions stirred up are deeper and stronger. But they are not emotions backed up by committing personal resources. They do not involve real or potential sacrifice, except by professional troops.

(Mann 1988: 184–185)

The idea of spectator-sport warfare was further developed by Colin McInnes (2002). In contrast to the dynamic of escalation that provided the backdrop for fears of total warfare, McInnes argued that contemporary wars waged by Western states have been localized in both their conduct and impact. This was because (1) there was no global conflict into which they can be subsumed (unlike the Cold War with its ideas of containment and expansionism); (2) Western definitions of the enemy have changed from the opposing state and its citizens to a narrower concern to change a particular regime or leader; and (3) with civilians no longer seen as legitimate targets there has been an effort to minimize 'collateral damage'. Obviously, since McInnes wrote his book, a debate has developed over the extent to which the US-led 'global War on Terror' has indeed replaced the Cold War as a global conflict into which local conflicts are increasingly connected (see Freedman 2001/02, Barkawi 2004).

The other key contrast is that the West's contemporary wars don't involve high levels of societal participation but are instead fought by a small number of its professional representatives (i.e. the armed forces). As a consequence, in wars of choice rather than survival, a relatively small number of casualties can have dramatic political repercussions, even for a military superpower like the United States. In Somalia, for example, the 18 US soldiers killed in a firefight in Mogadishu in October 1993 were enough to induce a strategic retreat from the country by Washington and its allies. Less than two weeks later, in Haiti, just the sight of paramilitary thugs on the Port-au-Prince dockside was enough to trigger the *USS Harlan County*'s retreat. This low tolerance of casualties is related to the fact that the wars waged by Western states in places like Bosnia, Somalia, Kosovo and Sierra Leone have been wars of choice to help achieve liberal policy objectives rather than wars of survival. When core national security interests are perceived to be on the line, as in Afghanistan or Iraq, tolerance of casualties will be much higher.

In this context, McInnes has identified several key characteristics of spectator-sport wars. First, these wars are expeditionary; that is, they are based on the localization of the conflicts concerned and a desire to fight away from the Western homeland. Second, the 'enemy' in these wars is narrowly defined as the leadership/regime of the target state rather than the whole of the enemy state's society. In a radical departure from past practice, even the enemy's military forces are no longer always a target for destruction per se. Indeed, engagement with the main body of the enemy's military is no longer necessary or desirable. A third characteristic of spectator-sport wars is the desire to minimize collateral damage because only small elements of the enemy society are identified as legitimate targets. Finally, force protection – that is, the need to minimize risks to Western forces – is a significant priority. The intention is to avoid both the 'body bag' syndrome, which might damage domestic support for the war, and to protect the West's investment in its military professionals.

In pursuing these wars, Western states have emphasized the importance of airpower. This is because airpower is easy to deploy compared to land and sea forces; it allows quick and direct access to enemy leadership; it can be very accurate; the West enjoys a massive comparative advantage in this branch of warfare; and airpower can attack the enemy's centre of gravity directly without engaging the mass of enemy forces. In practice, however, there are significant limitations to thinking of airpower as an ideal instrument to conduct 'humane' and 'risk-free' war (see Pape 1996, McInnes 2001). First, while the separation of combatants and civilians might sound easy in theory it is often difficult in practice. Second, targeting errors, operational mistakes and technical mal-functions produce civilian deaths. Third, many 'strategically' significant installations are part of the civilian economy. Fourth, even 'surgical' strikes on cities terrorize civilians because of the constant fear of errors. Finally, the protection afforded to pilots by flying at high altitude is offset in terms of efficiency by the presence of such awkward phenomena as clouds!

Of course, the spectator-sport approach is only applicable to a small number of states and hence is not very useful for understanding the dynamics of warfare in the rest of the world. Nevertheless, it highlights some significant trends in official Western thinking and therefore provides important clues for under-standing how the West wants to fight, and how its enemies will try to fight against it.

Conclusion

Although the Clausewitzean, or political, philosophy of war has traditionally held sway in much of the security studies literature it is important to remember that warfare can be conceived of in many different ways. In several respects, other ways of thinking about (and practising) war are gaining the ascendancy. On the positive side, the evidence compiled by some prominent datasets suggests that armed conflicts are decreasing in both frequency and intensity, especially interstate warfare. But other trends, particularly war's terrible impact upon civilians and the potential for actors to unleash nuclear weapons many times more powerful than those used against Japan, provide a sober reminder that warfare remains an important source of insecurity across many parts of the globe. Understanding the extent to which patterns of warfare are changing and what political consequences might follow should therefore remain near the centre of the agenda for security studies.

Further reading

Tarak Barkawi, *Globalization and War* (Lanham, MD: Rowman and Littlefield, 2006). An excellent discussion of the relationship between these two crucial concepts in security studies.

Carl von Clausewitz, *On War*, edited and translated by Michael Howard and Peter Paret (Princeton, NJ: Princeton University Press, 1976). The seminal discussion of the political philosophy of war.

Human Security Centre, *Human Security Report 2005* (New York: Oxford University Press, 2005). A useful survey of broad trends in organized violence from 1945.

Mary Kaldor, *New and Old Wars: Organized Violence in a Global Era* (Cambridge: Polity Press, 2nd edition, 2006). An important statement of the argument that the processes of globalization have fundamentally changed the nature of some armed conflicts.

Rupert Smith, *The Utility of Force: The Art of War in the Modern World* (London: Allen Lane, 2005). A sophisticated attempt to answer when, why and how to use military force in contemporary world politics by one of Britain's most experienced military commanders.

Charles Townshend (ed.), *The Oxford History of Modern War* (Oxford: Oxford University Press, new edition, 2005). This book provides a useful historical discussion of the evolution and contemporary elements of modern warfare.

Terrorism

Paul Rogers

▌ Abstract

This chapter provides an overview of the definitional debates surrounding the concept of terrorism and different types of terrorism, notably the difference between state terrorism and sub-state terrorism or terrorism from below. The chapter analyses trends in state terrorism and sub-state terrorism, in the context of other more substantive threats to security. It then examines the main responses to sub-state terrorism and assesses the response to the 9/11 attacks, the state of the 'Global War on Terror' after six years and the likelihood of a reconsideration of the nature of the response.

▌ Introduction

The 9/11 attacks in New York and Washington in 2001 brought the issue of terrorism to the forefront of Western security thinking and resulted in the declaration of a 'Global War on Terror' by the George W. Bush administration. Due to the suddenness of the attacks, the large numbers of people killed and the targeting of two hugely important symbols of American life, the World Trade Center and the Pentagon, the reaction was both vigorous and extended, leading on to the termination of regimes in two states, Afghanistan and Iraq. To some extent this concentration on the incidents and on retaliating against the al-Qa'ida movement has resulted in a concern with terrorism that may not be justified, given the many other problems of human and state security affecting the world. It therefore makes sense to seek a broader assessment of the phenomenon of terrorism, bearing in mind that it can be undertaken by states against their own populations as much as by sub-state actors, even if the latter forms of terrorism currently dominate the security agenda.

Terrorism in perspective

Excluding the very high levels of non-combatant casualties in Iraq since 2003, terrorist activities conducted by sub-state actors across the world result in the deaths of, at most, a few thousand people each year. While this is appalling for the victims and for their families and friends, it does mean that terrorism is one of the minor causes of human suffering in the world. Far more significant are the problems arising from poverty and underdevelopment, from natural disasters, from wars, from crime and even from automobile accidents. Even so, the 9/11 attacks have resulted in an extraordinary concentration on a particular form of transnational political violence, focusing mainly on the al-Qa'ida movement and associated Islamic jihadist groups.

The 9/11 attacks killed nearly 3,000 people in just one day, but at least that number of children die every day across the South from avoidable intestinal diseases including diarrhoea and dysentery, brought on mainly by impure water supplies. In Iraq in the closing months of 2006, the monthly death-toll of civilians in the insurgency and in sectarian violence was very nearly the same as the losses in the 9/11 attacks. In Rwanda in the mid-1990s, close to a million people died in genocidal attacks, and continuing conflicts in the Great Lakes region of Africa have since killed even more people. In the mid-1970s, it was estimated that over 400 million people suffered from malnutrition, but today this has risen to at least 700 million. Across the world, more than two billion people survive on the equivalent of two US dollars a day or less. The diseases of poverty are mostly avoidable yet kill millions of people each year.

In spite of this, the global War on Terror has been elevated to the principal challenge to security. Two regimes have been terminated, partly on claims of sponsoring terrorism, the US military budget is now approaching the level of the peak years of the Cold War and the term 'War on Terror' has itself been transformed into the 'long war against Islamofascism'. In its most extreme representation in some influential US political circles, this war is understood as the 'Fourth World War', and is just as much a matter of the survival of civilization as were the previous world wars, including the 'Third World War' against the Soviet Union.

Any dispassionate analysis would question the centrality of the current War on Terror, at least in terms of overall human well-being, but it is necessary to accept this representation given its potency and centrality in international security thinking since 2001. There are three elements that together offer some degree of explanation for this concentration. One is that the 9/11 attacks were deeply shocking to the USA in that a small group armed only with parcel knives could use civil aircraft as flying bombs to destroy a world-class financial centre and attack the headquarters of the US military. Moreover, the attacks came as a complete surprise to most people and their effects were witnessed live on television.

The second element that helps explain the response is that the Bush administration in mid-2001 was beginning to pursue its vision of a New American Century with some success. Unilateral stances on certain key issues were being developed and there seemed every prospect that the international community would come to accept American leadership as being essential for international security – a 'benign imperium' was said to be no bad thing (Krauthammer 2001). Finally, the almost inevitable focus of state-centred security, given the status of the USA as the world's sole military superpower, was that it was essential to regain control by destroying a dangerous sub-state movement and any state sponsors, not least because the al-Qa'ida movement and its presumed sponsors were based in the Middle East and South West Asia. This was a region of long-term security interest to the USA due to the critical importance of its energy resources and the close American ties to the state of Israel.

The end result of these factors is a situation that, in the absence of fundamental changes in policy, is likely to be a core feature of international security for many years to come. Yet terrorism is still a minor issue in terms of global human security, and an aim of this short contribution is to provide a wider perspective. This will involve a brief examination of definitions of terrorism, an analysis of state and sub-state terrorism, an overview of the main forms of terrorism in recent years and a discussion of the main responses to terrorism leading to a review of the counter-terrorism methods used specifically in response to 9/11.

Definitions

A succinct definition of terrorism is 'the threat of violence and the use of fear to coerce, persuade, and gain public attention' (NACCJSG 1976). A more complete definition, which brings in a political dimension and thereby excludes the use of terror in ordinary criminal activities such as protection rackets, is that:

> Political terrorism is the use, or threat of use, of violence by an individual or a group, whether acting for or in opposition to established authority, when such action is designed to create extreme anxiety and/or fear-inducing effects in a target group larger than the immediate victims with the purpose of coercing that group into acceding to the political demands of the perpetrators.
>
> (Wardlaw 1982: 16)

A definition used by the US government is 'premeditated, politically motivated violence perpetrated against non-combatant targets by subnational groups or clandestine agents, usually intended to influence an audience' (US Department of State 2001: 13).

Both of these definitions are concerned with the intention to have an effect on an audience that is larger than the group actually targeted. It follows that terrorism works through fear, but it is also the case that acts of terror may have distinct political aims rather than being, for example, acts of revenge. Moreover, the specific inducement of fear in a larger audience may be intended to ensure that a particular political response ensues, when it might not be stimulated by an act that does not elicit a wider response. The element of inducing fear in a larger population than that targeted is a key aspect of terrorism and is one explanation why it attracts so much attention compared with the many other forms of violence as well as suffering due to natural disasters or poverty and underdevelopment.

State and sub-state terror

There is one fundamental difference between the definition given by Wardlaw and that used by the US government in that the latter is concerned with sub-state actors, even if they may be supported or sponsored by a state, whereas Wardlaw's definition embraces the actions of states against their own populations. In broad terms, state terrorism is actually far more widespread in its effects, both in terms of direct casualties and in the inducing of fear.

Some of the most grievous examples of state terrorism have been the purges of Stalin's Soviet Union in the 1930s and Mao's China in the 1950s, but most colonial powers have used terror tactics to maintain control of colonies, especially during the early phases of colonization but also in response to the demands for independence in the early post-war years. More recently, states have readily used a wide range of terror tactics against their own populations. These have ranged from detention without trial through to torture and summary execution, but have also involved disappearances and the use of death squads. In Latin America in the 1960s and 1970s frequent use was made of such tactics, with persistent claims that the USA was involved at least indirectly (George 1991).

Even within the restricted 'sub-state' definition, which is the main concern of this chapter, there will be many controversies over who is a terrorist. Two examples illustrate this. During the long period of violence in Northern Ireland, the British government and most British people regarded the Provisional Irish Republican Army (Provisional IRA or PIRA) as a terrorist organization seeking to achieve a united Ireland by a sustained campaign of violence. Against this, though, many political supporters of Irish unity, in Northern Ireland and the Republic of Ireland, saw the PIRA volunteers as freedom fighters trying to liberate Northern Ireland from British rule. Such support extended to many members of the Irish-American community in the USA. Furthermore, when the peace process in Northern Ireland finally made progress in the period 1997 to 2007, some of those with close links with PIRA became accepted members of a power-sharing system, translating from perceived terrorists to legitimate political figures in a matter of years.

A second example is the use of terror and violence against black Americans across the southern states by white supremacist organizations for more than a century, right up to the 1960s and even more recently. Such groups were not, at the time, considered to be terrorists by most Americans but they would fit in with any of the three definitions given above. By a combination of beatings, torture and lynchings, a substantial sector of American society was terrorized into accepting its inferior place in society.

Sub-state terrorism can originate in very different societies and with highly variable motivations and underlying drivers. Although firm categorization is not easy, terrorism may be loosely divided into two orientations. One is terrorism that seeks fundamental change in a state or in society. Such revolutionary terrorism might be based on a political ideology of a radical persuasion that may be either left- or right-wing in nature, or it might be based on religious commitment. It may even combine the two. Either way, it aims for fundamental change, usually within a particular state but with this quite commonly being seen as a prelude to an international transformation. Baader Meinhof, Action Direct, Brigate Rossi and other European groups would be examples in the 1970s. More recently, the al-Qa'ida movement combines revolutionary change with religious belief.

The other form of terrorism seeks particular change for an identifiable community. This rarely has international ambitions but may link up with similar groups elsewhere. It is frequently separatist in nature but may have elements of revolutionary politics embedded in its thought. ETA in Spain and the LTTE Tamil Tigers in Sri Lanka are examples. Radical groups of this nature often arise in response to substantial political change that has damaged the prospects of the community from which they arise. Many radical Palestinian factions, for example, developed in direct response to the occupation of Palestinian territory by Israel in the Six Day War of June 1967, even if the Palestinian communities had previously been under the control of the Egyptians or Jordanians.

Responding to terrorism

There are three broad approaches to responding to sub-state terrorism (see also Chapter 25, this volume). The approach most commonly used may best be described as traditional counter-terrorism rooted principally in policing, intelligence and security. Paramilitary groups are identified and taken into custody before they can carry out attacks, or if this fails then those responsible for the attacks are detected, detained and subsequently brought to justice. In addition, improved security is directed at providing increasing levels of protection for perceived targets. The second approach is more overtly military and involves direct military action against paramilitary organizations, especially when they have distinct physical locations. If they are clearly seen to be sponsored by a state, that state may itself be targeted for punitive action or even regime termination.

The third approach concentrates on the underlying motivations of terrorist groups and the environment from which they draw support. While there may be a belief that the leaders and the most dedicated cadres of a paramilitary organization may have a degree of motivation and determination that is difficult to undermine, this approach is rooted in the idea that most paramilitary groups have evolved and are operating within a much wider context. They do not exist in isolation but depend for support on a sector of a particular society that shares their aims and approves, to an extent, of their methods. This approach also recognizes that there are conditions in which negotiations with paramilitary leaders may become possible, often with the utilization of mediators acceptable to both parties.

Most responses to terrorist campaigns employ a combination of these methods, but the balance may vary widely. Many of the middle-class left-wing revolutionaries in 1970s Europe that included the Baader Meinhof Gang in West Germany and Brigate Rossi in Italy believed that their violent actions would provoke an uprising of the masses leading to a working-class revolution. Even so, their campaigns did nothing to persuade the authorities to make any major changes in wage agreements or working conditions. The authorities did not see such movements as presaging a wider revolution and in this assessment they were correct. Instead, the response was very much one of intensive policing and intelligence-gathering, coupled with some degree of increased security for potential targets, especially senior politicians and industry leaders.

Between 1968 and 1972 there were widespread activities by a number of radical Palestinian groups, some of them working in association with paramilitary movements in Western Europe and Japan. While Israeli security forces sought to kill some of those responsible, the greatest concern for most Western states was the development of aircraft hijacking as a means of gaining attention and, on some occasions, attempting to negotiate prisoner release. Although there were intensive efforts to identify and detain those responsible, the most substantial response was to invest in a massive increase in security measures for air travel.

In the long-running Northern Ireland conflict, all three approaches to counter-terrorism were adopted by the British authorities. Intensive policing and intelligence-gathering, in Northern Ireland and also in Britain, were accompanied by new legal regulations, including courts that sat without juries and, for one period, internment without trial. These methods were paralleled by an intensive counter-insurgency posture by the British Army and local Northern Ireland forces, mainly in Northern Ireland itself but sometimes in cooperation with the Republic of Ireland. Even as these methods were being used, not always with success, there was a recognition that much of the support for the republican movement came from within the Catholic nationalist minority community in Northern Ireland, largely because it had been in an inferior socio-economic position and had had little political power for generations. Indeed, the origins of the violence in the 1960s came largely from a robust response from the Protestant unionist government to a civil rights movement from within the nationalist community that was partly modelled on the US civil rights movement.

Because of this underlying support for the republican paramilitaries, the British authorities worked towards the greater emancipation of the nationalist community, not least through a number of economic and social measures. This was a difficult process considering the suspicions of the unionist majority, itself vulnerable through seeing itself as a minority in the island of Ireland as a whole, even if it was the controlling majority in Northern Ireland. Nevertheless, the position of the nationalist community did improve over more than two decades and was one of the main reasons why a peace process became possible in the mid-1990s, even if particular tactics from the Provisional IRA directed at economic targeting in Britain almost certainly increased the British government's commitment to a peace process (see Box 12.1).

BOX 12.1 ECONOMIC TARGETING

Paramilitary organizations tend to be relatively conservative in their tactics, staying with particular methods that have been tried and tested. These may involve bombings, assassination, kidnappings, punishment beatings or combinations of these. This conservatism is often a reflection of the difficult environment in which they are operating and which makes it necessary to rely on those methods in which they are most practised. On occasions, changes in strategy and tactics can be significant in the effectiveness of an organization, and one of the developments of the two decades after 1990 was a tendency for a number of paramilitary groups to engage in the targeting of the economy of a target state in addition to more traditional targets such as the police and military forces and the political leadership.

Economic targeting has been practised to some extent by many paramilitary groups, with recent examples being the LTTE (Tamil Tigers) in Sri Lanka, the persistent attacks on Iraqi oil pipelines since 2003 and parallel attacks on Saudi facilities, most notably the attempt to disrupt the Abqaiq oil-processing plant in Saudi Arabia, the world's largest, in February 2006.

Economic targeting was developed, in particular, by the Provisional IRA in Britain between 1992 and 1997 at a time when there was a stalemate in the long-lasting violence in Northern Ireland. The campaign was not designed to cause mass casualties but rather to attack the financial centre of the UK, the City of London, which was then competing with Frankfurt to be the financial hub of Europe. Two large truck bombs were used to cause substantial damage in the heart of the city in 1992 and 1993 and another targeting a major road interchange. At least three other bombs were intercepted but the impact of the bombing was such that rigorous countermeasures were put in place in the City while the British government looked more favourably on the possibility of negotiations.

Apart from a temporary ceasefire, the period 1992 to 1997 saw many more attacks, some of them large, as in Canary Wharf and Manchester in 1996, with other small attacks causing substantial disruption to roads, railways and airports. PIRA tended to target facilities away from the centre of London because of improved security there, but still had a substantial impact on UK government attitudes. While other factors were involved, this change of tactics was influential in encouraging the Labour government from 1997 to devote considerable effort to resolving the conflict.

The 9/11 response and the War on Terror

The response to the 9/11 atrocities was unusual in that it placed far greater emphasis on military action compared with other forms of counter-terrorism. Other approaches such as improved homeland defence were utilized, but the primary focus was on the military with the main response being developed over the first six years into a global War on Terror. It was a particularly robust response for reasons already discussed above. In the first six years of this war, major military campaigns were mounted against presumed state sponsors of the al-Qa'ida movement in Afghanistan and Iraq leading to regime termination in both cases, and military operations were undertaken in a number of other countries, including Pakistan, Yemen and Somalia. Since the post-9/11 response has become a dominant feature of international security in general, and terrorism in particular, and is likely to remain so for some years to come, it is appropriate to examine this in some depth.

The group responsible for the 9/11 attacks, the al-Qa'ida movement, is a dispersed and very broadly based movement that is not narrowly hierarchical but does have clear aims and intentions. It is not a nihilistic collection of insane extremists, even if that impression is frequently given, but a rational movement involving an unusual combination or revolutionary political fervour rooted in a fundamentalist orientation of a major religion – Islam – rather than in a political ideology or nationalism. The movement has its theoretical origins in the writings of a number of radical Islamic thinkers, notably the Egyptian Sayidd Qtub, who was tortured and executed by his own government in 1966. In more practical terms, al-Qa'ida can be traced back to the success of the *Mujahiddin* fighters in Afghanistan and their opposition to Soviet occupation in the 1980s. Aided by the US Central Intelligence Agency and the Pakistani Inter-Services Intelligence Organization, the paramilitary and guerrilla fighters were eventually able to force the Soviet Union to withdraw from the country, and many within the movement see this as leading to the collapse of the Soviet system.

Following the eviction of Iraqi forces from Kuwait in 1991, substantial US military forces remained in the region, including Saudi Arabia – the Kingdom of the Two Holy Places (Mecca and Medina). This resulted in a revitalization of elements of the anti-Soviet movement of the 1980s, with the main focus being on evicting such 'crusader' forces, especially from Saudi Arabia. Central to this were two individuals. One was Osama bin Laden, a wealthy Saudi of Yemeni abstraction, who had been active in Afghanistan. The other was the Egyptian-born strategist Ayman al-Zawahiri. During the 1990s, the movement developed a more comprehensive strategy, rooted largely in Qtub's ideas of a revival of 'true' Islam following its corruption by Western culture. By the end of the twentieth century, al-Qa'ida had developed a number of short-term aims together with an overarching long-term vision.

There are six short-term aims. One was the eviction of US military forces from Saudi Arabia, an aim that the movement claimed to have achieved by 2005 when the last of the major US bases in the Kingdom was evacuated due to concern of the Saudi authorities over the US presence. A second is the eviction of foreign forces from the Islamic world. A third is the replacement of the House of Saud by a 'genuine' Islamist regime, the Saudi royal family being seen as corrupt, elitist and excessively linked to the USA. The fourth aim is the replacement of other corrupt, elitist and pro-Western regimes across the region, with an initial focus on Egypt and Pakistan but extending later to Iraq and Afghanistan. Fifth, there is deep antagonism to the Zionist state of Israel and support for the Palestinian cause and, finally, there is support for other Islamist movements such as the Chechen rebels and the southern Thailand separatists. Beyond this lies the long-term aim of establishing a pan-Islamic Caliphate, developing in the Middle East but extending eventually to other parts of the world.

In the context of these aims there is a broad distinction between the 'near enemy' which comprises the unacceptable regimes and their supporters across the Middle East and the 'far enemy', this being the USA and its coalition partners such as the United Kingdom. A further core aspect of the strategy of the movement is the question of time scales. The short-term aims are seen as being achieved progressively over a period of several decades and the long-term aim of establishing Islamist governance through a Caliphate may take 50–100 years. This is a fundamental issue as it differs so markedly from the typical time scales of Western political and economic institutions.

The 9/11 attacks were designed to demonstrate an ability to attack the far enemy of the USA, not least to increase support for the movement. It would also serve to attract US forces into Afghanistan in large numbers, enabling a guerrilla war to develop over a number of years with a similar effect on US resilience to that on the Soviet Union two decades earlier. Al-Qa'ida failed initially in this second aim in that the USA initially used a combination of airpower, Special Forces and a re-arming of the Northern Alliance to terminate the Taliban regime. Even so, by 2007 a Taliban revival was in progress and was tying down over 40,000 US and coalition forces in an evolving insurgency.

Following the apparent success in Afghanistan the Bush administration developed the War on Terror to encompass pre-emptive military action against what it called an 'axis of evil' of states believed to be developing weapons of mass destruction and sponsoring terrorist organizations. The principal members of the axis were declared to be Iraq, Iran and North Korea, with Iraq being the first candidate state for regime termination in 2003. While the Saddam Hussein regime was ended within three weeks, a complex insurgency then developed which eventually combined with a degree of sectarian conflict to produce a highly unstable and violent country. Four years after regime termination, at least 100,000 Iraqi civilians had been killed and close to four million were refugees. The USA lost over 3,000 troops killed and 25,000 wounded, many of the latter maimed for life. In spite of using a wide range of tactics, the US-led forces were unable to contain the violence and there was abundant evidence that the insurgents were able to develop techniques at a rate at least as fast as they could be countered. A marked tendency of US forces to use their overwhelming firepower against urban insurgents might be understandable from their own perspective but could be seen by opponents as little short of terror (see Box 12.2).

BOX 12.2 WHOSE TERRORISM?

The difficult issue of who is the terrorist is well illustrated by the US military action in the Iraqi city of Fallujah in November 2004. Seven months earlier there had been a US attempt to gain control of the city following a particularly brutal paramilitary action when four American security guards were killed, mutilated and their bodies burned before being hung from a bridge. The first assault failed but Fallujah was then seen as a centre of terrorism. The November assault was covered in detail by TV channels operating with US forces, and there was stark footage of the very heavy use of ordnance against the city. This was seen as an utterly just cause in the USA, and there was great satisfaction when the city was brought fully under control by the US Army and Marine Corps.

Across the Middle East, on the other hand, regional TV news stations (see Box 12.3) were reporting the effects within the city, where several thousand people were killed in the assault, many of them civilians, and most of the public buildings and more than half of all the private houses in the city were destroyed or severely damaged. Fallujah was known as the City of Mosques and the damage done to many of the mosques was a particular affront. For the US forces, though, mosques were often used by the insurgents and represented legitimate targets.

For the USA, the taking of Fallujah was an essential and fully justified military operation against a dangerously evolving insurgency that was already killing and injuring hundreds of American troops. Across the Middle East and the wider Islamic world, Fallujah was nothing less than an act of state terrorism conducted by an occupying power that was on a par with the 9/11 attacks. American opinion would be almost entirely unable to comprehend such a view, just as Arab opinion would find it extraordinary that the assault could in any sense be justified.

Perhaps most important of all was the status of Iraq as providing a jihadist combat training zone, an aspect of huge advantage to the al-Qa'ida movement and its associates. Moreover, Iraq represented a combat training zone that was far superior to Afghanistan in the 1980s in that young paramilitaries could gain experience against well-armed and well-trained US soldiers and Marines in an urban environment – far superior in paramilitary terms than poorly trained Soviet conscripts in rural Afghanistan two decades earlier. Given al-Qa'ida's decades-long time scale and its concern with terminating unacceptable regimes in the Middle East, ten years or more of combat experience against US forces in Iraq seemed likely to provide a new generation of jihadists. In that sense, the US decision to occupy Iraq may be seen as an historic error of quite extraordinary magnitude. Furthermore, the extensive coverage of the carnage in Iraq, both by regional satellite TV news channels and through propagandistic outlets, has done much to increase support for radical Islamist movements (see Box 12.3).

BOX 12.3 TERROR AND THE NEW MEDIA

One of the most striking developments in paramilitary movements has been the use of new media to publicize their actions, promote their cause and air their grievances. New versions of old media such as television in combination with new media and communications systems such as the internet, broadband, cellphones and DVDs have all made these aspects more effective. While the major changes have come about since the mid-1990s, they are not entirely new – television coverage of aircraft hijackings in the late 1960s and early 1970s was influential in bringing the activities of Palestinian paramilitary movements to world attention.

For television, the main change has been the development of new 24-hour regional satellite TV news stations. While these may be financed or owned by local elite rulers, as in the case of Al-Jazeera and Al-Arabiya, they portray a news agenda from a strongly regional perspective rather than an Atlanticist outlook as is the case with CNN and other US and European-owned outlets. Stations such as Al-Jazeera maintain high professional standards and are exceptionally popular across the Middle East for their independence from narrowly focused and often propagandistic state broadcasting networks. Prime time news bulletins attract viewing audiences in their tens of millions, a level that is far higher than the main channels in countries such as Britain, France or Germany. They are increasingly available worldwide to diaspora audiences and are notable for their coverage of the effects of conflicts in Iraq and Afghanistan. As such, they illustrate the effects of Western interventions with persistence and with little self-censoring of the impacts.

Beyond this extensive conventional TV coverage, many jihadist groups have become adept at videoing their activities and using them as part of highly propagandistic packages distributed by VC, DVD and, in particular, the internet. The widespread availability of broadband makes it possible to distribute detailed coverage of paramilitary actions within hours of the events. Furthermore, statements by leaders such as Osama bin Laden and Ayman al-Zawahiri are distributed by all the major means. Some of the outputs are in the form of extensive lectures that demonstrate a thorough familiarity with Western policies and attitudes, and are attuned to have a maximum effect among target audiences.

In the global War on Terror as a whole, six years into the war, well over 100,000 people had been detained without trial, for various periods, with at least 25,000 detained at any one time. Prisoner abuse, torture and rendition were being used and the detention centre at the US military base at Guantanamo in Cuba was widely criticized. Nevertheless, and despite increasing public opposition in the USA, there was little sign of any substantive change in policy. Furthermore, the importance of Persian Gulf oil was such that the region was considered to be essential to the maintenance of US security (Kubursi 2006). With well over 60 per cent of world oil reserves located in and around the Gulf, and the USA and China increasingly dependent on oil imports, a withdrawal of US forces from Iraq seemed highly unlikely. At the same time, the difficulties being experienced by the USA in its pursuit of the War on Terror would appear to make it appropriate to rebalance the approach away from military action towards a policy that recognizes the motivations of, and support for, the al-Qa'ida movement.

Trends in terrorism

In the years after 1990 there were a number of developments in terrorism and political violence that are likely to be significant in the longer term.

Terrorism and insurgency

The practice of employing regime termination as a major response to terrorism has produced a complex reaction that effectively mixes terrorism with insurgency. This has evolved in Afghanistan and Iraq into a form of warfare that may be concentrated in the two countries concerned but has a much wider impact, particularly in terms of increased support for the al-Qa'ida movement and its associates.

Internationalism

Although there has long been an element of transnational capabilities in paramilitary movements, this has evolved rapidly in recent years. In the first six years of the War on Terror, for example, the al-Qa'ida movement and its loose affiliates were able to carry out attacks in Egypt, Indonesia, Jordan, Kenya, Morocco, Pakistan, Saudi Arabia, Spain, Tunisia, Turkey, the United Kingdom and Yemen, quite apart from Iraq and Afghanistan, with attacks prevented in a number of other countries including France, Italy, Singapore and the USA.

Suicide terrorism

As with internationalism, suicide attacks as a facet of terrorism are not new, but the intensity of the attacks in many countries, and the willingness of so many people to engage in martyrdom, is novel. Suicide attacks are intrinsically more difficult to counter as an aspect of any form of political violence. Moreover, while most of the relatively rare incidents of suicide attacks until 2001 were by people with deep political or ethnic motives, such as the LTTE in Sri Lanka, the current trend is for suicide attacks to draw on religious motivation, especially within Islam, and for there to be a substantial increase in the numbers of motivated individuals.

Speed of learning

Most paramilitary groups in the past have been relatively conservative in their operations, tending to stay with methods they have developed and have become experienced in using. The intense environments of the insurgencies in Afghanistan and especially Iraq have forced paramilitary groups to learn fast in order to survive and thrive. There is abundant evidence that these learning environments have combined with the internationalization of terrorism to allow the far more rapid spread of tactics than in the past – advanced fusing for improvised explosive devices and the production of explosively formed anti-armour projectiles being just two examples.

Media developments

Regional satellite TV news channels, the use of the internet, VCRs, DVDs and mobile phones have all increased the ability of paramilitary groups to promote their causes (see Box 12.3).

Economic targeting

The development of sophisticated economic targeting strategies by groups such as the Provisional IRA (see Box 12.1) and insurgents in Iraq has provided a new avenue of influence and effect. Given the numerous nodes of power and economic activity in urban/industrialized societies, it is probable that this development is still in its early stages.

Mass casualty attacks and weapons of mass destruction

Although there has been no single instance of the large-scale use of nuclear, chemical, biological or radiological weapons, the increased use of mass casualty attacks has raised fears that weapons of mass destruction will ultimately be used by some terrorist organizations. While there is clearly a risk, it remains the case that conventional forms of destruction can readily lead to casualties on a very substantial scale, as in the 9/11 attacks.

Conclusion

The War on Terror as a response to the 2001 attacks in New York and Washington came to dominate international security, not least by embracing robust military operations as the principal responses to the attacks. Given the failure of such responses to have the intended effects, it is possible that there will be a rebalancing of counter-terrorism strategies, although the long time scale of the al-Qa'ida strategy and the long-term importance of the Persian Gulf region to the USA may militate against this. Given the developments in terrorist tactics and the factors aiding movements such as al-Qa'ida discussed above, it would appear that it would be wise to embrace a fairly fundamental rethinking of Western policies in general, and US policies in particular.

Further reading

Charles Allen, *God's Terrorists, The Wahhabi Cult and the Hidden Roots of Modern Jihad* (London: Abacus, 2006). Focuses on the long-term development of jihadism.

Sean K. Anderson and Stephen Sloan, *Historical Dictionary of Terrorism* (London: The Scarecrow Press, 2002). The most comprehensive coverage of sub-state terrorist movements available.

Jonathan Barker, *The No-nonsense Guide to Terrorism* (Oxford: New Internationalist Publications, 2003). A succinct analysis.

Jason Burke, *Al-Qaeda, the True Story of Radical Islam* (London: Penguin Books, 2007). The best single account of the development of the al-Qa'ida movement.

Alexander George (ed.), *Western State Terrorism* (Cambridge: Polity Press, 1991). A critical analysis of Western involvement in political violence.

John Horgan, *The Psychology of Terrorism* (London: Routledge, 2005). One of the few examples of an analysis of motivation.

Bruce Lawrence (ed.), *Messages to the World: The Statements of Osama bin Laden* (London: Verso, 2005). Essential reading in understanding the al-Qa'ida movement.

Genocide and Mass Killing

Adam Jones

▌ Abstract

This chapter will introduce students to the concept of 'genocide' – the destruction of human groups – and the place of genocide in human history. Key modern instances of genocide and mass killing are described, along with the range of interventionist and preventive measures adopted to confront the phenomenon. Central debates in the rapidly growing literature of 'comparative genocide studies' are also examined.

▌ Introduction

'The word is new; the concept is ancient', wrote Leo Kuper in his field-defining treatise, *Genocide: Its Political Use in the Twentieth Century* (1981: 9). The argument is not uncontested. A substantial current in comparative genocide studies contends that genocide is an inherently modern phenomenon, tied to the emergence of the 'modern' world, beginning around the fifteenth century. Such scholars emphasize certain features of modernity as indispensable to an understanding of genocide and mass killing. These include structures of bureaucratic organization (and the psychological 'distancing' from complex tasks that accompanies them); technologies of mass killing, such as gas chambers and intercontinental missiles; the rise of global empires, and ideologies of race and racial superiority that sought to justify them; and modern conceptions of 'nationhood' and mass democracy which, defined in ethnic terms, allowed only a marginal place for minorities.

The vulnerability of ethnic and religious minorities in the modern state system evoked mounting humanitarian concern in the late nineteenth and early twentieth centuries. It was decisive in the formation of Raphael Lemkin, a Polish Jew who was powerfully moved by anti-Jewish pogroms in Eastern Europe, and by the slaughter of Armenians and other Christian minorities in the Ottoman Empire during the First World War. But Lemkin's investigation of such persecutions extended far beyond the modern era. He grew up reading works like Henryk Sienkiewicz's *Quo Vadis*, and listening to stories about the Roman campaigns against early Christians.

While attentive to the distinctive features of modern genocides, most genocide scholarship has likewise adopted Lemkin's broad view, conceptualizing genocide as something deeply embedded in human society, indeed in the human psyche. The subtitle of Ben Kiernan's recent book, *Blood and Soil* – 'Genocide and Extermination from Carthage to Darfur' – captures this sense of historical sweep (Kiernan 2007). Kiernan defines the Roman destruction of Carthage in 146 BC as 'the first genocide'; but the further historical inquiry reaches back, the harder it becomes to isolate a primary instance of the phenomenon. One account suggests that the disappearance of the Neanderthals of what is today Southern Europe, tens of thousands of years ago, may in fact mark the onset of genocidal practice – or at least the first instance of which a faint historical trace survives.[1]

What is genocide? It is simultaneously an empirical phenomenon, an analytical-legal concept – and an argument for intervention. In developing his 'catalysing idea', Raphael Lemkin was motivated above all by a need to protect threatened minorities, and to develop a legal instrument capable of mobilizing the international community in their defence. This activist and interventionist dimension has characterized all subsequent applications of the term.

Lemkin was one of the great 'norm entrepreneurs' of the twentieth century. In casting about for a word to convey some of the horror of group destruction, and the damage done to the fabric of human civilization, he experimented first with 'barbarism' and 'vandalism'. In the end, he settled on a neologism combining the Greek *genos* (race, tribe) with the Latin-derived suffix *cide* (killing). The continuing power of the word 'genocide' is such that governments and other actors will turn cartwheels to avoid being tarred by it – as may be seen, for example, in the perpetual propaganda campaign by the Turkish authorities to discount claims of Ottoman genocide against the minority Armenian population nearly a century ago.

'Genocide' first appeared in *Axis Rule in Occupied Europe*, the book that Lemkin published in 1944, in exile in the USA after fleeing the Nazi invasion of Poland (Lemkin 1944). Only four years later, thanks largely to Lemkin's indefatigable lobbying at the nascent United Nations, his word had given rise to an international convention: the Convention on the Prevention and Punishment of the Crime of Genocide, passed in 1948 and ratified by a critical mass of member states by 1951.

For Lemkin, 'genocide' consisted of:

> a coordinated plan of different actions aiming at the destruction of essential foundations of the life of national groups, with the aim of annihilating the groups themselves. The objectives of such a plan would be disintegration of the political and social institutions, of culture, language, national feelings, religion, and the economic existence of national groups, and the destruction of the personal security, liberty, health, dignity, and even the lives of the individuals belonging to such groups. Genocide is directed against the national group as an entity, and the actions involved are directed against individuals, not in their individual capacity, but as members of the national group.
>
> (Lemkin 1944: 79)

As is immediately evident, the popular notion of genocide as physical extermination – even *total* physical extermination of a group – is far less prominent in Lemkin's formulation. He was preoccupied above all with the loss to humanity that the destruction of group identity and culture represented. Physical killing was one element of that destruction, but only one. The language of the Genocide Convention of 1948 accorded primacy to killing, but only as the first of five genocidal strategies that, 'whether committed in time of peace or in time of war', were outlawed:

> *Article II*. In the present Convention, genocide means any of the following acts committed with intent to destroy, in whole or in part, a national, ethnical, racial or religious group, as such:
>
> (a) Killing members of the group;
> (b) Causing serious bodily or mental harm to members of the group;
> (c) Deliberately inflicting on the group conditions of life calculated to bring about its physical destruction in whole or in part;
> (d) Imposing measures intended to prevent births within the group;
> (e) Forcibly transferring children of the group to another group.

As with all such treaties, the Genocide Convention was the product of protracted negotiations and intensive haggling over language. The result was an instrument that was both revolutionary – in establishing a new standard for 'civilized' behaviour in international society – and profoundly vexing. What was meant by 'destroy'? Why was genocide limited to 'national, ethnical, racial

[and] religious' groups – ignoring the vulnerabilities of political groups, social classes and gender groups, to name just three? What 'part' of a designated group had to be destroyed in order for the destruction to qualify as genocide? How severe did 'bodily or mental harm' have to be before it could be considered genocidal? And how did the mysterious reference to the destruction of groups 'as such' shape and limit the Convention's application?

For better or worse, however, the Convention has remained unaltered since its inception. In the mid-1980s, the UN commissioned an Englishman, Benjamin Whitaker, to prepare an assessment of the Convention and offer constructive proposals for change. Whitaker (1985) duly issued a report suggesting, among other things, that the question of including political groups in the Convention be reconsidered, and recommending that 'sexual group[s] such as women, men, or homosexuals' be added. His report was duly swallowed up by the UN bureaucracy, and not considered again. When the time came to draft the founding statutes of the International Criminal Court (ICC), the Genocide Convention was incorporated word-for-word.

Difficulties of definition and application contributed to the Convention's sidelining as a legal instrument for several decades after it came into force. Lemkin himself died in obscurity in 1959. More significant than its wording, however, was the challenge the Convention posed to the essential norm of the international system: state sovereignty and the right to non-interference in one's domestic affairs. This was precisely the norm that Lemkin had hoped to displace, by challenging the unlimited right of governments to persecute national minorities. But this was obstructed by the United Nations Charter, which anchored itself in traditional conceptions of state sovereignty. Interventions in genocide, sometimes successful, did occur between the 1950s and the dawn of the 1990s: for example, in East Pakistan/Bangladesh in 1971, Cambodia in 1978–1979, and Uganda in 1979 (see Wheeler 2000). But in no case did those mounting the interventions cite, even rhetorically, the Genocide Convention – or any other humanitarian grounds – to justify their actions. In general, as Leo Kuper wrote in his 1981 volume, a 'right to genocide' was observed in the domestic practice of states. The guiding understanding of 'security' was the security of states and their leaders – not that of the security of the civilian populations whose putative guardians were often their worst persecutors, despoilers and destroyers.

Genocide: key cases

The main spur to the international community in drafting not only the Genocide Convention, but also the whole range of post-war rights instruments, was the Nazi Holocaust – those 'barbarous acts which have outraged the conscience of mankind', in the language of the Universal Declaration of Human Rights (1948). The Nazis were promiscuous in their hatred. Where ethnic minorities were not slated for outright extermination, they generally figured as nothing more than slaves and helots in the Nazis' grand scheme.

Only two groups were explicitly designated for extermination down to the last child, woman and man: the Roma and Sinti (the so-called Gypsies), and European Jews, who had occupied a special place in Nazi thinking from the earliest years of Hitler's movement. The annihilation of up to six million Jews, the majority of them in institutions (death camps) purpose-built for mass killing, so boggled the mind that even American Jewish leaders resisted acknowledging the scale of the atrocities while they were underway. When realization sank in, it was the fate of the Jews, above all, that prompted the international community to take action (including by supporting the creation of Israel as a homeland for Jews). And after Lemkin coined the term 'genocide' in 1944, it was the Jewish Holocaust that came to be viewed as the paradigmatic instance of genocide.

Comparative genocide studies is likewise the outgrowth of Jewish Holocaust studies, which date approximately to the publication of Raul Hilberg's *The Destruction of the European Jews* in 1961 (now in its third edition – see Hilberg 2003), and to the trial of Adolf Eichmann in Jerusalem that same year. As scholarly research and public education about the Holocaust expanded in the 1970s, scholars – the majority of them American Jews – began to cast their analytical net more widely, to include other groups targeted by the Nazis, and other instances of genocide in modern history. Education and outreach efforts by members of the Armenian diaspora, paralleling and derived from those of Jews, meant that many early investigations sought to compare and contrast the Jewish Holocaust with the destruction of the Ottoman Armenian minority – some 1.5 million people in all – during the First World War. It was likewise the highly visible mobilizations and demands for restitution by North American Indians that prompted a growing recognition of the destruction wreaked upon indigenous populations in the Americas and Australasia – though perhaps only in the past decade or so have these cases achieved canonical status in comparative genocide studies.

The 1990 publication of Frank Chalk and Kurt Jonassohn's *The History and Sociology of Genocide* provided a model for the subsequent evolution of the field. Chalk and Jonassohn's reach extended back to the dawn of recorded history; they cited examples of genocide from biblical and classical civilizations, as well as from the medieval and early modern eras. The explosion of violence in the wars of Yugoslav succession in the early 1990s concentrated scholarly attention on the Balkans region and its blood-soaked history. But it was the apocalyptic events in the small Central African country of Rwanda, from April to July 1994, that lent a decisive impetus to comparative study. For the preceding 15 years or so, much ink had been spilled debating whether the Jewish Holocaust was in fact unique – or 'uniquely unique' – in the history of genocide. The argument that the destruction of European Jews was, in fact, 'phenomenologically unique' reached its apotheosis with the publication of the first (and so far only) volume of Steven Katz's *The Holocaust in Historical Context* (Katz 1994). But in the same year that Katz's massive volume appeared, its thesis of Holocaust uniqueness was severely challenged by the Rwandan events, which appeared to have distinctive and even 'unique' aspects of their own. The

Rwandan genocide was much more rapid than the Jewish Holocaust, with a million people killed in just 12 weeks; it murdered a larger proportion of the target group (Rwandan Tutsis versus European Jews) than had the Nazis; it featured the broad conscription of the population as perpetrators, which the Holocaust did not; and it offered the searing spectacle of the outside world looking on, not from a relatively distant vantage point, but from the edge of the killing fields themselves. Subsequent academic investigation, and soul-searching by the United Nations and others, has enshrined the Rwandan holocaust in something of the pivotal position for today's genocide scholars and students that the Jewish Holocaust held for an earlier generation (see Prunier 1995, Melvern 2000, 2006).

A vital element in the evolution of genocide studies is the increased attention devoted to the mass killing of groups not primarily defined by ethnic or religious identities. Most vulnerable minorities around the world *had* been so defined when Lemkin was crafting his genocide framework, and when UN member states were drafting the Genocide Convention. Such groups continued to be targeted in the post-Second World War period, as in East Pakistan/Bangladesh in 1971, or Guatemala between 1978 and 1984. But it became increasingly apparent that *political* groups were on the receiving end of some of the worst campaigns of mass killing, such as the devastating assault on the Indonesian Communist Party in 1965–1966 (with half a million to one million killed), and the brutal campaigns by Latin American and Asian military regimes against perceived dissidents in the 1970s and 1980s.

One result of this re-evaluation was that the mass killing by the Khmer Rouge regime in Cambodia between 1975 and 1978, previously ruled out as genocide or designated an 'auto-genocide' because most victims belonged to the same ethnic-Khmer group as their killers, came to be accepted as a classic instance of twentieth-century genocide. Detailed investigations were also launched into the hecatombs of casualties inflicted under Leninism and Stalinism in the post-revolutionary Soviet Union, and by Mao Zedong's communists in China. In both of these cases – and to some degree in Cambodia as well – the majority of deaths resulted not from direct execution, but from the infliction of 'conditions of life calculated to bring about [the] physical destruction' of a group, in the language of Article II(c) of the Genocide Convention. In particular, the devastating famines that struck the Ukraine and other minority regions of the USSR in the early 1930s, and the even greater death-toll – numbering tens of millions – caused by famine during Mao's 'Great Leap Forward' (1958–1962), were increasingly, though not uncontroversially, depicted as instances of mass killing underpinned by genocidal intent.

Challenges of intervention

A number of factors contributed to a resurgence of interest in genocide from the 1970s to the 1990s, and its growing use as a buttress for legal, rhetorical and military intervention. These included the continuing evolution of the human rights regime, demonstrated by the Helsinki Accords of 1975 and the UN conventions against apartheid (1976) and torture (1985); the growing influence of non-governmental organizations such as Amnesty International and Helsinki Watch (later Human Rights Watch); and the mass movement against nuclear weapons and the 'omnicide' (destruction of all life) that they threatened to inflict. Equally significant was the end of the Cold War – which separated issues of humanitarian intervention from the previous East–West competition – and the complex nature of national and international violence in the post-Cold War period. On the one hand, the decline of (or interregnum in) Russia's confrontation with the West allowed for a negotiated end to bloody conflicts in Southern Africa, Central America and South Asia. On the other hand, the breakup of the Soviet empire produced a wave of wars of succession, predominantly in Central Asia, some with genocidal overtones (as between Armenia and Azerbaijan, or in Chechnya in the 1990s and into the 2000s).

The death of communism spilled over to Yugoslavia. Following the death of Marshal Tito in 1980, the Yugoslav Federation had experienced economic decline and a growing crisis of political legitimacy. With the renewed impetus for national self-determination in the wake of the Soviet collapse, a generation of nationalist politicians worked to undermine the federation and to establish ethnically dominated nation-states. In 1991, Yugoslavia erupted into open war – first with a brief conflict over the secession of Slovenia, and then into a vicious trilateral conflict among Croatians, Serbs and Bosnian Muslims. By 1992, it was clear that a genocidal dynamic had developed. This was especially (but not exclusively) true of the Serbian 'ethnic cleansing', conducted by local militias supported from Belgrade, of areas of Bosnia-Herzegovina in which Muslims constituted a substantial minority or outright majority.

The apparent return of genocide to the European heartland, half a century after the vanquishing of Nazism and in the very Balkans region where conflict had sparked the epic conflagration of the First World War, prompted urgent debate among European and North American governments about how a successful 'humanitarian intervention' could be mounted.[2] Western European countries experimented with a variety of measures, including diplomatic pressure and UN resolutions; imposition of a uniform arms embargo; creation of an International Criminal Tribunal for the Former Yugoslavia (ICTY) to try accused war criminals and *génocidaires* on all sides of the conflict; and the dispatching of UN peacekeepers (the 'blue helmets' who had made their first appearance after the 1956 Suez Crisis), in part to protect designated 'safe areas' for displaced civilians. These measures produced little in the way of positive results. The siege of the Bosnian capital, Sarajevo, became institutionalized, despite a small UN presence and a trickle of outside aid. The uniform arms embargo favoured the Serbs, who had inherited most of the stockpiles of the Yugoslav National Army (JNA), over the landlocked and militarily strapped Bosnian Muslims. The peacekeeping contingents were vulnerable to humiliation by the Serbs, who occasionally seized them as hostages to force NATO countries to suspend or forgo airstrikes on Serb positions. Finally, the 'safe area' policy proved a grim chimera. When Serb forces chose, in mid-1995, to eliminate these areas, the desultory peacekeeper presence proved wholly inadequate to impede Serb designs. The 'safe area' at the town of Srebrenica was overrun in July, and the result was the worst massacre in Europe since the Second World War. Some 8,000 Bosnian men and adolescent boys were rounded up or hunted down, and slaughtered in scenes often reminiscent of the Nazi mass killings of civilians on the Eastern Front in 1941.

Srebrenica, however, did prove a catalyst for a resolution of the primary Balkans conflicts – in part because the elimination of the safe areas ratified 'ethnic cleansing' by creating a patchwork of geographically contiguous and ethnically homogeneous territories. In the aftermath of the massacre, NATO launched its most vigorous airstrikes on Serb strongholds. Croatian forces – which had rearmed with covert US assistance – launched a lightning assault on the majority-Serb Krajina region abutting Bosnian Serb territory. Some 200,000 Serbs fled (today they constitute the largest refugee population in Europe); and with Belgrade unwilling to intervene, the Bosnian Serbs were forced to the negotiating table. The signing of the Dayton Peace Accords in late 1995 led to the influx of 60,000 NATO troops to oversee the fragile peace, and to help build new and, where possible, non-sectarian institutions to stave off future genocidal outbreaks.

Intervention in the Balkans was thus generally slow, halfhearted, and ineffectual – even counterproductive – when it mattered most. But this was as nothing compared to the stunning abdication by the international community when not just genocide, but a full-blown holocaust, descended upon Rwanda in the spring of 1994. When systematic killing of ethnic Tutsis and moderate Hutus began in April of that year, and ten Belgian peacekeepers were murdered by the 'Hutu Power' regime, Western countries *did* intervene – but only to rescue their own (white) nationals, leaving black Africans at the mercy of the Rwandan army and *interahamwe* militia. Government officials in the USA and elsewhere bent over backwards to avoid applying the word 'genocide' to what was in fact the most rapid and intensive genocide in recorded history. To have done so would have activated the obligation to intervene and suppress the mass killing, and that was hardly conceivable. In the scathing assessment of human rights researcher Alison Des Forges, 'Rwanda was simply too remote . . . too poor, too little, and probably too black to be worthwhile' (quoted in National Film Board 1997). Especially shocking was the fact that forces capable of staging such an intervention, the 2,500 peacekeepers deployed following an interim peace accord in 1993, were on the ground when the genocide erupted. The response of the UN Security Council was to pull the bulk of them out, leaving only a skeleton force under Lt.-Gen. Roméo Dallaire to do what little it could to protect the Tutsi population. Dallaire's troops succeeded heroically in saving tens of thousands of lives, but the outside world abandoned a million other helpless victims to their deaths.

Rwanda was an abysmal low point, but it was not the final word in humanitarian intervention. It was followed several years later, in fact, by one of the most successful, and in many ways remarkable, of contemporary interventions – in September 1999, in the tiny Southeast Asian territory of East Timor. In

1975, the same year that Cambodia fell under the sway of the tyrannical Khmer Rouge, East Timor – previously a Portuguese colony – was invaded and occupied by the military regime in Indonesia. There ensued a scorched-earth campaign of suppression that killed fully one-third of the East Timorese population (some 200,000 people): by ground-level massacres; in bombing raids; and by starvation and destitution as crops were burned and civilian populations fled into inaccessible and infertile mountain regions. While the simultaneous atrocities of the Khmer Rouge aroused international condemnation and Hollywood film treatments, however, the suffering of the East Timorese was ignored by all but a tiny international network of scholars and activists, who worked tirelessly to keep the issue alive. They, along with the nascent Timorese independence movement, confronted a seemingly impossible task: to undermine the powerful position of Indonesia in the strategic *realpolitik* of the West, and to assert the right of Timorese to self-determination.

In 1999, the military regime under Indonesian President Suharto collapsed. Suharto was replaced by an elderly civilian leader, B.J. Habibie, who surprised many by approving a referendum on independence for East Timor. Before the vote, the still-powerful military mobilized pro-Indonesian militias across East Timor, who launched a campaign of terror against independence activists. Nonetheless, when Timorese went peacefully to the polls in August 1999, they voted overwhelmingly for independence. The generals responded with a murderous crackdown. Thousands of Timorese civilians were killed, and much of the territory's infrastructure was burned to the ground. As the small corps of international observers huddled terrified in the UN compound in Dili, machete-wielding thugs and pyromaniacs roamed beyond the walls. It seemed that, just as in Rwanda, the UN would abandon the field; the international community would decline to intervene; and genocide would reign unconstrained.

The violence, though, erupted scant months after the Kosovo crisis. The conflict in Kosovo was a holdover from the larger Balkans wars of the 1990s: formally part of Serbia, it had an overwhelming ethnic-Albanian majority which had long agitated for freedom from Serb subjugation – first peacefully, and then via an armed rebel movement, the Kosovo Liberation Army (KLA). In April 1999, Serb forces conducted a systematic campaign, murdering thousands of ethnic Albanians, and expelling some 800,000 to neighbouring countries. With memories of the Srebrenica debacle still relatively fresh, media airwaves and government press conferences resounded to Western leaders' lofty declarations that the rights of Kosovar Albanians had to be protected. The result was a sustained air campaign against Serb forces, and eventually the withdrawal of the Serb military from the province. In February 2008, Kosovo unilaterally declared itself independent, and was promptly recognized by the United States and major Western European countries, though Russia and China – and of course Serbia – objected vigorously. If the plight of Kosovar Albanians in Europe was sufficient to spark a major Western intervention, why should the plight of Timorese in Southeast Asia be insufficient? The well-established Timor solidarity network organized popular demonstrations that were astonishing in their size, with hundreds of thousands taking to the streets in major Australian cities alone.

The *realpolitik* equation had not changed. It behoved the world's most powerful countries to avoid antagonizing Indonesia, especially its still-dominant military, and to leave Timorese to their fate. But the combination of popular pressure and moral suasion, with the Kosovo precedent still fresh in public consciousness, trumped narrower conceptions of the 'national interest'. The USA intervened to place strong pressure on its erstwhile clients in the Indonesian Army. The Australian government announced its willingness to lead a military expedition to occupy the territory. Three weeks after the outbreak of mass violence, the first Australian soldiers stepped ashore at Dili, and a UN-sponsored protectorate took shape that oversaw the withdrawal of Indonesian forces and ushered East Timor towards its status (in 2002) as the world's newest independent state.

The Timor case suggests that the tolerance of the international community of states, and their publics, for genocide and mass atrocity may be declining, and the notion of a 'responsibility to protect' – in the catch-phrase propounded by a Canadian-sponsored commission – may be gaining ground (see ICISS 2001, and Chapter 28, this volume). Mitigating such optimism, however, was the pallid response of the international community to the burgeoning crisis in Darfur, a territory the size of France in western Sudan. When rebel movements in Darfur demanded autonomy, the authorities in Khartoum responded as despotic regimes often have: by mobilizing military and paramilitary forces to wage a brutal counter-insurgency, featuring widespread and indiscriminate violence against Darfurese civilians. In September 2004, US Secretary of State Colin Powell announced his government's conviction that the atrocities constituted 'genocide'. The declaration, however, was accompanied by little meaningful action. Three years later, at the time of writing, the USA and other governments were still debating whether to impose sanctions on the Khartoum regime (which was otherwise a valued ally in the 'War on Terror'). A small and ill-equipped African Union peacekeeping force watched ineffectually as populations were uprooted, civilian men and adolescent boys were murdered, and women and girls were raped. The only truly encouraging sign was the outburst of protest on university and high school campuses in the USA and elsewhere. By urging their academic institutions to divest from companies linked to Sudan, staging sit-ins and street demonstrations, and working to pressure the Chinese government to withdraw its vital political and economic support from the Sudanese regime, the movement energetically countered the stereotype of the current generation of students as apathetic, narcissistic and ill informed about the world beyond their iPods.

Conclusion: the way forward – and back

Amidst this shifting terrain of interventionist strategies and policies, genocide scholars and activists have played an important role. Their challenge has been twofold: to isolate the variables and circumstances that contribute to genocidal outbreaks, and to propose measures to confront them either before they occur, or while they are underway. A rich body of research now exists on genocide's causes and contexts. We understand, better than before, that societies with a prior history of genocide, where the state machinery has collapsed, or been 'captured' by a particular ethnic group and directed to sectarian ends, and where democratic institutions and practices have been suppressed, are all more likely to produce genocidal outcomes. We can more easily recognize patterns of discriminatory legislation, outbursts of hate propaganda, and lower level campaigns of political repression as potential early-warning signs of genocidal outbreaks. And we seek more readily to intervene, at least by witnessing, denouncing, shaming and sanctioning the actors responsible.

Where such measures do not succeed in preventing genocidal outbreaks, discussion continues – both within and outside genocide studies – about the most effective methods of direct military intervention. The examples of Kosovo and East Timor provide useful signposts, though the Darfur imbroglio demonstrates that ad hoc measures are rarely decisive. What is required is the institutionalization, both of an early-warning apparatus within the United Nations, and of a rapid-response military capability along the lines of the 'International Peace Army' proposed by genocide scholar Israel Charny (Charny 1999). (For some baby steps towards establishing such a body within the UN system, see Pippard and Lie 2004.)

On an intellectual plane, the study of genocide has experienced a number of significant transformations in recent years. It has become truly and broadly *comparative*, rather than serving as a limited offshoot of Holocaust studies. In so doing, it has opened up for examination a number of lesser known genocides – often taking a cue from struggles by survivors and their descendants for acknowledgement and restitution. A notable instance is the genocide that swept German South West Africa, today's Namibia, in the first decade of the twentieth century. Sparked by colonial seizures of fertile land and the erosion of traditional livelihoods, the Herero and Nama peoples rose up against their oppressors. Kaiser Wilhelm II dispatched a hardline officer, Lt.-Gen. Lothar von Trotha, to quell the revolt. Von Trotha issued an infamous 'annihilation order' (*Vernichtungsbefehl*), and combined direct massacres with a policy to drive the rebellious African populations into the barren Namib desert. Thousands died there of starvation, thirst and exhaustion. When Namibia gained its independence from South Africa in 1990, descendants of the Herero and Nama petitioned Germany for a formal apology and payment of reparations. The struggle continues, but has already scored one notable success: the 2004 visit, on the centenary of the uprising, by the German development aid minister. Heidemarie Wieczorek-Zeul declared that 'We Germans accept our historic and moral responsibility and the guilt incurred by Germans at that time' through the infliction of 'atrocities . . . [that] would have been termed genocide' (quoted in Meldrum 2004).

Inspired by such movements for recognition, and working to bolster them, genocide scholars have greatly increased our understanding of these distant events. Not only has the Namibian genocide now displaced its Armenian counterpart as the 'first' genocide of the twentieth century, but its links to subsequent German practice during the Nazi era have also been exposed. The connections include not only some of the same personnel, but racist ideologies, wars of extermination against *Untermenschen* ('subhumans'), grisly anthropological and pseudo-medical experiments, and the building of an infrastructure of concentration camps. As the colonial origins of the Nazi Holocaust have become plain, so too has the colonial nature of Nazi expansionism (*Lebensraum*) into Central and Eastern Europe.

The example of Namibia, obscure though it may still be, attests to the capacity of genocide studies to assist in reviving nearly forgotten atrocities, and to explain both their inner dynamics and their contemporary relevance. In this and other endeavours, genocide scholarship has been bolstered by contributions from an ever-wider range of social-scientific disciplines. A field that emerged with a concentration in history, sociology and psychology continues to produce groundbreaking contributions from those perspectives. But these have been supplemented by the work of anthropologists (including forensic anthropologists), conflict theorists, demographers, and scholars of gender and sexuality, to cite only a few.

The geographical breadth of the field has also expanded. What was once very much a US-centred inquiry has established flourishing bases in Western Europe (notably France, Germany and the UK); Australasia, with a particular focus on colonial genocides in the Antipodes and elsewhere; and now Latin America. The new geographical reach is accompanied by fresh framings of genocide. Australian scholars, for example, have explored the forcible transfer of (Aboriginal) children as a genocidal mechanism, while Latin American scholars have focused on the targeting of political dissidents under military or civilian dictatorships, as in Argentina and Mexico.

The future of genocide studies, and of genocide itself, is inevitably a matter of speculation. Scholarship on the subject will likely continue to draw on an expanding range of disciplinary and interdisciplinary contributions. One can expect continued definitional debates, the unearthing of new cases from past and present, and attempts to forge new strategies of intervention and prevention. Raphael Lemkin's original emphasis on cultural, not only physical, destruction as inherent to genocidal processes seems to be staging a comeback. And there is a growing tendency to view genocide not as something that occurs 'out there', in dictatorial societies and the developing world, but as a phenomenon integral to the Western (including liberal-democratic) experience.

A theme that has moved to the forefront in the recent literature is the element of *dynamism* and *contingency* in genocide. As noted earlier, for many years the field was strongly focused on the Jewish Holocaust, and on a particular vision of the Holocaust. This was the so-called 'intentionalist' framing, according to which Hitler and other Nazis intended from the earliest stage of their movement to exterminate European Jews, and worked inexorably and consistently to realize that ambition. There is no shortage of evidence that a profound hatred of Jews (in part due to their imputed political connection with Bolshevism) animated Nazism from the beginning. The policies it eventually implemented were predictably, and uniformly, hateful and persecutory. But the route from that core ideological orientation to the gas chambers and crematoria of the death camps was a long and winding one. A contending school of thought, the so-called 'functionalists', has emphasized the way that after 1933 Nazi policy evolved from boycott, to expropriation, to forced expulsion, to ghettoization, and finally to full-scale extermination. Each policy initiative was deemed the most viable option at the time, and each responded to a range of constraints: by German and international public opinion, by Jewish resistance, and by the challenge of implementing the Nazis' racist vision in the midst of the most destructive war the world has ever known.

This emphasis on the dynamic and contingent aspects of Nazi policy is increasingly echoed in studies of comparative genocide. Early on, the tendency was to view most genocides as intensively pre-planned and carefully prepared; killing campaigns that evolved more slowly, or with less general direction, were often not acknowledged as 'genocides'. Over the past few years, however, scholars have grown more attuned to the ways in which genocide may be chosen as a 'final solution' to a consuming crisis, almost always one linked to a civil or international war. Perpetrators rarely view genocide as a leisure activity. They are motivated instead by a psychological stew of fear, hubris, and past or looming humiliations; by a pervasive sense of *insecurity*, both personal and structural; and by rational, if evil, calculations of the policies most likely to produce desirable outcomes. This has important implications for the utility of security studies as a lens through which to examine genocide, and for effective strategies of intervention and prevention. A better understanding of genocidal dynamics and their evolution offers a rich analytical terrain for students of genocide, and for policy-makers as well. The more accurate our phase models become, and the better our academic discoveries are translated to the policy sphere, the greater will be the opportunities for constructive and timely interventions.

Since the early 1990s, much attention has focused on the diverse legal and quasi-legal mechanisms established to confront genocide – usually, and inevitably, *post facto*. Institutions such as national and international tribunals, truth and reconciliation commissions, and 'citizens' tribunals' will doubtlessly undergo further evolution in coming decades. As John Quigley's (2006) recent analysis of the Genocide Convention makes clear, case law at the national and international level is now adding flesh to the bare bones of the 1948 instrument. Understandings of the group identity of victims (whether subjectively claimed, or imputed by perpetrators); the nature and scope of genocidal 'intent'; the requisite scale of human destruction; the function of the 'genocidal rape' of women and the 'gendercidal' slaughter of civilian males – all have been clarified by recent legal decisions, especially those of the international criminal tribunals for Rwanda and the former Yugoslavia.

At the same time, many of the constraints of genocide's legal framing have become evident. These pertain, above all, to the difficulty of documenting 'intent' to 'destroy' a group 'as such'. Prosecutors have increasingly turned to the language of 'crimes against humanity', including the crime of *extermination*, which draws its international-legal definition directly from Article II(c) of the Genocide Convention. Convictions for crimes against humanity tend to produce similar gaol sentences as for genocide, without requiring a demonstration of intent strictly construed, or establishment of clear boundaries of group identity among targeted civilian populations. This trend will probably continue. It may be that within several decades will predominate, and we will view the principal utility of the 'genocide' framework not as a legal instrument, but as a tool for shaming perpetrators and mobilizing public opposition to their destructive designs. The international campaign underway at the time of writing, to rebrand China's 'One World' Olympics as the 'Genocide Olympics' (and thereby pressure the Chinese government to pressure in turn the government of Sudan, its close business partner), may serve as a harbinger of this future prioritization.

What of the prominence of genocide in human affairs? A recent and well-publicized study (Human Security Centre 2005) suggests that it may be declining, as the 'degenerate wars' of the late- and post-Cold War period also ebb (see Shaw 2003). If the trend exists, however, it is hardly uniform. The calamitous events in Iraq, now spilling over to other Middle Eastern states; ongoing carnage in the Democratic Republic of the Congo and Darfur; the pervasive brutality of regimes in Burma and North Korea; and worrying signs in Haiti and the Dominican Republic – all caution against facile optimism. Moreover, the pressures now building on land and sustainable resources, as global warming and other environmental transformations take hold, will likely fuel the conflicts born of material scarcity that have long been a hallmark of genocidal outbreaks. Staging meaningful 'interventions' thus requires more than developing a standing UN force or an effective regime of economic sanctions. Useful though these may be, the genocides of the twenty-first century will require a more nuanced understanding of the structural and institutional features of human society and economy. The range of necessary interventionist measures will be correspondingly wider, and probably more amorphous, than those practised or debated in the past. This will in central respects parallel the shift in security studies from a limited framing of 'national security' to a broader understanding of 'human security', and the multi-faceted threats that confront it at both national and international levels.

Notes

1   See Wright (2004: 25):

> If it turns out that the Neanderthals disappeared because they were an evolutionary dead end, we can merely shrug and blame natural selection for their fate. But if they were in fact a variant or race of modern man, then we must admit to ourselves that their death may have been the first genocide. Or, worse, *not* the first – merely the first of which evidence survives. It may follow from this that we are descended from a million

years of ruthless victories, genetically predisposed by the sins of our fathers to do likewise again and again.

2   The concept of humanitarian intervention may be traced at least as far back as the proclamations issued by Western European governments in the latter half of the nineteenth century, asserting the rights of Christian minorities in the Balkans and Middle East – while those same European countries were trampling, often genocidally, the rights of non-Christian populations in their colonial possessions.

Further reading

Alex Alvarez, *Governments, Citizens, and Genocide: A Comparative and Interdisciplinary Approach* (Bloomington, IN: Indiana University Press, 2001). A concise account, especially strong on the sociological variables underpinning genocide.

Frank Chalk and Kurt Jonassohn, *The History and Sociology of Genocide* (New Haven, CT: Yale University Press, 1990). Early and eclectic study, still popular as a textbook.

Adam Jones, *Genocide: A Comprehensive Introduction* (London: Routledge, 2006). Attempts to capture the interdisciplinary breadth of genocide studies in a student-friendly volume.

Leo Kuper, *Genocide: Its Political Use in the Twentieth Century* (New Haven, CT: Yale University Press, 1981). The foundational text of comparative genocide studies.

Manus Midlarsky, *The Killing Trap: Genocide in the Twentieth Century* (Cambridge: Cambridge University Press, 2005). Analysis of genocide from a political science and International Relations perspective.

CONTENTS

Ethnic Conflict

Stuart J. Kaufman

▌ Abstract

Ethnic groups are ascriptive groups – most people are born into them, rather than choosing them voluntarily – and they are usually distinguished from other groups by some combination of language, race and religious affiliation. These differences are not 'natural' or 'primordial'; they are 'socially constructed', so that people are divided in different ways depending on the social beliefs summarized in their group's 'myth-symbol complex'. Most countries are multiethnic, and most ethnic relationships are peaceful. However, some ethnic conflicts do become violent, often enough that ethnic wars represent a sizeable fraction of all wars that occurred in the twentieth century. Ethnic conflicts are most likely to result in serious violence when government is weak; the groups' myth-symbol complexes lead them to see each other as hostile; they fear for the survival of their group; and the competing sides demand political dominance over some disputed territory. Violent ethnic conflicts have important international dimensions: they are often encouraged by hardline émigré groups, they can cause very large flows of refugees across international borders, and they inspire international intervention ranging from diplomatic efforts to military force. While power-sharing and compromise are the internationally preferred formula for resolving ethnic conflicts, in practice most of them end only when one side wins militarily.

Introduction

Ethnic identities have existed throughout recorded history. Even in ancient times, ethnic groups such as the Hebrews, Babylonians and Egyptians were important political actors (Smith, A. 1986), just as contemporary Serbs and Kurds are. Most ethnic conflicts are peaceful, however: while political issues inevitably arise when different linguistic and religious groups mix, they are typically managed peacefully. The Soviet Union, for example, is said to have included 120 ethnic groups; yet with all of these points of friction, in only a handful of cases did ethnic groups clash violently when the Soviet Union collapsed (Fearon and Laitin 1996). Still, especially when the issue at stake is the political dominance of one group over another, violent ethnic clashes do sometimes occur. These ethnic wars are sometimes of critical international importance: Pakistan's effort to repress the Bengalis of East Pakistan in 1971, for example, provoked an Indian invasion that led to East Pakistan's becoming the independent country of Bangladesh, changing permanently the balance of power in South Asia.

In the twentieth century, ethnic civil wars – indeed, civil wars of all kinds – were more important than ever before. In fact, though they were overshadowed by the two World Wars and then the Cold War, civil wars were more common than international wars throughout the twentieth century. The disparity became particularly stark in the 1990s: one study identified over 50 armed civil conflicts ongoing in that decade, and only two international armed conflicts (Wallensteen and Sollenberg 1999). While classifications of these conflicts vary, about half of the civil wars and other internal armed conflicts were, to a large extent, ethnic conflicts. Ethnic conflict has long been one of the major sources of insecurity in the world, and it is becoming more so.

On one list of the 10 bloodiest civil wars of the twentieth century (Sarkees 2000), half of the cases were ethnic conflicts: the civil war between Sudan's Muslim-dominated government and non-Muslim rebels in the south from 1983 to 2005; the secession of Bangladesh from Pakistan in 1971; the Rwandan civil war and genocide of 1994; Sudan's earlier round of north–south conflict between roughly 1963 and 1972; and Bosnia's civil war from 1992 to 1995. Nigeria's civil war of 1967 to 1970 was comparably bloody. Each of these conflicts is estimated to have cost upward of a quarter of a million lives, and each was not only a catastrophe for the country that became a battlefield, but also a major source of disruption, conflict, and refugees for neighbouring countries as well. As a result, each became a major international issue, together sparking every sort of foreign intervention from mediation efforts to direct military involvement. Ethnic conflict is therefore a central issue for security studies.

Even ethnic riots can be deadly on a large enough scale to constitute a problem for international security. Hindu–Muslim riots in India in 1947 killed between 100,000 and 200,000 people and generated about 10 million refugees. A series of riots in 1966 by Muslim northern Nigerians (mostly Hausa) against

Christian Ibos from the south displaced over a million people by 1967. Rioting by Sri Lankan Sinhalese aimed against the Tamil minority in 1977 killed only about 100 people but displaced over 50,000. In all three of these cases, the eventual result was civil war causing even more death and destruction. Other cases, such as later rounds of Hindu attacks on Muslims in northern India, do not themselves lead to war, but reflect and contribute to international tensions – in this case, between India and Pakistan (Horowitz 2000).

What is ethnic conflict?

Discussions of ethnicity and ethnic conflict are notoriously imprecise, because people disagree about what counts as an ethnic conflict. Are race relations between blacks and whites in the USA an example of low-violence ethnic conflict, or is racial conflict a different category altogether? If race is different, does the distinction extend to Rwanda, where Hutus and Tutsis – both black – referred to their difference as one of race? Are relations between Muslims and Hindus in India, or between Sunni and Shi'a Arabs in Iraq, cases of ethnic conflict, or do they belong in different categories as 'religious', 'communal' or 'sectarian' conflicts?

For an anthropologist, what these cases all have in common is that the groups involved are primarily ascriptive – that is, membership in the groups is typically assigned at birth and is difficult to change. In theory, Indian Muslims can convert and become Hindu, and Iraqi Sunnis can become Shi'a, but in practice few do, and the conversion of those few is not always accepted by their new co-ethnics. Identities of this kind are therefore 'sticky', hard to change even if they are not marked by the kind of obvious physical differences that distinguish African-Americans from white Americans. Based on this commonality, I will use the broader definition of ethnicity that encompasses all of these kinds of ascriptive groups. According to Anthony Smith (1986), a group is an ethnic group if its members share the following traits: a common name, a believed common descent, elements of a shared culture (most often language or religion), common historical memories, and attachment to a particular territory.

In the past, experts disagreed widely about where ethnicity comes from. Some, focusing on the evidence that many ethnic identities seem to go back hundreds or thousands of years, asserted that ethnicity was a 'primordial' identity, and implied that it was essentially unchangeable. They emphasized that groups often worked hard to make their identity unchangeable, sometimes carving that identity on to their bodies through tattoos or circumcision (Isaacs 1975). Even when they do not go that far, however, people tend to stick to the identities – especially the language and religion – they learn first from their parents. This view of ethnicity implies that ethnic conflict is based on 'ancient hatreds' that are impossible to eradicate and nearly impossible to manage.

There is another, more complicated side to ethnic identity, however. Most people have multiple identities that are either 'nested' (as subgroups within larger groups) or overlapping. The average Cuban-American is at the same time also an American Hispanic or Latino, an American Catholic, an American, and a member of the worldwide Catholic Church. Which identity is more important to her is likely to depend on the situation: when listening to the Pope, she is likely to respond as a Catholic; when watching the US President, as an American; and when thinking about US policy towards Cuba, as a Cuban-American.

Furthermore, identities do sometimes change, with new ones emerging and old ones disappearing, especially in times of crisis. For example, when the Soviet Union was breaking apart in the early 1990s, Ukrainians and Russians in the Transnistria region of Moldova came together as 'Russophones' – people who preferred to speak Russian rather than Moldovan – to resist the assertiveness of the ethnic Moldovans (Kaufman 2001). On the other hand, the 'Yugoslav' identity disappeared with the country of Yugoslavia in 1991, so people who formerly called themselves Yugoslavs had to shift to another identity as Serbs, Croats, or members of some other group.

Noticing that people shift their identity – or at least the identity they use politically – based on the situation, a second group of scholars emerged to argue that ethnic identity is not 'primordial' at all, but merely 'instrumental' (Hardin 1995). From this perspective, people follow 'ethnic' leaders when it is in their interests to do so, and leaders try to create ethnic solidarity when it works for them. This view of ethnic identity implies that ethnic conflict can be blamed primarily on selfish leaders who mislead their followers in pursuit of their own power.

A third point of view about ethnic identity mixes the other two views by emphasizing the degree to which people create their identities. Expressed in book titles such as *The Invention of Tradition* (Hobsbawm and Ranger 1992), this view points out that ethnic identities are 'socially constructed'. They are not 'natural' in the sense that a simple primordialist view would assume; even racial distinctions are just a matter of custom. For example, most African-Americans accept the label 'black', but in South Africa most of them would be classified as 'coloured' – of mixed race – rather than as the darker, purely African 'blacks'. Most Americans would hardly notice the difference, but in Apartheid-era South Africa, the difference would have shaped every aspect of people's lives.

Furthermore, constructivists pointed out, the source of these customs was 'invented traditions': writers or scholars who created what Anthony Smith calls a 'myth-symbol complex'. This myth-symbol complex establishes the 'accepted' history of the group and the criteria for distinguishing who is a member; identifies heroes and enemies; and glorifies symbols of the group's identity. In most cases, these mythologies 'mythicize' real history, taking real events but redefining them as the morally defining experiences of their people. In many cases, these events are what Vamik Volkan (1997) has called 'chosen traumas', such as the Holocaust for Jews or the 1389 Battle of Kosovo Field for Serbs. In some cases, however, histories and myths are simply made up to create new identities.

These constructivist insights may be viewed as a way to settle the argument between primordialists and instrumentalists, because constructivist ideas explain both the insights and the problems of the other two views. For example, most Serbs honestly believe that their identity is primordial, forged in the fires of battle against the Turks at Kosovo in 1389, so their perception is that their conflicts with Muslims are the result of primordial 'ancient hatreds'. In fact, though, that view of history was the result of late nineteenth-century Serbian politics and educational policy (Snyder 2000); before then, most Serbs did not think of themselves as Serbs at all. Similarly, Serbian politicians such as Slobodan Milosevic did indeed use Serbian ethnic identity instrumentally to pursue their own power in the 1990s, but that identity only 'worked' politically because it had been socially constructed before. Any old identity will not do.

Another question is how to tell whether a particular conflict is an ethnic conflict. Most African countries are multiethnic, for example, but African civil wars often involve warlords competing for control over resources such as diamond mines, so ethnicity has little to do with who is on which side. A conflict is ethnic only if the sides involved are distinguished primarily on the basis of ethnicity. Often one or both sides in an ethnic conflict will be a coalition of ethnic groups rather than a single one, but the conflict is still ethnic because the people involved choose sides on the basis of their ethnic group membership, rather than other considerations such as economic interests.

While most ethnic conflicts are peaceful, I focus in this chapter on the violent ones, because in most cases it is only violent ethnic conflicts that become problems relevant for security studies, the focus of this book. I will begin, however, with a brief overview of ethnic conflicts more generally.

An overview of ethnic conflicts

Ethnic groups and ethnic conflicts are everywhere. One comprehensive survey found a total of 275 ethnic or communal groups in 116 countries around the world that were socially disadvantaged in some way – 'minorities at risk'. Put together, the groups included more than a billion people, or about 17.4 per cent of the world's population (Gurr 2000: 9–10). Of the 50 biggest countries in the world by population, only four – Poland, Tanzania, Nepal and North Korea – did not have at least one 'minority at risk' (and Tanzania has many ethnic groups: they were merely judged not to be 'at risk'). Some of these groups are very small, in mostly homogeneous countries: Australia's lone 'minority at risk', the Aborigines, comprise only about 1 per cent of the country's population; while Japan's only minority, the Koreans, comprise only one-half of 1 per cent. Some of the groups are very large and important, however: Malaysia's Chinese minority comprises 27 per cent of the population, and India's oft-mistreated Muslims form 11 per cent of India's population. Overall, it is accurate to say that most countries in the world are ethnically diverse.

Most of the time, the existence of minority groups does not lead to violence or even to serious conflict. In 1995, most of the 'minorities at risk' (58 per cent) were either politically inactive or mobilized only for routine politics. Another 15 per cent were a little more volatile, engaging in demonstrations, rioting, or both. Still, violent ethnic conflicts were unfortunately plentiful: 49 (18 per cent) of the 'minorities at risk' were engaged in 'small-scale rebellion' in 1995, and another 22 (8 per cent) were fighting a 'large-scale rebellion' (Gurr 2000: 28). These numbers, however, were just about the worst ever: the long-term trend is that the number of violent ethnic conflicts increased fairly steadily from the end of the Second World War until the mid-1990s, but then it started to drop. A separate survey for 2003 lists only 11 'intermediate armed conflicts' or 'wars' that were more or less ethnic conflicts. Those conflicts were: the Taliban rebellion in Afghanistan, the Karen insurgency in Burma, Hutu–Tutsi conflict in Burundi, the Kashmir insurgency in India, Palestinian resistance against Israel, the Muslim rebellion in the southern Philippines, the Chechnya conflict in Russia, the Tamil separatist conflict in Sri Lanka, two separate wars in Sudan (one against southern Christians, another in Darfur), and the Kurdish insurgency in Turkey (Eriksson and Wallensteen 2004).

What are these violent conflicts about? The simplest answer is political power in a disputed territory. Most of the conflicts involve a regional minority who want to separate and form their own state, or at least their own autonomous region. The conflicts in Burma (Karens), India (Kashmir), the Palestinian territories (occupied by Israel), Philippines (Muslims), Russia (Chechnya), Sri Lanka (Tamils) and Turkey (Kurds) are more or less of this type. In other cases, the insurgent ethnic group wants to take over government of the whole country: thus Burundi's majority Hutus wish to take power from the minority Tutsi government.

The goals and stakes are often unclear, as rebels may disagree with each other. For example, some Palestinians want to establish their own state alongside Israel, but others are fighting to replace Israel with a Palestinian state. The Afghanistan case is only partially ethnic: the rebel Taliban define themselves by their ideological aims – creation of an Islamic state – but in practice, virtually all of their support comes from the Pashtun ethnic group, while the Tajik, Uzbek and Hazara minorities generally oppose them.

Only rarely are these conflicts 'religious' in the sense of one group trying to impose its religion on another – even when the groups in conflict differ in religion. Thus even though Sri Lanka's Tamils are Hindu while the majority Sinhalese are Buddhist, neither group wants the other to convert. Rather, the rebel Liberation Tigers of Tamil Eelam want to establish their own state (Tamil Eelam) in northern and eastern Sri Lanka, while the Sinhalese-dominated government wants to prevent that outcome. The Kashmir, Chechen, Palestinian and Philippine–Muslim conflicts have a similar flavour. The biggest exception is Sudan, where the main grievance of the Christian and animist southerners was the attempt by the Sudanese government to impose Islamic law on the whole country, including them.

Another misconception is that ethnic conflicts are 'merely' economic. Some scholars argue that the statistical link between ethnic diversity and civil war is weak, and that the main causes of civil war are poverty, weak governments, and other factors that make it easy to start a guerrilla campaign (e.g. Fearon and Laitin 2003). The truth, however, is that while economic grievances are always present, in ethnic conflicts they are expressed in ethnic terms. In Mindanao in the southern Philippines, for example, the poor – Christians as well as Muslims – are all disadvantaged by inadequate government spending on education and infrastructure. But the Communist New People's Army, which tries to exploit such rich/poor distinctions to gain support, has had little luck in Muslim areas. Rather, Muslims there respond to specifically Muslim rebel groups who emphasize the differences between Muslims and Christians, not between rich and poor (McKenna 1998). In other cases, it is not the poor ethnic group but the rich one that rebels: in Yugoslavia, for example, it was the relatively prosperous Slovenes and Croats who first tried to secede, because they felt they were being held back by the more 'backward' ethnic groups in the rest of the country.

Causes of violent ethnic conflict

In the statistics about ethnic conflicts quoted above, the violent conflicts fell into two broad categories: riots, and armed conflicts or civil wars.

Deadly ethnic riots have occurred all over the world, but how and why they occur seems puzzling. Such riots typically begin suddenly, soon after a seemingly minor triggering incident. Once they begin they mushroom in size, yielding widespread violence across a city or an entire country. Furthermore, even though many such riots involve little or no planning, they almost always entail careful selection of victims: rioters seem to be in unspoken agreement about whom they want to kill. Yet together with this focus on whom to kill is often unspeakable brutality in how they are killed, with rape, torture and mutilation not uncommon. In addition, there is frequently no discrimination between ages and sexes: children, women and men of all ages may be targeted for torture and murder. After the killing is done, there is usually no remorse on the part of the killers or their co-ethnics: 'they had it coming' is the attitude typically expressed by rioting communities all over the globe (Horowitz 2000).

One comprehensive survey, which takes a social psychological approach, finds three main factors that lead to deadly ethnic riots (Horowitz 2000). First, there needs to be a hostile ongoing relationship between the groups – tensions of long standing to motivate the killing. Second, there needs to be authoritative social support: potential rioters need to be assured by public statements from community leaders in their group that the leaders agree killing members of the other group is justified. At the same time, this support usually extends to the security forces: riots usually become large only if the police are sympathetic, or at least do not make determined efforts to stop the killing.

Finally, there needs to be a stimulus, some event – usually implying some sort of threat – that provokes fear, rage or hatred in the rioting group. For example, a report (true or not) of a violent attack by one of 'them' against one of 'us' might spark a widespread cry to 'teach them a lesson'. Alternatively, a political change – even a potential one – might provoke a similar outburst. In 1958, for example, Sri Lankan Prime Minister S.W.R.D. Bandaranaike, a Sinhalese, signed a power-sharing deal with the leader of his country's Tamil minority, but quickly backed away under political pressure. *After* the deal was abrogated, ordinary Sinhalese vented their wrath at the very idea of such power-sharing by attacking innocent Tamils in a large-scale riot.

Another approach to explaining ethnic riots focuses not on psychology but on social organization. In India, for example, hostile relations between the Hindu and Muslim communities are common, but most of the riot violence is concentrated in just a few cities. Why? The riot-prone cities, it turns out, have 'institutionalized riot systems': community activists and extremist organizations that benefit from keeping tensions high, politicians who benefit from occasional violence, and criminals and thugs who can profit from it (Brass 1997). On the other hand, Indian cities with little or no riot violence have community organizations (e.g. business groups, labour unions) that cross communal lines, bringing Hindus and Muslims together instead of driving them apart (Varshney 2002).

Explanations of ethnic civil wars divide along similar lines: social psychology approaches, social mobilization approaches and instrumentalist approaches. Instrumentalist approaches start with what creates the opportunity for rebels to act: weak governments, large populations and inaccessible terrain create the opening extremists need to act (Fearon and Laitin 2003). Also important in most instrumentalist arguments are extremist leaders seeking to grab or hold on to power, who stir up ethnic disagreements and provoke violence to create a 'rally around the flag' effect uniting their group around their own leadership (Gagnon 1995). A key role, from this perspective, is played by extremist media, which seek popularity by appealing to group loyalties, presenting the news in terms of 'us' against 'them' (Snyder 2000). These two factors work together: extremist leaders provide heroes for the extremist media to promote, while one-sided media portrayals seem to validate the extremist leaders' claims that their group must unite against the 'enemy'. The most prominent example of extremist leaders of this kind is Slobodan Milosevic, who headed the upsurge of Serbian national identity that led to the breakup of Yugoslavia in 1991.

Social mobilization approaches consider these leadership roles, but are also interested in how ethnic groups mobilize – that is, how do members of the group get together the people and resources needed for collective action? The answer, these theorists point out, is that people use social organizations and networks that already exist, such as political parties and labour unions. Successful mobilization efforts find 'brokers', people who can link different groups and networks together to help them cooperate in a single movement (McAdam *et al.* 2001). This provides one answer to the question: Why do people mobilize as *ethnic* groups instead, for example, of organizing as economic interest groups? It is because people's social networks tend to be mostly within their ethnic group; barriers of language or religion typically separate them from members of other groups.

Social psychological approaches focus on a different puzzle: Why do people follow these extremist leaders? Even if people mobilize as ethnic groups to look out for their interests, why do they follow extremist leaders who want violence, instead of following moderate leaders who will work for peace? One answer is proposed by symbolic politics theory, which emphasizes the roles of group myths and fears. Remembering that a group is defined by its myth-symbol complex – the stories it tells about the group's history and identity – symbolic politics theory suggests that when the group's myth-symbol complex points to the other group as an enemy, its members will be predisposed to be hostile to the other group. Politicians will then be able to appeal to symbols of past hostility – such as Slobodan Milosevic referring to the Battle of Kosovo Field – to rouse people's emotions against the enemy which that symbol brings to mind (Muslims, in the case of Kosovo). If the group are at the same time convinced that they are in danger of extinction – of being wiped out as a group – they can be persuaded to back extreme measures that are justified as 'self-defence' (Kaufman 2001).

To see how these complex processes play out in practice, let us consider in detail two examples of the bloodiest ethnic conflicts in recent decades: Sudan's north–south civil wars, and the three-sided fight in Bosnia.

Sudan

Sudan is one of the less sensible results of map-making by colonial powers in Africa. Northern Sudan is overwhelmingly Muslim in religion and is led by a long-dominant Arab elite; the south is a mixture of Christian and animist groups, of which the largest are the Dinka and the Nuer. During and before the Mahdiyya (1885–1898), a period of Muslim fundamentalist rule, southerners' main contact with northerners came when northerners raided their lands to collect slaves. In colonial times (1899–1955) the British, nominally in partnership with Egypt, ruled the two regions separately, with the north under a form of Islamic law (Kaufman 2006).

Sudan had the preconditions for ethnic war from every perspective. Instrumentalists would note that its large population, huge land area (the biggest in Africa), hostile neighbours and weak government provide ample opportunity for rebel groups to form. Symbolists point out that northerners' myth-symbol complex glorifies the Mahdiyya as a basis for an Islamic identity for Sudan; while southerners see Islamist rule as a disaster for themselves, and they fear northerners' efforts to spread Islam as a threat to their own identities. North and south were thus primed for mutual hostility.

When Sudan gained its independence in 1955, northern elites – led in part by descendants of the Madhiyya's leader, the al-Mahdi clan – gained almost all government jobs and benefits, and they formulated a Muslim and Arab national identity to try to unite northerners behind their rule. They attempted to impose this identity on the south, swiftly sparking violent resistance that escalated to full-scale civil war in the early 1960s. A military coup in 1969 brought to power the secularist colonel Jaafar al-Nimeiri, who signed a peace agreement in 1972 granting autonomy to the south.

By the late 1970s, however, Nimeiri's secular coalition began crumbling under pressure from traditional northern elites like the al-Mahdi clan, while Sudan's economy sagged. To maintain his power, Nimeiri began appealing to Islamist symbols, dressing like an Arab sheikh, publicizing his mosque attendance, and forming a coalition with the Muslim Brotherhood and al-Mahdi clan leader Sadiq al-Mahdi. As part of this campaign, he revoked in 1983 the southern autonomy he had granted a decade before, and imposed Islamic law throughout the country. Since southerners' identity was threatened by this programme of forced Islamization, they immediately rebelled again.

Nimeiri was right that his programme of appeals to symbols of Islam was popular, but it did not save him. He was overthrown in 1985, and in the brief period of democracy that followed, the group with the most enthusiastic following was the Muslim Brotherhood, which convened huge rallies promoting such slogans as 'No alternative to God's law!' to block any suggestion of compromise with the south. When a new military dictatorship took power in 1989 under General Omar al-Bashir, it maintained Islamic law and the coalition with the Islamists – and continued the war in the south for another 16 years. Tragically, as the war in the south wound down after the 2005 Comprehensive Peace Agreement, a new civil war had begun in Sudan's western region of Darfur.

Yugoslavia

Yugoslavia, formed in the aftermath of the First World War, was a multiethnic state with no majority group. The three largest groups all spoke the same language, Serbo-Croatian, but differed in their religious tradition among Serbs (Orthodox Christians), Croats (Catholics) and Bosnian Muslims. The fourth largest group, the Slovenes, are Catholics but speak a different (though related) language; the next largest, the Albanians, are Muslims who speak a wholly unrelated language. Before the Second World War, Yugoslavia was ruled by a Serbian king and dominated by Serbian politicians.

During the Second World War, the Germans conquered the country and placed Croatian fascists, the Ustashe, in power in the regions of Croatia and Bosnia, where they engaged in genocidal violence against the Serbs. As the war ended, communist partisan leader Josip Broz Tito took power in Yugoslavia, massacring the Ustashe and re-creating Yugoslavia as a nominal federation of six Republics: Serbia, Croatia, Bosnia-Hercegovina, Slovenia, Macedonia and Montenegro (Kaufman 2001).

When Tito died in 1980, the loss of his charismatic authority severely weakened Yugoslavia's government, creating the permissive conditions for war emphasized by instrumentalist theorists. The republic governments, growing in power, now increasingly allowed the kind of mutually hostile myth-making that Tito had tried to stamp out. For example, nationalist Serbs began talking about the menace of the Albanians who formed the majority in the symbolically important Kosovo region, while labelling any Croatian disagreement as evidence of resurgent Ustashe fascism. As symbolists would note, ethnic myths and fears were growing.

The leader of Serbia's League of Communists, Slobodan Milosevic, noticed the power of this nationalist sentiment and in the late 1980s became its spokesman, repressing the Albanians and attempting to impose Serbian control on the whole of Yugoslavia (Gagnon 1995). In response to this Serbian threat, voters in Slovenia, Croatia and Bosnia turned to supporting their own nationalist leaders – with the Croatian nationalists reviving the national symbols last used by the Ustashe fascists, raising alarm among Serbs and making Milosevic's appeals ever more plausible. Yugoslavia was dying. Slovenia moved first, declaring independence on 25 June 1991. The Croats quickly followed, sparking a months-long war in which the Yugoslav army conquered areas in Croatia inhabited by Croatia's Serbian minority.

The agony of Bosnia-Hercegovina was to be longer. Home to a mixture of Bosnian Muslims, Serbs and Croats, Bosnia was torn three ways. Serbs wanted to remain in Yugoslavia; but fearing Serbian domination, the Muslims wanted to secede and form an independent Bosnian state, while Croats wanted their areas (especially western Hercegovina) to join Croatia. In 1992 a coalition of Muslims and Croats therefore declared Bosnian independence, sparking a three-sided civil war in which Serbia and Croatia – trying to take over chunks of Bosnian territory – provided military assistance to their co-ethnics in Bosnia, while the Muslims were the principal victims. Under the slogan, 'Only Unity Saves the Serbs', Serbs exaggerated the disadvantages of separation from Serbia into a threat to their national existence, and used this invented threat to justify – and invent – the term 'ethnic cleansing': the Serbs' programme of massacring enough of their ethnic enemies to force the rest to flee any territory they claimed. Finally, in 1995, a Croatian military counter-offensive backed by NATO airpower prompted the Serb side to agree to stop the fighting.

International security dimensions of ethnic conflicts

As these two examples illustrate, ethnic conflicts often have important international effects. The Bosnian case illustrates a wide range of such effects. First, the politics of ethnic conflict transcends national boundaries, with ethnic diasporas often playing an important role. For example, the Croatian émigré community in the USA provided lavish funding for national leader Franjo Tudjman in Croatia, giving his party a significant edge over moderate rivals in Croatia's first free elections in 1990. In 1991, a politically influential Croatian minority in Germany tilted German foreign policy towards support for the Croatian cause. This support undermined international efforts to head off war: US Secretary of State James Baker visited Yugoslavia shortly before war broke out in 1991, but his efforts to restrain the Slovenes and Croats were undercut by the Germans. Croatian émigrés in the West thus played an important role in causing Yugoslavia's breakup and the wars that followed.

A second international effect of ethnic civil wars is the creation of refugees. Any warfare generates displacement, as civilians sensibly flee for their lives from combat areas. Ethnic civil wars, however, produce particularly large numbers of refugees because such wars are often about which group will control disputed lands, so massacres and evictions – ethnic cleansing – are frequently-used weapons. When the victims stay within their own country, as did most of Bosnia's 1.8 million homeless, they are technically 'internally displaced persons' rather than refugees, and their international effect is limited. Presenting a humanitarian problem, they often receive humanitarian aid, but provoke little more reaction.

If, however, they do cross international borders, refugees may be seen as threats to international security in several different ways. For example, when Serbia began an ethnic cleansing campaign in Kosovo in 1999, the hundreds of thousands of ethnic Albanian refugees who flooded across the border into Macedonia threatened to destabilize the tenuous ethnic balance between ethnic Macedonians and the Albanians already there. Alternatively, refugees might turn their refugee camps into bases from which to attack their former homeland. For example, in 1994, hundreds of thousands of ethnic Hutus (many involved in committing genocide) fled from Rwanda to Zaire when their Tutsi rivals took power. They quickly began launching attacks against Rwanda's Tutsi-led government, using international humanitarian aid to supply their war effort. These attacks finally provoked Rwanda and its allies into invading Zaire, not only stopping the attacks but also toppling President Mobutu's government, sparking what came to be known as 'Africa's first world war'.

Another effect of ethnic civil wars is that they often become a major issue for international diplomacy. As the crises in Croatia and Bosnia grew in 1991 and 1992, respectively, diplomats wrangled over how best to avoid war. As Bosnia's agony mounted in the mid-1990s, Western governments came under increasing pressure to act to stem the humanitarian emergency generated by ethnic cleansing. At the same time, the fact that Europeans initially split over the Yugoslav crisis, with the French and British at first tilting towards the Serbs, spurred the European Union to upgrade its efforts to form a common foreign and security policy.

The result of such pressure is sometimes effective diplomatic intervention, and sometimes tragically unsuccessful diplomacy. On the one hand, the short war between Slovenia and Yugoslavia was ended through mediation of European Community (EC) leaders in talks on the island of Brioni in 1991. Similarly, the war between Croatia and the rump Yugoslavia was ended in early 1992 through a ceasefire brokered by United Nations (UN) special envoy Cyrus Vance (a former US Secretary of State), building on the efforts of EC mediators. On the other hand, German pressure pushed the EC into formal diplomatic recognition of Croatia and Slovenia, and into consideration of recognition for other Yugoslav republics declaring independence, in January 1992. This position faced Bosnia with the perception that it was now or never for its own prospects for independence. Bosnia went ahead, declaring independence and sparking its agonizing three-year civil war. Thus the same diplomatic moves that helped to end the war in Croatia helped to start the much more violent one in Bosnia (Cohen 1995: 238).

When diplomacy alone is not enough, international actors sometimes resort to sending peacekeepers to try to manage ethnic violence. If there is a ceasefire in place, peacekeepers can be effective in helping to maintain it, especially if the warring factions are physically separated with the peacekeepers posted in between. In a situation such as this, UN peacekeepers have successfully policed a ceasefire between ethnic Greeks and Turks on the island of Cyprus since 1974. On the other hand, this conflict has still not been finally resolved, and it may be that the peacekeepers have done their job too well: by preventing bloodshed, they have made the current situation of neither peace nor war an easier option than the tough compromises that a final peace agreement would require.

Bosnia, however, is a prominent example of the ineffectiveness of peace-keepers if they are introduced in the wrong circumstances. The UN Protection Force (UNPROFOR) was originally sent into Yugoslavia in early 1992 to monitor the ceasefire between the Croats and Serbs in Croatia. This it was able to do. But as the fighting in Bosnia escalated, the UN voted to increase UNPROFOR's size and expand its mission to guarantee the provision of humanitarian aid to beleaguered Bosnian towns. The whole idea was self-contradictory: while pretending to be neutral and refusing to engage in combat, UNPROFOR was acting to undermine the Bosnian Serbs' strategy of block-ading Bosnian Muslim towns to starve them out. Not surprisingly, the Serbs obstructed UNPROFOR's efforts whenever they could.

The futility of UNPROFOR is illustrated by the fate of the town of Srebrenica: declared a UN 'safe area' in April 1993, it was intermittently supplied by UN convoys and protected by a small UNPROFOR garrison. But when an all-out Serb offensive came in July 1995, the UNPROFOR troops stood aside, the town was captured, as many as 8,000 Bosnian Muslim males were slaughtered by the victorious Serb troops, and the rest of Srebrenica's civilians were forced to flee. Srebrenica was 'ethnically cleansed' (Rieff 1996).

Because international interest in ethnic conflicts is often intense, and because peacekeepers are not always effective, international actors often resort to violent intervention, either directly or indirectly. Indirect intervention in ethnic civil wars is common: foreign countries frequently provide supplies, weapons and military training to the sides they favour. In many cases this international aid is also ethnically motivated, with countries backing the side more closely related to them (Saideman 2001). Thus in the Yugoslav conflicts, Russia armed their fellow Eastern Orthodox Slavs, while the Bosnian Muslims received arms and volunteer fighters from the Muslim Middle East. The Christian United States, similarly, not only provided arms for Catholic Croatia, but also paid a US-based private firm to train the Croatian army, readying it for the 1995 offensive that threw the Serbs out of Croatia. Similar patterns occur all over the world: Christian Kenya and Ethiopia helped the partially Christian southern Sudanese against their Muslim adversaries, for example, while Muslim Libya and other Muslim states aided the Muslims of the southern Philippines in their war against the Christian-dominated Philippine government.

Sometimes these interventions are purely opportunistic rather than ethni-cally based. For example, in the war in the mountainous Karabagh region of the former Soviet Republic of Azerbaijan in the early 1990s, Russia switched back and forth between aiding the (Muslim) Azerbaijanis and the (Christian) Armenians, depending on which side was more pro-Russian at the time.

When indirect military intervention is not enough and interests are strong, foreign actors sometimes resort to the direct use of force to influence ethnic civil wars. In the Bosnian case, the USA and its NATO allies had only to launch a limited air campaign in 1995 to end the war, as the main effort on the ground was carried out by the US-trained Croatians. Four years later, a 78-day NATO bombing campaign against Serbia was required to persuade the Serbs to stop their campaign of ethnic cleansing in Kosovo. Turkey took even more direct action in Cyprus in 1974: when Cyprus' ethnic Turks were threatened with being forcibly united with Greece, Turkey invaded the island, occupying the northern 40 per cent of its territory and creating a 'Turkish Republic of Northern Cyprus' for the Turkish Cypriots. Ethnic civil wars are dangerous in part because there is often the danger that they will turn into international wars.

Resolution of ethnic civil wars

Because of the danger that ethnic civil wars may spread, international intervention is often aimed at stopping the fighting, or even at resolving the underlying disputes. Some theorists argue that the best way to stop an ethnic conflict is to arrange a compromise settlement, usually with a mixture of power-sharing in the central government and regional autonomy for dis-gruntled minority groups (Lijphart 1985). Others maintain that ethnic civil wars end only when a rebel minority is either repressed by military force or granted its own separate state by partitioning – dividing up – the existing country (Kaufmann 1996). Either way, in this view, ethnic civil wars end only when one side wins: usually the government, but occasionally the rebel ethnic group.

In most cases, peace does result from a military victory. The most effective foreign intervention is therefore to help one side win. One analysis of 27 ethnic civil wars resolved between 1944 and 1994 found that 16 of the cases, or 59 per cent, ended either in a military victory or in a partition that stemmed from a military victory (Kaufmann 1996). The most prominent government victory was in Nigeria, which crushed the effort of its Ibo minority to create the separate state of Biafra in the late 1960s. In other cases, though, the rebels attracted enough foreign aid to win: in 1971, India went to war against Pakistan to help the ethnic Bengalis create the separate state of Bangladesh (an example of partition); and in 1994, Rwandan Tutsi rebels backed by Uganda defeated the genocidal Hutu leadership of Rwanda. In Bosnia, the result was for all practical purposes a partition: the Serbian bid to dominate most of the country was defeated by Croatian and NATO military force, but each of the three groups received its own autonomous area under a very weak Bosnian federal government.

Some ethnic conflicts are settled in a compromise deal among the parties involved, but all too often these agreements collapse later. As mentioned above, Sudan's first civil war was settled in 1972 in a deal that gave autonomy to the non-Muslim southerners, but that deal collapsed into renewed fighting in 1983. Some experts point to peace agreements in Lebanon in 1958 and 1976, but each of them also collapsed later into even worse fighting than before. Similarly, the highly touted Oslo accords of 1993 that seemed to put the Israeli–Palestinian conflict on the road to resolution collapsed into renewed fighting in 2000.

One way of bringing these two perspectives together is to think about conflicts in terms of whether they are 'ripe for resolution' (Zartman 1985). In this view, the best chance for negotiations to succeed comes when the conflict reaches a hurting stalemate, a situation in which neither side seems likely to win, but both sides are suffering. This was the case before each of Sudan's peace agreements, and before each of Lebanon's. The Bosnian war, too, ended more in a stalemate than in a victory for one side: each side succeeded in gaining control of a share of the territory, but NATO forced all sides to recognize that they would not be able to win decisively. The Dayton Accords, the compromised Bosnian peace deal of 1995, were the result.

Power-sharing advocates can point to a few cases in which violent conflicts did end in a successful power-sharing deal. The most important case is South Africa, which in 1994 ended decades of apartheid – oppressive white minority rule over the country's black majority – in a peace deal that guaranteed the white minority a share of power during the transitional period, and the opportunity to elect its own representatives in the future, democratic South Africa. In an initiative that soon inspired many imitators, the new government worked to address the legacy of past oppression and discrimination by establishing a Truth and Reconciliation Commission to collect and publicize information about all of the apartheid government's misdeeds, many of which had been kept secret or denied.

A second prominent case of power-sharing is in Northern Ireland, where the Good Friday Accords of 1998 called for power-sharing between the local Protestant majority (who wanted to remain united with Britain) and the Catholic minority (who preferred to become part of the Irish Republic). The accord resulted in the Provisional Irish Republican Army (IRA) finally laying down its arms, and in 2007 after years of delay a power-sharing government uniting the region's bitterest rival leaders finally took shape. Although Northern Ireland remained politically united with Great Britain, the Republic of Ireland was also given a role in the new order.

Sometimes, international efforts to promote power-sharing can go terribly wrong. The 1994 Rwanda genocide, for example, was carried out by Hutu extremists trying to prevent the implementation of a UN-sponsored power-sharing deal with a minority Tutsi-led rebel group. Similarly, East Timor received its independence from Indonesia in another UN-sponsored deal in

1999, but not before militia groups sponsored by the Indonesian military massacred thousands of east Timorese. In both cases, as in the case of UNPROFOR, the UN peacekeepers had neither the mandate (that is, the assignment) to stop the killing, nor enough military power to do so.

It is fitting that this chapter should end with these negative examples of international involvement. Even though the number of violent ethnic conflicts in the world is starting to decline, the ongoing conflicts remain extremely difficult to settle, and many of those that have been settled are at risk of recurring. While international involvement can help, the good intentions of international actors do not guarantee that their efforts will improve the situation: misfired peace plans and ineffective peacekeepers may not only fail, but also prolong the agony or even cause it to worsen.

Further reading

Michael E. Brown (ed.), *Nationalism and Ethnic Conflict*, revised edition (Cambridge, MA: MIT Press, 2001). This collection of excellent articles from the journal *International Security* on the causes and management of ethnic conflict includes prominent statements of the instrumentalist approach, and a famous argument in favour of partition as the best way to resolve ethnic wars.

Ted Robert Gurr, *Peoples Versus States* (Washington, DC: US Institute of Peace, 2000). The leader of the Minorities at Risk research team outlines the detailed results of their statistical data collection and analysis effort, presenting evidence for all three approaches to explaining ethnic violence.

Donald Horowitz, *Ethnic Groups in Conflict* (Berkeley: University of California Press, 1985). Horowitz's book is the classic statement of the social psychological approach to explaining ethnic conflict and conflict management, with myriad examples from across Asia, Africa and the Caribbean.

Stuart J. Kaufman, *Modern Hatreds: The Symbolic Politics of Ethnic War* (Ithaca, NY: Cornell University Press, 2001). This book sets out the symbolic politics theory about the causes and avoidance of ethnic war, with a set of case studies from the former USSR and former Yugoslavia.

David A. Lake and Donald Rothchild (eds), *The International Spread of Ethnic Conflict: Fear, Diffusion and Escalation* (Princeton, NJ: Princeton University Press, 1998). In this collection of articles the leading instrumentalist and rational-choice scholars offer their insights for understanding ethnic conflict and its international dimensions.

Coercion

Lawrence Freedman and Srinath Raghavan

▌ Abstract

This chapter considers coercion as a distinctive type of strategy, in which the intention is to use threats to put pressure on another actor to do something against their wishes (compellence) or not to do something they had planned to do (deterrence). The chapter considers the different forms coercion can take in terms of the ambition of the objective, the methods used (denial versus punishment) and the capacity of the target for counter-coercion. It will also examine how perceptions of an actor's strategic environment are formed and the extent to which these perceptions are susceptible to targeted threats as part of another's coercive strategy.

▌ Introduction

Coercion or the use of threats to influence another's conduct is a ubiquitous phenomenon in social and political intercourse. Activities as diverse as child-rearing, controlling crime and nuclear strategy involve an element of coercion. This chapter considers coercion as a distinctive type of strategy, in which the intention is to use threats to pressurize another actor to do something against their wishes, or not to do something they had intended to. The chapter will consider the different forms coercion can take in terms of the objective being pursued, the methods used and the capacity of the target for counter-coercion. It will also consider how strategies of coercion could influence the relationship between the protagonists from a long-term perspective.

Strategy

The concept of strategy as used in this chapter is closely related to the concept of power, understood as the ability to produce intended effects. Power is often considered merely as capacity, usually based on military or economic strength. However, confronted with certain challenges or in the pursuit of some objectives, much of this capacity may be useless. It takes strategy to unleash the power inherent in this capacity and to direct it towards specific purposes. Strategy is thus the creative element in any exercise of power.

Strategy is about choice. It depends on the ability to understand situations and to appreciate the dangers and opportunities they contain. This in turn calls for an understanding of the choices available to others and of how this might frustrate or enable one's own choices. The essence of strategy is therefore the interdependence of choice.

Strategies may be understood as falling under three broad categories along a spectrum. A *consensual* strategy involves the adjustment of strategic choices with others without the threat or use of force. By contrast, a *controlling* strategy involves the use of force to restrict another's strategic choice, for example, by defending disputed territory against any attempted seizure. A *coercive* strategy (or strategic coercion) involves deliberate and purposive use of overt threats of force to influence another's strategic choices.

Some important aspects of strategic coercion might be noted. Central to the concept is the notion of the target as a voluntary agent. It is presumed that the opponent will retain a capacity to make critical choices throughout the course of a conflict. Whether a threat succeeds in influencing the target's strategic choices will depend on the target's perception of the threat and on the other factors that go into its decision calculus. Furthermore, the threat must be both deliberate and purposive: it must be issued intentionally, and with some aim. *B* may feel threatened by *A*, although *A* may not be interested in threatening it. This cannot be considered a case of strategic coercion. Finally, although coercion is defined in terms of threats of force, it does not preclude the actual use of force, if only to reinforce the threats.

Deterrence and compellence

Thus defined, strategic coercion may be divided into two subcategories in terms of the objective. Deterrence is the use of threats to dissuade an adversary from initiating an undesirable act. Strategies geared to coercing an adversary to do something or to stop doing something have been described as compellence or coercive diplomacy (Schelling 1966, George and Simons 1994).

Deterrence and compellence differ on several counts: initiative, time scale and the nature of demands. Deterrence involves making clear through explicit threats what the coercer considers undesirable and then waiting, leaving the overt act to the adversary. The coercer would need to act only if the adversary makes the forbidden move. Compellence, on the other hand, involves initiating an action that stops or becomes harmless, only if the target responds. Compellence, then, might require the coercer to punish until the target acts, unlike deterrence, which requires administering punishment only if the adversary carries out the undesirable act.

Deterrence has no time limit. The threat will be carried out whenever the adversary acts undesirably. Indeed, the coercer would prefer to wait forever. Compellence, however, requires a clear deadline. In fact, if the adversary is not given a specific time limit by when to change his behaviour, the threat could become irrelevant.

Deterrent threats are usually clear because they aim at preserving the existing situation, which may be observed with a reasonable degree of confidence. Compellent threats, by contrast, 'tend to communicate only the general direction of compliance, and are less likely to be self-limiting, less likely to communicate in the very design of the threat just what, or how much, is demanded' (Schelling 1966: 73). A corollary to this is the role of assurances. Every coercive threat carries with it an implicit assurance that if the adversary behaves as desired, the threat will not be implemented. Since the demands of a compellent threat are not as evident as those of a deterrent threat, the former may need to be accompanied by overt assurances. In addition, with deterrence compliance is literally a non-event; it does not require any special rationalization by the target. With compellence, however, compliance will be blatant, and will carry with it the added reputational significance of humiliation. Compellence, therefore, may be more difficult than deterrence.

Notwithstanding these differences, the distinction between deterrence and compellence is not watertight. The two might merge when B starts doing something that A has urged it not to do in the first place and the situation has to be retrieved. Another example might be a conflict in which both sides can hurt the other, but neither can forcibly accomplish its purpose. In such a situation what is compellent and deterrent can shift for both sides over time. Once an engagement has begun, the difference between the two, like the difference between defence and offence, may disappear. Consider the Cuban Missile Crisis of 1962. The USA was at once warning the Soviet Union to stop constructing missile sites in Cuba (compellence) and not to pass ships carrying any more missiles through the American blockade (deterrence). When it was deciding what steps to take, Moscow in turn warned Washington that if its threats were implemented then terrible consequences would ensue. This was therefore a case of both sides trying to coerce the other, with deterrence and compellence underway at the same time.

Designing coercive strategies

The central challenge with both deterrent and compellent strategies is to find ways of ensuring that the opponent receives the threat, relates it to his proposed course of action, and decides as a result to change his behaviour. But what the coercer intends to convey may not be what the target receives. This problem would be minimized if it could be assumed that the adversary would act according to the dictates of rationally determined self-interest. This usually turns out to be difficult, if only because different actors have different views about what constitutes rational behaviour. For deterrence to work, A must persuade B to act to serve the interest of them both, but according to B's conception of rationality. Even if both sides share the same framework of rationality, deterrence may still fail because B may misinterpret the signals sent by A or, even if he understands them correctly, he may be inclined to believe that A will not implement his threat. There are examples of misunderstanding and confusion resulting either in a failure to deter someone who needs deterring, or in provoking someone who was inclined to be cautious, thereby aggravating a crisis.

The construction of effective military threats depends on two factors. First, because military signals are notoriously ambiguous, they need to be supplemented by some more direct forms of communication to ensure that the opponent receives the message being sent without distortion. The problems of interpretation grow in the psychological intensity of the crisis to the point where even interpreting straightforward communications can become problematic. In the later stages of the Cuban Missile Crisis, for instance, there was a moment when the USA received two communications from Moscow in quick succession, the second more hawkish. President Kennedy had to judge what this confusing development revealed about the real objectives of his Soviet counterpart, Nikita Khrushchev, and what pressures were working on him. At the same time, he had also to decide whether the attack on an American U2 aircraft that same day was a separate incident or part of a new stage in the Soviet Union's strategy.

Second, the coercer's threats must be credible. This, at one level, will depend on the costs associated with implementing them, which might simply reflect the amount of resource and effort entailed. But, more seriously, it may also reflect the ability of the target to respond and impose costs on the coercer. The problem of credibility was central to nuclear deterrence during the Cold War. Since both sides possessed nuclear capabilities, the possibility of retaliation could never be eliminated. In effect, the basis of deterrence was not so much a credible threat to use decisive force if the opponent overstepped some mark, but the possibility that some force might be used, to which a response was all but inevitable, so setting in motion an inexorable process of escalation to nuclear war.

Thus when threats are no more than hints and are couched in vague terms, a coercive strategy may become feeble and unconvincing. Then again, even if threats are well constructed and are perfectly understood, they may form only one part of the target's decision calculus. His response will have to factor in all the pressure to which he is susceptible. The threat itself will be one variable among many and not necessarily the most important.

In consequence, proving that strategic coercion works is challenging, especially with deterrent strategies. The failure of deterrence is evident. *B* has been told not to engage in a particular action if he wishes to avoid dire consequences, but he goes ahead with it. But when deterrence succeeds, all that is known is that *B* did not take the proscribed step. This could well be because *B* never intended to do it in first instance, or was only suggesting that he might do so for bargaining purposes. If he had the intention and then refrained, this could be due to a whole range of factors, both external and internal. Apart from threats of punishment, these might include the probability of being able to accomplish the act, the resources required, the opportunity costs, domestic opposition, problems of securing support from allies and other important but uncommitted actors, and uncertainties over the benefits.

Punishment and denial

Coercive strategies could differ from one another not only in the objective (deterrence or compellence) but also the in the methods used. Coercion is usually associated with the threat of punishment. The early use of the term *deterrence* in twentieth-century strategic vocabulary, for instance, in connection with air power, was close to the Latin root – *deterre* or to frighten from or away. The word has seemed most apposite when being used to convey the idea of scaring off a potential aggressor by using threats of consequential pain.

This definition, however, is restrictive in that it only touches upon one aspect of the cost/benefit calculation that the adversary must make (Snyder 1958). If one can pocket the gains without too much difficulty, then one may be more willing to risk costs in retaliation. But if moving forward is going to be extremely difficult due to the obstacles erected directly in one's path, then the costs of surmounting these – in the form of more troops, better equipment, greater logistical effort – will intermingle in one's mind with costs resulting from the opponent's reprisal. These types of strategies have been called *denial*.

A strategy of denial is potentially more reliable than a strategy of punishment because its quality can be measured in more physical terms and thus more confidently. Calculating the amount of military effort required to hold on to a piece of territory may not be an exact science, but it is still more straightforward than an attempt to discern the effect of prospective punitive measures on an opponent's decision-making. Furthermore, it offers a greater hope of retrieving the situation if the opponent presses on regardless.

Defences can be passive or active. During the Cold War the former were also known as civil defences. In practice, faced with a nuclear attack, they involved running for shelter or evacuation, and so were hardly passive. Active defences referred to the anti-aircraft or anti-ballistic missile systems designed to bring down the enemy offensive before any targets were reached. Nevertheless, in the nuclear context reliance on defences never really appeared as a credible option; for only even a few nuclear weapons out of the thousands in existence could cause unconscionable devastation.

Coercion by denial has had many proponents. John Mearsheimer (1983) has argued that conventional deterrence essentially depends on the coercer's ability to convince the adversary that a blitzkrieg-type offensive would be foiled. More recently, Robert Pape has picked up this debate on denial versus punishment. He argues that the most effective coercive strategies will be directed against the benefit side of the opponent's cost/benefit calculus (Pape 1996). Pape, however, is more concerned with conventional war and battlefield success. Thus he describes the purpose of coercion as obtaining concessions without having to pay the costs of a military victory. He further sees denial in terms of influencing the opponent's capacity to engage in battle while punishment is largely linked to the use of airpower to impose civilian suffering. But, as he acknowledges, 'the distinction between coercion by denial and the pursuit of military victory is more ambiguous, for both present the target state with military failure.'

The difference between denial and war fighting may be better understood in terms of control and coercion. War fighting aims at imposing control, whereas denial threatens to impose control. Yet if denial is pursued to the bitter end, it will result in control. So long as denial falls short of this, the target has a choice; hence, denial is a coercive strategy. With punishment, the target continues to retain choice even after the coercer inflicts some pain. In this sense, denial is closer to control than is punishment. Denial is evidently a better strategy than punishment: even if the target fails to be coerced, the coercer can proceed to impose control. Viewing denial and punishment in this fashion clarifies yet another issue. There is no reason why we should consider punishment in terms of civilian damage alone: losses imposed on the target's armed forces can also constitute punishment as long as the target is not deprived of choice. The loss of the major part of one's army may have all sorts of dire consequences – related to internal as much as external threats. For instance, during the war in Kuwait, Saddam Hussein was anxious to protect his Republican Guard from being annihilated by the allies because of the role he envisaged for it in the preservation of his regime against Kurdish and Shiite rebels.

In practice, denial and punishment may not necessarily lead to an altogether different use of force. This point is obscured by the excessive focus on nuclear deterrence in the strategic studies literature. The problems with preventing a successful nuclear strike made it possible to think of punishment that did not involve a prior battle. The enemy would not have to be overcome: the pain would follow minutes after the decision to inflict it. But in a non-nuclear context, in order to damage an opponent's society or state, its armed forces must first be defeated in battle. The target will take steps to avoid hurt, and this can lead to a trial of strength not very distinct from a trial over the seizure of territory. Irrespective of whether the coercer aims at punishment or denial, the adversary will still be relying on radar, interceptor aircraft, anti-aircraft guns and so on to thwart this application of force.

Types of costs

To understand the relative efficacy of coercive strategies, let us consider the two types of costs with which the coercer might threaten his target: *resistance* costs and *compliance* costs. Resistance costs are those involved in defying the coercer's demands, i.e. the costs the target will incur should the coercer implement its threat. Resistance costs have two components. First, the costs involved in trying to prevent the coercer from executing the threat; second, the pain imposed by the coercer's action. Much of the literature tends to equate resistance costs with the latter alone. This is a valid assumption when studying nuclear coercion, since the target cannot hope to resist a nuclear strike. But when examining non-nuclear coercion, we cannot overlook the costs attached to resisting the coercer's attempts to punish non-compliance. Even if the target succeeds in thwarting the coercer's efforts, it would have incurred some costs. The target, then, suffers even before the coercer fully implements its threat. If the target fails to foil the coercer's efforts, it will have to incur the compliance costs. These are costs associated with forgoing benefits or accepting losses by acquiescing in the coercer's demands.

In military terms, the forms of the resistance are obvious: the destruction of civilian centres from the air first requires the penetration of enemy air defences; the imposition of a blockade at sea may require the confirmation of 'command of the sea' in a naval battle; territory may not be acquired until the defending army has been overwhelmed. These battles may not be once-and-for-all affairs, matters being settled after a single encounter. During the course of a campaign there may be many battles, which will allow the two sides to refine their assessments of their future prospects. The use of the term *battle* does not refer only to classic encounters between armies to establish local supremacy, but any trial of strength. In fact, the same issues occur with non-military forms of pressure, such as trade boycotts. There are resistance costs in trying to circumvent economic sanctions, in setting up routes for smuggling or paying above-market price for essential goods.

The resistance and compliance costs reflect the central calculation which is at the heart of coercion. Coercion may thus be understood as an attempt by *A* to present *B* with a choice between two types of costs: that of resisting *A*'s efforts to punish and incurring the subsequent pain that *A* threatens to cause, and that of complying with *A*'s demands. In the simplest version, coercion is likely to succeed if *B* is convinced that the resistance costs exceed the compliance costs.

The difference between denial and punishment may be understood in terms of these costs. Both threaten the target with resistance and compliance costs; the difference lies in linkage between the two sets of costs in each strategy. In denial, the target is presented with resistance and compliance costs *together*. The coercer threatens the target that if its resistance fails, compliance costs will automatically follow; since control will be imposed on the target, leaving it with no choice. In punishment, the two sets of costs are uncoupled: even if resistance fails, the target still has the option of choosing whether or not to comply. As long as the coercer has not got what it wants, the target may have a way out. Viewed in this framework, it is all the more clear why denial is preferable to punishment.

Two questions arise from the preceding discussion: If denial is so obviously better than punishment, why resort to the latter at all? And if denial is a feasible strategy, why not take control? In answering these questions, we must consider a third variable in the framework of costs – enforcement costs. As opposed to resistance and compliance costs that the coercer presents to the target, enforcement costs are those that the coercer himself has to bear. These are costs associated with overcoming the target's resistance and with incurring the pain or damage the target is likely to inflict on the coercer. Enforcement costs are an integral part of the calculations involved in coercion.

Coercion is a dynamic process: the target, too, will attempt to influence the coercer's cost calculus. We may call this *counter-coercion*. In framing a coercive strategy, the coercer will have to consider the enforcement costs, which will indicate the effort required to render the threat credible and to implement it if necessary. The target will invariably try to increase the coercer's enforcement costs. This could be done in many ways. The target may issue a deterrent threat to the coercer; it may strengthen its own defences; it may escalate militarily or invoke the support of a powerful patron to convince the coercer to back down. In most conflicts, mutual coercion, even somewhat one-sided, is much more likely than a wholly asymmetric relationship. Indeed, such an asymmetric relationship would imply scant freedom of manoeuvre for the target and hence control.

Enforcement costs play an important role in deciding which variant of coercion to employ. If enforcement costs were comparable, denial would be preferable to punishment. Yet, because of the effort and costs involved in denial, punishment, at times, may seem a less costly and risky option. This, of course, was the basis of the original theory of strategic bombardment. It was assumed that mounting air raids would be much more straightforward, and much less easy to resist, than launching ground invasion. This was also the calculation that led NATO to adopt a strategy of deterrence by punishment against the Warsaw Pact during the Cold War. Despite the obvious merits of denial, in that the threat would be more credible and carry far fewer risks of an escalation to a nuclear exchange, it was always undermined by the cost that was expected to be involved in building NATO's forces up to Warsaw Pact levels.

Even in situations where imposing control is a possibility, a strategy of denial may be preferred. For the coercer might reckon that the difference in enforcement costs between control and denial exceeds the difference in compliance benefits arising out of control and denial. For example, the US-led coalition in 1991 assumed that while Iraqi forces might not put up a serious fight to hold on to Kuwait, they might be more committed to the defence of their own homeland. In such situations, it may be worth offering the opponent a deal on the basis that his alternative is still defeat and that some form of conditional surrender will at least provide relief from the costs of resistance. This can be offered right up to the edge of victory – the victim's choice is purely whether to continue to resist or to yield.

With denial the opponent only retains choice over whether or not to engage in battle; with punishment the choice remains even after the battle is finished, since the coercer has still not got direct access to what he is after. Put in this fashion, denial appears to be the least interesting form of coercion because the choice is so circumscribed; and it becomes even less interesting the more irresistible the coercer appears. The interesting cases are those where either denial is not an option, or at least difficult, but where there are other possibilities for imposing costs.

How do these costs affect each other and the outcome of coercion? In the simplest setting, coercion is likely to succeed when resistance costs exceed compliance costs. The latter are also related to enforcement costs. If compliance costs are low, i.e. if the target does not consider the magnitude of the coercer's demands to be high, then it might not be inclined to much resistance. In consequence, enforcement costs are likely to be proportionately low. This explains why deterrence may be relatively easier than compellence.

Conversely, if enforcement costs for the coercer are high, then the value of the target's compliance should also be correspondingly high. This may seem obvious, but in practice cumulative enforcement costs over time may exceed the potential benefits arising from the target's compliance. America's strategy in Vietnam is a case in point. To avoid this, the coercer may have to offer inducements to the target. These may help reduce the target's determination to resist, which in turn could lead to a reduction in enforcement costs. Inducements could thus play an important role in coercive strategies. Alternatively, if enforcement costs seem unacceptably high, the coercer may have to settle for a less satisfactory outcome. Political objectives may need to be modified to take into account what military means can achieve.

Enforcement costs are also related to resistance costs. A threat will be credible only if resistance costs for the target exceed enforcement costs for the coercer. This indicates the importance not only of threatening the target with high costs, but also of denying it the opportunity to neutralize the coercer's efforts to impose costs or to present effective threats to the coercer in turn.

Multiple audiences

Coercion does *not* refer to a type of strategic relationship between two sides, but only to one aspect. Most strategic relationships are rather complex and are unlikely to be governed by a single type of communication, however severe its implications. The fact that the Cold War involved a bipolar relationship gave an impression that the situation to be examined was stark and simple. There was, however, an inherent unreality in the presumption of a dyadic relationship involving only two actors. The circumstances in which threats were issued and received, even during the Cold War, were far more complex. To understand how coercion works in practice, we need to have a sense of how this political context impacts on the formulation and efficacy of strategic threats.

Contrary to the impression conveyed by formal theories of deterrence and compellence, threats are often issued to impress domestic audiences as much as the notional target. India's decision to resume nuclear testing in 1998 was widely understood as being aimed at keeping Pakistan in place, but it transpired that one of the motives was also to shore up the government's domestic position. Decision-makers will invariably be subject to such pressures, and in consequence coercive strategies may be fashioned to meet political as well as functional criteria, though these often tend to pull in different directions.

Similarly, international factors could be an important aspect of a coercive process. They could affect the coercer's assessment of the enforcement costs attached to a threat. On the one hand, these costs might be increased if there were a possibility of external powers supporting the target. The coercer might then be impelled to take steps to reassure these powers of its aims and intentions. On the other hand, the coercer's estimate of enforcement costs might be reduced by its expectation that external powers would keep the target in check. For instance, during the India–Pakistan crisis of 2001 to 2002, the expectation that the USA would help rein in Pakistan was an important factor in India's calculus. Furthermore, both the coercer and the target could try to use the external actors to convey a sense of urgency to the other or to enhance the credibility of their threats. They could also try to persuade the external actors to intercede with the target in order to achieve the desired outcome. This in turn might force the external actors to clarify their own interests at stake in the crisis.

Reputations

Another complicating factor is the impact of one act of coercion for those that might follow. In principle, every act of foreign policy has some significance for the creation of expectations of future performance. Compliance may be a form of humiliation and an acknowledgement of submission. This can have long-term consequences. From the coercer's standpoint, this might mean that a desire for a reputation for resolve may override the interests involved in a dispute. In other words, even if enforcement costs exceed compliance costs, it might be worth persisting in order to reduce the potential enforcement costs in any future attempt at coercion. Similarly, owing to concerns about reputation the target may remain defiant despite the costs threatened by the coercer. How one coerces now will have an impact on how much one might have to coerce in the future.

The most notorious statement of this view came from Thomas Schelling, who wrote that 'face' is 'one of the few things worth fighting over'. Although 'few parts of the world are intrinsically worth the risk of serious war by themselves, especially when taken slice by slice,' he argued that 'defending them or running risks to protect them may preserve one's commitments to actions in other parts of the world at later times' (Schelling 1966: 124). The world, in this view, is closely interconnected. A state's behaviour during an encounter could influence the outcome of another encounter, as other states will scrutinize its behaviour for signs of resolve or lack thereof. Thus, if a state retreated in one area of contention, it would acquire a reputation for weakness or for lacking resolve. This in turn would lead its adversaries to doubt the credibility of its threats in other areas of contention, so rendering the state incapable of preserving its commitments by using coercive strategies.

The risk involved in this line of argument lay in creating a vital interest where none truly existed or in persisting with a flawed course despite mounting costs. Not only was this idea undermined by what appeared to be its consequences in Vietnam, but empirical analysis seemed to lend it little support. Paul Huth, for instance, found no evidence to suggest that losing a war against one country led another to assume a lack of resolve against them (Huth 1988). Reputation, however, is intangible, and difficult to measure and identify. It provides an intuitive test of the quality of a policy rather than a specific goal itself. The evidence, moreover, suggests that the issue of reputation might have a greater salience in protracted regional rivalries involving the same pair of adversaries (Shimshoni 1988, Lieberman 1995).

Long-term impact

In principle, every act of foreign policy has some significance for the creation of expectations of future performance. Coercion might influence the development of the power relationship between the protagonists. The party that emerges worse off from a crisis may want to ensure that it will fare better in any future confrontation. It could do so either by augmenting its own military capabilities or by allying itself with a powerful third party. At least in theory, then, successful coercion could drive the target to fortify itself, and so set the stage for a failure in the future.

Furthermore, acts of coercion may have a wider impact on the management of conflict between the adversaries. Even if they do not generate a 'reputation' for the coercer, they may convince the target that certain actions are best avoided owing to the likely reaction of the coercer. Over time, this perception might become ingrained: the target might desist from certain courses despite the absence of an ever-present threat from the adversary. Land may be coveted but not grabbed; the unacceptable practices of foreign governments denounced but no further action taken; inconveniences, disruptions, outrages are tolerated; punches are pulled. All of these might result from the sensible application of what should always be the first principle of strategy: anticipate the probable responses of the opponent. This sort of deterrence is far more regular than the sort that academics and policy-makers tend to focus on, where a determined effort is made to dissuade another party from taking action one judges harmful to one's interests. Only on occasion is it necessary to resort to the explicit threats related to specific prospective acts we commonly associate with a deterrent strategy. This perspective is critical to any understanding of how deterrence might work as a political strategy. We can call this *internalized* deterrence.

An actor may be deterred even if there is no direct interaction with the one doing the deterring. But in terms of strategy this is less important than those cases where there is such an interaction. From a longer term perspective, the real challenge for strategic coercion is to create internalized deterrence in its targets.

Conclusion

The study of coercion is concerned with the role of threats in international politics. The distinguishing feature of coercion is that the target always retains choice, but must weigh the choices between the cost of compliance and non-compliance. Nonetheless, because this is a bargaining situation the target may in turn be able to threaten the coercer. The negotiation in each instance will essentially be over what may be deemed acceptable compliance and over the costs of enforcement of, or resistance to, the coercer's will. In practice, however, strategic threats may be issued by *A* for a variety of reasons, not all connected with the expected behaviour of *B*; multiple audiences are being addressed at all times. The political context, both domestic and international, will impact upon the construction of coercive strategies, and their outcome. Furthermore, every act of coercion feeds into the set of assumptions and expectations about the behaviour of others, which conditions all power relationships in international politics. The study of coercion, therefore, is not simply about the design of effective threats. It must also consider how perceptions of a state's strategic environment are formed, and how susceptible these are to manipulation by another's coercive strategy.

Further reading

Many of the ideas developed in this chapter are set out in Lawrence Freedman, *Deterrence* (Cambridge: Polity Press, 2004).

Lawrence Freedman (ed.), *Strategic Coercion: Concepts and Cases* (Oxford: Oxford University Press, 1998). This book also contains a number of studies seeking to apply the concept to a number of regional cases.

The two classic books on strategic coercion are the collection of case studies edited by Alexander George and William E. Simons (eds), *The Limits of Coercive Diplomacy*, 2nd edn (Boulder, CO: Westview Press, 1994), which is largely concerned with the problems of US crisis management, and the more theoretical work by Thomas C. Schelling, *Arms and Influence* (New Haven, CT: Yale University Press, 1966).

Daniel Byman and Matthew Waxman, *The Dynamics of Coercion and the Limits of Military Might* (Cambridge: Cambridge University Press, 2002). This book provides a more contemporary analysis of the issues, although again largely from a US perspective.

An excellent discussion of the range of issues concerned with deterrence is found in Patrick M. Morgan, *Deterrence Now* (Cambridge: Cambridge University Press, 2003).

Human Security

Fen Osler Hampson

▌ Abstract

This chapter reviews recent academic and policy research on human security. It first summarizes the various definitions and conceptions of human security informing current academic research and thinking. It then offers a brief overview of some recent contributions to the human security literature. The final section identifies some of the key debates and issues currently at the centre of human security research.

▌ Introduction

There is little doubt that human security studies are attracting growing attention in the wider International Relations and social science literatures. The expanding UN agenda of human security concerns (among them war-affected children, racial discrimination, women's rights, refugees), coupled with former UN Secretary-General Kofi Annan's personal interest in and commitment to human security activism, catapulted these questions to the forefront of the scholarly and policy research agenda in the 1990s (see MacFarlane and Khong 2006). This agenda accompanied the long-standing human security concerns of students and practitioners of international development – an agenda that has generally tended to focus on the ways that globalization dynamics have damaged the prospects for human development and the provision of basic human needs.

Despite the growing investment of research and interest in human security, to date, there is no real consensus on what can or should constitute the focus of what are still loosely termed human security studies. There continues to be considerable methodological, definitional and conceptual disquiet about the real meaning of human security, and about the implications of the human security paradigm for the study or the practice of International Relations. This should come as no surprise, given the nature of the academic enterprise and the different disciplinary and methodological backgrounds informing the work of scholars engaged in human security research. (Even so, the evident inability of scholars to advance beyond theoretical debates over definitions towards practical policy recommendations understandably frustrates practitioners in the policy community.)

There is also a great unevenness in the depth (and breadth) of research on particular themes. Some issues, such as anti-personnel landmines or small arms, are well ploughed; the literature on these subjects is rich not only in analysis of particular problems and causes, but also in implications for public policy. Other problems, such as gender-directed violence, are only just beginning to receive the sort of attention they deserve as evils in their own right and as sources and symptoms of human insecurity.

This chapter reviews recent academic and policy research on human security. It first summarizes the various definitions and conceptions of human security informing current academic research and thinking. It then offers a brief overview of some recent contributions to the human security literature. The final section identifies some of the key debates and issues now at the centre of human security research.

Understanding the scope of human security

There are arguably three distinct conceptions of human security that shape current debates. The first is what might be termed the natural rights/rule of law conception of human security, anchored in the fundamental liberal assumption of basic individual rights to 'life, liberty, and the pursuit of happiness', and of the international community's obligation to protect and promote these rights (Alston 1992, Lauren 1998, Morsink 1998). A second view of human security is humanitarian. This is the view of human security that, for example, informs international efforts to deepen and strengthen international law, particularly regarding genocide and war crimes, and to abolish weapons that are especially harmful to civilians and non-combatants (Boutros-Ghali 1992, Moore 1996, UN 1995, 1999, UNDP 1997). This view lies at the heart of humanitarian interventions directed at improving the basic living conditions of refugees, and anyone uprooted by conflict from their homes and communities. On those rare occasions when military force has been used ostensibly to avert genocide or ethnic cleansing, it has also been justified usually on rather specific humanitarian grounds such as the need to restore basic human rights and dignity.

These two views of human security, which focus on basic human rights and their deprivation, stand in sharp contrast to a broader view, which suggests that human security should be widely constructed to include economic, environmental, social and other forms of harm to the overall livelihood and well-being of individuals. There is a strong social justice component in this broader conception of human security, as well as a wider consideration of threats (real and potential) to the survival and health of individuals. According to this third view, perhaps the most controversial of the three conceptions of human security, the state of the global economy, the forces of globalization, and the health of the environment, including the world's atmosphere and oceans, are all legitimate subjects of concern in terms of how they affect the 'security' of the individual (UNDP 1994, Nef 2002).

The 'broadeners' have attracted sharp criticism. Yuen Foong Khong (2001) warns that making everything a priority renders nothing a priority – raising false hopes in the policy realm and obscuring real trade-offs between rival human security objectives. Similarly, Andrew Mack (2001, 2005) makes the sound methodological point that overly broad definitions of human security can block investigation of the very phenomena that need to be understood. Examining the relationship between poverty and violence, for example, requires us to treat them as separate variables. A definition that conflates dependent and independent variables will confound analysis of causal connections between them.

As a practical matter, many human security initiatives, such as the international campaign to ban trafficking in small and light weapons, generally, fall between the narrower and the broader definitions of human security. But, there is a lively debate among scholars and practitioners as to what legitimately should be the scope of efforts to promote and advance human security at the international level, and as to whether we should define human security in more restrictive or broader terms (Khong 2001, Paris 2001, Hampson *et al.* 2002, MacFarlane and Khong 2006).

How should human security be defined? One way is to define it negatively, i.e. as the absence of threats to various core human values, including the most basic human value, the physical safety of the individual. Alkire (2002: 2) offers a more positive definition of human security: 'The objective of human security is to safeguard the vital core of all human lives from critical pervasive threats, and to do so without impeding long-term human flourishing.'

The definition offered by the Report of the Commission on Human Security (2003: 2) is even more expansive: 'to protect the vital core of all human freedoms and human fulfilment.' What is this vital core? Does it represent all human freedoms? And should personal fulfilment be placed alongside freedom as a basic right and public responsibility? The same paragraph goes on to embrace almost every desirable condition of a happy life in its description of human security:

Human security means protecting fundamental freedoms. ... It means protecting people from critical (severe) and pervasive (widespread) threats and situations. It means using processes that build on people's strengths and aspirations. It means creating political, social, environmental, economic, military, and cultural systems that together give people the building blocks of survival.

Underlying much of the human security literature is a common belief that human security is critical to international security, and that international order cannot rest solely on the sovereignty and viability of states – that order depends as well on individuals and their own sense of security. This is clearly a departure from traditional liberal internationalism, which sees international order as resting on institutional arrangements which, in varying degrees, help secure the integrity of the liberal, democratic state by reducing threats in the state's external environment (see Chapter 3, this volume). Placing the individual as the key point of reference, the human security paradigm assumes that the safety of the individual is the key to global security; by implication, when the safety of individuals is threatened, so too in a fundamental sense is international security. In this view, global challenges have to be assessed in terms of how they affect the safety of people, and not just of states. Proponents of the enlarged or maximalist conception of human security also argue that these threats arise not only from military sources; non-military causes such as worsening environmental conditions and economic inequalities can, in some instances, exacerbate conflict processes (UNDP 1994, Paris 2001, Nef 2002).

Setting the boundaries of human security

Not surprisingly, problems of definition and boundary-setting have dominated much of the recent literature in human security research. To some degree, these uncertainties simply reflect the state of the art; these are, after all, relatively new approaches. But it is also fair to say, as do King and Murray (2001/02), that these definitional and conceptual arguments echo turmoil experienced since the Cold War in schools of both development and national security – two important sources of human security scholars and scholarship.

King and Murray responded with a bold answer of their own, what they call 'a simple, rigorous, and measurable definition of human security'. They define human security as 'the number of years of future life spent outside the state of "generalized poverty"'. Generalized poverty, in this definition, occurs when the individual falls below a specified threshold 'in any key domain of human well-being'. Operating the definition therefore requires choosing domains of well-being, constructing practical indicators, and specifying threshold values for each. King and Murray find their domains mainly in the

UNDP's Human Development Index (per capita income, health, education), and add 'political freedom' and 'democracy' (for example, by applying Freedom House measures of voting and legislative conduct).

Human security in this scheme is thus expressed as a probability – the expected number of years of life spent outside 'generalized poverty', whether for an individual or aggregated across an entire population. Leaving aside other questions of domain choice and threshold selection, the King–Murray equation (they frame it mathematically) raises provocative issues of methodology and policy. Mack (2005), on the other hand, measures human security in terms of the costs of war on human suffering. The Liu Institute's Report on Human Security documents in vivid detail the impact that war – measured in terms of civilian casualties – has had on different countries and regions of the world.

Some of the recent literature has attempted to define human security by integrating its disparate dimensions. Hazem Ghobarah (with Huth and Russett 2001) explored long-term health effects of civil wars with a cross-national analysis of World Health Organization (WHO) statistics on death and disability. The immediate harms done to health by specific wars are familiar; in contrast, Ghobarah and his colleagues tracked the delayed after-effects and their mechanisms: rising crime rates, property destruction, economic disruption, diversion of health-care resources and so on.

In *Madness in the Multitude* (2002) Fen Hampson and others situated human security approaches in the long history of liberal democratic theory, but concentrated on the distinguishing features of human security as a global public good. Among other advantages, the lens of public goods analysis focuses attention on certain recurring issues in the human security discourse – namely problems of under-provision, collective governance and operational delivery.

Ongoing debates and unresolved issues

A number of key debates and/or unresolved issues are reflected in the scholarly and the policy-oriented human security literature. One of the burgeoning areas of research, especially among students of international development, involves the relationship between globalization (in its various meanings) and human security – or insecurity. There is more or less general agreement that the forces of economic globalization are transforming international politics and recasting relationships between states and peoples with important implications for human security: globalization is not only intensifying trade and economic connections, but also accelerating the pace of economic and social change. Further, it is not just goods and capital that are exchanged across borders, but ideas, information and people.

On one side of this argument, enthusiasts of globalization argue that the breakdown of national barriers to trade and the spread of global markets are processes that help to raise world incomes and contribute to the spread of wealth. Although there are clear winners and losers in the globalizing economy, the old divisions between the advanced 'Northern' economies and 'peripheral'

South are breaking down and making way for an increasingly complex architecture of economic power (Held *et al.* 1999: 4). On the other side, globalization's critics argue that although some countries in the South have gained from globalization, many have not, and income inequalities between the world's richest and poorest countries are widening. They suggest that trade and investment flows are intensifying between those countries that can compete in the global economy while leaving behind those that cannot. As income gaps and deep-seated social and economic inequalities widen, so the argument runs, so do the prospects for violence and civil strife.

The latter point is argued most convincingly in the World Bank's report, *Global Economic Prospects 2007*. This reports that globalization, which is contributing to the rapid growth in average incomes over the next 25 years, with developing countries playing a central role, will be accompanied by growing income inequality and potentially severe environmental pressures. The greatest danger is that some regions, notably sub-Saharan Africa, will be left behind. There is also a growing risk of rising income inequalities within countries – a factor that some scholars argue contributes to the likelihood of civil unrest, especially in the world's poorest countries (Stewart and Brown 2007).

Marshall (2007) and his colleagues at the University of Maryland offer a similar conclusion in their own research. According to Marshall,

> the most troubling regional sub-systems in the Globalization Era are the regions constituted by the sub-Saharan African countries and the pre-dominantly Muslim countries, which stretch from Morocco and Senegal in the west to Malaysia and Indonesia in the east. The Lorenz curves for these two regions are roughly equivalent; income inequality among African countries is only slightly greater than income inequality among Muslim countries.

It is also apparent that 'although the general magnitude of armed conflict in both regions has diminished substantially since the end of the Cold War, the overall decrease in warfare in Africa has fallen more slowly than the general global trend'. Muslim countries, however, 'are the sole region [*sic*] where there has been an increase in armed conflict in recent years, possibly levelling, or even reversing, the general downward [global] trend'.

Globalization raises new dangers to human security as patterns of world trade, production and finance morph into new relationships which, if left unregulated, can further impoverish the world's poor – with dire social and political consequences (Kay 1997, O'Neill 1997, Willett 2001). Nowhere is this more evident than in the area of public health. There is growing recognition that declining levels of health and epidemic diseases such as AIDS, which are ravaging many developing countries, are partially rooted in the workings of the global economy, and in externally imposed structural adjustment policies that have directly contributed to a deterioration in public health delivery and in overall living standards (Leon and Walt 2001).

Much work remains to be done on the positive and negative consequences of globalization for human security, and on how globalization affects the capacity of various international, national and subnational actors and institutions to provide for human security. There also needs to be a better appreciation of the distribution of gains and costs resulting from specific globalization processes, and whether, to quote Caroline Thomas, there is a requirement for 'different development strategies from those currently favoured by global governance institutions', i.e. 'strategies that have redistribution at their core' (2001: 174). Macro-oriented studies of the globalization–human security nexus should be complemented by case studies of specific countries or globalization processes (e.g. Ball 2001, Muggah 2001, Hendrickson and Ball 2002). This will advance understanding of how best to address the consequences of various globalization processes for human security and help identify response strategies and institutional arrangements best suited to particular development contexts.

Value trade-offs among the separate dimensions of human security are also receiving greater attention. Normative concerns typically surface when the imperative of human security is invoked in cases of humanitarian intervention (ICISS 2001, Holzgrefe and Keohane 2003; see also Chapter 28, this volume). There is obviously a continuing debate on whether force should be used in support of particular human security objectives. At one level, the dispute is about the proper hierarchy of humanitarian goals and international norms of state sovereignty and non-intervention. But it is also a debate about whether or when it is right to use violence against individuals – especially non-combatants who find themselves in harm's way – when force is exercised for human security purposes. Where human security concepts challenge traditional notions of what constitutes a 'just war' or a just cause, and test our sense of what are tolerable degrees of 'collateral damage' – this is fertile terrain for ethicists and others concerned with the deeper ramifications of evolving human security norms.

These debates underscore the tensions between diverse conceptions and priorities in the human security agenda. But exploring these tensions within explicit ethical and normative frames of reference can itself yield new knowledge and understanding – if not always agreement. Not only will such analysis render explicit the kinds of value trade-offs involved, but it may also help societies to make more ethically informed choices as they respond to the human security threats they face.

The concept of human security also poses an interesting challenge to traditional notions of democratization, civil society development and peace-building. Some scholars, citing familiar post-colonial history, hold that liberal democracy and economic liberalization by themselves will not suffice to ensure human security – especially not the security of vulnerable communities. The argument is that historical patterns of human settlement and lingering colonial legacies have too often marginalized large numbers of peoples from social, economic and political development processes. As Swatuk and Vale report, the people of the South African homelands and townships still suffer the insecurities of poverty and pains of incorporation into the political economy of South Africa. The power of 'vested interests and established social relations in support of neocolonial political economies', along with 'fissures of identity' reflected in 'race, class, state, nation, and tribe' pose a major if not insurmountable barrier to the advancement of human security – not just in South Africa but throughout the whole region (Swatuk and Vale 1999: 384).

There are clearly different understandings of human security particular to different social, political and economic contexts – details that raise important questions about the limitations of traditional liberal assumptions about democratization and political development. Increasingly, scholars and practitioners are beginning to ask difficult but essential questions about the proper sequence and priorities to be adopted in peacebuilding and democratic development, and how to ensure that these processes are informed by indigenous perspectives of what human security requires in their own lives. Negotiated political transitions (from communist dictatorship or from apartheid, from oppressive military or from one-man rule) impose a sharp focus on the significance of these issues. Given the predominant role of Western governments and publics and Western-oriented intergovernmental and nongovernmental organizations in the peacemaking and peacebuilding field – and the reality that colonial legacies are seldom erased easily in developing countries – there is considerable potential for a collision between opposed human security values and priorities.

The literature also reveals telling differences in national and regional perspectives – different assessments of the subject, and different judgements on policy and political performance. Khong (2001) (with others) has speculated that the human security agenda grew out of the particulars of Canada's own history and circumstances – if not as a 'fireproof house', at least as relatively safe from the world's troubles and decently governed:

> In a world consisting primarily of Canadas, human security might command a consensus; and the kind of intrusiveness associated with implementing such an agenda might be acceptable. . . . However, too many individuals in the twenty-first century reside in makeshift shelters and thatched homes. What difference will it make to their lives for us to insist that they have become the referents of security? Not very much.

Asian perspectives command considerable attention in the literature on human security (e.g. Tow *et al.* 2000). More than one observer has remarked on the policy divergence between Canada and Japan on human security. Acharya (2001) has outlined a more expansive (but less intrusive) view of human security that goes beyond conventional issues of violence to matters of politics, culture, dignity and freedom – a definition expressed most comprehensively, of course, by the late Mahbub ul Haq at UNDP. Furtado (2000) looked to specific Asian states and reports on their particular responses to financial shock. Applying yet another perspective, Cocklin and Keen (2000) have described threats to human security (or well-being) characteristic of urbanization on South Pacific islands. These examples suggest how human security takes on different attributes in micro-level examinations.

Geisler and de Sousa (2001) have raised an awkward case of human security endeavours working disastrously at cross-purposes in Africa. They examine so-called 'ecological expropriation', namely the creation of millions of refugees by the closure of lands for purposes of environmental protection and repair. 'Human security and environmental security, often reinforcing, can be at odds', they note. Human security can no doubt be enhanced by environmental protection – or imperilled by it.

The 1994 UN Human Development Report identified drug trafficking, migration, terrorism and weapons of mass destruction (WMD) as major threats to human security. In the case of terrorism, it pointed out – rather presciently it would seem – that although the observable number of terrorism incidents was dropping in the early 1990s, the number of casualties remained high, and the focus of terrorist activity was increasingly global rather than regional in orientation (1994: 36). Although there is a sizeable and growing literature on these threats, much of it has a decidedly 'national security' outlook. The specific linkages of these threats to human security – or how a human security approach to these threats would differ from existing measures and approaches – remain unexplored.

Interestingly, these threats were largely omitted from the mandate of the Independent Commission on Human Security (2003), which chose to focus on a narrower set of issues. These include the ways internal conflicts threaten the physical security of non-combatants; human insecurities stemming from preventable diseases, injury or chronic ill health; insecurities flowing from a lack of basic literacy, access to education and innumeracy; and the insecurities of poverty and economic, social and gender inequalities.

There is growing evidence that transnational organized crime (especially in narcotics, human trafficking, and counterfeiting) transnational terrorism and transnational migration flows all have destabilizing consequences for sending and/or recipient countries – and they are on the rise (Helsinki Process 2005). Further, the risk that WMD may be used in terrorist attacks or interstate wars also appears to be increasing as more states and nonstate actors learn how to make or acquire these weapons (Kemp 2001: 78).

It is still an open question whether there is a distinctive value added in a human security approach to these problems – which traditionally have been the purview of more conventional national security studies. One promising example of how human security concepts can shed new light on the problems of nuclear proliferation is found in the work of Itty Abraham (1999). He argues that traditional, interstate nuclear deterrence models ill-suit South Asia. Because 'domestic populations of nuclear weapons states are the principal victims of nuclearization,' he says, 'international pressures must be replaced by domestic groups acting internationally' (Abraham 1999: 10). His intriguing argument, that 'domestic legal and moral constraints are the most appropriate means for controlling the anti-democratic and militaristic tendencies of the nuclear complex', contains more than a residual echo of the work of John Mueller (1989, 2004, 2005) and Richard Price (1997) on how social and political norms can change and be changed.

Human security risk assessment

Much of the human security literature uses the language of 'threats' to characterize a wide – and, it would seem, always growing – list of challenges to human security. To group all of these problems – from pandemic diseases to human-induced environmental catastrophes, to population displacements to terrorism, to the proliferation of nuclear or small arms – on the same long list, as if the costs (immediate as well as long-term) and probabilities (present and future) of each were the same, is needless to say a doubtful project. There is clearly a need to disaggregate (and carefully specify) the costs and probabilities associated with each of these distinct problem areas. Changing rates of infection and mortality rates only tell us the direct, human costs of diseases like AIDS, for instance; as some scholars now argue, there are profound, longer term social, economic and potential political consequences of these diseases as well. Once these costs are identified, it will be important to consider their longer term implications for public policy and for preventive and mitigation strategies, especially if long-term social and economic costs are significant and widespread.

Mortality rates or poverty 'thresholds' are only one benchmark of human security. Although some 'threats' have major human security costs attached to them (the terrorist detonation of a nuclear bomb in a city, for example), the actual probability associated with these events may be quite low (Mueller 2006a, 2006b), especially when compared to the array of human security risks that most people confront in their daily lives. Nor do probabilities remain constant; on the contrary, some can rise suddenly, and others will fall. Resources and policy attention need to be re-allocated to those human security risks that are increasing, but only after undertaking a serious comparative assessment of relative risks (importantly including an identification of which population groups face the most risk).

The report on *Global Risks 2007*, which was presented at the World Economic Forum (2007: 4) in Davos, Switzerland, argues that 'there has been a major improvement in the understanding of the interdependencies between global risks, the importance of taking an integrated risk management approach to major global challenges and the necessity of attempting to deal with root causes of global risks rather than reacting to the consequences'. The report documents 23 core global risks which include energy supply disruptions, climate change, natural catastrophes, international terrorism, interstate and civil wars, pandemics and infectious diseases, and the breakdown of critical information infrastructures. The report measures the probabilities and costs associated with these risks on the basis of qualitative and quantitative data. In assessing severity, two indices – 'destruction of assets/economic damage and, where applicable, human lives lost' – were considered. It also offers a number of institutional recommendations on how businesses and governments can best mobilize resources and attention in order to 'engage in the forward action needed to begin managing global risks rather than coping with them'.

The relationships between political and economic variables, and their impact on conflict processes and so-called 'state failure', have also been examined in risk-assessment frameworks. The 'failed state index' developed by Fund for Peace and *Foreign Policy* (2006) magazine finds that some 60 countries in the world are dysfunctional because the government does not effectively control its territory, provide basic services to its citizens, or the country is experiencing some kind of internal unrest.

There is also currently a great deal of work on organized violence and its causes (Duffield 2001b, Cleves *et al.* 2002, Collier 2007, Stewart and Brown 2007). Three explanations dominate this literature:

1 those that stress the importance of group-based inequalities as a source of conflict, i.e. conflicts are based on 'creed';
2 those that focus on private gains, i.e. conflicts are driven by 'greed';
3 explanations which stress the failed social contract thesis, i.e. conflicts are really about 'needs'.

Those who have looked at these explanations closely find that it is not *absolute* poverty, but *relative* poverty that matters most. That is to say, poor countries where some groups are, relatively speaking, much better off than others due to caste or creed are much more predisposed to experience violent conflict.

The policy implication of this research is that development strategies must be tied not simply to alleviating poverty in the poorest countries, but also to addressing the horizontal inequalities that divide those societies through, for example, redistribution of land, privatization schemes, credit allocation preferences, educational quotas, employment policies that stress balanced employment, and public sector infrastructure investment that advantages the disadvantaged (Stewart and Brown 2007). Research also shows that economic development is critical to sustaining the peace in states that have just ended a civil war (Paris 2004). Economic development is necessary to restore a state's human capital and infrastructure, raise the opportunity costs of conflict, and get buy-in from the local populace by raising their standard of living.

The subjective aspects of risk are another potentially promising research venue. We now know that most people tend to discount risks they consider controllable, while exaggerating risks they think are uncontrollable. (This may explain why some people have a fear of flying.) People also tend to discount – and usually quite heavily – future risks even though the probabilities associated with them are high, as against imminent risks that are relatively low. This is all to say that there is a substantial literature in psychology on the cognitive biases that come into play as individuals confront the ordinary risks of daily life (Tversky *et al.* 1982, Tversky and Kahneman 2000). However, there has been little direct application of this research to human security concerns. Do individuals in different societies perceive common human security threats through similar or different cognitive frames of reference? Are there significant cross-cultural barriers that stand in the way of coordinated policy responses to shared human security risks? To what extent are perceptions about different kinds of risks to human security at variance with more 'objective' assessments of those risks? Are there cultural taboos that stand in the way of efforts to reduce certain kinds of human security risks (family violence, violence against women, infanticide), and what kinds of strategies are appropriate to changing social attitudes? Are some social institutions better able to manage certain kinds of risks? And are there lessons to be learned about ways to reduce risk exposure for the most vulnerable groups in society? (For a fascinating discussion about how Americans, for example, came to see technology itself as a 'threat' see Douglas and Wildavsky 1982.) These are some questions that warrant further study.

Governance and human security

The literature continues to display the tension between still new human security concerns and still standing institutions and categories that continue to shape academic and political assumptions. There is an extensive consensus that prevailing institutions – state, interstate, nonstate – are performing inadequately. There is noisy disagreement on explanations and remedies.

Hampson *et al.* (2002) explored adaptations by international financial institutions (IFIs) to the human security agenda, and find them partial and unreliable: constrained by bureaucratic divisions or inertia, and by conflicts among their own (state) donors, IFIs 'have tended to adopt those elements among the different conceptions of human security that are most compatible with *existing* organizational mandates'.

Again, in the development discourse, there has been an early and fundamental dispute about the place of the state in the human security universe. Griffin (1995) had concluded by the mid-1990s that it was essential 'to construct new, post-Cold War structures for global governance and cooperation among peoples,' and to 'shift the emphasis from national sovereignty and state security to individual rights and human security'. In an instant and spirited counter-argument, Bienefeld (1995) held that states themselves are a precondition to successful global governance – and to the achievement by any society of democracy, human security and sustainable development: 'Therefore we cannot abandon the sovereign state and strive for global governance. Instead, we must seek to protect the sovereign state in order to use it to fashion a system of global governance.'

Former Canadian foreign minister Lloyd Axworthy (2001) found it possible to resolve this polarity in the imagery of interdependence-driven coalition-building among states, NGOs, intergovernmental organizations, businesses and others. The Landmines Convention and the Rome Statute demonstrated the possibilities of diplomacy to advance human security (McRae and Hubert 2001). But even Axworthy himself acknowledged the current operational inadequacies of governance in some critical human security activities – dramatically in the realm of coercive international intervention, where norms remain inchoate or contradictory and institutions weak.

Several authors have applied human security analysis to the governance of refugee problems. Adelman (2001) has detected a shift in emphasis at UNHCR, away from legal asylum issues and towards human security protection of refugees and refugee operations (including protection of internally displaced people). But he does not diagnose this as a radical departure: 'It was built into the possibilities of the UNHCR from the beginning.' Again on refugees, Schmeidl (2002) found confirming evidence that refugee flows themselves can constitute a menace to human security – but especially when states encourage the transformation of refugee populations into 'refugee warrior communities'. Her assessment of the Afghan refugee experience in South Asia leads to the conclusion that 'the way local, regional and international actors responded to the refugee crisis seems to have contributed equally, or more to the security dilemma, than the migration itself'.

Towards a theory of human security

Running through the human security literature is a recognition – not always explicit – of the difficulty in grounding these subjects in cohesive theory or methodology. Indeed, conventional realist frameworks of International Relations theory prove quite inhospitable to human security approaches – one reason, no doubt, why the treatment of human security in the prominent journals of security studies has so far seemed brief and dismissive (Mack 2001). Systematic attempts to develop theory and methodology helpful to understanding human security ultimately appear to involve the abandonment, if not outright repudiation, of the various realist schools of International Relations theorizing. Some scholars have turned instead to feminist critiques to address human security questions, and more generally to constructivism (see Chapters 5 and 8, this volume).

For Newman (2001), 'constructivist international relations theory is not a single unified movement'. Still, 'the underlying argument is that behavior, interests, and relationships are socially constructed, and can therefore change. Values and ideas can have an impact upon international relations; norms, systems, and relationships can change.' Constructivism thus helps explain phenomena to which realism (neo or not) is blind or indifferent. Moreover, constructivism shares fundamental assumptions with human security approaches – the assumption, for example, that threats are constructed, not inevitable, and that they can be altered or mitigated. The acknowledgement by states that certain forms of economic and political organization facilitate domestic peace and stability, and that domestic conditions affect the international system, are characteristically constructivist insights.

As Newman (2001) observes, 'there are methodological confusions about constructivism', especially as it is associated with feminism and other meta-theoretical challenges to mainstream realist and neoliberal theory. Nonetheless, tenets of constructivism easily resonate in feminist theory-building – especially in the affirmation that social, political and economic relations are constructed and changeable.

Hyndman (2001) has formulated this approach as 'a feminist geopolitics'. This is 'not an alternative theory of geopolitics,' she says, but 'an approach to global issues with feminist politics in mind.' It is also explicitly about political action, 'the possibility of "doing something": of normative engagement and action within a given context'. As meta-theory, it draws expressly from the broader scholarship of 'critical geopolitics' – 'less a theory of how space and politics intersect than a taking apart of normalized categories and narratives of geopolitics'.

Both as methodology and advocacy, Hyndman's feminist geopolitics addresses familiar human security issues: shifting scales, from household to substate to global; breaking down dichotomies, as between public and personal, national and international; and acknowledging mobility, whether of refugees or fugitives from human rights law. Throughout, there is in feminist analysis a sharp and careful attention to unequal and violent relationships in families, communities or transnational systems – the kinds of relationships that often define human insecurity.

Taken together, constructivist and feminist analyses offer promising methodologies for examining exactly the phenomena that concern human security scholars. By reorienting the research focus to life as it is lived by the most insecure in any society (women, the poor, minorities, aboriginal communities), these methodologies can advance research and make for more productive human security policy.

Conclusion

For all their inconsistencies and uncertainties, human security studies are growing demonstrably stronger and more abundant. In fact, the diversity of disciplinary foundations accounts for some of the strength in human security scholarship. There is a kind of evolutionary advantage in drawing from a wide variety of intellectual method and tradition. That same variety goes some way towards explaining a profusion of research activities that can sometimes look like incoherence.

Some scholars are still busy trying to define the boundaries of human security, organizing a discipline, arranging typologies. Meanwhile, others are exploring human security issues on the ground – and beginning a serious scholarly contribution to the design and execution of human security policy.

In all of this, policy-makers and scholars are bound to find each other at odds from time to time. Practitioners, hard-pressed to prevent the crises not already exploding on CNN, and to cope with crises under way, show understandable impatience with scholarship that renders any problem more complicated – or worse, that does not evidently address any recognizable problem at all. Policy-makers (some of them scholar *manqués* themselves) would do well to remind themselves that scholars honour their own obligations and professional standards; they are neither desk officers at the beck and call of foreign ministries nor cheering spectators at the policy sidelines. Equally, scholars ambitious to affect policy are wise to understand the constraints of politics and resources that act on policy in every phase. They should also respect the dictatorship of deadlines that practitioners face – and the low tolerance among practitioners for elegant definitional argument. When a theory collides with reality, busy practitioners may want to know why; they will show no detectable excitement when a theory collides with another theory. In the best sort of dialogue – frank, timely, open-minded – academic and policy communities can collaborate to their lasting and shared advantage. More to the point, together they may advance the progress of human security.

Further reading

Fen Osler Hampson *et al.*, *Madness in the Multitude* (Toronto: Oxford University Press, 2002). Provides an overview of the history and evolution of different conceptions of human security and key policy initiatives.

International Commission on Intervention and State Sovereignty (ICISS), *The Responsibility to Protect* (Ottawa: International Development Research Centre, 2001). A key policy document that discusses the challenges of humanitarian intervention and offers major recommendations to strengthen the capacity and will of international institutions to intervene when there are major violations of human rights.

Neil S. MacFarlane and Yuen Foong Khong, *Human Security and the UN: A Critical History* (Bloomington: Indiana University Press, 2006). Discusses the history and evolution of the contribution of the United Nations to human security.

Jorge Nef, *Human Security and Mutual Vulnerability* (Ottawa: International Development Research Centre, 2002). One of the earliest and most definitive discussions of the meaning of human security and its importance in international development.

Report of the Commission on Human Security, *Human Security Now: Protecting and Empowering People* (New York: UN, 2003). A key report of an international commission that discusses the different aspects of human security and the ways to address different human security challenges.

CONTENTS

Poverty

Caroline Thomas

■ Abstract

This chapter argues that fundamentally, the pursuit of security is about individual human beings – i.e. human security – and the protection and fulfilment of their human rights. The pursuit of other levels of security – for example, global, regional or national – has legitimacy and relevance to the degree to which it supports human security, and the latter cannot be defined or contained within the territorial boundaries of an exclusive political unit. Working with this understanding of security as being a priori about human beings, it becomes clear that poverty is of direct relevance for security studies; indeed, poverty and human insecurity are in many respects synonymous. Both refer to a human condition characterized by the lack of fulfilment of a range of human entitlements such as adequate food, healthcare, education, shelter, employment and voice; a life lived in fear of violence, injury, crime or discrimination; and an expectation that life will continue in this way. The connections between poverty and security have been recognized by mainstream development and security analysts since the early 1990s. While this is welcome, it has not yet resulted in a sustained critique of neoliberal development policy, but rather a reassertion of it. Tackling the poverty–conflict–poverty trap will require a different approach to development.

Introduction

Despite 60 years of official development policies, as well as the commitment made in 2000 by 189 states at the UN to the Millennium Development Goals (MDGs), a billion people continue to live in extreme poverty. Almost half of the world's six billion people live on $2 a day or less. Poverty is the cause of far more deaths than armed conflict. This human insecurity occurs against the backdrop of a growth in global military spending (reaching an estimated US$1,058.9 billion in 2006, or 15 times annual international aid expenditure) (Control Arms Campaign 2006: 6), a growth in the arms trade, and the significant proliferation in small arms and light weapons which account for the majority of violent deaths and maiming.

In addition, this routine insecurity occurs in the context of global and national political and economic systems which many believe perpetuate not only poverty but also deepening inequality. If nobody had to endure a life of poverty, then the fact that 1 per cent of the global population earns annually as much as the poorest 57 per cent of humanity might not be an issue. However, given the current scale of global poverty and the spectre of increased numbers living in poverty, the continuation and arguably the intensification of inequalities should be of concern. These trends are evident in increased differentiation and polarization within and between states, world regions and globally, and raise fundamental questions about the appropriateness of global and national economic, social, political and security structures, policies and values.

Globally, the political and economic challenge is defined in limited terms of 'poverty reduction' via quantitative targets set out in the MDGs. Yet with the global population on course to reach eight billion by 2025, even the limited goal of poverty reduction appears to be a very ambitious target in many parts of the world. Moreover, if we continue on the current development trajectory – which equates neoliberal economic policy with development policy – it is reasonable to expect that even the limited MDG targets, if met, will be unsustainable over time. In other words, what is being sold as the solution to global poverty – neoliberal economic policy – is actually part of the problem.

BOX 17.1 THE MILLENNIUM DEVELOPMENT GOALS, 2000

Goal 1 Eradicate extreme poverty and hunger

Targets: Halve, between 1990 and 2015, the proportion of people whose income is less than one dollar a day; and halve, between 1990 and 2015, the proportion of people who suffer from hunger.

Goal 2   Achieve universal primary education

Target: Ensure that by 2015, children everywhere – boys and girls – will be able to complete primary schooling.

Goal 3   Promote gender equality and empower women

Target: Eliminate gender disparity in primary and secondary schools by 2005, and all levels of education by 2015.

Goal 4   Reduce child mortality

Target: Reduce by two-thirds (1990–2015) the under-5 mortality rate.

Goal 5   Improve maternal health

Target: Reduce by three-quarters (1990–2015) the maternal morbidity ratio.

Goal 6   Combat HIV/AIDS, malaria and other diseases

Targets: Halt and begin to reverse spread of HIV/AIDS by 2015, and the incidence of malaria and other diseases.

Goal 7   Ensure environmental sustainability

Targets: Integrate sustainable development principles; halve the proportion of people without sustainable access to safe drinking water; achieve a significant improvement in the lives of 100 million slum dwellers by 2020.

Goal 8   Develop a global partnership for development

Targets: Further develop a rule-based non-discriminatory financial and trading system; address needs of least developed countries, small island and landlocked states; make debt sustainable; employment for youths; access to medicines; share benefits of new information and communications technologies.

Is poverty an appropriate concern for security studies?

Over the past two decades, interest has grown in the relationship between security and poverty. Prior to that, 'experts' such as practising diplomats, government leaders and mainstream academics in security studies generally thought of these areas as separate. Of course, it is unlikely that their view was shared by ordinary citizens throughout the world, since their direct experience would have suggested otherwise. Security for the 'experts' was understood narrowly as protecting the national interest, defined foremost as upholding the physical, territorial integrity of the state against external military attack, but in reality often involving protection against internal fragmentation or challenge to the ruling elite. Economic issues, insofar as they were considered at all by this group, were very much low order issues. Poverty was relegated to the domain of development practitioners and development academics, who shared the state-based approach of their security colleagues. They understood and measured development in terms of national achievements.

During the 1990s, the mainstream security agenda merged with the mainstream development agenda under the mantle of global governance. Global political changes post-Cold War, the shift in conflicts mainly to poorer regions of the world (particularly Africa), the scale of humanitarian emergencies, the perceived threat of global terrorism, and deepening global economic integration with its attendant inequalities and political protests, created space for the exploration of the relationship between poverty and security within mainstream analysis. Nowadays, mainstream academics, diplomats and politicians speak openly of the need to integrate approaches to poverty and security. Leaders of the G8, the International Monetary Fund (IMF) and World Bank, for example, have spoken forcefully about a possible link between poverty and conflict.

The acknowledgement of connections between poverty and security is welcomed by those who have long advocated a holistic approach, but a word of caution is in order as such analysts remain sceptical about the direction of travel. The new global political focus on poverty reduction is seen by some as a means to ensure that opposition to global economic integration is neutralized, and the economic liberalization project continued unimpeded.

Whose poverty? Whose security? Placing human beings at the centre of our concern

One of the first problems a student of poverty and security encounters is the contested nature of the key terms of the debate. In other words, what precisely are we talking about? Security means different things to different people, as has been demonstrated ably in this book. Likewise, poverty has different meanings, and these are often understood within the larger concept of development – itself a heavily debated term. Both have been analysed and measured in terms of individual human beings, sub-state regions, the state level, continental regions and even at the global level; both have also been thought about in terms of specific groups or categories of people who may be contained within or spread beyond a single state.

The term 'conflict' crops up in discussions of poverty and security, and this equally takes on many different meanings according to the perspective of the respective author. It often refers to wars, for example: interstate wars, proxy wars, internal wars fought to gain regional independence or to gain political supremacy, wars initiated by outside powers (Stewart 2003: 329–330). Yet conflict is also experienced at the individual level, particularly among poor communities where, for example, a gun culture can flourish aided by the easy availability of small arms and light weapons, and also in the domestic setting where gendered power relations underpin domestic violence. In addition to all of these complexities, there is the challenge of understanding the term 'violence': for many authors it is physical; for some, such as Galtung, it is structural, exemplifying the condition of living perpetuated by the development of the global economy over the past 500 years, whereby swathes of humanity are disenfranchised, living in routine poverty and exploitation (see Chapter 6, this volume).

These conceptual and theoretical debates are rehearsed extensively in the academic literature, and they are not repeated here; but it is important to be aware of the many claims to 'truth', and the role that perspective and position play.

For this author, security at its very core is about the condition of individual human beings and humankind, rather than geographical, administrative, economic or political units, or faceless others. Fundamentally, the pursuit of security is about individual human beings – i.e. human security – and the protection and fulfilment of their human rights. (It is noteworthy that even the recent term 'human security' is generating a voluminous literature, as its meaning is contested, just as has been the notion of human rights over many years. See Chapter 16, this volume.) The pursuit of other levels of security – for example, global, regional or national – has legitimacy and relevance to the degree to which it supports human security, and the latter cannot be defined or contained within the territorial boundaries of an exclusive political unit. Thus, for example, the pursuit of national security by a state must not compromise the human security either of its citizens or indeed of people living beyond the boundaries of the state.

Working with this understanding of security as being a priori about human beings, it becomes clear that poverty is of direct relevance for security studies; indeed, poverty and human insecurity are in many respects synonymous. Both refer to a human condition characterized by the lack of fulfilment of a range of human entitlements such as adequate food, healthcare, education, shelter, employment and voice; a life lived in fear of violence, injury, crime or discrimination; and an expectation that life will continue in this way. All of these elements are to varying degrees dependent facets, and the loss of one often leads to the loss of/decline in enjoyment of others (e.g. undernourishment and poor housing contribute to ill-heath, which itself prevents productive work, and this affects the ability to grow or purchase food, which contributes to further malnutrition); living without title to land or housing opens the way to physical insecurity and the feeling of hopelessness, for example as slums are cleared; living in fear of arbitrary violence from gangs, or even from those acting in the name of or in the payroll of the government, undermines voice and obstructs economic and political development.

Improvements in human security necessarily involve poverty reduction, and likewise, poverty reduction will decrease human insecurity. Such improvements may also be seen as synonymous with improvements in the experience of human rights – economic, social, civil, political and cultural – by individual human beings.

Thus poverty is not simply a relevant area of concern for security studies; rather, it is a central concern for those who believe that security is a priori about human beings, and that it is about states, world regions and the global political system only to the extent that they help or hinder the primary goal of human security.

Therefore, in a world where half of humanity lives in a condition of poverty (read: human insecurity or lack of enjoyment of basic human rights), understanding the national and global structures and policies which sustain this situation is crucial for the articulation of policies supportive of the enhancement of human security. Thus a critique of current development policy, and the articulation of alternative pathways to development, is a key focus for security studies. Indeed, the continuation of entrenched academic silos which differentiate between and create 'experts' in the study of security, or poverty/development or human rights, obstructs the growth of knowledge and understanding about the human condition, and the enormous challenges to be faced. The need for an inclusive, integrated approach is clear.

What do we know about the poverty–security nexus?

Defining security in human terms, we know that the current model of development is failing to deliver to the majority of people across the world, and in some cases, such as across sub-Saharan Africa, it actually seems to be making a significant contribution to the deterioration of the human condition.

For the one billion people living below the internationally identified poverty line of $1 a day, and the next two billion living on $2 a day, poverty is a chronic condition; for others it may be transient, for example, following a specific, one-off crop failure. Specific disadvantaged groups exist within these figures (e.g. the elderly, disabled, youths, refugees, internally displaced persons, HIV/AIDS sufferers). Also hidden within these figures are the poor who are made even poorer and more vulnerable by some specific event (e.g. the Asian tsunami (December 2004); or the Pakistan Kashmiri earthquake (October 2005), which rendered 2.5 million people homeless and devastated the livelihoods of subsistence farmers who lost a harvest and their livestock (Ozerdem 2007)).

Those in chronic poverty lead wholly insecure lives, routinely lack voice, basic needs, work and opportunity, often living in fear, subject to physical abuse, forced eviction and so forth. In addition to arbitrary violence often perpetrated by the authorities, those living in poverty face violent crime. In

BOX 17.2 THE BLUEPRINT FOR DEVELOPMENT: NEOLIBERAL ECONOMICS, OR 'THE WASHINGTON CONSENSUS'

By the early 1980s, with changes in the domestic politics of leading industrialized countries, the post-war liberal principle of state-guided markets gave way to the rise of neoliberal economic policy. This signalled a fundamental shift in development policy from state-led to market-led.

'The Washington Consensus' as it came to be known was promoted as a universal blueprint for development by an increasingly coordinated set of actors – public and private international financial institutions (e.g. IMF and World Bank, private banks), think-tanks and political leaders in Washington DC, other OECD governments, all keen to ensure the repayment of Third World debt.

The causes of poverty and underdevelopment were identified as internal to the state, rather than external/structural or a combination of both. Export-led growth would generate foreign exchange necessary for debt repayment, and benefits would occur throughout society by the 'trickle-down' effect. The role of the state was redefined as the enabler of the private sector, facilitating privatization, liberalization and deregulation. Good governance was crucial for competitive elections, enforcing property rights, tackling corruption and so on. Global economic integration through trade and investment liberalization was the best way to promote economic growth, which in turn would deliver improvements for all worldwide.

While on paper the theory may have looked convincing to some, when applied in the real world it has not been without problems. The reform of domestic economies across the developing and transition countries, with an emphasis on rolling back the state in favour of market-led development, trade and investment liberalization, has not resulted in benefits for all. Indeed, many in the former Soviet bloc and East Asia have been thrown into poverty following particular crises of liberalization, while in Africa poverty has deepened routinely as anticipated growth has failed to materialize through the combination of structural adjustment policies, plus increasing debt, falling commodity prices and disappointing levels of aid. State infrastructures have declined.

Voices of opposition from development NGOs have grown louder, criticizing the imposition and questioning the appropriateness of a universal blueprint recommended and applied irrespective of local conditions or wishes. Increasingly, criticisms have been heard within the IMF and World Bank, and have resulted in significant resignations (e.g. Joseph Stiglitz left the World Bank in 2000).

By the late 1990s, the key advocates of neoliberalism were supporting a change of emphasis: growth alone is not enough; it must be 'pro-poor', and locally owned by national governments and civil society. Yet in reality, post-2000, the emphasis on domestic reform in support of the private sector plus trade liberalization remains.

major cities they endure the normalization of the gun culture (e.g. in Lagos, Rio de Janeiro and Nairobi). The perpetrators and the victims are generally young unemployed male youths without hope. This hopelessness among youths is particularly worrying, given the evolving age profile of the global population, and the fact that young people are the next generation of social and economic actors (World Bank 2006). Opportunities missed, and behaviours/cultures developed early on in life can be very difficult to reverse.

The direct experience of poverty is often linked to significant vertical inequalities based on income, and/or horizontal social, economic and political inequalities (i.e. differences across geographical regions or social groups) which may occur within the national or global context, and are often played out over generations (UN Development Programme 2005: 163). These inequalities don't just happen. Rather, they are the result of actions or inactions by human beings in government or in international institutions. They are created, sustained, made worse or better, or ignored by human beings in positions of authority and/or power and influence, who choose to promote certain rules of the economic and political game over others. These inequalities erode the

BOX 17.3 RESULTS OF APPLYING THE WASHINGTON CONSENSUS MODEL OF DEVELOPMENT

▌ Economic growth lower than expected, and of poor quality (e.g. neither job-creating nor poverty-reducing).

▌ Trickle-down failed to occur – inequalities increased within and between states, including those of the developing world.

▌ Debt remained a serious problem, especially for the most heavily indebted countries for whom debt as a percentage of external exports rose from 38 per cent in 1980 to 1984, to 103 per cent in 1995 to 2000.

▌ Trade liberalization – developing countries which relied on the export of primary commodities (i.e. the poorest) suffered a continuous, significant decline in market share – they were more open to trade, but earned less (UNCTAD 2006: 20).

▌ In countries with low per capita income, benefit from trade openness accrued to the rich not the poor.

▌ Social problems increased as market-based entitlement deprived poor people of access to essential services (e.g. healthcare to meet HIV/AIDS emergency in Africa).

▌ Official development assistance was disappointing, with the expected new money failing to flow in; indeed, after the deduction of debt relief, there was a decline in aid to the poorest countries between 1996 and 2000; thereafter, increases were absorbed by Iraq and Afghanistan.

▌ Foreign direct investment – poorest countries lost out, with 49 of them attracting just 2 per cent of FDI to the South, or 0.5 per cent of global FDI, in 2001.

BOX 17.4 PROGRESS ON THE MILLENNIUM DEVELOPMENT GOALS

Progress in achieving the Millennium Development Goals has been far from uniform across the world. The greatest improvements have been in East Asia and South Asia, where more than 200 million people have been lifted out of poverty since 1990 alone. Nonetheless, nearly 700 million people in Asia still live on less than $1 a day – nearly two-thirds of the world's poorest people – while even some of the fastest growing countries are falling short on non-income goals, such as protecting the environment and reducing maternal mortality. Sub-Saharan Africa is at the epicentre of the crisis, falling seriously short on most goals, with continuing food insecurity, disturbingly high child and maternal mortality, growing numbers of people living in slums and an overall rise of extreme poverty despite some important progress in individual countries. Latin America, the transition economies, and the Middle East and North Africa, often hampered by growing inequality, have more mixed records, with significant variations in progress but general trends falling short of what is needed to meet the 2015 deadline (Annan 2005: 11).

All regions are off-track to meet the target for reducing childhood mortality; nutrition is a major challenge, with half of all children in developing countries underweight or stunted; and half the people in developing countries lack access to improved sanitation (World Bank 2007c: 1). The largest 'MDG deficit' is in states with weak institutions and governance, and often in conflict – the 'fragile states' (World Bank 2007c: 3).

political legitimacy of government in both the developed and the developing world, and of global governance through institutions such as the World Trade Organization (WTO) and IMF.

These horizontal inequalities may play out within a state's borders (e.g. in Sudan, Nepal, China, Russia, India, or Mexico), where particular regions and/or groups of people feel disadvantaged by the state and a conflict situation exists. Governments can play a role in alleviating or exacerbating vertical and horizontal inequalities, and therefore human insecurity, within their states. It is noteworthy that in terms of deaths through violent physical acts, more people are killed by their own governments than by foreign armies. For example, it has been estimated that in the twentieth century, while approximately 40 million people were killed in wars between states, more than four times that number – some 120 million people – were killed by their own governments (Rummel 1994: 21). Deprivation resulting from acts or omissions of government via their policies adds to the citizens' death-toll. Often, economic and social policies pursued by governments are heavily influenced from outside (e.g. IMF, WTO, or a major power which ties aid to specific domestic policy reform (see below)).

Within the half of humanity living in poverty, there are an estimated 25 million internally displaced people, beyond UN assistance, including 5 million in Sudan, of whom 2.3 million are from the Darfur region. Globally, there are an estimated 12 million refugees, at the present time including several hundred thousand who have fled/are fleeing from Darfur to Chad (UNDP 2005: 154). Statelessness and mass denial of effective citizenship by governments threatens the security of individuals, and groups, and this can have a detrimental effect beyond borders. In Africa, for example, an estimated 17.3 million migrants and pastoralists are without effective citizenship from governments (CRAI 2007). Another contemporary example is the Chechen inhabitants of Chechnya in the Russian Federation who feel terrorized, experience unemployment, hopelessness, massive internal displacement, with the entire population living below the poverty line (UNDP 2005: 160, CICS 2005: 64–66).

Horizontal inequalities can also be detected from a global perspective, with entire world regions and their inhabitants disadvantaged or advantaged by the particular global rules within which all must operate, yet few set. For example, the vast majority of HIV/AIDS sufferers live in sub-Saharan Africa, yet they and their governments have no voice in developing the global rules which determine access to drugs. A further example involves the rules which determine the benefits of the globalization process in which sub-Saharan Africa and its people have been marginalized; these are legitimated by international financial institutions and the G8 governments. Another example is a system of trade that fails to take into account the needs of the poorest, especially rural agricultural workers. These inequalities are created, they are intentionally or unintentionally made worse, or simply ignored by major governments or external agents such as the IMF, the WTO or aid donors. Through their policies these actors can create, promote and sustain or simply even permit human insecurity, to devastating effect. The tragic history of debt accumulation and repayment by African governments (read: poor inhabitants of African states) is testimony to this.

Let us take the example of food insecurity. This is one of the defining features of existence for people living in poverty. Three-quarters of poor people live in rural areas, yet rural livelihoods in agriculture are being destroyed by the unfolding of global economic integration, and inadequate alternative opportunities are being created in urban areas. The progress of trade liberalization means that food produced using huge subsidies in rich countries such as the USA and within the EU finds it way to markets in poor countries where local farmers lose their livelihoods and are left without the means to buy the imported foodstuffs. In Haiti, for example, poor rice farmers have lost their means of subsistence as US rice has flooded the national market and they have no alternative means of subsistence. Similarly, poor farmers in tropical countries who depend on the sale of their agricultural products in northern markets – such as coffee, tea or cotton farmers – find their livelihoods are completely insecure. Eleven million cotton farmers in West Africa, and 20 million coffee farmers, faced devastation in recent years.

While the contemporary effects of economic liberalization on food security are clear, it is also noteworthy that governments that have chosen over the past 60 years to prioritize food security have been able to lift their populations out of food insecurity. Diverse examples exist: Sri Lanka, countries of South East Asia, Cuba. Governments are not without choices, but it remains to be seen to what degree they will have leeway with the progression of rules on trade liberalization.

What do we know about poverty–violent conflict?

While poverty causes more deaths than violent conflict, it may itself contribute to violent conflict and therefore to further human insecurity. Likewise, violent conflict may contribute to poverty. What do we know about this relationship? In the post-Cold War period, and particularly since the mid-1990s, there has been a significant scaling-up of research on the poverty–violent conflict nexus by universities, institutes, NGOs and even governments. These investigations range from large projects offering detailed data-gathering and analysis (e.g. Uppsala Conflict Data Programme working in partnership with the Human Security Centre, University of British Columbia; Stockholm International Peace Research Institute), political economic analysis and econometric modelling (e.g. Queen Elizabeth House, Oxford and WIDER), or case studies of regions or issues (e.g. Centre for International Cooperation and Security (CICS), Bradford University, Amnesty International, the International Action Network on Small Arms, and Oxfam International), to more theoretical critiques of the broad area (Duffield 2001b, Stewart and Fitzgerald 2001, Wilkin 2002). Of course, many citizens on the ground would doubtless suggest that these findings simply confirm what they already knew from direct experience.

Effect of poverty on conflict

While it is often not possible to completely disentangle a whole range of factors which may contribute to a conflict (e.g. environmental, social, economic, political, historical), the growing body of knowledge has provided evidence in a previously data-light area that 'poverty and falling incomes are critical drivers for violent conflict in less developed countries' (Miguel 2006: 1). Nafziger and Auvinen (2002: 153) have shown that 'stagnation and decline in real GDP, high income inequality, a high ratio of military expenditures to national income, and a tradition of violent conflict are sources of emergencies'. Collier *et al.* (2003) have shown that there can be a variety of economic motivations for conflict, born out of poverty, including economic grievance, greed and even opportunity. Econometric studies have shown that poverty feeds insecurity, and insecurity feeds poverty, both at the level of the state and the individual. The UNDP has summed this up as 'the conflict trap is part of the poverty trap' (UNDP 2005: 157).

The UN categorizes states according to their per capita income, and has identified poor countries – and therefore their inhabitants – as being far more likely to experience violent conflict than rich countries. In 2006, 50 least developed countries (LDCs) were identified, each exhibiting a per capita income under $750, human resource weakness (poor health, nutrition, education, adult literacy), and economic vulnerability. Of these, 16 were landlocked and 12 were small islands. Such low-income countries accounted for over half of countries experiencing violent conflict between 1990 and 2003. What is more, countries with per capita income of $600 are half as likely to experience civil war as countries with per capita income of $250. In other words, the poorer the country, the more likely its people are to experience civil war.

The majority of countries listed by the UN as LDCs are in sub-Saharan Africa, and the problems of poverty and conflict affect Africa disproportionately. The region is caught in a trap of poverty–conflict–poverty.

> Almost every country across the middle belt of the continent – from Somalia in the east to Sierra Leone in the west, from Sudan in the north to Angola in the south – remains trapped in a volatile mix of poverty, crime, unstable and inequitable political institutions, ethnic discrimination, low state capacity and the 'bad neighbourhoods' of other crisis-ridden states – all factors associated with increased risk of armed conflict.
>
> (Human Security Centre 2005: 4)

The issue of how to lift these countries and their peoples – most of whom depend on the production of basic commodities – out of the poverty trap is pressing. Those commodities have experienced a long-term decline in value compared with manufactured goods. G8, IMF and World Bank structural adjustment policies call for increased exports of such commodities to generate foreign exchange which may be used towards debt repayment. Yet more and more of these very products have to be produced and sold in order simply to stand still. And then there is the additional problem of governments of many low-income states spending more on weapons than on healthcare (e.g. Burundi, Ethiopia, Nepal, Bangladesh (UNDP 2005: 160)).

Effect of conflict on poverty

Mounting evidence shows the negative effect of conflict on development and poverty alleviation. The 13 case studies published by CICS in 2005 illustrate the vast range of possibilities, which may be short- or long-term, local, regional, national or even international. Examples include:

- depletion of the productive workforce through direct involvement in conflict and indirectly through displacement, hunger, injury and disease;

■ destruction of physical and social infrastructure, including transport, power, education and health;

■ destruction of the agricultural base and therefore of subsistence and livelihoods, plus a loss of local expert farming knowledge with subsequent movement of displaced into urban areas;

■ disruption and destruction of markets;

■ diversion of young children into military roles;

■ expansion of youths in urban areas turning to crime and acceptance of violence as a legitimate way to settle differences;

■ decline in economic growth and export revenues;

■ rise in military expenditure by governments;

■ negative effect on growth nationally and in neighbouring states.

At a human level, conflict exacerbates the human insecurity of those directly involved or caught in the cross-fire, many of whom already do not routinely enjoy basic entitlements and rights. It is a cruel irony that for some, conflict is seen as the route to secure rights and entitlements which they see their government as denying them.

The diplomatic agenda on poverty and security

At the academic level, data-gathering and analysis regarding poverty, security and their interlinkages, as well as theoretical critique, is proceeding rapidly. What of the diplomatic level? The poverty–security connection was under the spotlight in the 2005 World Summit at the UN General Assembly, which considered the report of the High-level Panel on Threats, Challenges and Change, *A More Secure World: Our Shared Responsibility*.

The report defines a threat to international security as 'any event or process that leads to large-scale death or lessening of life chances and undermines States as the basic unit of the international system' (UNGA 2004: 25). It details a number of threats, including poverty, infectious disease and environmental degradation; conflict between and within states; nuclear, radiological, chemical and biological weapons, terrorism and transnational organized crime. Kofi Annan, in his note before the body of the report, has commented:

I support the report's emphasis on development as the indispensable foundation stone of a new collective security. Extreme poverty and infectious diseases are threats in themselves, but they also create environments which make more likely the emergence of other threats, including civil conflict. If we

> are to succeed in better protecting the security of our citizens, *it is essential that due attention and necessary resources be devoted to achieving the Millennium Development Goals.*
>
> (UNGA 2004: 2 para. 7)

But is the focus on the MDGs appropriate? Of course they should be met, and their fulfilment will enhance the human security of some of the world's poorest people. And yes, conflict will make their achievement more difficult. Yet the mere existence of those goals is testimony to the failure of development policy to date. The fundamental issue is whether the current approach to development (read: economic neoliberalism) is appropriate for meeting the challenge of human security or poverty eradication or human rights – today and tomorrow. The evidence suggests that it is not. Rather, a radical critique of that policy and the development of an alternative should be at the heart of diplomatic endeavour.

Consider this: a 2003 UNDP report contended that if sub-Saharan Africa continues on its current course, it will take another 150 years to reach the MDG target of halving poverty, and the hunger situation will continue to worsen (UNDP 2003). In addition, the World Bank (2007b:1) notes that sub-Saharan Africa 'now accounts for 30% of the world's extreme poor, compared with 19% in 1990 and only 11% in 1981'.

At the broadest level, the failure of development post-1945 must be acknowledged, and the values underpinning the approach must be brought into question (see Stewart 2004). There are no signs that this development model is about to be overturned. The modifications of the existing approach evident in the post-Washington Consensus are not likely to deliver poverty eradication or human security for all, or result in a sustainable future for the eight billion people who will inhabit our planet by 2025. The pursuit of growth without equal attention to equity and sustainability will perpetuate the current poverty–conflict–poverty trap.

For the countries of sub-Saharan Africa, their specific circumstances mean that the continuation of trade openness will contribute to further poverty, inequality and insecurity. These are the very countries which are currently the most conflict-ridden. In particular progress must be made on commodities – especially basic agricultural commodities – if the world's governments are serious about the eradication of hunger and malnutrition, and improving human insecurity. Progress on the trade rules governing arms flows is also vital: human security rather than liberal free trade principles must inform the development of the rules. The signs are a little more positive on this than on commodities: in June 2006, 42 governments signed up to the *Geneva Declaration on Armed Violence and Development*. This committed them to 'promote sustainable security and a culture of peace by taking action to reduce armed violence and its negative impact on socio-economic and human development'. This was followed in October 2006 by a UN General Assembly resolution (A/c.1/61/L.55) to start a process to develop an Arms Trade Treaty. This had been given great impetus by the Million Faces campaign launched by NGOs. The UN committed to establish a Group of Governmental Experts to scope 'a comprehensive, legally-binding instrument establishing common standards for the import, export and transfer of conventional arms' to be reported on at the UN General Assembly 62nd session in 2007. The resolution was carried with 139 votes in favour out of a possible 164, with only the USA voting against.

Likewise with aid: the very countries which are currently the most conflict-ridden – those in sub-Saharan Africa especially – are missing out under the current aid regime. Despite the promises made by the G8 at Gleneagles in July 2005, a tiny number of recipients outside the continent are the greatest beneficiaries of aid. The African Progress Panel was launched in April 2007 to ensure accountability of the donors – a sure sign that delivery is not matching promises.

While developments at Gleneagles looked promising, it remains the case that one year after the summit, low-income countries still had debts of $380 billion, and middle-income countries $1.66 trillion. But where debt had been cancelled, real improvements in the lives of the poor had been achieved (e.g. in Zambia, the cancellation of $5 million debt was followed rapidly by the introduction of universal basic healthcare).

Human security must drive trade, aid and foreign investment, as well as domestic reform, and we must measure their legitimacy by their contribution to it. The contribution of internal factors to current insecurity must be matched by due acknowledgement of the role of external/structural factors. A development strategy for human security must embrace both.

Conclusion

This chapter has explored the relationship between poverty and security. Defining security at its core in human terms, the chapter suggests that poverty is not only an appropriate concern for students of security – it is an essential part of their study. A significant proportion of humanity is caught in a poverty–insecurity–poverty trap. Poverty and insecurity are two sides of the same coin. A person who experiences one will likely be familiar with the other. If governments and international institutions tackle one, they will impact upon the other. Serious students of one necessarily need to study the other. All need to think about development, for without that there cannot be poverty eradication or sustainable human security.

Further reading

Centre for International Cooperation and Security (CICS), *The Impact of Armed Violence on Poverty and Development* (Bradford University: CICS, 2005, www.bradford.ac.uk/cics). An accessible collection of case studies examining the effect of armed violence on poverty and development across the world.

Human Security Centre, *Human Security Report 2005* (New York: Oxford University Press, 2005). A rich, authoritative compilation of data which suggests a dramatic, and unnoticed, decline in the number of wars, genocides and human rights abuse over the past decade, due it suggests in large part to the unprecedented upsurge of international activism, spearheaded by the UN.

Paul Rogers, *Losing Control: Global Security in the Twenty-first Century* (London: Pluto Press, 2nd edn, 2002). An engaging and accessible read which calls for a radical rethinking of Western perceptions of security, and highlights the need to address the core issues of global insecurity, including poverty and inequality.

Frances Stewart, 'Conflict and the Millennium Development Goals', *Journal of Human Development*, 4(3) (2003): 325–351. Shows the relationship between conflict and the fulfilment (or not) of the Millennium Development Goals.

Peter Wilkin, 'Global poverty and orthodox security', *Third World Quarterly*, 23(4) (2002): 633–645. A critique of orthodox security analysis and its failure to address global social crises afflicting the twenty-first century world.

CONTENTS

Environmental Change

Simon Dalby

▌ Abstract

This chapter introduces students to the environmental security debate and how it has changed since the environment was first discussed in the 1980s as a matter requiring attention by security agencies. While popular author Robert Kaplan prompted widespread concern with his ideas about environmental change and poverty causing political disruptions in the mid-1990s, sceptical scholars suggested that Kaplan's links between environmental change and large-scale conflict were dubious, and even if they were established then the military was an inappropriate agency to deal with such problems. In recent years climate change has again raised concerns about environment as a cause of geopolitical conflict, but what has also become clear is that these potential disruptions are a matter of environmental damage caused by affluence not poverty. Security for all requires cooperation in the face of environmental change and not the traditional strategies of geopolitical rivalry that used to be at the heart of security studies.

Introduction

In the late 1980s as the Cold War confrontation came to an end, environmental themes reappeared on the international agenda. In some discussions environment was explicitly linked to matters of international security. It seemed obvious to some commentators that matters of ozone holes, the destruction of the tropical rainforests, and the possibilities of climate change disruptions were serious enough that they needed to be treated as security threats by governments around the world. While some authors had speculated about environment as a matter of security in the 1970s, it was only in the late 1980s that such thinking started to frequently shape policy discussions, media alarms and then scholarly investigations.

The debate on 'environmental security' has been going on ever since (Dalby 2002). Looking carefully at the discussion allows us to see the assumptions built into contemporary security thinking, raises many concerns about the appropriateness of extending the remit of security, and poses the big questions about who decides what matters are serious enough to require attention from either the security apparatuses of states or students studying security. Indeed, as the rest of this chapter suggests, how environment is portrayed and how it is presented as a potential future danger in need of security policies tells us a considerable amount about both the geopolitical imagination in Washington and how security studies works in universities.

Environmental security

Environmental security ideas came from many sources although prominent among them were think-tanks such as the World Resources Institute and World Watch Institute in Washington DC. The Soviet Union, in its dramatic 'new thinking' on security in the late 1980s, also suggested that environmental security was now very important. The Chernobyl nuclear reactor accident in 1986 had focused the attention of many Soviet thinkers in a way that many in Washington failed to perceive at the time. Since he left power after the end of the Cold War Mikhail Gorbachev, former head of the Soviet Union, has devoted much of his attention to these matters. In arguing for the need to think about global environmental security the Soviets were in tune with discussion of ozone holes as well as rising concern about climate change. Tropical deforestation, in Brazil in particular, and the hot summer of 1988 in the USA, when the Mississippi river flow was so reduced that commercial navigation was disrupted, garnered their share of attention too.

Simultaneously the World Commission on Environment and Development was focusing attention on the need to rethink development in ways that would alleviate poverty without further degrading numerous landscapes. In the pages of its 1987 report on *Our Common Future* the authors had taken for granted that environmental degradation and shortage of resources would lead to political instability and conflict in many places as poor people struggled to find the means of subsistence. Fear of conflict over inadequate resources was one of the reasons for thinking in terms of 'sustainable development'. Frequently referred to as the Brundtland Commission after its Norwegian chairperson Gro Harlem Brundtland, the Commission laid much of the intellectual groundwork for the huge United Nations 'Earth Summit' on Environment and Development held in Rio de Janeiro in 1992 (Chatterjee and Finger 1994).

In the 1990s, following the Cold War and in the absence of any obvious contenders to challenge American power, numerous new dangers appeared on the geopolitical agenda in Washington. Drugs, migration, terrorism, population growth, globalization and the environment fed into discussions of risk and threat, and the apparently overarching need for surveillance and monitoring in the event that these matters might threaten the USA and the mode of economy that its political power supported. Not all of these security concerns required the exercise of much military might, but in a society in which matters of security remained important, environment was part of this policy agenda. In the 1990s Vice President Al Gore was influential in drawing attention to the matter of 'failed states' and the possible environmental causes of their political collapse.

The debate about environment and conflict suggested that environmental degradation was likely to cause conflict in many places in the global South (Kahl 2006). Lack of development was related specifically to environmental scarcities; the poor are hungry due to a lack of food, not because of poverty. Shortages of agricultural land and rainfall are supposedly to blame. In short, so the thinking of the time suggested, there is a clear geopolitical divide between those in direct danger of environmentally induced political problems in the South and the prosperous populations in the North. But what, the arguments then asked, if those problems spilled over into Northern states? This would then, surely, require a security response.

Robert Kaplan's 'coming anarchy'

Probably the most influential single publication on all this was Robert Kaplan's essay in the February 1994 issue of the *Atlantic Monthly*. More than any other contribution this article focused attention in Washington, and subsequently elsewhere, on the debate about post-Cold War security concerns tied to environment. Kaplan's prose is very dramatic:

It is time to understand 'the environment' for what it is: *the* national-security issue of the early twenty-first century. The political and strategic impact of surging populations, spreading disease, deforestation and soil erosion, water depletion, air pollution, and possibly, rising sea levels in critical overcrowded

> regions like the Nile Delta and Bangladesh – developments that will prompt mass migrations and, in turn, incite group conflicts – will be the core foreign-policy challenge from which most others will ultimately emanate, arousing the public and uniting assorted interests left over from the Cold War.
>
> (Kaplan 1994: 58)

In many of the environmental security discussions, and in Kaplan's popular articulation of these themes in particular, there is nonetheless cause for alarm in the North. This is because of the potential that instability in the South may spill over into the zones of prosperity in the North; hence its formulation in the environmental security literature as a matter that 'we' – security scholars and policy-makers in the North – ought to monitor.

Not least this is so because environmental degradation as a cause of political instability, and hence as a security threat, apparently rarely occurs in the developed North. In Kaplan's article and much of the rest of the literature in the 1990s, environmental degradation is a matter of Southern states and poor populations, not an issue directly concerning affluence (Dalby 1999). Environmental difficulties in the North are a matter for government regulation and of course technical innovation, but not a matter usually understood to have consequences in the South. Political instabilities might be expected in the South, especially in those areas not yet blessed by the political stability that supposedly comes from technological sophistication and democratic governance.

Translated into Kaplan's journalistic style,

> We are entering a bifurcated world. Part of the globe is inhabited by Hegel's and Fukuyama's Last Man, healthy, well fed, and pampered by technology. The other, larger, part is inhabited by Hobbes's First Man, condemned to a life that is 'poor, nasty, brutish, and short.' Although both parts will be threatened by environmental stress, the Last Man will be able to master it; the First Man will not. The Last Man will adjust to the loss of underground water tables in the western United States. He will build dikes to save Cape Hatteras and the Chesapeake beaches from rising sea levels, even as the Maldive Islands, off the coast of India, sink into oblivion, and the shorelines of Egypt, Bangladesh, and Southeast Asia recede, driving tens of millions of people inland where there is no room for them, and thus sharpening ethnic divisions.
>
> (Kaplan 1994: 60)

But some researchers at least were unconvinced by Kaplan's lurid prose and other expressions of alarm by policy-makers and pundits. Policy debates continued while the scholarly research began to explore the evidential basis for the alarmist claims. Daniel Deudney (1999), perhaps the most notable sceptic, argued that environmental concerns and military matters were so different that confusing them was doing just that – causing conceptual confusion. If environmental matters were a matter of security concern, then they should be understood as just another cause of warfare and hence should be added into the existing scholarly investigation into the causes of warfare. Further, he argued, if environmental degradation did not necessarily cause conflict anyway then invoking security was simply confusing everything and actually making it more difficult to deal with important matters of environmental management. Likewise even if it did cause conflict then what needed attention were matters of environmental change, not the kind of policy issue which military and security agencies were in any way equipped, organized or trained to handle. Each of these arguments is worth paying some attention to because they go to the heart of the matter of the subject and nature of post-Cold War security studies. But they come down to two questions, the first an empirical one as to whether environmental change causes conflict, and the second, a policy debate about the appropriate place, if any, of environment in security discussions.

Environmental threat: science?

Is there evidence that environmental matters actually do cause conflict? This was repeatedly assumed in the 1980s; it seemed to be common sense that environmental shortages would lead to conflict as people fought over resources. Hence, in the Brundtland Commission report the need for sustainable development is partly justified by the fear of conflict if it isn't provided. Kaplan explicitly said that Thomas Malthus, the country parson turned economist, who two centuries ago published his essay on 'The Principle of Population' wherein he argued that people always breed faster than they expand their food supply, and hence misery and disaster result, was effectively the prophet of the future in Africa in particular and elsewhere too. But a 200-year-old text in economics isn't exactly scholarly evidence on which to build a contemporary policy agenda, however convenient its arguments may appear to be.

This was Thomas Homer-Dixon's point of departure, effectively asking the question about how environmental change leads to conflict. Or to be more precise, in a series of studies through the 1990s Homer-Dixon tried to show plausible connections between the two. It turned out to be much more difficult that many initially thought. Reviewing a huge amount of scholarly literature in disciplines including political science, history and economics he came to the initial very important conclusion that while environmental matters were probably related to conflict in some circumstances, there was little evidence that they had caused wars in the past, and hence little good reason to assume that they would do so in the future. On questions such as ozone depletion and climate change it was not clear that there was any way states could form coalitions to fight about any aspect of these phenomena (Homer-Dixon 1994).

Homer-Dixon went on to investigate the causal dynamics that might link environmental change and 'sub-national diffuse' conflicts and suggested some plausible connections. But in the process he also emphasized that the ability of states and institutions to manage social stress was important in dealing with conflict. He also showed how complicated such broad notions as environment actually are in these discussions and how important clarity is when it comes to defining what a resource is. Finally, he pointed to the need for societies to show ingenuity in responding to environmental stress. Adaptation will be needed if societal breakdowns are to be avoided. While he did show linkages between environmental change and conflict, he also showed that simple Malthusian assumptions don't hold; complex social arrangements matter as causes of conflict much more than any simple assumptions about scarcity (Homer-Dixon 1999).

While Homer-Dixon (1994) had dismissed the likelihood of war being caused by environmental change early on, the International Relations researchers who studied the causes of wars examined their databases, ran complicated statistical tests using a variety of data on environment and resources, and concluded that there was little in their research to support the argument that environmental change caused wars either (Gleditsch 1998). More recently the quantitative analysis of environmental security literature has confirmed the argument that environmental resource shortages rarely lead to violence, conflict or the collapse of states. Examining states with high population growth, high rates of urbanization or housing large numbers of refugees shows that they don't seem to have any higher prevalence of either violence or state collapse. Neither is agricultural land availability clearly related to violence (Urdal 2005).

But, as it turns out, what is related to violence in many important cases is resource abundance. The opposite argument to the Malthusian one seems to explain more of the violence, at least in the poorer developing states in the South. Where states are not strong, economic development is at an early stage, and valuable resources including minerals, oil and sometimes timber are easily available, there is a very large incentive on the part of people and ethnic groups to use violence to try either to gain control, or to keep control of the resource revenues generated when they are exported to the larger world economy (de Soysa 2002). In short, rich resources are worth fighting for if one has few other economic opportunities; resource wars are the result where states are unable, or leaders unwilling to share the wealth and use the revenues to ensure development.

This finding connects the violence in the South directly into the larger global economy. Policy efforts that attempt to deal with resource wars include boycotts of such things as diamonds mined in conflict zones, and campaigns to certify ethical production practices which in turn become part of the marketing campaigns of major corporations in some cases (Le Billon 2005). What is interesting about these campaigns is that they show clearly that there are connections between Northern consumption and the disruptions and violence in the South. Although not often thought of in this manner the politics around 'resource wars' make clear that there are numerous inter-connections in the global economy that are an important part of any discussion of security. In the earlier discussions of Malthusian fears of population growth in the South the geographical divide between North and South was frequently reinforced by the attribution of all responsibility for environmental difficulties to the poor in the South. But resource wars make it clear that this division is untenable in serious thinking about global or human security.

Environmental threat: policy options?

This brings us to the second big question in the whole discussion of environmental security: the assumption that security is a useful way of thinking about environmental difficulties and the related assumption that invoking the language of security will facilitate intelligent policy-making to deal with the dangers so specified. Assuming that environmental change is actually a major and imminent problem, what agencies should deal with it, and why is security a good way to think about all this anyway?

Gwyn Prins posed this question very clearly in choosing the title 'Top Guns and Toxic Whales' for his documentary film and companion book on the subject in the early 1990s. The Top Guns are the fighter pilots flying hugely sophisticated planes that supposedly provide national security for modern states by shooting down any potential invaders. But they are powerless to do anything about the poisoning of the seas which affect whales, which ingest the polluted seafood and concentrate the contaminants in their flesh to such a degree that they are considered toxic waste when they die. Someone has to deal with the whale carcasses washing up on the beach, but fighter pilots and their expensive machines are not going to be much help. The military is not apparently the kind of agency that is needed to deal with environmental threats to well-being (Prins and Stamp 1991).

Daniel Deudney (1999) explored this line of argument further in his writings and raised the additional point that invoking national security is actually counterproductive given that international cooperation is what is needed to deal with most environmental difficulties. Invoking nationalism and thinking in military terms only makes matters worse. The threats from traditional military concerns of security are different from environmental ones and hence traditional ways of thinking are inappropriate. Military threats are usually from states; they are violent and direct intentional acts; environmental threats tend to be diffuse, indirect and international, originating both inside and outside the state concerned. Military threats are occasional and unusual events; environmental degradation is a long-term process usually derived accidentally from routine economic activities. As we have seen in Robert Kaplan's representation of the poor states of the South as a threat to the North, geopolitical reasoning is more likely to lead to policies that try to limit migra-tion or use violence to control change, than it is to getting at the root causes of poverty and the global disruptions of natural systems.

If, as Deudney concluded, you add into the whole argument the point that wars are unlikely to be caused by environmental difficulties anyway, as other scholars point out (Homer Dixon 1999, Kahl 2006), the logic of linking security to environment collapses and the case for changing what we mean by security and how we think about achieving it becomes unavoidable. Deudney concludes his argument by putting the matter very directly:

> Nationalist sentiment and the war system have a long-established logic and staying power that are likely to defy any rhetorically conjured redirection toward benign ends. The movement to preserve the habitability of the planet for future generations must directly challenge the power of state centric nationalism and the chronic militarization of public discourse. Environmental degradation is not a threat to national security. Rather, environmentalism is a threat to the conceptual hegemony of state centered national security discourses and institutions. For environmentalists to dress their programs in the blood-soaked garments of the war system betrays their core values and creates confusion about the real tasks at hand.
>
> (Deudney 1999: 214)

However, regardless of Deudney's passionate warnings about conceptual confusion and inappropriate policy formulation, discussions of all this continue and notions of environmental security appear repeatedly in foreign policy discussions in Washington, in international reports and policy discussions in the United Nations and in the World Bank. Only sometimes is the geography in these matters made explicit. But when it is, it usually specifies matters of threats and instabilities in terms of endogenous causes of political instability in particular poor regions where environmental degradation is a problem. In American policy debates, the notion of key pivotal states in the South in need of attention by foreign policy-makers attracted considerable attention in the late 1990s (Chase *et al.* 1996). The Clinton administration took such matters seriously enough to establish a series of environmental 'hubs' in Southern states to focus aid projects designed to thwart imminent environmental dangers.

While much of this was subsequently eclipsed by concerns about terrorism and 'rogue states' for some years after 11 September 2001, nonetheless the discussion of environment and political stability in the South remains part of the larger discussion of American policy and global politics more generally. As fears of repeated terrorist attacks on the USA faded in the years after 2001 and American military campaigns in the Middle East changed the political landscape, environmental concerns gradually moved back on to the geopolitical agenda, not least because of the confused debate about the role of petroleum in the causes of the American invasion of Iraq in 2003. But now, in the latter part of the first decade of the twenty-first century, climate change has become the most prominent cause of concern, and at least a few in the Pentagon have once again posed the question of the importance of environmental matters for American national security.

Ten years after: the Pentagon climate scenario

A decade after Robert Kaplan's dystopian 'Coming Anarchy' crystallized the environmental security literature for the policy community in Washington, the environment, disaster and insecurity were once again under discussion in these now very different political circumstances. In February 2004, exactly ten years after Kaplan's essay had first appeared in the *Atlantic Monthly*, there was a brief flurry of media attention to criticisms of the Bush administration for its failure to deal with climate change. This time there was a much more scientific basis to the analysis than in Kaplan's article, and in much of the early writing on all this where vague and general arguments about deteriorating environments were usually enough to generate concern. The renewed attention to these matters in 2004 was triggered by the publication of a consultant report by Peter Schwartz and Doug Randall, written in 2003 for the Pentagon, on possible threats to the USA as a result of relatively sudden changes in the climate system.

The geological record shows that past climate change has sometimes been sudden rather than gradual. There is no reason to suspect that future changes of the Earth's climate system, already under stress by the rise in carbon dioxide and other 'greenhouse' gases, will be either slow and smooth or precisely predictable (Flannery 2006). One of the mechanisms that may explain many of the rapid shifts in the climate system in the past is disruption of the so-called 'thermohaline conveyor' ocean current system. Sometimes known simply as the Gulf Stream, the most important part of this current flows from the Gulf of Mexico across the Atlantic, past the British Isles and Iceland. In doing so it keeps the climate of Northern Europe much warmer than other places of similar latitude. Once these waters flow close to the Arctic they sink into the ocean depths and flow back around the planet in a complex pattern that effectively keeps all the world's oceans moving, and the climate pattern relatively predictable in many places. What makes the waters of the Atlantic part of the conveyor belt, which sinks as it gets into high latitudes, is their relative temperature and salinity. Current conditions make these waters marginally more dense than other Arctic waters, so they sink. Minor changes, either increased temperature or decreased salinity due to increased freshwater run-off from Greenland, might cause the conveyor to slow or even stop, inducing numerous climate changes in various parts of the world.

The Pentagon report took this science and projected what a disruption in this thermohaline circulation might mean for the USA in terms of its national security. (Hollywood moviemakers also used this science as a base from which to provide the greatly exaggerated fictional scenario for the 2004 summer season disaster movie *The Day after Tomorrow*. Two years later these themes were also a small part of Al Gore's popular documentary movie *An Inconvenient Truth* and accompanying book (Gore 2006) about climate change.) The authors examined the implications of a parallel climatological event to one which occurred approximately 8,200 years ago, an event that suggests the following changes:

1 Annual average temperatures drop by up to 5 degrees Fahrenheit over Asia and North America and 6 degrees Fahrenheit in Northern Europe.
2 Annual average temperatures increase by up to 4 degrees Fahrenheit in key areas throughout Australia, South America and Southern Africa.
3 Drought persists for most of the decade in critical agricultural regions and in the water resource regions for major population centres in Europe and eastern North America.
4 Winter storms and winds intensify, amplifying the impacts of the changes. Western Europe and the North Pacific experience enhanced winds.

The ability of many societies to adapt to quick changes in environment is in doubt. Such changes might lead to conflict and possibly war as a result of '1) Food shortages due to decreases in net global agricultural production; 2) Decreased availability and quality of fresh water in key regions due to shifted precipitation patterns, causing more frequent floods and droughts; 3) Disrupted access to energy supplies due to extensive sea ice and storminess' (Schwartz and Randall 2003: 2). The report argues that many of the poorer parts of the world will have populations more vulnerable to changed climates and less capable of adapting than the richer parts of the world. Hence migration of large numbers of people seeking to survive in those parts of the planet that are rich enough to adapt is a plausible outcome, but one that might generate very considerable political violence if the rich attempt to use military force to prevent this migration.

Rich states are likely to move to protect themselves from the disruptions. Thus war is part of the future if climate change strikes suddenly. The scenario might unfold thus:

> The United States and Australia are likely to build defensive fortresses around their countries because they have the resources and reserves to achieve self-sufficiency. With diverse growing climates, wealth, technology, and abundant resources, the United States could likely survive shortened growing cycles and harsh weather conditions without catastrophic losses. Borders will be strengthened around the country to hold back unwanted starving immigrants from the Caribbean islands (an especially severe problem), Mexico, and South America. Energy supply will be shored up through expensive (economically, politically, and morally) alternatives such as nuclear, renewables, hydrogen, and Middle Eastern contracts. Pesky skirmishes over fishing rights, agricultural support, and disaster relief will be commonplace. Tension between the U.S. and Mexico rises as the U.S. reneges on the 1944 treaty that guarantees water flow

> from the Colorado River. Relief workers will be commissioned to respond to flooding along the southern part of the east coast and much drier conditions inland. Yet, even in this continuous state of emergency the U.S. will be positioned well compared to others. The intractable problem facing the nation will be calming the mounting military tension around the world.
>
> (Schwartz and Randal 2003: 18)

The picture of a warring future as a result of climate change is highly reminiscent of Robert Kaplan's language from a decade earlier. It suggests that the USA in particular is well placed to survive such a crisis but that poor and marginal populations in many places are much less likely to be so lucky. But quite how this mounting military tension might play out around the world isn't so clear. Who threatens whom in this scenario and who might launch what kind of military action to respond to the crisis?

The Pentagon scenario is interesting because it partly changes the focus of the cause of danger from indigenous causes in the South to disruptions caused by global climate change; while the poor in the South are seen as a threat to the citadels of prosperity inhabited by Kaplan's rendition of the 'Last Man' it is no longer quite so clear that they are the authors of their own misfortune. Nonetheless, once the focus comes on the military dimension of this, the disaster of rapid climate change which is caused much more by the historical actions of the affluent than by the poor, once again the poor are presented as a threat to the rich rather than the other way around. Insofar as the violent imposition of political order is the first priority of security agencies this is merely business as usual. But if more critical voices are to intrude on the discussion of security the assumption of business as usual is one of the things that will have to be fundamentally challenged.

Human security and global ecology

While Kaplan was busy with his coming anarchy essay, the authors of the annual United Nations Development Report (UNDP 1994) produced a rather different analysis of the human condition and the causes of insecurity in many places. They argued that security needs a radical update and a shift from state centrism and territory to people (see Chapter 16, this volume). 'The concept of security has for too long been interpreted narrowly: as security of territory from external aggression, or as protection of national interest in foreign policy or as global security from the threat of a nuclear holocaust. It has been related more to nation-states than to people' (UNDP 1994: 22). In contrast, human security has two main aspects: 'It means first, safety from such chronic threats as hunger, disease and repression. And second it means protection from sudden and hurtful disruptions in the patterns of daily life – whether in homes, in jobs or in communities' (UNDP 1994: 23).

In formulating these ideas of human security the report's authors looked to the conditions that rendered people insecure and noted that the causes of insecurity were numerous, environmental security being but one of seven components. Environmental damage at the global scale, ozone depletion, greenhouse gases, biodiversity decline and the destruction of both oceanic and terrestrial habitats all contribute in various ways to human insecurity whether indirectly through potential climate disruptions and reduced nutrition or more directly through health effects of ultraviolet exposure. The point is not that all, or the worst, environmental dangers are global, but clearly they add to the local difficulties of pollution and are a matter beyond the capabilities of individual states to rectify. They require a more explicit focus on the conditions of human existence which now requires that we take seriously the changes that we are, mostly inadvertently, introducing into the biosphere, which is the shared home of all humanity (McNeill 2000). These changes, only the most obvious of which is captured in the current debate about climate security, are the environmental context within which human security is now increasingly discussed.

The World Wildlife Fund and numerous other organizations now make it clear that humanity has so altered the natural conditions of our existence that we have qualitatively changed the biosphere (WWF 2006). We have moved mountains, dammed most large rivers, cleared vegetation off much of the most fertile soil on the planet, and in the process of removing their habitat killed off numerous species in addition to the ones we have directly hunted to extinction. The atmosphere we breathe is now measurably different from that which our grandparents inhaled, to the extent that we have increased the concentration of carbon dioxide beyond the levels known to have existed for the past half a million years, a period that has seen a number of ice ages come and go.

Much of this activity has been undertaken either directly by the rich consumers of Northern states or by their agents in the more remote parts of the world harvesting and mining commodities for consumption in the shopping malls of suburbia. Only the most obvious commodity in all this is the petroleum that literally fuels most of contemporary civilization and the car-driving inhabitants of contemporary cities. It is this industrial urban society, now spreading to all corners of the globe, that is ironically threatening everyone's human security, and doing so by the simple mundane everyday actions of driving, shopping and heating homes. As such the causes of insecurity are now less the deliberate actions of governments using military power for various purposes, than the unintentional changes wrought by people enmeshed in the new ecological condition we call the global economy. Because that global economy, the increasingly artificial context of our lives, is what is changing the biosphere and threatening to unleash the kind of dramatic climate disruptions that worried the Pentagon consultants in 2003; industry and consumer lifestyles are now the cause of environmental threats.

Dealing with these new threats makes it clear that Daniel Deudney's (1999) warning about grafting environmental concerns on to national security is ever more important. Shifting security studies away from geopolitical pre-occupations with competing nation-states and towards the difficulties of reforming the global economy so that it no longer produces many dangerous things, all the while ensuring that people get food, water, shelter and can live meaningful lives is a tall order, especially in a world that now frequently focuses on the threat of terrorism as though it were the most important contemporary security challenge (see Chapter 12, this volume). Doing so reinforces the state nationalism and militarization that has perpetuated many modern forms of insecurity (Klare 2004). Doing so also reinforces precisely the current global order that is based on the economy and mode of development that the Brundtland Commission understood, 20 years ago, to be unsustainable.

The dilemmas for security studies are thus palpable when environmental matters on the largest scale are juxtaposed with the agenda for human security (Dodds and Pippard 2005). If our actions in generating greenhouse gases are, as the scientific community is now fairly clear is the case, causing more extreme weather events and increasing the severity of storms, then the 30,000 people who died in the heatwave in Europe in the summer of 2003 (ten times the number who died on 9/11) can plausibly be understood as victims of global environmental insecurity. How might we then understand the victims of Hurricane Katrina and the property damage in New Orleans caused by inadequate dykes to protect the city? Or for that matter the numerous casualties in the early years of this century in floods and landslides in Latin America, or those killed in huge storms in Bangladesh in the late 1990s (Abramowitz 2001)?

But the most important assumption buried at the heart of the Pentagon's analysis, and prominent in Kaplan's writing too, is the one shared with most security practitioners. It is the assumption that in a crisis people will fight rather than trade and cooperate. That's not all the Pentagon study suggests, but it is a key part of the analysis. In contrast the focus on human security makes it clear that cooperation is needed to ensure security; and nowhere more so than across the many facets of environmental insecurity. Likewise the environmental problematique reinforces the key point brought out by the resource wars finding that resources tied into the global economy are more likely to be related to violence in the South than local changes in environment there.

However, as has been clear for quite some time now, it is the affluent states and their citizens who have caused most of the environmental changes and it is within those states that many of the solutions will have to be found (Sachs et al. 1998). Solutions that don't blame the poor and marginal for their fate, and that understand that we now live in new circumstances of globalization that require us to recognize our interconnected fates in a biosphere that humanity is changing quite drastically (Pirages and DeGeest 2004). Otherwise the nightmare geopolitical scenarios that inform both Kaplan and the Pentagon consultants may come to pass, but not because of any intrinsic causes over there in the South from whence supposedly the threat emanates, but precisely because of the disruptions caused by the modes of consumption enjoyed by the affluent populations who pay for armies to keep the poor at bay, and for the universities that study security threats to the political order which keeps them affluent in the first place.

Further reading

Simon Dalby, *Environmental Security* (Minneapolis: University of Minnesota Press, 2002). An overview of debates on environmental security.

Felix Dodds and Tim Pippard (eds), *Human and Environmental Security: An Agenda for Change* (London: Earthscan, 2005). Discussions of the policy options linking security to more ecologically sensitive modes of living.

Colin Kahl, *States, Scarcity, and Civil Strife in the Developing World* (Princeton, NJ: Princeton University Press, 2006). This book summarizes and extends the discussion about conflict and environment in states in the South.

Michael Klare, *Blood and Oil: The Dangers and Consequences of America's Growing Dependence on Imported Petroleum* (New York: Metropolitan, 2004). Discusses the importance of petroleum in contemporary security policy.

J.R. McNeill, *Something New Under the Sun: An Environmental History of the Twentieth-century World* (New York: Norton, 2000). An excellent overview of the numerous ways in which humanity has altered the biosphere.

D.C. Pirages and T.M. DeGeest, *Ecological Security: An Evolutionary Perspective on Globalization* (Lanham, MD: Rowman and Littlefield, 2004). An ambitious examination of how environmental changes are linked to globalization.

CONTENTS

Health[1]

Colin McInnes

▌ Abstract

In this chapter, students will learn why health has not traditionally been seen as a security issue and why this began to change. They will look at the main health issues on the security agenda: the spread of infectious disease, especially to the West; the impact of HIV/AIDS, especially on state stability; and the risk of bioterrorism. Questions which arise include whether some of these risks have been overstated, whose interests are being served by securitizing health, and whether health should be a concern for security policy or development policy.

▌ Introduction

At the end of 2006, UNAIDS estimated that 39.5 million people were living with HIV/AIDS. In that year alone, between 2.5 million and 3.5 million were believed to have died from AIDS-related illnesses, while an additional 4.3 million people had been infected with the disease.[2] The estimate of AIDS-related deaths is roughly double that of a decade ago, and is likely to double again by 2030. The scale of suffering caused by this single illness is immense and the number of deaths dwarfs that of more traditional security crises such as those in Iraq and Afghanistan, or the War on Terror. Moreover, HIV/AIDS is only one of a number of communicable diseases, many of which are preventable, which each year kill millions of people. These include long-established diseases such as malaria and TB as well as new diseases such as SARS and H5N1, which threaten to become global pandemics with the potential to kill millions in a relatively short space of time. Further, non-communicable diseases such as tobacco-related illnesses and cardio-vascular disease again kill millions each year – indeed, tobacco-related diseases account for more deaths each year than any other non-natural cause. In sum, the lives and livelihood of the overwhelming majority of people on this planet are at greater risk from disease than from war, terrorism or other forms of violent conflict. But does this make global health a security issue? Indeed, given the links between poor health and poverty, is global health more properly a subject for development studies than International Relations? And should it be the focus of government ministries such as the Department for International Development in the UK, rather than the Foreign Office or Ministry of Defence?

For much of the past 50 years the relationship between health and security has been limited and unidirectional: conflict has caused health problems. These problems have been both a direct result of conflict (largely in the form of combat casualties) and indirect (e.g. the destruction of infrastructure affecting the ability of hospitals to keep working, increased prevalence of water-borne diseases as a result of disruption to the water supply, refugee flows leading to the spread of infectious disease or the overburdening of public health systems). But this was not always the case. In the nineteenth century, as trade between Europe and the rest of the world increased, so did the risk of infectious disease being brought into Europe from elsewhere. Disease was viewed as an exogenous threat which had to be dealt with by means of international cooperation and the introduction of internationally agreed health regulations. Thus the origins of international cooperation on public health lie in the security concerns of Europe in the nineteenth century. After the Second World War however, this relationship disappeared for two main reasons. First, health was presented not as a security issue but as a human right. This move was seen in the constitution establishing the World Health Organization (WHO) in 1948 and reached its high point in the 1970s with the WHO's 'Health for All' initiative. Second, during this period the perception grew that infectious diseases were being conquered, especially through the use of antibiotics. The number of deaths in the West from infectious diseases fell dramatically in the early decades following the Second World War, while in the late 1960s for the first time in history a major infectious disease, smallpox, was effectively eradicated. These successes prompted the US Surgeon General in the late 1960s to declare (perhaps apocryphally) that communicable disease had been conquered, at least for the West. What was patently clear was that this was not the case elsewhere, where living conditions and levels of poverty were much worse. Therefore global health became for the West less of a security concern than one of development.

By the late 1990s however this had begun to change. Two examples of this are the 1999 US National Intelligence Estimate on the global threat of infectious disease to the United States, and the January 2000 meeting of the

UN Security Council on HIV/AIDS. On the first, in 1999 the Central Intelligence Agency (CIA) identified a number of risks to US security arising from infectious disease, risks exacerbated by rapid globalization and the increased movement of goods and people. These included not only risks to US citizens travelling abroad, but to citizens in the US itself given the potential ease with which diseases could spread internationally as a result of travel and trade. Crucially however the CIA went further than this, arguing that infectious disease also posed a risk to international stability and to economic growth, placing it firmly in the territory of national security (CIA 2000). On the second, at its first meeting of the new millennium, the UN Security Council discussed the threat of HIV/AIDS to Africa and in Resolution 1308 warned 'that the HIV/AIDS pandemic, if unchecked, may pose a risk to stability and security'. In particular the Security Council drew attention to the effects of HIV/AIDS on social stability and on peacekeeping missions.[3] This debate raised the global political stakes on HIV/AIDS, and in subsequent years HIV/AIDS was framed not only as a humanitarian catastrophe but as a risk to national security and international stability. In the early years of the twenty-first century, health issues began to appear in statements from foreign and security ministers, while global health was discussed at a number of G8 summits, including Genoa, Gleneagles and St Petersburg, in the context both of humanitarianism and security. By the middle of the first decade of the twenty-first century a variety of health issues were therefore beginning to appear on the foreign and security agendas of Western states. Why was this?

Health as a security issue

Two factors facilitated the emergence of health as a security issue. The first of these was the growing acceptance during the 1990s of a broadened security agenda. The end of the Cold War saw security analysts shift their focus away from threats, especially military threats, to more diffuse risks. This opened the door for a more eclectic range of issues to be considered as security concerns. Further, the shift from threat to risk allowed security's focus to shift from the idea of a 'clear and present danger' to more probabilistic assessments of potential hazards. Both of these moves opened up a space whereby public health issues could be raised as security concerns. Moreover, questions were raised not only over the security agenda – those issues which were to be considered as security concerns – but also over the referent object: whose security was to be protected? Whereas the Cold War had prioritized national security, in the post-Cold War world global and human security began to be considered as legitimate concerns. Although definitions of human security varied, the very idea that risks to the individual from macro-level developments could be part of the security agenda again allowed a space for the inclusion of health as a security issue. After all, individuals generally were more likely to be at risk from new infectious diseases spread as a consequence of globalization than from ethnic conflict, environmental disasters or terrorism.

The second facilitating factor was human agency. A number of prominent individuals used their positions of power and influence to place health on the foreign and security policy agenda. Two examples of this are the former head of the World Health Organization, Gro Harlem Brundtland and President Clinton's ambassador to the UN, Richard Holbrooke. As WHO's Director General, Brundtland emphasized the changing nature of public health in a globalized world, and argued that global public health could not be divorced from broader social and political trends. Significantly it was during Brundtland's tenure that WHO coined the term 'global health security'.

The second example of individual agency is that of Richard Holbrooke, who is widely acknowledged as a key player in the securitization of HIV/AIDS. According to Barnett and Prins (2006: 360), when visiting Africa in 1999 Holbrooke realized not only the scale of the HIV/AIDS pandemic but also that existing aid-based approaches were failing to deal with the crisis. Moreover the potential social consequences of the pandemic were beginning to become apparent, including state instability. On his return to New York, Holbrooke was instrumental in placing HIV/AIDS on the Security Council's agenda. What is unclear is whether Holbrooke saw his actions as motivated solely by security concerns, or whether he saw the securitization of HIV/AIDS as a way of achieving greater political prominence and global action to help deal with the crisis. This potential for the securitization of health to act as a Trojan Horse for greater attention and assistance to the most needy is an important theme in the debate over health and security.

Neither the broadening of the security agenda nor individual agency however can explain the emergence of health as a security issue. If it was simply a by-product of the broadening agenda, then this move would have been

BOX 19.1 BRUNDTLAND ON GLOBAL HEALTH AND SECURITY

In a speech to the US Council on Foreign Relations in 1999, Gro Harlem Brundtland, Director of the World Heath Organization, argued that 'With globalization – on which [the US's] prosperity so much depends – all of humankind today paddles in a single microbial sea – and we have to conclude: there are no health sanctuaries. ... The levels of ill-health in countries constituting a majority of the world's population pose a direct threat to their own national economic and political viability, and therefore to the global economic and political interests of the United States and all other countries. Territorial dispute is no longer the prime source of conflict. It is increasingly rooted in human misery, aftermaths of humanitarian crises, shortage of food and water and the spreading of poverty and ill-health. So investing in global health is investing in national security.

(Brundtland 1999)

expected in the early to mid-1990s when the broadened agenda was being developed, not the late 1990s/early twenty-first century when it did eventually appear. And agents cannot act successfully without issues of substance with which to make their case. Rather three substantive health issues contributed to the emergence of health on the security agenda: the spread of infectious disease; the HIV/AIDS pandemic; and bioterrorism. Moreover, these three issues continue to dominate the thinking of security analysts with regard to health, though not necessarily public health specialists.

The spread of infectious disease

New infectious diseases have been emerging at an accelerated rate over recent years, averaging one a year for more than two decades. These new diseases include HIV/AIDS, SARS and H5N1, all of whose impact has been, or has the potential to be global in nature. Although this phenomenon of increased numbers of new diseases may be a by-product of the increased speed of movement of goods and people and their interaction over wider geographical areas, it may also be that changes are occurring in the microbial world which are independent of these social forces. In addition to new diseases, previously contained diseases have begun to spread and have been seen in the West. Over the past decade, for example, the USA saw its first cases of ebola, West Nile virus and monkeypox. Finally, new strains of diseases are appearing which are resistant to existing drugs, including antibiotics. Perhaps the most serious of these is TB, with cities such as New York already experiencing epidemics of this new form of the disease.[4]

But why have these developments triggered concerns in the security community? There are broadly three reasons for this. First, the spread of these diseases could pose a direct threat to the health and well-being of the very people that states are there to protect, and for the first time in perhaps half a

---

BOX 19.2 INFECTIOUS DISEASE AND GLOBALIZATION: SARS

The outbreak of SARS (severe acute respiratory syndrome) in 2002 to 2003 is a good example of the extent and speed with which new diseases can spread. The disease appears to have originated in Guandong province in southern China in November 2002 and began to spread internationally in February 2003. The World Health Organization issued global alerts on 12 and 15 March 2003, by which time the disease had already spread from China to Taiwan, Singapore, Vietnam and Canada. By the time the disease came under control in August 2003, 8,422 cases had been identified in 29 countries with 908 fatalities (WHO 2003).

century, this includes the populations of Western states. Estimates of the impact of an outbreak of avian flu transmitted from human to human suggest that perhaps 25–30 per cent of people living in the West could contract the disease, with perhaps 300,000 in the UK dying.[5] Infectious disease therefore poses an exogenous threat to the people of a state. Second, a pandemic may cause social disruption and threaten the stability of a state: confidence in the state may be reduced if it cannot provide a basic level of protection against disease; social inequalities may be highlighted as the rich or privileged obtain access to better drugs or healthcare, potentially leading to public disorder; if large numbers of people die or are unwilling/unable to go to work, public services may be placed at risk threatening the functioning of a state; violence and disorder may appear if the authorities become unable to cope and if groups feel they have nothing to lose. Thus a state may begin to fail threatening its own security. Moreover, as the US *National Security Strategy* put it, 'America [and the West] is threatened less by conquering states than we are by failing ones' (White House 2002: 1). Third, a large-scale epidemic may also contribute to economic decline by: forcing increased government spending on health as a percentage of GDP; reducing productivity due to worker absenteeism and the loss of skilled personnel; reducing investment (internal and external) due to a lack of business confidence; and by raising insurance costs for health provision. For the state involved, the costs may be highly significant, but in a globalized world the effects may be felt around the world. The relatively short-lived SARS outbreak of 2002 to 2003 led to less than a thousand deaths – individually tragic but, compared to annual deaths from HIV/AIDS, TB or malaria, statistically relatively insignificant; but the loss in trade and investment was calculated to be as much as $30 billion for the economies in Asia. The macro-economic effects of a major epidemic may therefore be very significant, threatening to make the relatively affluent poor and the already poor poorer, with a consequent impact upon the ability of states and individuals to provide for their security and well-being.

HIV/AIDS as a security issue

The HIV/AIDS pandemic has not only led to widespread humanitarian concerns, but – uniquely for a single disease – has been identified as a security issue, most significantly by the UN Security Council. The claims made in 2000 by the Security Council in Resolution 1308 have set the agenda for the subsequent debate on HIV/AIDS as a national security issue: that HIV/AIDS poses a risk to stability, to uniformed militaries and to peacekeepers, and that the spread of HIV/AIDS is exacerbated by conditions of violence. On the first of these, the effects of the disease on economies and on governance have been consistently highlighted. HIV/AIDS poses particularly severe economic problems due to the cumulative effects of the disease over a number of years; because its full effects are postponed as those infected become ill only gradually but then pose an increasing economic burden on society; and because of its disproportionate impact upon workers in what should be the most productive period of their lives (ICG 2001: 9–13, UN Secretariat 2003: xiii–xiv). Such economic decline may increase income inequalities and poverty, exacerbating or creating social and political unrest. HIV/AIDS may also lead to social and political problems. HIV infection rates are unusually high among skilled professionals (including civil servants, teachers, police and health workers) and young adults, threatening 'the very fibre of what constitutes a nation' (ICG 2001: 1). Democratic development may be harmed if societies become polarized as a consequence of HIV/AIDS, if disaffection with the political process sets in, or as a consequence of aid-dependency. The stigma of AIDS may also lead to exclusion from work and/or society, creating alienation, fatalism and anger among people, especially young people, living with HIV/AIDS. These people may become prone to criminal violence or to following violent leaders (CIA 2000, Justice Africa 2004).

The second concern focuses on the high rates of HIV infection among security forces, including the military – typically cited as being up to five times that of the general population. In sub-Saharan Africa in particular, infection rates among the military are often cited as being especially high, with a number of militaries experiencing rates above 50 per cent, those of Malawi and Zimbabwe believed to be in the order of 75–80 per cent, and elements of the South African military believed to be perhaps 90 per cent. Moreover, during periods of conflict it is believed that the risk of infection may be as much as 50–100 times that of the civilian population. The consequences of this include its impact on combat readiness and military performance. Of particular concern appears to be the potential loss of experienced military and technical specialists with 8–15 years service, the 'middle management' and technical glue which holds an organization together. Morale may also deteriorate as workloads are increased to cover for the ill; as the progressive deterioration of comrades due to AIDS is witnessed; or due to the fear of infection and the stigma associated with it. The pool of recruits may diminish as HIV+ youngsters are turned away, while the cost of treating those in the military may pose a major burden on defence budgets. If military effectiveness is reduced as a result of HIV/AIDS, or even if it is perceived to have been affected, then states may be at greater risk from internal conflict or external aggression. Moreover, there is some evidence to suggest that conflicts may be prolonged either to defer the return of HIV positive troops, or to enable them to gain sufficient money (legally or otherwise) to allow them to purchase anti-retroviral drugs to combat the disease (Elbe 2002, 2003, Heinecken 2003, ICG 2001, UNAIDS 2003).

The third concern is the impact of HIV/AIDS on peacekeeping. Peace-keepers may be at increased risk from HIV since many of the world's conflicts are in regions with a high prevalence of HIV. They may also act as vectors for the spread of the disease, especially since the top 10 contributory nations to peacekeeping operations include states with high HIV prevalence rates (such as Kenya, Nigeria and Ghana), as well as a number perceived to be at high risk (such as Ukraine, Bangladesh, Pakistan and India) (UNAIDS 2003: 6). HIV may also make it difficult for some armies to deploy peacekeeping forces, especially at short notice. In particular the attempt to devolve peacekeeping to regional powers may be hamstrung by high HIV prevalence, particularly among key African armies such as South Africa and Nigeria (Elbe 2002, Heinecken 2003).

Finally, there is a concern that conflict acts as a vector for the spread of HIV/AIDS. Soldiers, already a high-risk group, are willing to engage in even more risky behaviour in conflict regions; incidents of sexual violence increase in conflict; combat injuries may be treated in the field with infected blood; health education and surveillance may be poor in zones of conflict; soldiers returning from conflicts may bring HIV with them; conflicts create migration which may facilitate the spread of HIV; and refugee camps may have poor health education and access to condoms, but are also areas where sexual violence is rife. In addition, HIV/AIDS may act as a disincentive to end conflicts because of fears that troops from low prevalence areas may act as a Trojan Horse for the spread of the disease on their return (UNAIDS 2003).

By the middle of the first decade of the twenty-first century however, the evidence supporting these four concerns had begun to appear less clear-cut, more complex and case sensitive. For example, evidence began to appear that conflict might also constrain the spread of HIV/AIDS by limiting the ability of people to move; with the exception of Sierra Leone, there appeared to be little empirical evidence linking UN peacekeeping missions with high HIV prevalence; and AIDS awareness programmes in the military have significantly reduced the disparity in infection rates (de Waal 2005, McInnes 2006). Moreover, the causal links between HIV/AIDS and insecurity appear less robust. It is unclear how high HIV prevalence will transform societies; what intervening variables will determine the nature of such transformations; and how significant such transformations will be. Nor is it apparent that the weakness of a state's armed forces is a causal agent in either internal or external aggression. It appears far more likely to be a contributory factor, and even then secrecy over combat readiness and HIV prevalence may limit the impression of weakness.

It is tempting to argue that some of the dangers identified have been averted through preventative action, not least AIDS awareness programmes; but in retrospect the case made in 2000 was somewhat speculative, while worst case thinking and snowballing subsequently led these concerns to a position of orthodoxy which now appears less assured. This is not to say that HIV/AIDS does not create security problems. Indeed, as Laurie Garrett has commented, 'the lack of demonstrable proof of a security threat currently in place against any given state, regional, or transnational system does not mean the danger is nonexistent, or that it will not emerge as a pandemic'(Garrett 2005: 15). Rather it is to suggest that the case is at the very least more complex than originally articulated, that the threat may be less direct.

Bioterrorism

The idea of using biological agents (or pathogens) to cause disease as a weapon of war goes back several hundred years, and was a major source of concern not least during the Cold War. Following the terrorist attacks of 11 September 2001 and the mailing of anthrax spores in the USA later that same year, the possibility of a major terrorist attack using biological or chemical weapons has loomed large in the minds of Western security analysts. In its assessment of risks to the USA through to 2020, for example, the CIA concluded that a terrorist attack using biological weapons represented a major threat (CIA 2005). This risk has forged a close link between public health and national security. The covert and potentially global nature of terrorist activities, the relative ease with which materials to produce such weapons can be acquired, and the comparative simplicity in their use, have created new risks. These cannot be addressed by military means alone and have led to a flurry of national, regional and international activity aimed both at preventing the development and use of such weapons, and at improving policy responses should they be deployed. Crucial to the latter has been the development of a closer relationship between national security and public health, using public health both as a defence against such attacks and conceivably as a deterrent to the use of such weapons.

Renewed concerns over biological weapons began to emerge in the early to mid-1990s, supported by intelligence reports of a potential proliferation of materials to produce such weapons following the breakup of the Soviet Union. Political and economic instability in the region, accompanied by growing lawlessness and the rise of organized criminal groups, raised fears that materials were being sold to terrorist organizations and 'rogue states' such as Iraq, Iran, Libya, Syria, Cuba and North Korea. Suspicions were already rife that Iraq had been stockpiling anthrax, botulinum toxin, smallpox and other agents prior to the Gulf War of 1990 to 1991. Of particular concern were the relatively low costs compared to other 'weapons of mass destruction' and their comparative ease of use, making them not only a cheap alternative to nuclear weapons for states but also accessible by sub-state groups including terrorist organizations. Moreover, the use of biological weapons by Iraq against its Kurdish population in 1988, the attempt by followers of Rajneesh Bhagwan to spread salmonella in the USA, and the attack on the Tokyo subway using sarin by the Aum Shinrikyo cult in 1995, suggested a willingness to use such weapons.

Even before the events of 11 September 2001 there was a growing discussion, in the USA and other major Western countries, between the public health and security communities, of the need to improve measures to prevent and respond to a major bioterrorist attack. Efforts continued both to strengthen the 1972 Biological and Toxin Weapons Convention (BWC) and to gain intelligence, not least on potential suppliers and their customers. Attention however was also focused on public defence: on how to improve response measures, recognizing that 'we will not be able to prevent every act of

BW (biological weapon) terrorism' (Simon 1997: 428). Measures included drawing up contingency plans, identifying key targets, stockpiling vaccines and training key personnel.

The use of anthrax spores in letters to US news media and congressional offices shortly after 9/11 however brought into sudden focus the potential risks from terrorists wielding biological weapons. Initially anthrax preoccupied popular attention, but fears of other infectious agents were soon raised. High among these was smallpox, already a concern of the US government which had ordered 40 million doses of vaccine in April 2001. These heightened concerns led to a step change in activity. At the national level, Western states examined their procedures for dealing with such attacks, most significantly with the 2002 signing of the US Public Health Security and Bioterrorism Bill formally placing public health in the realm of homeland security. US efforts to improve domestic capacity included improved inspections of food entering ports, tracking biological materials, strengthened communication networks, stockpiling vaccines, and the development of new medicines (Bush 2002). Other states including the UK, Canada and Australia explored similar domestic strategies. International cooperation was demonstrated by a series of meetings addressing response and preparedness, while the WHO encouraged states to strengthen both regional and global surveillance and response measures through the Global Outbreak Alert and Response Network (GOARN, later used successfully during the 2003 SARS outbreak). In addition, a wide range of studies were commissioned by governments and other organizations into how best to meet a bioterrorist attack. The unifying themes of these actions were that the risk of attacks on the West had greatly increased, and that public health would play a key role in defending against such attacks.

Three problems however have emerged in responding to the risk of bioterror. First, there have been clear tensions between an internationally versus domestically focused strategy. Following the anthrax attacks, the USA stepped up its stockpiling of the smallpox vaccine, soon joined by other countries including the UK. Given the large-scale purchasing by a few states of the vaccine, supplies worldwide were soon scarce. Similarly, worldwide supplies of the antibiotic Cipro used to treat anthrax rapidly became scarce. This national strategy of stockpiling vaccines raised international concerns over hoarding by a few states to the detriment of others. Tensions also arose over the US government's decision to pull out of negotiations on the BWC. The priority of the USA appeared to be to focus on domestically based security measures, while others argued that a more international approach would yield better results.

This tension is also revealed in the second problem – whether it is better to try to prevent such attacks from happening or whether the priority should be on defence. The former suggests that attention should be given to international cooperation on intelligence and to the use of diplomatic efforts (including arms control) to make the supply and production of such weapons more difficult. In this, public health would be important in monitoring and surveillance of activities, but not the key element in an international strategy. The alternative approach however accepts that attacks are likely to be attempted and that a much more nationally focused strategy would be more appropriate. This would use domestic counter-terrorist agencies and 'at the border controls' to prevent biological weapons from entering the country, but would also make much greater use of public health systems in defending against such attacks.

The third problem is whether the risk has been overstated. Despite the comparatively recent use of such weapons in Iraq, Japan and the attempt to use salmonella in the USA, there remain doubts both over how easy it is for sub-state groups to gain access to or produce effective weapons and over how easy it is to use them in a manner which may cause significant loss of life. The failure to discover such weapons in Iraq only added to doubts over whether the extent of the problem had been overstated. Moreover, as Malcolm Dando has pointed out, using biological agents as weapons of mass destruction would require their use as an aerosol over large areas. The means to do this – especially against Western states – is almost wholly the preserve of states with relatively advanced militaries, not small terrorist groups (Dando 2005).

A not so perfect partnership?

Health affects every one of us – our state of well-being affects individual life, lifestyle and livelihood. Moreover, our health is often intertwined with that of the communities in which we are located, either geographically or as part of a socio-economic group. Poor communities, for example, are more likely to be at risk from TB; malaria is common in certain parts of the world but not in others. Thus health officials have long understood that well-being is as much socially determined as it is a bio-medical condition. These social determinants have an international dimension – infectious diseases, for example, can cross state boundaries. But the process of globalization has raised awareness that this international dimension is becoming more important and that the ability of national health services to protect their populations is partial in the face of such change. Health is therefore increasingly globalized (Lee 2003). With this recognition has come an increased interest on the part of the public health

---

BOX 19.3 DANDO ON BIOTERRORISM

There can be little doubt that a terrorist group at the present time could carry out some small to medium-scale biological weapons attacks. The situation in regard to a massive WMD aerosolised attack is quite different. All the technical literature and opinion maintain the view that although the problems of production and dissemination have been solved in state programmes in the past it is presently unlikely that a sub-state group would have the necessary capabilities and resources.

(Dando 2005: 40)

community in foreign and security policy – an awareness both of shared interests between these different communities and the possibilities of health issues gaining increased attention and resources through 'piggy-backing' on foreign and security policy. Simultaneous to this, security communities have become increasingly aware of health issues as security risks, most notably the three issues identified above. Thus the prospect has developed of a mutually beneficial partnership between health and security. For those on the security side of this partnership, health (and in particular public health) brings valuable tools and expertise to a range of novel problems; for those on the public health side, securitizing health raises its political profile, leading to the prospect of greater resources being devoted to urgent health needs.

This securitizing move is not unproblematic however. Three issues in particular have proved worrying, especially for the health side of the partnership. The first of these is: Who controls the agenda? At present it is clearly security policy, with global well-being lagging as a policy driver. The debate at present is dominated by those health risks which are seen as threatening the national interest, regional stability or international security; it is not about promoting a healthier world. Thus diseases which kill millions each year – including TB, malaria and diarrhoeal diseases – are not considered security risks, while bioterror (which does not rank on the list of major causes of non-natural death) dominates. Moreover, it is an agenda dominated by the West – how international health issues threaten the security interests of the West – even though the majority of those who die of preventable illnesses do so outside the West. This is not to say that Western policy more generally does not have a humanitarian dimension, though the impact of policies tends to be limited. Rather it is to say that in securitizing health, the national security interests of the West have been prioritized over the human security of the poor elsewhere.

The next two problems both follow from this control of the agenda. The second is the relatively narrow range of issues which are considered part of the global health security agenda. Infectious diseases such as TB and malaria, as well as non-communicable diseases such as tobacco-related illnesses and cardiovascular disease, are not considered to be part of the agenda despite the fact that they kill millions each year and may be mitigated by concerted international action. Tobacco sales, for example, have increased dramatically as a consequence of Western-prompted policies on the liberalization of international trade. The UK MP Frank Dobson has referred to tobacco as a 'weapon of mass destruction', but the Framework Convention on Tobacco Control provides only limited controls on the promotion and sale of tobacco. This is partly the result of the lack of an agreed conceptual basis for what is and what is not a global health security issue. But it is also a consequence of the third problem, that of the referent object – whose health is at risk and whose security? Despite health being a risk to individuals, the human security dimension has not been dominant. Rather, national security perspectives have prevailed. Tobacco is not considered a global health security issue because, despite the number of individuals who die from tobacco-related illnesses each year, there are no national security implications. On the other hand, although deaths from bioterrorism are speculative rather than real, the risk to national security is such that it is clearly entrenched on the agenda.

Conclusion

Over the past decade health issues have begun to appear on the security agenda. This has been aided by the post-Cold War shift away from military threats which pose a 'clear and present danger', to more diffuse and conceivably long-term risks. To date this attention has focused on three health-related risks: the spread of infectious disease, HIV/AIDS, and bioterrorism. With the possible exception of bioterrorism, none of these yet dominate security agendas in the West, and indeed there are still debates there over whether global health security is more of an issue for international development policy than for national security; but elsewhere in the world, particularly in those areas where HIV/AIDS prevalence is high, the risk to states is much more serious, while from a human security perspective, health risks rank among the highest causes of non-natural death. The agenda to date however has been dominated by national security concerns, and particularly those of the West, such that the WHO's term 'global health security' is in danger of meaning the national security of Western states from health risks rather than the promotion of well-being globally.

Notes

1   I would like to thank Kelley Lee for her advice and willingness to discuss with me many of the issues discussed in this chapter.
2   UNAIDS produces an annual update on HIV/AIDS infections available on its website, http://unaids.org/en/. Estimating the number of cases of HIV infection is notoriously difficult, not least because of the social stigma associated with the disease in many parts of the world.
3   The Security Council session was followed by a special session of the General Assembly on HIV/AIDS in 2001.
4   In 1991 New York City Hospital reported a series of nosocomial outbreaks of multidrug-resistant TB (MDR TB). The city had already been experiencing a growth in TB associated with high numbers of people living with HIV/AIDS and immigrants to the USA.
5   Estimates at this stage are very uncertain and depend both on the effectiveness of public health responses and the nature of the mutation allowing the disease to spread – most mutations reduce the potency of a virus.

Further reading

Stefan Elbe, *The Strategic Implications of HIV/AIDS* (Adelphi Paper 357. Oxford: Oxford University Press for IISS, 2003). A classic orthodox account of HIV/AIDS as a security problem.

David Fidler, 'Fighting the axis of illness: HIV/AIDS, human rights, and U.S. foreign policy', *Harvard Human Rights Journal*, 17 (2004): 99–136. Compares US strength and global leadership with its failure to address the HIV/AIDS pandemic in Africa, and raises the question of material might and the responsibility to protect others against illness.

Ilona Kickbusch, 'Influence and opportunity: reflections on the US role in global public health', *Health Affairs*, 21 (2002): 131–141. Influential article arguing that the USA could use health as a tool of 'soft power' in addition to its humanitarian benefits.

Kelley Lee, *Globalization and Health* (Basingstoke: Palgrave Macmillan, 2003). An excellent introduction. Although its focus is an examination of how different aspects of globalization have impacted upon health, its utility is much broader than that.

Colin McInnes and Kelley Lee, 'Health, security and foreign policy', *Review of International Studies*, 32(1) (2006): 5–23. Begins by examining the rise of health as a foreign and security policy issue before critiquing its narrow focus and questioning who is served by this move.

PART 3
INSTITUTIONS

ALLIANCES

REGIONAL INSTITUTIONS

THE UNITED NATIONS

Alliances

John S. Duffield with Cynthia Michota and Sara Ann Miller

▌ **Abstract**

This chapter explores the concept and theories of alliances, paying particular attention to the question of alliance persistence and disintegration. After discussing what alliances are, the chapter surveys the scholarly literature on why alliances form and fall apart. It then reviews the somewhat puzzling case of NATO, which many observers expected would not long outlive the Cold War. The chapter asks how well existing theories explain NATO's persistence and concludes with theoretically informed observations about the alliance's future prospects.

▌ **Introduction: Why study alliances?**

Alliances are one of the most significant phenomena in security studies and world politics more generally. Indeed, the eminent American political scientist George Modelski once described alliance as 'one of a dozen or so key terms of International Relations' (1963: 773). For hundreds of years, great powers, and many smaller ones as well, have regularly formed, acted through, and sometimes broken alliances. Alliance diplomacy has typically constituted a major component of states' external policies.

Why is this so? Because alliances are one of the most valuable instruments for advancing a state's interests. In particular, alliances are a primary tool for enhancing a state's security in the face of external and sometimes internal threats. Focusing on the international realm, Kenneth Waltz (1979: 118) has noted that the means available to states for achieving their ends fall into just two categories: internal efforts and external efforts, including moves to strengthen and enlarge one's own alliance or to weaken and strengthen an opposing one. And for smaller states with limited resources, reliance on alliances may be the only option. Thus the formation and use of alliances is a frequent response to the dangers of aggression and the opportunities for aggrandizement present in the international system.

Not surprisingly, alliances have been quite common in modern history. The most comprehensive database on alliances, based on the Alliance Treaty Obligations and Provisions (ATOP) project, lists a total of some 648 alliances between 1815 and 2003 (Leeds *et al.* 2002).[1] Most alliances have been quite small, with the average number of members being just over three. But the major powers and European states have turned to alliances quite frequently. Just six European powers – the United Kingdom, France, Germany, Austria-Hungary, Italy, and Russia/Soviet Union – account for one-quarter of all alliance memberships during that period.

Arguably, alliances have also had a major impact on international relations. After all, states would presumably not form or maintain alliances if they were not thought to serve the states' interests in ways that were otherwise impossible or less cost-effective. In addition, a number of studies have established that alliances have been an important determinant of the outbreak, spread and results of militarized conflicts. As Stephen Walt has written, 'The formation and cohesion of international alliances can have profound effects on the security of individual states and help determine both the probability and likely outcome of war' (1997: 156).

This chapter explores the concept and theories of alliances, paying particular attention to the question of alliance persistence and disintegration. After surveying what the scholarly literature has to say about the issue, it examines the case of the North Atlantic Treaty Organization (NATO) after the Cold War.

Definitions: What is an alliance?

The conclusions that one draws about the causes and effects of alliances depend very much on what one counts as an alliance. Unfortunately, the process of developing theories of alliances has been complicated by the use of widely varying definitions.

A number of influential definitions of alliances have been overly broad. For example, Walt, in his seminal study of the origins of alliances, defined alliance as 'a formal or informal relationship of security cooperation between two or more sovereign states' (1987: 1). An almost identical definition was used by Michael Barnett and Jack Levy in their path-breaking work on the domestic sources of alliances (1991: 370). More recently, Patricia Weitsman has described alliances as 'bilateral or multilateral agreements to provide some element of security to the signatories' (2004: 27).

Such broad definitions are reflected in quantitative coding schemes. In their efforts to be comprehensive, the most complete alliance databases have grouped together defensive alliances, offensive alliances, non-aggression pacts, neutrality pacts and consultation agreements. Further complicating matters is the fact that a high percentage of these so-called 'alliances' – more than half (364 of 648) in the case of the ATOP dataset – consist of two or more types.

There are at least two potential problems with such broad definitions of alliances. First, they may be so expansive as to encompass just about any imaginable security arrangement between states. Of particular concern is the fact that they blur the important distinction between alliances, on the one hand, and collective security arrangements, on the other, which involve fundamentally different orientations. Alliances are primarily, if not exclusively, outwardly oriented, intended to enhance the security of their members *vis-à-vis* external parties. In sharp contrast, collective security arrangements and related phenomena such as arms control agreements are designed to enhance the security of their participants *vis-à-vis* each other.

The other problem is the failure to distinguish between various forms of security cooperation. The above definitions would seem to embrace all manner of security cooperation, no matter how innocuous. Thus they include alliances that might be limited to supportive diplomacy or economic aid with security objectives. What has traditionally distinguished alliances from many other security arrangements between states, however, is the emphasis that they place on military forms of assistance, especially the use of force.

Such considerations suggest the need for a subset of alliance definitions that take these important distinctions into account. Four decades ago, Robert Osgood defined alliance as 'a formal agreement that pledges states to co-operate in using their military resources against a specific state or states and usually obligates one or more of the signatories to use force, or to consider (unilaterally or in consultation with allies) the use of force in specified circumstances' (1968: 17). Similarly, Glenn Snyder, in his magnum opus *Alliance Politics*, wrote that 'Alliances are formal associations of states for the use (or nonuse) of military force, in specified circumstances, against states outside their own membership'. He went on to emphasize that '[t]heir primary function is to pool military strength against a common enemy, not to protect alliance members from each other' (1997: 4). Even Walt later amended his conception of alliances, noting that 'the defining feature of any alliance is a commitment for mutual military support against some external actor(s) in some specified set of circumstances' (1997: 157).

These definitions clearly exclude a number of agreements that have sometimes been treated as alliances. In particular, they would seem to militate against the inclusion of pledges by states to refrain from engaging in aggression against one another, promises to remain neutral in the event of a military conflict with a third party, and commitments to consult in the event of a crisis that threatens to lead to war. Nevertheless, hundreds of security arrangements meet the more stringent criteria contained in them.

Before proceeding, it may be useful to consider one further distinction. Even these more restrictive definitions encompass both defensive and offensive alliances. Primarily offensive alliances, however, are relatively rare and almost always short-lived. Of the 277 offensive and/or defensive alliances listed in the ATOP database, only 14 were purely offensive. Of those 14, moreover, only four lasted more than two years, and all began and ended during the nineteenth century.[2] In view of these considerations, the remainder of this chapter will focus on alliances with a defensive purpose, including those that might also have had an offensive element (about 25 per cent).

Even when the focus is limited to defensive international military alliances, there are a number of possible important issues to explore. Among the topics that have received the most attention from scholars are the following:

- *Alliance formation*: Under what conditions do states form alliances? Who aligns with whom?

- *Alliance dynamics*: How are alliance policies and strategies determined? How are burdens shared among alliance members? What determines the relative degree of alliance cohesion?

- *Alliances and state behaviour*: Do states honour their alliance commitments when called upon to do so?

- *Alliances and war*: Do alliances make war more or less likely? In particular, do alliances deter aggression against their members? Do alliances embolden their members to act with less restraint? When war occurs, do alliances improve their members' prospects of victory?

Clearly, these are far too many questions to explore thoroughly in a single book, let alone in a short chapter such as this. Motivated by what some would describe as NATO's puzzling persistence after the Cold War, the remainder of this chapter will focus on the question of why some alliances endure while others disintegrate.

Explanations of alliance persistence and collapse

Most international military alliances have ended at one point or another, but some have lived to a ripe old age while others have quickly fallen apart. How long have alliances tended to last? Of the approximately 263 defensive alliances (both purely defensive and with a combination of both defensive and offensive elements) in existence between 1815 and 2003, the mean duration was 13.4 years with a standard deviation of 13.1 years. Interestingly, defensive alliances with no offensive component have tended to last nearly twice as long on average as those with an offensive component, with average life spans of 15.1

years versus 8.2 years. This striking difference exists even though some 42 of the 197 purely defensive alliances in the ATOP database had not yet terminated as of 2003.

Have more recent alliances tended to last longer than earlier ones? Although such longitudinal comparisons may be problematic, there is some evidence to suggest that they do. Consider the periods 1815 to 1865 and 1945 to 1995. Both are long intervals of relative peace immediately following a major power war. During the first period, the mean alliance duration was 8.7 years, with a standard deviation of 10.3 years. During the latter period the average life span was 17.7 years, with a standard deviation of 13.7 years. Similar differences in durability are found even if one considers only purely defensive alliances, even though more than one-third (42 of 124) of those between 1945 and 1995 were ongoing as of 2003.

What factors cause alliances to persist or to collapse? And can they account for this seeming temporal shift in alliance longevity? One obvious factor is major war and the shifts in the map of international politics that such wars can occasion. Of the approximately 40 alliances formed before 1870, only two outlived the wars of German unification. Likewise, only two of the alliances in existence before the First World War remained after that conflict was over. And only five of the alliances formed before the Second World War, including such peripheral pairings as Turkey–Afghanistan and Russia–Mongolia, remained standing when the conflagration came to an end. In other words, major wars tend to sweep the landscape clean of alliances.

Of greater interest, then, are the factors other than war that help alliances to endure or cause them to fall apart. The following subsections examine a number of such factors. The analysis is limited, however, to those theories that seem most relevant to the question of NATO's persistence following the Cold War. It does not aspire to provide a truly comprehensive survey of the causes of alliance persistence and collapse that have been hypothesized, although it encompasses most of the prominent ones.

Theories of alliance formation

The first place to look is at explanations of alliance formation. Such an approach may at first seem counter-intuitive. But, arguably, as long as the factors that caused the alliance to form in the first place remain in place, then the alliance will endure. Should those conditions change, however, the alliance may lose the glue that held it together and fall apart.

In principle, states can freely join alliances. In practice, however, they do not enter into such arrangements lightly, since alliance membership has costs as well as potential benefits. Among those costs may be the loss of autonomy and the creation of dependence. Thus, we need to ask, under what circumstances are states willing to assume and bear these costs? For the purposes of this chapter, the most relevant theories of alliance formation fall into two categories: those that emphasize international determinants and those that focus on domestic factors.

INTERNATIONAL DETERMINANTS: CAPABILITIES AGGREGATION MODELS

The most prominent international explanations of alliance formation are associated with the realist school of International Relations. Also known as capabilities aggregation models, they emphasize how states form alliances in order to combine their military capabilities and thereby improve their security positions. But when precisely will states do so?

The most parsimonious explanation is balance-of-power theory (Waltz 1979: 117–123). It posits that states form alliances to balance the power of other states, especially when they are unable to balance power through their individual efforts or when the costs of such internal balancing exceed those of alliance membership. From this perspective, unbalanced power alone represents a threat to the survival of less powerful states. Therefore, two or more relatively weak states, when confronted with a much more powerful state, will ally.[3]

Clearly, balance-of-power theory can also serve as a theory of alliance persistence and disintegration. In this case, shifts in the international distribution of power may threaten the existence of established alliances. For example, the previously predominant state may decline, to the point where an alliance of other states is no longer required to balance its power. Indeed, with the passage of time, an alliance member may become the most powerful state, prompting its erstwhile allies to cut their ties and perhaps even to form counterbalancing alliances against it.

An important refinement of balance-of-power theory is balance-of-threat theory. Sometimes, alliances appear to be unbalanced in terms of power. For example, during much of the Cold War, the alliances centred on the USA were more powerful, as measured on a number of indices of capability, than those revolving around the Soviet Union. Walt addressed such apparent anomalies by arguing that states form alliances in response to common threats, not just power. Although aggregate power is an important component of threat, it is not the only one. How threatening a particular state appears to be is also a function of its geographical proximity, its offensive capabilities and the aggressiveness of its intentions. Thus the Soviet Union, by virtue of its relative proximity, its massive ground forces and its hostile ideology, seemed to pose much more of a threat to its strong but less powerful neighbours, such as France, West Germany, Japan and Britain, who chose to ally instead with the USA (Walt 1985, 1987).

By the same token, balance-of-threat theory should also illuminate the question of alliance durability and collapse. A decline in the magnitude of the threat posed by an adversary will cause an alliance to weaken or dissolve. This may happen, moreover, even in the absence of any shift in overall power, if, for example, an adversary significantly mutes its offensive military capabilities or seems to moderate its intentions.

Some scholars have noted that states may also use alliances to manage, constrain and control their partners (Osgood 1968, Schroeder 1976, Weitsman

2004). Obviously, this function is contingent upon the existence of some external balancing purpose; otherwise, we could not speak of the arrangement as an alliance. However, assuming that the condition of a more powerful or threatening third party is met, this function can nevertheless be an important, albeit secondary, one. Although this perspective may not be especially helpful for explaining alliance formation, it may shed additional light on the dynamics of alliance disintegration. In this case, if the ally that the alliance is intended, at least in part, to contain becomes too threatening or too powerful to manage successfully, then the alliance will not long survive.

DOMESTIC DETERMINANTS

Balance-of-power theory may be excessively crude as an explanation of alliance formation, persistence and collapse. In contrast, balance-of-threat theory represents a more nuanced approach, but this refinement comes at the cost of other analytical problems. After all, is it always so obvious which state will be regarded as a threat by others? In particular, when will a state be regarded as harbouring aggressive intentions? Threat perception may depend as much, if not more, on the internal characteristics of states, a subject to which we now turn.

Fortunately, scholars have been equally productive at identifying possible domestic determinants of alliance formation. One set of explanations focuses on similarities and differences in the culture, ideologies and political institutions of states. The general argument is that, other things being equal, states will tend to ally with states whose political orientations are similar to their own (e.g. Walt 1987). Thus conservative monarchies will prefer alliances with other monarchies, dictatorships with dictatorships, liberal democracies with liberal democracies, and so on.

Scholars have advanced several interrelated reasons for this tendency. Similar value systems may generate common interests and common interpretations of what constitutes a threat. In the case of states sharing a formal ideology, such as Marxism-Leninism, they may even be operating under an explicit injunction to join forces in the face of a hostile international environment. Not least important, forming an alliance with like-minded states may enhance the domestic legitimacy of a weak regime by suggesting that it is part of a broader, popular movement (Walt 1987: 34–35).

Such arguments also suggest possible causes of alliance disintegration. Most obviously, a sudden regime change in one partner or another as the result of a revolution, coup or other internal upheaval will immediately loosen the bonds of affinity that held the alliance together. Even more gradual changes in political outlook can have the same effect over a longer period. And in some cases, tensions may arise even among states with a common ideology, since it may dictate that national interests must be subordinated to a single authoritative leadership (Walt 1987: 35–36).

In view of such considerations, scholars have suggested that alliances among liberal democratic states are likely to be especially strong and resilient (Gaubatz

1996). One reason is the relative stability of public preferences and the greater continuity of national leadership. Although different administrations may come and go, the democratic process ensures that leadership transitions occur smoothly and abrupt policy shifts are unlikely. In addition, the international commitments associated with alliances become more deeply embedded in domestic law and institutions. That tendency, combined with a more general respect for legal commitments, enhances the ability of leaders in liberal democracies to tie the hands of their successors.

Alliance institutionalization and socialization

Thus far, the discussion has been limited to explanations of alliance formation that may also shed light on the question of alliance duration. Despite their differences, these theories have in common the idea that when the conditions that promoted the creation of an alliance are no longer present, we should expect the alliance to dissolve. There is, however, another set of factors and processes that can promote alliance persistence even in the face of significant changes in those formative conditions.

INSTITUTIONALIZATION

One of these is alliance institutionalization. Some alliances are endowed with important institutional characteristics from the outset, and some may become increasingly institutionalized over time, with important implications for their staying power. Two particular dimensions of alliance institutionalization stand out.

First, alliances may include or develop intergovernmental organizations to facilitate cooperation among their members. These organizations often include a formal bureaucracy with a staff, budget and physical location. Although presumably of use to the alliance members, such bureaucracies are also actors in their own right with some degree of autonomy and an inherent interest in perpetuating themselves (Bennett 1997, Walt 1997). As Robert McCalla (1996) has noted, such actors may engage in various types of behaviour to ensure the organization's survival. For example, they may actively resist change; they may affirm the necessity of the organization; and they may try to manage change by promoting modifications in the alliance's roles and missions that will maintain member state support while not threatening the organization's core functions.

Second, alliances may contain or acquire institutional capabilities that can be used for tasks beyond those for which they were originally designed (Walt 1997, Wallander 2000). Thus even when an alliance's original *raison d'être* fades, member states may find that they can readily employ such institutional assets to address new threats and security concerns. This tendency will be especially pronounced when states are risk averse or the costs of maintaining pre-existing capabilities are clearly less than those of creating new ones from scratch.

The overall implication of such reasoning is that alliances characterized by high levels of institutionalization will last longer on average. Of course, some scholars may reply that the level of institutionalization of an alliance is itself a function of other determinants of alliance formation and persistence. For example, states facing particularly acute threats may choose to create especially capable alliance organizations, or liberal democracies may find it easier to establish and abide by the additional constraints associated with alliance institutions. Once established, however, such alliance institutions may assume a life of their own and exert an independent impact on subsequent member behaviour. Their consequences cannot simply be reduced to the influence of other factors.

In fact, there has been considerable variation in the initial level of institutionalization of alliances. Of the agreements establishing the 263 defensive alliances in the ATOP dataset, 70 have contained a named organization with regularly scheduled meetings or a stand-alone organization with a permanent bureaucracy; 28 agreements provided for an integrated military command among the allies; and 63 have called for official contact among national militaries during peacetime or committed the members to conducting a common defence policy.

Moreover, the initial degree of alliance institutionalization has tended to increase over time, suggesting a possible explanation for the greater longevity of more recently formed alliances. Although some 150 (57 per cent) of the 263 defensive alliances were established following the Second World War, 36 (88 per cent) of the 41 with a permanent bureaucracy date from the post-war era, as do 21 (75 per cent) of those providing for an integrated military command and 49 (78 per cent) of those calling for close military contacts. Nevertheless, such indices of institutionalization leave much to be desired, since they do not directly measure organizational autonomy or the fungibility of institutional assets. Moreover, the existing data do not yet capture changes in the level of institutionalization that may occur after the alliance is established.

SOCIALIZATION

Another process that can promote alliance longevity is the socialization of member states, or more precisely, of their political elites and possibly their general publics. Alliance-related social interactions can lead to the development of more similar worldviews and even a common identity. Thus, as Walt has noted, an alliance may persist because its members come to see themselves as integral parts of a larger political community (1997: 168).

Scholars have lamented that the processes of socialization in international relations are undertheorized and poorly understood (Johnston 2001, Checkel 2005). Nevertheless, it is possible to identify a number of mechanisms through which alliances might promote the socialization of their members, both directly and indirectly. For example, institutionalized alliances may facilitate substantial contact among elites through regular meetings. Within formal organizational structures, both civilian and military personnel seconded from member governments will often work side-by-side with their counterparts from other countries. In addition, similar to the organizational arguments presented above, international civil servants may actively seek to cultivate a sense of community among elites and attentive publics through their pronouncements and lobbying activities.

Socialization need not be limited to highly institutionalized alliances, however. The existence of even a weakly institutionalized alliance between two states may reinforce or lead to other connections between the members that facilitate socialization. Because allied states have less to fear from one another than from third parties, other things being equal, they may be more likely to engage in trade and to be receptive to the exchange of capital, technology, information, ideas and people. And as the eminent political scientist Karl Deutsch (1957) argued some five decades ago, it is through such mundane material and ideational flows that political communities may be forged.

The case of NATO after the Cold War

What light does alliance theory shed on the important case of NATO? And what can an examination of NATO after the Cold War contribute to alliance theory?

Background: NATO's origins and evolution during the Cold War

NATO, along with a handful of other alliances formed in the years immediately following the Second World War, is one of the longest lived alliances. It dates back to 1949, when the North Atlantic Treaty was signed in Washington DC, and then ratified by the 12 original members. Although the treaty does not refer to any particular adversary, it was clearly a response to the growing threat that appeared to be posed by the hostile ideology and military power of the Soviet Union. At the same time, at least some members also viewed the alliance as an insurance policy, provided primarily by the USA, against the then admittedly distant prospect of a resurgent Germany. As NATO's first Secretary General, Lord Hastings Ismay, reportedly remarked, the purpose of the alliance was threefold: to keep the Russians out, the Americans in, and the Germans down.

The alliance's initial organizational expression was extremely modest. The treaty called for only a council and a defence committee. In contrast, the Brussels Treaty Organization, founded a year earlier, had a much more elaborate organization, including a military command structure and regional planning groups. And so things remained until mid-1950, when the Korean War abruptly altered Western attitudes about the imminence of the military threat.

In response, the members quickly put the 'O' in NATO. They established a council of representatives in permanent session in Paris and, over time, an increasingly complex intergovernmental apparatus for consultation and joint decision-making. They created an international staff, headed by a secretary general, to serve the council. And, not least important, they set up a military committee and an elaborate integrated military planning and command structure, the most prominent officer of which would be the Supreme Allied Commander Europe (SACEUR).

This is not the place to go into detail about the first four decades of NATO's history. Suffice it to say that the alliance suffered its share of internal stresses and strains. Indeed, disagreement on one important matter or another was a nearly constant theme (e.g. Osgood 1962, Daalder 1991, Duffield 1995). There were intense debates on such questions as how much emphasis to place on nuclear versus conventional weapons in NATO's military strategy, how many conventional forces each member should provide, and whether and how to modernize the alliance's nuclear arsenal. In the 1960s, France withdrew from the alliance's military structures, precipitating the sudden transfer of NATO's civilian and military headquarters to new quarters in Belgium.

What appears most important in retrospect, however, is that the alliance survived the many challenges to its internal cohesion that arose during those decades and even outlasted the Soviet Union itself. Indeed, NATO's persistence during the Cold War is rarely, if ever, discussed, perhaps because it has subsequently seemed inevitable. After all, the Soviet Union continued to pose a serious political-military threat to the alliance's members, and, secondarily, NATO proved to be an effective vehicle for harnessing West Germany's tremendous military potential without re-creating destabilizing security dilemmas in Western Europe.

The puzzle of NATO's post-Cold War persistence

Instead, what has seemed most puzzling and, as a result, has been the object of considerable inquiry has been NATO's survival after the Cold War. Even before the disintegration of the Soviet Union and especially thereafter, some International Relations scholars argued that the alliance's days, or at least its years, were numbered and that it would sooner or later fall apart (e.g. Mearsheimer 1990, Waltz 1993). The principal argument offered was the absence of a compelling external threat. With the end of the Cold War and the Soviet Union, the NATO members would no longer see any imperative to maintain the alliance, and it would soon lapse into ineffectuality, even if it continued to exist on paper. Later in the 1990s, Walt offered the more general argument that alliances will tend to be less robust in a multipolar world because major powers will possess more options as their numbers increase (1997: 163). Thus, he concluded, 'prudence suggests that existing alliance commitments can no longer be taken for granted' (1997: 164).

These predictions proved, at a minimum, to be premature. Rather than go out of business, NATO has, at least in some ways, thrived since 1990. It has added 11 new members, nearly doubling in size. Forces under NATO command have engaged in extensive combat operations in places such as Bosnia, Kosovo and Afghanistan. Indeed, the core operational element of the treaty, Article V, which obligates members to provide assistance should one or more of them be the object of an armed attack, was invoked for the first time, following the terrorist actions of 11 September 2001. All in all, NATO has exhibited what might be regarded as a surprising degree of durability and robustness.

Explaining NATO's persistence

Can NATO's post-Cold War persistence be accounted for in terms of the existing explanations of alliance persistence identified above? Are there any aspects of the alliance's recent history that do not fit these theories? What other explanations may be adduced to account for these anomalies?

Before proceeding, there is one methodological issue that should be aired. Some of the explanations of alliance persistence have in fact been developed with the case of NATO after the Cold War in mind. Since the goal of this chapter is not to test theories but rather to use them to illuminate a particular instance, this circularity poses no troubling methodological issues. But it does, at a minimum, raise the question of whether such explanations are in fact likely to find applications elsewhere, even though their underlying logic may be sound.

Some might argue that there is no puzzle to be explained because NATO is no longer an alliance. Rather, it has been transformed into something else, perhaps a regional collective security arrangement or what Wallander and Keohane (1999) have called a security management institution. Such an argument, however, would still beg the question of how and why NATO was able to perform this feat of re-inventing itself.

The first place to turn for answers is the explanations that emphasize the international determinants of alliance persistence. Here we might note three principal reasons for NATO's longevity. One is the residual threat posed by the remnants of the Soviet Union, notably Russia. Although greatly diminished in power and geographically separated from NATO Europe by an additional layer of buffer states, Russia nevertheless continued to possess a military capability second to none on the continent and by far the most lethal nuclear arsenal. Compounding this enduring disparity in raw capabilities was much uncertainty about Russia's future intentions. Russia's experiment with democracy was troubled from the outset, and recent years have been marked by renewed efforts by Russia to assert itself, sometimes by coercive means, on the world stage.

A second external factor was the emergence of new threats that were largely shared by NATO members. The first to emerge, even before the Cold War was officially interred, were instability and bloody civil conflicts on or near NATO's borders, especially in the Balkans. Apart from the humanitarian imperatives that such conflicts generated, some had the potential to spill over into or draw in neighbouring states, raising the possibility of a wider conflagration. Concern about regional conflicts was followed by the growing threat of international terrorism. To be sure, NATO as an organization has thus far played a relatively minor role in the overall efforts of its members, chiefly the USA, to combat terrorists (de Nevers 2007). Nevertheless, it has made important contributions, most notably its assumption of the command of the International Security Assistance Force in Afghanistan.

Not to be overlooked is the continuing intra-alliance function that NATO has played in ensuring friendly relations among its members. Certainly, this function is less important than it was during the early years of the Cold War, when memories of the Second World War were still fresh, and it has been increasingly assumed by the European Union. Still, NATO's post-Cold War role in this regard has not been insignificant, especially its role in allaying potential concerns about a newly unified Germany. By increasing transparency, further denationalizing security policies and subtly balancing power, the alliance has helped to assure its members that they have nothing to fear from one another (Duffield 1994/95). German leaders in particular have recognized the value of maintaining NATO as a vital organization for the purpose of reassuring their neighbours (Duffield 1998).

What about NATO's institutionalization and the socialization of its members over time? Clearly, NATO has acquired a substantial organizational structure. Overall, more than 5,000 civilians work for NATO, with 1,200 of them concentrated in an international staff at the alliance's headquarters in Brussels. There is little evidence to suggest, however, that this bureaucracy has exercised much influence over the relevant actions of the member countries (McCalla 1996). Although the secretary general and his staff have sometimes played a critical role in facilitating cooperation among members (Hendrickson 2006), the key decisions concerning the perpetuation of the alliance since the end of the Cold War have been entirely consistent with pre-existing national interests and priorities.

Arguably more important in explaining NATO's persistence has been the fungibility of its institutional assets (Wallander 2000). In addition to the civilian bureaucracy, NATO had developed an elaborate integrated military planning and command structure and associated joint military assets, which made it unique among peacetime alliances. Although these assets were developed with Cold War challenges and contingencies in mind, they have proved to be remarkably adaptable to the new threat environment. In particular, they have enabled NATO and its members to take a number of actions, such as the operations in Bosnia and Kosovo, that other alliances or ad hoc groupings would have found difficult, if not impossible, to mount. Here, however, we must acknowledge a close, if not symbiotic, relationship between the emergence of new threats and NATO's institutional ability to deal with them. Neither factor by itself would have provided a sufficient rationale for maintaining the alliance.

Finally, we turn to the question of socialization within NATO. This is perhaps the most difficult explanation to evaluate. There is some evidence that the views of government officials and military commanders have been altered by their close association with alliance counterparts (Tuschhoff 1999). It is not clear, however, how extensive or consequential such changes may have been. Certainly, it would be difficult to conclude that interpersonal intra-alliance interactions have altered national identities or worldviews in ways that may be said to have had a measurable impact on national policies towards NATO since the end of the Cold War. Perhaps more important have been the broader contacts, especially those of a transatlantic nature, that have been facilitated and nurtured by the existence of NATO over the years. The substantial movement of goods, investments, ideas and people has created close societal ties between the two sides of the Atlantic. But here, too, it would be nigh impossible to draw a direct link between them and NATO's persistence.

Of course, numerous though they be, the above explanations do not exhaust the possibilities. Thus before concluding, it is worth considering some additional reasons that may be unique to the case of NATO and thus impossible to generalize to other alliances. One is NATO's utility as a tool for political reform. Since the breakup of the Soviet empire, NATO countries have employed the prospect of membership to promote liberal democratic practices and institutions, such as civilian control of the military and transparency in defence budgets, in the countries of Central, Eastern and Southeastern Europe. Although these efforts may be viewed as part of the alliance's overall strategy for enhancing the security of its members, they constitute an unconventional approach by historical standards, to say the least.

Another reason for NATO's longevity may be its usefulness as an enforcement arm of the UN Security Council. During the Cold War, the two security organizations had little or nothing to do with one another, and it took the trauma of the conflict in Bosnia to prompt the first halting steps towards coordination. Now, however, NATO has a long track record of enforcing Security Council resolutions. To be sure, the member countries have used the alliance in this way only where doing so served their interests, but these interests may be increasingly broadly defined, as suggested by the assistance that the alliance has provided in a situation as geographically remote and as unrelated to traditional security concerns as Darfur.

Conclusion: alliance theory and the future of NATO

The above analysis, despite its necessary brevity, suggests the usefulness of alliance theory for illuminating the reasons for NATO's persistence after the Cold War and, more generally, for understanding international relations. Indeed, alliance theory may be too useful, insofar as the case of NATO tends to affirm the utility of multiple approaches. Typically, social scientists search for cases that will differentiate more decisively among alternative theories on the basis of their explanatory power. But that was not the goal of this chapter. Rather, the NATO case was chosen because of its practical importance in a world where significant threats to the security of states still exist. Whether or not one can draw broader conclusions about the conditions influencing the longevity of alliances is beside the point. Indeed, given the many unusual, if not unique, features of NATO, any attempts to generalize are likely to be misleading.

Instead, we might content ourselves by concluding with some discussion of what alliance theory can say about the future of NATO. Here, the theory is less useful, although no less useful than other theories when it comes to prognostication. Perhaps the best that it can do is to draw attention to the types of factors that are likely to be determinative, even if no particular weights or probabilities can be attached to them. Among the most important will be the presence or absence of threats that are sufficiently shared and intense so as to cause the NATO countries to continue to see value in addressing those threats in a collective manner. Closely related will be the ability to adapt NATO's institutions, especially in ways that are less costly than institutional alternatives, so that they can continue to address the evolving spectrum of threats.

From this perspective, NATO faces at least two significant challenges. One is a growing divergence in the principal security concerns facing NATO members. This divergence is partly a result of the alliance's successful enlargement after the Cold War, which necessarily widened the range of concerns. While older members may especially value NATO for its role in promoting stability beyond the alliance's borders, some of the newer members may view it primarily as a means of providing security in the face of a potentially revanchist Russia. Although these varying motives for maintaining NATO may complement one another, they can nevertheless generate strains when it comes to establishing alliance priorities and deciding on concrete courses of action. Further complicating matters is the emergence of new threats that may not always, or even often, be best addressed through NATO. Most obvious here is the challenge posed by international terrorism, which has prompted rather divergent responses among the members of the alliance.

The other challenge is the existence of promising institutional alternatives, especially for the European members of NATO. Since the early 1990s, the European Union (EU) has made great strides towards the development of common policies and policy-making structures in the areas of foreign, security and even defence policy. Thus far, the leaders of NATO and EU countries (many of whom are one and the same) have succeeded in ensuring that the two sets of institutions and their activities remain compatible with one another. But in view of the many tensions that have roiled transatlantic relations in recent years, it is not difficult to imagine circumstances in which European leaders would decide to assign clear priority to the use of EU structures, calling into question the preservation of NATO in anything like its present form.

Notes

1   The ATOP data are available at http://atop.rice.edu/.
2   The mean duration of the 14 purely offensive alliances was 4.4 years, with a standard deviation of 6.5 years.
3   An important exception to this general rule may occur when one state becomes so powerful that no combination of other states can balance its power. In that case, other states may choose to 'bandwagon' with the predominant state (Waltz 1979: 126).

Further reading

The best recent overview of the subject of alliances is Glenn Snyder, *Alliance Politics* (Ithaca, NY: Cornell University Press, 1997).

A much earlier, but still useful, survey is George Liska, *Nations in Alliance: The Limits of Interdependence* (Baltimore, MD: Johns Hopkins Press, 1962).

The two most thorough examinations of alliance formation and persistence are Stephen Walt, *The Origins of Alliances* (Ithaca, NY: Cornell University Press, 1987), and Patricia A. Weitsman, *Dangerous Alliances: Proponents of Peace, Weapons of War* (Stanford, CA: Stanford University Press, 2004).

Perhaps the most authoritative and up-to-date history of NATO is Lawrence S. Kaplan, *NATO Divided, NATO United: The Evolution of an Alliance* (Westport, CT: Praeger, 2004).

CHAPTER 21

Regional Institutions

Louise Fawcett

CONTENTS

Abstract

This chapter considers the role of regional institutions in the provision of international security. It looks at the history and development of regionalism in the security sphere, and the evolving relationship between the United Nations (UN) and regional institutions. Employing a wide historical and comparative perspective, it considers both the conditions behind the growth of regional security projects, and explanations for their success and failure. Although there has been increasing demand for regional security provision, reflected in the growth and development of institutions, their record is mixed, showing considerable variation from region to region, depending on both local conditions and interests of external powers. It is also subject to debate: there is little consensus about the value of international institutions in security affairs on the one hand, and the comparative advantage of regional institutions over global actors such as the UN on the other. Despite such limitations however, regional institutions have become increasingly important in security provision worldwide, and their roles are recognized by multilateral institutions, states and non-state actors.

Introduction

Viewed from the perspective of the early twenty-first century, the rise of the regional security institution over the past half century looks impressive. Prior to the Second World War, there were few formal international institutions and even fewer dealing explicitly with security matters: the main exception was the League of Nations. Since then their numbers have grown steadily if unevenly. By the end of the twentieth century, of a growing array of intergovernmental regional organizations (Diehl 2005), over 25 included a commitment to security provision – in Europe, Africa, the Americas, Asia and the Middle East/Islamic world (see Table 21.1). When one considers that much earlier institutional growth was identified primarily with economic integration this is particularly notable.

Equally impressive is the range of their activities: from peacekeeping and dispute settlement to arms control and foreign policy coordination. Box 21.1 highlights the diverse security roles of a selected group of regional organizations.

Further, while they have become more active in their own right, more and more regional institutions have also become involved in collaborative security ventures, typically with the UN, but also with other regional/cross-regional institutions, and an array of non-governmental organizations (Pugh and Sidhu 2003). This collaboration is particularly evident today in the area of peace operations (see Chapter 27, this volume). Since the 1990s a growing number of major peacekeeping operations have counted on the participation of the UN and a variety of regional organizations. At the end of 2005, some 15 regional organizations were involved in collaborative peacekeeping/peacemaking activities (CIC 2006). Member states of the African Union (AU) in 2006 provided over 75 per cent of all UN peacekeepers in Africa, as well as running their own operations.

Finally, these new security roles of regional organizations, though still relatively understudied, have been increasingly recognized by states, the UN and other actors. Earlier and widely expressed scepticism about the values of such institutions has given way to acknowledgement of their potential. They are part of the 'explosion of international activism', highlighted by the Human

Table 21.1 Major regional institutions with security provision, 1945–2007

Africa	OAU/AU, IGADD/IGAD, ECOWAS, SADCC/SADC, CEMAC
Europe	EC/EU, WEU, NATO, (Warsaw Pact) OSCE, CIS, CSTO
Asia	(SEATO), ASEAN, SAARC, ARF, SCO, CACO, ICO
Middle East	LAS, (CENTO), GCC, AMU, (ACC), ECO, ICO
Americas	OAS, CARICOM, OECS, MERCOSUR
Australasia	ANZUS, SPF/PIF

Note: ( ) defunct institutions / name change

BOX 21.1 SECURITY ACTIVITIES OF SELECTED REGIONAL INSTITUTIONS

- Confidence-building measures
- Defence of sovereignty and territorial integrity
- Peacekeeping
- Security and economic development
- Peaceful settlement of disputes
- Foreign policy coordination
- Security cooperation
- Resolution of border disputes
- Disarmament and arms control
- Preventive diplomacy
- Freedom, security and justice
- Safeguarding of national rights
- Combating terrorism, drugs and weapons trafficking
- Peace enforcement
- Election monitoring
- Institution building
- Non-proliferation

Security Report (2005), that is seen as responsible for the overall decline in conflict. In the words of former UN Secretary-General Kofi Annan, 'multi-lateral institutions and regional security organizations have never been more important than today' (UN/SG/SM/8543: 9/12/2002).

What do the above developments amount to in real terms and how can they be explained? While a 'new wave of regionalism in security affairs' can readily be identified (Lake and Morgan 1997), it is harder to demonstrate that it has established deep or enduring roots or significantly altered the contours of world politics. Indeed, the real significance of the current regional wave, like the previous waves discussed here, remains a matter of debate.

First, the evidence of its impact itself is mixed. The number of institutions in existence tells us little about their remit and effectiveness. The lofty rhetoric found in their charters and mission statements is often unmatched in practice, and practice itself varies widely. Some well-established regional organizations have registered important advances in the security domain, whether in Africa, Southeast Asia, Latin America or Europe; the record of others – in the Middle East, South or Central Asia, for example – remains limited. There is no regular or easily identifiable pattern or process to the development of security regionalism. Latin American, South Pacific and Southeast Asian countries have successfully established and maintained a nuclear-free zone throughout their regions. In South Asia, the two major regional powers, India and Pakistan, have gone nuclear, while the commitment of the League of Arab States (LAS) to remove all weapons of mass destruction (WMD) from the Middle East has failed, with Israel's nuclear capacity well established and Iran moving closer to becoming a nuclear power.

Second, the very value of such institutions, whether international or regional, is subject to different interpretations (Higgott 2006). At one end of the spectrum, scholars argue that institutions have helped to shape the way states think about security and community. Institutions promote dialogue and learning among states allowing them to rethink their security priorities and behaviour, and embark upon collaborative ventures (Deutsch 1957). In these accounts regional identities may play important roles in determining how states choose partners in cooperation and over which areas they choose to cooperate (Barnett 1998). In the middle ground are those who see institutions as serving useful purposes in situations of interdependence, allowing states to benefit from common rules and procedures. In this rational actor model regional identity is incidental to cooperation. At the other end of the spectrum are those who express scepticism as to whether institutions, of any type, promote security and international order (Mearsheimer 1994/95). Institutions are transient and reflect current power balances in the international system. The idea of the region is only important inasmuch as strong regional states, or alliances of states, may be instrumental in trying to achieve a more favourable balance of power for their members.

Third, even the desirability of regionalism, in theory or in practice, is contested. Although some argue that regional security might be the gateway to global security, that peace might be obtained 'in parts' to quote the title of an early work by Joseph Nye (1971), an equally strong body of opinion supports the view that regionalism should be considered at best complementary and secondary, at worst detrimental to global efforts to promote peace and security. Drawing on early idealist thinking about international organization, which promoted universal over particularistic values, there is still a wide consensus that the UN, or some universal body, should be the main security provider. In this account, the promotion of regional security contradicts the search for global security; regional organizations cannot be impartial and will be susceptible to the ambitions of strong regional powers (Dorn 1998). In other words, if international security institutions have value, this should be sought and promoted at the global level by a truly international not regional society.

Organization of the chapter

Against this background of ambivalence about the nature and significance of regionalism, this chapter examines the existing evidence and offers some tentative conclusions about the current and future roles of regional institutions in security affairs. The following section looks at the history and evolution of regional security institutions since the Second World War. The third section surveys some aspects of the contemporary regional security arena, looking at the role of institutions in peace operations and their relations with the UN. It also considers how institutions have fared in dealing with the 'latest' security threats of terrorism and the spread of WMD. The final section assesses the growth of security regionalism, and concludes with a consideration of its contemporary significance and future prospects.

Note on terms

What is a regional institution and what defines the security component of a regional institution? All three terms – 'regional', 'security' and 'institutions' – are subject to differing interpretations, so a note of clarification on their use here is needed. In International Relations, institutions refer to formal organizations with 'prescribed hierarchies and capacity for purposive action' and to international regimes with 'complexes of rules and organizations, the core elements of which have been negotiations and explicitly agreed upon by states' (Keohane 1988). Regional institutions are regimes and formal organizations comprising a membership which is limited to a particular geographical region, or perhaps to two or more proximate regions (e.g. NATO or ARF), though other definitions based more loosely around issues, activities and ideas have also be used (e.g. Nye 1968, Russett 1967, Katzenstein 1996b). Although such institutions may be formal or informal and include state or non-state actors, the focus here, for reasons of precision and economy, is on formal state-based regional, or cross-regional, organizations (see Hettne (2004) for contrast), a choice justified by noting that the state remains the gatekeeper of most global security activity (Russett and Oneal 2001).

The *security* dimension of regional institutions may be understood in two different, though related ways. First, it could be interpreted as the attempt to promote peaceful and predictable relations among its members, to build security and community through cooperation (Adler and Barnett 1998). This loose understanding of security may be said to apply to any regional organization. Second, and more formally, a regional security institution may be understood as an organization whose charter contains an explicit reference to security *provision* through the coordination of defence, security and foreign policy at some level. This distinction may be understood by contrasting the early European Community (EC) project with that of the later European Union (EU). Security provision is designed to meet threats arising from inter- and intra-state conflicts. The focus here will be principally on the more measurable forms of security provision, less on security understood as community building, though the two are often linked.

The origins and development of regional security institutions

The growth of regional institutions dates from the Second World War and is part of a general pattern of growth in international institutions. Three main types of early regional institution may readily be identified: first, multipurpose institutions, such as the LAS, Organization of American States (OAS) or

Organization of African Unity (OAU); second, those with principally an economic focus, such as the EC; and third, security alliances, such as NATO, SEATO and CENTO. The emphasis here is on institutions with an explicit security component, or the first and third types. Even if the different functions of regional institutions may be closely related, with security regionalism perhaps springing from economic regionalism, there is no necessary link or 'spillover' effect as some early integration theorists predicted (Haas 1958). Not all regional economic institutions have developed security provision, nor do all regional security institutions have provision for economic cooperation (NATO is one example). Security cooperation is not necessarily harder (or easier) to achieve than economic cooperation.

In the area of regional security, three broad waves of institutional growth may be identified from 1945 to the present: the first coinciding with the immediate post-Second World War and early Cold War period (see Table 21.2), the second occurring in the mid- to late Cold War period (Table 21.3), and the third, and most recent wave, in the first post-Cold War decade (Table 21.4). There has been little *new* institution-building since the turn of the century, though a number of institutions have continued to expand and develop their capacity in different areas. For each wave, institutional growth correlates with change and development in the international system and with state formation and breakdown. The last major systemic change, which saw both the birth and death of a number of institutions, was the end of the Cold War and the breakup of the Soviet bloc.

Prior to the Second World War, formal security institutions were few and regional security institutions non-existent. The Inter-American system, with its roots in the late nineteenth century, was not a formal security institution, though it embodied the idea of a security regime expressed, for example, in the Monroe Doctrine, which singled out the Americas as part of a US sphere of influence. Other security regimes were evident in nineteenth-century Europe, where the idea of a 'concert' or balance of powers clearly informed understanding of regional order. It was only when this loose regime was finally broken by the onset of the First World War that international statesmen, led by US President Woodrow Wilson, made the first sustained attempt at constructing a formal security institution: the League of Nations.

The League experiment, though intended to be universal, betrayed a number of regional features, not least that its dominant members were all European. A reference in the Covenant, in Article 21, to 'regional understandings' was included to attract the USA, which did not become a member, and the Monroe Doctrine was the only understanding actually mentioned (Zimmern 1945). More broadly, the League period set the tone for a wider and ongoing debate about how to deal with the problem of integrating regional arrangements into the framework of a general security organization. This debate was overtaken by the events of the 1930s when Europe, and much of the rest of the world, became embroiled in a new war. By this time it was evident that the League had failed as a security institution, and regionalism had been negatively associated with Japan's pan-Asian project, or the Nazi's European one.

Regional security institutions in the Cold War

It was against this backdrop that the UN was constructed and the first wave of regional institution-building took place. The League's example, both positive and negative, informed the development of a new set of international institutions after 1945. At one level such institutions were constructed precisely to prevent the social, political and economic upheavals that had taken the world to war after 1939, and hence to do better than the League. At another, not entirely complementary level, they were designed to make new and old states feel more secure. If few states thus questioned the need for a more ambitious universal security organization, many sought to protect their own interests through regional or cross-regional groupings (Table 21.2).

Already by 1945, the first such regional institutions, representing not only the Americas, but also the Commonwealth, and Arab states had come into being, in a pattern that would soon be replicated in Africa with the creation of the OAU in 1963. The final design of the UN Charter, like the League Covenant before it, was strongly influenced by states with investments in such institutions. Despite the widely expressed reservations by UN founding fathers (notably US President Roosevelt) about diluting its universal aspirations and competence, regional interests were simply too strong to be ignored. The UN Charter thus endorsed the principle of regional partnership and action, though always within the framework of the global security organization.

The provisions regarding the role of regional agencies, and their relationship with the UN, are clustered in Chapter VIII, Articles 51–54, though a number of references may also be found elsewhere in the Charter. They focus almost exclusively on their contribution to peace and security. Article 51 endorses the right of states to collective self-defence; in Article 52, regional agencies are called upon to 'make every effort to achieve peaceful settlement of local disputes . . . before referring them to the Security Council'. The Charter is ambiguous as to which types of regional actors and institutions are appropriate for Chapter VIII partnerships, leaving this open to a variety of interpretations, though in time different agencies would be periodically singled out and praised for their roles (Schreuer 1995, Sarooshi 1998).

The construction of the first formal regional organizations, and their acknowledgement by the UN, were responses to impending and actual changes in the international system, brought about both by the war itself and the end of European empires. Now these institutions had to readapt to a new international environment characterized by the Cold War. In this environment it

Table 21.2 Cold War regional security institutions: the first wave, 1945–1965

Multi-purpose institutions	Security alliances/institutions
(Commonwealth), LAS, OAS, OAU	NATO, Warsaw Pact, SEATO, Baghdad Pact/CENTO, ANZUS, WEU

was clear that the power of regional actors, particularly where new Third World states were concerned, would be severely constrained. Their very newness and lack of diplomatic expertise were part of the problem, and resources were scarce. Cold War 'overlay' also further reduced the autonomy of weaker states (Buzan 1991). While the USA was able to maintain its privileged position within the new American institutions, weaker states in the new regional institutions had less room for manoeuvre.

For different reasons, the early general-purpose organizations are often regarded as failures, at least in the short term (Haas 1993). They were unable, for example, to foster regional security whether understood as securing their regions against external threats on the one hand, or promoting ideas of regional community on the other. Their regions suffered from civil wars and external intervention. On the other hand, these new institutions, given the obvious difficulties they faced, were not wholly unsuccessful in forging common positions on issues of great importance to their members such as decolonization and apartheid (in the African case) or support for Palestine (in the Arab sense). Peacekeeping roles were also played by the OAU, OAS and the Arab League in conflicts over Chad, Dominican Republic and Kuwait and Lebanon respectively. Institutions thus had an early role to play in assisting the 'weak in the world of the strong' and states were inclined to support them (Rothstein 1977).

The rise of the Cold War alliance system undoubtedly complicated this picture. On the one hand, it may be argued that by far the most successful regional security institutions were those on either side of the East–West divide: the Warsaw Pact and NATO respectively. If the Cold War has been characterized as the 'The Long Peace' (Gaddis 1987) it was the role of these two institutions and their superpower patrons that was critical in keeping that peace through the maintenance of a stable balance of power. On the other hand, these security alliances and the bilateral and multilateral arrangements they promoted bypassed the UN system and influenced both the global and regional security picture, offering very little scope for regional organizations either to develop their own arrangements, or the type of security relationships detailed in Chapter VIII.

Neither NATO nor the Warsaw Pact were designed as Chapter VIII institutions; they retained full autonomy of action, bypassing the careful wording of Article 103, on the primacy of UN obligations over 'any other international agreement'. If the very presence of NATO was a major factor in removing security from the agenda of the West European states, thus helping to explain the EC's early successes in economic integration, the same could not be said to apply to other regions. Efforts by the USA to create regional security organizations to serve similar Cold War purposes, whether in Southeast Asia (SEATO), the Middle East (Baghdad Pact/CENTO) or Australasia (ANZUS), were far less successful except for the latter, and even divisive in the case of CENTO. Ultimately, Cold War security on the periphery was achieved through bilateral alliances rather than formal institutional arrangements. Japan, for example, through its bilateral security treaty with the USA, was arguably far more secure than most of the states that formed part of either SEATO or CENTO.

It was in reaction to this superpower dominance of the regional security arena, the disappointing early results of multi-purpose institutions and the changing regional security environment itself, that a second wave of institution-building occurred, mainly among developing countries (Table 21.3). This new wave of security regionalism, which took place between 1966 and 1986, should be distinguished from the earlier wave of mostly economic regionalism that had been inspired by the creation and successful early years of the EC (Nye 1968). It was similar in that it was mostly subregional in scope (with subregional here meaning subcontinental, or at least encompassing a smaller geographical space and fewer states than the earlier pan-regional groups), though it also included both a pan-European security institution, the Conference on Security and Cooperation in Europe (CSCE), and a pan-Islamic institution, the ICO.

Overall, this second wave was characterized by small steps to improve regional self-sufficiency and cooperation in a changed regional and global environment which afforded a little more flexibility to regional actors. Bipolarity had somewhat loosened in the détente era of the late 1960s to mid-1970s, while many developing countries had consolidated their statehood and autonomy. Not all these new institutions immediately assumed security roles; a number had ostensibly more economic functions and purposes: the GCC is an interesting case of an institution designed to meet a security threat whose charter is couched in mainly economic and cultural terms (see Article 4, www.gcc-sg.org/CHARTER). However, there was a clear security dimension to this second wave of institution-building. In fact many of these second-wave security institutions were constructed with a particular local threat in mind: for ASEAN it was Vietnam, for the GCC, revolutionary Iran; for SADCC, apartheid South Africa. The short-lived Arab Cooperation Council (ACC) was conceived as a vehicle for the containment of Iraq. However, the overlay features of the Cold War were also present, and continued to restrict options. This was of course true for the CSCE, a quite different pan-European security enterprise, which by encouraging East–West convergence in several areas played a facilitating role in the end of the Cold War.

The results of this second wave, like the first, were mixed, but a couple of points should be noted. As in the first wave, institutional survival rates were high: few institutions died (except for the security pacts, CENTO and SEATO, and the short-lived ACC), showing how they were valued by their members. They were also flexible: as their *raison d'être* was increased by the new balance of power at the end of the Cold War, many went on to expand their security roles.

Table 21.3 Cold War regional security institutions: the second wave, 1966–1986

Subregional institutions	Pan-regional institutions
ASEAN, CARICOM, SPF, ECOWAS, OECS, SADCC, ECO, GCC, SAARC, (ACC)	CSCE, ICO

Regional security institutions since the Cold War

The international system had closely defined the parameters and possibilities of security regionalism in the Cold War. It was system change that also helps explain the post-Cold War changes and developments. The very growth and expansion of regional security projects cannot be understood without reference to the post-Cold War environment, which changed the parameters of the security domain and made regional security both more vulnerable and more accessible to local actors. This exposure of the 'regional security complex' (Buzan and Wæver 2003) gave rise to a new wave of regionalism (see also Chapter 5, this volume). Like earlier waves, the post-Cold War regionalism has been the subject of much debate and a growing literature, but the evidence on the security side merits examining on its own terms (Lake and Morgan 1997).

At first, there was a distinctly universal flavour to the post-Cold War order which did not immediately suggest an important role for regional institutions. Just as the two World Wars had seen the birth and rebirth of universal paradigms of global order, reflected in the early ethos of the League and the UN, the end of the Cold War era was similarly informed by idealized notions about the possibilities of global institutions and projects, even global peace. This was picked up in the rhetoric of the 'New World Order' articulated by US President George Bush Sr., after the 1991 Gulf War, and in popular works on the end of history, ideology, geography and so on. These big ideas were captured by different understandings of the term *globalization*. As in the past, regionalism was viewed by some as a mere stepping stone, and by others as potentially obstructive and damaging to broader global processes.

Two things illustrated regionalism's potential and possible trajectory. First was the experience of Western Europe. Although the evidence from Europe on the eve of the Maastricht Treaty (1992) was mixed, the European process could not easily be disregarded. Even if the experience of the EU was not readily or immediately exportable, it still represented an important model of how cooperation might be conducted at the regional level, and non-European institutions did start to grow quickly after the Cold War ended. The EU was also poised to move away from a predominantly economic focus to one which also emphasized security cooperation.

Second, and less tangible, was the so-called 'clash of civilizations' thesis (Huntington 1993). This clumsy characterization made the point that 'civilizations', often loose regions, could not be homogenized and had creative and fragmentary power. In a somewhat related vein, Ian Clark (1997) showed how processes of globalization and fragmentation had competed and coexisted historically and were likely to continue to do so in the future. In this sense regionalism, construed as a response to the global other, merely extended the project that had commenced with the early Third World regionalisms and the second wave of regionalism in the latter decades of the Cold War.

From a practical perspective, it quickly became clear that the post-Cold War multilateral structures, given the huge demands placed upon them, would need buttressing. Nowhere was this more apparent than in the area of conflict resolution. In calling for the revival of Chapter VIII provision, UN Secretary-Generals were not advocating regionalism per se, but burden-sharing (Boutros Ghali 1992). The UN, despite the euphoria that accompanied its early post-Cold War years (a euphoria which peaked in the Gulf War of 1991), lacked the resources and the commitment of major states to act as a global security provider, creating vacuums that regional powers and institutions sought to fill (Weiss 1998, Price and Zacher 2004). Hence the new wave of security regionalism must be understood in terms of UN capacity, the relative disinterest of great powers in costly external interventions and former alliance systems. It represented the further development of a self-help system for weaker states to cope with the new security environment. It also permitted stronger regional powers the scope to set local agendas within a legitimate institutional framework.

The third wave of security regionalism was characterized by two main developments: the upgrading of security provision in existing institutions and the creation of new ones (Table 21.4). Like the third wave of democratization, there were few regions which did not participate in this new wave. New institutions were formed in the Asia-Pacific region and in the former Soviet space. China entered into regional security arrangements for the first time. Major reforms were introduced in a number of existing institutions, notably in Europe, the Americas and Africa, where additional protocols, treaties and conventions were signed relating to conflict prevention and management, human rights and democracy. A great deal has already been written about the nature and purpose of this 'new' regionalist moment, and its varied and arguably novel dimensions (e.g. Soderbaum and Shaw 2003). However one regards it – and there is a case to be made for continuity as well as change – the quantitative evidence is noteworthy.

A brief glance at some of these institutions helps to illustrate this point. First, in Europe the EU's moves, since 1992, to develop a Common Foreign and Security Policy (CFSP) and then a European Security and Defence Policy (ESDP) have been well documented. Forces from EU member states have been involved in a growing number of peace operations inside and outside Europe and discussions continue on the establishment of an EU rapid reaction force and battle groups (Dinan 2005). The wider Europe has seen the development of the CSCE into the OSCE, following the Paris Summit of 1990, marking its move from a more informal conference to a formal organization, acquiring permanent institutions and operational capabilities. Comprising 56 member states it was, in 2006, the largest regional security organization in the world, followed by the African Union (www.osce.org).

Table 21.4 Post-Cold War regional security institutions: the third wave, 1987–2007

New institutions	Renamed institutions/new agenda
CIS, CSTO, SCO, ARF, APEC, MERCOSUR, NAFTA, CACO	OAS, ECOWAS/ECOMOG, CSCE/OSCE, UDEAC/CEMAC, EC/EU, SPF/PIF, OAU/AU, IGADD/IGAD, SADCC/SADC

NATO has overcome early doubts about its post-Cold War future, attracting new members and engaging in 'out-of-area' operations from Kosovo to Afghanistan. Within the former Soviet bloc there has been institution-building (CIS, CSTO, CACO) to fill gaps left by the demise of Cold War structures. East European and Baltic states have also looked West for association and membership of existing structures such as the EU and NATO. Russia was party to the establishment of the Shanghai Cooperation Organization (SCO) in 2001 (successor to the Shanghai Five), which has provided a forum where Central Asian states can engage with China (Allison 2004). Less well known was the expansion, in 1992, of the Economic Cooperation Organization (ECO) to include Afghanistan and the six Muslim republics of the former USSR.

Moving to the Asia Pacific, the creation, in 1994, of the ASEAN Regional Forum (ARF), a cross-regional association of 25 states including China, Russia, Japan, the EU and the USA, gave substance to ideas of a broader multilateral security forum in Asia. ASEAN, with the admission of Cambodia in 1999, now includes all Southeast Asian countries, no small feat considering the severity of earlier regional rivalries.

Important changes have taken place in African institutions. In its 1991 summit the OAU made regional integration a priority and established mechanisms for conflict management. During the 1990s, ECOWAS, SADC, IGAD and CEMAC underwent major restructuring, all assuming greater politico-security roles including peacekeeping. Finally, in the Constitutive Act of the African Union (AU), the framework was laid for an African Parliament, Court of Justice, Peer Review Mechanism and African Standby Force, providing the pillars for a potentially far more robust pan-regional institution.

Latin America has also seen important new institutional developments. MERCOSUR was set up in 1991; initially as a trade agreement, but one which expanded by 1998 to include commitments to regional democracy in the 'compromiso democratico' and peace (see www.mercosur.int/msweb/). The OAS Santiago Declaration (June 1991) also made the link between democracy and security; followed up by the Interamerican Democratic Charter in 2001. CARICOM in 2001 established a Regional Task Force on Crime and Security to address the security issues arising from illicit drugs, arms and money laundering. NAFTA has no explicit tripartite security mechanism, though from a community perspective it has been instrumental in consolidating Mexican democracy. Security, though, given border and illicit trafficking concerns, is an inescapable feature of US–Mexico relations.

Contemporary challenges

In examining the capacity and achievements of the contemporary regional institutions in the security domain, two areas may be singled out: peace operations and the coordination of anti-terror and WMD policies. These by no means exhaust the different types of security activities undertaken by institutions since the Cold War, but provide some useful indicators of their roles and effectiveness.

Peace operations

Regional actors, not always formal regional institutions, have been active in a variety of solo and joint peacekeeping operations since the 1990s, many in conjunction with the UN (Weiss 1998). This is in sharp contrast to the Cold War. Figure 21.1 illustrates the significant rise in what are now termed 'peace operations' conducted by UN and non-UN actors, a large proportion of which are regional organizations. The range of these operations is wide: from enforcement missions like that of NATO in Kosovo, to election monitoring or institution-building, like those of the EU or OSCE in Bosnia-Herzegovina (see CIC 2006).

The high demand for peacekeeping and the fact that the UN is not always the 'mediator of choice' (Hampson 2004) has encouraged regional organizations to take on more roles in this area. Again, a review of the range of their activities is illustrative.

Starting from the involvement of ECOWAS in the Liberian conflict in 1990 leading to a joint UN peacekeeping operation in 1993 (UNOMIL), there has been steady and growing involvement of regional organizations in different aspects of peacekeeping in Africa. Peace operations have been undertaken in Burundi, the Comoros, Côte d'Ivoire, Central African Republic, DR Congo, Guinea-Bissau, Lesotho, Sierra Leone, Somalia and Sudan under the auspices of ECOWAS, SADC, CEMAC and the AU.

The same is true of the wider Europe. Since the early 1990s the UN and European groups such as the EU, OSCE, CIS and NATO have been involved in numerous peacekeeping and peace support missions in the Yugoslav and Soviet successor states. Such groups were brought together in Bosnia in the

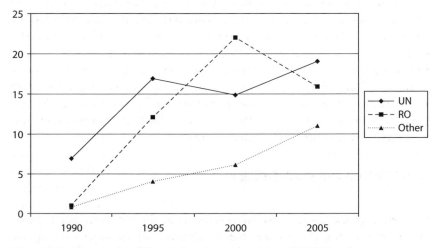

Figure 21.1 UN and non-UN* peacekeeping operations, 1990–2005

Note: *regional organizations and other peacekeeping/monitoring groups

1995 Dayton Accord, and in 1999 in Kosovo, where NATO was the major security provider, with the OSCE and EU working in the areas of democratization, institution-building and economic reconstruction. In Georgia a UN mission works with the OSCE and CIS; the latter has also been involved in operations in Moldova and Tajikistan.

Outside Europe, EU forces have been engaged in monitoring missions in Indonesia and peace support operations in the DR Congo: Operation Artemis and EUFOR RD. Under a UN mandate, NATO took over the coordination of the International Security Assistance Force in Afghanistan in 2003, its first mission outside the Euro-Atlantic area. In the Americas, OAS action has supported democratic governments in Haiti, and since 2004, in Colombia, the organization has been involved in monitoring the demobilization of paramilitary groups. The Pacific Islands Forum in 2003 authorized the sending of a Regional Assistance Mission to the Solomon Islands to restore order following inter-communal violence in the late 1990s.

In the Middle East two peace operations, legacies of the Arab–Israel conflict, continue, but the region has seen little action by its own regional institutions, despite LAS efforts to mediate during the Lebanese crisis in 2006. The EU, in contrast, launched a mission in Palestine in 2006. The ICO has yet to take on a major peacekeeping role, though it has provided observers and monitoring missions to Islamic countries in conflict.

In 2006 to 2007, after a short-term decline in the numbers of regional peacekeepers and operations, there was a new phase of growth driven by the start-up of new missions and the expansion of NATO and EU operations in Afghanistan and the DR Congo respectively. With the AU's role in Darfur, Sudan, the role of regional institutions in ever more complex peace operations looked set to continue. This situation is not just the result of incremental growth and development in the post-Cold War period, but rather due to the severity of regional security concerns and the absence of other security providers, generating a high demand for regional action. Core states, aware of the opportunities and constraints of a regional security policy, have been willing to provide leadership.

A number of doubts have been expressed about the growth of security regionalism, both inside the UN and in the wider policy-making community (Job 2004). Issues of legitimacy and impartiality, as well as that of primacy in the relationship between the UN and regional actors, have been raised. In the latter case the problem has been that regional organizations have conducted operations without prior authorization of the UN Security Council. Questions have also been asked about the tendency of strong regional states to impose their own security agendas: Russia in the CIS, Nigeria in ECOWAS, Australia in the PIF, or the USA in NATO are some examples. Accepting the precedent of regionalization of security may produce the dangerous precedent of excluding areas like Africa from high-quality peace operations (Bellamy and Williams 2005). Setting such problems aside, and given the current international environment and the limited capacity of multilateral institutions, the search for 'regional solutions to regional problems' is likely to continue.

The post-2001 security environment

The kinds of peace operations described above represent the most important element of the security agenda of regional institutions in the early twenty-first century. Another is the more recent concern about the spread of terrorism and WMD. Such security issues are nothing new; their novelty lies in the way that they have been identified as core security threats by dominant states and thus captured the centre of the security debate, demanding institutional responses. This has posed new challenges to security institutions, already in the process of readjustment after the Cold War.

A number of established regional institutions – NATO, the OAS, the OAU and the EU – already had anti-terrorist provision in place. The founding document of the SCO, drafted before the events of 9/11, singled out terrorism, separatism and extremism as 'three evils' to confront, reflecting the concerns of members like Russia and China. Regions are arguably well positioned to react to, monitor and deter terrorist activity, and most regional organizations have responded to recent events, by incorporating new mechanisms to deal with terrorist activity. The OAS has a sophisticated mechanism in the Inter-American Committee Against Terrorism; the AU has adopted an additional protocol on the prevention and combating of terrorism; NATO has endorsed a new Concept for Defence against Terrorism; finally the EU in 2004 appointed a Counter-terrorism Coordinator.

The potential for regional organizations to act in this area is again highlighted by the difficulties faced by the UN in articulating a common position. As in the case of peace operations, however, the results are mixed. There is also the question as to the extent to which states really wish to entrust such high politics (yet often domestic) security concerns to international institutions. Note, for example, how differences between NATO's new concept and the 2006 US National Strategy for combating terrorism demonstrate the role of dominant states (de Nevers 2007). For developing countries, the emphasis on terrorism may be regarded as distracting attention from other more pressing regional security and development goals, a further argument for regionalism perhaps, but one that also demonstrates the way in which key system players continue to dominate and constrain local agendas.

The issues regarding WMD are similar in some ways, though this has long been the domain of multilateral action and treaties, less of regional agencies. Many regional institutions publicize commitments to non-proliferation and uphold the enforcement of existing treaty regimes. The EU, since 2003, has had in place an anti-proliferation policy to strengthen and universalize the existing multilateral system, though two EU states are themselves nuclear powers (European Security Strategy 2003).

ASEAN, South Pacific and Latin American states are exceptional in supporting nuclear-free zones through long-standing treaties. Twenty-four Latin American countries in 1967 signed the Latin American Nuclear Free Zone Treaty at Tlatelolco. ASEAN's summit in 1995 saw the signature of the Treaty on Southeast Asian Nuclear Weapons Free Zone (SEANWFZ). African states, signatories to the Pelindaba Treaty, are also close to agreeing a nuclear-free zone. While there are rational arguments supporting such cooperation for the regions in question, one must ask what role in enforcing such regimes has been played by external actors (the US or China, for example), and whether or not regional regimes could ever be effective in fully restraining the ambitions of an aspiring nuclear state.

Although the issue of WMD, like terrorism, could represent a new growth area with great possibilities for cooperation, evidence shows that in this high politics arena, security matters are still more likely to be handled outside regional frameworks – by the P-5, strong regional powers and multilateral institutions.

Assessing the growth of regional security institutions

This chapter has outlined the main developments in regional security institutions from 1945 to the present, with a view to understanding and demonstrating their contemporary significance. It has sought to throw more light on an important but still understudied aspect of regionalism, and one in which explanations for cooperation differ: international security is an area in which institutionalist theories expect that cooperation will be hardest to achieve.

Yet security cooperation has been achieved across a wide range of issues and regional institutions have generated more orderly relationships between states. Two features of this cooperation stand out. First, a major driver of regionalism in security affairs has been changes in the international system requiring states to respond to shifts in the global and regional balances of power. This is well illustrated by considering the timing and content of three waves of security regionalism. All were responses to the new balance of power in the international system with institutions designed to enhance and consolidate the position of both strong and new/weak states. Cooperation has been a means of increasing security, but also influence and bargaining power. The latest developments in the third wave, post-9/11, again suggest how regional organizations, in adapting to recent threats, are responding to the security imperatives of the dominant global powers – those most threatened by terrorism.

Second, states value institutions. If explanations of power balancing are useful in explaining the start-up and changing functions of institutions, they are only part of the story. Institutions are not mere epiphenomena. They have survived and developed new functions, adjusting to changing conditions, including regime change and state type. In providing more predictable bases for cooperation and negotiation in an interdependent world, they have become invaluable tools of diplomacy and statecraft (Duffield 2006).

The above developments are less the result of a natural growth in functions and ideas about cooperation, an ongoing process of learning and dialogue, or deep-seated regional preferences, as new institutions or charters for new purposes in a changing world order. Neither ECOWAS nor SADCC nor IGADD had 'succeeded' as economic or development institutions before they developed a security profile. They responded to new demands. The same is also true of Europe. If security spill-over has occurred, this development has as much to do with local threats, and the desire of the EU to reposition itself as a great power and counterbalance the USA, as it has to do with fostering common identity and purpose.

The notion of a European, Asian or African style of crisis management is not without significance. It is currently fashionable to consider how the language and form that regionalism takes reflects the identity and culture of states (Acharya 2000). Regions and regional security are self-evidently what states want to make of them, but what most states want is achievable security against external threats. The history of regionalism in security affairs suggests that one should be cautious about attributing too much significance to concepts of regional identity. More important is the need for regions to project their power and influence, however limited, while attending to their own security concerns in a way that preserves regional autonomy and order. The pro-sovereignty norm in ASEAN, the non-intervention tradition in the Americas, the expansion of AU instruments are about self-help and awareness that collective action is more likely to achieve results. Regional institutions are vehicles for coping with a security predicament, for alleviating state weakness in a hostile international environment (Ayoob 1995). Here, it is worth recalling the influential report 'Responsibility to Protect' (ICISS 2001), which highlights the salience of security regionalism: 'Those states which can call upon *strong regional alliances*, internal peace and a strong and independent civil society seem best placed to benefit from globalization' (italics added).

In concluding, this chapter has argued that a useful distinction can be made between regionalism under bipolarity and regionalism under unipolarity. In both cases, regionalism in security affairs must be understood as a response to the dominant security order – whether balancing against large powers or bandwagoning with them. The way in which the functions of regional organizations and their memberships have shifted in line with dominant security trends supports this. Regional institutions do condition the behaviour of their members and provide parameters for action, but the propensity of institutions to switch roles in response to systemic changes suggests also the close correlation between material interests and collective behaviour. On the other hand, their survival and maintenance indicate that states value institutions and are willing to bear their costs even during periods of uncertainty and failure.

Under unipolarity the trend towards further regional conflict management is set to continue. The UN, as highlighted in the *2005 World Summit Outcome* document, is likely to encourage rather than supplant the roles of regional organizations in the near future. The consequences of the overextension of US power may be seen in Iraq and elsewhere, demonstrating the demand for alternative sources of action. Strong states will continue to find useful legitimizing roles for regional institutions, and weak states will benefit from their security umbrella. To some extent then, security regionalism is on a path-dependent trajectory that is unlikely to change unless and until some new critical turning point is reached.

▌ Further reading

Centre for International Cooperation, *Annual Review of Global Peace Operations* (Boulder, CO: Lynne Rienner, 2007). An annual statistical review of peace operations (both UN and non-UN) with short analytical essays discussing particular themes and missions.

Paul F. Diehl and Joseph Lepgold (eds), *Regional Conflict Management* (New York: Rowman and Littlefield, 2003). A useful survey of different regional approaches to conflict management from around the world.

Margaret P. Karns and Karen A. Mingst, *International Organizations. The Politics and Processes of Global Governance* (Boulder, CO: Lynne Rienner, 2004). An excellent introduction to how international organizations have dealt with a wide range of challenges, including global security issues.

David Lake and Patrick Morgan (eds), *Regional Orders. Building Security in a New World* (Pennsylvania, PA: Pennsylvania State University Press, 1997). One of the earlier attempts to theorize about regional security institutions illustrated with some case studies from around the globe.

Richard Price and Mark Zacher (eds), *The United Nations and Global Security* (New York: Palgrave, 2004). An excellent survey of how the UN has attempted to tackle a variety of security challenges.

CHAPTER 22

The United Nations

Thomas G. Weiss and Danielle Zach Kalbacher

Abstract

This chapter discusses the principal organs of the United Nations (UN) and their role in maintaining international peace and security – the world body's primary mandate. It provides an overview of the UN system as well as a short history of its contributions to security studies. It also addresses key threats confronting the globe at the dawn of the twenty-first century, such as terrorism and weapons of mass destruction, and assesses the UN's capacity to meet these security challenges.

Introduction

The United Nations was born in June 1945 from the ashes of the Second World War. This second experiment in universal international organization followed the failed League of Nations that had emerged after the First World War – the so-called war to end all wars. The mass death and destruction, unconscionable atrocities and human suffering caused by a further round of great-power armed conflict prompted a further effort to institutionalize collective security. The UN embodies the latest attempt at international co-operation 'to save succeeding generations from the scourge of war'.

The world organization's hierarchy of functions and tasks is reflected in the principles and values of the UN Charter – the world organization's 'constitution' (Simma 2002). The Preamble expresses the main purpose, the maintenance of international peace and security, and to that end it outlawed the use of force except in self-defence. Indeed, such other main tasks as ensuring respect for human rights and promoting economic development were seen as instrumental to the primary security function rather than being crucial in themselves. The Charter's foundation is state sovereignty – the sanctity of a state's monopoly on the use of force and authority over a defined population within territorial borders. As Article 2(7) clearly states, 'Nothing contained in the present Charter shall authorize the United Nations to intervene in matters which are essentially within the domestic jurisdiction of any state'.

While the UN's founders had high hopes that the world body would play a central role in managing the majority of the globe's security affairs, the onset of the US–Soviet rivalry quickly dashed such aspirations. Other than buffer forces and observers, or 'peacekeepers', the UN's security machinery was essentially marginalized for most of the Cold War. It was not until the Iron Curtain fell and later the Soviet Union imploded that the UN assumed a substantial role in international peace and security.

At the dawn of the twenty-first century, the UN comprises nearly every country on the planet. To be precise, 192 states are members, a nearly fourfold increase from the original 51 in 1945. The organization's global legitimacy constitutes one of its fundamental strengths.

When discussing the past, present and future of the United Nations, a crucial distinction is between the intergovernmental institution, the 'first UN', and the administrative entity, the 'second UN' (Kennedy 2006, Weiss and Daws 2007, Weiss *et al.* 2007). The former is an arena for state decision-making and negotiation. Member states constitute the world organization and fund its activities. Although actors other than states are increasingly involved in security issues (as part of the problem and the solution), states remain the dominant actors in the realm of international peace and security.

The second UN comprises myriad departments, agencies, programmes and commissions. The Secretariat, headed by the secretary-general, is the core of the administrative apparatus. The lack of commitment, resources and political will among member states often inhibits the international civil service's ability to effect change. The second UN nonetheless wields considerable moral force and has some autonomy and marked achievements.

This chapter begins with a lengthy discussion of the Security Council followed by shorter examinations of the General Assembly and the Secretariat and its secretary-general. In relationship to security studies, these are the three most relevant of the UN's six principal organs. The Economic and Social Council (ECOSOC), the International Court of Justice (ICJ) and the Trusteeship Council are treated briefly as are other relevant parts of the UN system, or its 'extended family'. An analysis follows of contemporary security threats – including failed states, terrorism, nuclear proliferation and genocide – and the UN's capacity to grapple effectively with these grave challenges to international peace and security. To facilitate understanding of the UN's complex web of relationships and acronyms, an organizational diagram is given in Figure 22.1.

At the outset, it is important to circumscribe the term 'security' given considerable debate, in this book and elsewhere (MacFarlane and Khong 2006), about the distinction between the more traditional notion of military security from threats external to the state and the more comprehensive notion of human security that uses individuals as the metric. The latter usage connotes a broad range of issues affecting human well-being – including development and sustainability – but is not the focus here, which is the UN's efforts to address immediate and violent threats to human life.

The Security Council

The pre-eminent UN organ with responsibility for maintaining international order, as stated in Charter Article 24(1), is the Security Council. Unlike its defunct predecessor the League of Nations, the UN was designed to have military 'teeth' to ensure compliance with its decisions about security (Bailey and Daws 1998, Malone 2004, Luck 2006). This section details the council's composition and powers; the post-Cold War expansion of tasks; the impact of US hegemony; and the increased access of nonstate actors.

Composition

Unlike the General Assembly, which includes all member states, the Security Council is an exclusive forum. The victors of the Second World War have always comprised the five permanent members (P-5): China, France, Russia (formerly the Soviet Union), the United Kingdom and the USA. In addition to not needing to be elected (i.e. occupying permanent seats), they can also veto any resolution. This special status was a tactical compromise to avoid the pitfalls of the League of Nations – to ensure great-power cooperation and to avoid making matters worse by launching war against a major power. The Security Council now also includes ten rotating members (there were six from 1945 to 1965) that are elected for two-year, non-renewable terms and cannot veto decisions.

Given the fundamental changes in world politics over the past six decades, it is no surprise that the council's permanent membership does not mirror the contemporary distribution of power, globally or regionally. While defeated and occupied in 1945, Germany and Japan are now world heavyweights – the second and third largest financial contributors to the UN's regular budget after the USA – but do not have a commensurate voice in the Security Council. Neither do such regional powers as Brazil, India, Nigeria, Egypt and South Africa. Over the years, the council's anachronistic composition and veto privileges have been heatedly debated and targeted for reform. Given the political impossibility of garnering consensus on proposed reforms, however,

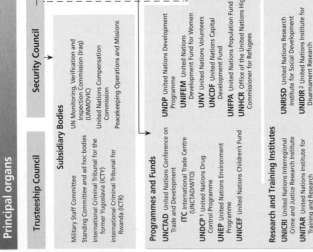

Figure 22.1 The United Nations system

such efforts have been futile – as the outcome of the 2005 World Summit vividly illustrates (Weiss 2005).

Powers

The Security Council's specific powers are codified in Chapters VI–VIII of the Charter. Chapter VI, 'Pacific Settlement of Disputes', invests the council with the authority to call disputing parties to resolve their conflict through peaceful means such as fact-finding, good offices, negotiation, arbitration and judicial settlement. It further grants the council the right to investigate disputes that might endanger international peace and security and to recommend terms of settlement.

By contrast, decisions under Chapter VII – 'Action with Respect to Threats to the Peace, Breaches of the Peace, and Acts of Aggression' – are compulsory rather than voluntary. Unlike the League of Nations, which had none, Chapter VII endows the Security Council with coercive authority – that is, it can compel compliance through decisions binding on member states and not merely proffer pious recommendations. In response to what the council deems a threat to international peace and security, it may impose diplomatic and economic sanctions on belligerents or even authorize military force. Article 43 envisaged that members would enter into special agreements with the UN to make available armed forces, assistance and facilities on call; and Article 46 called for the creation of a powerful overseer, the Military Staff Committee. Neither has materialized. Military forces are assembled on a case-by-case (or ad hoc) basis.

Chapter VIII, 'Regional Arrangements', encourages such organizations to engage in peaceful dispute settlement before involving the Security Council and requires that they seek the council's authorization before undertaking coercive action. It also grants the council the power to delegate enforcement to regional bodies, which the UN has increasingly done over the past two decades to compensate for its own lack of military wherewithal.

The Security Council's task expansion

Excessive veto use, mostly by the Soviet Union for the first half of the Cold War and the USA for the second, stymied the Security Council. However, the UN was able to carve out a role in security matters through the invention of so-called peacekeeping operations. These were dubbed 'Chapter VI and a half' operations because such measures were not explicitly mentioned in the Charter, but they fall somewhere between Chapters VI and VII. Comprised of civilians and borrowed soldiers and police from member states under the command of the United Nations, the goal of such operations is to help keep a lid on conflicts by monitoring cease-fires, interpositioning troops between belligerent forces and maintaining disengagement zones. UN peacekeepers are also known as 'blue berets' or 'blue helmets' because of their distinctive headgear (such soldiers otherwise wear national uniforms). They are deployed with the consent of warring parties and do not use force except in self-defence.

Between 1948 and 1988, the Security Council approved 13 operations. Over that four-decade period, the UN deployed some 500,000 peacekeeping personnel to places as far-flung as West New Guinea, Cyprus, India and Pakistan, Israel, Egypt, Syria, Lebanon and the Dominican Republic. While not all operations were successful, blue berets were crucial to sustaining peace in many places, and in 1988 they received the Nobel Peace Prize.

By contrast, the Security Council invoked Chapter VII a mere five times in that same period. Twice it authorized the use of force: in 1950 on the Korean peninsula in defence of the south against the communist north – only possible because the Soviet Union had boycotted the council; and in 1960 in newly independent Congo – an outpost where major powers had few strategic interests. Once it invoked Chapter VII to impose a cease-fire between Israel and its Arab neighbours and twice to impose sanctions – against Rhodesia and South Africa – motivated largely by human rights violations by white-minority regimes. The latter two cases may be seen as a precursor to the council's intimate linkage of human rights with international peace and security in the post-Cold War era.

The end of the East–West rivalry made cooperation among the P-5 more feasible, thus revitalizing the Security Council as the guardian of world peace. Several new operations began in 'flashpoints' of the East–West struggle (Afghanistan, Cambodia, Angola, Namibia, El Salvador and Nicaragua), but the real breakthrough came from the invocation of Chapter VII authorizing military force to roll back Iraqi aggression against Kuwait in 1990. The dramatic decline in vetoes is also illustrative of changes in council dynamics in the new era: between 1946 and 1986 the veto was wielded 212 times, as compared to 38 times between 1987 and 2005. The number of resolutions also doubled in half the time, 593 in 40 years versus 1,010 in 20.

What became known as 'second-generation' peacekeeping included electoral assistance, human rights monitoring, and even weapons collection, activities once seen as within the domestic jurisdiction of states. However, these operations were still based on the principle of consent, and peacekeepers remained bound by restrictions on the use of force.

The 1990s witnessed a radical shift in the nature of UN operations, from peacekeeping to peace enforcement, as well as an ever widening scope for what the council judged to be a 'threat to international peace and security' (the basis for decisions; see also Chapter 27, this volume). Breaking new ground, the council called interference with humanitarian action and violence against civilians 'threats to international peace and security'; it authorized military operations to such war-torn places as Bosnia, Somalia, Rwanda, Kosovo and the Democratic Republic of the Congo (DRC). In Haiti, the council even determined that the overthrow of a democratically elected president and accompanying instability were a threat to the peace. In contrast to earlier peacekeeping, these new operations were authorized under Chapter VII and thus were coercive rather than consensual.

Lacking its own capacity to deploy military operations, the world body often authorizes coalitions of the willing or regional bodies – such as the African Union, Economic Community of West African States and the North Atlantic Treaty Organization (NATO) – to assume command of such missions. At the end of 2006, these organizations had 68,000 peacekeepers in the field (CIC 2007). Extending beyond any traditional interpretation of Chapter VII, the world body has even assumed what some see as 'neo-colonial' administrative and coercive responsibilities of a state, as in post-conflict East Timor and Kosovo. European organizations have been especially helpful partners in the UN Interim Administration Mission in Kosovo.

In addition to the use of military force, the Security Council has increasingly relied on two other coercive measures – economic sanctions and international criminal prosecution. Indeed, in the post-Cold War period, the council imposed dozens of sanctions against 16 entities, including such nonstate actors as the Union for the Total Independence of Angola and al-Qa'ida. First levied in this period against Saddam Hussein's Iraq in 1990, blanket trade sanctions were at the centre of controversy due to their devastating humanitarian impact. In response, the council began applying only targeted sanctions via arms embargoes, financial asset freezes, travel bans and commodity boycotts (Cortright and Lopez 2000).

International criminal tribunals were another invention. In the wake of genocide and other crimes against humanity in the former Yugoslavia and Rwanda, the council established judicial bodies to try those responsible for heinous acts in the conduct of war. These tribunals have had mixed results. After ten years, neither has completed more than 30 cases, while many of the key perpetrators remain free. In addition to criticisms about effectiveness and costs, some have questioned whether they actually inhibit peace building and national reconciliation. Nonetheless, the war crimes tribunals have contributed to the development of international criminal law – for example, that rape can be a form of genocide – as well as the 1998 creation of the International Criminal Court and other judicial efforts in East Timor, Cambodia and Sierra Leone.

In sum, an increasingly active council in the post-Cold War era was willing to consider massive human rights abuses, forced displacement, purposeful starvation, and even the overthrow of an elected government as threats to international peace and security. In January 2000, the HIV/AIDS pandemic was identified as a threat to international peace and security (see Chapter 19, this volume), and in April 2007 the council debated whether climate change constituted such a menace (see Chapter 18, this volume).

The definition of what is 'essentially within the domestic jurisdiction' of states is changing, and the principle of state sovereignty along with it. This was evident at the 2005 World Summit, when some 150 heads of state and government endorsed the 'responsibility to protect', which re-frames sovereignty as contingent rather than absolute (see Chapter 28, this volume). If a state is unwilling or unable to protect its people from ethnic cleansing or mass killing, it forfeits its sovereignty; and the responsibility for protecting citizens falls on the international community of states.

US hegemony

The end of the Cold War facilitated Security Council action, but the switch from a bipolar to a unipolar world left the USA unchallenged as the remaining superpower. With military expenditures equal to the rest of the world combined, US hegemony meant that Washington's approval, or at least acquiescence, was essential to the functioning of the world body in the security arena.

The reality of asymmetric US power is that a hegemon may indeed choose to 'go it alone', which generates legitimacy crises for the United Nations. The US-led invasion of Iraq in 2003 without council approval, and in the face of worldwide opposition, is a vivid illustration. The George W. Bush administration in fact returned to the Security Council for its blessing in rebuilding Iraq, showing that even the lone superpower needs the world body on occasion. The conundrum for the UN was whether it should help bail out the US-led coalition that had gone to war after ignoring the council, a situation that will undoubtedly appear again as domestic pressures increase for an American withdrawal.

Finessing the council in the Iraq case, however, should be seen in historical context. The USA has vacillated between multilateral and unilateral urges not merely since 1945 but since the Senate refused to join the League of Nations, the brainchild of US president Woodrow Wilson (Luck 1999). Addressing a number of priority security threats (including terrorism and nuclear proliferation) would seem, by definition, to require multilateral cooperation even for a superpower.

Increased access by actors other than states

While states remain the gatekeepers of international peace and security, NGOs and other actors have become more visible and numerous in the post-Cold War era, and the Security Council has responded by providing them with more access. In contrast to ECOSOC, which through Charter Article 71 can grant NGOs consultative status – thereby allowing these groups to attend meetings and even make statements and propose agenda items – no equivalent arrangement exists between such groups and the Security Council. Thus, while civil society organizations were for decades engaged in UN activities, their official participation until recently was limited to matters pertaining to development, human rights, humanitarianism and environment.

The council's expanded definition of threats to international order to include human rights violations and humanitarian disasters opened up avenues for NGOs to have a voice in security matters. The council in the early 1990s initiated greater dialogue between states and nonstate actors. The so-called Arria formula (named after the Venezuelan ambassador who launched the experiment during his presidency) has become a standard procedure, and humanitarian and human rights organizations have been able to offer country-

and issue-specific knowledge, practical expertise and information about on-the-ground developments.

In the early post-Cold War period, council presidents also began briefing the media, thereby drawing public attention to the body's negotiations and decisions. Celebrities have contributed to enhancing the council's visibility, as they have used their status to cast a spotlight on issues such as humanitarian crises and the plight of women and children in armed conflict. At the end of 2006, one prominent movie star even made a statement before the Security Council, urging members to halt Khartoum's atrocities in Darfur.

The General Assembly

The General Assembly is a more inclusive arena for deliberations by states than the Security Council. Indeed, each UN member state has equal status in the body and one vote – concrete evidence of the 'sovereign equality of all its Members' called for in Article 2(1). Unlike the Security Council's decisions that are binding, however, the General Assembly's resolutions are 'recommendations'. They are adopted by a simple majority, except for those identified as concerning 'important questions', which require two-thirds of the members present and voting. According to Article 18, these include 'recommendations with respect to the maintenance of international peace and security [and] the election of the non-permanent members of the Security Council'.

Charter Articles 11–12 grant the General Assembly the ability to discuss such issues and make recommendations to states and to the council, but not while a dispute or situation is being considered by the Security Council. In practice, the assembly has considered conflicts regardless.

When the council is unable to act due to actual or threatened vetoes, the General Assembly has served as an alternative avenue for addressing security issues (Peterson 2005). Resolution 377(V), titled 'Uniting for Peace' (UfP), was a watershed. It created a parallel authority in the assembly by establishing:

> procedures by which a simple majority of the Security Council on a procedural vote (not subject to veto) or a majority of UN member states can convene the Assembly in 'emergency special session' on twenty-four hours' notice to consider and develop collective responses to a crisis when the Security Council has been unable to act (Peterson 2007: 104).

While the assembly cannot make binding decisions, through UfP it can endorse coercive actions. Adopted in 1950, it was a means to allow what many saw as 'blue-washed' US military action in Korea – originally authorized under Chapter VII – to continue despite the Soviet Union's return to the council after an earlier boycott due to Taiwan's occupancy of the 'Chinese seat'. Over the years, this procedure has been used sporadically (ten instances to be exact), the last time being against Israel in 1997 for its policies in the occupied territories.

Since decolonization, the Third World constitutes a strong majority in the General Assembly. Thus, smaller and weaker member states – and even middle powers when not elected to the council – prefer the democratic assembly in which they have a role in security matters. In particular, the Non-Aligned Movement NAM – the 115 developing countries that form a bloc – has staunchly defended self-determination, sovereignty and nonintervention, which are linked to many Security Council deliberations. Moreover, Third World resistance to white-minority rule in Rhodesia and South Africa was important in mobilizing international action against those rogue regimes, which eventually led to action by the council. Similarly, the Third World has consistently advocated in the assembly for the Palestinian cause in spite of council action (or inaction); over the past six decades, the assembly has passed a never-ending stream of resolutions concerning Israel and the occupied territories.

The Secretariat

International civil servants comprise the UN's administrative apparatus, or Secretariat. At the helm is the secretary-general, who is appointed by the assembly on the recommendation of the council. In reality, the P-5's veto power makes the selection process for the secretary-general into an exercise in geographic horse-trading (the position rotates from region to region, usually after two terms) in which the qualifications of the individual candidates are a secondary concern (Newman 1998, Gordenker 2005). Indeed, as Brian Urquhart has argued, efforts are made to select a candidate who 'will not exert any troubling degree of leadership, commitment, originality, or independence' (Urquhart 1987: 227–228). Charter Article 100, however, requires that the organization's top civil servant and other UN personnel perform their duties independent of governments, and it obliges member states 'not to seek to influence them in the discharge of their responsibilities'. In order to fulfil his (not yet her) mandate for security matters, it is essential that the secretary-general does not incur the wrath of any of the P-5. The ill-fated first incumbent Trygve Lie – who resigned after Moscow's opposition to his conduct in Korea – once described the post as 'the most impossible job in the world' (Rivlin and Gordenker 1993) (see Table 22.1).

While the largest financial contributors to the world body often complain that the second UN is a sprawling bureaucracy, such criticisms are exaggerated. The UN Secretariat itself employs some 30,500 personnel to administer the affairs of the globe. If one considers the nine bodies of the UN proper that have special status in matters of appointment – the largest being the UN Children's Fund (UNICEF), UN Development Programme (UNDP), UN High Commissioner for Refugees (UNHCR), and World Food Programme (WFP) – the international civil service comprises about 56,000 staff worldwide. Similarly, the UN's regular budget is limited in light of the tasks

Table 22.1 Secretaries-general of the United Nations, 1946–2007

Trygve Lie (Norway)	February 1946–April 1953
Dag Hammarskjöld (Sweden)	April 1953–September 1961
U Thant (Burma, now Myanmar)*	November 1961–December 1971
Kurt Waldheim (Austria)	January 1972–December 1981
Javier Pérez de Cuéllar (Peru)	January 1982–December 1991
Boutros Boutros-Ghali (Egypt)	January 1992–December 1996
Kofi Annan (Ghana)	January 1997–December 2006
Ban Ki-moon (Republic of Korea)	January 2007–

Note: *Acting Secretary-General, November 1961–November 1962

that fall under the organization's purview. Although it has risen over the past six decades from $21.5 million in 1945 to $1.9 billion in 2007, when adjusted for inflation, the change is not nearly as substantial (Myint-U and Scott 2007: 126–128). The regular budget certainly appears paltry when compared to annual US confectionary and alcohol expenditures – $27 billion and $70 billion, respectively.

For security studies, it is important to note that these figures do not include the world body's peacekeeping personnel and budget. At the end of 2006, the UN had 81,000 troops, military observers and police engaged in 18 operations. If all current mandates were staffed to authorized levels, this figure would reach 140,000, nearly double the previous peak of 77,000 during the tumultuous early 1990s (CIC 2007: 2). Meanwhile the July 2006 to June 2007 peace-keeping budget reached an all-time high of $5.4 billion – about one month's expenditures by the USA in Iraq or less than half the annual budget of the New York City Board of Education. Despite the magnitude of operations, the Department of Peacekeeping Operation's (DPKO) staff represent just 5 per cent of total Secretariat personnel, a mere 507 employees; and the Department of Political Affairs (DPA) has only 182 employees. Together they have fewer employees than the Department of Public Information (Myint-U and Scott 2007: 127).

The Secretariat and the secretary-general play crucial roles in security matters because they are charged with carrying out Security Council decisions. The organization's executive head routinely engages in preventive diplomacy, dispute mediation, negotiations and fact-finding, and is the person to whom UN-sponsored forces report. His authority derives from Charter Article 99, which grants him the power to call the Security Council's attention to 'any matter which in his opinion may threaten the maintenance of international peace and security'. Article 99 has been invoked on only three occasions – by Dag Hammarskjöld in 1960, in the wake of decolonization in the Congo; by Kurt Waldheim in 1979, in response to the Iranian hostage crisis; and by Javier Pérez de Cuéllar in 1989, in the escalation of armed conflict in Lebanon. Given the fruitlessness and potential embarrassment of invoking the article without P-5 support, secretaries-general have usually pursued 'quiet diplomacy', pressing their position with states behind the scenes.

Some have played more visible roles in enhancing the Secretariat in matters of international peace and security, partly because of their personalities but also the international political context during their tenures (Ramcharan 2008). Despite Cold War constraints, Lie managed to bolster his investigatory and conflict prevention responsibilities. Hammarskjöld was the intellectual force (along with Canadian minister Lester Pearson) behind the creation of Chapter VI peacekeeping operations. Under his direction, the first ever armed peace mission, the UN Emergency Force, was launched in 1956 in response to the Suez Canal crisis. Meanwhile, U Thant carved out a role for the secretary-general as an independent mediator, while Pérez de Cuéllar – whose tenure extended into the post-Cold War period – enhanced the 38th floor's (the top floor of the UN's headquarters in New York) capacity for fact-finding and observation, oversaw the initial expansion of peacekeeping, and helped quell turmoil in such Cold War flashpoints as Central America, Afghanistan, Cambodia and southern Africa. He was in office when UN peacekeepers were awarded the 1988 Nobel Peace Prize.

Boutros Boutros-Ghali, the sixth head of the world body, was one of the most influential in the security arena. His intellectual contribution was the forward-looking *An Agenda for Peace* – following the first ever meeting in his first month in office of the Security Council at the level of head of state and government – that 'still defines the conceptual framework through which (for better or worse), the UN thinks about its work in the political field, formalizing concepts such as peacebuilding, early warning, preventive deployment and peace enforcement' (Myint-U and Scott 2007: 94). He oversaw the development of more muscular peace missions and was responsible for pushing the council to action in Somalia – where the first enforcement mission under UN command and control was launched – and pushing for the first ever preventive deployment mission in Macedonia. He also reorganized the Secretariat, including the establishment of two crucial departments: the Department of Political Affairs – responsible for conflict prevention and political analysis – and the Department of Peacekeeping Operations – responsible for the operational dimensions of UN missions.

Secretary-General Kofi Annan, who received the Nobel Peace Prize in 2001, also left a considerable legacy. As under-secretary-general for peacekeeping operations in the 1990s, he had more direct experience with the operational dimensions of peace operations than his predecessors and devoted the bulk of his time to peacekeeping management rather than mediation and diplomacy. He was intimately involved in the dramatic expansion in peace operations, taking a leading advocacy role in calling for humanitarian intervention and in overseeing the UN's quasi-state role in post-conflict Kosovo and East Timor (Annan 1999c). The widespread opposition to the US-led war in Iraq without Security Council approval, instances of peacekeepers' sexual exploitation of women and children, and the Oil-for-Food Programme scandal involving his son, however, clouded the end of Annan's second term. In January 2007, Ban Ki-moon became the eighth secretary-general.

Other UN organs and actors

The three other principal organs – ECOSOC, the ICJ and the Trusteeship Council – are less central to understanding the UN's relevance for security studies. ECOSOC's purview spans economic, social, cultural, education and health as well as human rights. Charter Article 65 grants ECOSOC the power to 'furnish information' to the Security Council and requires it to assist the council upon request. Historically the link between these two bodies has been weak, even non-existent.

In the late 1990s, however, the Security Council sought to engage ECOSOC with a possible role in the UN's post-conflict peace building. Resolution 1212 of November 1998 formally called upon ECOSOC to assist Haiti with a long-term sustainable development programme, and in response ECOSOC created an Ad Hoc Advisory Group to make recommendations and implement them. In collaboration with the Security Council, ECOSOC also created a working group on Guinea-Bissau. However, ECOSOC's ineffectiveness prompted the High-level Panel on Threats, Challenges and Change (2004) to recommend the creation of a new body. In late 2005 the Security Council and General Assembly approved similar resolutions calling for the creation of the Peacebuilding Commission to address coordination problems that often hamper efforts at building lasting peace.

The International Court of Justice may be considered as part of the world body's peaceful settlement of disputes machinery. However, disputing states must voluntarily consent to the court's jurisdiction, and decisions normally take years. Given that states generally consider peace and security matters too important to be settled by 15 jurists and too urgent to wait, the ICJ has not handed down decisions or opinions that have actually resolved armed conflicts. Even when such cases are brought before the court, moreover, compliance with the ICJ's ruling is not obligatory – as illustrated by the US's refusal to implement the judgment of *Nicaragua vs. the United States*.

The Trusteeship Council, the successor of the League of Nations Mandates system, was established to oversee the transition from foreign to self-rule in colonies, a topic linked to international peace and security. For decades it worked closely with the General Assembly and, in areas designated as 'strategic', the Security Council. The last remaining 'trust territory', Palau, became independent in 1994, and so this principal organ is now dormant. The 2005 World Summit agreed to eliminate the Trusteeship Council, but this would require a Charter amendment, hardly likely.

The UN's own funds and programmes – especially the largest humanitarian players UNDP, UNICEF, UNHCR and WFP – are often present on the landscape in security crises and work side-by-side with UN soldiers. The host of specialized agencies depicted in Figure 22.1 are part of the UN system; but they are more peripheral to security studies for two reasons: they are not directly responsible to the UN secretary-general, and their main activities are in economic and social development.

Twenty-first-century challenges

In the new millennium, the UN finds itself amidst a sea change in security affairs. While interstate disputes (its original justification) will always pose threats to international order, intrastate conflicts – often linked into global arms, trade and drug trafficking networks – are widespread and constitute substantial threats to regional and even global stability. Alongside changes in warfare and the security problems posed by so-called failed states, the world organization confronts the intertwined threats of terrorism and weapons of mass destruction (WMDs).

Changes in the nature of war and UN responses

The UN's mechanisms to prevent and confront armed conflict were conceived in the aftermath of two large-scale wars involving world powers. Since 1945, however, intrastate conflicts have become commonplace and lethal. One explanation is the end of the superpower rivalry, which dried up the abundant financial and military aid flowing from the USA and Soviet Union to their respective Third World allies. Hence, the resources used to sustain fragile regimes through coercion and patronage led to turmoil in some parts of the South and even state collapse, as in Somalia. The implosion of Yugoslavia and the Soviet Union, moreover, produced some 20 new countries, and the redrawing of territorial boundaries generated tensions within and between successor states. A second explanation for intrastate wars is globalization, particularly technological change and rapid economic interactions, which have made borders porous. Neoliberal structural adjustment policies similarly have curtailed resources for patronage, by requiring cuts in public sector employment, collective goods and subsidies.

Contemporary conflicts are thus waged and funded differently from most previous interstate wars. In contrast to hierarchically organized standing armies, a variety of actors participate directly in warfare – including such entities as criminal gangs and militias – via decentralized networks. Belligerents fight for control over territory and access to resources in the midst of civilian populations who are often the targets of violence rather than so-called collateral damage. In fact in many recent wars, civilians constitute 90 per cent of victims, a reversal from the beginning of the twentieth century when the ratio of military to civilian deaths typically was 9:1 and a change from the Second World War when similar numbers of civilians and soldiers died. Ethnic cleansing, forced displacement, mass rape, scorched earth campaigns, purposeful starvation and attacks on humanitarian aid workers are a standard bill-of-fare. These tactics are not 'new', but their coming together and intensity are more apparent than in the past, and this quantitative change is often sufficient enough to constitute a qualitative change.

The accompanying humanitarian emergencies adversely affect the security of neighbouring countries. Massive refugee populations are financially burdensome and menacing; and camps may serve as grounds for launching cross-border attacks – as illustrated by the concept of the 'refugee warrior'. In countries that already have precarious ethnic balances, the influx of particular groups may be destabilizing – a key concern, for instance, surrounding the influx of Kosovar Albanians into Macedonia in 1999.

Another source of instability arises from the economics of financing such violence. The war economies sustaining many civil wars reflect plunder, smuggling, drug trafficking and the sale of other illicit commodities. Those who benefit have an interest in continued violence not peace, especially because criminal trade networks operate globally. Failed states, moreover, can serve as havens for terrorists whose calculations are not based on cost–benefit analysis.

Peace enforcement operations were a key UN response to the actual and potential international instability emanating from war-torn societies (see also Chapter 27, this volume). As mentioned earlier, the UN itself is incapable of launching its own military operations or commanding borrowed soldiers – vividly illustrated by the failures to halt massive killings and displacement in Bosnia and Somalia. The United Nations has relied on coalitions of the willing and regional organizations – options that are not without their problems. With the exception of NATO and the European Union, regional bodies are ill-equipped militarily. In addition to operational issues, making use of sub-contracted forces also raises questions of accountability. The involvement of regional heavyweights in neighbouring country conflicts can shift local balances of power and serve interests other than human protection. NAM rhetoric often emphasizes, for example, that humanitarian intervention may be veiled neocolonial tactics.

In places where valuable natural resources, such as diamonds, constitute the basis for sustaining war economies, the Security Council has imposed commodity embargoes on states as well as nonstate actors, and investigative panels have been created to monitor compliance. Here as elsewhere, however, noncompliance with council sanctions is a considerable obstacle to their effectiveness.

In addition to addressing conflicts once they erupt, the UN has attempted to focus on the phases before and after wars. Over the past decade, the world body has increasingly engaged in conflict prevention, particularly since the council's failure to respond to the Rwandan genocide. UN secretaries-general have been at the forefront of such efforts. Boutros-Ghali's seminal *An Agenda for Peace* emphasized the importance of preventive diplomacy, while Secretary-General Kofi Annan's *Prevention of Armed Conflict* pledged to 'move the United Nations from a culture of reaction to a culture of prevention' (Annan 2001: 1).

A crucial component of conflict prevention entails tackling the so-called root causes of conflict, which have economic, social, environmental and institutional origins. Hence, structural prevention involves efforts to foster socioeconomic development and good governance. In a 2006 report, Annan expanded the concept to include 'systemic prevention', which aims to address international-level factors that enhance the risk of conflict such as the global illicit trade in small arms. Given the extensive scope, structural prevention is a nebulous concept that is hard to implement; it involves virtually every acronym in the UN system.

At the other end of the spectrum, post-conflict peacebuilding missions aim to assist countries to make the transition from violence to peace and prevent the recurrence of warfare. Core tasks include: weapons collection; elections monitoring; assistance with rebuilding governmental institutions; judicial reform; training of police forces; and human rights monitoring. In the most drastic cases, the UN along with other international organizations has sometimes assumed core state functions.

The record of such efforts is seen by many to be positive – if one measures success as the absence of recurrent large-scale violence. However, in some places, such as Central America, crime is endemic and levels of socioeconomic inequality have increased, while in others, such as Cambodia, democratic rule is precarious. Overall, the extent to which peace building missions have created conditions for lasting peace is mixed, and a general conclusion is that longer term commitments are required (Paris 2004).

Terrorism

Al-Qa'ida's attacks on US territory brought into stark relief the destructive capacity of nonstate actors in a globalizing world. Terrorism, however, has been on the UN's agenda for decades. Indeed, the General Assembly – serving as the lead UN actor due to the Cold War stalemate in the Security Council – has addressed it since 1972. Although unsuccessful in reaching an agreed-upon definition of terrorism, the assembly, particularly its Sixth Committee, has facilitated 13 international legal conventions spanning such issues as hijacking, bombings and use of nuclear material.

The spate of terrorist bombings in the late 1980s and 1990s spurred the Security Council to act. It imposed sanctions on rogue states such as Libya – which was shielding suspects in the bombing of Pan-Am flight 103 – and Afghanistan – which was providing sanctuary to Osama bin Laden and al-Qa'ida. In the wake of 11 September, the council for the first time deemed self-defence a legitimate response to a terrorist attack in resolution 1368, thereby endorsing the US war in Afghanistan to change the Taliban regime. Subsequently, resolution 1373 required all states to implement specified measures to combat terrorism, including changes to national legislation, and established the Counter-Terrorism Committee (CTC) to monitor their implementation. In 2004, the council was concerned about terrorists' acquiring nuclear capabilities. It passed binding Chapter VII resolution 1540 that requires states to ensure appropriate measures to control and account for nuclear, biological and chemical weapons. Kofi Annan established a Policy Working Group to explore how the UN should respond to terrorism. He also convened the High-level Panel on Threats, Challenges and Change (2004) to recommend a comprehensive UN approach to security, including anti-terrorism. He also called attention to human rights violations perpetrated in the name of fighting terrorism – Guantánamo Bay and Abu Ghraib being hallmarks.

After three decades of grappling with this issue, the 2005 World Summit still could not agree on a definition of terrorism. The lack of consensus among member states is especially problematic in light of the Security Council's authorization of self-defence as a response to terrorism (Boulden and Weiss 2004).

Disarmament and non-proliferation

Disarmament and non-proliferation were central at the UN's establishment. The Charter refers to the regulation of armaments, specifying roles for the General Assembly, Security Council and Military Staff Committee, while Articles 11 and 47 allude to disarmament.

Key components of the UN's machinery are the General Assembly, the Disarmament Commission, and the permanent Conference on Disarmament, which is an autonomous forum that reports to the assembly and is linked to the Secretariat. The UN, however, has not been a major player, although it has been crucial in the development of norms. Its main contribution has been facilitating the negotiation of international treaties, the most important being the Nuclear Non-Proliferation Treaty (NPT), the Chemical Weapons Convention (CWC), and the Biological Toxins and Weapons Convention (BWC). In 1996, the General Assembly adopted the Comprehensive Test Ban Treaty (CTBT), but it has not yet entered into force. The world body also cooperates with the International Atomic Energy Agency (IAEA), a specialized agency, which conducts inspections to verify that nuclear materials and activities are not used for military purposes, the Organization for the Prohibition of Chemical Weapons (OPCW), and the Prep Com for the Nuclear-Test-Ban-Treaty Organization (CTBTO) (see Chapter 24, this volume).

The United Nations directly engaged in a coercive disarmament operation in Iraq following the Gulf War, when the Security Council established intrusive weapons inspections bodies, first the UN Special Commission (UNSCOM) and subsequently the UN Monitoring, Verification and Inspections Commission (UNMOVIC). Given the USA's failure to locate WMDs in Iraq following its invasion in 2003, the world body was seemingly successful in overseeing the destruction of Saddam Hussein's arsenal.

The majority of contemporary war-related deaths stem from small arms (see Chapter 23, this volume). Since the late 1990s, the UN has stepped up its non-proliferation efforts in this arena. The world body, however, has been unsuccessful in negotiating a legally binding treaty. By contrast, parallel advancements took place outside the UN to ban anti-personnel landmines, which culminated in the Ottawa Convention. This initiative was spearheaded by nongovernmental organizations and negotiated outside of the Conference on Disarmament.

Conclusion

Dag Hammarskjöld is widely reported to have remarked, 'The purpose of the UN is not to get us to heaven but to save us from hell.' The United Nations has played an essential role in diffusing interstate and intrastate disputes, responding to humanitarian emergencies, and elaborating norms for human rights. Over the past six decades, the world organization has demonstrated considerable creativity in navigating the constraints of power politics. However, so long as states fail to provide requisite resources and delegate authority, the UN's capacity to fulfil its mandate will remain circumscribed.

Further reading

Thomas G. Weiss, David P. Forsythe, Roger A. Coate and Kelly-Kate Pease, *The United Nations and Changing World Politics* (Boulder, CO: Westview Press, 5th edn, 2007). An up-to-date text about the world organization.

Thomas G. Weiss and Sam Daws (eds), *The Oxford Handbook on the United Nations* (Oxford: Oxford University Press, 2007). A compendium of 40 original essays as Secretary-General Ban Ki-moon takes the helm.

For concise and current treatments of the three principal organs discussed here with relevance for security studies, see the volumes from the Global Institutions Series: Edward C. Luck, *UN Security Council: Promise and Practice* (London: Routledge, 2006); M.J. Peterson, *The UN General Assembly* (London: Routledge, 2005); Leon Gordenker, *The UN Secretary-General and Secretariat* (London: Routledge, 2005).

Center for International Cooperation, *Global Peace Operations 2007* (Boulder, CO: Lynne Rienner, annual). A statistical and analytical overview of the UN's military efforts.

PART 4
CONTEMPORARY CHALLENGES

The International Arms Trade

William D. Hartung

▌ Abstract

The dynamics of the global arms trade have changed substantially from the end of the Cold War to the new era marked by the 9/11 terror attacks. Sales of major combat equipment continue to pose the greatest challenge in managing relations between states. But as the proportion of wars carried on within states rather than between states has accelerated, small arms and light weapons (SALW) have become the tools of choice in most of the world's conflicts. In an era of asymmetric warfare, the 'high end' of the weapons spectrum has also become cause for increasing concern as some regional powers seek the technology to produce nuclear, chemical and biological weapons. Using shifting US policies as a primary example, this chapter traces the political, economic and strategic factors driving these three strands of the arms trade: major combat systems, small arms, and technology suited to building nuclear weapons.

▌ Introduction

The international arms trade is intimately linked to issues of peace and security, justice and injustice, and development and underdevelopment. Arms sales can fuel regional and local conflicts, or help create balances of power that head off conflict. They provide repressive regimes with the tools they need to suppress democratic movements and commit human rights abuses. They can be used to facilitate terrorist acts, or to support oppressed populations in fighting off genocide and ethnic cleansing. They can fuel technological growth or undermine economic development. They can serve as an independent variable fuelling conflict, or merely as a tool used by both sides in a pre-existing conflict driven by other causes. The impacts of exported weapons depend on the forces driving the trade and the circumstances under which they are used.

The dynamics of the global arms trade have changed substantially over the past five decades, from the Cold War to the War on Terror. The rationales for the trade have ranged from geopolitics (cementing relations with key strategic allies) to geoeconomics (securing substantial weapons deals that serve to subsidize the defence industrial bases of arms-exporting countries). These shifting justifications have mirrored changing global circumstances, as analysed below. However, before addressing that crucial set of issues, a few definitions are in order.

Three channels for arms transfers

The global arms trade is composed of three different elements: (1) the trade in major systems such as combat aircraft, tanks and warships; (2) the trade in small arms and light weapons, from AK-47s to shoulder-fired missiles (see Hartung 2000); and (3) the trade in 'dual-use' items with both civilian and military applications, including everything from shotguns and unarmed helicopters to equipment that may be used to manufacture nuclear, chemical and biological weapons.

The trade in major conventional weapons is the best-known, most lucrative and best-monitored element of the global arms business. Major arms manufacturing states such as the USA, Russia, the United Kingdom, France and China – the five permanent members of the UN Security Council – generally control between two-thirds and three-quarters of all global weapons sales in a given year. Table 23.1 shows that between 1996 and 2005, for example, these states accounted for between 64 per cent and 84 per cent of total global arms sales agreements (Grimmett 2006: 81).

The pursuit of exports of fighter planes, tanks, military helicopters and combat ships to states in Europe, Asia and the Middle East sparks intense competition among major suppliers. There are clear economic incentives for pursuing these deals. Sales of major combat systems not only generate revenues and profits for military firms, they also contribute to the balance of trade and provide jobs in key regions and localities of the exporting state.

While economics is one driver of the trade in major conventional weapons, politics and security often have an even more important role to play. During the Cold War, the USA used arms exports to cement relationships with key regional allies such as Iran, Indonesia, Taiwan and Brazil. These relationships

Table 23.1 Arms transfer agreements, Permanent Five Members of the UN Security Council 1996 to 2005 (in millions of dollars)

	1996	1997	1998	1999	2000	2001	2002	2003	2004	2005
USA	10,527	7,187	9,457	11,673	11,158	11,573	13,129	14,576	12,820	12,758
Russia	4,900	3,400	2,200	4,600	6,500	5,500	5,600	4,400	5,400	7,400
France	2,500	4,900	6,300	1,700	4,600	4,200	1,200	2,000	2,100	7,900
UK	4,900	1,000	2,000	1,500	600	600	700	300	6,400	2,800
China	1,000	1,300	700	3,100	500	1,100	400	500	700	2,100
World Total	31,827	21,287	29,457	35,173	31,358	30,973	28,929	27,476	38,920	44,158
P-5 as %	(75%)	(84%)	(70%)	(64%)	(74%)	(75%)	(73%)	(78%)	(70%)	(75%)

Sources: Grimmett (2003: 79, 2006: 81)

involved tacit or explicit commitments to promote US security interests in their region; to develop the capacity to operate smoothly alongside US military forces in the event of a conflict; and, in a number of key cases, to provide access to military bases in the recipient country (Klare 1984: 29–30, 35). Without arms sales as a tool, it would have been difficult for the USA to develop the 'global reach' that it achieved during the Cold War, and that it has maintained ever since.

During this same period, the Soviet Union made substantial arms exports, often in the form of military aid. From supporting national liberation movements in South Africa, Angola and Central America to courting nationalist regimes in Egypt and India, Soviet exports were even more driven by political considerations than those of the West. The USSR's range of clients was much smaller than the US's, with just 20 major clients in the global South for most of the Cold War period. By the mid-1980s, just five clients – Angola, India, Iraq, Libya and Syria – accounted for 75 per cent of Soviet weapons exports. Of these, three – India, Iraq and Syria – had Treaties of Friendship with the USSR (Anthony 1989: 200).

More details of the incentives for and impacts of conventional weapons sales will be supplied below. But now we must look at the second major channel of arms transfers, the supply of dual-use items. In the 1980s, the sale to Iraq of equipment and materials useful in the development of everything from medium-range Scud missiles to nuclear, chemical and biological weapons was a classic case of the 'boomerang effect' – the tendency of arms and military technology transfers to be used against the states that supplied them. Some of the supplies came from nominal Iraqi allies such as Russia and China, but large flows of dual-use items also came from the USA, France, Italy, the United Kingdom and Germany – the states that led the opposition to Iraq in the 1991 Gulf War. Since dual-use transfers generally involve arms-making *technology* rather than finished weapons systems, they are generally harder to track, even when exporting states put their minds (and resources) to the job. The stage for arming Iraq was set during the Iran/Iraq war (1980–1988), when a wide range of countries supplied one or both sides of the conflict including not only the major suppliers but also smaller suppliers such as Brazil, North Korea, Egypt, Jordan and Syria. Even so, major suppliers dominated in the value of arms transferred. France (over one-quarter) and the USSR (nearly one-half) supplied the bulk of Iraq's weapons imports; on the other side of the ledger, China supplied about one-half of Iran's imports during the war (Anthony 1989: 196–197).

The third channel of arms flows – one that has taken on particular prominence since the end of the Cold War – is the trade in small arms and light weapons (SALW). The vast majority of combat deaths in the world's annual roster of two to three dozen conflicts are inflicted with these systems, which are loosely regulated and were largely ignored as a proliferation problem until the late 1990s. SALW are easy to maintain and transport, relatively cheap to purchase, and notoriously hard to track. For all of these reasons they are the weapons of choice for terrorists, separatist movements, militias, warlords and other nonstate groups that are central players in the wars of the post-Cold War period, the vast majority of which are fought within countries, not between countries (see Boutwell et al. 1995). Control of SALW is further complicated by the fact that armed factions can seize control of natural resources like gold, diamonds and timber and sell them illicitly to garner funds to buy another round of armaments (see UN Security Council 2000: 11–20, 30–38, 50–61). These weapons may in turn be used to capture more territory and control more resources. This vicious cycle has had a devastating effect on a wide range of countries, and it can operate in significant part without the participation of major governments.

Arms sales take-off: the 1970s and 1980s

Arms sales and military aid have been tools of warfare and diplomacy from the outset of the Cold War, from US aid to Greece and Turkey to fight pro-communist partisans after the Second World War to British, French and Soviet bloc exports to both sides of the 1956 Suez crisis. But weapons exports really took off in the 1970s and 1980s, when the total value of the global trade increased threefold (US ACDA 2004: 53).

The increase in arms sales was driven by two major factors. On the geopolitical side, US President Richard Nixon was looking for a way to promote US interests around the world without resorting to another major military intervention as was the case in Vietnam. The result came to be known as the Nixon Doctrine. It was first elaborated in a 1969 speech in Guam in which he announced that from there forward it would be US policy to arm regional allies to protect US security interests rather than sending US troops to confront those threats directly (Nixon 1971: 544–549).

The second major factor driving the increase in arms sales was the rise in oil prices fostered by the formation of the Organization of Petroleum Exporting Countries (OPEC) in 1974. Oil revenues created purchasing power that was used by Saudi Arabia, Iran, and other oil-exporting states to purchase top-of-the-line fighter planes and combat vehicles from the USA, Britain, France, and other suppliers (Klare 1984: 33). And the Nixon Doctrine spurred sales not only to major oil exporters but to regional allies such as Anastasio Somoza in Nicaragua as well as the regimes in Brazil, South Korea and Taiwan. In some cases these transfers involved not only the weapons themselves but also extensive training packages and the knowledge and technology needed to produce comparable systems.

During this period, the USA, the Soviet Union and Western Europe slugged it out to see which area would dominate the global trade; in most years the split was about one-third each, with the large caveat that many of the Soviet sales were in the form of military aid, not cash sales. Economic incentives to export arms rivalled geopolitical drivers during this period. One such incentive was the felt need by the Western powers to 'recycle petrodollars' – to recapture additional monies spent to purchase higher-priced oil by selling expensive weapons systems to the oil-exporting states. In the USA, increased arms sales also helped smooth out the dip in military spending that came with the end of the Vietnam War; as US procurement for the war declined from 1973 to 1975, arms sales rose substantially, creating an alternative market that partly made up for declining Pentagon spending.

The administration of Jimmy Carter tried to change the dynamics of the global trade by promoting a policy of arms sales restraint. The Carter initiative built on the actions of the post-Vietnam, post-Watergate Congress, which passed the Arms Export Control Act (AECA) in 1976 in response to runaway US arms sales (see Hartung 1995: 56–62). The mid-1970s saw the USA offering excessive arms transfers to Saudi Arabia and Iran, arming both sides of the war between Greece and Turkey over Cyprus, and arming right-wing rebel groups in Angola which were allied with the apartheid regime of South Africa. The AECA gave Congress veto power over major sales of military equipment; put forward the principle that US-transferred arms should be used for defensive purposes; and stated that it would henceforth be the policy of the USA to adopt a leadership role in promoting arms sales restraint.

In line with this framework and in pursuit of his own beliefs, Jimmy Carter campaigned for president on a pledge to take the lead in curbing the international weapons trade (United States 1978: 266–275). His most promising initiative in this regard was the Conventional Arms Transfer (CAT) talks between the USA and the Soviet Union. The talks appeared to be making progress as each major supplier honed in on regions in which it would pledge to reduce the size and scope of its arms transfers. But late in Carter's term, his National Security Adviser Zbigniew Brzezinski pulled the rug out from under the talks, in part to clear the way for the USA to offer military technology to China as part of the ongoing normalization of US–China relations. President

Carter's own commitment to arms sales restraint waned as he warmed to the idea of using arms transfers as tools to reward friends and intimidate adversaries (Blechman and Nolan 1987).

In keeping with Carter's shift in emphasis, the USA armed the Shah of Iran right up until the end of his regime in 1979, when he was overthrown and replaced with a regime headed by the Ayatollah Ruhollah Khomeini. The US arms relationship with the Shah continued despite the repressive character of his regime, in which the US-trained SAVAK intelligence service engaged in kidnappings, torture and murder in its efforts to suppress anti-regime activists (Sick 1985: 24–25).

In addition, the Carter administration offered arms packages to a wide range of states in the Persian Gulf and the Horn of Africa – including Kenya, Egypt and Saudi Arabia – in exchange for access to military facilities that could be used by the newly forming Rapid Deployment Force, designed to ensure that there would be 'no more Irans' and 'no more Afghanistans' in the Persian Gulf region. Even Carter's greatest foreign policy achievement – the Camp David peace accords between Israel and Egypt – was sealed with a multi-billion-dollar military aid package for each party to the talks. In short, Jimmy Carter was ultimately seduced by the short-term benefits of arms transfers in securing political and military support, and allowed them to trump concerns about human rights, democracy and the fuelling of regional conflicts (Hartung 1995: 82–83).

While Jimmy Carter came late to the business of promoting arms sales, Ronald Reagan was a major booster from the outset of his administration. One of his first major efforts was to lobby Congress to approve a $9 billion-plus sale of Airborne Warning and Control System (AWACS) radar planes to Saudi Arabia, a fight which he won when the Senate voted 52 to 48 to support the sale (Klare 1984: 148–154). This was followed by a sale of F-16 combat aircraft to Venezuela, in contravention of a policy introduced during the Carter years that called for a virtual ban on sales of advanced US combat aircraft in Latin America. But perhaps the most important aspect of the Reagan arms sales policy was his support for covert arms sales to movements in Afghanistan, Angola, Cambodia and Nicaragua, all of whom he described as 'freedom fighters' regardless of their actual ideologies and practices.

In Afghanistan, the US funnelled over $2 billion in weapons and training to the mujahadin dedicated to ousting Soviet occupiers from their country (Katzman 1993: 15). Equipment ranged from automatic rifles, to military trucks, to shoulder-fired missiles. While there is no question that these supplies aided the efforts of Afghan rebel groups to defeat the Soviet Union, they had a significant aftershock. Much of the weaponry destined for Afghanistan was siphoned off by the ISI, Pakistan's military intelligence service, and transferred into conflict zones in Kashmir, India, Tajikistan, and other hot spots around the globe (Chris Smith 1995). Osama bin Laden, who went on to found the global terrorist group al-Qa'ida, used contacts with CIA-trained and armed mujahadin that he made during the Afghan war to build the foundations of his organization.

Perhaps the most publicized arms scandal of the 1980s was the Iran/Contra affair, in which the Reagan administration bartered arms with Iran to raise funds to arm the anti-government Contra militia force in Nicaragua. The operation violated a Congressional ban on aid to the Contras, and demonstrated what a determined administration can do when it chooses to use arms sales to perform an 'end run' around legal restrictions. The operation was revealed to the public after Eugene Hasenfus, a low-level operative involved in delivering weapons via air to the Contras, was captured by the Sandinista government and acknowledged his role in the pro-Contra operation. A bipartisan Congressional committee which investigated the case found that Col. Oliver North had coordinated a multinational arms supply operation out of his offices around the corner from the White House. Among the other players in the scandal were Saudi Arabia, which put up $32 million to help arm the Contras, along with a 'rogues' gallery' of middlemen that ranged from ex-CIA and Pentagon officials to international arms dealers such as the Saudi Adnan Khashoggi and Iranian Manucher Ghorbanifar. While the scandal was ultimately uncovered, punishments for the participants were minimal and it was not at all clear that steps had been taken to prevent such an operation in the future (see Draper 1987). In fact, Richard Gadd, who served as a pilot in Oliver North's covert 'air force' that was used to arm the Contras, later received a contract to ship weapons to the Colombian government as part of the US 'war on drugs'.

Post-Cold War dynamics

With the end of the Cold War, economic motives moved to the forefront in the Clinton administration's arms sales policy, which explicitly cited the importance of weapons exports in supporting the US defence industrial base. Even before he was elected president, Bill Clinton showed a penchant for supporting major arms deals as a way of currying favour in key states. His opponent, the incumbent George Herbert Walker Bush, announced several large deals during the stretch run of the campaign, including a $5-billion sale of F-15 combat aircraft to Saudi Arabia and a $9-billion sale of F-16 combat aircraft to Taiwan. While the Bush I administration went through the motions of presenting strategic rationales for each of these deals, the real motives were made clear when candidate Bush announced the deals at major rallies in front of cheering workers in St Louis (home to production of the F-15) and Fort Worth, Texas (where F-16s are manufactured). In Fort Worth, Bush made his remarks amidst signs saying 'Jobs For America – Thanks Mr. President' (Wines 1992). In St Louis, he asserted that 'in these times of economic transition, I want to do everything I can to keep Americans at work' (Bush 1992).

Candidate Bill Clinton immediately put out a press release supporting the F-15 sale to the Saudis (despite objections by Israel, one of the USA's strongest allies), in no small part because the planes are built in Missouri, an important 'swing state' that could have gone Democratic or Republican in the 1992 elections. Clinton's support for the Saudi sale was no anomaly; US arms sales nearly tripled in his first year in office, to $33 billion (US DoD 2003). And he sent his Secretary of Commerce, the late Ron Brown, to the 1993 Paris Air Show, where he secured a sale of radar aircraft to France and stopped along the way to convince the Saudis to 'stay the course' on tens of billions of arms deals with the USA, despite concerns in Riyadh about whether the Saudi kingdom could afford them all.

One of the most embarrassing – and instructive – arms sales developments of the Bush/Clinton years was the revelation that the USA and its allies had been major suppliers of arms and arms-producing technologies to Iraq in the run-up to the 1991 Gulf War. While countries like France, the United Kingdom and Italy provided finished weapons systems to Saddam Hussein's regime – not to mention the then Soviet Union, the largest supplier – the USA primarily supplied arms-making technologies, from equipment used in Iraq's missile production factories to materials applicable to the production of biological weapons (Wines 1991). Indirect US impacts on the Iraqi arsenal included the transfer of US-designed cluster bombs to Baghdad via Chilean arms dealer Carlos Cardoen (Pastzor 1991).

In the wake of the 1991 war, US President Bush and British Prime Minister John Major pledged to do something to curb the burgeoning (and destabilizing) weapons trade to the Middle East. Talks were commenced involving the five permanent members of the UN Security Council (China, France, the Soviet Union, the United Kingdom and the USA). All of these states had armed Iraq in the run-up to the Gulf War. The aim of the talks was to reduce the levels of sales to regions of tension and to place specific curbs on the sale of ballistic missiles. Unfortunately the talks broke down when China withdrew in 1993, in part because of US and French sales of advanced combat aircraft to Taiwan, and in part due to its own specialization in missile exports, the very systems targeted for curbs in the arms sales talks (Oberdorfer 1992). One small bright spot in the post-Gulf War period was the establishment of the UN Arms Register, a voluntary system of reporting arms exports and imports which helped focus attention on the issue of the weapons trade while providing information not always available from existing governmental and non-governmental sources.

Post-9/11 arms exports

The 11 September 2001 terror attacks on the Pentagon and the World Trade Center created yet another shift in arms sales policy. In the name of fighting the 'global War on Terror' (GWOT), the Bush administration lifted human rights and nonproliferation restrictions on sales to countries like Pakistan, Yemen, Kazakhstan and Indonesia, and increased military aid to Georgia, the Philippines and other states viewed as potential allies in fighting terrorist networks (Hartung and Berrigan 2005: 7). The number of states receiving US military aid doubled from 2001 through 2005, and nearly three-quarters of US arms recipients were either undemocratic regimes or major human rights abusers, through criteria established by its own State Department (Hartung and Berrigan 2005: 4, 36).

This shift towards explicitly arming repressive governments in pursuit of the War on Terror did not initially lead to major increases in the dollar value of US weapons sales, but by 2006 such sales had doubled, from about $10 billion per year to over $20 billion, the highest levels since the wake of the 1991 Gulf War. Major drivers of the increase in the arms market included a major sale of F-16 combat aircraft to Pakistan, a plan for re-equipping and retraining the Saudi National Guard (SANG), and substantial sales to Turkey, Egypt and Israel (Wayne 2006).

The trade in small arms and light weapons

As noted above, the trade in SALW is a major focus of recent analysis and activity related to the global arms trade due to its centrality in enabling current conflicts and its potential and actual role in arming terrorist groups. In order to look more closely at these phenomena, it is necessary to provide a more detailed definition of the trade.

Most writing on SALW uses as its point of departure the definition developed by the *Report of the Panel of Governmental Experts on Small Arms* (UN General Assembly 1997). The most comprehensive assessment of the global trade, global stockpiles, and global impacts of small arms and light weapons is the Small Arms Survey. The survey defines small arms and light weapons as follows:

- Small arms: revolvers and self-loading pistols, rifles, and carbines, assault rifles, submachine-guns and light machine-guns.

- Light weapons: heavy machine-guns, handheld under barrel and mounted grenade launchers, portable anti-tank and anti-aircraft guns, recoilless rifles, portable launchers of anti-tank and anti-aircraft missile systems, and mortars of less than 100mm calibre (Small Arms Survey 2002: 10).

According to a rough estimate by the Small Arms Survey, there are 639 million small arms in the world. This estimate covers firearms only, not light weapons such as mortars or rocket-propelled grenades. Compared to the approximately eight million new small arms produced each year, the market in second-hand weapons is dominant, due to the sheer size of the stockpiles.

The bulk of the world's small arms stockpile – 378 million, or nearly 60 per cent – are owned by civilians. Many of these are handguns, some of which have been acquired by terrorists or insurgents purchasing weapons from US-based gun dealers, taking advantage of the relatively lax gun control laws that prevail in the USA.

Starting in the late 1980s the Colombian government has repeatedly called for the US government to take steps to restrict the ability of Colombian drug cartels to purchase pistols and firearms in the USA. According to the head of the US Bureau of Alcohol, Tobacco and Firearms (BATF), 87 per cent of a sampling of 292 firearms seized from Colombian drug traffickers during 1988 and 1989 were of US origin (Isikoff 1989b). During that same time period the *Washington Post* reported that '[l]aw enforcement officials report growing evidence that agents of the cartels operating in the United States have made major new efforts to purchase large caches of semi-automatic weapons – including AR-15 and Uzi assault guns – since the August 18 [1989] assassination of Colombian presidential candidate Luis Carlos Galan.' As Jack Killorin, then spokesperson for the BATF, put it, 'what we have is a constant flow of guns out of the country using the same trail that drugs are coming into the country . . . the cocaine traffickers are not going back empty handed' (Isikoff 1989a).

The flow of weapons from the USA to Mexican drug syndicates appears to be even larger than in the Colombian case. A 1993 article in the *Cleveland Plain Dealer* (18 October 1994) reported that in 1992 and 1993 the Mexican authorities identified over 8,700 guns from the USA, noting that 'officials on both sides of the border say the real numbers are far higher'. Among other crimes, US-origin guns were used in the March 1994 killing of Mexican presidential candidate Luis Donaldo Colosio; the September 1994 murder of Jose Francisco Ruiz Massieu, the Secretary-General of Mexico's Institutional Revolutionary Party (PRI); a Roman Catholic cardinal in 1993; and in a slaughter of 19 men, women and children in Ensanada, Mexico.

In addition to guns in civilian hands, an additional 241 million firearms – about 38 per cent – are controlled by traditional military forces (i.e. uniformed military forces answerable to states, not private militias or other military or paramilitary organizations) (Small Arms Survey 2002: 63, 75, 79). Some of these weapons also end up in the hands of terrorists or insurgents, either through capture, theft or corruption (i.e. sales to the groups by members of regular military forces). For example, it is suspected that weapons accumulated by al-Qa'ida members involved in the May 1993 bombing of three residential compounds in Saudi Arabia were sold to them by members of the Saudi Arabian National Guard (Finn 2003). On a larger scale, it is believed that much of the weaponry used by Chechen rebels at the height of their war with the Soviet military in the mid-1990s were *bought* from those very same Soviet personnel in a sort of 'weapons for food' programme. As one Soviet soldier asserted, 'The Chechens bought all of their weapons from us; otherwise, we wouldn't have had money to eat' (Klare 1995: n. 20).

It is believed that there are 70 to 100 million copies of just one type of automatic weapon – the Russian-designed AK-47 (and its variants) – worldwide. The AK is a popular weapon with insurgents, terrorists and armed forces alike. For example, when the USA went about building a new Iraqi military in the wake of the overthrow of Saddam Hussein, it was initially decided to arm them with AK-47s, which many Iraqis were already used to – and which were less likely to jam in the windy, dusty climate of Iraq.

How do nonstate groups get their hands on SALW? Two important avenues are theft or purchase from government forces, and taking advantage of lax local gun laws. But another major source of SALW destined for terrorist and insurgent groups comes from illegal, clandestine sales, commonly referred to as the black market. This market operates on a global scale, taking advantage of state-of-the-art communications, transportation, banking and brokering services.

Under this definition, covert arms transfers of the kind that the USA made to Afghan rebel groups during their war against the Soviet occupation of their country would fall into a grey area – clandestine, but permissible under US law, and sought by rebel groups seeking to oust an illegal occupying force. But even in these cases, the weapons supplied as covert sales are often left behind to become ready stockpiles for sale on the global black market. The amounts involved can be immense. For example, according to an estimate by the Congressional Research Service, the USA funnelled $2 billion in arms and training to the various Afghan rebel factions during the 1980s alone (Katzman 1993: 15). These systems were redistributed throughout South Asia and beyond, to the point where researcher Chris Smith asserted that '[t]he single most important factor in the introduction of small arms and light weapons into South Asia was the effort by the US and Pakistan to arm the Afghan mujahadin resistance' (HRW 1994: 5).

Although no comprehensive figures are available, it is widely believed that the bulk of the small arms and explosives being used by the insurgency against the US/UK-led coalition in Iraq came from internal sources. Analysts for the Small Arms Survey have written:

> [a]s the forces of Saddam Hussein collapsed in April 2003, there was little left of his armies but one of the largest small arms inventories in the world. With a large proportion of these weapons already gone and the rest unguarded, the collapse precipitated what was almost certainly one of the largest and fastest transfers of small arms ever.
>
> (Small Arms Survey 2004: 44)

There is evidence to suggest that members of Iraq's armed forces distributed the country's weapons stockpiles to locations throughout the country prior to the US intervention on the assumption that they would end up fighting a guerrilla war after US forces toppled the regime itself. To give a sense of the scale involved, the Small Arms Survey (2004: 46) has estimated that as many as 4.2 million firearms were in the hands of Iraqi military and reserve forces prior to the March 2003 US invasion, and that 'many of these largely military weapons were abandoned, pilfered, looted and sold to the Iraqi public after Saddam Hussein's defeat and disappearance'.

As journalist George Packer (2005: 299) noted, '[b]etween August 2002 and January 2003, Iraqi commanders had removed weapons and equipment from bases and hidden them in farms and houses all over the countryside.' In addition, there was considerable looting of warehouses that contained these materials. One of the most deadly weapons of the war – the improvised explosive device (IED) – is described by Packer (2005: 299) as 'a home-made bomb composed of an artillery shell or other military munitions (available at unguarded factories and ammo dumps throughout Iraq)'. Last but not least, several hundred thousand members of the Iraqi army – disbanded by Paul Bremer, head of the Coalition Provisional Authority in Iraq, in May 2003 – took their weapons with them when they left military service.

A UN panel of experts that investigated violations of the arms embargo against Liberia – which has since been lifted with the advent of a democratic government there – shed further light on methods used to transport illicit weaponry. For both aircraft and ships, Liberia had long provided a lax registration process that allowed middlemen and third countries to transport weaponry and other illicit items under Liberian 'flags of convenience'. This lax system 'enabled arms trafficking networks to camouflage their operations through fake registrations, document fraud and . . . the setting up of a mystery airline with the full knowledge of Liberian authorities in order to avoid detection' (UN Security Council 2001: 33).

One of the most important needs of arms brokers and their governmental or nongovernmental clients seeking illicit weaponry are real or forged end-user certificates. These allow weapons shipments to clear customs in any country on their transport route, after which they are either delivered to the country listed on the certificate and then transferred to a third country, or sent directly to a third country not listed on the certificate. Once again, the best documented cases come from West Africa. For example, a popular mechanism for getting 'small arms, missiles, helicopters and cargo aircraft' to Liberia from Eastern Europe was by using forged end-user certificates indicating that the weapons were destined for the armed forces of Guinea. In late November 2000, the Ugandan government impounded 1,250 submachine-guns allegedly destined for Guinea when authorities decided, based on the plane's flight plan, that the shipment was heading to Liberia (UN Security Council 2001: 36, 39).

This seemingly straightforward deal involved a long chain of front companies and illicit transport operators. Among the companies involved in the attempted shipment of the 1,250 submachine-guns to Liberia were Centafrican Airlines, registered in Bangui, Central African Republic, and operating out of the United Arab Emirates; Pecos, an arms-dealing company based in Conakry, Guinea; Vichi, 'a private agent for the Moldovan Ministry of Defence', and MoldTransavia, companies that were chartered to fly the aircraft used in the arms shipments. The UN panel of experts that investigated the incident also learned that the aircraft used in the transfer was owned by the arms dealer Victor Bout, and leased from his company Transavia Travel Agency of the United Arab Emirates. San Air, another UAE-registered company, supplied insurance for the deal. The majority of the companies involved were ultimately owned either by Victor Bout, his brother Sergei, or current or former associates of Victor Bout (UN Security Council 2001: 39–42). Bout is one of the most active players in the illicit arms trade, with involvement in deals to UNITA in Angola, the Charles Taylor regime in Liberia, and the rebels in Sierra Leone. In addition, according to intelligence documents uncovered by the International Consortium of Investigative Journalists (ICIJ 2002: 147), Bout was involved in supplying $50 million in weaponry to the Taliban during the period that they were hosting and supplying al-Qa'ida.

Dangers of dual use: the A.Q. Khan network

While the transfer of SALW to terrorist organizations and other nonstate actors is a going concern, their pursuit of weapons of mass destruction – and nuclear weapons in particular – is of even greater long-term concern. Even if the probabilities of terrorists getting control of a nuclear weapon are low, the consequences of their acquiring these weapons could be catastrophic, costing tens or hundreds of thousands of lives and rendering large parts of major cities or other targeted areas uninhabitable for years to come. One model for how a nuclear black market operates is the extensive nuclear smuggling network established by Pakistani nuclear scientist A.Q. Khan.

Khan is known as the father of Pakistan's nuclear bomb. Using plans he developed while working at a nuclear facility in Europe – along with a blank cheque from the Pakistani government of Zulfikar Ali Bhutto – Khan built a vast centrifuge facility at Kahuta, near Islamabad. By the early 1980s the facility was able to enrich significant quantities of uranium. By 1984, Khan claims he completed work on a nuclear bomb. He later boasted about this feat in the context of his country's lack of development, saying, 'A country which could not make sewing needles [or] good bicycles . . . was embarking on one of the latest and most difficult technologies' (Edidin 2004). But he did not do it alone. He took advantage of weak export controls and loopholes in national and international regulations that focused on plants and complete systems rather than components. Using this approach, Khan was able to purchase much of what was needed for the Pakistani bomb on the open market. By the late 1970s, the US State Department was regularly expressing its concerns to European officials about particular sales to Pakistan. In addition, the CIA was monitoring Khan's dealings and subsequently revealed that Pakistan obtained one or more of almost every component needed to build a centrifuge enrichment plant (Weissman and Krosney 1981).

Sellers from all over the world congregated in Pakistan to offer price lists for high-technology goods applicable to Pakistan's nuclear programme, according to the *New York Times*. 'They literally begged us to buy their equipment. . . . My long stay in Europe and intimate knowledge of various countries and their manufacturing firms was an asset', Khan bragged (Broad *et al.* 2004). Once Pakistan had the bomb and the capacity to enrich uranium, Khan 'reversed the network' he had developed to bring nuclear components and materials into Pakistan, using the same illicit channels to disseminate nuclear know-how and plans throughout the world.

International Atomic Energy Agency director Mohamed ElBaradei (2004) describes the elaborate model Khan perfected for disseminating nuclear materials – 'nuclear components designed for one country would be manufactured in another, shipped through a third country (which often appeared as a legitimate user) assembled in a fourth and designated for eventual turnkey use in a fifth'. The network included suppliers from all over the world – including Switzerland, the United Kingdom, the United Arab Emirates, Turkey, South Africa and Malaysia. It was responsible for the transfer of nuclear weapons-related technology, centrifuge parts and blueprints to Iran, North Korea, Libya and elsewhere (Lin 2004).

According to Christopher Clary (2004) from the Center for Contemporary Conflict, Iran was Pakistan's first major customer and Libya was its most recent. Clary asserts that Pakistan's proliferation grew steadily more complex, noting that 'sharing with Iran was fairly limited, Pakistani–North Korean cooperation was more significant, while Libya was in the midst of acquiring the most extensive "package" when it made the strategic decision to forgo weapons in 2003'.

By the time Khan supplied materials to Libya, Khan Research Laboratories was reportedly able to offer a 'turnkey' nuclear package. Robert Joseph, a nonproliferation expert serving on the US National Security Council, asserts that 'A.Q. Khan and company' was 'the principal supplier for the entire program. Khan provided the design, the technology, the expertise, and the equipment, primarily for the centrifuges. He also provided the warhead design' (in Motta 2006).

While Khan asserts that he 'transferred nuclear technology so that other Muslim countries could enhance their security', money was also a factor: Khan spent millions buying up homes and properties, including a tourist hotel in Africa that he named after his wife Henny (Broad *et al.* 2004). Officials within the Bush administration estimate that the Khan network netted $100 million for the technology it sold to Libya alone (Broad and Sanger 2004). In early 2004, the world learned what the intelligence community had long known: A.Q. Khan oversaw what Dr ElBaradei called the 'WalMart of private sector proliferation'.

Khan was dismissed from his post amid what Pakistan's government termed an 'investigation into alleged acts of nuclear proliferation by a few individuals'. At the beginning of February 2004, Khan and as many as six nuclear scientists were detained and questioned by the military's Inter-services Intelligence Agency. Pakistani President Pervez Musharraf vowed to punish 'with an iron hand' anyone who leaked nuclear weapons secrets to foreign governments, but by 5 February Khan had been pardoned, and dubbed a national hero in Pakistan. Even worse, Musharraf announced that he would block any international probe into Pakistan's nuclear programme. Khan lives in comfortable house arrest (estate arrest) and even the text of his 12-page confession has not been made public. The IAEA does not have direct access to Khan and is only able to submit written questions for the scientist to answer.

Apparently Khan's network did not function wholly independently. A study by the US Congressional Research Service concluded that 'A.Q. Khan must have had significant logistical support from elements in the Pakistani military and the civilian nuclear establishment' (Cronin *et al.* 2005).

Prospects for restraint

The role of arms transfers in fuelling conflict and enabling terrorist networks has driven the international community to seek measures to curb the trade. While past efforts such as the Conventional Arms Transfer talks between the US and the Soviet Union ended in failure, the new initiatives have a broader constituency and are seeking a wider range of controls. This suggests that there is a greater chance that at least some of these new initiatives could be implemented.

The most extensive efforts to curb military exports have come in the area of SALW, propelled by pressure from a broad network of NGOs ranging from arms control and human rights groups to organizations representing the handicapped to humanitarian aid and global development groups. The landmark 2001 UN Conference on Curbing Illicit Trafficking of Small Arms and Light Weapons in All of Its Aspects produced a programme of action calling on UN member states to undertake voluntary efforts to institute better internal controls on the export of SALW; consider ways to mark and trace weapons so that arms involved in conflicts and human rights abuses can be traced to their source countries; and increased intelligence and law enforcement cooperation in tracking small arms transfers. There are also separate initiatives underway to curb the trade in 'conflict diamonds' and other natural resources that have been illicitly acquired and traded as a source of revenue for buying small arms and light weapons.

The most ambitious undertaking in the field of arms trade regulation is the proposal for a global Arms Trade Treaty, which has initial support from 153 of the 192 UN member states. The treaty would set standards for denying sales based on violations of human rights, enforcement of existing embargoes, and destabilizing supplies to areas of conflict. Major obstacles to the treaty to date have been open opposition by the USA – which voted against even exploring the parameters of an agreement – and tacit opposition from Russia and China, which abstained on the same vote. Arguments against the treaty include the assertion that existing regulations should be better enforced first; and the claim that decisions on arms transfers should be the sovereign prerogative of individual states. Unstated rationales for opposing the treaty, from preserving 'freedom of action' to arm key allies regardless of their human rights performance to garnering the economic benefits of weapons exports without legal impediments, may be even stronger barriers to a global agreement. However, a paradigm shift may be underway which can overcome even these vigorous objections.

Conclusion

Whether or not additional restrictions are developed, the global arms trade will continue to be a major factor in the spheres of human rights, war and peace, and the economics of international trade. For this reason, it bears greater scrutiny and transparency to enable better decision-making on when arms sales are an appropriate foreign policy tool, and when they may do more harm than good.

Further reading

Gordon Corera, *Shopping for Bombs: Nuclear Proliferation, Global Insecurity, and the Rise and Fall of the A.Q. Khan Network* (Oxford: Oxford University Press, 2006). The most detailed account yet of the workings of the A.Q. Khan network, a private web of manufacturers and middlemen that provided nuclear weapons technology to Libya, Iran and North Korea, among others.

Lora Lumpe (ed.), *Running Guns: The Global Black Market in Small Arms* (London: Zed Press, 2000). Uncovers the anatomy of the illicit trade in small arms and light weapons, including analyses of small arms manufacturing, supply networks, sources of financing, and policy issues raised by the trade.

Andrew J. Pierre, *The Global Politics of Arms Sales* (Princeton, NJ: Princeton University Press, 1982). A primer on the motives driving major arms suppliers and recipients to engage in the weapons trade.

Anthony Sampson, *The Arms Bazaar: From Lebanon to Lockheed* (New York: Viking Press, 1977). The classic treatment of the often corrupt politics of international arms sales, grounded in pathbreaking government investigations of the mid-1970s.

John Tirman, *Spoils of War: The Human Costs of America's Arms Trade* (New York: The Free Press, 1997). Tracks the causes and consequences of two major US arms deals as a window on to the moral and economic dilemmas posed by the US role as the world's number one arms-exporting nation.

CONTENTS

Nuclear Proliferation

Waheguru Pal Singh Sidhu

Abstract

The post-Cold War world has witnessed the emergence of three challenges related to the proliferation of nuclear weapons. First, there is the challenge posed by states within the existing non-proliferation regime. The second set of challenges comes from states outside the present non-proliferation regime. The third and perhaps the most formidable challenge comes from non-state actors, including but not limited to terrorist groups. These three sets of challenges have led the international community to follow at least three different approaches: first, the traditional multilateral institutional approach anchored in treaty-based regimes; second, non-treaty-based multilateral approaches initiated by the UN-based international community; and third, a set of ad hoc, non-institutional, non-conventional approaches to address the immediate challenges of proliferation. These approaches, in turn, have led to several significant consequences for proliferation in future. This chapter examines all of these aspects related to proliferation.

Introduction

Soon after nuclear weapons first made their appearance in 1945, they emerged as the principal guarantors of international peace and security and underpinned world order during the Cold War. Indeed, it was the possession, or protection under the umbrella of nuclear weapons that was regarded as one of the primary factors behind the long period of relative peace and stability in the international system following the Second World War. Even in the post-Cold War period, the possession of and protection by nuclear weapons remains the fundamental basis for world order, evident from the continued dependence on nuclear weapons by states already possessing them and the acquisition of these weapons by new states. And yet, at least since 1 July 1968 when negotiations of the nuclear Non-proliferation Treaty (NPT) were completed and only five states (the United States, the Soviet Union, the United Kingdom, France and the People's Republic of China) were known to possess nuclear weapons, there has been a desire to prevent new states from acquiring nuclear weapons and also to curb the unfettered buildup of nuclear weapons among possessor states with the ultimate objective of eventually eliminating all nuclear weapons. Thus, ironically, the NPT has the unenviable task of preventing proliferation and disarming the very weapons upon which the present world order and international security continues to be based.

Predictably then, some scholars have argued that the NPT has been far from effective in the objective of preventing proliferation and the disarmament of nuclear weapons. They point to the existing global nuclear arsenal of over 27,000 weapons and the increase in the number of states known to possess nuclear weapons from the original five in 1968 to nine in 2007 (with Israel, India, Pakistan and the Democratic People's Republic of Korea (DPRK) joining the nuclear club) as proof of the failure of the NPT. However, some other scholars argue that the NPT has in fact been relatively effective in curbing proliferation. They note the dramatic decline in the number of nuclear weapons from around 80,000 in the late 1980s to less than half that number today and the fact that only four new states (three of which – Israel, India, Pakistan – have still not signed the NPT) have acquired nuclear weapons instead of nearly 20 states that some analysts had predicted. Indeed, several states, including Bulgaria, Canada, Germany, Italy, Japan, the Netherlands, Norway and Spain, did not pursue a nuclear weapons programme despite having the technical wherewithal to do so. In addition, other states, including Argentina, Australia, Brazil, Egypt, Poland, Romania, the Republic of Korea (South Korea), Spain, Sweden, Switzerland, Taiwan and Yugoslavia which had nuclear weapons programmes during the Cold War eventually abandoned them. Similarly, Libya, which was suspected of having started a clandestine nuclear weapons programme at the end of the Cold War, terminated it in 2003. Moreover, in the post-Cold War period other states, including South Africa, Belarus, Kazakhstan and Ukraine, which possessed nuclear weapons also gave them up. Clearly, the NPT has been more successful in preventing new states from acquiring nuclear weapons than it has been in either slowing down or disarming states that already possess nuclear weapons. The latter objective is likely to be met only when nuclear weapons are decoupled from the present world order; an unlikely eventuality given the interest of nuclear weapons states in maintaining the status quo despite the current unipolar moment.

Three caveats

This chapter is based on three essential caveats. First: contrary to conventional approaches which club nuclear weapons, along with biological and chemical weapons, into a convenient but specious category of so-called 'weapons of mass destruction' (WMD), this chapter will deliberately focus only on nuclear weapons. This is primarily because biological, chemical and nuclear weapons do not belong to the same conceptual category. The lethality of chemical weapons is not significantly different from that of conventional explosives. Similarly, a variety of protective measures exist to mitigate the effects of a biological attack. In contrast, there are no effective preventive or protective measures that can mitigate a nuclear attack. Besides, although nuclear weapons are not forbidden by international law (as is the case with biological and chemical weapons), given their cataclysmic nature, the taboo against their use is so strong that it is difficult to imagine their use other than against enemy nuclear weapons. In this context, the creeping tendency to redefine the mission of nuclear weapons to counter *all* WMD has two consequences: it lumps together biological, chemical and nuclear weapons into one fuzzy conceptual category, and it weakens the nuclear taboo. If nuclear weapons are accepted as having a role to counter biological-chemical warfare, then by what logic can nuclear weapons capability be denied to a country like Iran which has actually suffered chemical weapons attacks? Therefore, this chapter appropriately focuses only on nuclear proliferation.

Second caveat: proliferation should include both vertical (qualitative and quantitative improvement in the arsenals of states that already possess nuclear weapons) and horizontal (the quest of new states to acquire nuclear weapons) proliferation. In this context, proliferation of weapons among new nuclear states, such as the DPRK and, possibly, Iran, is as much of a concern as the ongoing improvement of the nuclear arsenals of the five original nuclear weapons states, evident in programmes such as the USA's 'reliable replacement warhead' (RRW) programme, and the United Kingdom's decision to update its *Trident*-based nuclear force. Moreover, today there appears to be a direct correlation between vertical and horizontal proliferation: both Iran and North Korea often cite the presence of nuclear-equipped US military forces in their respective regions as one of the primary motives behind Tehran's perceived and Pyongyang's evident quest for nuclear weapons.

Third caveat: as represented in the NPT package nuclear non-proliferation should be linked to nuclear disarmament. However, in the recent past, efforts have been made to delink non-proliferation and disarmament, with non-proliferation only. This is apparent in the demand for complete, verifiable and irreversible disarmament for new proliferators, such as the DPRK, without applying similar standards to the original five proliferators.

With these three caveats this chapter will begin with a brief overview of the three key nuclear proliferation challenges confronting the international community in the post-Cold War world. It will then examine the three approaches being followed by the international community to address these proliferation challenges. Finally, the chapter will offer some broad conclusions related to the likely consequences of the three approaches and what more could be done to facilitate non-proliferation.

Non-proliferation regime

At this point it would be worthwhile to elaborate on the non-proliferation regime. Although the NPT is the linchpin of the non-proliferation regime, the regime itself is much broader and is considered to comprise the following elements: the Partial Test Ban Treaty (PTBT) and the Comprehensive Test Ban Treaty (CTBT), both of which sought to prevent nuclear proliferation by banning nuclear tests; the proposed Fissile Material Cutoff Treaty (FMCT), which seeks to ban the production of fissile material; bilateral negotiations and agreements to limit nuclear arsenals, particularly of the USA and the Soviet Union/Russian Federation such as SALT I and II, the Anti-Ballistic Missile (ABM) Treaty, START I, II and III, the Intermediate-Range Nuclear Forces (INF) Treaty, and the Strategic Offensive Reductions Treaty (SORT); nuclear technology denial regimes such as the Nuclear Suppliers Group (NSG) and the Missile Technology Control Regime (MTCR); ensuring compliance of the NPT provisions through the safeguards of the International Atomic Energy Agency (IAEA); and Nuclear Weapon Free Zones (NWFZs).

Three challenges

The post-Cold War world has witnessed the emergence of three challenges related to the proliferation of nuclear weapons. While some of these, clearly, date back to the Cold War they nonetheless remain of particular import even today while others are more recent and might be related to the end of the Cold War.

First, there is the challenge posed by states within the existing non-proliferation regime. Here states that announced their intention to withdraw from the NPT, built and tested a nuclear weapon, such as the DPRK, pose as much of a challenge as nuclear weapons states which are seeking to develop a new generation of potentially usable nuclear weapons as outlined in the USA's National Nuclear Security Administration 'Complex 2030' plan (NNSA 2005), and the United Kingdom, which is updating its *Trident* strategic deterrence system (BBC 2007). Indeed, while much attention has been devoted to both Iran and the DPRK (Chubin 2006, Cha and Kang 2003), not as much attention has been paid to the huge combined arsenals of the five nuclear weapons states within the NPT.

As official data of national nuclear weapon stockpiles are shrouded in secrecy, there are no accurate nationwide or worldwide figures for the total number of nuclear weapons (see Table 24.1 based on open sources reflecting

BOX 24.1 MISSILES: BLIND SPOT OR ALLEY?

Nuclear weapons and missiles have a direct correlation: all the nine known nuclear weapons states possess missiles capable of delivering nuclear weapons. While all nuclear weapons states already have nuclear-tipped ballistic missiles, almost all of them also possess or are in the process of acquiring nuclear-capable cruise missiles. 'A ballistic missile is a weapon-delivery vehicle that has a ballistic trajectory over most of its flight path. A cruise missile is an unmanned, self-propelled weapon-delivery vehicle that sustains flight through the use of aerodynamic lift over most of its flight path' (UN Report 2002: para. 19). Conversely, however, not all ballistic and cruise missile possessing states have nuclear weapons. This poses a particular dilemma for non-proliferation: Is the possession of missiles, particularly ballistic missiles, an indication of the aspiration of states to acquire nuclear weapons? The answer would have to be a qualified maybe.

In the early days of the nuclear era, missiles were seen as a *blind alley* – a distraction from the primary objective of arms control, non-proliferation and disarmament of nuclear weapons. Today, however, missiles and efforts to manage and control them are seen as a *blind spot* – a crucial gap in the existing panoply of arms control and non-proliferation that needs to be addressed (Sidhu and Carle 2003).

However, unlike the nuclear weapons they are associated with, '[n]o universal norm, treaty or agreement governing the development, testing, production, acquisition, transfer, deployment or use specifically of missiles exists' (UN Report 2002: para. 32). Even more significantly, there is no universal norm, treaty or agreement to rid the world of missiles. Indeed, the rare cases of missile disarmament (the Intermediate Range Nuclear Forces (INF) Treaty, Iraq, South Africa and Libya) were the result of particular circumstances and not in adherence to any global norm or regime.

Against this backdrop and the growing salience of missiles, two trends have become evident among the international community. The first is a series of political and diplomatic initiatives (such as the INF Treaty, Missile Technology Control Regime, the Hague Code of Conduct, the Global Control System, and the three United Nations Panel of Governmental Experts) at the bilateral, regional and global levels. The second is a number of military and technological initiatives (such as the war to disarm Iraq, missile defence and the Proliferation Security Initiative). While both approaches have been limited in their effectiveness, the former is more in line with the desire for nuclear disarmament while the latter is likely to perpetuate the continued possession of nuclear weapons in the hands of some states.

Table 24.1 Estimates of nuclear weapons in the possession of known nuclear weapons states

Nuclear weapons states	Arms Control Association	Bulletin of Atomic Scientists	SIPRI	Nuclear Threat Initiative
USA	9,968 (5,968 strategic, 1,000 tactical, 3,000 stockpile)	10,104 (5,735 plus about 5,000 in reserve)	10,000 (5,521 plus 5,000 in reserve)	10,000 (6,000 strategic, 800 tactical, 3,200 stockpiled)
Russian Federation	19,478 (4,978 strategic, 3,500 tactical, 11,000 stockpile)	16,000 (5,830 plus 10,000 in storage)	16,000 (5,682 plus 10,000 in storage)	20,000 (no accurate count of tactical nuclear weapons)
UK	Less than 200 strategic warheads	200	185	Less than 160 warheads (also 110 US tactical bombs based)
France	~ 350 strategic warheads	350	348	~ 350 warheads
China	More than 100 warheads	200	130	400 (250 strategic, 150 tactical)
Israel	~ 75–200 warheads	~ 60–80	~ 100–200	100 to 200 warheads
India	~ 45–95 warheads	~ 50–60	~ 50	40 to 90 warheads
Pakistan	~ 30–50 warheads	~ 40–50	~ 60	30 to 50 warheads
DPRK	1 to 2 (with material for 6 weapons)	~ 5–10		1 possibly 2 warheads

this wide disparity). However, it is estimated that around 97 per cent of the world's nuclear arsenal of 27,000 weapons are in the stockpiles of the US and the Russian Federation alone (Norris and Kristensen 2006). Even more troubling, several thousands of these weapons remain on hair-trigger alert and could be launched within minutes, causing unimaginable death and destruction on a global scale.

While there is no doubt that all five nuclear NPT states have made significant cuts in their arsenals, the lack of transparency makes it very difficult to assess accurately whether these reductions are complete, verifiable and irreversible. For instance, the NNSA Report on Plans for Future of the Nuclear Weapons Complex notes that as per the Strategic Offensive Reductions Treaty (SORT) between the USA and the Russian Federation, '[b]y 2012, the U.S. nuclear weapons stockpile will be reduced by nearly 50 per cent from the 2001 level, making it the smallest stockpile since the Eisenhower administration' (NNSA 2007) but does not provide any specific numbers. Moreover, as some non-nuclear NPT states point out, SORT 'does not require the destruction of these weapons, does not include tactical nuclear weapons and does not have any verification provisions. The process is neither irreversible, nor transparent' (*International Herald Tribune* 2004).

Besides, despite these significant reductions in the actual number of nuclear weapons, the five nuclear weapons states are nowhere near meeting their disarmament commitments under Article VI of the NPT, which calls on these states to 'pursue negotiations in good faith on effective measures relating to cessation of the nuclear arms race . . . and to nuclear disarmament' (Treaty on the NPT 1968). Indeed, even though the United Kingdom has been the most forthcoming and today has the smallest arsenal among the NPT nuclear states, its decision to upgrade the *Trident* system means that it will retain nuclear weapons at least until the middle of this century. Similarly, both the USA and the Russian Federation, despite the massive cut in their arsenals, are likely to retain nuclear weapons until 2012 and beyond. The same is true of both France and China which remain the least transparent of all the five NPT nuclear states in terms of their nuclear disarmament commitments.

As one senior US official argued, echoing the sentiments of the other NPT nuclear states: 'Nuclear weapons continue to have relevance in today's world . . . several national nuclear weapons programmes were never initiated, or were halted, because security guarantees provided by a nuclear armed United States convinced these states not to seek nuclear weapons' (Rocca 2007). This view, however, has been challenged by four former senior US officials who argued in an op-ed that 'reliance on nuclear weapons for this [deterrence] purpose is becoming increasingly hazardous and decreasingly effective' (Schultz *et al.* 2007). One area where the former officials agree with the current US perspective on non-proliferation is the need for 'effective measures to impede or counter any nuclear-related conduct that is potentially threatening to the security of any states or peoples'.

In light of this statement, will the conditions ever prevail for complete nuclear disarmament? Or, is the presence of some nuclear weapons in the hands of some states essential to prevent proliferation? Finally, in the absence of nuclear guarantees, do states have the right to build nuclear weapons to ensure their own security? These dilemmas relate not only to the first set of challenges posed to the non-proliferation regime from within but also to the second set of challenges posed from states without.

The second set of challenges comes from states such as India, Israel and Pakistan which have not signed the NPT but also states such as China, DPRK, Egypt, Iran, Israel and the USA, which have still to ratify the CTBT. There are a variety of reasons why these states either never joined these treaties or having signed them did not ratify them, or having joined them decided to opt out and withdraw from the treaty. These reasons could vary from domestic political, technological or economic factors to regional security concerns to prestige and the desire to have a greater say in global governance. In the case of Israel and Pakistan (Cohen 1998, Weissman and Krosney 1981), both the quest for nuclear weapons and the desire to stay outside of the non-proliferation regime were driven primarily by security concerns. In the case of India, however, the reasons were apparently more complex (Perkovich 1999); they were partly related to security concerns, partly to display domestic technological prowess and partly to acquire a prominent seat in determining world affairs. In the case of the DPRK the primary factor for its apparent withdrawal from the NPT and staying out of the CTBT was probably driven by security concerns in the changed international scenario after the Cold War when it lost the protection of a collapsing Soviet Union and felt increasingly threatened by an unchecked USA. In the case of the USA the change in its attitude towards the non-proliferation regime in general and the CTBT in particular came in the wake of a regime change in Washington DC. The George W. Bush administration remains suspicious of international treaties and arrangements, and fears that these are designed to bind the USA into unacceptable commitments. Irrespective of their motives, the presence of states with nuclear weapons outside the non-proliferation regime poses a peculiar and unique challenge. Can the regime make non-members comply with the norms and principles of the treaties even if they are not legally bound to the rules and regulations? On the other hand, can non-members behave like members of the regime in spirit if not in law? Would that be acceptable to the regime?

The third and perhaps the most formidable challenge comes from non-state actors, including but not limited to terrorist groups. According to UN Security Council Resolution 1540 of 28 April 2004, a non-state actor is defined as an 'individual or entity, not acting under the lawful authority of any State in conducting activities which come within the scope of this resolution'. This would include the quest of transnational or subnational fundamentalist or cult groups, such as Aum Shinrikyo and al-Qa'ida, to develop nuclear weapons, as well as the antics of nuclear scientists and entities, such as Dr A.Q. Khan, to hawk their materials and expertise. The Khan episode in particular indicates a triple proliferation threat. First, there is a real concern about the ability of a weak state like Pakistan to manage and control its nuclear establishment and scientists and, as a corollary, its nuclear weapons. Second, it also highlights the possibility that states seeking a nuclear arsenal now have access to another unchecked network for acquiring nuclear weapons technology (see also Chapter 23, this volume). Third, there is also the serious possibility that armed transnational non-state actors seeking nuclear weapons (such as al-Qa'ida) might also receive the necessary know-how and expertise from the elaborate Khan network (Albright and Hinderstein 2005, Corera 2006).

Although non-state actors were known to have used biological and chemical weapons as early as the mid-1980s and sought to acquire nuclear weapons

---

BOX 24.2 THE MAKING OF NUCLEAR WEAPONS

All nuclear weapons are made out of fissile materials which are so-called because they are composed of atoms that can be split by neutrons in a self-sustaining chain reaction to release enormous amounts of energy. The key fissile materials for nuclear weapons are plutonium-239 and uranium-235. While uranium occurs in nature, plutonium normally does not.

Natural uranium comprises about 99.3 per cent of uranium-238 and 0.7 per cent of uranium-235. For the purposes of making nuclear weapons this natural uranium is 'enriched' so that it comprises 90 per cent of the uranium-235 isotope. About 15 to 25 kilograms of highly enriched uranium is required to make one nuclear bomb.

Plutonium-239 is a man-made element and is the by-product of burning uranium-238 in a nuclear reactor. However, the plutonium recovered from a nuclear reactor has to be 'reprocessed' chemically before it can be used to build bombs. About six to eight kilograms of plutonium are required for one bomb. Unofficial estimates of the world stockpile of fissile material are put at 1,830 metric tons of plutonium and 1,900 metric tons of highly enriched uranium – enough for over 300,000 nuclear bombs.

The explosive power of nuclear weapons is based on either splitting atoms through a process called 'fission' or combining atoms through a process called 'fusion'. The former is possible only with fissile material, such as plutonium-239 and uranium-235, while the latter requires light atoms with very small mass, such as deuterium or tritium, both isotopes of hydrogen; hence a 'fusion' bomb is also called a hydrogen bomb or a thermonuclear bomb. While conventional explosives form the trigger for a 'fission' bomb, a nuclear explosion is required to trigger a 'fusion' bomb.

Since the first nuclear test on 16 July 1945 over 2,000 nuclear tests have been carried out worldwide up until now. The latest nuclear test was conducted by DPRK on 9 October 2006. However, nuclear weapons have not been used since 1945 when the USA dropped a uranium bomb on Hiroshima on 6 August and a plutonium weapon on Nagasaki on 9 August 1945.

thereafter, this concern was accentuated following the events of 11 September 2001 when the phenomenon of mass terrorism became more apparent. Expert opinion is sharply divided over the threat posed by non-state actors, particularly armed non-state actors. According to Graham Allison, 'In sum, my best judgement is that based on current trends, a nuclear terrorist attack on the United States is more likely than not in the decade ahead. . . . Former Defense Secretary William Perry has said that he thinks I underestimate the risk' (Allison 2006: 39). This alarmist view is challenged by other scholars who argue that 'nuclear terrorism is a less significant threat than is commonly believed, and that, among terrorists, Muslim extremists are not the most likely to use nuclear weapons' (Frost 2005: back cover).

These differences notwithstanding, it is important to note three characteristics of the use of biological, chemical and nuclear weapons by non-state actors. First, so far biological and chemical weapons have been used by non-state actors operating in the territory of their own state and *not* by transnational groups such as al-Qa'ida in the territory of another state. This was true of the Rajneesh group's attack in Oregon, the Aum Shinrikyo's assault on the Tokyo subway and the so-called Amerithrax attack in the USA. Second, casualties caused by the use of chemical, biological and nuclear weapons by non-state actors have been minimal (far less than the daily death-toll in Iraq caused by conventional means): in the Rajneesh case, while 751 people were affected by salmonella poisoning, there were no deaths. The Aum Shinrikyo attacks affected 5,000 people and led to 12 deaths. In the Amerithrax case where letters containing anthrax were posted to several locations in the USA, 22 people were affected and five died. Third, so far there has been no known case of terrorism successfully using nuclear material. While one plot in England planned to use radioactive material in a conventional bomb, this 'dirty bomb' plan was nipped in the bud (BBC 2006).

To consider this threat realistically, five factors would have to be taken into account. These include motives of the outfit (whether they are religious terrorists); their methods (whether they have a propensity for indiscriminate and mass killings); access to nuclear material; the necessary monetary resources to buy nuclear material; and the necessary expertise to manufacture and use such weapons (Zaman 2002). Given what we do know about transnational armed non-state actors, such as al-Qa'ida, and if we consider their outlook in terms of the five factors listed above, we can conclude that while there is certainly a high risk of nuclear terrorism, the probability of its occurrence is low. However, there is a higher risk and probability of the use of a radiological dispersal device (popularly called a 'dirty bomb' because it combines conventional explosives with other radioactive material, such as that used for medical or industrial purposes). Such a device when detonated would not cause a nuclear explosion but would cause radioactive material to scatter and fall over a large area, increasing panic and radioactive risk.

Three approaches

These three sets of challenges from state parties, states not parties as well as non-state actors to the non-proliferation regime have led the international community to follow at least three different approaches to address them.

First, there are the traditional multilateral institutional approaches anchored in negotiated treaty-based regimes, such as the Partial Test Ban Treaty (1963), the NPT (1968) and the CTBT (1996). All these treaties were concluded after a long-drawn-out negotiating process. In the case of the CTBT, for instance, the idea was first proposed in the 1950s but was only taken up seriously in the early 1990s. This long delay may have been on account of the ongoing Cold War as well as the impetus of the NPT nuclear states to continue testing; the end of the Cold War and the cessation of tests by at least three of the five NPT nuclear states paved the way for the CTBT negotiations to begin. Given the complexity of negotiating treaties, such treaties are also not amenable to amendments and cannot be altered to adjust to the new realities. Finally, these treaties are invariably strong in setting norms and principles and in international law, but they tend to be relatively weak on enforcement. For instance, the NPT is as incapable of dissuading states from exercising the right to withdraw under Article X as it is of enforcing nuclear disarmament under Article VI.[1]

Despite these drawbacks the post-Cold War period was regarded as one of opportunity to strengthen the treaty-based regime. This promise was partly fulfilled in the mid-1990s following the indefinite extension of the NPT in 1995, the successful culmination of the CTBT in 1996 and adoption of the so-called '13 steps' in the 2000 NPT Review Conference. The '13 steps' suggest a set of practical measures for the 'systematic and progressive efforts' to implement Article VI of the NPT. They call for, among other things, a moratorium on nuclear testing, further unilateral reductions in the nuclear arsenals of nuclear weapons states, a reduced role for nuclear weapons in security policies, and an unequivocal undertaking by the NPT nuclear weapons states to the total elimination of their nuclear arsenals (NPT Review Conference 2000: 14 para. 15). Simultaneously, the promise was also belied by the failure to make substantive progress on the Middle East resolution (a critical element of the 1995 deal to indefinitely extend the NPT), the inability to ensure the entry into force of the CTBT (partly on account of the shift in US policy and partly as a result of the Indian and Pakistani tests in 1998), and a retreat on the commitment to the '13 steps', especially by the NPT nuclear states. The diminishing role of the multilateral approach was highlighted by the debacle of the 2005 NPT Review Conference, which 'foundered on procedural wrangling' and failed not only to produce a substantive consensus Final Document but also retracted from some of the significant agreements made in the 1995 and 2000 NPT Review Conferences, particularly the '13 steps' (Johnson 2005). If the treaty-based regime was ineffective in holding member states to their commitments, it was even weaker in its efforts to deal with both non-member states as well as non-state actors.

Second, partly on account of these inherent weaknesses in the treaty-based regime, in the post-Cold War world the international community embarked on a series of non-treaty-based multilateral approaches, such as the various declarations and resolutions made by the UN Security Council (UNSC) and the UN General Assembly (UNGA). This, of course, was not the first time that such an approach was followed: in the 1960s the UNGA passed several resolutions supporting the NPT and, after further revision (concerning mainly the preamble and Articles IV and V), the General Assembly commended the draft text of the NPT, which is annexed to UNGA resolution 2373 (XXII). Similarly, it was the UNGA that resurrected the CTBT (after it had been blocked at the Conference on Disarmament in Geneva) by adopting a resolution (A/RES/50/245) on 10 September 1996. In April 2005 the UNGA also adopted the *International Convention for the Suppression of Acts of Nuclear Terrorism* which addresses non-state actors.

In contrast, the UNSC, which had been in a debilitating paralysis during the Cold War, also became active on the issue of nuclear proliferation. The first indication of this was the various resolutions related to Iraq's invasion of Kuwait, which also established the UN Special Commission (UNSCOM) to disarm Iraq's nuclear, biological and chemical programmes. Another significant step was the UNSC Presidential Statement of 31 January 1992 which stressed that 'proliferation of all weapons of mass destruction constitutes a threat to international peace and security' and with specific reference to nuclear weapons noted 'the decision of many countries to adhere to the [NPT] and emphasise the integral role in the implementation of that Treaty'. Ironically, this statement also highlighted the failure of the NPT nuclear states (which are also the permanent members of the UNSC) to keep their commitments to the Treaty. Subsequently, the UNSC passed several other resolutions related to state actors and nuclear proliferation including 1172 (1998), 1696 (2006), 1718 (2006), 1737 (2006), 1747 (2007) and 1803 (2008). In addition, the UNSC also passed several resolutions related to non-state actors and nuclear proliferation including 1373 (2001), 1540 (2004) and 1673 (2006).

The latter sets of resolutions are particularly innovative for two reasons: first, they seek to deal with non-state actors and, second, they seek to provide stopgap arrangements to plug existing loopholes in the present treaty-based regime. UNSCR 1540 in particular is far-reaching because it calls on all UN member states to 'adopt and enforce appropriate effective laws which prohibit any non-State actor to manufacture, acquire, possess, develop, transport, transfer or use nuclear, chemical or biological weapons and their means of delivery' as well as to 'take and enforce effective measures to establish domestic controls to prevent the proliferation of nuclear, chemical, or biological weapons and their means of delivery'. While the resolution has been generally welcomed given that current treaty-based regimes do not address this aspect of pro-liferation, there is concern that this approach of using the UNSC to legislate, if exercised often enough, would circumvent the negotiated approach to developing treaty-based regimes.

Third, of even greater concern to some members of the international community, there are a set of ad hoc, non-institutional, non-conventional approaches led by individual states or a group of states to address the immediate challenges of non-proliferation. These include the so-called preventive war against Iraq's nuclear, chemical and biological weapons in 2003, which was probably the first (and last) non-proliferation war; the US-led Proliferation Security Initiative (PSI); the EU3's negotiations with Iran; the six-party talks to address the DPRK's nuclear ambitions; and the Indo–US civilian nuclear initiative. All of these arrangements tend to be stronger on the enforcement dimension but are relatively weak in international law as well as establishing norms and principles. Indeed, all of these initiatives are discriminatory and, predictably, do not enjoy universal adherence. Although the states behind these initiatives – primarily the NPT nuclear weapons states – have attempted to seek greater legitimacy for their actions by having these initiatives endorsed by the UNSC, there is concern that these initiatives may deal a fatal blow to the already weakened treaty-based non-proliferation regime. Nonetheless, given the inability of the existing formal regime to address many of the proliferation challenges of today, these ad hoc initiatives are likely to flourish.

Based on the above overview, it is evident that the liberal and institutional school would prefer strengthening the multilateral treaty-based institutions to address the non-proliferation challenges rather than opt for ad hoc and military options to deal with the present set of proliferation challenges. In contrast, the realist school would appreciate the ad hoc and unilateral or 'coalition of the willing' approaches, including the use of force, to ensure the security of the state *vis-à-vis* other states as well as non-state actors. However, it is equally clear that ad hoc approaches alone are unlikely to be effective either in the short or the long term unless they are intrinsically linked to the universally applicable treaty-based regime. This is possible only if the realists and liberals bridge their differences and seek a middle ground. Is such a compromise possible?

Way forward

Scholars and practitioners from both the liberal and the realist schools believe that while in the short term ad hoc and innovative approaches are likely to be preferred in addressing the most immediate challenges, such approaches should be dovetailed with the medium- to long-term objective of strengthening the global non-proliferation regime by eventually decoupling nuclear weapons and international peace and security. For instance, among the proposals made by Schultz *et al.* (2007) are:

- Changing the Cold War posture of deployed weapons to increase warning time and reduce the danger of accidental or unauthorized use of nuclear weapons.

- Continuing to reduce substantially the size of nuclear forces in all states that possess them.

■ Eliminating short-range nuclear weapons designed to be forward deployed.

■ Achieving ratification of the [CTBT].

■ Providing the highest possible security standards for all stocks of weapons . . . [and fissile material] . . . everywhere in the world.

■ Halting the production of fissile material for weapons globally.

■ Resolving regional confrontations and conflicts that give rise to new nuclear powers.

Most of these proposals are neither radical nor new but their authors are converts from the original nuclear weapon state and, therefore, this message carries greater weight than that of other analysts. However, in a new op-ed by Schultz et al., which was endorsed by over 30 other former officials and leading scholars, the emphasis appears to have shifted from disarmament to non-proliferation (Schultz et al., 2008).

In addition, countries which are currently under the extended nuclear umbrella of nuclear weapons states might consider whether their dependency on such weapons is posing a challenge for nuclear disarmament. What are the likely implications for such countries to reconsider their position and move out from under the nuclear umbrella? Would it really make them more vulnerable or less vulnerable? Would such vulnerability be worth it to start the process of nuclear disarmament rolling? What is the likely critical mass of countries required to ensure that the process of disarmament could begin and be sustained? Yet another approach to delinking nuclear weapons and world order would be for one of the current permanent members of the UN Security Council and nuclear weapons states to give up their arsenals and become the Council's first non-nuclear weapons permanent member. What are the prospects of one of the nuclear weapons states considering that their security is unaffected even if they were to give up their nuclear arms? It would also, inevitably, set the stage for the creation of a new world order not based on nuclear weapons and would have a lasting impact on the reform of the UNSC. These ideas are compelling and the only missing element is the will to operationalize them. This is, perhaps, the mother of all challenges.

Note

1   Article X of the NPT gives each signatory the 'right to withdraw from the Treaty if it decides that extraordinary events . . . have jeopardised the supreme interests of its country', while Article VI calls on members to 'pursue negotiations in good faith on effective measures relating to the cessation of the nuclear arms race at an early date and to nuclear disarmament'.

Further reading

Disarmament Diplomacy available at www.acronym.org.uk/dd/index.htm. An independent, quarterly journal of the Acronym Institute which provides some of the best in-depth and critical coverage of developments in disarmament negotiations, multilateral arms control and international security.

The Bulletin of Atomic Scientists available at www.thebulletin.org/. The oldest (founded in 1945 by atomic scientists involved in the Manhattan Project) and most respected journal on all things nuclear, especially non-proliferation. Its data on nuclear arsenals of nuclear states (prepared by the Natural Resources Defense Council) is regarded as one of the most reliable.

Nuclear Threat Initiative (NTI) available at www.nti.org/ is a one-stop website for nuclear, biological and chemical weapon programmes of different countries. The website also hosts an innovative online tutorial (WMD 411) which provides essential information on nuclear weapons and efforts to disarm them.

Jozef Goldblat, *Can Nuclear Proliferation be Stopped?* (Geneva: Geneva International Peace Research Institute (GIPRI), 2007). An excellent, concise overview of the current state of nuclear proliferation. It includes recommendations that build on, and go beyond, the '13 steps'.

Waheguru Pal Singh Sidhu and Ramesh Thakur (eds), *Arms Control after Iraq* (Tokyo: UN University Press, 2006). Offers global and regional perspectives to examine the impact of the ongoing Iraq crisis on nuclear proliferation and stresses a central role for the UN in non-proliferation.

Counterterrorism

Paul R. Pillar

▌ Abstract

This chapter discusses the several different elements involved in combating international terrorism, including dissuading individuals from joining terrorist groups, dissuading groups from using terrorism, reducing the capability of terrorist groups, erecting physical defences against terrorist attacks, and mitigating the effects of attacks. Reducing terrorist capabilities in turn requires the use of several instruments – each with its own strengths and limitations – including diplomacy, intelligence, financial controls, criminal justice systems and military force. Counterterrorism unavoidably raises difficult and often controversial policy issues, including conflicts with other values such as personal liberty and privacy.

▌ Introduction

The increased prominence of counterterrorism during the past few decades obscures the true age of the underlying challenges. Terrorism dates back to ancient times. Counterterrorism, as a concerted and cooperative effort by governments to combat this tactic, is not that old, but it long pre-dates any 'war on terror' aimed at the Islamist variety of international terrorism that is the most recent focus of attention. What could be called the first international conference on counterterrorism took place in Rome in 1898, to deal with a wave of anarchist assassinations that had been going on worldwide for several years.

Interest in counterterrorism has waxed and waned significantly throughout modern history. That pattern has partly reflected the rise and demise of different types of terrorist threat, such as the anarchism of the 1890s or the leftist violence that beset Europe in the 1980s. It has also reflected the political mood and milieu in individual countries. Terrorist attacks were occurring in the USA in the mid-1970s, for example, at a pace that would cause public alarm if replicated there today. But because the American public then – having just lived through the wrenching Watergate affair – was more concerned about excesses and abuses by its own government, the attacks did not stimulate major new counterterrorist initiatives (Jenkins 2003). Understanding counter-terrorism requires awareness of such swings in public mood and attention, but it also requires focusing on the essential elements and issues of counterterrorism that are present regardless of the political environment.

Basic elements

Not everything that can be done to combat terrorism ordinarily bears a label of 'counterterrorism'. Anything that cuts the roots or attenuates the causes of terrorism is properly viewed as being at least partly a counterterrorist measure, even if it is not commonly called that and even if other policy goals are involved. Scholars and politicians often disagree about the roots of terrorism. Some focus on the conditions in which would-be terrorists live. Others point to particular conflicts that become sources of rage. Still others emphasize the allure of extremist ideologies propounded by terrorist leaders and groups. Despite these differences in emphasis, they all have to do with one of the basic elements of counterterrorism, which is to address whatever it is that leads individuals to join terrorist groups.

Counterterrorist policies that reflect the different ways of looking at the causes of terrorism mentioned above are not mutually exclusive. A government may, for example, promote political and social change to weaken what it regards as roots of terrorism as well as waging a battle of ideas against extremist ideologies. These two approaches have both been facets of US counterterrorist strategy focused on the Middle East, especially in the wake of al-Qa'ida's attacks in September 2001.

For several European governments, attention to the roots of terrorism has more to do with their own Muslim populations. High-profile terrorist attacks such as those against transit systems in London and Madrid have heightened attention to the status of European Muslims. Here, too, there are disagreements and differences in approach, such as between the British concept of multi-culturalism and the French emphasis on assimilation. But in either case, reducing the chance that young members of these communities will gravitate towards terrorism is a goal of government policy.

Another fundamental element of counterterrorism focuses on decisions by groups whether or not to conduct more terrorism. It has to do with shaping the incentives for groups to use peaceful rather than violent means to pursue their objectives. This element is not germane to all terrorist groups. It is irrelevant to a group such as al-Qa'ida, whose ultimate goals – the overthrow of most of the political order in the Muslim world – are so sweeping that they could never be assuaged by any negotiations, concessions or change of policy by a government. Even with groups whose goals are more circumscribed – such as the Liberation Tigers of Tamil Eelam and its objective of an independent Tamil state carved out of Sri Lanka – the conflicts of interest may still be so acute that it is extremely difficult to divert the group from its violent path.

In some instances, however, a negotiated resolution of issues in conflict can be a major part of inducing a group to cease terrorism. The most conspicuous case is the Good Friday agreement on Northern Ireland reached in 1998. Despite many fits and starts over the subsequent decade, the peace process centred on that agreement was instrumental in inducing the leadership of the Provisional Irish Republican Army to give up terrorism.

The remaining elements of counterterrorism are more commonly labelled as such. One is usually called 'incident management', which includes anything done, once a terrorist incident occurs, to mitigate its effects. The concept of incident management first arose in response to attacks in which hostages are seized and their lives kept in jeopardy as the terrorists voice demands, such as for the release of previously jailed comrades. Management includes communications or negotiations with the terrorists. Expertise has been developed over the years (and has been applied by police services and private security firms to terrorist as well as non-terrorist hostage situations) on how best to deal with hostage-takers. The principal objectives are usually to weaken the will of the terrorists while avoiding any move that could stimulate rash action and harm to the hostages. Ultimately, however, the outcome of such incidents depends heavily on the policy of the authorities involved towards making concessions under duress to terrorists. Some governments (e.g. Italy) have been willing to make concessions in the interest of securing safe release of hostages. Others (e.g. the USA) are opposed to such concessions on the grounds that they encourage further terrorism.

Another aspect of managing such incidents involves communications with the public and the role of the press. An objective of terrorists in staging such incidents – at least as much as the specific demands they make – is to gain attention for their cause. Partly because of this, some counterterrorist officials consider it important to restrict the release of information on such incidents and to limit public attention to them. Any such restrictions, however, raise issues of freedom of the press and of the responsibility of the press and government alike to inform citizenry about important events.

A third aspect of the management of such incidents is the possible use of force to rescue the hostages. A successful rescue operation avoids the difficult choices of whether to make concessions to terrorists, as well as constituting a dramatic blow against terrorism and immediate punishment of terrorists. Past failures at hostage rescue have stimulated the development of highly skilled forces trained to conduct rescue operations. Germany developed such a force after its failure to rescue Israeli athletes taken hostage at the Olympic games in Munich in 1972, as did the USA after its aborted attempt to rescue diplomatic hostages in Iran in 1980. Even well-trained forces, however, face an extremely difficult task because the terrorists have the advantage of being able to inflict immediate harm on hostages. Because of this inherent difficulty, the record of hostage rescue attempts will always be mixed (see Box 25.1).

In recent years, most major terrorist incidents have involved not the seizure of hostages and the threat of inflicting harm on them, but instead the direct and unprovoked killing of innocent people, usually with bombs. In this context, 'incident management' has come to acquire a different meaning, referring primarily to emergency responses designed to tend to the wounded and to deal with any continuing hazards at the scene of the attack. The underlying purpose is still to mitigate effects of the attack; prompt medical attention for the wounded, of course, can minimize the number of deaths. Particular emphasis is now placed on responding to terrorist attacks using unconventional weapons or materials. Despite what is still the relative rarity of

---

BOX 25.1 SUCCESSFUL AND UNSUCCESSFUL RESCUE ATTEMPTS

Attempts to rescue hostages taken by terrorists have ranged from brilliant successes to tragic failures. Some countries have experienced both types of outcome.

An example of how a rescue attempt can go horribly wrong involved the hijacking by the Abu Nidal Organization of an Egyptian airliner in 1985. A team of Egyptian commandos attempted a rescue while the plane was on the ground in Malta, beginning their operation by using explosives to blow open doors of the aircraft. In an ensuing exchange of grenades and gunfire, the interior of the plane caught fire. Fifty-six out of 88 passengers died, as did two crew members.

A conspicuous success ended one of the last of the major hostage-takings, which began in late 1996 when the Tupac Amaru Revolutionary Movement (MRTA) seized the Japanese ambassador's residence in Lima, Peru. The Peruvian government negotiated with the terrorists for four months while secretly digging tunnels underneath the residence and making other preparations for a military raid. The raid began with an explosion that collapsed part of the ground floor of the building (where the MRTA members were playing a soccer game, with their 72 hostages being kept on an upper floor). All but one of the hostages were rescued unharmed. Two members of the rescue force and all 14 terrorists were killed.

such attacks, the emphasis is warranted because quick measures to contain or neutralize a biological, chemical or radiological hazard could make a substantial difference in minimizing casualties beyond those sustained immediately in the attack itself.

The measures that are most often thought of explicitly as counterterrorism – and that are the focus of the remainder of this chapter – concern efforts to curb the *ability* of terrorists to conduct attacks. These include defensive security measures designed to protect potential targets from attack. They also include a variety of offensive measures intended to reduce terrorist capabilities.

Defence

Defensive security measures (which sometimes bear the label 'anti-terrorism') are applied at several different levels. Most specific is the protection of individual sites, be they office buildings, military bases, embassies, or any other facility that could become a target of terrorist attack. Much site-specific security is the business of the private sector – of the owners or managers of the facilities being protected. Government facilities tend to have more security per site because the security also serves other purposes (such as preserving the secrecy of sensitive activities) and because, in the eyes of terrorists, official facilities are likely to have greater symbolic value as targets for attack. Related types of security include special short-term protection provided to high-profile events such as inaugurations or major sporting events and personal security given to governmental leaders or other prominent persons.

The next level of defensive measures is security provided to entire systems. The systems-level security that has played the greatest role in counterterrorism is that surrounding civil aviation. The inherent vulnerabilities and mobility of airliners will always make them tempting terrorist targets. The protection given to commercial aviation today demonstrates two principles of systems-level security. First, a chink anywhere in the armour can provide an opening for attackers – which is why reported weakness in security procedures at any one airport is legitimately a concern for people elsewhere in the system. Second – and partly in recognition of the first principle – security must be multi-layered, which in the case of aviation includes everything from x-ray inspection of baggage to hardening of cockpit doors. No other systems have received as much counterterrorist attention as aviation, but obvious vulnerabilities have increased questions in recent years about the need for additional protection to other systems such as public transit and electrical power grids. Electronic systems, such as those that support banking and financial transactions, have also received added scrutiny.

The most general level of defensive security measures is the protection of an entire country, particularly by keeping terrorists, and to some extent the wherewithal for conducting terrorist attacks (especially nuclear material) outside its borders. The USA, following the 9/11 attacks, greatly increased its emphasis on homeland security. This included not only a substantial increase in expenditures but also the creation – in the largest US governmental reorganization in over 50 years – of a Department of Homeland Security. The geographic and other circumstances of each country, however, make the homeland security task different for each. For most European countries, free cross-border movement within the European Union would make it impossible for individual states to approach homeland security in the same way that the USA does. Even the USA, given its long undefended border with Canada, must consider how much emphasis to place on stopping terrorists at its own borders and how much to keeping them out of North America altogether.

Defensive countermeasures work in several ways. The most obvious is the direct foiling of an attempted terrorist attack. Even if defences do not defeat an attempted attack, however, they may deter terrorists from attacking. Terrorist preparations typically include substantial study and surveillance of the intended target, to identify vulnerabilities and possible avenues of attack but also to assess security measures. Sometimes terrorists conclude from such study that the security protecting their intended target is too tight, and they stand down from their planned attack. Of course, this does not necessarily mean that they forgo terrorism altogether; they may look for an alternative target. But at least the defences have complicated their planning and forestalled whatever specific objective they had hoped to achieve by hitting their primary target.

Complicating terrorists' planning like this also slows them down, providing more time in which they might be detected. This raises another general way in which security countermeasures work, which is to complement other counterterrorist efforts. Defences that force terrorists to prepare their operation in ways they might not otherwise have used may increase the chance that they will be caught. Besides lengthening the time to prepare an attack, another possibility is the need to build a bigger bomb to overcome security such as blast-resistant walls or barriers that create a standoff distance. The purchases and fabrication needed for a larger bomb may be more conspicuous and detectable than the making of a smaller device.

Mention of large bombs raises a final way in which defensive measures can save lives even if they do not prevent attacks. The truck bomb that terrorists used to attack the US military housing facility at Khobar Towers in Saudi Arabia in 1996 was so powerful that it killed 19 servicemen, even though it exploded some distance away in the street. In a sense, perimeter security at the facility worked; if the truck had been permitted to enter the compound, the casualty toll would have been far higher.

Defensive security measures have several inherent limitations. They are expensive. The costs are measured not just in direct monetary expenditures for security, although some commonly used methods – such as machines that are both effective and efficient in screening large volumes of luggage of air passengers – are indeed expensive. The less measurable but still significant costs come in the form of unavoidable inefficiencies imposed on the people being protected and higher costs of doing business stemming from such issues as longer travel time. Some legitimate business, including government business, may be more difficult to do at all. The type of embassies that can most readily be protected from terrorist attack – for example fortress-like compounds located away from city centres – also make it harder for the diplomats who work there to do the parts of their job requiring free and easy interaction with the local population.

The most important limitation is that not everything can be protected, even though everything is a potential terrorist target. Terrorists will always have the advantage of choosing where to attack, with that choice reflecting in part where security is strong and where it is weak. In that sense the strengthening of security countermeasures has a self-negating aspect. Whatever the form of competition, the offence always has this advantage over the defence.

Going on the offence

Offensive counterterrorist operations have this intrinsic advantage over defensive measures: going on the offensive means not surrendering the initiative to terrorists and not trying to guess where and how they will strike next. A successful security countermeasure saves from attack whatever target or potential target is being protected. A successful offensive operation that puts a terrorist cell out of business prevents it from ever attacking *any* target. This does not mean that offensive operations are an alternative to defensive efforts. Rather, they are complementary parts of a comprehensive counterterrorist programme.

Offensive counterterrorism itself involves the use of several different tools. Again, they are complements rather than alternatives to each other. Each tool has its own advantages and limitations.

The transnational nature of modern terrorism makes *diplomacy* an important tool. Enlisting the cooperation of other governments is critical to countering terrorist operations that cross international boundaries. Diplomacy's most immediate use is to obtain cooperation on specific cases. A diplomatic demarche is the channel through which to get another government to arrest a suspected terrorist, to raid a terrorist cell, or to turn over a suspect. Diplomacy can also help to drive and guide cooperation more generally between military, security and intelligence services. As such, it provides important support to all of the other counterterrorist tools. Finally, diplomacy is the main means for containing and confronting state sponsors of terrorism.

Counterterrorist diplomacy can be either multilateral or bilateral. Multilateral diplomacy is most useful in creating a worldwide climate that recognizes terrorism as a shared problem and that is supportive of counterterrorist efforts. (Public diplomacy – communication through mass media to publics rather than to governments – is also used for this purpose.) Multilateral diplomacy has succeeded in making that climate much more conducive to counterterrorism than it was a quarter of a century ago, when much terrorism got overlooked or condoned out of a disinclination to criticize 'national liberation movements'.

Multilateral diplomacy also has a more practical side, in the form of a series of international conventions on terrorism that have been negotiated over the past 40 years and that establish rules and procedures on such matters as jurisdiction over hijacking incidents and the tracing of explosives. Most practical international cooperation on terrorism, however, is bilateral. Individual terrorist cases typically involve only two or three states at a time, and the handling of secret material becomes more difficult the more states that are involved.

Another tool that diplomacy has been instrumental in supporting is *financial control* in the form of freezing or seizing of terrorist assets. Getting at terrorists' money has received increased emphasis in recent years, although legal instruments for doing so have existed for much longer. The US Treasury has long had the statutory authority to freeze the financial assets of states, groups or individuals associated with terrorism. Except for states, however – whose financial accounts are more readily identified than those of groups or individuals – the haul of frozen assets was meagre until after 9/11, when the assistance of other governments became easier to obtain. US legislation in 1996 that created a formal list of foreign terrorist organizations also made it a crime to contribute financially to any organization on the list.

Despite frequently expressed hopes of curbing terrorism by removing its 'lifeblood' of money, the contribution of financial controls to counterterrorism will always be limited, for two reasons. One is that much of the money associated with terrorist activity flows through channels that are extremely hard to detect and intercept. This is particularly true of the informal money transfer networks known as *hawala* that are prevalent in the Middle East and South Asia. The other reason is that most terrorism is cheap. It simply does not cost much to assemble a truck bomb or many other means of inflicting heavy casualties.

The tool that has perhaps received more emphasis than any other in discussions of counterterrorism is *intelligence*. Inquiries in the USA following the 9/11 attacks focused primarily on intelligence. One of the principal legislative responses to the attacks was a reorganization of the intelligence community that created an additional counterterrorist centre and an additional layer of supervision over the entire community. The sentiment to which such measures are a response has more to do with defence than with offence: the hope that intelligence will uncover enough details of the next major terrorist plot to enable the authorities to roll the plot up before it can be executed.

That hope, although an understandable reaction to tragic events and a widespread perception of what intelligence ought to do, is largely misplaced. Unearthing the tactical details of terrorist plots must always be one of the missions of intelligence, and the occasional successes in doing so are among the most satisfying counterterrorist triumphs. But such successes always will be rare. Some terrorist plots, including some major ones, always will go undetected no matter how skilled and assiduous the intelligence operations aimed against them may be. Terrorist plots – which typically involve small numbers of operatives who can conduct their operations in secret, avoid communications or any overt actions that could reveal their plan, are highly conscious of operational security, and are ruthless towards anyone suspected of betraying them – will always be extremely difficult targets for intelligence.

Intelligence performs three other functions that make larger contributions to counterterrorism. One is to provide a more strategic sense of terrorist threats – are they increasing or decreasing, which groups or states pose the greatest dangers, which areas of operation are of most concern, and so forth. Such strategic appraisals help to guide policy-making on all aspects of counter-terrorism, including security countermeasures as well as offensive operations. A second function is to provide detailed support to all the other tools. Diplomatic demarches about terrorism, for example, are nearly always based on – and very often convey – information collected by an intelligence service. Intelligence is also important in identifying and locating terrorist financial assets. And intelligence provides critical input to law enforcement and military operations, discussed below.

The third function is clearly offensive and in many ways the most important. This is the collection and analysis of information on terrorist organizations and infrastructures, enabling them to be disrupted. The information concerned is specific but not plot-specific. It involves the names and biographic data of suspected terrorists, the location and strength of terrorist cells, the location of safe houses, and the operational connections among cells and groups. Intelligence services themselves may not accomplish the actual disruption, but the information they provide enables police or internal security services to conduct raids, arrest suspects and confiscate material. Such actions often provide leads for collecting more information, which in turn facilitates further disruption of terrorist infrastructure. This type of offensive action does not always generate headlines, unless a particularly well-known terrorist is taken into custody. But it probably accounts for the largest portion of counterterrorist successes, including successes against important groups such as al-Qa'ida.

Law enforcement and military force

A common, but misleading and useless, frame of reference often invoked in discussion of counterterrorism is to ask whether the problem should be considered as one of 'crime' or 'war'. Nothing inherent to terrorism warrants either posing such a choice or selecting one of these labels as an alternative to the other. Terrorists clearly commit crimes (such as murder), while their political objectives give them something in common with warfare and distinguish their actions from non-political crimes motivated by greed or passion. Counterterrorist policies and practices also do not provide a basis for any 'crime versus war' choice. Both criminal justice systems and military services appropriately play roles in counterterrorism. The establishment by the USA of military tribunals to determine the guilt or innocence of terrorist suspects – a system that is inseparably part of the realms of both 'crime' and 'war' – illustrates the falsity of the dichotomy.

Most proponents of the 'crime versus war' formulation are really just arguing in code for greater emphasis to be placed on one or the other of the associated counterterrorist tools: *criminal prosecutions* or *military force*. Most often, it is proponents of military force who invoke that formulation, because 'war' has the added favourable connotation of taking the problem seriously and giving it high priority. A more useful perspective, however, is to discard the metaphysical and semantic debates and realize that criminal justice and military force are simply two additional offensive counterterrorist tools. Like the other tools such as intelligence or diplomacy, each tool has its peculiar strengths and weaknesses. And as with the others, they are best used as complements to each other as part of an integrated counterterrorist programme.

Arrest of suspected terrorists and their prosecution in a criminal court can accomplish several things. Incarcerating (or executing) a terrorist obviously prevents him from committing further attacks. A well-publicized prosecution can help to demonstrate governmental resolve. It may also strengthen deterrence of other terrorists apprehensive about getting caught. Even if not deterred, the fear of getting caught may impede or restrict their operations. A successful prosecution can satisfy the public's appetite for punishment of wrongdoers, but it does so in an orderly and peaceful framework that upholds respect for the rule of law.

Use of a criminal justice system also has significant limitations. A terrorist first has to be caught, of course, before he can be prosecuted. Senior leaders who plan and direct terrorist attacks are less likely to be caught than underlings who must be at the scene of the attack. In the case of state-directed terrorism, the leaders most responsible are unlikely ever to be arrested. Deterrence may be ineffective – particularly inasmuch as leaders tend to go free – and is irrelevant to suicide bombers. A legal case that establishes beyond reasonable doubt that someone has committed terrorist crimes is more difficult to make than an intelligence case that someone is probably a terrorist. There is thus the risk of acquittal, an outcome less favourable to counterterrorism than if a terrorist had not been arrested in the first place. Accused terrorists may use a public trial as a platform for propaganda. Incarceration of convicted terrorists may stimulate further attacks, perhaps in the form of hostage-taking aimed at bargaining for the prisoners' release.

With terrorists moving and operating across international boundaries, jurisdictional issues also complicate the application of criminal justice. This has partly involved the assertion by the USA of extra-territorial jurisdiction of terrorist crimes against US interests in other countries, an assertion that is questionable under international law and that comes into conflict with the laws of the countries on whose territories the crimes were committed. Disagreements over the death penalty – opposed by the European Union, still used in the USA – have been an added complication that has impeded the extradition of, and even sharing information about, some terrorist suspects.

Some have looked to the International Criminal Court (ICC), the founding statute of which was ratified by enough states to enter into force in 2002, as a place to prosecute international terrorists while pre-empting some of these jurisdictional issues. There remain problems, however, of distinguishing terrorist crimes to be tried in the ICC from ordinary crimes that would still be tried in national courts. The handling of sensitive security-related information, which is often involved in terrorism cases and is difficult enough to use as evidence even in national courts, is another complication for the ICC.

The most successful use of military force for counterterrorist purposes was the US-led intervention in the civil war in Afghanistan following al-Qa'ida's attacks in the USA in September 2001. Notwithstanding the subsequent continued security problems in Afghanistan (where command of the international forces was later turned over to the North Atlantic Treaty Organization), the intervention did force al-Qa'ida from its main sanctuary and ousted the Taliban regime, which, as a close partner of al-Qa'ida, had become a major state sponsor of terrorism. This success helped to raise expectations, especially in the USA, about how a more aggressive use of military force might be effective in combating terrorism.

Some of the principal attractions of military force for this purpose are stronger versions of the attractions of using a criminal justice system. A military strike can be an even more dramatic demonstration of resolve than a prosecution. It can immediately disrupt or destroy terrorist capabilities, such as training camps, and possibly kill key terrorists. It may have deterrent effects not just on terrorist groups but also on states. And it can do all this without the administrative, evidentiary and other legal complications that often impede criminal prosecutions.

The principal limitation of the counterterrorist use of military force is that international terrorism simply does not present very many good military targets. Afghanistan of the Taliban was a unique case. Even state sponsors in general have become a significantly smaller part of international terrorism than they were two decades ago. And with groups rather than states, most of the important preparations for terrorist attacks occur not in open-air training camps but in places not readily targeted for military strikes, such as apartments in cities.

Further limitations parallel some of those associated with criminal prosecutions. A military attack may serve more to provoke than to deter. The US military strike on Libya in 1986 in response to a terrorist attack in Germany may have helped to provoke the much deadlier Libyan bombing of Pan American flight 103 two years later. Being subject to a military attack may rally support for an extremist group's leader, among the group's membership and possibly among a wider constituent population. Military strikes also have their own practical problems, such as access to bases and overflight of third countries.

Other drawbacks stem from the inherently destructive nature of military force. Collateral damage, including the loss of innocent lives, is almost inevitable. Such damage can alienate civilian populations, as it has to some degree as a result of military operations in Afghanistan. Some will always regard the use of military force as excessive, making it at least as prone to controversy as any other counterterrorist instrument.

Issues and choices

The expansion of counterterrorist powers and functions, even if not involving military force, frequently gives rise to public debate. This partly reflects disagreement over the effectiveness of particular measures in curbing terrorism. It also stems, however, from unavoidable conflicts and trade-offs between counterterrorism and other public values and goals.

The treatment of suspected terrorists has been one focus of controversy in the USA and Europe in the years since the 9/11 attacks. The controversy comes not from any reservoir of sympathy for terrorists but instead from concerns over human rights and the principle that even the guilty should be treated humanely. Another concern is that not all suspects are in fact guilty.

Issues involving the handling of suspected terrorists have spilled over international boundaries and have included reports of secret prisons in which detainees have been held incommunicado indefinitely, as well as 'renditions' in which suspects are turned over from one country's custody to another without any open legal procedure to authorize the process. Renditions have been used for many years as an efficient way to transport suspected terrorists to the countries where they are most wanted for their crimes, without the pitfalls associated with a formal extradition process. They have become more controversial largely because some of the receiving countries have been known for their rough handling, including torture, of prisoners. Torture in general, even with detainees who have not been subjects of rendition, has also become a more prominent issue of debate in recent years. The relevant questions include not only whether human rights are being violated but also whether torture is effective in eliciting accurate information.

Beyond torture is the issue of assassinating individual terrorist leaders, often referred to as 'targeted killings'. Some argue that this kind of decapitation of a terrorist group or cell can be effective in preventing terrorist attacks, and that the procedure should not be considered functionally or morally different from many conventional military operations. Others emphasize what can go and has gone wrong in clandestine assassinations, including the killing of innocent people through mistaken identity or collateral damage. Moreover, such assassinations may constitute a stooping to the same level as terrorists, by using a procedure that in some contexts may be considered to be terrorism itself. Both sides can find much to adduce in the experience of Israel, which has made extensive use of targeted killings as a counterterrorist tool (Byman 2006).

Most citizens never experience directly anything having to do with the controversial procedures mentioned above, but they do experience other conflicts between counterterrorism and important public values. There is unavoidable conflict with two values in particular: liberty (absence of restrictions on daily life) and privacy (avoiding governmental scrutiny of personal matters). Liberty is curtailed every time one is denied access to a formerly public place in the interest of security, or one has to empty pockets and detour through a metal detector to enter a building. Privacy is compromised when government agencies collect and exploit financial, travel or other data on individuals in the interest of identifying possible terrorists. Issues of privacy became especially acute in the USA with the expansion of investigative activities following the 9/11 attacks. Debate centred on, for example, the Federal Bureau of Investigation's new power to require public libraries to identify which books an individual had borrowed, or the National Security Agency's interception of telephone conversations without a court warrant.

There is no single, optimum formula for resolving these conflicts. Counterterrorism is not the only objective in public policy, nor should it be. It is up to each nation's citizenry, preferably acting through a fair process of representative government, to decide where it wishes to strike a balance between safety from terrorism and other interests and values.

A citizenry's confidence that this balance has been struck properly and in a way consistent with its values is important for the final, critical ingredient in counterterrorism: informed and sustained public support. This type of support is difficult to obtain. Public interest in counterterrorism is high after a major terrorist attack, but tends to wane if time passes without more such attacks. A counterterrorist programme can be effective only if government officials and private citizens alike understand that the programme must be applied consistently, coherently and over a long period of time.

Further reading

Audrey Kurth Cronin and James M. Ludes (eds), *Attacking Terrorism: Elements of a Grand Strategy* (Washington, DC: Georgetown University Press, 2004). This book surveys the principal counterterrorist instruments and some of the major issues that arise in applying them.

Philip B. Heymann and Juliette N. Kayyem, *Protecting Liberty in an Age of Terror* (Cambridge, MA: MIT Press, 2005). This book examines the most difficult issues of civil liberties, privacy and treatment of detainees.

Paul R. Pillar, *Terrorism and U.S. Foreign Policy* (Washington, DC: Brookings Institution Press, 2003). This is a general treatise on counterterrorism that also places the subject in a broader policy context, with particular reference to the USA.

Richard A. Posner, *Preventing Surprise Attacks: Intelligence Reform in the Wake of 9/11* (Lanham, MD: Rowman & Littlefield, 2005). This book analyses the challenges of applying intelligence to counterterrorism.

Counterinsurgency

Joanna Spear[1]

Abstract

Counterinsurgency is an old issue with new currency in the twenty-first century. The ongoing campaigns in Afghanistan and Iraq are leading to a new generation of writings on counterinsurgency drawing comparisons and contrasts to the campaigns of the past. Counterinsurgency is an issue area where there are many scholar-practitioners (in contrast to other areas of security studies) which gives their writings a certain immediacy and applicability. Many of these scholar-practitioners are engaged in trying to change the way that militaries understand and fight these 'hearts and minds' campaigns.

Introduction: the current discourse on counterinsurgency

I live in Washington, DC and it is a city currently obsessed with counter-insurgency. It is the main topic of international affairs conversation in the Executive Branch of the US government, in Congress, in the media, and in bars around town (or so they tell me). The reasons for this obsession are not hard to fathom; the ongoing campaigns in Afghanistan and Iraq are leading Americans to ask important questions about how to defeat determined but illusive opponents in challenging environments where superior technology does not seem to be the answer.

For a European eavesdropping on these discussions there are a number of very interesting aspects. First is the fact that many Americans seem to be discovering the issue for the first time despite the fact that the successful campaign against the Huq rebels in the Philippines and the unsuccessful Vietnam conflict were both counterinsurgencies. Rarely, until President Bush's speech in late August 2007, was America's own experience of battling a highly motivated, low-tech local insurgency in Vietnam discussed. So deep is the post-Vietnam self-induced amnesia of America that when the issue is discussed, the historical parallels generally make reference to *European* – not American – experiences of counterinsurgency.

Despite this brief presidential allusion, 'Vietnam syndrome' – usually defined as the fear of politicians of losing American lives in futile overseas operations – seems to have a new aspect that makes any attempt to discuss or learn from this US experience of counterinsurgency beyond the pale. Thus, interestingly, the first book-length consideration of the parallels between the two counterinsurgencies has actually been produced in Europe (Dumbrell and Ryan 2007).

Part of the reason for the recent American 'discovery' of counterinsurgency is that at the outset of the Iraq War the Bush Administration had no expectation that they would need to fight insurgents; rather they expected it to be a 'cakewalk' in the words of Defense Science Board member Kenneth Adelman (*Washington Post*, 12 February 2002) and assumed that the US would be welcomed as 'liberators' (Vice-President Dick Cheney on *Meet the Press*, 16 March 2003). Given this expectation, there was little planning for extensive post-conflict reconstruction, let alone for counterinsurgency! Thus, America is trying to get up to speed fast on counterinsurgency – both its theory and its practice.

A second notable feature of the discourse over counterinsurgency is that it does not appear to be happening to the same extent nor with the same hand-wringing in other countries engaged in the same campaigns. There has not been the same level of rediscovery of counterinsurgency in Britain, Canada, Australia, Poland and so on. This may be partly a reflection of the fact that the US has born the brunt of the casualties of Iraq (though not necessarily in Afghanistan) and the US, because of lingering 'Vietnam syndrome', is particularly traumatized by the deaths of its troops. That said, the number of casualties taken by the smaller forces of the allies is not out of proportion to those of the US, and in the case of the Canadians in Afghanistan, their casualty rates have been heavier than the norm.

Part of the reason for the difference is because all of these allies have militaries that have been accustomed to participating in multinational peace-keeping and peacebuilding operations, which require a comparable range of skills and attitudes. More than that, these are considered major missions for these forces, so training and doctrine have led everyone to value and expect to be using these skills. I will expand on this point below.

A third notable feature of the American discourse on counterinsurgency is the fact that it is often also linked to a discussion of military learning – or, more accurately, not learning (Nagl 2005). This goes back to my observation about American amnesia on counterinsurgency. This is not confined to the public, but is evident in the American armed services as a whole (albeit with pockets of expertise on the issue in units such as the Special Forces). Counterinsurgency is a mission that politicians and the military largely turned their back on after Vietnam, and the military had devalued or forgotten much of what it knew. It is now in the process of relearning counterinsurgency.

A fourth point about the discussion concerns the need for soldiers to be able to act with a degree of autonomy and to use initiative to assist in the counter-insurgency mission, to become what has been called 'strategic corporals' (Krulak 1999). This runs up against traditional military practice which relies upon hierarchies and minimizes the independence of soldiers. Here, however, counterinsurgency has a potential ally; the US agenda of force 'transformation' has a similar aim to somewhat flatten organizational hierarchies and empower those on the ground to make decisions (regardless of the fact that commanders now have more battlefield information available to them than ever before).

A final facet of the discourse in Washington is the battle going on within the Department of Defense (DOD) to win recognition that counterinsurgency is going to be an important mission for decades to come and that DOD needs to therefore prioritize it over more traditional Cold War missions and weapons platforms. Just as in the 1990s when the 'airpower lobby' waged a bureaucratic campaign in the Pentagon (aided by a number of scholars, people from think-tanks and aerospace industry executives) to prioritize airpower over land warfare capabilities – with significant success – so there is a new battle for supremacy being waged (Pape 1996). Those arguing that counterinsurgency is the most likely future of conflict are meeting stiff opposition to their claims. Part of the battle here comes down to concerns about the allocation of budgets. Despite US defence spending being at a historic high in terms of constant dollars (though not in terms of percentage of gross domestic product), the various services are concerned that prioritizing counterinsurgency, combined with the heavy costs of the campaigns in Iraq and Afghanistan, may lead to the diversion of funds away from their pet projects and desired military spending for the future (Bennett 2007).

Having briefly laid out the discussions on counterinsurgency currently gripping America (and to a lesser extent its allies), this chapter will now examine some of the key aspects of counterinsurgency. In the first section I discuss the state of the field and highlight some contrasts between it and other areas of security studies. In the second section I examine insurgency, which is the problem that counterinsurgency is designed to check. Here I discuss the differences between 'classic' insurgencies and those taking place today and the implications of this for how armies must fight counterinsurgency. The third section looks at an enduring aspect of counterinsurgency: the battle for hearts and minds. The fourth section looks at the role of force in counterinsurgency (and the debate over it), and the strategies and tactics that are often involved.

BOX 26.1 KEY DEFINITIONS

Insurgency

Insurgency is defined in British military doctrine as 'an organized movement aimed at the overthrow of a constituted government through the use of subversion and armed conflict' (UK Ministry of Defence 2004: 4). The same definition is used by the North Atlantic Treaty Organization (NATO) and the US military.

Counterinsurgency

Counterinsurgency is defined in British and NATO military doctrine as 'those military, paramilitary, political, economic, psychological, and civic actions taken to defeat insurgency' (UK Ministry of Defence 2004: 4). The US definition is subtly different: 'Those military, paramilitary, political, economic, psychological, and civic actions taken *by a government* to defeat insurgency' (DOD 2007; emphasis added). Thus, for the USA, counterinsurgency is a solely government activity, whereas Britain and NATO have a rather more free-wheeling attitude.

The fifth section discusses military learning in general while the sixth looks at doing counterinsurgency in an age of a global media. The seventh section draws comparisons between counterinsurgency and so-called 'post-conflict peace-building'. The final section considers whether counterinsurgency is a major mission for the future.

The state of the field

Writings on counterinsurgency differ in one crucial respect from most of the writings in the field of security studies: a much higher percentage of the writers are both scholars *and* practitioners. This has certain advantages; for example, the writers often display a deep understanding of military practice, communicate a sense of what the operational environment is like and have spent many hours pondering the successes and failures they experienced. The down-side can be that they are writing primarily for a military audience (and this can make it hard to follow), that they tend to assume that what works for them in one country will automatically work elsewhere, and – particularly in the case of those who fought in Algeria and Vietnam – some of them are embittered by their counterinsurgency experiences and treat writing as a form of therapy.

BOX 26.2 COUNTERINSURGENCY SCHOLAR-PRACTITIONERS

T. E Lawrence: Also known as 'Lawrence of Arabia' for his role in leading an Arab revolt against the Ottoman Turks in the Middle East (to provide help to Lord Kitchener by defeating this ally of Germany). More of an insurgent than a counterinsurgent, his book *Seven Pillars of Wisdom* is a valuable account of the problems of insurgency and has been studied by those seeking to understand the psyche of insurgents.

Roger Trinquier: First practised counterinsurgency with the French in Indochina before moving to Algeria in 1957 as a Lieutenant Colonel. Algeria was the inspiration for *Modern Warfare: A French View of Counterinsurgency* (1961) which stressed the importance of winning the support of the people. He believed victory would come through: securing an area to operate from, good intelligence, gaining support in the government and general population, maintaining the initiative, and carefully managing propaganda (Tomes 2004: 18). He advocated a 'gridding system' of dividing territory into sectors that can be swept clear of insurgents, a *quadrillage* strategy used by the French in Algeria that had the effect of tying down over 300,000 troops (Alexander and Keiger 2002: 15, 21).

David Galula: Completed *Counterinsurgency Warfare: Theory and Practice* in 1964. In it he distilled his experiences in China, Greece, Indochina and Algeria into a series of principles for counterinsurgency from which strategies and tactics could be derived. He concluded that in counterinsurgency 'most of the rules applicable to one side do not work for the other' (cited in Tomes 2004: 20). He also stresses the dynamic nature of insurgency and the ways in which it will adopt new injustices to reinforce its cause. In response the counter-insurgent must be alert to potential problems and proactively solve them. Galula conceives of counterinsurgency as demanding primarily political responses.

Frank Kitson: Rose to the rank of Commander-in-Chief of the British Land Forces and was knighted. He fought insurgencies in Kenya, Malaya, Cyprus and Northern Ireland. His controversial work *Low Intensity Operations: Subversion, Insurgency and Peacekeeping* published in 1971 put particular stress on psychological operations against insurgents.

David Petraeus: A West Point student, he was the top graduate of the US Army Command and General Staff College Class of 1983 and won all three of the available class prizes when he attended Ranger School. His career has alternated between command and staff assignments and working as an aide to some of the Army's most prominent generals. Along the way he attended Princeton University and obtained a Masters in International Relations and completed a Ph.D. thesis on 'The American Military and the Lessons of Vietnam'.

His first combat was in Iraq in 2003 and he later won praise for his handling of the Mosul area during the first year of occupation. He was subsequently charged to train the Iraqi security forces (a poison chalice of a job) and then went back to Fort Leavenworth. He is the intellectual inspiration for and a major contributor to the new US Army and Marine Corps *Counterinsurgency Field Manual* (2007). In January 2007 he was appointed by President Bush to oversee operations in Iraq and instigated the 'surge' strategy to provide greater security to Baghdad's residents.

John Nagl: An active duty officer in the US army who took time out to complete a thesis at Oxford University and then found himself in Iraq practising what he had written about. The introduction to *Learning to Eat Soup with a Knife* is a reflective discussion of how well his theoretical insights stood up to the reality of counterinsurgency practice. He worked with General Petraeus on the Army's new counterinsurgency manual and instigated its wider publication, recognizing the importance of the general public accepting counterinsurgency as a key US mission. He is quite the media darling, having been profiled by the *New York Times Magazine* and appeared on the popular satirical show *The Daily Show with Jon Stewart* (Maass 2004).

David Kilcullen: An Australian currently working in Baghdad with General Petraeus. He previously served in the Middle East, Southeast Asia and the Pacific and in the counterinsurgency in East Timor. He is a prolific author and a thoughtful commentator on the situations he encounters and on the bigger strategic picture.

The problem that counterinsurgency responds to – insurgency

Insurgency is not a new form of violent opposition to rule by a stronger force. If you look at the history of the Roman Empire it is clear that they faced a number of insurgent movements. The same may be said of the opposition that the British forces encountered in the American colonies in the eighteenth century and the French resistance to Nazi rule during the Second World War.

In the 'classical insurgencies' of the late colonial era (*c.* 1944–1980) – when much of the initial formulation of counterinsurgency took place – the insurgent groups were intent on expelling foreign forces from their territories and establishing their own sovereign states. In Latin America, where Che Guevara both practised and wrote about guerrilla warfare, the emphasis was on deposing local elites and replacing them with a socially just (i.e. leftist) system of government. As he wrote of guerrilla warfare in 1963, 'this form of struggle is a means to an end. That end, essential and inevitable for any revolutionary, is the conquest of political power' (Guevara 1963: 1). Thus, insurgents had clear political agendas, involving gaining control of the state, and, following Mao Zedong's strategy, often sought to prove they were fit to rule by providing an alternative authority structure to that of the colonialists/oligarchs.

The tactics employed by insurgents were – and still are – necessitated by their military weakness; they could not confront the opposing power directly and therefore attacked vulnerable points and then retreated among the local population (moving as 'fishes to the water' in Mao's classic analogy) so that they were hard to detect and punish. These insurgent tactics were hard to counter. Attempts at mass punishment of populations in response to insurgencies had the counter-productive aim of alienating the local population from the authority trying to maintain its power and legitimacy. As a consequence, a body of knowledge began to be built up – primarily by colonial militaries – about how best to deal with these difficult insurgent tactics. Knowledge was often the result of painful learning even in ultimately successful operations; for example, the British in Malaya suffered real problems in the early years of the campaign before they honed a successful strategy.

David Kilcullen (one of our scholar-practitioners) has made a number of useful observations about contemporary insurgencies as compared to those that formed the basis for many of the 'classical' works on how to understand and prosecute counterinsurgency. He warns against simply transferring practices from history to the counterinsurgencies of today.

Kilcullen points out that unlike traditional insurgencies (which he defined as those occurring between 1944 and 1980 aiming to overthrow colonial authority), contemporary insurgents are not all seeking to take over and establish their own state. Rather in some cases, 'insurgency today follows state failure, and is not directed at taking over a functioning body politic, but at dismembering or scavenging its carcass, or contesting an "ungoverned space"' (Kilcullen 2006: 112). Moreover, some religiously motivated insurgencies may not have a political aim; the very act of insurgency may be seen as earning God's favour (Kilcullen 2006: 116). Nevertheless, even if an insurgency lacks political motive, it will have political consequences.

He also highlights another contrast; in a classical insurgency, the insurgent is the instigator (catalysing a counterinsurgent response), whereas 'in several modern campaigns – Iraq, Afghanistan, Pakistan and Chechnya, for example – the government or invading coalition forces initiated the campaign', making the insurgents reactive rather than pro-active (Kilcullen 2006: 113). A profound consequence of this change is that whereas in the past it was the insurgency that was the revolutionary force, today it is often the insurgents who are fighting to preserve the status quo.

In the classical model the insurgents live off the population, so a key aim is to isolate the insurgents from these sources of support. This would not – in itself – be a successful tactic today as, in direct contrast to times past, the insurgents in Afghanistan and Iraq are often better off than the population because they receive outside funding (Kilcullen 2006: 119). By contrast, today insurgents sometimes provide resources to the local population in exchange for services such as planting roadside bombs. Nevertheless, the local population remains an important source of camouflage and intelligence-gathering for the insurgents, so the aim of isolating them from the people still has value.

The classical counterinsurgencies were primarily rural affairs but this is not true today, where the insurgencies of Iraq and Afghanistan are fought in urban areas, causing new headaches for the counterinsurgency forces:

> engagements are short range and fleeting as in traditional insurgencies, but bystanders are now always present and cleverly exploited by insurgents. Media presence is greatest in the cities, fuelling propaganda-based tactics that target the population to generate shock and provoke sectarian unrest. Traditional counterinsurgency methods like fencing villages, cordon and search, curfews and food control ... have drawn sharp criticism in Iraq and Afghanistan because of the enhanced disruption they cause in urban neighbourhoods.
>
> (Kilcullen 2006: 120)

Classical insurgencies were usually confined to one state or region and involved one insurgent group and one government. This is far from the case with today's insurgencies where in Afghanistan and Iraq the array of forces that the USA and its allies are facing is very complex and the relationship of local groups to one another fluid and shifting (International Crisis Group 2006). Indeed, a particular feature is that local groups are not only fighting against the external occupiers but are also fighting among themselves, making conflicts less binary struggles than multi-sided violent interactions.

The positive side of this is that there will be some opportunities for counterinsurgents to ally with local forces; for example, the alliance struck between US forces and the tribal groups of Tal Afar against units of 'Al-Qa'ida in Iraq'. These shifting alliances make it even more important for force to be used on the basis of good intelligence and to be used discriminately and well, so that future functional alliances remain possible.

The negative side is that just as alliances can shift one way, they can also shift another. The experience of the USA in backing counterinsurgents in Afghanistan (including Osama bin Laden) in the 1980s shows that an alliance at one point is no guarantee of an alliance in the future. Moreover, 'field experience from Iraq suggests that it may be harder, not easier, to defeat such a complex, inchoate and disorganised swarm of opponents' (Kilcullen 2006: 116).

Another side of this complexity should be noted; it is no longer a traditional military handling all aspects of the counterinsurgency mission. Who does counterinsurgency is now more complex too, with private security companies, aid agencies, nongovernmental organizations, the media and a host of other actors playing a role (sometimes unwittingly) in the counterinsurgency campaign. This has led to clashes of organizational culture in the field, as a group pursues its activities unaware (or unconcerned about) the wider counterinsurgency mission. For example, in Iraq the second largest outside force in the country (after the USA) are private military contractors. Their missions are specific and limited, often as simple as 'convey person A to point Y safely'. Their only concern is to complete that mission and they will run cars off the road, stop the traffic and annoy Iraqis and not worry about it, even though it counteracts the larger counterinsurgency mission of winning 'hearts and minds' by treating the locals with respect and minimum inconvenience. This has led contractors into conflicts with military and civilian authorities.

Kilcullen warns of the dangers of applying wholesale lessons from classical counterinsurgency to contemporary situations, since the nature of the insurgents, the complexity of local environments and the degree of globalization of the international system require a careful adaptation of counterinsurgency to the contemporary era. That said, he is clear that one key aspect of insurgency and counterinsurgency has not changed; it is a battle for the support of the people.

'Hearts and minds'

It is now a truism that successful counterinsurgency involves winning the 'hearts and minds' of the local population. This reflects the fact that there is a competition going on for the allegiance of the people. Scholar-practitioner Frank Kitson made the insightful comment that 'Insurgents start with nothing but a cause and grow to strength, while the counterinsurgents start with everything but a cause and gradually decline in strength and grow to weakness' (Kitson 1971: 29, cited in Nagl 2005: 23).

The phrase 'hearts and minds' was initially coined by High Commissioner Gerald Templer and reflected the transformation he brought to British strategy in Malaya. His changes involved listening and responding to some of the insurgents' demands – therefore taking away from their cause and source of popularity – and ensuring the British became genuine protectors of the local population and therefore winning local support against the insurgents.

Despite most discussions of counterinsurgency giving a prominent place to 'hearts and minds', the mantra does not always get translated into policies on the ground in a timely fashion. Thus, we have seen a number of counterinsurgencies lose valuable psychological ground by initially focusing on the use of force (discussed more below) and neglecting the aspect of listening to and wooing the local population.

There is a second front in the battle for 'hearts and minds' that is sometimes under-appreciated: the battle on the home front in the state conducting the counterinsurgency. Interestingly many insurgent groups have ultimately triumphed not because they won but because the counterinsurgents lacked the will to carry on, having lost the hearts and minds of their constituents. This was even true for the Soviet Union in Afghanistan. Despite the fact that it was not a democracy, the Soviet government realized that there was insufficient popular support for continuing to prosecute the conflict (Savranskaya 2001).

Time is often on the insurgents' side, because the stakes are much higher for them and they can wear down the support of the home population for the counterinsurgency. The faltering domestic support for the current conflicts in Afghanistan and Iraq in many of the countries with forces there – and the number of states that have withdrawn forces altogether in response to domestic opinion – points to the importance of the hearts and minds at home.

The role of military force in counterinsurgency

Another scholar-practitioner is Robert Thompson who focused more on strategy than tactics and created what he called the *Five Principles of Counterinsurgency*:

1 The government must have a clear political aim: to establish and maintain a free, independent and united country which is politically and economically stable and viable.
2 The government must function in accordance with the law.
3 The government must have an overall plan.
4 The government must give priority to defeating the political subversion, not the guerrillas.
5 In the guerrilla phase of insurgency, a government must secure its base areas first (Thomson 1972: 50–60, cited in Nagl 2005: 29).

Even bearing in mind the points made by David Kilcullen about how the insurgents and the counterinsurgents have changed, there is still much of value here. In particular, the principle of securing base areas first and then spreading outward – the so-called 'ink blot' (British term) or 'oil-spot' (American term) strategy was used successfully in Malaya and is currently being employed in Afghanistan and latterly in Iraq (having been advocated by many Vietnam-era veterans) under the leadership of the scholar-practitioner General David Petraeus (Krepinevich 2005).

In terms of tactics, an important part of counterinsurgency is actually *not* using force. David Galula (1964: 89) suggested that the ideal counter-insurgency campaign would be '80% political, 20% military'. He contended that the point of military power was to create the space for political progress (Galula 1964: 88). Given the centrality of 'hearts and minds' this makes perfect sense; a counterinsurgency campaign should involve politics, economics, psychology and, as necessary, military force. As Kilcullen concluded, 'This certainly remains relevant to modern counterinsurgency in the sense that non-military elements of national power remain decisive, though less well resourced than military elements' (2006: 123).

In the case of Iraq, there was recognition by the Bush Administration that non-military issues were important and that infrastructure mattered. 'The

United States intended reconstruction as a Marshall Plan for Iraq. Clean water, communications, sanitation and power were intended to win the hearts and minds of the Iraqi people' (Bowman 2007: 5). However, planning for reconstruction was inadequate, piecemeal, uncoordinated and ultimately undermined by Iraqi insurgents, as the Special Inspector General for Iraq Reconstruction has documented (Special Inspector General for Iraq Reconstruction).

In the Iraq campaign the Pentagon initially had the lead role in reconstruction – arguably something not suited to its skills – and this led to inter-agency disputes and problems on the ground in Iraq. For example, the Pentagon's Task Force to Support Business and Stability Operations in Iraq has largely failed in its task of helping the Iraqi manufacturing sector (White 2007: A1, A11). This raises the wider question of why on earth the military was undertaking tasks better suited to other parts of government or the private sector. The many failures of the reconstruction effort meant that many Iraqi 'hearts and minds' were hardened against the American forces.

Clearly, in situations where you are trying to win the support of the local population, the heavy-handed use of military power is likely to be counter-productive. As Montgomery McFate and Andrea Jackson (2006: 15) note, 'A direct relationship exists between the appropriate use of force and successful counterinsurgency.' Thus when force is used it must be precise, discriminating and accurate. All of this points to the crucial role of good intelligence in ensuring the appropriate use of force. Yet this is often a real shortcoming of counterinsurgency efforts, at least in the early stages and sometimes throughout the campaign. Moreover, intelligence is more than situational information; it is also about understanding the culture, workings and priorities of the local population. A classic feature of unsuccessful counterinsurgencies is either an underestimation of the will of the people (for example, President Johnson declared that the USA could not be defeated by the 'bicycle powered economy' of Vietnam), or its motivation (the USA failed to see conflict in Vietnam as an ongoing anti-imperialist struggle, viewing it through the Cold War lens of virulent communism and assuming that if Soviet and Chinese support was ended, the war would be won).

For the US military fighting the counterinsurgency campaign in Iraq one of the major points of discussion is how much to prioritize force protection as compared to protecting the local population. In the early days of the operation in Iraq the American military gave clear priority to force protection, in comparison to the British military operating in the (much more benign) atmosphere of Basra. Thus whereas the British were patrolling on foot and wearing berets, the American military were patrolling in armoured vehicles with heavy weaponry (Brown 2004). Although this was partly a question of differing security situations, there was also a different set of priorities for the two; the British tradition of imperial policing led them towards a model that put security of the local population as the key mission, whereas the US military prioritized force protection above all else (possibly another manifestation of 'Vietnam Syndrome'?). However, when General David

Petraeus took command in Iraq, priorities shifted and protecting the population became the ultimate aim. One consequence of this has been a rising number of American military deaths and injuries, but there seem to have been some concomitant gains in security for the Iraqi population.

Another facet of the use of military force is the US military's general preference for conventional warfare fought with high-technology weapons systems. As the initial invasion of Iraq showed, the USA is a formidable fighting machine, but in the words of a senior British officer, it is one which 'is fascinated by electronics, PowerPoint and the rhythm of battle' (Mills 2004). One of the problems of counterinsurgency is that these weapons are generally not useful in fighting urban insurgencies.

Learning on the ground

According to David Kilcullen, 'the nature of counter-insurgency is not fixed but shifting' and this is because 'it evolves in responses to changes in insurgency' (2006: 112). On a micro-scale this may be seen in Iraq and Afghanistan where the insurgents' tactics have evolved. For example, the use of improvised explosive devices (IEDs) has become more extensive, has evolved to include follow-up small arms fire, is now often videoed for propaganda use, and has spread to Afghanistan and Thailand (Waterman 2006). In response the counterinsurgency has shifted to try to meet these new and difficult challenges, but it is not yet evolving at a faster pace than insurgent tactics.

One of the key aspects of counterinsurgency is to allow the forces on the ground to use their best judgements in responding to the situations they encounter; to be 'strategic corporals'. In the UK this is generally more easily achieved due to the anti-doctrine bias in the British armed forces, where there is a tradition of having a basic set of rules, the interpretation and implementation of which is left to commanders in the field. This is believed to give British counterinsurgency flexibility and to encourage initiative (Thornton 2000). There is also a certain tradition of regimental 'lore' which is often unique to a particular regiment and reflects their history, approaches and tactics and is informally passed down to new soldiers.

For the much larger American military this is more of a challenge; the very size of the force means that there is greater reliance upon hierarchies and written doctrine and therefore traditionally there are fewer roles for individual initiative (Aylwin-Foster 2005). Moreover, whereas Nagl defines the British as a 'learning military' he sees the US military as failing to learn and adapt (2005: 191–208). This does not mean that there is not learning at the tactical level in the US military – the Iraq counterinsurgency is replete with examples of learning on the ground – but that this does not percolate upward into doctrinal and strategic change (Gavrilis 2005). The new counter-insurgency manual – which Nagl contributed to – is a direct attempt to change this situation (US Army 2007).

Over the past decade, however, there has been an effort afoot to 'transform' the US military. In its original conception and interpretation this was an attempt to undertake a 'Revolution in Military Affairs' (RMA) that transformed the way the US fought by taking advantage of very advanced technologies. The 1991 Gulf War saw some of the potential of the RMA, with the air war constituting the majority of the conflict. A large part of the RMA is about providing and using information to disadvantage enemies by achieving 'information dominance'. As the RMA advocates within the Pentagon – latterly led by Secretary of Defense Rumsfeld – sought to implement the RMA they ran into problems. One in particular was that the provision of the same information to the soldier on the ground as goes to the Chair of the Joint Chiefs of Staff was democratizing the battlefield in ways that made the military hierarchy uncomfortable. As the discourse shifted away from technology and the RMA it has focused more on the 'transformation' of the military; a key aspect of this agenda involves a flattening of these hierarchies and a greater role for individual initiative. Thus, a success in 'transformation' should technically assist the US military in undertaking successful counterinsurgency.

In Iraq and Afghanistan soldiers have been using the World Wide Web to share information and tactics on dealing with insurgents. This has proved invaluable when one military unit is rotating out of a theatre and wishes to pass on information to the incoming units (sometimes information that their leaders do not want them to know). However, the American authorities became concerned about who else was reading these blogs and web-posts and watching the YouTube videos, and imposed restrictions on what can be posted and when – in an attempt to protect operational security (OpSec). They argue that insurgents could glean valuable intelligence from these sources (Shane 2005). Interestingly, the British military have not done the same and seem to regard new technologies as an excellent means of ensuring quick learning about evolving insurgent tactics.

To indicate the extent of the learning challenge that the US military has faced, according to Nigel Aylwin-Foster, in 2005 there were no courses in the DOD military education system (which is extensive) focused solely on counterinsurgency (Aylwin-Foster 2005: 9). There are a number of institutional attempts to help US forces learn on the ground. Initially this involved creating a counterinsurgency academy in Iraq for newly arrived forces and was designed specifically to pass on best practices fast. This learning has been placed earlier in the training for those to be deployed and now takes place in the USA. An important initiative is at Fort Leavenworth, where there is a Center for Lessons Learned, staffed by 200 researchers and personnel who seek to answer questions from soldiers on the ground who need help fast. The Center has prepared *A Soldier's Handbook: The First 100 Days* for those going to deploy to Iraq. It covers what to be alert for, IEDs, avoiding routines and complacency, how to face the dead and the injured and so on (WBEZ 2007).

What difference does it make to be doing counterinsurgency in the media age?

Given the centrality of the 'hearts and minds' of the local and the home populations, the media is an essential sinew of a counterinsurgency campaign. Back in the 1930s T.E. Lawrence wrote that 'The printing press is the greatest weapon in the armory of the modern commander' (cited in Nagl 2005: 24). The media has become another arena of competition between insurgents and counterinsurgents, with each trying to convince key constituents of its positions. With the globalization of the media and the technologies that facilitate it, it has become harder to control. A lot of counterinsurgency practice now is about 'spin control'; attempting to influence how events, campaigns and progress are reported, both locally and at home.

A consequence of the increasing democratization of the media (anyone with a cell phone, access to the internet or a camera can be a reporter) is that everything the counterinsurgent does may be observed. This goes from the very macabre – jihadists taking videos of the destruction they cause – to citizen/journalists providing a 'bird's-eye' view of what they see of the counterinsurgency. One of the consequences of this is that every move the individual soldier, contractor and official makes has to be calibrated in terms of the overall counterinsurgency; something that was desirable anyway but has become crucial, though difficult to achieve.

In the 1960s the important role of the individual soldier was termed the 'strategic corporal' and the phrase was revived in 1999 by Charles Krulak, a Marine General (Krulak 1999). As Robert Kaplan (2005: 5) explained, 'while generals were involved in the tactical level as never before, the actions of the lowliest corporals and privates could be of great strategic impact under the spotlight of the global media'. However, there is more to the idea of the 'strategic corporal' and it refers to the reality that those on the ground have to make decisions and act in ways compatible with the main mission – using their own judgements. This can be very challenging for large armies that for decades have relied on hierarchies and strict adherence to doctrine, but is less so for smaller armed forces that have had to adapt to taking on multiple tasks (including ostensibly non-military ones) and consequently 'making it up' as they go along. The new US counterinsurgency manual is clear on the importance of the individual stressing the need to 'empower the lowest levels' (US Army 2007).

Similarities to post-conflict peacebuilding

There are a number of comparisons to draw between counterinsurgency operations and post-conflict peacebuilding which are worth noting.

First, in both situations the ideal ratio between force (kinetic) and non-violent (non-kinetic) activities is the same: 20 per cent military to 80 per cent non-military elements. In each type of operation there are the same questions over the suitability of the military for doing some of these tasks – particularly the economic and political elements. In both situations the military are often the only group present in strength and inevitably find themselves completing tasks they are not trained for.

Second, both operations are aimed at standing up and supporting weak governments. Often the situation they encounter is where informal authorities are the only game in town and society works through patrimonial networks (tribes and clans). Consequently, some of the same dilemmas are involved, in particular the tension between doing things efficiently (that is, by the outsiders doing it – be it armies, international organizations or NGOs) and enabling local ownership. T.E. Lawrence said of the Arabs in 1917: 'better [they] do it tolerably well than you do it perfectly.' We can see this dilemma clearly in Iraq and Afghanistan where there is concern over the ability of the local police forces to effectively fulfil their duties. In peacebuilding operations the temptation to take over from the locals is usually overwhelming, particularly as missions often have only one year to achieve 'peace' before they leave.

Third, in both counterinsurgency and peace-building operations there is a lot of knowledge at the tactical/operational level, but less at the strategic level, leading to a tendency to apply 'standard models' with very mixed results. In both counterinsurgency and post-conflict peacebuilding, efforts are often undermined by the same problems of lack of cultural knowledge, which rarely get fixed in time. In both situations there are attempts to learn from past operations; for example, the United Nations had a 'lessons learned' unit (which was subsumed within the Best Practices Unit in 2001), but these efforts are not very successful. Consequently, there is the same kind of sporadic learning – especially in the USA which does not regard either operation as a core mission (even though the US military ends up doing both).

Fourth, in both post-conflict peacebuilding and counterinsurgency there are similar mixes of actors involved in the operations: NGOs, international organizations, private firms, military and civilian authorities, contractors, local civil society and so on. This leads to parallel problems of coordination and the difficulty of ensuring that all elements are pursuing the same agenda.

Finally, the Disarmament, Demobilization and Reintegration (DDR) campaigns that are an important part of peace-building face the same problem as counterinsurgency: how to drain away the uncommitted supporters from the fanatical ones who will not be swayed by alternative employment and economic opportunities.

Clearly, there are many similarities between these two types of operations. This helps to explain why forces that are regularly involved in post-conflict peace-building operations find the move to counterinsurgency less traumatic than do militaries who are primarily focused on missions involving major wars with high-technology opponents.

Conclusion

An important question in modern counterinsurgency is: 'What constitutes victory?' A quote from Donald Rumsfeld sums up the dilemma: 'We know we are killing a lot, capturing a lot, collecting arms. We just don't know yet whether that's the same as winning' (Rumsfeld, cited in Hoffman 2004: 16).

Kilcullen points to the fact that in contemporary insurgencies the continued existence of even a few insurgents armed with modern communications technologies could mean that they continue to cause significant problems, so it may not be enough to destroy an organization. Therefore, 'In modern counter-insurgency, victory may need to be re-defined as the disarming and reintegration of insurgents into society, combined with popular support for permanent, institutionalized anti-terrorist measures that contain the risk of terrorist cells emerging from the former insurgent movement' (Kilcullen 2006: 123). This is interesting, as it reinforces the parallels between counterinsurgency operations and post-conflict peacebuilding noted above.

Within the US military there is a lively campaign being conducted to have counterinsurgency recognized as a core mission for the future. Those evangelizing for counterinsurgency want to ensure that the USA does not have to go through the same painful relearning experience in the future, but is ready, trained and able to take on the missions. Among the key counter-insurgency advocates are people like scholar-practitioners John Nagl, James Gavrillis, Thomas Hammes and David Petraeus.

These advocates are meeting spirited opposition and there are a number of reasons for this. First, counterinsurgency is not a mission that the military necessarily likes; operations are messy, inconclusive, can cost lives and are in many ways 'post-heroic'. Second, the military culture of efficiency, organization and clear missions is somewhat at odds with what it takes to practise successful counterinsurgency: empowering locals (even at the cost of efficiency), not really using force and stepping outside of usual roles. Third, counterinsurgency is a mission that gives the lead to the Army and Marines and that is never going to please the Air Force and the Navy (even though both branches are providing personnel for counterinsurgency operations today). Fourth, counterinsurgency is a mission that does not require any major advanced weapons platforms (e.g. fighter aircraft, aircraft carriers, big tanks) and this will make it more difficult to advocate for these types of weapons platforms – and the US military loves its high-technology weapons systems. Fifth, the US record in counter-insurgency does not encourage making it a core mission; at best the record is decidedly mixed. Sixth, the US military has not recently shown itself to be a 'learning military' and this is a tremendous obstacle to making counter-insurgency a core mission (Aylwin-Foster 2005). Finally, there is the political question of whether, after the bruising experience of Iraq – which was a war of choice – the USA will be willing to take on new insurgencies or will it be deterred? David Kilcullen (who works for General Petraeus) has suggested that the USA will be called upon to fight insurgencies until it finds a way to defeat them, so they will not have a choice.

The issue is clearer for other states, such as Britain and Canada, that expect to be involved in peacebuilding, but have no expectation of fighting a major war alone. For these states, their training and planning in encompassing peacebuilding puts them in a good position to adapt to counterinsurgency as necessary.

Note

1   I would like to thank Dr Sean Edwards for his comments on an earlier draft of the chapter.

Further reading

A good starting point is *The U.S. Army and Marine Corps Counterinsurgency Field Manual* with Forwards by General David H. Petraeus, Lt. General James F. Amos and Lt. Colonel John A. Nagl, and by Sarah Sewall (Chicago, IL: University of Chicago Press, 2007). This is the first time that a field manual has been published by a mainstream press and this speaks to the current interest in the issue (and may be viewed as part of the 'hearts and minds' campaign at home). A notable feature is the emphasis on understanding local culture.

John A. Nagl, *Learning to Eat Soup With A Knife: Counterinsurgency Lessons from Malaya and Vietnam* (Chicago, IL: University of Chicago Press, 2005). The title is taken from T.E. Lawrence who said, 'To make war upon rebellion is messy and slow, like eating soup with a knife.'

John Dumbrell and David Ryan (eds), *Vietnam in Iraq: Tactics, Lessons, Legacies and Ghosts* (London: Routledge, 2007). This book contains a number of interesting essays investigating the comparisons and contrasts between US involvement in these two counterinsurgencies.

As with many contemporary security topics, there is a lot of 'noise' about the issues in the 'bloggosphere' but its quality is really variable. However, I do recommend the Small Wars Journal blog: http://smallwarsjournal.com/blog/. This is both a good round-up of recent events and gets good-quality contributions from those serving in Iraq such as David Kilcullen.

Other internet sites of value are the horizontal networking sites www.company command.com and www.platoonleader.org.

A US radio programme called 'This American Life' did a show on the Center for Lessons Learned on 25 May 2007. This Podcast may be downloaded at: www.thislife.org/Radio_Archive.aspx#5.

The Battle of Algiers (Directed by Gillo Pontecorvo, 1966). This film is set during the 1954 to 1962 Algerian War and follows French efforts to roll up an insurgent cell. It has great *verity* as many of the actors in the film were locals who had lived through the civil war. The film does not flinch from showing both the violence perpetrated by the insurgents and that by the counterinsurgents. It is said that the film was watched by military officials of the Bush Administration in the aftermath of the 2003 Iraq invasion.

The War Tapes (Directed by Deborah Scranton, 2006). Filmed by members of Charlie Company stationed in Iraq, it shows the day-to-day progress of the war and the strain it places on soldiers there.

CONTENTS

Peace Operations

Michael Pugh

▌ Abstract

Peace operations range from observation and monitoring to peace-building in war-torn societies. At one extreme, some observers contend that it includes combat falling short of outright belligerency: peace enforcement. This chapter traces the shift in peace operations discourse and packaging since the mid-1990s. Reforms that make peace operations a handmaiden to 'human security', enlightened governance and liberalization have as much to do with ideological conviction and the quest to maintain hierarchy as with technical and operational requirements. Peace operations reflect power distribution in the international system and, as a form of crisis management, serve to sustain rather than transform the global system.

▌ Introduction

This chapter focuses on the agency of peace operations. It contends that while peacekeeping by blue berets was largely a vision-less response to international crisis management, peace operations have been increasingly co-opted into grand intentions to bring about liberal peace. This is a highly problematic enterprise, in terms of both meaning and practice. In part this expansiveness occurs in a permissive environment because peace missions are ill-defined, have various purposes (from preventing conflict to transforming war-torn societies), and are undertaken by a bewildering range of actors, from the Commonwealth of Independent States (CIS) to the African Union (AU). For Western states and the UN, the expansion of peace missions forms a key part of a broad project to confer liberal privileges on societies at war by implementing 'responsibility to protect civilians', 'good governance', 'human security' and 'capacity-building'.

The circumstances and nature of peace operations have changed considerably since the Cold War. First, because informed consent by hosts was such a critical variable in the deployment of peacekeepers, it could be convincingly argued that state sovereignty was left intact, indeed protected by restrictive status of forces agreements and memoranda of understanding. However, sovereignty is now considered contingent on unthreatening behaviour, human rights and 'good governance'. Weak and failed states are to be relieved of sovereignty and accorded 'shared sovereignty' (Krasner 2005). Second, the small post-war missions – 45 observers along the 500-mile ceasefire line in Jammu and Kashmir after 1949; the modest six-month executive role in West New Guinea when a UN 'tsar' ran the territory without a budget backed by only 1,500 troops – have been eclipsed by ambitious deployments. Only the 20,000-strong Congo mission in the 1960s seems to be regarded as a precursor of current deployments, and is cited as a Cold War oddity. The contrast has been starkest in the Lebanon where 4,500 UNIFIL troops were operating under a broad 1978 mandate until after Israel's aggression in 2006, when the guarantors of a ceasefire decided that a 15,000-strong force was needed. Third, there are many more actors competing for roles and claiming special dispensations arising from regional interest or expertise, from a high moral ground or from a particular use of power. Fourth, in contemporary operations, peacekeepers are seemingly engaged in everything from civilian protection to conflict resolution, support for police raids on fraudsters to backing up 'peace' agreements with a coercive presence.

The chapter begins with a discussion of language and typologies to show that peacekeeping has been subsumed into peace operations, constructing a discourse framework that facilitates the imposition of liberal norms and values to sustain Western hegemony in the international system, irrespective of the nationalities contributing. The subsequent section provides a snapshot of peace operations from the mid-1990s and discusses the reforms instigated to cope with the predicaments presented by civil wars and the resurgence of demand from 2003. The reforms led to peace operations having a more visionary rationale than old-style peacekeeping by blue berets. Three issues that exercise policy-makers and practitioners in contemporary operations are discussed – standards of professionalism, hybrid missions and the so-called public security gap. Finally, the chapter considers the future prospects of this activity. First, however, it is important to unpack the confusion of terminology.

Language and meaning

In this field, language and meaning has particular importance for three main reasons. First, use of the term 'peace' as an adjective clothes 'operations' in a normative garb of beneficence and as something distinct from war. Indeed, US military doctrine fashioned 'peacekeeping' as a category of 'Operations Other Than War', but managed also to make it a subcategory of 'stability operations' – which in Iraq and Afghanistan are possibly destabilizing and barely distinguishable from combat. François Debrix (1997) points out that this labelling is designed to camouflage the inadequacies of such operations in bringing about either an absence of war (negative peace) or contributing to structural change that will embed non-violence in the system (positive peace). In his view, peace operations represent a simulacra, or image, of peace. Some so-called peace operations may of course bring respite from violent conflict but this is by no means assured and such interventions may make matters worse, as clearly happened in Iraq. In similar vein, Oliver Richmond concludes that peace has not been imagined in a way that avoids hegemonic imposition: peace operations bring about a 'virtual peace' (Richmond 2005). David Chandler formulates a more radical critique, basing his thesis around Zaki Laïdi's notion of post-ideological meaningless and weakness (Laïdi 1998: 8–9, 110). Laïdi's argument that commitments are contingent, and that states interact to evade rather than engage, is applied by Chandler to demonstrate that engagement in the name of good governance and other vague agendas facilitates the evasion of both responsibility and the discharge of power (Chandler 2006: 18). Otherwise, why would potential contributors have to be bullied and cajoled into sending troops to the Lebanon, Afghanistan and the Sudan?

On the contrary, however, peace operations may be considered as agencies of liberal peace, contributing to the prevailing structures of power, not least when reifying technical and administrative involvement in so-called weak or failed states. As with Cold War peacekeeping, peace operations engage in ordering and tidying up violent conflict in the international system. By the turn of this century, however, more expansive peace operations were co-opted into ambitious designs based on liberal norms and values (Jacoby 2007).

Second, such operations have been deployed where there is no peace to secure, where ceasefires break down or, as in Afghanistan, where war continues in some areas if not in all. And so the adjective can be a misleading signifier of the conditions into which operations are inserted, and which have to use violence 'to bring peace'. The oxymoron then commonly employed is 'peace enforcement'.

Third, for practical operational reasons, especially in multinational contexts, it is essential to clarify the meaning of such operations so that military and civilian personnel have common frames of reference. But the linguistic grounds have been shifting. The UK's Ministry of Defence and Foreign and Commonwealth Office, for example, use the term Peace Support Operations, implying that such operations are not ends in themselves but supportive – whereas the US uses the term Peace Operations. Even more confusing, the annual review of UN peace-keeping, sponsored by the UN Department of Peacekeeping (formerly Peacekeeping) Operations is entitled *Annual Review of Global Peace Operations* (Center on International Cooperation 2006). Finally, the incoming UN Secretary-General Ban Ki-moon has proposed that the Department of Peacekeeping Operations (DPKO) be dismantled and split into two: a Department of Peace Operations (not peace-keeping, peacekeeping or peace support) and a Department of Field Support. It is thus possible to detect a trend whereby peacekeeping has been subsumed under something much broader and ill-defined – peace operations.

The umbrella term 'peace operations', therefore, includes a wide range of activities. UK government departments categorize them according to general objectives: conflict prevention; peacekeeping; peacemaking; peace enforcement; and peacebuilding. As some of these issues are discussed elsewhere in this volume, the analysis here will be confined largely to the use of uniformed (military and police) forces for peacekeeping and enforcement missions permitted under Chapter VI and Chapter VII respectively of the UN Charter (items 3 and 4 in Box 27.1).

BOX 27.1 THE UK'S CATEGORIES OF PEACE SUPPORT OPERATIONS

1 **Conflict prevention**: Identifying causes of conflict and preventing its occurrence, persistence or resumption (for example, through having a military presence).
2 **Peacemaking**: Securing through diplomacy a ceasefire or peace settlement to bring about an end to violence.
3 **Peacekeeping**: Military forces and police operating with host consent to underpin a peace settlement or ceasefire, using force impartially and with severe restrictions (for example, in self-defence).
4 **Peace enforcement**: Force used coercively to get compliance with agreements, impose a peace or protect civilians from hostilities.
5 **Peacebuilding**: Support to the long-term regeneration of war-torn societies and for establishing sustainable peace through administrative, judicial, military, economic and political capacity-building.

Surge, retraction, resurgence

The pattern of UN deployments changed dramatically in the decade after the mid-1990s. In July 1993, the UN was deploying 78,444 uniformed personnel, one-third of them in the Balkans. The number fell away after the debacle in

Somalia and the Dayton accords for Bosnia, where NATO took responsibility for military forces. By the late 1990s the number of personnel on UN operations had fallen to below 15,000. Clearly, the UN had found it extremely difficult to adjust to the demand for peace enforcement in internal conflicts. Beginning in October 2003, however, five major ventures were underway in Liberia, Côte d'Ivoire, Haiti, Burundi and the Sudan. The Democratic Republic of Congo operation (MONUC) was expanding and a considerable expansion of UNIFIL in the Lebanon in the wake of Israel's aggression in mid-2006 resulted in a further increase (see Figure 27.1).

At the start of 2007, the UN was deploying 69,146 troops, 2,527 military observers and 8,695 police, a total of 80,368 personnel in 15 missions (with additional personnel in three political/peacebuilding missions: see Figure 27.2). Only the US has a greater global deployment than the UN. Of the 112 contributing countries, the main suppliers continued to be Pakistan, Bangladesh and India with about 9,500 each, followed by Jordan and Nepal with about 3,500 each, and then Ghana, Uruguay, Ethiopia and Nigeria with about 2,500 each. Some previously supportive participants in UN peacekeeping had virtually dropped out, or confined their contributions to military observers and police. At the start of 2007, New Zealand had only one soldier on UN service, Australia nine and Canada a mere 15. The US supplied only nine troops (but almost 300 police). These risible troop contributions were completely overshadowed by those of relative newcomers such as China (1,400) and Namibia (600). The UK with 275 soldiers provided a similar number to

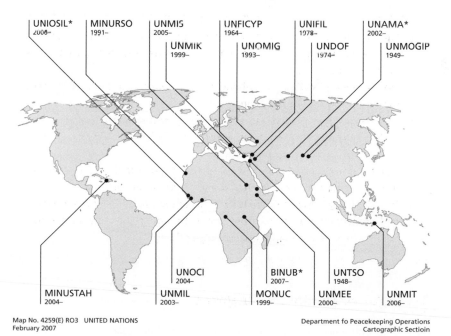

Figure 27.1 Missions administered by the Department of Peacekeeping Operations

Note: *political or peace-building mission

Mongolia, Rwanda and Slovakia. The US, the UK and its former 'dominions', along with some European states, were of course otherwise engaged in (largely fruitless) non-UN warlike operations in Afghanistan and Iraq.

Lack of resources has been an abiding concern of the UN, as demands rose and states were reluctant to participate in risky ventures. The budget for operations had grown from US$1.5 billion in 2000 to $5.25 billion in 2007, about one-hundredth the size of the US defence budget. The only states allocated more than 5 per cent of the peacekeeping budget were: the USA (unilaterally and progressively reducing its contribution from 31.7 per cent in 1993 to 25 per cent for 2007), Japan (19 per cent), Germany (9 per cent), the UK and France (7 per cent each) and Italy (5 per cent). But $2.5 billion in contributions was outstanding. The US had fallen $505 million in arrears from before 2005 as a result of its unilateral capping, and another $117 million from 2005 to June 2007 (US GAO 2007: 4). Indeed, UN operations are conducted on the cheap, the US Accountability Office estimating that to run the Haiti mission would cost double if conducted unilaterally (US GAO 2007: 2).

Under such pressures, accompanied during the Bush Administration by the scarcely concealed contempt and hostility of the USA towards the global organization, and Kofi Annan in person, the UN could be more easily kept on a leash. Nevertheless, the UN strived to catch up with the evolving conflict environment and attempted to institute reforms congenial to its most powerful member states.

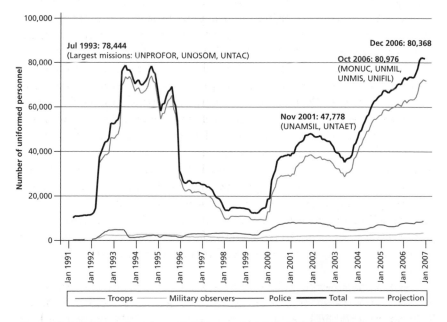

Figure 27.2 Uniformed personnel in UN peacekeeping, 1991–2006

Source: Prepared by the Peace and Security Section of the United Nations Department of Public Information in consultation with the Military Planning Service of the Department of Peacekeeping Operations (DPI/2444, 22 January 2007).

Reforms

As a consequence of the surge in the early 1990s and the bruising experiences in Somalia, Rwanda and Bosnia, Kofi Annan, himself a former Under Secretary-General for Peacekeeping, gave full support to a reconceptualization of peacekeeping. He pronounced in July 1997 that without sufficient resources or political will to endow the UN with capabilities to act under Chapter VII of the Charter, ad hoc coalitions of 'the willing' would be the most effective mechanism for enforcement missions. Reiterating the view of his predecessor Boutros Boutros-Ghali, Annan argued that: 'Cooperation with regional organizations will be intensified and regional organizations will increasingly become partners of the United Nations in all activities related to the maintenance of international peace and security' (Annan 1997). In part, the future of intervention would lie in hybrid operations, or contracted-out enforcement as in the Balkans. This was reinforced by an interrogation of peacekeeping in 2000 by the Secretary-General's experienced Special Representative and Special Adviser, Lakhdar Brahimi.

Brahimi's report

First, Brahimi contended that UN forces must be able to defend themselves effectively, and that this should include impartial defence of the mandate. In the light of Lt. Gen. Roméo Dallaire's distressing experience in Rwanda (Dallaire 2004), Brahimi suggested that peacekeeping needed to be more flexible and robust. If peacekeeping forces could move up a gear to enforcement and back again without losing their impartiality and without having to rely on the wholesale consent of all parties in a host country, this, it was imagined, would answer the Rwandan problem of low-level, but effective, resistance to feeble UN missions by determined armed groups. Second, if flexible toughness was the new mantra, then far more consultation with troop contributors had to be instituted to avoid 'taxation without representation'. This could side-step disputes about the use or misuse of national units in fraught situations, such as that which arose in Srebrenica, Bosnia, when Dutch troops compounded the Bosniak government's abandonment of this designated 'safe area' by failing to protect the civilian population. Third, mandates would need to reflect the resources available. Funds should be released for the planning and start-up of missions, even before a mandate had been agreed. If commitments by states were not forthcoming then mandates should be limited.

The Brahimi concept, welcomed by those Western militaries engrossed in doctrine development such as the French and British, was seriously flawed in its assumptions. First, it assumed that a strategy could be devised for both peacekeeping and enforcement by the same forces, as if they were part of a spectrum of force (whereas peacekeeping is on a spectrum of non-force). Moreover, the analysis rested on a misrepresentation of the potential effectiveness of enforcement, when the critical failure was not operational but political will (see Berdal 2001: 67, Johnstone 2006: 5). Second, based on a dubious projection of the Rwanda model of conflict it assumed that peace could be secured by military means and without widening resistance. Subsequently, robust forces spent as much effort on force protection as on protecting civilians. The UN Mission in Sudan originally aimed to have 10,000 peacekeepers, of whom 4,000 were for force protection (UNMIS 2006).

Third, the concept ran foul of nationalism, especially the unwillingness of states to see their forces put in harm's way under a UN command – an issue that almost paralysed NATO strategy when the US–UK aerial bombing in Kosovo would have put any ground troops at risk of Serbian retaliation. The Clinton Administration had already signalled disengagement after its disaster in Mogadishu by issuing Presidential Decision Directive 25 of 22 February 1996, which reinforced US opposition to placing troops under UN control.

Fourth, as Bellamy, Williams and Griffin point out (2004: 170), if international forces were to plan for their exits, an imposed peace would have to be part of a broad strategy involving multiple agencies that would address root causes and establish a non-violent future in war-torn societies. A liberal ideology had to be activated with a package of transformation policies – construed by academics as the 'liberal peace' (see Richmond 2005). Concerned with democratization, rule of law and economic reconstruction, the roots of liberal peace are traceable to a global modernization project of the early Cold War years in US foreign policy (Jahn 2007), or even further back to Woodrow Wilson after the First World War. Where the UN or non-UN coalitions had administrative control, as in Bosnia, Kosovo, Timor Leste and Afghanistan, the ideology could be applied directly, the presence of military forces providing the means to enforce it (Chesterman 2004). Enforcing preferred norms of governance and socio-economic development was a grave contravention of norms declared since the Second World War that asserted the right of every state to 'choose its political, economic, social and cultural system, without interference in any form by another State' (Declaration 1965). A normative shift towards a less pluralist conception and more universalistic and individualistic conception of rights appears to have occurred in the late 1990s. It culminated in a consensus that states had a moral duty, though not a legal right, to protect civilians from gross abuse in other countries if their own state failed to do so (see Chapter 28, this volume).

Coalitions were taking matters into their own hands anyway and bypassing UN peacekeeping. Sierra Leone was a case in point. In February 2000, the UN Assistance Mission for Sierra Leone (UNAMSIL) was provided with a Chapter VII mandate to protect civilians, though without sufficient resources to do so. The Revolutionary United Front (RUF) took some 500 peacekeepers hostage in May 2000. But rather than strengthen UNAMSIL, the UK sent an independent combat force of paratroopers and marines to secure Freetown and drive the RUF back. This division of labour, with the UN subcontracting, underwriting or turning a blind eye to enforcement by freelance entrepreneurs seemed a practical solution. Indeed, the Annan/Brahimi reforms acknowledged a growing division of labour between 'enforcers' and 'peacekeepers' as the spectrum strategy proved untenable in Sierra Leone. It also enabled states such as Canada and Australia to be more selective about contributing forces to the UN and perhaps to have a louder political voice in regional frameworks than was the case in New York.

Guéhenno's goals

Towards the end of 2005 the Under Secretary-General for Peacekeeping, Jean-Marie Guéhenno, noted that the Brahimi reforms were intended to give the UN the capacity to launch one new large operation a year. There were three in 2004 (Côte d'Ivoire, Haiti and Burundi), and between 2000 and 2005 there had been a fivefold increase in personnel in the field (Guéhenno 2005). In addition, the safety of mission personnel was being strained in attempting to meet the challenge of armed groups, including armed children, looters and criminal gangs. In the 44-year period 1948 to 1992, there had been 925 fatalities. In the fourteen and half years from January 1993 to June 2007 there were 1,454 (UNDPKO 2007).

Guéhenno's five-year plan, *Peace Operations 2010*, had five goals relating to personnel, doctrine, cooperation with other bodies, resources and integrated structures (see Box 27.2). Personnel policies would focus on selection, training and a review of conditions of service. Doctrine reform would focus on the elaboration of guidelines, codes and best practices through enhanced production of policy directives, standard operating procedures and manuals. Improved partnerships with other UN and non-UN agencies and organizations would be achieved by integrated planning with these other bodies from the start of a mission, and establishing clear lines of authority. In particular it would be vital to establish *modus operandi* with the newly established Peacebuilding Office and Commission and with partners in hybrid operations. The DPKO

BOX 27.2 PEACE OPERATIONS 2010

Goal 1: Recruit, prepare and retain high-quality personnel.

Goal 2: Set out doctrine and establish standards.

Goal 3: Establish effective partnerships, integrated missions and predictable frameworks of cooperation.

Goal 4: Secure essential resources to improve operations, notably in rapid response and policing.

Goal 5: Establish integrated organizational structures at headquarters and in the field.

was committed to supporting the African Union's capacity-building, to procedures for dealing with the EU's proposed 'battle groups' in support of peace missions, and to cooperation with NATO and the World Bank. Resources were needed to strengthen operational capacity in three areas: policing (with a 25-person Standing Police Capacity), rapidly deployable military forces and enhanced information production in the field and in communicating with publics in host and troop contributing countries. Integrated organizational capacity would be achieved by establishing 'backstop teams' in DPKO for each mission, comprising specialists in political, military, police, civilian, logistic, financial, personnel and public information, and by establishing joint operation centres in the field.

Ban's plans

These steps to deal with overstretch, underperformance and lack of resources were certainly necessary but would take five years to implement in full. In 2007, the new Secretary-General, Ban Ki-moon, proposed a more radical restructuring to cope with the expansion and complexities of peace operations. The DPKO would not only lose its 'peacekeeping' designation to become the Department of Peace Operations, it would also lose its Mission Support Unit to a new Department of Field Support, which would also gain resources from other parts of the UN. The role of the Field Support Department would be to administer and manage field personnel, procurement, finances and information/communications technology. The General Assembly accepted this restructuring as an attempt to improve planning, responsiveness and resource efficiency, but most of the state representatives re-emphasized Ban's proviso that unity of command and integration of effort would need to be guaranteed. Given that the proposal would reverse a merger of the political and logistic components of peacekeeping in 1993 to 1994, designed to achieve better planning and integration, this plan has to be considered a potentially risky revival of fragmentation. Ban's decision to head both departments with Under Secretaries-General but to have the head of Field Support reporting to and taking direction from the head of Peace Operations seems more like a recipe for confusion and disintegration. Further, the General Assembly financed the Field Support Department for only a year with 284 temporary posts, as against Ban's request for 400. Nor did developing countries allow the new department to acquire the procurement function: it being one of the powers they had left in the Department of Management.

Standards

Reports of corruption and human rights (including sexual) abuse damaged the reputation of peace operations in the 1990s. For example, women subject to sexual violence in conflict (inflicted on men too) were also vulnerable through poverty and diminished status to the aggressive masculinities of male-dominated peace missions (Olsson and Tryggestad 2001). In 2000, for the first time, the UN Security Council passed a resolution (1325 of 31 October) insisting on mainstreaming gender sensitivity in peace operations. Following further reports of sexual abuse by civilians as well as troops in the Balkans, the DRC and elsewhere, an investigation was led by Prince Ra'ad Zeid, who recommended legal steps to stamp it out (Zeid 2005). National forces, regional bodies and international training centres had invested in raising professional standards and producing manuals and codes of conduct. In November 2006, DPKO also sent Conduct and Discipline Units to the largest UN operations to instil high standards of behaviour. Thanks to resolution 1325 and Guéhenno's reforms the missions should become more professional, better trained and more effectively deployed.

But as scholars have pointed out, the issue is not resolved by legal measures, manuals and training alone. To begin with, fewer than 1,500 women were in uniform in UN service in 2007, and often had to be kept apart from their male colleagues (Valenius 2007). An Indian paramilitary police unit of 105 women joined the Liberian mission in 2007 for crowd control and robust policing in an environment where rape has been endemic – but they did not mix with the local population either (Grewal 2007). To some extent the increased robustness expected of peace operations may have inhibited women's inclusion. However, there are two deeper causes. First, the cultural power of aggressive masculinities and essentialist views of the roles of women as victims, or the pacifying dimension of peace operations, hinders inclusiveness – and needs to be destabilized. Second, the privileging of liberal internationalism as an apolitical and benign enterprise, while powerful UN member states engage in power politics and technical fixes, helps to maintain silences around gendered power relations – and these need to be disturbed (Whitworth 2004). In sum, although training, codes and standards of conduct, not only on gender issues, have probably had an impact, militaries and civilian police have to confront challenges to their own social norms. Furthermore, it is clear that, in general, peace operations are presented as so rational and sagacious that they tend to lack an ethic that incorporates an understanding of the images of peace operations held by those subjected to them (see Pouligny 2006).

Hybrid operations

The UN has no monopoly in peace operations, or even peacekeeping, and never has done. Freelance missions have been an element in International Relations, at least since the nineteenth-century coalitions were formed to manage the prolonged dismantling of the Ottoman Empire, including the international military administration of Shkodër, Albania in 1913 to 1914. Under the UN system, the US-sponsored Multinational Force and Observers in the Sinai after the Egypt–Israel Peace Treaty of 1979 is a prominent example of a non-UN mission. Although, as Trevor Findlay (2002) demonstrates, UN missions have used force, sometimes beyond self-defence, the trend has been for the UN to opt out of operations likely to involve combat, and has allowed groups of states to act as proxies. The Dayton Peace Agreement

Implementation Force (IFOR) in Bosnia originally comprised 60,000 from NATO-led states; its successors, the Stabilization Force (SFOR), and EUFOR, conducted by the EU (with only 2,500 troops by 2007) also had Chapter VII mandates. NATO also supplies the troops for the UN Mission in Kosovo (UNMIK). The Economic Community of West African States has launched five operations; the Russian-dominated CIS has 18,000 troops in Georgia and Tajikistan; the AU has 6,500 troops and police in Sudan; and Australian-led forces operate in the southwest Pacific.

Hybrid operations, in which regional or freelance organizations operate alongside one another, may reduce the problems arising from groups of self-appointed states policing their own interests that, wittingly or not, add to the dynamics of conflict. For example, NATO, the EU, OSCE and the UN have worked jointly, if dysfunctionally at times, as part of UNMIK. The UN Mission in Sudan (UNMIS) operates under the overall command of the AU's African Mission in Sudan (AMIS). Many developing states, but also others such as Japan, continue to regard the UN as the most appropriate body to safeguard international peace and security because all states are represented and it embeds even the most powerful members in a system of checks and balances. Two heads of peacekeeping at the UN, Sir Marrack Goulding and Guéhenno, have expressed concern that beyond Europe regional organizations are either not politically willing to conduct multilateral missions in their region (Asia and Southeast Asia) or (like AMIS) do not have the resources and infrastructure to match the UN (Goulding 2002: 17, Guéhenno 2003: 35–36). However, the support to emerging multinational infrastructures may reduce the huge disparities between capacities in Europe and elsewhere (see Bellamy and Williams 2007: 343). Nevertheless, hybrid operations place a high premium on effective coordination, even integration, which has not often been apparent.

Although the UN has promoted hybridity, its universal legitimacy and a trend towards increased professionalism should continue to make peace missions a core function of the organization. Freelance peace missions will be only one of a range of international responses to wars and complex emergencies. Coalition forces engaged in coercion to provide security may be accompanied by UN missions. They may be followed up by UN forces for the long-term regeneration of societies in the voids created by coalitions bent on exit or unable to cope. UN deployments will still be needed where regional bodies are overstretched, lacking in infrastructure or requiring legitimacy.

Public security gap

Given the predilection of interventions to emphasize the establishment of rule of law, a third thorny issue became apparent in Bosnia: how to deal with civil unrest and public disorder (see e.g. Oakley *et al.* 1997). Soldiers are usually the first element to arrive in a war-torn society but are inadequate for democratic policing and send a signal to local populations that brute force is the ultimate arbiter of social conflict. One answer was to send in paramilitaries, such as the Italian *carabinieri*, operating under military control and rules of engagement.

Another, with a long-standing pedigree since the peacekeeping mission in Cyprus, has been to send in civilian police. Rarely have they engaged in executive roles, Kosovo being an exception. Rather, they have concentrated on modernizing, training and supervising local police services. However, unlike many military forces, the national police forces of contributing states have not traditionally required threats abroad to justify their existence. Consequently, obtaining commitments and contributions of well-qualified officers has been highly problematic. The EU has developed expertise and a degree of competence in this field but Guéhenno's proposal for a standby capacity at the UN indicates the perceived need to strengthen this component of peace missions. However, the intrusion into rule of law issues in war-torn societies also reinforces the liberal framework of what constitutes peace and the normative values to be imposed.

Conclusion: future prospects

Peace operations are assumed to have a role in bringing about or maintaining conditions that reduce or eliminate violent conflict. There is some evidence for this claim. The authors of the 2005 *Human Security Report* argue that purposeful international activism, including peace operations, has been responsible for the decline in deadly civil conflicts (Human Security Centre 2005: 155). However, the evidence is largely circumstantial and one is still entitled to ask: what do peace operations represent in the early twenty-first century? Are they evidence of a grand design to simulate peace? Or are we about to witness a post-Iraq retreat into scaled-back pragmatism? To help answer these questions it is tempting to boil down the impulses that construct an imagined peace, to which peace operations contribute.

For a self-styled pragmatic view we can turn to George Pratt Schultz, the neoliberal economist and Cold War diplomat who tolerated or supported dictatorships in Chile, the Philippines, Nicaragua and Haiti. Former economic adviser to Eisenhower and Nixon, Reagan's Secretary of State (1982-1989) and a Republican Party strategist, Schultz characterized his approach to Cold War politics as problem-solving. International Relations, in his view, required constant attention to the obstacles, frictions and crises that arose in the quest for peace, similar to weeding a garden. The weeds are almost entirely produced by unruly others, which in the Schultz worldview included US allies who fell out of line. Cold War peacekeeping was also problem-solving, but without so much partiality as to the origins and outcomes of disputes.

Peace operations, modern-style, are more ambitious. And for a visionary perspective we can also turn to Schultz, honorary co-chair and subscriber to an influential Princeton University project, *Forging a World of Liberty under Law*, published in September 2006 (Ikenberry and Slaughter 2006). Signalling a retreat from the polarizing unilateralism of the Bush Administration, the Princeton strategy has the same Wilsonian vision of a global order based on the spread of liberal democracy. In this respect the thinking behind the *Liberty under Law* strategy is the latest manifestation of the liberal peace, in which the weeds of the international system have to be killed off and unruly others have to be administered and controlled to protect peace. Certainly, the strategy bids to fuse hard and 'soft power', relies less on military solutions and proposes a rediscovery of international law by the US. But it also proposes a permanent Concert of Democracies led by the US to help create a 'better and safer world'. *Liberty under Law* clearly retains the rhetorical impulse for changing the world in the liberal image.

In practice as well as in rhetoric, engagement in peace is accompanied by dogmatism and zeal. In addition to the co-option of peace missions into the wider project of promoting a liberal global order, authority figures have made strong efforts to embed ideals in their work. Lord Ashdown, High Representative in Bosnia and Herzegovina in the period 2002 to 2006, exemplifies the point. His reflections on his tenure in office are instructive because he lays considerable emphasis on the need for divided communities to seek a common vision beyond their immediate concerns. In the case of Bosnia, the goal is membership of the EU (Ashdown 2007). The vision provides a rigorous form of conditionality introduced from the outside with no organic foundations, and serves as a rescue package that requires deferred gratification, since membership lies well into the future. An even more egregious instance, a component of so-called 'peace stabilization' that followed the illegal freelance invasion of Iraq, was the lengths to which Paul Bremer, the second US head of the Coalition Administration in the first half of 2003, pursued a vision of economic development that swept aside indigenous forms of production, exchange and regulation. Bremer's fetish for deregulation, foreign direct investment, privatization (including privatization of the privatization process) and anti-protectionism was so severely disruptive and punitive against the most vulnerable sections of society that it had to be abandoned (Klein 2005).

Since the end of the Cold War UN and non-UN peace missions continue to effect repairs, put conflicts on ice or try to resolve local and immediate issues, as they did in the past. However, they have also been co-opted into bold schemes for transformation. These have met resistance or lacked sustainability because they have been devoid of secure political foundations in war-torn societies. There is thus an emerging debate about whether the liberal peace can continue as a fantasy based on a flawed, perhaps meaningless, concept of change that actually inhibits political accountability, or whether an aggressive 'shared sovereignty' and cosmopolitan views of 'human security' and 'the responsibility to protect' will dominate the framing of peace operations. The meanings of peace missions continue to be framed as meeting threats that are the product of others, usually in failed states. They represent a constancy of assumption in many quarters that the world is available for liberating by liberalism. However, the power to implement this is attenuated, and expressed by evasion of responsibility and claims of immunity from accountability. A nervousness about sending and keeping forces in Iraq and southern Afghanistan merely underlines the crisis of meaning among the technically powerful.

Further reading

Alex Bellamy and Paul Williams (eds), *Peace Operations and Global Order* (London: Cass, 2005). This collection of articles covers a range of conceptual and practical issues confronting peace operations in the international system. It contains various perspectives on the role of peace operations in global order by some of the foremost non-American scholars in the field.

Adekeye Adebajo and Chandra Lekha Sriram (eds), *Managing Armed Conflicts in the 21st Century* (London: Frank Cass, 2001). This collection of articles contains excellent analyses of the context in which peace missions operate.

Center on International Cooperation, *Annual Review of Global Peace Operations* (Boulder, CO: Lynne Rienner, annual starting 2006). This is an encyclopaedic annual review of UN and non-UN missions with plenty of maps, statistical tables, charts and diagrams and photos. In addition to analyses of case studies there are thematic chapters.

François Debrix, *(Re-)envisioning Peacekeeping: The United Nations and the Mobilization of Ideology* (Minneapolis: University of Minnesota Press, 1997). A challenging and critical analysis of how visual simulation is disseminated to represent effectiveness and order through peace operations. Debrix shows that liberal ideologies of governance are promoted through media strategies that had no relation to actual situations in the areas of operations in the 1990s.

Béatrice Pouligny, *Peace Operations Seen From Below* (London: Hurst, 2006). A remarkably original insight into the interactions between staff on UN operations and local interlocutors. Pouligny's research in six conflict areas investigates how local people interact with peace missions and how their daily lives are affected.

Sandra Whitworth, *Men, Militarism and UN Peacekeeping. A Gendered Analysis* (Boulder, CO: Lynne Rienner, 2004). The abuses committed by Canadian peacekeepers in Somalia provide a backdrop for this interrogation of 'peace militarism' from a gender perspective. The cultivation of particular kinds of masculinity in national contributions to peace operations is dissected to demonstrate the limitations of the worldviews present in such missions.

The Responsibility to Protect

Alex J. Bellamy

Abstract

In this chapter, students will learn about the 'responsibility to protect' principle, which seeks to rethink the relationship between security, sovereignty and human rights. It looks at the origins of the principle and the politics behind its adoption by the UN in 2005, focusing on its three main components: the prevention of humanitarian catastrophes, the world's reaction to those events and the level of commitment to rebuilding political communities afterwards. Key questions include whether sovereignty should entail the protection of a state's citizens and whether states can be persuaded to take responsibility for protecting human rights overseas.

Introduction

For both realists and liberals alike, security has traditionally been understood as the purview of states, and two of the principal guarantors of state security are the principles of sovereignty and non-interference. According to this perspective, security is best achieved by establishing a basic degree of international order based on each state's recognition of every other state's right to rule a particular territory and engage in external relations. This is often labelled 'Westphalian sovereignty', referring to the 1648 Peace of Westphalia which is commonly reckoned to have instituted a world order based on the right of sovereigns to govern their own people in whatever way they saw fit (Beaulac 2004, Gross 1948). This idea sits at the heart of contemporary international society's rules governing relations between states. Article 2(7) of the UN Charter prohibits states from interfering in the domestic affairs of other states, while Article 2(4) prohibits the threat or use of force except in self-defence or with the approval of the UN Security Council.

The value of this Westphalian system of security rests on the assumption that sovereign states are the best guardians of human security. The challenge for security studies is to explore how best to respond when sovereign states are unable to protect their citizens from genocide, mass killing or ethnic cleansing or engage in these practices themselves. This is no idle puzzle, nor is it a peripheral problem for the Westphalian system of security. According to one study, in the twentieth century alone some 262 million people were killed by their own government. This figure is six times greater than the number of people killed in battle by foreign governments during the same period (Rummel 1994). Most recently, the Sudanese government and its *Janjawiid* militia have been responsible for the killing of at least 250,000 and forced displacement of over two million Darfuri civilians. This is just the latest in a string of recent cases of killing conducted, sponsored or acquiesced in by the host government. Other recent cases include mass killing in East Timor and the Balkans and the 1994 Rwandan genocide in which approximately 1 million people were slaughtered in 100 days. Should states lose their sovereign rights in such circumstances and be subject to legitimate humanitarian intervention? Do other states have a duty to do whatever is necessary to protect imperilled people in distant lands?

At the UN's Millennium Summit in 2000, Canada's Prime Minister Jean Chretien announced the creation of an International Commission on Intervention and State Sovereignty (ICISS) charged with the task of finding a global consensus on humanitarian intervention. In 2001, the Commission – chaired by Gareth Evans and Mohamed Sahnoun – delivered a landmark report entitled *The Responsibility to Protect*. The Commission argued that states have the primary responsibility to protect (hereafter, R2P) their citizens. When they are unable or unwilling to do so, or when they deliberately terrorize their citizens, 'the principle of non-intervention yields to the international responsibility to protect' (ICISS 2001: xi). This involved not only the responsibility to react to humanitarian crises but also the responsibility to prevent such crises and transform failed and tyrannical states afterwards.

At the 2005 World Summit, the UN General Assembly committed itself to the R2P, pledging that all states have a responsibility to protect their citizens from genocide, mass killing and ethnic cleansing and that this responsibility transfers to the society of states as a whole in cases where the host government manifestly fails to discharge its duty. For the first time, governments collectively agreed that in some circumstances the security of individuals and groups should be prioritized over the security of states, rejecting the logic of Westphalian sovereignty described earlier.

The purpose of this chapter is to understand the thinking behind the R2P, the politics behind its adoption at the 2005 World Summit, and what it means for the security of the world's most imperilled people. To that end it is divided into four parts. The first provides an overview of the transformation of thinking about sovereignty. The second section outlines the main findings of the ICISS. The third section focuses on the political debates surrounding R2P's adoption at the World Summit. The fourth section looks at the ways in which R2P has been put into practice and how it might be strengthened.

Sovereignty and responsibility: from the American Revolution to the ICISS report

The idea that sovereignty entitles governments to treat their citizens however they see fit is based on a common misunderstanding of the meaning of 'absolute sovereignty', a doctrine that prevailed in Europe until the nineteenth century.[1] 'Absolute sovereignty' is commonly understood as providing a government with *carte blanche* within its internationally recognized borders. However, in the sixteenth century, when the doctrine of absolutism was first espoused, sovereigns and lawyers distinguished between two different meanings of 'absolute sovereignty'. Yes, sovereigns had exclusive jurisdiction in their territory but they were not entitled to rule arbitrarily because sovereignty entailed responsibilities to God. While citizens enjoyed no right of rebellion, it was commonly accepted that the manner of a sovereign's rule would be judged by God (Onuf 1991).

At the beginning of the industrial age in the late eighteenth century, liberals and republicans guided by beliefs in rationalism and science refused to accept that sovereigns were only answerable to God. Beginning with the American Revolution in the early eighteenth century and culminating in the principle of self-determination set out by the Versailles treaty at the end of the First World War, they insisted that sovereignty derived from the people within a state (Bukovanksy 2002). According to this doctrine, states draw their right to rule from the consent of the governed and this consent may be withdrawn if the sovereign abuses its citizens or fails to guarantee their basic rights.

Following this, the horrors of the Second World War produced a somewhat contradictory response from international society because of three key factors pulling in different directions. First, the war created a strong impetus for the outlawing of war as an instrument of state policy enshrined in Article 2(4) of the UN Charter. Second, the belief that peoples had a right to govern themselves gave impetus to decolonization under Article 1(2) but posed the problem of how to protect newly independent states from interference by the world's great powers. In addition to the ban on force, the key protection afforded to new states was the principle of non-interference set out in Article 2(7). Finally, the Holocaust and other horrors persuaded international society to place aspirations for basic human rights at the heart of the new order (as set out in Articles 1(3), 55 and 56). The tension this created is evident in the preamble of the UN Charter. On the one hand, it promises to 'reaffirm faith in fundamental human rights, in the dignity and worth of the human person'. On the other hand, states pledged to 'practice tolerance and live together in peace with one another as good neighbours'. Thus the Charter reflected a pivotal political dilemma: How should states behave in cases where maintaining faith in human rights means refusing to be a good neighbour to a tyrannical regime? For this reason, the question of humanitarian intervention was often portrayed as a debate over the priority that should be accorded to either sovereignty or human rights.

There is no space here to rehearse the debates about humanitarian intervention (see Bellamy and Wheeler 2007). Suffice it to say that during the Cold War, no right of humanitarian intervention was permitted because states were primarily concerned about maintaining as much international order as possible through adherence to the rule of non-interference. There were also deep and well-founded concerns among post-colonial states that the great powers would abuse any such right of humanitarian intervention to justify neo-imperialist activities. After the Cold War, the horrors of northern Iraq, Somalia, Bosnia and Rwanda brought a subtle but important change whereby states agreed that the UN Security Council was entitled to use its Chapter VII enforcement powers to authorize humanitarian intervention. However, a strong commitment to non-interference remained and at no time did the Security Council authorize interventions against fully functioning sovereign states which abused their citizens.

Two events in the 1990s prompted academics, politicians and international organizations to revisit the meaning of sovereignty. In 1994, the world stood aside as the Rwandan armed forces and Hutu militia massacred approximately 1 million Tutsi and Hutu civilians. The Rwandan genocide raised questions about how international society should make good its promise to affirm human rights by preventing genocide and mass killing and how individual states might be persuaded to commit troops and money to protect imperilled foreigners in such cases. Importantly, although there was no humanitarian intervention, no governments argued that Rwanda's sovereignty should be privileged over concern for its citizens. In 1999, NATO bombed the Federal Republic of Yugoslavia to coerce its leader, Slobodan Milosevic, into ceasing the ethnic cleansing of Kosovar Albanians. NATO was forced to act without a UN mandate because Russia and China believed that the situation in Kosovo was not serious enough to warrant armed intervention. This case also raised two important questions: Is it legitimate for states or groups of states to intervene without UN approval and, to put it crudely, how are we to make judgements about whether there has been enough killing to warrant intervention?

It was questions like these that prompted a rethink about the nature of sovereignty. An important contribution to this line of thinking was made by Francis Deng, a former Sudanese diplomat who was appointed the UN Secretary-General's special representative on internally displaced people in 1992. In a book published in 1996, Deng and his co-authors argued that:

> sovereignty carries with it certain responsibilities for which governments must
> be held accountable. And they are accountable not only to their own national
> constituencies but ultimately to the international community. In other words,
> by effectively discharging its responsibilities for good governance, a state can
> legitimately claim protection for its national sovereignty.
>
> (Deng *et al*. 1996: 1)

According to Deng, legitimate sovereignty required a demonstration of responsibility. Troubled states faced a choice: they could work with international society to improve their citizens' living conditions or they could obstruct international efforts and forfeit their sovereignty (Deng *et al*. 1996: 28). Seeing sovereignty as responsibility removed the validity of objections to international assistance and mediation based on the principle of non-interference. But at what point could a state be judged to have forfeited its sovereignty and what body has the right to decide? Deng *et al*. were sketchy on these points but they did suggest that sovereignty as responsibility implied the existence of a 'higher authority capable of holding supposed sovereigns accountable' and that this dominant authority should place collective interests ahead of the national interests of its members (Deng *et al*. 1996: 32). Clearly, the UN Security Council most closely resembles this description, though it falls a long way short of Deng's ideal.

The divisiveness of NATO's operation in Kosovo prompted UN Secretary-General, Kofi Annan, to enter the debate in 1999. In his annual address to the General Assembly, he insisted that 'state sovereignty, in its most basic sense, is being redefined by the forces of globalization and international cooperation'. He continued,

> the state is now widely understood to be the servant of its people, and not vice
> versa. At the same time, individual sovereignty – and by this I mean the human
> rights and fundamental freedoms of each and every individual as enshrined in
> our Charter – has been enhanced by a renewed consciousness of the right of
> every individual to control his or her own destiny.
>
> (Annan 1999b)

Concluding, Annan pointed to three concerns that he considered essential to moving the debate forward, all of which were taken up by the ICISS. First, intervention should be understood broadly to cover the wide range of measures short of armed force that could be used to prevent and halt humanitarian emergencies. 'It is a tragic irony,' he argued, that 'many of the crises that continue to go unnoticed and unchallenged today could be dealt with by far less perilous acts of intervention.' Moreover, the need for intervention should be seen as evidence of a failure of prevention. Second, it should be recognized that sovereignty alone was not the principal barrier to effective action to uphold human rights. Just as significant, Annan argued, was the way in which member states defined their national interests. Third, international society needs to make a long-term commitment even after the violence has stopped. It is well known that the countries most likely to descend into war are those that recently endured violence. In order to demonstrate their humanitarian credentials, potential interveners should be prepared for the long-haul process of rebuilding war-shattered states.

Together, Deng and Annan pointed towards a new way of conceiving the relationship between sovereignty and human rights which recalled the long-forgotten idea that sovereignty entailed responsibilities as well as rights. It was at this point in the debate that the Canadian government commissioned the ICISS to produce a systematic study of the relationship between sovereignty and human rights.

R2P

As noted above, the ICISS report is premised on the notion that when states are unwilling or unable to protect their citizens from grave harm, the principle of non-interference 'yields to the responsibility to protect'. The concept of R2P was intended as a way of escaping the logic of 'sovereignty versus human rights' by focusing not on what interveners are entitled to do ('a right of intervention') but on what is necessary to protect people in dire need and the responsibilities of various actors to provide such protection. Taking a lead from Annan and Deng, the ICISS argued that R2P was about much more than just military intervention. In addition to a 'responsibility to react' (inter-vene) to massive human suffering, international society also had responsibilities to use non-violent tools to prevent such suffering and rebuild polities and societies afterwards. Rather than viewing sovereignty and human rights as antagonistic, R2P sees them as mutually supporting, insists that international society has a responsibility to ensure and enable this relationship to flourish, and sets out a number of ways in which this might be achieved. The following discussion is organized around the three sets of responsibilities identified by the ICISS.

Responsibility to prevent

The prevention of deadly conflict is one of the fundamental goals of the UN. Indeed, the whole endeavour of UN peacekeeping grew out of the Secretary-General's belief that the primary contribution that the world organization could make to international peace and security was in the prevention and resolution of armed conflict. The ICISS likewise concluded that prevention was the most important aspect of R2P. The need for the world to do better in relation to prevention was a constantly recurring theme of the Commission's global consultations (ICISS 2001: 19). Reflecting long-standing views about the different types of prevention, the Commission divided its recommendations into the areas of early warning, tackling root causes, and direct prevention.

In relation to early warning, the ICISS noted that failings associated with early warning are often overstated. The nub of the problem, the Commissioners argued, tends to lie not in the failure to predict the outbreak of mass killing but in the failure to generate the political will to effectively respond to those predictions. The carnage of Bosnia, genocide in Rwanda and reign of terror in Darfur were all predicted before the event – the latter two cases by senior UN officials. In all three cases, however, states valued the protection of their own troops and financial interests more highly than the protection of endangered civilians. In two of the three cases (Bosnia and Darfur), many states argued that sovereignty mitigated against collective international action without the consent of the governments that were primarily responsible for the problem in the first place (Yugoslavia and Sudan). However, the Commission found that more accurate analysis of warning signs might identify earlier opportunities for constructive third-party engagement and recommended that UN headquarters develop the capability to collate this information, including sensitive intelligence, from member states (ICISS 2001: 21–22).

Given the sheer diversity of the potential root causes of mass killing, it is not surprising that the Commission's recommendations in this area were somewhat opaque. In keeping with the overall tenor of its findings, the ICISS called for the UN Security Council to play a leading role and identified four key dimensions of root cause prevention:

- Political (relating to good governance, human rights, confidence-building).

- Economic (relating to poverty, inequality and economic opportunity).

- Legal (relating to the rule of law and accountability).

- Military (relating to disarmament, reintegration and sectoral reform).

These four dimensions also shaped the Commission's recommendations in relation to direct prevention. In this regard, the political dimension referred to the Secretary-General's preventive diplomacy; the economic dimension to the use of positive and negative inducements; the legal dimension to a range of measures from mediation to legal sanctions; the military dimension – considered the most limited in scope – to preventive deployments. To actualize this agenda, the ICISS called for the creation of a pool of unrestricted development funding that might be used for root cause and direct prevention and the centralization of efforts at UN headquarters, making it a 'repository of best practice tools and strategies' (ICISS 2001: 26).

Despite stressing the critical importance of conflict prevention, the Commission stopped short of making extensive proposals other than the call to centralize the world's conflict prevention efforts and to develop capacity in relation to early warning. It also stopped short of offering guidelines for prevention equivalent to its guidelines for intervention set out below, probably because this is a wide and complex question that requires much further study. What is more, the Commission avoided explicit discussion of the single most pressing dilemma in relation to the 'responsibility to prevent': how to translate early warning signs into a commitment to act on the part of specific actors and consensus about how to act.

Responsibility to react

On the specific question of humanitarian intervention – what the ICISS labelled the 'responsibility to react' – two crucial aspirations informed the Commission's approach. First, it wanted to avoid future situations like Kosovo, where the UN Security Council was paralysed by division. Second, it wanted to avoid future disasters like Rwanda, where the world stood aside as genocide unfolded. I will briefly discuss the remedies proposed by the ICISS for both sets of problems.

There are two competing accounts of the causes of deadlock in the Kosovo case. According to one perspective, put forth in the Security Council by the ambassadors of Slovenia and the Netherlands, deadlock was caused by unreasonable threats of Security Council vetoes by Russia and China. The competing view holds that Russia and China had genuine concerns about the use of force, based on their view that the level of killing and ethnic cleansing was not bad enough to warrant intervention. To help prevent future Kosovos, therefore, ICISS needed to make it more difficult for Security Council members to use the veto capriciously, particularly in the face of humanitarian emergencies, while also making it harder for states to abuse humanitarian justifications. The principal device for achieving this goal was a set of criteria that governments and other observers could use to evaluate whether humanitarian intervention would be legitimate in particular cases. These criteria are set out in Box 28.1.

ICISS argued that if states committed to these principles, it would make it easier to build consensus on how to respond to humanitarian emergencies. On the one hand, it would be harder for states like China and Russia to oppose genuine humanitarian intervention because they would have committed themselves to a responsibility to protect in cases of large-scale loss of life and ethnic cleansing (just cause thresholds). On the other hand, it would be harder for states to abuse humanitarian justifications because it would be very difficult to satisfy all the criteria in non-genuine cases.

Preventing future Rwandas can be boiled down to overcoming a single obstacle: how to persuade states, particularly powerful states, to risk troops to save strangers in distant lands where few strategic interests are at stake. Overcoming this obstacle requires that two fundamental problems be addressed: first, identifying precisely which actors should assume the responsibility to protect; and second, persuading those actors to accept their responsibility to act in certain circumstances.

BOX 28.1 THE RESPONSIBILITY TO PROTECT: PRINCIPLES FOR MILITARY INTERVENTION

1 The Just Cause Threshold

Military intervention for human protection purposes is an exceptional and extraordinary measure. To be warranted, there must be serious and irreparable harm occurring to human beings, or imminently likely to occur, of the following kind:

A **large-scale loss of life,** actual or apprehended, with genocidal intent or not, which is the product either of deliberate state action, or state neglect or inability to act, or a failed state situation; or

B **large-scale 'ethnic cleansing',** actual or apprehended, whether carried out by killing, forced expulsion, acts of terror or rape.

2 The Precautionary Principles

A **Right intention:** The primary purpose of the intervention, whatever other motives intervening states may have, must be to halt or avert human suffering. Right intention is better assured with multilateral operations, clearly supported by regional opinion and the victims concerned.

B **Last resort:** Military intervention can only be justified when every non-military option for the prevention or peaceful resolution of the crisis has been explored, with reasonable grounds for believing that lesser measures would not have succeeded.

C **Proportional means:** The scale, duration and intensity of the planned military intervention should be the minimum necessary to secure the defined human protection objective.

D **Reasonable prospects:** There must be a reasonable chance of success in halting or averting the suffering which has justified the intervention, with the consequences of action not likely to be worse than the consequences of inaction.

3 Right Authority

A There is no better or more appropriate body than the United Nations Security Council to authorize military intervention for human protection purposes. The task is not to find alternatives to the Security Council as a source of authority, but to make the Security Council work better than it has.

B Security Council authorization should in all cases be sought prior to any military intervention action being carried out. Those calling for an intervention should formally request such authorization, or have the Council raise the matter on its own initiative, or have the Secretary-General raise it under Article 99 of the UN Charter.

C The Security Council should deal promptly with any request for authority to intervene where there are allegations of large-scale loss of human life or ethnic cleansing. It should in this context seek adequate verification of facts or conditions on the ground that might support a military intervention.

D The Permanent Five members of the Security Council should agree not to apply their veto power, in matters where their vital state interests are not involved, to obstruct the passage of resolutions authorizing military intervention for human protection purposes for which there is otherwise majority support.

E If the Security Council rejects a proposal or fails to deal with it in a reasonable time, alternative options are:

I consideration of the matter by the General Assembly in Emergency Special Session under the 'Uniting for Peace' procedure; and

II action within area of jurisdiction by regional or subregional organizations under Chapter VIII of the Charter, subject to their seeking subsequent authorization from the Security Council.

F The Security Council should take into account in all its deliberations that, if it fails to discharge its responsibility to protect in conscience-shocking situations crying out for action, concerned states may not rule out other means to meet the gravity and urgency of that situation – and that the stature and credibility of the United Nations may suffer thereby.

4 Operational Principles

A Clear objectives; clear and unambiguous mandate at all times; and resources to match.

B Common military approach among involved partners; unity of command; clear and unequivocal communications and chain of command.

C Acceptance of limitations, incrementalism and gradualism in the application of force, the objective being protection of a population, not defeat of a state.

D Rules of engagement which fit the operational concept; are precise; reflect the principle of proportionality; and involve total adherence to international humanitarian law.

E Acceptance that force protection cannot become the principal objective.

F Maximum possible coordination with humanitarian organizations.

Source: ICISS (2001).

If the responsibility to protect is spread too widely, for example, by saying that the 'international community' has responsibility, the concept is likely to become meaningless because no actors or groups are given specific duties. Powerful states are also wary of responsibility being spread too narrowly, placing an unrealistic burden of expectations on a small number of actors. Apportioning responsibility too narrowly would also raise difficult questions about who has the right to authorize humanitarian intervention. To get around this problem, the ICISS linked the question of where responsibility lay to an intervention's authorization (see 'right authority'). Thus after the host state, the UN Security Council has the primary responsibility to act and if it fails to do so, the ICISS argued that it would lose credibility and legitimacy. In such cases states could approach the UN General Assembly and, failing that, relevant regional organizations. This suggests a hierarchy of responsibility, starting with the host state, then the Security Council, the General Assembly, regional organizations, coalitions of the willing and finally individual states.

How, though, are governments to be persuaded to abandon the narrow self-interest that caused the world to stand aside in Rwanda and, more recently, Darfur? The ICISS answer to this lay in the commitment to the just cause thresholds, which would create expectations among domestic publics about when their governments ought to act to save imperilled people. Thus, in cases of mass killing and ethnic cleansing, governments would be put under pressure to act because they had already committed in principle to doing so.

Responsibility to rebuild

The label 'responsibility to rebuild' is something of a misnomer because the aim after an episode of genocide, mass killing or ethnic cleansing is not to 'rebuild' a society by returning it to its pre-war state but to transform it into something new. After all, the pre-war society contained within it the seeds of mass killing and destruction. The ICISS argued that potential interveners should have a strategic plan about how they intend to transform societies. In so doing, interveners were required to consider three sets of issues: security, justice and reconciliation, and development (ICISS 2001: 40). In relation to security, the ICISS argued that interveners acquired a moral duty to protect those in their care and should also work towards disarming and demobilizing former combatants and establishing effective and legitimate national armed forces. To engender justice and reconciliation, peace-builders should establish a local judicial system, foster local opportunities for reconciliation and guarantee the legal rights of returnees – people forced to flee their homes. Finally, military interveners are required to use all possible means to foster economic growth (ICISS 2001: 42).

The transformation of war-torn societies has long been a hotly contested topic. On the one hand, neo-liberals argue that economic liberalization and rapid democratization are central. Their critics insist that it is most important to establish effective infrastructure and institutions first (see Paris 2004). The ICISS did not further this debate, choosing to limit itself to arguing that interveners acquired responsibilities for the post-war society. At face value this is relatively uncontroversial but it leaves many questions. First, there are questions about how best to pursue this exercise, highlighted by the problems of post-war Iraq. Second, there are unresolved questions about moral responsibility. Does a failure to rebuild delegitimize an intervention that halted genocide? What if a weak and poor state had intervened to stop the Rwandan genocide but was unable to fulfil its responsibility to rebuild? Finally, there are political questions. Who decides what sort of society ought to be built? How long does the responsibility endure?

From ICISS to the World Summit

The 2005 World Summit adopted a declaration committing the UN to the R2P. The declaration comprised four main elements: (1) states recognized their responsibility to protect their own citizens from genocide, war crimes, crimes against humanity and ethnic cleansing; (2) they pledged to help states fulfill their primary responsibility; (3) the international community will take a host of non-coercive measures to prevent genocide and mass atrocities; (4) in extreme situations, where a government is manifestly failing to protect its citizens, the UN Security Council stands ready to intervene using the full range of its powers. It also contained a number of other provisions relating to the prevention of humanitarian catastrophes and peacebuilding. Some lauded these measures as a major breakthrough because they confirmed the reconfiguration of the relationship between sovereignty and human rights. Others argued that the ICISS report's findings had been watered down to such an extent that it would not, in practice, afford greater protection to imperilled peoples. Of the three elements of the R2P, the 'responsibility to rebuild' was relatively uncontroversial as it involved the reconstruction of sovereign states. However, the responsibilities to prevent and react provoked fierce international debate.

The ICISS report was received most favourably by 'like-minded' states including Canada, the UK and Germany which had, since the Kosovo intervention, been exploring the potential for developing criteria to guide global decision-making about humanitarian intervention. The USA rejected the idea of criteria on the grounds that it could not offer pre-commitments to engage its military forces where it had no national interests, and that it would not bind itself to criteria that would constrain its right to decide when and where to use force (Welsh 2004: 180). China insisted that all questions relating to the use of force should defer to the Security Council, making criteria irrelevant. Russia agreed, arguing that the UN was already equipped to deal with humanitarian crises and suggesting that, by countenancing unauthorized intervention, the *Responsibility to Protect* risked undermining the UN Charter. Opinion outside the Security Council was also sceptical. The Non-Aligned Movement (NAM) rejected R2P, though the 'Group of 77' (G77) developing states was more equivocal. Offering no joint position on the concept, the G77 nevertheless suggested that R2P be revised to emphasize the principles of territorial integrity and sovereignty (Bellamy 2006: 151–153).

The 'responsibility to prevent' met with a similarly lukewarm response. Once again, like-minded liberal democracies argued in favour. The USA and some members of the UN Secretariat advocated a narrower version, focusing specifically on the prevention of genocide. Inspired by the ICISS recommendations, in 2004 the UN created a Special Adviser on the Prevention of Genocide charged with alerting others to potential future cases and managing coordinated responses to prevent genocide. This narrower understanding of the responsibility to prevent was endorsed by both the NAM and African Union, both of which continued to defend a traditional understanding of the relationship between sovereignty and human rights by arguing that the scope of prevention should be limited because preventive action infringed on state sovereignty and should be reserved only for the worst cases (AU 2005, NAM 2005). Other states rejected the idea entirely: Pakistan insisted that the responsibility to prevent could only be enacted after a 'right to develop' had been enshrined, while China argued that the best path to conflict prevention lay in rigid adherence to the rules of sovereignty and non-interference (Reform the UN 2005: 5, PR China 2005: 10–12).

As a result of these doubts, significant changes had to be made to persuade the UN's member states to adopt the R2P. In particular, references to making conflict prevention the centrepiece of the UN system were dropped, the criteria guiding decisions about the use of force were removed, R2P intervention was made dependent on UN Security Council authorization, the thresholds at which crises would become matters of international concern were raised to cover only governments 'manifestly' failing to protect their citizens, and caveats were added to give the Security Council the flexibility to choose not to act. On the positive side, the Summit agreed to institute a 'culture of prevention' (something initially called for by Annan in 2001) and support the Special Adviser on Genocide. Most significantly, it created a Peacebuilding Commission designed to spearhead efforts to transform war-torn communities. Specifically, the Commission was given three roles: to provide a forum for the coordination of international agencies involved in peacebuilding; to provide financial and political support for troubled countries; and to advise the central organs of the UN on peacebuilding matters (Almqvist 2005: 2).

The Summit declaration was momentous in that this was the first time the society of states had formally declared that sovereignty was related to human rights. The R2P declaration and Peacebuilding Commission are practical manifestations of the overall ambition of R2P to change the relationship between sovereignty, human rights and international society, where the role of the latter is understood as being to enable sovereigns to fulfil their human rights responsibilities. Indeed, in April 2006, the Security Council adopted resolution 1674 committing itself to protecting civilians and punishing those responsible for acts of violence against them. However, the 2005 declaration was also more limited in scope than the ICISS report. This raises the question of how the principle might be strengthened and put into practice, the topic for the final section of this chapter.

Turning ideas into actions?

How is R2P being put into practice? The two most noticeable ways are in the fields of conflict prevention and the protection of civilians by peace operations. Other than reshaping the language used in policy debates about whether or not to intervene in humanitarian crises, R2P has exerted little influence on the way states actually behave, as the world's decision not to intervene in Darfur demonstrates only too well. Partly thanks to the R2P, there is today greater recognition of the fact that genocide and mass killing tend to take place in wartime and that therefore the best way to prevent them is to prevent the outbreak and escalation of violent conflict. In addition to the creation of the Special Adviser on Genocide, the R2P has given impetus to a range of conflict prevention initiatives undertaken by the UN, individual states, groups of states and NGOs. In relation to early warning, the World Bank and ReliefWeb have developed mechanisms that try to predict as precisely as possible where and when conflicts are likely to erupt or escalate. In addition, states have committed to establish processes for working towards cooperative agreements on the management of natural resources, commonly touted as one of the major sources of future conflict. They have also agreed to revisit the question of regulating the trade in small arms, and to provide the UN Secretariat with more resources to lead and coordinate multi-faceted conflict prevention efforts. In addition, the rapid proliferation of peace operations in recent years suggests a growing acknowledgement of the role peacekeepers can play in preventing and managing violent conflict (see Chapter 27, this volume).

The second key way in which the R2P has impacted on practice relates to the protection of civilians. In particular, it has helped to strengthen the idea that peacekeepers must be prepared to use force to protect endangered people irrespective of what their mandate says. This idea was first touted by the so-called Brahimi Report on peace operations (2000) and has been embraced to some extent by the Security Council, which has included civilian protection roles in a majority of its peacekeeping mandates handed down since 2000. This in turn has raised three problems. First, even those states most committed to R2P and civilian protection have yet to develop clear guidelines on how best to protect civilians. In order to remedy this problem a number of scholars and organizations have begun to think seriously about this and to make proposals about the best way to protect civilians (Holt and Berkman 2006). Second, the Security Council has been reluctant to fully embrace civilian protection. Where it has mandated protection, as in the UN missions in Sudan, Liberia and Democratic Republic of Congo, the Security Council has added caveats such as limiting the geographical scope of protection or instructing peacekeepers only to protect civilians when they have the capability to do so rather than ensuring that they do have the necessary capabilities (Williams and Bellamy 2007: 9). Finally, many developing states are deeply sceptical about the use of force for civilian protection, seeing it as a creeping infringement on sovereignty. Speaking for the NAM, Morocco argued that UN peacekeepers should only use force in self-defence (Williams and Bellamy 2007: 9).

Ultimately, however, it is governments that will determine whether or not the R2P translates into real protection for the world's endangered peoples. After all, political interests not sovereignty determine whether or not states will prevent and halt human disasters and transform war-torn societies. One problem is that democratic governments tend to be risk-averse, not least because voters tend not to elect or reject governments on the basis of whether or not they save imperilled foreigners. Voters do, however, sometimes change the way they vote if governments deploy troops overseas and sustain casualties. In order to persuade democratic governments to assume their R2P, it is first necessary to change the way they calculate their interests. This could be done by a range of measures such as making governments more accountable by offering alternative policy plans, educating the public about the nature of overseas crises and the potential for positive intervention, and building coalitions of governments other than those usually turned to in dire emergencies. Measures such as these may help tip the balance of national interests in R2P's favour.

Conclusion

The R2P is an attempt to reconfigure the relationship between sovereignty, human rights and international society. Traditionally it was assumed that the demands of international order required strict adherence to the principles of sovereignty and non-interference and that in cases where the security of states and individuals collided, the former should be privileged. After the Cold War, many governments and scholars argued that in grave circumstances sovereignty should be suspended and intervention permitted. This produced a complex debate about who had a right to authorize such interventions and in what circumstances. This debate pitted sovereignty against human rights. In doing so, however, it played down both the original meaning of sovereignty and two centuries of republican thinking. From the republican perspective, sovereignty resides with the people and governments may only claim sovereign rights if they fulfil certain basic responsibilities to their people. It is this approach to sovereignty and human rights that underpins the R2P. If sovereignty is understood as interdependent with human rights, then the role of international society becomes one of enabling and supporting sovereigns in the discharge of their responsibilities to their citizens. R2P suggests that this is not just a matter of charity but also a matter of responsibility, because the very foundations of sovereignty and international society are individual human rights. As a result, international society has a responsibility to ensure that sovereigns fulfil their duties to their citizens by preventing and reacting to cases of genocide, mass killing and ethnic cleansing and helping to transform societies afterwards. This responsibility was acknowledged at the 2005 World Summit, but there remains much work to be done by states, international organizations and NGOs to ensure that all this makes a difference to those in need.

Note

1   I am grateful to Luke Glanville for these insights.

Further reading

Alex J. Bellamy, *The Responsibility to Protect: The Global Effort to End Mass Atrocities* (Cambridge: Polity, 2009). A detailed account of the emergence of R2P and its operationalization.

Victoria Holt and Tobias Berkman, *The Impossible Mandate? Military Preparedness, the Responsibility to Protect and Modern Peace Operations* (Washington, DC: The Stimson Center, 2006). An excellent account of the potential and problems associated with putting the R2P into practice.

International Commission on Intervention and State Sovereignty, *The Responsibility to Protect* (Ottawa: ICISS, 2001). The ICISS report setting out the R2P in detail.

Ramesh Thakur, *The United Nations, Peace and Security: From Collective Security to the Responsibility to Protect* (Cambridge: Cambridge University Press, 2006). An overview of the UN's approach to peace and security that puts the R2P into broader context.

Thomas G. Weiss, *Humanitarian Intervention: Ideas in Action* (Cambridge: Polity Press, 2007). An insightful account of the origins and rise of R2P.

Nicholas J. Wheeler, *Saving Strangers: Humanitarian Intervention in International Society* (Oxford: Oxford University Press, 2000). Still the best book on the norm of humanitarian intervention prior to 2000.

Private Security

Deborah D. Avant

▌ Abstract

In this chapter, students learn about the growing trend towards private security – security allocated through the market. The chapter explains why this development is important for the control of force and outlines a debate over its costs and benefits. It also describes the current market, compares it to other markets for violence in the past, and explores its origins. The chapter encourages students to think about how the market for force poses trade-offs to the state and non-state actors that seek to control it and how a market for force challenges central assumptions in security studies.

▌ Introduction

It has long been common sense in security studies that the control, sanctioning and use of violence fall to states. Private security activity in the past two decades, though, lays waste to this conventional wisdom. When the USA won a resounding victory against the Iraqi army in 2003, more than one out of every ten people it deployed to the theatre during the conflict were employed by private security companies (PSCs) performing the work (logistics, operational support of weapons systems and training) that used to be done by military personnel.[1] As lawlessness followed the fall of the Iraqi government and coalition forces were stretched thin, an 'army' of private security personnel flooded into the country. Some were hired by the Coalition Provisional Authority (CPA) to train the Iraqi police force, the Iraqi army, and a private Iraqi force to guard government facilities and oilfields. Other PSCs worked for the US army translating and interrogating prisoners, or for Parsons providing security for employees rebuilding oilfields, or for ABC News or the Research Triangle Institute or any of a number of international non-governmental organizations (NGOs) working in the country. By spring 2004, it was esti-mated that in excess of 20,000 private security personnel, mostly retired military or police from countries as varied as Chile, Fiji, Israel, Nepal, South Africa, the United Kingdom and the USA, employed by some 60 different PSCs worked for the US government, the British government, the CPA, private firms and NGOs in that country. A 2006 US Department of Defense census of contractors in Iraq showed over 100,000 working alongside the 133,000 US troops (Merle 2006). The role of PSCs in the Iraqi occupation was thrust into the public eye when four private security personnel working for the US PSC, Blackwater, were killed and mutilated on 31 March 2004 and when contracted interrogators working for CACI and Titan were among those implicated in the abuses at Abu Ghraib prison.

The role of private security in Iraq is simply the latest chapter in the private security boom. While the state's monopoly on the use of force which Max Weber (1964) wrote about was exaggerated from the start and there has been a role for the private sector in security for some time, in the past two decades that role has grown and is larger and more different now than it has been since the foundation of the modern state. PSCs now provide more services and more kinds of services including some that have been considered core military capabilities in the modern era. In addition, changes in the nature of armed conflicts have led tasks less central to the core of modern militaries (such as operating complex weapons systems and policing) to be subcontracted to PSCs. Furthermore, states are not the only organizations that hire security providers. Increasingly transnational non-state actors (NGOs, multinational corporations and others) are financing security services to accomplish their goals. In sum, a burgeoning transnational market for force now exists alongside the system of states and state forces.

This chapter analyses these issues in five sections. The first explains why this development is important for the control of force and outlines the debate over the market's costs and benefits. The second section describes the current market for force and provides some examples of how it works. The third section compares today's market for force to other markets for violence in the past. The fourth section explains the origins of the current market. Finally, the chapter concludes with some thoughts about how the market for force poses trade-offs to the control of force and changes the role of both states and non-state actors in security studies.

Private security and the control of force

Why should we worry – or even care – about this transnational market? The answer is simple: private security may affect how and whether people can control violence. The existence of this market also raises some important questions for students of security studies: Does the privatization of security undermine state control of violence? Can the privatization of security enhance state control of violence? Does the privatization of security chart new ways by which violence might be collectively controlled? How does private security affect the ability to contain the use of force within political processes and social norms?

Private security even raises questions about the language we use to talk about and analyse these developments. In keeping with the most common usage, I will use 'private' to refer to non-governmental actors. Commercial entities and NGOs thus fall into this category – however, so do vigilantes, paramilitaries and organized crime bosses. Although many use 'public' to denote government institutions of whatever sort, it is important to distinguish between governments that have the capacity and legitimacy to claim to work towards collective ends (strong states) and those that do not (weak states).

The implications of privatizing security for the control of force have been hotly debated. Pessimists claim that the turn to private security threatens to undermine state control and democratic processes (e.g. Silverston 1998, Musah and Fayemi 2000). In Africa, for example, Musah and Fayemi (2000: 23–26) argue that the consequences of privatizing security can be severe. Although contemporary mercenaries attempt to distinguish themselves from the lawless 'guns for hire' that ran riot over Africa during the Cold War, their consortium with arms manufacturers, mineral exploiters, and Africa's authoritarian governments and warlords is said to sustain the militarization of Africa. This poses 'a mortal danger to democracy in the region'. Unregulated private armies linked to international business interests threaten to undermine democracy and development in Africa.

Optimists, however, declare that private options offer solutions to intractable security problems that can operate within national interests and/or the values shared by the international community (e.g. Shearer 1998, Brooks 2000). David Shearer (1998) argues that in Africa and elsewhere PSCs willing to take on messy intervention tasks that Western militaries are eager to avoid can help end civil conflicts that would otherwise be intractable. He argues that rather than outlawing PSCs, the international community should engage them, give them a legitimate role and expect them to operate as professionals, according to the values held by the international social system. Doug Brooks (2003) proposes that a consortium of PSCs could bring years of peacekeeping experience and NATO-level professionalism to protect vulnerable populations in places like the Democratic Republic of the Congo (DRC) or Darfur, Sudan; they could also train local gendarmes in policing and human rights so as to build a more professional local force.

Who is right? Depending on the context in question, both could be 'right' because their arguments hinge on different conceptions of 'control' and often hold private security alternatives to different comparative standards. This means that we must be aware that privatization's effect on the capability of forces and the values they serve should vary depending on the issue and context in question. Privatization sometimes leads to greater capabilities, other times to lesser capabilities and sometimes leads to more, sometimes less integration of violence with prevailing international values. Inevitably, however, privatization should involve the redistribution of power over the control of violence, both within states and between state and non-state actors. In effect, the shift to private guardians changes who guards the guardians.

When considering the varied effects of privatization in different settings, a fundamental intervening variable is the capacities of states. Strong states that are coherent, capable and legitimate to begin with are best able to manage the risks of privatization and to harness the PSCs to produce new public goods but sometimes risk corruption of democratic processes. Weak states with ineffective and corrupt forces potentially have the most to gain (or the least to lose) from the capacities offered by the private sector, but also are the least able to manage private forces for the public good. For the regimes in such weak states efforts to harness the private sector for state building are often desperate gambles.

A transnational market for military and security services

Private security companies provide military and security services to states, international organizations, NGOs, global corporations and wealthy individuals. For instance, every multilateral peace operation conducted by the UN since the 1990s included the presence of PSCs, and companies such as Shell have regularly hired PSCs to guard personnel and installations.

The number of private security providers burgeoned during the 1990s with well over 200 such companies making the news between 1995 and 2004. Private firms trained militaries in more than 42 countries during the 1990s. Some claim that several hundred companies globally operate in over 100 countries on six continents (Singer 2003b: 2).

Not surprisingly, the market also grew substantially. One set of projections within the industry suggested in 1997 that revenues from the global international security market (military and policing services in international and domestic markets) would rise from US$55.6 billion in 1990 to US$202 billion in 2010 (see Vines 1999: 47). Estimates suggest that the 2003 global revenue for this industry was over US$100 billion (Singer 2003b: 2). Some PSCs were also valuable commodities in their own right with companies that publicly traded stocks growing at twice the rate of the Dow Jones Industrial Average in the 1990s. Between 1994 and 2002 US-based PSCs alone received more than 3,000 contracts worth over US$300 billion from the US Department of Defense (ICIJ 2002: 2).

BOX 29.1 CLASSIFYING A PRIVATE SECURITY COMPANY: THE EXAMPLE OF ARMORGROUP (FORMERLY DSL)

ArmorGroup began as DSL, a British firm founded in 1981. DSL was purchased by a publicly held American conglomerate called Armor Holdings in 1997. Most of its employees who operate out of its London office are former British Special Air Services (SAS), but the company also draws on retired US military personnel and local personnel in its offices all over the world. In 2000 Armor-Group had offices in the USA, the UK, South Africa, DRC/Zaire, Mozambique, Kenya, West Africa, North Africa, Zimbabwe, Uganda, Hong Kong, Nepal, Asia, the Philippines, France, Bosnia-Hercegovina, Russia, Kazakhstan, Ukraine, Columbia, Ecuador, Venezuela and Brazil, and regional managers in Europe and the CIS, Russia, Latin America, Southern Africa, Central Africa, North Africa, the Far East and the Middle East. In most of the regional offices, a small expatriate core with a largely British military background employs predominantly local personnel. ArmorGroup works according to local laws and with local personnel, but its behaviour in one area affects its reputation worldwide. The company's leadership claims to be keenly aware of the need to have professional standards for behaviour and to monitor them closely.

ArmorGroup works for a variety of customers including private businesses, INGOs and states. It provided security and logistics personnel to the UN mission in the former Yugoslavia from 1992 to 1995, protected BP oil property against attacks in Colombia, provided security for Bechtel in Iraq, and has also worked for such clients as De Beers, Shell, Mobile, Amoco, Chevron, CARE and GOAL.

DSL was privately held until 1997, but was publicly traded as part of Armor Holdings from 1997 to 2004. In January 2004, US-based ArmorGroup informed the Securities and Exchange Commission that it intended to sell off its London-based affiliate DSL (renamed ArmorGroup International) to a group of its own staff. With that sale complete, it was again a privately held company. Like all PSCs ArmorGroup fills contracts from its database, supplemented by advertisements. That is, it has a small contingent of full-time employees and a large database of individuals from which to fill specific contracts. These databases are not exclusive – persons may appear on the databases of several different firms. This means that someone could be working for ArmorGroup one week and Control Risk Group, Erinys, or one of a dozen others the next.

Sources: O'Brien (1998), ArmorGroup company literature, author's interviews.

What kinds of services do these firms provide? Despite the media hype, few contracts promise participation in ground combat. Instead, PSCs offer three broad categories of external security support: operational support, military advice and training, and logistical support. PSCs also offer internal security services ranging from site security (armed and unarmed), crime prevention and intelligence. Singer (2003a) has disaggregated these firms by the relationship of their primary services to 'the tip of the spear' in 'battlespace'. Services closest to the tip of the spear are those on the front lines of battle, typically the most deadly and dangerous. According to Singer, this leads to distinctions between type one firms that provide implementation and command, type two firms that provide advice and training, and type three firms that provide military support. While the distinction between service type makes sense, the same PSC may provide 'type one' services in one contract and 'type three' in another. Indeed, given the way service firms fill contracts from databases and advertising, it is easy for them to move from one service type to another. Thus it makes more sense to use contracts rather than firms as the unit of analysis. Figure 29.1 draws on Singer's battlespace analogy, substituting contracts for firms and extending the categorization to internal as well as external security services.

A small number of contracts have stipulated services at the very tip of the spear that most closely resemble 'core' military competencies – armed operational support on the battlefield. Sandline and Executive Outcomes (EO) (both now defunct) became famous for missions that included the deployment of armed personnel on the battlefield: Sandline in Sierra Leone and Papua New Guinea and EO in Angola and Sierra Leone. EO closed its doors for business after the South African government passed legislation ostensibly designed to

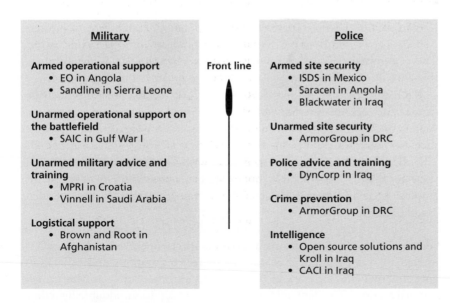

Figure 29.1 Contracts in battlespace

Source: Avant (2005: 17)

regulate the export of military services but believed by many to try to outlaw this kind of activity. Although EO employees now operate or work for a variety of firms – some new, some outside of South Africa – the firms are less public about their dealings.

Many more contracts do not raise troops or deploy personnel on the battlefield, but offer advice and training to military forces. The training programmes vary widely from the high end where PSCs are reorganizing the force structure and training officers in battlefield scenarios to more mundane troop training, simulations and peacekeeping training. Examples of such firms in the USA include MPRI, Booz Allen and Hamilton, Cubic and DynCorp. UK examples include ArmorGroup, Aims Limited, Gurka Security Guards, WatchGuard International and Sandline. Similar firms may also be found in Canada, France, Israel, Australia and Belgium.

There are also firms that offer operational support in the form of command and control, transport and weapons systems. Both Sandline and MPRI suggested that they could offer command and control support to UN peace missions. More common are contractors that provide support for or operate weapons and information systems on the battlefield. As the technological sophistication of weapons systems and platforms has grown, more and more contractors have been hired to work with troops to maintain and support these systems. During the 2003 war with Iraq, for instance, PSCs also provided operational support for the B-2 stealth bomber, the F-117 stealth fighter, Global Hawk UAV, U-2 reconnaissance aircraft, the M-1 tank, the Apache helicopter, and many navy ships.

Logistics support for militaries in the field is another significant market for the private sector that has many providers. A wide variety of PSCs offer transport, telecom, food, laundry, and other administrative services as well as setting up and taking down temporary bases and camps. Halliburton subsidiary, Kellogg, Brown and Root (a US company) has a huge presence in this market. They supported American troops in Somalia, Haiti, Bosnia, Afghanistan and the 2003 war with Iraq.

PSCs also offer internal security services, closer to what police routinely do, such as site security, international civilian police, police training, crime prevention and intelligence. They include decades-old private security companies such as Pinkertons and Wackenhut as well as new firms in South Africa, the UK, the USA and all over Europe. For instance, virtually all US contributions to international civilian police units in the 1990s were DynCorp employees. DynCorp was also responsible for protecting Afghan President Hamid Karzai.

Harder to categorize are the contracts that offer operational capacity in counter-insurgency, anti-terrorism and other special operations. These services, offered to states as well as to multinational corporations and other nongovernmental entities, work in the nebulous area that connects external and internal security. The demand for these kinds of services undoubtedly reflects the increasing concern with international criminal threats and the blurring of internal and external security (Andreas 2003).

The role of PSCs in Iraq has yielded insights into the blurring of lines between policing and combat and the general blending of roles that accompany operating in a combat zone. For example, Blackwater employees, under contract to the CPA to provide security to US administrator Paul Bremer and five outposts, carried weapons, had their own helicopters and fought off insurgents in ways that were hard to distinguish from combat (Priest 2004).

A helpful way to think about the contours of the market for force is set out in Table 29.1. This makes use of the distinction between the financing and delivery of security services. As the shaded boxes in Table 29.1 indicate, I will use the term *privatization* to refer to decisions to devolve *delivery* or *financing* of services to private entities – the two outermost rows and columns in Table 29.1. Although conventional wisdom suggests that traditional military forces are the norm, the last century has provided cases that fit in almost every box. The not-for-profit financing column is the most problematic, conceptually, as it encompasses a range of possibilities from NGOs to rebel, paramilitary and militia forces. It is also, however, one of the more important columns. During the post-Cold War era, private (for- and not-for-) profit financing and delivery have been significant areas of growth.

The current market compared

This is not the first market for force. Markets for allocating violence were common before the systems of states came to dominate world politics. Feudal lords supplemented their forces with contracted labour from the beginning of the twelfth century, and from the end of the thirteenth century through the Peace of Westphalia in 1648 virtually all force was allocated through the market. Furthermore, the rise of the state did not immediately preclude the market allocation of violence. Early modern states both delegated control over force to commercial entities and participated in the market as both suppliers and purchasers.

Chartered companies, prominent in the seventeenth and eighteenth centuries, such as the East India Company, were an instance of state-delegated commercial control over violence. Chartered companies were state-designated entities for engaging in long-distance trade and establishing colonies. The Dutch, English, French and Portuguese all chartered companies during this time. French companies were state enterprises forged by the king and designed to increase state power later in the game. Dutch companies were private wealth-seeking enterprises that were organized in a charter so as to enhance the Dutch profit relative to the English or (particularly) the Portuguese. The crown chartered the English companies for similar reasons. These forces were both an army and a police force for establishing order and then protecting both trade routes and new territory. Also during the early period of the state, states rented out their forces to other friendly states. These troops would arrive equipped and ready to fight under the command of the contracting government.

Table 29.1 The variety of arrangements for allocating violence

	Financing for security services				
	National financing	Foreign national financing	Multinational financing	Private financing (for profit)	Private financing (not for profit)
National delivery	USA in WWII	German troops in the American Revolution	The first Gulf War	Shell financing Nigerian Forces	WWF financing park guards in DRC
Foreign national delivery	German troops in the American Revolution	Korean troops fighting for the USA in Vietnam	The first Gulf War	Branch group contributing to Nigerian forces in Sierra Leone	
Multinational delivery	NATO in Kosovo	Muslim states' contribution to Western military aid in Bosnia	UN Peacekeeping		
Private delivery (for profit)	MPRI's provision of ROTC Trainers to the USA	MPRI's work for Croatia	MPRI's work for Bosnia	DSL working for Lonhro in Mozambique	DSL working for ICRC around the world
Private delivery (not for profit)			'Green Cross'	BP financing Columbian paramilitaries	Wildaid in Asia

Source: Avant (2005: 25)

Even in the modern system, some states have relied on the private sector, for weapons, particularly, but also for logistics support, and for a variety of services idiosyncratic to a particular conflict. The US government, for instance, has a long history of looking to the market for military services. Up until the beginning of the Second World War, most of these services were in the area of logistics support and weapons procurement. During the Cold War, however, the USA hired firms to perform military training missions as well. The British government hired from the market for military services less frequently in the modern period than the USA, but allowed its citizens to sell their services abroad. The commercial sale of security services by British citizens abroad can be traced back through the centuries (Thomson 1994: 22). More recently UK Special Air Services (SAS) personnel formed firms to sell military and security services during the Cold War. For instance, in 1967 Colonel Sir David Stirling founded WatchGuard International (O'Brien 2000). And, of course, individuals acting on their own sold a variety of services in Africa during the Cold War. In addition, states still do 'rent out' their forces – to UN peace-keeping units or to other states. In the first Gulf War, for instance, US forces were subsidized by Japan. In the 2003 war with Iraq, the USA paid forces from other countries to participate in the coalition.

While market allocation of security was never completely eliminated in the modern era, it was frowned upon. This led private security to be informally organized, secretive, and directed to a specific customer base. Soldiers of fortune operated in the shadows – as did the covert private military services provided to individual governments. In the current system, though, PSCs have a corporate structure and operate openly, posting job listings on their websites and writing papers and articles mulling over the costs and benefits of the private sector in security (see, for example, IPOA 2007). They have sought, and received, some degree of international acceptance.

The corporate form, relative openness, acceptance and transnational spread of today's security industry bear many similarities to the late Middle Ages and early modern period. There are some features of today's market, though, that are unique. First, unlike the military enterprises of the late Middle Ages today's PSCs do not so much provide the foot soldiers, but more often act as supporters, trainers and force multipliers for local forces. PSCs, then, are different from private armies – when they leave, they leave behind whatever expertise they have imparted – subject to whatever local political controls (or lack thereof) exist. Second, unlike the period of the chartered companies, states do not authorize private takeover of other territories, even though transnational corporations and INGOs finance security on their own – either by subsidizing weak states or hiring PSCs. Thus chartered companies provided a more specific administrative and legal framework for the private use of force than is the case with private financiers today.

Why the current market?

As would be the case in the development of any market, the increase in private security can be tied to supply and demand. In the 1990s, the supply factors came from both local (the end of apartheid in South Africa) and international (the end of the Cold War) phenomena that caused militaries to be downsized in the late 1980s and early 1990s. Military downsizing led to a flood of experienced personnel available for contracting. Concomitant with the increase in supply was an increase in the demand for military skills on the private market – from Western states that had downsized their militaries, from countries seeking to upgrade and Westernize their militaries as a way of demonstrating credentials for entry into Western institutions, from rulers of weak or failed states no longer propped up by superpower patrons, and from non-state actors such as private firms, INGOs and groups of citizens in the territories of weak or failed states.

The downsizing of these militaries took place in an ideological context where liberal capitalist ideas were in the ascendancy. Initially, prevailing ideas about the benefits of privatization were associated with the powerful conservative coalitions in the USA and the UK in the 1980s, but the collapse of the Soviet bloc, the ensuing privatization of state-owned industries across Europe, and the endorsement of these principles by international financial institutions such as the International Monetary Fund and the World Bank led privatization to be endorsed much more widely. The appeal of privatization ideas both led people to see private alternatives as obvious and affected the growth of private supply.

The end of the Cold War also had important political repercussions which influenced the market for force. Just two years into what US President George H.W. Bush called the 'New World Order', a rash of smaller scale conflicts unleashed disorder and demands for intervention. As the clamour for a Western response grew just as Western militaries were shrinking, nascent PSCs provided a stop-gap tool for meeting greater demands with smaller forces. For example, according to Robert Perito (2002), who served as Deputy Director of the International Criminal Investigative Training Assistance Program at the US Department of Justice during the 1990s, this was the logic for the initial use of DynCorp to mobilize a small group of international civilian police to send to Haiti. The USA had no such force and DynCorp could provide one.

The Cold War's end had a different impact in the former Eastern bloc (where it led to defunct governance structures and forces, new opportunities and a sudden opening to global flows) and in the developing world (where it abruptly ended superpower patronage – revealing the enduring difficulties of these governments and their militaries – corruption, poor standards, poor management, ethnic rivalries and so on). In each instance, the potential for violence increased. Weak governments paved the way for ethnic mobilization, transnational criminal activity, warlords, rebels and paramilitaries, and the result ravaged civilians, enslaved children, destroyed the environment, and otherwise disrupted order and violated global norms (see Fearon and Laitin 2003). In some cases PSCs provided tools for weak governments in the Eastern bloc and the developing world (e.g. Angola, Papua New Guinea and Sierra Leone) to shore up their capabilities.

But it was not just states that took advantage of the market for force. Transnational firms in the extractive industry, particularly, are often likely to remain in dangerous areas if that is where the resources are. Unable to rely on weak states for security and often unwilling to leave, these actors have provided another pool of demand for non-state protection that PSCs have exploited. The reason why PSCs – and not multilateral armed responses, such as those provided by the UN – have thrived is because multilateral forces have been much harder to deploy and (often because of problematic mandates) are seen as less effective.

Thus, both material and ideational changes placed private security options on the agenda. The reluctance of states to take on the variety of missions that people have felt moved to respond to, and the poor performance of multilateral institutions, have made the private alternative appear more workable as have prevailing beliefs that private means cheaper and better.

Conclusion

Global forces, new ideas and political choices have combined to enhance the opportunities for private delivery of and private financing for security services. As a result, a growing market for force now exists alongside, and intertwined with, state military and police forces.

This development holds significant implications for students of security studies. It also has implications for the control of force that poses states, firms and people with a number of trade-offs. Individual states can sometimes enhance the capacity of their forces, and thereby increase functional control. At the same time, though, the market undermines the *collective* monopoly of the state over violence in world politics, and thus a central feature of the sovereign system. Without that collective monopoly, states face increasing dilemmas about whether to hire from the private sector for security and how best to regulate the export of security services.

The existence of an extensive market alternative for military services changes the options available to states for the conduct of foreign and security policies. The use of market alternatives, however, through government contracts or regulation, operates differently from using modern military organizations, and advantages some portions of the government more than others. In particular, using market allocation generally advantages executives relative to legislatures, reduces transparency, and reduces the mobilization required to send public forces abroad. Furthermore, the use of market alternatives often involves the private sector in decision-making – giving those with commercial interests in policy influence over its formation and implementation. Because of these changes, the market option makes it easier to undertake adventurous foreign policies – or actions that do not have widespread support in a polity – and more likely that such action will be taken.

The USA has taken particular advantage of this market. PSCs have been vital to US efforts in Iraq, where they not only supported US troops via logistics and operational support missions, but also deployed quickly to the country to train Iraqi forces and provide security as stability unravelled in the wake of Saddam Hussein's fall from power. Sometimes these choices have been more costly than using US military forces, other times less, but as one US official told me in 1999, 'it is easier to get money out of the Pentagon than people'. The USA can thus use PSCs as force multipliers for its own troops, to train and supervise other troops, and even as a tool for recruiting something resembling an imperial force.

But not all states have reacted to the market in the same way. For example, the US strategy *vis-à-vis* the market for force is strikingly different from South Africa's eschewing of the private security sector. South Africa's efforts to sideline the market have not only led it to forgo new policy tools, it also decreased its ability to control the violent actions of its citizens abroad. This is particularly poignant as South African personnel and PSCs have poured into Iraq under contract with the USA to support stability operations in the wake of a war that the South African government did not support (*The Star* 2004).

Whether privatization of security in states like the USA will lead to disruptive change in military effectiveness or be folded into a new process of control is the $64,000 question. In the recent Iraqi conflict, well-publicized cost overruns from outsourcing, dramatic scenes of private personnel abused and abusing, unclear coordination between public and private forces and a higher than average separation of special forces personnel from both the USA and UK to take higher paying private security jobs, all seem to point towards an eroding process of control. At the same time, however, if using PSCs allows the USA to withdraw from Iraq more quickly, the potential for high salaries in the private sector prompts an upsurge in military recruitment, Americans' stock portfolios rich with defence services companies continue to rise, and private security is associated with effective action, perhaps private forces will be folded into the future of American foreign policy as a necessary dimension in a new military era.

As well as offering states new foreign policy choices, privatization also shifts power over violence outside the bounds of state machinery. This is most obvious when non-state actors finance security, which accords influence over security decisions to actors both outside the territory of the state and outside of government. In individual instances, transnational financing often diffuses power over the control of force. From a broader perspective, this diffusion of power should also lead us to expect a greater variety of actors to have influence over the use of force, should predict a furthering of competing institutions with overlapping jurisdictions over force, and thus accords with many who have argued that the world is entering a neo-medieval period (see Bull 1977: 254–255, Cerny 1998).

What is often lost in contemporary commentary is the notion that the 'ideal' form of markets can only function effectively when the state is also playing its 'ideal' role. Similarly, NGOs, to play their ideal role, rely on a government. In this sense, the privatization of security does not so much transfer power from one institution (the state) to another (the market) so much as pose challenges to the way both states and markets have functioned in the modern system. Instead of focusing on ideal types of states and markets (which have little basis in historical fact), it would be more prudent to examine the variety of institutional forms that are emerging, the way they are functioning, and think about their viability in terms of the degree to which they generate mechanisms that work together, potentially generating reinforcing processes, or chafe against one another, generating continued change.

The market for force has loosened the ties between states and force and undermined states' collective monopoly on violence in the international system. This has not made states, per se, less important, but has opened the way for changes in the roles states and other actors play in controlling force on the world stage. The rush to normative judgement about whether the privatization of security was 'good' or 'bad' has impeded analysis of the range of privatization's effects, the trade-offs associated with private security, and the choices available for its management. Both policy-makers and their constituents, however, would be well served by refocusing on these issues now.

Note

1   There is a debate over how to identify companies that provide violent services. David Shearer coined the term 'private military company' and the acronym, PMC, which has become a common descriptor of these firms. Some argue that there is a clear distinction between PMCs and private security companies (PSCs) – PMCs do military tasks, PSCs do policing tasks. The distinction between PMCs and PSCs is hard to maintain, though, given the variety of services that any given company may provide and the increasing blur between traditional military and other security tasks in today's wars. Most recently, Peter Singer (2001/02, 2003a) has introduced 'privatized military firm' (PMF). I use PSC to denote the whole range of for-profit security companies because it both more aptly describes the range of services these companies provide and avoids adding a new acronym to the list.

Further reading

Deborah Avant, *The Market for Force: The Consequences of Privatizing Security* (Cambridge: Cambridge University Press, 2005). This book provides an overview of the global market and its implications.

Simon Chesterman and Chia Lehnardt (eds), *From Mercenaries to Markets: The Rise and Regulation of Private Military Companies* (Oxford: Oxford University Press, 2007). This book brings together a range of analysts and participants in the market to examine the potential for regulation.

P.W. Singer, *Corporate Warriors: The Rise of the Privatized Military Industry* (Ithaca, NY: Cornell University Press, 2003). This book suggests a typology of military firms and gives a good history of three: Executive Outcomes, MPRI and Halliburton.

ArmorGroup website (www.armorgroup.com/) As described in this chapter, ArmorGroup is among the largest of the transnational firms. Contrast its website with Blackwater's.

Blackwater, USA website (www.blackwaterusa.com/). The Blackwater website gives a good description of the company and services it provides.

Transnational Organized Crime

John T. Picarelli

Abstract

This chapter provides an introduction to the world of transnational organized crime, one of the progenitors of the move towards the notion of homeland security. It examines transnational organized crime groups, their activities and the efforts made to stop them worldwide. The goal is for students to gain an understanding of the depth and breadth of the complexities transnational organized crime raises for national and international security planners, as well as the way these criminals threaten individuals on a daily basis.

Introduction

Since the 1990s, security experts have viewed transnational organized crime as a rising security threat. Some see crime groups as a direct challenge to the state, usurpers of state authority and threats to the well-being of their citizens. The Clinton Administration agreed with this outlook, declaring international organized crime a national security threat in Presidential Decision Directive 42 in October 1995. Another focus is the corrosive power of transnational crime on international norms and stability. The signing of the United Nations (UN) Convention against Transnational Organized Crime in 2000 is a prime example of how multilateral organizations seek to coordinate state responses and preserve international norms. A third camp of security experts view transnational organized crime as one of many challenges that threaten the well-being of individuals throughout the globe. Crime groups spreading corruption, fuelling conflict, damaging ecosystems, poisoning lives and exacerbating poverty have thus landed in the sights of non-governmental organizations such as Human Rights Watch and the International Crisis Group as well as major commissions looking to improve human security.

Transnational organized crime is a complex security threat that demands a multi-layered approach and response. In this chapter, you will come to terms with transnational organized crime as an issue of security studies. The opening section will explore transnational crime groups, focusing on their definition, their origins and their organizational composition. The next section explores the wide breadth of transnational criminal activities that form the illicit political economy, economic flows that mimic legal ones but that fall under the control and regulation of crime groups rather than states and firms. The third section synthesizes these descriptions to explore how transnational organized crime threatens the security of individual human beings, nation-states and even the international system. The final section briefly introduces you to the depth and breadth of the response to transnational organized crime.

Transnational criminal organizations

According to the UN Convention, a transnational crime group is one comprising three or more members who are organized for a set period of time before and after they act in a coordinated manner to commit a 'serious crime' for the purpose of obtaining financial or other benefit. By and large, one can find two forms of criminal organizations. Mafias are a specific form of crime group that sell private protection, sometimes have close links to government officials or agencies and often assume quasi-governmental roles within society. Mafias are difficult to root out since they replace the state in the social contract, often requiring significant efforts on the part of civic institutions to bring down. Examples include the Sicilian Mafia (see Box 30.1), the American La Cosa Nostra and the Japanese Yakuza. Other organized crime groups, on the other hand, are more akin to international businesses, operating one or more cross-border criminal acts in order to acquire illicit profits. Organized crime groups rarely have strong ties to the state outside of the use of corruption to protect themselves. Examples range from Nigerian fraud rings to Albanian people smugglers to Indonesian pirate groups.

Despite the flurry of attention that transnational criminal groups garnered after the end of the Cold War, they are not a recent phenomenon. Criminal groups operating across distances existed prior to the emergence of the modern nation-state. Groups of highwaymen robbed and extorted money from

BOX 30.1 THE FIGHT AGAINST THE SICILIAN MAFIA

For over a century, a score of civic and religious groups struggled mightily to turn Sicilian society against the Mafia. When in 1992 Mafia assassins struck down two Italian prosecutors, Giovanni Falcone and Paolo Borsellino, it brought the anti-Mafia movement to a head. Italian authorities were quick to retaliate. Exploiting the groundwork these civic groups had laid and leveraging the public outcry over the killing, Italian investigators quickly rounded up scores of Mafiosi and placed them on trial. So shaken were the Mafia that they resorted to terrorism, bombing even the Uffizi Museum in Florence. The bombings backfired, further driving the public away from the Mafia. By the end of the 1990s, a score of the major Sicilian crime families had lost their grip on Sicilian society. In recognition, the signing ceremony for the UN Convention Against Transnational Organized Crime was held in Palermo, the ancestral home of the Mafia, and the central square of Corleone was renamed for Borsellino and Falcone. Today, anti-Mafia groups are reclaiming land the Mafia once controlled for the cultivation of durum wheat and transforming their villas into hotels.

travellers in Europe, often using the borders between European city-states and regal territories to their advantage. Nor did these groups end with the emergence of the nation-state in the seventeenth century. One study revealed multiple crime groups operating in both urban and rural areas of the Netherlands in the seventeenth and eighteenth centuries (Egmond 2004). The roots of organized crime in Russia, China and Japan date back centuries as well.

The label 'transnational' is therefore not used to designate a new form of regional or global criminality. Rather, the term is a recognition of how these groups have successfully leveraged recent technological and political changes. The emergence of new forms of instantaneous, global and secure forms of communication is the foundation of the global spread of criminal networks that exist simultaneously in multiple countries (see Box 30.2). High-powered computers and information networks provide crime groups with new tools for old crimes as well as new criminal opportunities. As anyone with an email account by now knows, transnational crime groups seeking the proverbial 'sucker-born-every-minute' continue to solicit banking information in return for significant deposits. The tectonic shifts in geopolitics that have occurred in the past 20 years have also facilitated the formation of transnational criminal groups. The fall of the Soviet Union, the formation of the Schengen zone within the European Union, the emergence of global cities and the vast improvement in international passenger travel have all contributed to the creation of criminal organizations that can operate across borders in numerous countries without increased cost or risk. In sum, those forces that have 'flattened' the world and revolutionized international corporations have had

BOX 30.2 CRIME GROUPS COMPARED

When most people think of an organized crime group, the vision that comes to mind is that of Marlon Brando's portrayal of Vito Corleone in *The Godfather*. Crime groups with a hierarchical structure of capos, lieutenants and foot soldiers are only one model of organized crime today, however. Increasingly, crime groups have adopted a networked form of organization that is less hierarchical and better positioned to operate across political borders. Networked groups are able to rely on resources like document forgers, money launderers and smugglers on a case-by-case basis, and are also better able to insulate themselves from law enforcement raids. The most significant consequence of the rise of networked criminal groups is that it has led to the growing recognition of the links between crime groups and other transnational threats such as terrorists and weapons proliferators.

the same impact on the formation of truly *transnational* criminal organizations. It is ironic, therefore, that the most common method of cataloguing trans-national criminal organizations is by their perceived ethnic membership or cultural origins. While this is a common and easy way of portraying the global nature of transnational crime, it tends to vastly oversimplify the complexities found within these groups. For example, many of the 'Russian Mafia' groups located in New York City are not Russian at all, but rather are Russian-speaking groups drawn from the various ethnic groups from across the former Soviet Union. The same 'Russian Mafia' groups found in New York City quite often have subgroups in Ukraine, Moldova, Georgia, Turkey, Italy, Spain and numerous other cities in the USA (Finckenauer and Waring 1998). The use of ethnic labels to catalogue transnational criminal organizations also does not reflect how frequently these groups cooperate with one another. The cocaine trade into Europe is managed through a cooperation of numerous ethnic crime groups, not just the Colombian cartels with which it is so often associated.

The illicit political economy

Transnational organized crime is a label which also applies to sophisticated criminal activities that cross the borders of states. Such criminal activities are frequently estimated to consume between 5 and 20 per cent of GDP per annum, making the illicit political economy a significant source of global revenues. While forced labour, small arms and illicit drugs are the three largest illicit markets globally, they reside within a plethora of other criminal activities. Such criminal markets are closely associated with increasing levels of money laundering and the spread of political corruption. The combinations of criminal activity, financial malfeasance and political corruption are just some of the reasons why the illicit political economy is also known as the dark side of globalization.

The big three: drugs, people and arms

The trade in illicit drugs is most frequently cited as the largest sector of the illicit political economy. In 1999, Peter Reuter estimated the size of the illicit drug market as lying between $45 and $280 billion (Thoumi 2003). Using a different measurement, the UN's 2006 survey of the global drug trade noted that there were 200 million users of illicit drugs on an annual basis. But the drug trade is in fact not one but four overlapping markets, each with its own production, trading and consumption patterns. Cannabis and synthetic drugs are the most globally diffuse drug markets and thus rank first and second, respectively, in size and breadth. The UN estimated that in 2005 cannabis was produced in some 176 countries to meet a global demand of over 162 million users. The cannabis trade revolves around three major sources of demand. In Europe, domestic production is supplemented with trafficking in cannabis leaf from Morocco, Colombia, South Africa, Nigeria and India. The USA is the second major market, again supplementing domestic production with a trade that originates in Canada, Mexico and the Caribbean. Finally, a brisk trade in cannabis resin (hashish) originates in Afghanistan, Pakistan and Lebanon and supplies the Middle East and South Asia.

Turning to the market for synthetic drugs, the UN estimated that in 2004 over 480 metric tons of synthetic drugs were produced. The trade in amphetamines centres on three regional markets with significant linkages between them, forming a global diffusion of synthetic drugs. In East Asia, synthetic drugs produced in China, Taiwan, Myanmar and the Philippines are trafficked to markets in Thailand, Japan, Australia, New Zealand, Europe and North America. In North America, the USA produced a significant amount of synthetic drugs for domestic consumption and supplements its market with imports from Mexico. Finally, in Europe, the main production centres in the Netherlands, Poland, Belgium, Lithuania, Estonia, Bulgaria and Germany feed the European market.

Cocaine and heroin, while popular, are more regionally focused drug markets. Cocaine remains a popular drug in the USA and Western Europe. Although the days of the Medellin and Cali cartels have faded, the world's largest cocaine suppliers still reside in Colombia, followed by Peru and Bolivia. Two changes in cocaine trafficking in the past decade have led South American crime groups to 'outsource' the wholesale and retail distribution of cocaine and focus on production. In Mexico, the rise of groups such as the Tijuana cartel (aka the Arellano-Felix organization), the Golden Triangle Alliance (formerly the Juarez cartel) and the Gulf cartel have largely taken over the transport and wholesale distribution of cocaine in the USA. This in turn has led to sharply increased levels of violence and corruption in Mexico. South American cocaine producers are transshipping cocaine via the Caribbean (e.g. the Netherlands

Antilles and Jamaica) to wholesaling crime groups across Europe. While Africa is becoming a destination and transshipment point for South American cocaine, Asia constitutes a minor destination for cocaine. Heroin remains a potent drug in the Northern Hemisphere.

With some 16 million users worldwide, heroin and other opiates occupy a small but stable share of the global drug market. Afghanistan and Myanmar remain the two largest producers of raw opium and refined heroin, with Pakistan, Laos, Mexico and Colombia occupying a distant second tier. Heroin has three distinct markets. Afghan heroin is trafficked first to neighbouring countries, then to the Middle East and finally to Europe. Heroin from Southeast Asia is trafficked to neighbouring countries, especially China, and onwards to Australia. Finally, heroin from Colombia and Mexico supplies markets in the USA and Canada.

Trafficking in persons remains the second largest transnational criminal enterprise globally. Trafficking is the recruitment and movement of human beings for the purpose of slavery or slave-like practices such as debt bondage or involuntary servitude. While exact numbers of trafficking victims are difficult to come by, the US State Department estimates that between 600,000 and 800,000 persons are trafficked on an annual basis. Trafficking is most often associated with sexual exploitation such as prostitution, but labour trafficking is equally if not more prevalent throughout the globe. Other forms of exploitation associated with trafficking include domestic service, the trade in organs and even illicit adoptions and the sales of babies. The profits from trafficking are significant when one considers that a trafficking victim can earn profits on a day-to-day basis while other forms of crime, such as drug trafficking, are a point-of-sale model dependent on a constant replenishment to obtain profits.

Trafficking is a global criminal enterprise that defies easy summation. Trafficking routes crisscross almost every country worldwide. While the USA and Western Europe remain the largest destinations for trafficking syndicates, recent trends have begun to weaken the assumption that trafficking is purely an activity that runs along the development gradient from poorest to richest. Many states that were formerly seen as a source of supply for traffickers are now turning into destinations for trafficked victims. Sex tourism adds an additional layer of complexity as it brings the demand for sexual slavery to the supply, which is again located in the developing world. One final wrinkle is the fact that trafficking can occur entirely within the borders of a state, with transportation now taking on a local rather than international function.

The illicit trade in small arms is a profitable yet highly murky form of transnational crime. The illicit arms trade is estimated at approximately $1 billion per year. Unlike drugs or human beings, the trade in small arms and light weapons occurs in a three-level market: a regulated licit market, an unregulated grey market and an illicit black market. The grey market is the most difficult to control since it involves state authorities and appears legal until the final stage of the transfer. Groups involved in the many conflicts around the globe can avoid arms embargoes by transshipping weapons via a third country whose government officials will issue export licences for a bribe. But the outright black market for weapons, especially used weapons, is another source of arms. Numerous Warsaw Pact arsenals were looted after the fall of the Soviet Union, none more infamous than the 500,000 AK-47s taken from Albanian stores in 1997, and other thefts and diversions form a recurring supply for black markets. Arms are a frequent item for barter in the black market, swapped for illegally harvested commodities or illicit products such as narcotics.

The wide world of crime

Aside from the 'big three' issues of transnational crime, a litany of cross-border criminal enterprises lays plain the entrepreneurial spirit of contemporary organized crime. A veritable cornucopia of goods and resources are smuggled across borders on a daily basis. Stolen cars from Western Europe are resold in the Balkans and elsewhere in Eastern Europe. Europol estimates some 700,000 vehicles a year fall victim to these cross-border schemes. Other crime groups illegally harvest exotic plants for sale around the globe or poach protected species to suit the demand from cultures seeking a balm or increased virility from them. Alcohol and cigarettes remain staples of smuggling, with crime groups supplying black markets that avoid state regulations and taxes. Organized rackets steal fine art and illegally dig up antiquities. One group in Italy was found to have sold some 110 items of antiquity via the famous London auction house Sotheby's in 2005 alone, many of which wound up in the collections of major museums in Europe and the USA. Rising demand for natural resources has led to increased levels of smuggling and black marketeering that have, in turn, enticed criminal groups to become involved in these schemes. For example, crime groups have been linked to the harvesting and processing of rare hardwoods in Southeast Asia, oil in Nigeria and Angola, fish in Russia's Asian seas and precious metals such as nickel, silver, gold, platinum and palladium from across the globe. The most infamous criminal racket for natural resources remains the trade in 'blood' diamonds from West Africa, many of which provided cash and arms to ruthless rebel factions that continued conflicts for years. Finally, migrant smuggling remains one of the most lucrative criminal operations worldwide. Migrants seeking to enter the USA from China pay in excess of $40,000 to migrant smugglers dubbed 'snakeheads', while the 'coyotes' and 'polleros' charge thousands of dollars to cross into the USA from northern Mexico.

Fraud and counterfeiting are also significant categories of organized criminal activity. From music CDs to movie DVDs to computer software, criminal groups have engaged in wholesale piracy of intellectual property. Crime groups have also been linked to the counterfeit reproductions of high-end consumer products such as handbags and perfume. But law enforcement agencies have also found crime groups counterfeiting everyday items such as baby formula, prescription medication and even coupons. All told, the OECD estimated in 1998 that some 5 to 7 per cent of global trade involves counterfeit products –

a number measured in the hundreds of billions of dollars (though not all of this is attributable to crime groups per se).

The explosion of information technology has also helped spread the reach of fraud networks operating across borders. Most famous are the afore-mentioned advance fee fraud rings of West Africa. Starting first with faxes in the 1990s, these groups today use email and internet sites to solicit unsuspecting victims for their banking information so that they can receive a large deposit of money and retain some percentage of the amount (i.e. the advance fee) once the transaction is completed. Of course, after transmitting the banking information, victims will soon find their accounts cleaned out. Medical insurance fraud and financial frauds such as 'pump and dump' stock deals are also common rackets of organized crime. Finally, investigators of identity theft are beginning to see the involvement of transnational criminal organizations.

Finally, it would be remiss to overlook the traditional rackets that remain a staple of organized crime. The sale of private protection to business owners and others continued to plague many neighbourhoods globally. Private protection is at its essence extortion, hinging on the failure of the state to protect its citizens in certain regions such as émigré communities, urban neighbourhoods or rural districts. Most often, Mafia groups will charge a fee or a percentage of profits in return for 'ensuring' that harm does not come to the person or business, even though all involved know that the harm would come from the Mafia group charging the fee in the first place. Kidnapping for ransom remains a profitable venture as well, especially in the developing world. Some of the best analyses of the financing of the Iraqi insurgency have demonstrated that criminal groups are kidnapping Westerners and prominent Iraqis and selling them to the highest bidder, be they an insurgent group, a terrorist group or, with luck, government agents (Looney 2005). The hijacking of freight from trucks and, more recently, on the high seas continues as a staple of criminal groups. The embezzlement of public funds through dummy corporations and ghost employees is another popular racket. Criminal groups that specialize in providing services such as document fraud, contract killing and even hacking to other criminal groups continue to garner significant profits as well.

Money laundering and corruption

Money laundering and corruption are tangential to criminal enterprises yet are central to understanding the operation of modern criminal groups. Money laundering is quite simply the process by which money is hidden from government oversight such that its origins and destinations are no longer clear. Money being laundered might originate with tax evasion or corruption, but the form of money laundering that concerns us is the transformation of criminal profits into seemingly licit funds. Banking regulations and financial oversight make it difficult for anyone to deposit or draw upon thousands to millions of dollars without clear statements of the funds' origins. Money laundering provides a way for money obtained illegally to be transformed either to appear legitimate or to obfuscate attempts to trace the monies to their origin. The conventional wisdom is that money is most often laundered through offshore banking centres, but in fact most laundering uses the traditional banking system. Starting in 1995 and lasting 42 months, some 7 billion US dollars were laundered through the Bank of New York alone in one of the largest money-laundering schemes of recent memory. Other laundering methods include the use of front companies and properties, private banks, wire transfers and even the bulk shipment of cash offshore to jurisdictions with more lax deposit controls.

Corruption is vitally important to understanding organized crime. In many countries, mafias and other criminal groups are closely tied to political parties and influential business people. Crime groups can supply voters and employ political violence for politicians in return for impunity and, oftentimes, portions of proceeds from public works contracts. The Sicilian Mafia in Italy and numerous crime groups in the former Soviet Union follow this model. Crime groups have also worked closely with business people to ensure their oligopolistic control of certain industries in return for direct payments or shares of public contracts. La Cosa Nostra groups in New York City were a prime example of this merger of crime groups and business interests, using public unions as proxies to allow penetration of the sanitation, finance and fish markets of New York.

The dark side of globalization

Just as recent changes in global politics facilitated the transnational nature of criminal groups, the same forces aided in the emergence of an illicit political economy that is commonly described as the 'dark side of globalization'. Scholars of international political economy have theorized about this turn from two directions. Mittelman (2000) provides an excellent example of a top-down approach. Using Polanyi's notion of a double movement,[1] Mittelman demonstrates that the spread of transnational criminal activities is directly tied to the most recent phase of globalization. Mittelman posits that the spread of economic liberalization and market forces via globalization represents the first movement, while the growth and spread of transnational criminal groups and the informal economy are a form of resistance. Transnational crime is thus a way for members of societies to avoid the rules and norms of 'legal' globalization by turning to 'illegal' activities.

Passas (1999), on the other hand, employs a more bottom-up approach by focusing on how globalization impacts upon individuals and drives them towards transnational criminal activities. Using Durkheim's notion of anomie as his model, Passas sees globalization as driving increased consumerism globally but concentrating capital into fewer hands. The result is global anomie, anger arising from the inability of vast numbers to acquire that which is outside of their means. Unable to find legal ends to acquire the capital needed to meet these consumer wants, Passas finds that citizens lose faith in the state and turn instead to criminal activities. Thus whether top-down or bottom-up, globalization's impact on transnational organized crime is far broader than just supporting the formation of global crime groups.

Transnational crime as a security issue

The depth and breadth of transnational organized crime prove far too daunting for any one theory of international security to capture. Transnational criminal groups can sap the components of power so important to states. For example, transnational crime drains potential tax revenues from the coffers of the state while forcing the state to dedicate more financial and human resources to border control and law enforcement. Transnational crime can also impact upon a country's 'soft power'. States saddled with rampant and high-level corruption problems suffer significantly for want of trust and authority in the international system. Others have approached transnational organized crime from alternative security paradigms.

Transnational organized crime impacts upon security at three levels of analysis and thus requires a multi-layered approach to explanation. At the international level, crime undermines the norms and institutions vital to the maintenance of the international system. At the national level, transnational organized crime can destabilize the internal cohesion of the state and also undermine the components of power so important to realists and security planners. Finally, transnational organized crime has had a profound impact on human security, imperilling numerous individuals worldwide. Developing an understanding of transnational organized crime as a security issue thus requires a multi-layered approach.

International security

By its nature, transnational organized crime is a collective action problem. Given the fact that transnational crime groups operate across borders, states cannot fight these groups alone. The fight against transnational organized crime is thus by definition an issue of international security. More specifically, crime groups are often quick to take advantage of differences in legal codes or state capabilities across borders to accomplish their ends. Migrant smugglers often use countries with lax immigration controls as transit states, especially those who enjoy visa-free access to destination states (e.g. Puerto Rico and the USA). The theft and smuggling of automobiles from Western Europe exploded after the Schengen agreement brought some intra-European Union border controls to an end, which allowed criminals to drive stolen cars across Europe without having to stop for checkpoints.

Another way of viewing transnational organized crime as an issue of international security is that it challenges the norms and institutions that regulate the state system. Crime groups flout internationally negotiated environmental protections when they illegally harvest natural resources or dump waste products improperly. Money laundering and financial fraud force states to support more strident regulations that run counter to the *laissez-faire* demands of international markets. But the most transparent threat to international norms is the ways in which crime groups aid and enable violent groups worldwide. Criminals have collaborated with terror groups to provide them access to finances and arms. The trade in blood diamonds has prolonged conflicts in Africa. Smugglers have skirted arms embargoes to provide the tools of genocide in Sudan and elsewhere. Finally, and most controversially, is the involvement of organized crime in the theft and transfer of nuclear weapons or other strategic materials, undermining the most important of global taboos – that against the proliferation of strategic weapons.

National security

Organized crime is most often presented as a direct or even existential threat to the state. According to this view, crime groups are not only contributing to the decline of sovereignty as the central ordering principle for world politics but are also directly challenging the authority of states. Rosenau (1990) sees the rise of a parallel world of non-state actors (in his vernacular, sovereign-free actors) such as crime groups that is increasingly challenging the ability of states or sovereign-bound actors to achieve their goals. Cusimano (2000) approaches the problem in a similar fashion, viewing transnational organized crime as one of a number of challenges that states cannot solve among themselves and, if left unchecked, weaken their sovereignty and undermine their authority. Strange (1996) details how crime groups contribute to an atmosphere wherein the state is increasingly unable or unwilling to execute traditional regulatory functions, preferring instead to allow the market or private actors to handle them.

Transnational organized crime can also undermine the social, economic, political and military components of state power. Crime groups promoting a culture of corruption can have a deleterious impact on the social cohesion of states, undermining their ability to project power. Widespread corruption often leads to a breakdown of the trust and legitimacy publics have in states. Collaborative arrangements between the Christian Democrats and Italian criminal groups as well as those between the Liberal Democratic Party and Japan's Yakuza certainly fit this mould. Transnational organized crime can also undermine a state's economic resources. Crime groups maintaining economic cartels and enforcing protection rackets stifle the growth of new businesses and the expansion of the state tax base. Likewise, smuggling and laundering undermine the state's ability to regulate and tax flows of goods and services across its borders. Aside from the smuggling of small arms to prolong conflicts, transnational organized crime can also hamper military resources and readiness of a state. For example, the outgrowth of criminal groups from Russia's military and intelligence services has led many to question their readiness, while in Mexico the Gulf cartel has formed an elite unit of former military officers dubbed the Zetas to maintain security for their smuggling routes.

Human security

Transnational crime is a direct threat to individuals as well. One of the best ways to illustrate this is to use the novel conception of human security, which seeks to shift the referent of security away from the state to the individual. The 2003 Final Report of the UN Commission on Human Security arrived at ten ways to improve human security worldwide. Transnational organized crime actively or indirectly undermines half of them. Specifically, transnational crime runs counter to the Commission's desire to protect people in violent conflict, protect people from the proliferation of arms, support the security of people on the move, establish transitions for post-conflict situations and develop an equitable and efficient global system for patent rights.

Transnational organized crime thus undermines human security in a number of different ways. Criminal enterprises can impact upon the health and well-being of individuals. Regions laying astride narcotics smuggling routes often witness a precipitous rise in drug addition and the medical and social costs attendant to it. Sex trafficking and tourism lead to increased rates of narcotics addiction and HIV infections. Arms smuggling prolongs and intensifies conflicts. Contract killings and internecine feuds between crime groups victimize many with no involvement in criminal activities and can further foment a vicious cycle of violence in society. But most problematic is the general insecurity that organized crime has perpetrated on society. For example, migrant smugglers and human traffickers are frequent targets of other crime groups in home invasions and violent robberies in the USA, while the demand for stolen automobiles has led to increased rates of carjackings in Western Europe. In short, the potential for harm from transnational organized crime is acute.

Responses to transnational crime

Befitting the multiple layers of threat it represents, the response to transnational organized crime has come from multiple sources. At the international level, a number of international and regional organizations have formed to coordinate the fight against transnational crime. At the national level, states have focused on unilateral and multilateral measures to counter transnational crime. And a focus on approaching transnational crime as a threat to human rights has shown some promise in improving the security of individuals against crime groups. How well these efforts work in harmony will have a significant say in how transnational organized crime evolves in the years to come.

The root of any effort against transnational organized crime lies in co-operative measures. One form of cooperative measure is between states, and here international and regional organizations have taken the lead in co-ordinating the fight against transnational crime. In 1997, the UN Office for Drugs and Crime (UNODC) was founded to focus member state efforts against all forms of cross-border crime but specifically to improve the fight against transnational organized crime. To this end, the UNODC sponsored a series of working meetings that resulted in the UN Convention against

Transnational Organized Crime, which seeks to harmonize legal codes and improve law enforcement capabilities in order to curtail cross-border crime. Other international organizations that dedicate at least a portion of their resources to fighting transnational crime include the International Criminal Police Organization (Interpol; criminal intelligence sharing), the Financial Action Task Force (FATF; money laundering) and the International Organization for Migration (IOM; human trafficking and migrant smuggling).

Regional organizations have also begun to incorporate transnational organized crime into their mandates. The Organization of American States (OAS) has dedicated significant resources to improving regional cooperation against transnational organized crime, especially narcotics trafficking, migrant smuggling and the trade in human beings. The formation of the European Police Office (Europol) is rooted in the effort to fight transnational organized crime. In Asia, the member states of the Association of Southeast Asian Nations (ASEAN) have held numerous meetings focused on coordinating responses to transnational organized crime as well.

Aside from an institutional approach, a more interesting way of viewing the fight against transnational organized crime at the international level is through the lens of prohibition regimes. Detailing the rise of global prohibition regimes against specific types of transnational organized criminal activities, Nadelmann (1990) has demonstrated how countries such as the USA and European powers have worked together to engender a general consensus on transnational criminal activities. Global prohibition regimes act as a double-edged sword, however, as the inability to quell demand for prohibited goods among publics leads directly to the formation of black markets in which transnational crime groups thrive.

Responses at the national level have focused on two broad mechanisms. The first are bilateral and multilateral efforts to harmonize legal codes and build institutional capacity. Mutual legal assistance treaties (MLATs) between two or more states have flourished in the fight against transnational organized crime as these treaties seek to harmonize disparate legal codes and institutionalize cooperation over such issues as extradition, joint investigation and evidence collection. The joint construction of law enforcement capabilities is an equally important component of this effort. For example, the USA has placed hundreds of its law enforcement officials overseas to work directly with their foreign colleagues and has opened up law enforcement academies in Budapest, Bangkok and elsewhere that train foreign law enforcement officials to fight transnational crime.

Public–private partnerships are another interesting effort on the part of states to fight transnational crime (Cusimano 2000). Such partnerships are a pragmatic recognition that states cannot fight many forms of cross-border crime without the assistance of firms and other private organizations. For example, states cannot hope to end money laundering through regulation alone, but can make better headway working in cooperation with banks and other financial institutions. More often than not, these relationships are rooted in mutual benefit. For example, the American Container Security Initiative provides shippers with more predictable access to US ports of entry and US authorities with better intelligence on the contents of containers entering the USA, thus closing a significant loophole for smugglers.

Finally, the institutions of civil society have a significant role to play in containing transnational crime. Numerous Italian scholars of the Mafia have demonstrated that the absence of civil society is a factor in the formation of the Sicilian and other mafias. The experts also agree that a significant reason why the Mafia is in retreat today is that it lost touch with society when it began to assassinate Italian investigators and judges in the late 1980s and early 1990s. The Italian state was thus able to strengthen its ties with the citizens of Sicily, who rallied around the near century-long anti-Mafia movement for the first time. The efforts of numerous non-governmental organizations, watchdog groups and others thus have a sometimes unintended consequence – the construction of civil society buffers against the intrusion of transnational organized crime.

Conclusion

Transnational organized crime is one of the most complex threats facing security planners today. Spanning the globe, transnational crime is far from a homogeneous phenomenon. The impact of transnational criminal activities is perceived as a drag on financial markets, as a complication for global trade, as a threat to environmental health, as a threat to the authority of states, as a source of harm for individuals and so on. The growing network of local, national and international organizations dedicating their time and resources to fighting transnational crime is a testament to the multi-layered security problem which transnational organized crime represents. Regardless of how the globe continues to evolve, there is little doubt that transnational organized crime will remain a significant problem well into the future.

Note

1   A double movement occurs when the growth of economic markets breaks down societal norms and institutions (the first movement), which leads to the formation of resistance to the further intrusion of the market (the second movement).

Further reading

Peter Andreas and Ethan Nadelmann, *Policing the Globe: Criminalization and Crime Control in International Relations* (New York: Oxford University Press, 2006). One of the best views of transnational organized crime as an issue of illicit political economy and a function of historical evolution.

Mats Berdal and Monica Serrano (eds), *Transnational Organized Crime and International Security: Business as Usual?* (Boulder, CO: Lynne Rienner, 2002). One of the few books that engages transnational organized crime as a security threat, with strong contributions by a number of experts in the field.

Cyrille Fijanut and Letizia Paoli (eds), *Organized Crime in Europe: Concepts, Patterns and Control Policies in the European Union and Beyond* (Dordrecht: Springer, 2004). A thick tome with contributions from experts across Europe, this is the reference book to have to hand when trying to understand transnational crime in Europe.

James Jacobs, *Gotham Unbound: How New York City was Liberated from the Grip of Organized Crime* (New York: NYU Press 1999). A well-written examination of how the US government severed the grip of the Five Families on the commerce of New York City in the 1900s.

Ronen Palan, *The Offshore World: Sovereign Markets, Virtual Places and Nomad Millionaires* (Ithaca, NY: Cornell University Press, 2003). One of the better analyses of the complexity of 'offshore' zones and how they are used for money laundering, tax evasion, corruption as well as for legal purposes.

Williem van Schendel and Itty Abraham (eds), *Illicit Flows and Criminal Things* (Bloomington, IN: Indiana University Press, 2005). Provides an excellent analytical framework for understanding transnational crimes that states might view as being illicit but publics view as legal.

Contents

Population Movements

Sita Bali

▎ Abstract

This chapter will begin by examining why and how population movements have come to be seen as security issues. It will go on to outline the types of population movements and highlight the way states normally deal with them. Attention will then focus on the direct impact population movements can have on security, narrowly and traditionally defined: in the sense of security of the state from war, violence and conflict. Next, the effect of population movement on security, more widely defined, will be considered. This will include an assessment of the impact of migration and ethnic minority communities on a state's foreign policy, and its relationship with other states, particularly the countries of origin of its migrant communities. Finally the impact of ethnic minority communities on the internal social stability and cohesion of a state will be examined.

▎ Introduction

Population movement or the phenomenon of migration is as old as humanity itself, and has played a crucial role in shaping the world as we know it. In recent years such migration has gained prominence on the international agenda due to its increasing scale and the consequences such movements have for international affairs, including security concerns of states.

The increase in international population movements can be attributed to several factors. First, the ubiquitous nature of state control makes any international movement a matter of concern to at least two and sometimes more states. Second, there is the rapid increase in the world's population, which is still growing. Third, globalization has brought about a revolution in communications and transportation that has made people aware of vastly differing conditions and opportunities in other parts of the world, as well as making travel to those areas easier. Finally, the world is a turbulent and unstable place, and turmoil and uncertainty play a role in motivating people to move, to escape and/or search for a better life. This is best illustrated by the consequences of the end of the Cold War and the demise of the Soviet Union, which led to massive movements of people in Europe for the first time since the end of the Second World War. Ethnic Germans and others migrating to Germany and the West in search of a better life were joined by millions fleeing war and ethnic persecution in the former Yugoslavia, for example.

According to the International Organization for Migration (IOM), the number of international migrants in the world has increased from just 75 million in 1960, to 191 million in 2005, making up 3 per cent of the global population, or if they were a country, the fifth most populous country in the world. Among these were 8.7 million refugees. According to the UN High Commission for Refugees (UNHCR), another 6.6 million people were displaced from their homes but still living within their own countries (internally displaced people) at the end of 2005 (Table 31.1).

This chapter will examine the phenomenon of international population movement or migration, with a view to evaluating the extent and nature of the threat it represents to state security. It will of necessity concentrate on outlining and analysing the various ways in which population movements can constitute a threat to the security of states, societies, and the individuals within them. It is thus not called upon to make the positive case for migration, but this does

Table 31.1 World migrant numbers in selected years

Year	Number of voluntary migrants (millions)	Number of refugees (millions)	Total migrant number (millions
1960	64.2	1.8	66
1970	17.5	2	81.5
1980	91.4	8.4	99.8
1990	136.6	17.4	154
2000	162.8	12.1	174.9
2005	182.3	8.7	191

Source: UNHCR and IOM websites

Table 31.2 Remittances to developing countries (in billions of dollars)

Year	2000	2001	2002	2003	2004	2005	2006
Amount	85	96	117	145	163	188	199

Source: World Bank website

not mean that there is no case to argue or that population movements must always have a negative impact on sending and receiving countries, or their security. Migration can be economically beneficial to both sending and receiving countries and for the migrant. Sending Third World countries benefit hugely from remittances that migrants send home, and from the easing of pressure on employment, housing and other social facilities (Table 31.2).

The receiving country benefits from availability of labour at reasonable cost, increasing national productivity and economic growth. It acquires adventurous, entrepreneurially inclined individuals, determined to succeed in their new environment, who are more likely than average to become wealth creators and generators of employment. It may also acquire sorely needed highly trained and skilled personnel, such as doctors and software engineers, without having to invest in their skills. The migrants benefit from better standards of living, and fulfilment of their aspirations. Host countries become home to migrants with a variety of talents from business acumen to sporting prowess to musical, literary and theatrical abilities, and can become vibrant, open, multicultural, multi-ethnic, multi-faith societies with a flourishing cultural life. Migrants can contribute to building bridges between communities at home, and strengthening ties with their countries of origin abroad.

Population movements as a security issue

Over the past decade or so, a range of events in a number of countries have forced scholars to consider the importance of international migration in International Relations. The flight of East Germans to the West through Austria and Hungary, that ultimately resulted in the demise of the East German state, coups and political instability in Fiji and Pakistan, ethnic cleansing and refugee movements in the Balkans, the rise of right-wing political forces such as neo-nazis in Germany and Le Pen in France to name but a few, have contributed to this increasing interest. Changes to the international environment with the end of the Cold War and the re-envisaging of security with threats now perceived to emanate from a number of non-traditional sources such as environment and health, created space for rethinking the relationship between international relations and international migration. Within this context, there is also increasing recognition of the links between international migration and security.

The terrible events of 11 September 2001 dramatically reaffirmed the role international migration can play in international relations generally, and in security issues in particular. When it emerged that the perpetrators of 9/11 were all temporary or illegal immigrants, the USA began to treat their immigration service as part of their national security apparatus, with sections of the USA PATRIOT Act being devoted to immigration policy and process, and immigration coming under the supervision of the Department for Homeland Security. As the global aims, reach and spread of al-Qa'ida became clearer, so this approach was taken up in many other Western states. The case was further strengthened by the Madrid bombings (11 March 2004) and the London tube bombings (7 July 2005). It is now widely accepted in many Western states that the public policy process should explicitly treat immigration and security as intertwined, and bring a security focus to bear on matters of control and management of population movements.

Migration can pose a threat to the people and governments of both sending and receiving states, and to relations between these two countries. It can turn civil wars into international conflicts and it can cause the spread of ethnic conflict and civil unrest from one country to another. It can lead to some form of conflict, including full-scale war between countries. Migration can also play a role in facilitating terrorism. Population movements can become the cause of economic hardship and the increase in competition for scarce resources of various kinds from jobs to social housing, and can weaken existing power structures and institutions within countries, as well as threatening cultural identities and social cohesion.

Population movements categorized

All international migrations can be divided into two categories: involuntary or forced (also called refugee movements), and voluntary or free (also called economic migration) on the basis of the motivation behind the migration. Involuntary or forced migration refers essentially to refugee flows, where for reasons of natural disaster, war, civil war, ethnic, religious or political persecution people are forced to flee their homes. The flight of thousands of Afghans to Pakistan and Iran since 1979 or the desperate journeys of black African Sudanese from their homes in Darfur would fall into this category.

Voluntary migrations can be further subdivided into three main categories. The first is legal permanent settler migration of the kind that populated the USA or created the Asian and Afro-Caribbean minorities in Britain. This kind of migration has decreased most sharply in recent years. The second kind is legal temporary migration, and includes the bulk of the voluntary migrations. This category would include the movement of people for education, business, tourism and employment, such as the temporary workers admitted to the Gulf States to service the oil-powered economic boom in construction and other sectors. The third kind of voluntary migration is the illegal migration of people from one country to another, which may be temporary or permanent. This would include, for example, the clandestine movements of Mexicans and others across the long US–Mexican border. The relevance of this categorization is based on the existence of an international regime and norms to deal with involuntary or forced migrations, and the complete absence of the same with regard to voluntary or free migration.

Sovereignty is regarded as the defining characteristic of a state in our international system. It implies, among other things, that states have control and jurisdiction over what goes on within their territorial boundaries. One aspect of the exercise of sovereignty has always been a state's inviolable right to control who will enter and exit from their territory. Thus states have traditionally operated a system of border controls, with policies regarding who may enter, for how long and under what conditions. With regard to free or voluntary migration, states have the full authority to decide who they will accept as entrants or immigrants. They make their decisions based on a variety of criteria including the labour and skills needed by their economies and cultural and ethnic similarities with incoming migrants. But when it comes to involuntary or refugee movements, there are some limited constraints on a state's authority in the form of the obligations imposed on them by the 1951 Convention on the Status of Refugees.

This Convention obliges states to extend asylum and protection to those facing persecution, on grounds of religion, race, nationality or political opinion. Further, implicit in the meaning of refugee lies an assumption that the person concerned is worthy of being and ought to be assisted, and if necessary protected from the cause of flight (Goodwin-Gill 1983: 1). In

BOX 31.1 THE 1951 REFUGEE CONVENTION

The 1951 Convention relating to the Status of Refugees is the key legal document in defining who is a refugee, their rights and the legal obligations of states. It was created in the aftermath of the Second World War to deal with displaced people in Europe, and originally intended to last just three years. But the refugee issue was not so easy to solve, and it was given permanence through the 1967 Protocol, which removed geographical and temporal restrictions from the Convention. The Convention is based on the principle of non-refoulment, laying down that no state should return a refugee to a state where their life might be in danger. It also established the now universal definition of a refugee, both key principles of international law. The Convention provides the most comprehensive codification of the rights of refugees and lays down basic minimum standards for the treatment of refugees. The Convention is to be applied without discrimination as to race, religion or country of origin, and contains various safeguards against the expulsion of refugees. The Office of the UN High Commissioner for Refugees monitors states' compliance with the Convention.

practice the Convention commits states to ensure that no asylum seeker is sent back to any country where they are likely to face danger to life or liberty, without their application for refugee status being given due consideration. Also relevant is the Universal Declaration of Human Rights (1948), which states in Article 14 that everyone has the right to seek and enjoy asylum from persecution, in other countries.

However, none of these agreements or practices actually guarantees anyone the right to refugee status, only the right to seek it. This is because in practice there is total acceptance in international society of the right of every sovereign state to decide for itself who should be allowed entry to its territory. Thus, the question of whether someone is a refugee and should be treated as such by a state becomes an issue decided by the government and the courts of the country in which refuge is sought. Nevertheless, these instruments form a significant part of the international consensus on the treatment of refugees, and they lay down an important universal principle that most states have come to endorse, namely that people with a well-founded fear of persecution have a right to exit from their own country, cannot be returned to their country of origin, and have international status.

For an asylum seeker to be recognized as a refugee is a political decision, and depends to some extent on the relationship between the sending and receiving countries. For instance, during the Cold War, anyone who managed to escape from any Eastern Bloc country to the West was welcomed with open arms. In fact in the USA, under the terms of the McCarran-Walter Act (1952) up until 1980, a refugee was defined as a person fleeing communist persecution. Since the end of the Cold War, as erstwhile communist bloc citizens became free to exit from their countries, Western governments were no longer so hospitable.

Sometimes different streams of migration mix and merge over time. For example, the movement of Sikhs from the Punjab to the UK, USA and Canada since the 1960s was a classic free economic migration. But then in the 1980s, when the demand for an independent Sikh state in the Punjab arose, it was violently suppressed by the Indian government and a number of Sikh advocates of an independent Punjab were forced to leave their homeland and seek refuge elsewhere. Quite naturally, many of them found their way to the countries that were already home to Sikh migrants, where they could live among their kith and kin. One result of this kind of convergence of different types of migrations is that receiving state governments and their people are increasingly likely to treat all immigrants alike, once they are in the territory of the receiving state.

The one inevitable long-term consequence of international population movements, whether the movements of refugees or the free migration of people aspiring to a better life, is the creation of ethnic minority communities in the receiving countries. In most host countries, and certainly in democracies, it has become clear that once migration takes place, for whatever reasons, and whether intended to be permanent or temporary, it invariably results in at least some immigrants becoming citizens of the host country, and creating a cultural, linguistic, religious and possibly a racially distinct minority within the state.

The existence of these communities has a substantial impact on security, both in the traditional sense of security of the state from violence, war and conflict, to security in the wider sense of social stability, economic prosperity and the internal politics of states; as well as on the relationship of host states with the countries from where these communities originate.

Population movements and violent conflict

Large-scale refugee migration from one country to another usually raises serious security concerns. Refugee flows, by their very nature, are the result of conflict, social and political upheaval and turmoil. It is therefore hardly surprising that they may sometimes carry that instability with them to the host country. In such circumstances, the refugee flows are both a consequence of some sort of conflict, violence or repression as well as themselves becoming the cause of conflict between their country of origin and the receiving state. When a government becomes unwilling host to a large refugee population, it is likely to take steps to ensure that the stay of the refugees is temporary, and there is every potential for conflict between sending and receiving countries in this case. Examples include the flow of Palestinians into the neighbouring Arab states in 1948 when Israel was created; the migration of East Pakistanis into India to escape the brutal attentions of the West Pakistani army in the early 1970s; and the movement of Afghans from their country to Pakistan in the wake of the Soviet invasion in the 1980s.

The receiving state will try to bring about a change in the situation or policies of the sending country government that led to the exodus, or failing that, try to bring about a complete change of government there. This usually tends to lead to some sort of conflict between the sending and receiving states. Often, receiving states become involved in the conflict in the sending state, threatening to arm or actually arming the refugees; and sometimes deploying their own armed forces. Instances abound, with the actions of various Arab governments towards the Palestinians; Pakistani involvement (with Western help) in Soviet-controlled Afghanistan, Indian arming of the Sri Lankan Tamils being cases in point. The instance that had the most far-reaching consequences was the Indian intervention in East Pakistan in 1971, which came about as a result of ten million East Pakistanis fleeing the violent suppression of their rebellion by the West Pakistani army, resulting in the formation of Bangla Desh.

This strategy is not without risk. By strengthening a refugee group, the receiving country takes the chance that it will lose its ability to deal independently with the sending country, and that refugees will attempt to determine the host country's policies towards the sending country (Weiner 1995: 139). This has happened to the Arab governments who have supported the Palestinians, the Pakistanis who supported the Afghan Mujahidin, and to the Indians who supported the Tamils in Sri Lanka. The conflicts created by such movements can sometimes be protracted, often lasting as long as it may take for return of the refugees to their homeland, or the creation of some alternative permanent arrangement for their resettlement.

Recent events in Britain have illustrated that it does not take a large number of refugees to have a negative impact on the security of the receiving country. Britain had given refuge to a small number of high-profile charismatic and influential Islamist clerics when they sought to escape repressive Middle Eastern regimes who were targeting them for their extreme Islamist views. Among these was Sheik Omar Bakhri Mohammed who founded the Islamist student movement Al-Mohajiroun and radicalized British Muslim youth. There was Abu Hamza, the Afghan war veteran and extremist preacher who converted Finsbury Park Mosque into a haven for Islamists and a recruitment centre for al-Qa'ida. There was also Abu Quatada, the cleric who has been now named as al-Qa'ida's spiritual leader in Europe, whose speeches influenced several European suicide bombers including Zacharias Moussavi, the twentieth man involved in the 9/11 attacks, and Richard Reid, the shoe bomber. These extremist clerics helped radicalize many young British Muslims, recruited and sent British Muslims to fight in Bosnia and Chechnya, and arranged trips for terrorist training to Afghanistan for some. They and their associates must be seen as at least partly responsible for the radicalization that ultimately resulted in four young British Muslim men blowing themselves up on London's transport network on 7 July 2005, killing 51 members of the public and injuring hundreds more.

In recent years the War on Terror has focused attention in the West on the potential security threat from some among their Muslim residents and citizens of immigrant origin. However, attacks by Islamists based in the West go back to the first attack on the World Trade Center in 1993, and the bombing campaign by Islamist Algerians on the Paris Metro in the summer of 1995. Most of those involved in the attack on the Twin Towers of the World Trade Center were temporary migrants, resident in the USA ostensibly for education or business. A number of those involved in the Madrid bombings, terrorist trials in Germany (where some of the 9/11 bombers were resident) and currently detained in the UK, France and Italy, are Islamist residents of the countries they are now attacking. The fact that most of them are either refugees, immigrants themselves or of immigrant origin presents Western liberal democracies with a significant challenge.

Population movements and foreign policy

Immigrant or ethnic minority communities, formed by labour or refugee migration, can play a significant independent political role in world politics. Their continued political involvement in states in which they no longer live, and whose laws they are not subject to, presents a serious challenge to the sovereignty of that state. By the same token they challenge the ability of host states to exercise independent control over the direction of their own foreign and domestic policy.

Migrant communities tend to maintain a strong connection with their home countries, and turbulence or instability in those societies can find expression within the migrant community. When this happens, these communities will become involved in a range of political activities targeted at their home country. They will use all means at their disposal to influence events at home, which could be in support of, or (more often) against their home governments. They take advantage of their unique status, being outside their home country and not subject to its jurisdiction, to take those actions that people living in their country of origin cannot, due to fear of arrest, persecution or violence. In particular, they can join political groups proscribed in the home country, publicize the grievances, agendas and demands of these banned groups, be critical of home government actions and policies, and become the voice of a suppressed opposition. They can try and draw the attention of the wider world to the problems in their country of origin, causing at the very least embarrassment to the home governments. They raise funds within their diaspora community and provide financial support to like-minded forces, or victims of government persecution in their home country. Migrant communities will also try to enlist the support of the host government and population to further their particular political aims in their home country. Home country governments respond to all this offshore activity by putting pressure on the host state's government to restrict them and not allow them voice and succour. But if the migrant communities are acting within the laws of the host state, there may be little the host government can easily and legally do to restrict their activities. The consequence is deterioration in the relationship between the host and home states.

The case of the Sikh community in the UK acting in concert with the wider Sikh diaspora in other Western countries, including the USA and Canada, is a good example of the phenomenon. The Sikh populations in Britain, Canada and the USA were deeply influenced by the politics of the Punjab and the demand for independence from India in the 1980s and early 1990s. The diaspora communities were themselves divided along the same factional lines as politicians in the Punjab, and disputes between factions as well as between the Sikhs and the Punjabi Hindu community and the Indian government were reflected within the Sikh communities abroad, particularly in the struggle for control of wealthy and influential Sikh temples in major Western cities and in a deteriorating relationship between other Indian immigrant organizations and Sikh institutions. In Britain this did spill over on to occasional but limited violence in centres with large Sikh populations, as well as leading to some high-profile members of the Sikh and Punjabi communities being assassinated.

Sikh communities abroad contributed significantly to the violence in the Punjab which targeted Indian security forces and members of the Hindu community. Their major contribution was through the collection and illegal transfer of funds to the Punjab for those carrying out the secessionist violence in India. They also created serious problems for the Indian government by campaigning and publicizing the demand for secession and independence abroad as well as highlighting cases of human rights abuse carried out by the

Indian security forces. The diaspora Sikhs declared an independent state of Khalistan, established a government in exile in London, and began issuing passports and banknotes for their new country. In constituencies with large numbers of Sikhs, Members of Parliament were inundated with requests to raise these issues, and questions regarding the situation in the Punjab and censure of the Indian government were tabled in the Commons. The Indian government tried to put pressure on Britain by questioning the UK government on its provision of asylum and benefits to some Sikh refugees, and by trying to get the UK to restrict the activities of the Khalistan Council and agree to an extradition treaty with India. The British government was reluctant to go down this route. The Indian government then delayed or cancelled commercial orders for defence equipment and helicopters with British firms. In general, for a considerable period through the 1980s and early 1990s, the activities of the Sikhs in the UK had the effect of damaging the long-standing and generally amicable and close relationship between Britain and India.

The success of migrant communities' attempts to recruit their host governments and populations to their cause in their home country depends to a large extent on the nature of the political system in the host country. The more open the system and the more susceptible to lobbying it is, the more likely it is that minority communities will succeed in getting their concerns on the agenda. The USA is usually seen as being susceptible to such pressures, due to the openness of its political system to political lobbying. Thus, some American foreign policy stances are partially explained by the efficacy of minority community pressure on behalf of their home country. The unwavering support that the USA has given Israel since its inception is a reflection of the power of the Jewish lobby in American politics. Similarly, the Greek community in the USA successfully lobbied politicians to get Congress to embargo military assistance to Turkey, following the Turkish invasion of Cyprus.

Arguably, the presence of the Muslim minority population in Britain has become a factor to be considered in foreign policy decision-making. For example, the stance of the Muslim communities in various European states affected the policies of those states during the Gulf War (Collinson 1993: 15–16). In addition, the concerns of British Muslims may have helped draw attention to the suffering of Bosnian Muslims and Kosova Albanians, both situations in which Britain and other states ultimately intervened to protect the Muslims. The anti-war demonstrations in London prior to the 2003 invasion of Iraq saw the Muslim minority, in conjunction with other interest groups, make clear their opposition to Britain's participation in this action, and no doubt generated much mail for MPs in constituencies with large Muslim populations. Britain's participation in the invasion is understood to be one of the main causes of Muslim dissatisfaction and disenchantment with the present government.

Migrant communities may also be used by the government of the home country to pursue its own aims, *vis-à-vis* the host country government. The relationship between successive Israeli governments and American Jews illustrates this point. Host governments too will try to use their ethnic minority communities to achieve their own goals, particularly those in relation to events in the country of origin of that community, with Mafia leaders, for example, assisting the Allied invasion of Sicily during the Second World War.

Population movements and internal security

Admitting migrants has long-lasting social effects on receiving countries. It can turn more or less homogeneous societies into multicultural ones through the introduction of ethnically different people. Migrants raise social concerns because they potentially threaten to undermine the popularity and strength of the nation-state. At the moment nation-states remain the dominant unit of social organization across the globe with each state ostensibly forming a 'territorially based self-reproducing cultural and social system' (Zolberg 1981: 6). Their members are seen to share a common history, language, religion and culture that binds them into a cohesive integrated unit with a shared sense of nationhood. As citizens of one state moving to live and work in another, migrants clearly challenge traditional notions about membership of a state, the meaning of nationality and citizenship, and the rights and duties of citizens towards their state and vice versa. The fact that very few states fit the idealized picture of the homogeneous nation-state, and that most states are cultural and social products of earlier movements of peoples, fails to register in the popular consciousness.

Migration can become a threat to social cohesion and stability if migrants or minority communities are seen to be an economic burden on society. The perceptions of migrants as welfare dependent, or so numerous and needy as to stretch local resources in housing, education, healthcare and transportation can cause resentment and hostility. Migrants are also perceived to be criminals and carriers of infectious diseases in some quarters. In advanced industrial societies, concern with the cost of welfare provision to migrants, particularly asylum seekers and refugees, has become a major political issue. It is argued that the validity of the welfare state model in many of these countries, reliant on ordinary people's taxes, is threatened if the public begin to feel, rightly or wrongly, that their taxes are being used to subsidise foreigners' living expenses and healthcare, rather than taking care of those in need within the home society. Many European countries have seen a resurgence of the extreme right in politics as a consequence of this public unease about immigration and asylum. The rise of neo-nazis in Germany, Le Pen in France, Jorg Haider in Austria, Pim Fortuyn in the Netherlands and the British National Party in the UK are all examples of the domestic political forces pushing European governments to take an increasingly hard line on immigration. These pressures have also prompted collective action from Western European countries. European Union[1] states have tried to move towards a process of harmonization of their refugee and immigration policies. This has proved to be a more difficult and slower process than they envisaged, but some fundamental agreements are now in place. The 1990 Dublin Convention (which came into effect in 1997) provided that an asylum seeker who has had his or her application rejected in one European country cannot seek asylum elsewhere in the European Union. Thus rejection by one member state is to be seen as a rejection by all the established members of the Union.

Most Western European states (with the exception of Ireland and the UK) have further collaborated on developing a common visa and immigration policy, the Schengen Agreement, which harmonizes rules for visa requirements, travel within their borders and removes intra-European travel barriers. It also establishes a system of increased cooperation and information sharing between police and immigration authorities of member states, enabling states to cooperate on dealing with illegal immigrants, drug and people traffickers, and security threats. The Amsterdam Treaty of the EU further commits member states to striving towards developing a single European Refugee and Migration policy.

Most of the world's refugees originate from and remain in the developing world, and here large refugee inflows can be an immense burden in economic terms. In the short term they can cause quite serious distortions in the markets of the receiving countries, particularly with regard to escalating the prices of essential commodities. This is what happened in Iran in the aftermath of the Gulf War, when Kurdish and Shia refugees flocked into that country. In the long term, a developing state generally has to rely on international assistance, usually through the office of the UN High Commissioner for Refugees to alleviate the burden on the economy, but is susceptible to the internal political tensions that difficult economic situations bring.

Migrants are received with hostility if they are perceived as a threat to the culture and way of life of the people in the receiving country. This tends to happen when large numbers arrive in a short period of time or when migrants are seen as holding themselves apart and being reluctant to make any efforts to integrate into the host country's way of life.

Large long-term refugee populations can bring about significant changes in the social cohesion and stability of the host country. Pakistan's problems with increased drug addiction among its population, as well as the threats to law and order posed by the flourishing arms bazaars in Peshawar and elsewhere (what has been described as the 'Kalashnikov culture'), are laid at the door of their Afghan guests. Large numbers of refugees can also be a driving force for change within the receiving country, particularly if they are ethnically similar to their hosts, or speak a common language. The gradual 'talibanization' of parts of Pakistan, and the growing support attracted by the Islamic political parties, is at least in part a result of playing host, for nearly 20 years, to millions of Pashtuns from across the Durand line that separates Afghanistan from Pakistan. Similarly, the large Palestinian presence in Lebanon contributed towards the destabilization of that country during its long civil war, and continues to do so to the present day.

Further, migration can affect political and social conditions, and even, in rare instances, fundamentally alter the nature of society in receiving countries, many years after the actual movement of people has ceased. An illustration of this may be seen in Fiji, where indenture migration created an Indian immigrant community nearly a century ago. Indo-Fijians formed nearly half of the Fijian population by 1987, and an election brought an Indo-Fijian-dominated political party to power, and gave Fiji its first Indo-Fijian prime minister. The largely indigenous Fijian armed forces took power in a coup and tried to enshrine a new constitution ensuring political primacy for their ethnic group. The tussle for power between the two groups continues and Fiji has since experienced intermittent upheavals and further coups, the last being in 2006.

The extent and nature of integration of a migrant community, and the impact this has on 'societal security' as described by Ole Waever (Waever *et al.* 1993: 17–40), has recently come under the microscope, particularly in European countries such as Britain, France and Denmark. The substantial long-established Muslim community in these and other European countries is now, in light of the global War on Terror, being seen as a source of threat. There are approximately 20 million Muslims in Europe, with France having the largest numbers (5–6 million) forming 8 to 9 per cent of its population. Muslims make up from 5 to 1.5 per cent of the population of most other Western European countries. Events such as the attack on London, the murder of film-maker Theo Van Gogh in retaliation for making a 'blasphemous' film about Islam and women, and riots in the suburbs of Paris as well as controversy about the publication of cartoons depicting the Prophet Mohammed as a terrorist, the law banning the use of headscarves in state institutions in France, and the increasing use of the full-face veil by young Muslim women, to name but a few, have been bitterly divisive.

In Britain, the 7/7 attacks precipitated soul-searching and debate about the supposedly divisive nature of multiculturalism as a model of integration, the importance of migrants being fluent in the language of the majority, and the common values that needed to underpin a cohesive multi-ethnic multi-religious society. These debates are taking place against the backdrop of a difficult security situation, involving arrests and high-profile trials of some young Muslims. This has made the Muslim minority defensive and unable or unwilling to acknowledge and confront the extent of radicalization among their number. The economic and social marginalization of Muslims, particularly Pakistanis, who on virtually every social indicator lag behind other immigrant communities, including those from the Indian subcontinent, is evident in even a cursory examination of areas in which they are concentrated, such as Britain's northern mill towns. This lack of economic and social progress is clearly relevant to the ongoing discussion. The direction taken by this national debate is crucial to future social stability in Britain.

Conclusion

Until the world is free of repression, conflict, political instability and economic inequality it is certain that population movements will continue. In an increasingly globalized world, with easy access to information, instant communication and cheaper travel, the numbers of people on the move can only increase. While most free migration post-1945 has been from the developing world to the richer world, most refugee migration has taken place within the developing world itself. Thus there is no part of the globe that is untouched by migration and unconcerned with its impact. Migration reflects the unequal and volatile nature of our world, and brings the conflicts and instability of the poor world into the streets and ultimately the policy forums of the comfortable and comparatively secure developed world. It also adds to the deprivation, instability and violence of the developing world. It raises questions of human rights, international law and state sovereignty, and it is a hotly debated, live and difficult issue in the contemporary politics of many states, both rich and poor.

Population movements cast light on the divided nature of the contemporary world. In a larger part of the world, most of Africa, Latin America and Asia, there is considerable insecurity, violence, conflict, repression and deprivation. By contrast, in Europe and North America and a few other areas, including Japan, Australia and New Zealand, people enjoy prosperity and democracy. Such stark contrasts are a striking indictment of the present age and they contribute significantly to population movements. Such movements show that the rich Western countries cannot maintain their isolation from, and remain untouched by the deprivation and instability of the developing world. They provide a powerful argument for the sensible and whole-hearted participation of the powerful West in the development, both economic and political, of the rest of the planet.

The global War on Terror adds another dimension to this already divided world. The preoccupation in the West with preventing another 9/11 or 7/7 horror has led to the abrogation of long-established civil rights at home, and preventive military action abroad. These actions have arguably created more tensions than they have resolved, adding to destabilizing population movements in the Middle East and along the Durand line, as well as alienating different communities' own citizens from each other, thus increasing insecurity at home.

However, it would not be appropriate or realistic to conclude that the best policy for states would be to drastically restrict migration. First, that does not deal with the fact of past migrations and their consequences, and would, for example, do nothing to resolve the issues raised in the context of the War on Terror. Second, it would strongly signal that states see migration and migrants as a problem, which would make it more difficult to achieve desirable levels of integration of immigrants and may add to social insecurity. Opponents of immigration such as the extreme right would probably interpret such a signal as a licence to step up their divisive anti-immigrant activities. Third, as argued at the start, migration can have considerable economic and other benefits. Fourth, in a globalized world, open, free market societies will need to facilitate some migration to accommodate their demand for skills and labour, and to create the unrestricted environment in which cultural exchange, creativity, entrepreneurship and business can flourish. A balanced immigration policy, based on the needs of the economy and all citizens with fair and transparent rules, is the key to the management of migration in the contemporary era. This has to be combined with policies that allow existing migrant communities opportunities for economic self-improvement, and encouragement to integrate. Migrant communities need to have a stake in their host societies and see their own rights, best interests and prosperity dependent on and tied to the rights, interests and prosperity of the larger society around them.

Note

1   This does not yet apply to the 10 new members which joined the Union in 2004, or Romania and Bulgaria which joined in 2007.

Further reading

Stephen Castles and Mark Miller, *The Age of Migration* (Basingstoke: Palgrave Macmillan, 3rd edn, 2003). A very useful overview of the phenomenon of population movement and its impact on international politics.

Robin Cohen, 'Diasporas and the nation-state: from victims to challengers', *International Affairs* 72(3) (1996): 507–520. Focuses on the changing role of diasporas from forced migrants to challengers of the authority of nation-states.

Nana Poku and David Graham (eds), *Redefining Security: Population Movements and National Security* (Praeger, CO: Westport, 1998). A wide-ranging and useful collection, focused on various aspects of the security implications of migration.

Myron Weiner, *The Global Migration Crisis* (New York: HarperCollins 1995). Excellent, explicitly political analysis of the migration phenomenon with a special focus on security by one of the pioneers in the field.

Websites (all very useful for statistics, background and news):

■ European Union (http://europa.eu/)
■ International Organization for Migration (www.iom.int/)
■ UN High Commission for Refugees (www.unhcr.org/)
■ World Bank (www.worldbank.org/)

Energy Security

Michael T. Klare

Abstract

In this chapter, students will examine the various meanings of 'energy security' and consider why it has suddenly attracted so much attention from both policy-makers and the general public. In particular, international concern over the future availability of energy supplies is ascribed to doubts about the ability of energy producers to keep pace with rising world demand, the shift in the centre of gravity of world oil production from the global North to the global South, and the targeting of oil installations by terrorists, insurgents and ethnic separatists. Various strategies for enhancing energy security are also considered.

Introduction

To the array of significant forms of security that command the attention of policy-makers and citizens around the world – among them national security, international security, human security, economic security and environmental security – has now been added another pressing concern: energy security. A term almost unheard of outside the specialized analytical community until just a few years ago, energy security now figures prominently in the policy discourse of major government officials. 'Energy security', said President George W. Bush in March 2001, should be 'a priority of our foreign policy' and govern key elements of domestic policy (Bush 2001). Similar views have been expressed by senior officials of other industrialized states, thus highlighting the importance now being accorded the energy issue. This naturally invites a pair of obvious questions: What, exactly, is meant by energy security, and why has this aspect of security gained such prominence *now*?

Understanding energy security

To begin this discussion, it is necessary first to highlight the centrality of energy in all human endeavours. Even the most primitive humans must consume food in order to obtain the caloric energy to hunt, gather more food and other essential materials, build shelter, and defend against predatory animals and hostile tribes; more complex societies need energy to procure food and water and to construct cities, fortifications, factories, ships, roads, railways and so on. The more complex and productive a society, the greater its need for energy; without adequate supplies of basic fuels, a complex society cannot maintain a high rate of industrial output, provide a decent standard of living to its citizens, or defend itself against competing powers. 'Oil is not just another commodity,' Senator Richard G. Lugar of Indiana observed in November 2005. 'It occupies a position of *singular importance* in the American economy and way of life' (Lugar 2005, emphasis added). It is from this perception of energy's 'singular importance' to the functioning of modern industrial societies that the concept of energy security springs.

In most Western states, the task of procuring, producing and delivering energy to consumers is largely performed by private companies, which do so in the pursuit of profit; some of these companies, in fact, are among the most profitable in the world. However, because the acquisition and delivery of adequate supplies of energy is considered so essential to the economic health of the nation, governments also play a significant role in key aspects of the energy procurement process. The intervention of state authorities in the management of energy acquisition and distribution is typically justified in terms of 'energy security' – that is, ensuring that appropriate incentives and policy instruments are in place to impel private firms to take the steps needed to produce and deliver adequate supplies of energy to meet the nation's requirements; when the private sector proves unequal to this crucial task, the state must be prepared to step into the breach.

There is no standard, all-embracing definition of 'energy security'. Most analysts describe it as the assured delivery of adequate supplies of affordable energy to meet a state's vital requirements, even in times of international crisis or conflict. 'Put simply', explained a task force convened by the Council on Foreign Relations, 'energy security' constitutes 'the reliable and affordable supply of energy' on a continuing, uninterrupted basis (Deutch and Schlesinger 2006: 3). In practice, this is usually understood to encompass the dual functions of ensuring the procurement of *sufficient supplies* of energy to meet fundamental needs as well as ensuring their *unhindered delivery* from point of production to ultimate consumer (see also Kalicki and Goldwyn 2005).

Fulfilling these dual requirements has proven enormously challenging in recent years as the worldwide demand for energy has increased – and the task is expected to grow even more demanding in the years ahead. Obtaining sufficient supplies of energy to satisfy national requirements will become more demanding because the needs of most states will continue to expand as populations grow, urbanization and industrialization proceed, incomes increase, and ordinary citizens acquire additional energy-consuming devices (especially automobiles). According to the most recent projections from the US Department of Energy (USDoE), combined world energy consumption is expected to grow by an astonishing 72 per cent between 2003 and 2030, jumping from 421 to 722 quadrillion British thermal units (BTUs) per year (USDoE 2006: 83). Procuring all of this additional energy – an estimated 300 quadrillion BTUs – will prove a gargantuan task on a global scale, but it will be at the national and regional level that the job of actually generating all of the required additional fuels will largely be performed. For those officials who are delegated with responsibility for overseeing this crucial chore, energy security will to a considerable degree entail taking such measures as are deemed necessary to ensure that the supply of available energy keeps expanding in consonance with rising demand.

So far we have been speaking of energy in the *aggregate* – of the sum of all sources of energy, including oil, natural gas, coal, nuclear power, hydro-power, and traditional sources such as wood and charcoal. As indicated, policy-makers will feel compelled to increase the *net* supply of energy, in all its forms, to satisfy rising demand in the decades ahead. But these officials also seek to avoid over-reliance on any one or two of these sources, lest a future shortage of those materials causes a severe energy crisis and resulting economic disaster. Policy-makers are also aware that growing concern over global climate change could well lead to future restrictions on the use of fossil fuels – oil, coal and gas – whose consumption typically results in the release of carbon dioxide and other heat-trapping greenhouse gases. In terms of ensuring adequate supplies to meet future needs, therefore, energy security has also come to mean *diversifying* a state's primary sources of fuel and investing in climate-friendly alternatives – especially renewable forms of energy such as solar, biofuels and wind power.

The second major energy challenge, ensuring the unhindered *delivery* of crucial supplies, will also grow more demanding in the years ahead because the global energy supply system (like that for many other basic commodities) has become highly globalized, with numerous suppliers around the world contributing oil, natural gas, coal, uranium and electricity to extended, over-stretched and often fragile networks of pipelines, transmission lines and maritime trade routes. Aside from the normal wear and tear of overburdened infrastructure, these networks are often vulnerable to attack by terrorists, insurgents, pirates and criminal bands – making the safe delivery of energy increasingly problematic. As the worldwide demand for energy expands and reliance on these far-flung networks grows along with it, energy security will inevitably entail increased emphasis on the protection of global delivery systems.

The protection of overseas sources of energy extends to several forms of energy but places special emphasis on petroleum – the world's single most important source of energy. According to the USDoE (2006: 85), oil accounted for 38 per cent of the world's primary energy supply in 2003 and is expected to provide nearly as much in 2030. Although some large consumers of petroleum, including the USA and China, are able to draw on domestic oil reservoirs for at least some of their requirements, most industrial powers must import a large share of their supply, often from providers located half-way around the globe. As the demand for energy grows, the role played by these international petroleum transactions will assume ever greater significance in the energy calculations of the major energy-consuming states. The fact that so many of the supply routes used in the global transport of petroleum originate in or pass through areas of instability and conflict can only add to the degree to which the energy security problem is equated with the safe delivery of oil.

The challenge of securing sufficient energy to satisfy national needs and to ensure the safe delivery of imported oil faces many states, but arises with particular vehemence for the USA, which on any given day consumes approximately one-quarter of the world's total available energy supply – approximately 6.4 million tonnes of oil equivalent (BP 2006: 40). With its growing population and robust economy, the USA is also expected to account for a significant share of the *additional* energy that will be required to satisfy anticipated world requirements in the decades ahead. The problem of energy security has thus become a major policy concern in Washington, prompting debate and action at the very highest levels. In February 2001, President Bush established the National Energy Policy Development Group (NEPDG) to review the nation's long-term energy requirements and to devise a strategy for ensuring that its vital needs would continue to be satisfied in the decades to come. 'The goals of this strategy are clear,' he explained, 'to ensure a steady supply of affordable energy for America's homes and businesses and industries' (Bush 2001).

In its final report, *National Energy Policy*, the NEPDG concluded that the USA was not adequately developing domestic sources of energy to satisfy its future needs and was becoming excessively dependent on unreliable foreign suppliers, thus exposing the country to the threat of recurring supply interruptions. The report therefore called for increased emphasis on the exploitation of domestic sources of supply – including oil derived from protected wilderness areas, such as the Arctic National Wildlife Refuge (ANWR) – along with diminished reliance on overseas suppliers. Under the rubric 'Increased Energy Security', the NEPDG announced its intent to 'lessen the impact on Americans of energy price volatility and supply uncertainty' by 'reduc[ing] America's dependence on foreign sources of petroleum'. At the same time, however, the group acknowledged that the USA cannot eliminate its reliance on foreign suppliers altogether, and so indicated that 'energy security must be a priority of U.S. trade and foreign policy' (NEPDG 2001: xv).

For the USA, as for other industrialized states that rely on imported supplies of energy, energy security thus entails a conspicuous *foreign policy* dimension, in that a principal objective of its overseas diplomacy is to establish and sustain friendly ties with key providers of oil, gas and other fuels, thereby facilitating the procurement of these fuels by companies linked to the home country. In many cases, the maintenance of such ties has become a major responsibility of senior government officials – from the president or prime minister on down. President George W. Bush, for example, has conducted several meetings with President Vladimir Putin of Russia to discuss increased energy cooperation between the two countries, while President Hu Jintao of China has made several trips to Africa in pursuit of increased investment opportunities for African energy firms.

By the same token, energy security has acquired a significant *military dimension* for the USA and a number of other energy-importing states, in that senior officials perceive a need to protect overseas energy supply routes and to help defend their country's major foreign energy providers against rival forces that might seek to impose less favourable terms over the flow of oil. For Washington, the protection of friendly oil suppliers like Saudi Arabia and the defence of vital maritime trade routes – such as the narrow Straits of Hormuz between the Persian Gulf and the Arabian Sea – has become a major element of national strategy (Klare 2004, Palmer 1992).

The military dimension of energy security was first accorded high-level attention in the USA in late 1979 and early 1980, when Islamic insurgents overthrew the US-backed Shah of Iran and Soviet forces intervened in Afghanistan – in both instances threatening the safety of oil deliveries from the Persian Gulf to the USA and its allies. 'The Soviet effort to dominate Afghanistan has brought Soviet military forces to within 300 miles of the Indian Ocean and close to the Straits of Hormuz, a waterway through which most of the world's oil must flow,' then President Jimmy Carter told Congress on 23 January 1980. 'The Soviet Union is now attempting to consolidate a strategic position, therefore, that poses a grave threat to the free movement of Middle East oil.' This is a threat that the USA cannot abide, Carter affirmed. 'Let our position be absolutely clear: An attempt by any outside force to gain control of the Persian Gulf region will be regarded as an assault on the vital interests of the United States of America, and such an assault will be repelled by any means necessary, including military force' (Carter 1980). This principle – widely known as the Carter Doctrine – was invoked by President George H.W. Bush in August 1990 when announcing the decision to deploy American troops in Saudi Arabia and to commence what became known as the first Gulf War (see Klare 2004: 48–53, Woodward 1991: 224–273). Some analysts also believe that the *second* Gulf War – the 2003 US invasion of Iraq – was also triggered by the Carter Doctrine and its injunction to employ military force whenever deemed necessary to overcome threats to the free flow of Persian Gulf oil (see Klare 2004: 94–100, Phillips 2006: 68–96, Yergin 2002). This is energy security writ large.

But energy security can have yet another meaning, particularly for states that are highly dependent for their energy supplies on one or two suppliers but are in a weak bargaining position with respect to them and hence vulnerable to political pressure. This is the case, for example, of the former Soviet Republics that rely on Russia for much of their oil and natural gas supplies, especially Ukraine, Belarus, Georgia and the Baltic states. On several recent occasions, the Russians have threatened to or have actually cut off the flow of energy to these states, producing widespread economic hardship. Ostensibly, these actions were prompted by disputes over the *pricing* of energy, but most Western observers believe that Moscow undertook such action to punish an unfriendly government or to extract political concessions from the nation involved (Buckley 2005, Kramer 2006). For these countries, then, energy security has come to mean reducing their dependency on a single provider that can employ its dominant position in order to inflict punishment for an unwelcome decision or extract concessions of some sort.

Energy security, then, can have a variety of meanings, depending on the outlook of the particular state involved. For virtually every state on the planet, it means securing sufficient energy to meet vital needs, both now and in the future. This means, in most cases, diversifying the types of energy on which a state relies and investing in climate-friendly energy alternatives. In addition, for those states that rely to a considerable extent on imported sources of supply, energy security also incorporates a significant foreign policy dimension in terms of maintaining friendly ties with key foreign providers; these countries must also worry about threats to the unhindered delivery of their energy supplies, and this has led, in some instances, to a decision to employ military force in the protection of overseas supply routes. Energy security can also embrace efforts to reduce reliance on a single major supplier that uses its dominant position to extract concessions or otherwise manipulate its highly dependent clients.

Why now?

Concern over adequate supplies of energy has been a significant issue for many states for a very long time, but the concept of energy security has only gained widespread prominence and attention in recent years. Why is this? What explains the enormous attention now being devoted to the problem by senior government officials, military strategists, scholars and the general public?

Analysis suggests that the growing emphasis on energy security reflects widespread anxiety about both key aspects of the problem: whether there will be *sufficient* supplies of energy to meet national requirements in the years ahead, and whether the supplies that are available will be safely transported from point of production to point of need. This anxiety stems from three key recent developments in the energy field, largely concerned with the global availability of petroleum. These are: (1) fears of a slowdown in future world petroleum output; (2) a shift in the centre of gravity of world oil production from the global North to the global South; and (3) the explicit targeting of oil facilities by insurgents, terrorists and extremists.

Intimations of global petroleum insufficiency

The first and most important source of anxiety about the future availability of adequate petroleum supplies arises from concern about the ability of the global energy industry to continually increase crude oil output to satisfy ever rising levels of consumption. At present, the industry appears capable of satisfying global demand, which at the beginning of 2006 stood at an estimated 82.5 million barrels per day (mbd) (BP 2006: 11). But serious doubts have arisen in energy and policy-making circles about the industry's capacity to meet much higher levels of demand expected for the future, when many existing oilfields are expected to fall into decline. Even if net world oil output rises to a higher level in the years ahead – say, 100 mbd or more – the major consuming states will still experience a condition of petroleum *insufficiency* if global demand climbs to levels substantially above that figure and the industry proves unable to raise output to those elevated levels.

Consider the long-term projections provided by the USDoE (2006: 87, 155): according to the 2006 edition of its *International Energy Outlook* (IEO), world oil consumption is expected to jump from 80 mbd in 2003 to 111 mbd in 2025, an increase of 31 mbd. Fortunately, says the USDoE, global oil-production capacity will rise by a similar amount over this period, from 82 to 115 mbd. It is hard to argue with the projections for increased *demand*, as these are consistent with long-term trends regarding economic expansion, population growth, global motorization rates and so forth. Far more problematic, however, are the assumptions regarding future *production*: these are based on estimates of future output from existing wells along with predictions of new oilfield discoveries, and so entail considerably more guesswork. It is these latter calculations that have aroused scepticism and alarm among specialists in the field (Deffeyes 2001, Deutch and Schlesinger 2006, Goodstein 2004, Roberts 2004).

This scepticism arises from several observations regarding the world's net oil-production capacity. The first derives from evidence that many of the world's most prolific oilfields are nearing the end of their most productive years and are about to experience a substantial decline in output. This is said to be the case for many mature fields in the older producing areas, including those in North America, East Asia and Western Siberia – but is also thought to be true of Saudi Arabia, the world's leading producer. In a widely cited book on Saudi Arabia's long-term production prospects, investment banker Matthew R. Simmons (2005: xv) wrote that Saudi Arabian oil production 'is at or very near its *peak sustainable volume* . . . and is likely to go *into decline* in the very foreseeable future'. Although Simmons' conclusions have been contested by Saudi oil officials, it appears that his work, and that of other specialists who have raised doubts about the productivity of Saudi fields, has begun to influence the thinking of USDoE analysts, who have downgraded their projections of future Saudi output. In the 2004 edition of the IEO, for example, Saudi Arabian output was projected to reach 22.5 mbd in 2025; in the 2005 edition, its projected output was reduced to 16.3 mbd; in 2006, it had slipped again to 15.1 mbd. When combined with projected declines in production by other key producers, including Iran, Iraq, Kuwait, Libya, Mexico and Nigeria, this has prompted the USDoE to gradually lower its projections for future world oil-production capacity: whereas the IEO for 2005 had projected that total output would rise to 126 mbd in 2025, the 2006 edition projected output of only 115 mbd, a decline of 11 mbd. Rising oil prices were no doubt part of the explanation for this downward assessment, but it also reflects growing pessimism about the ability of the world oil industry to achieve heroic increases in production (Deutch and Schlesinger 2006: 14–23).

The second reason for anxiety about the future sufficiency of global production capacity arises from the steady decline in the rate of *new oilfield discovery*. If the global supply of petroleum is to satisfy anticipated world demand in the years ahead, we would need to see a volume of discovery that equates to both the decline in older fields and the added consumption prompted by global economic growth. However, that is not what is happening. According to the US Army Corps of Engineers, the peak level of oilfield discovery occurred in the 1960s, when new reserves with approximately 480 billion barrels of oil were identified. Since then, the rate of discovery has dropped in each succeeding decade while the consumption of existing reserves has continued to climb, with net extraction overtaking reserve additions for the first time in the 1980s; it now exceeds the discovery rate by a ratio of two to one (Deffeyes 2003: 47–51, Fournier and Westervelt 2005: 13). What this means is that the world is now relying on previously discovered reservoirs for an ever increasing share of its consumption – a pattern that can only result in the exhaustion of existing supplies and an inevitable contraction in supply.

A third and final reason for anxiety over the future availability of petroleum arises from the fact that whatever discoveries *are* being made today tend to be located in areas that are difficult to tap into for geographic, environmental or political reasons – and thus may not be developed to their full potential. This is hardly surprising: it is a common law of resource extraction that developers first pursue mineral deposits that are close at hand, easy to extract and relatively free of political impediments; only after all the easy-to-exploit reserves are exhausted do developers go after less appealing sites in more distant, less accessible areas. In the case of oil, with many of the world's mature fields facing decline and no new fields in familiar areas left to be tapped, producers see no choice but to pursue options in remote, hazardous areas, such as sub-Saharan Africa, the deep waters of the Gulf of Mexico and the Russian Far East. True, giant firms such as Chevron, Exxon and BP have the technical capacity to operate in remote, difficult locations, but will they (and their lenders) be willing to risk the many billions of dollars in new infrastructure that will be needed to develop these exceedingly demanding reservoirs? The answer may not always be 'yes'.

A shift in the centre of gravity of world oil production

The growing emphasis on energy security is also being driven by a perception that the centre of gravity of world oil production has irrevocably shifted from safe, friendly areas of the global North to more dangerous, unfriendly areas of the global South. For most of the petroleum era, the production of petroleum was largely concentrated in the North, especially the USA, Canada, Europe, and the European portion of the Czarist/Soviet Empire. Hence, as recently as 1950, approximately two-thirds of worldwide oil production was centred in these areas. This is hardly surprising, given the aforementioned tendency of resource producers to focus their initial efforts on the exploitation of the most readily accessible deposits, while leaving for later those deposits located in harder-to-reach, more remote locations. But precisely because the more accessible deposits were the first to be exploited, they are also among the first to be facing systemic exhaustion. As the demand for crude has grown, therefore, the consuming states have had no choice but to increase their reliance on providers in the global South. These producers generally entered the energy business later than their counterparts in the North, and so their fields – in some cases larger than those in the North to begin with – are at an earlier stage of development, and so are capable of sustaining higher levels of production in the future. As a result, the centre of gravity of world oil production has shifted decisively from North to South and will remain there for as long as we can see into the future.

Evidence of this shift is clearly seen in the projections on future global oil output supplied by the USDoE. In 1990, producers in the global North (including the USA, Canada, the North Sea states, Australia, Russia and a handful of others) jointly accounted for 39 per cent of total world oil output; by 2030, their combined share is expected to drop to 26 per cent. Meanwhile, the USDoE (2006: 87, 155) projects a significant increase in the share of world petroleum supply provided by key producing areas of the global South, notably Africa, the Caspian Sea basin and the Persian Gulf; together, the proportion of world consumption accounted for by these three areas is expected to jump from 31 per cent in 2003 to 48 per cent in 2030.

This shift in the centre of gravity of world oil-production capacity has profound implications for the energy-seeking states because it entails a heightened risk to the uninterrupted flow of energy supplies. Although not all states of the global North are peaceful and not all states of the global South are conflict-prone, there is a greater incidence of disorder in the South than in the North. This is due partly to the endemic poverty and the high rates of youth unemployment found in many developing states – a natural source of fodder for insurgency, ethnic extremism and criminal violence – and partly due to the legacies of colonialism, which in many cases include borders drawn to meet the convenience of imperial overlords rather than the aspirations of ethnic constituencies on the ground. These problems are often compounded by the discovery of oil in poor ex-colonial countries, where the inequitable allocation of oil revenues is often a significant factor in disputes between the central government and ethnic or regional enclaves – such as Aceh in Indonesia, Cabinda in Angola, Kurdistan in Iraq, the Niger Delta region in Nigeria, and the non-Muslim south in Sudan.

Many post-colonial states also suffer from weak governance structures and a tendency towards military strongmen and pervasive corruption; what sets the oil-producing countries apart from others like them, however, is the powerful attraction that oil revenues (or rents) have for all aspirants to state rule. Once in power, the leaders of these 'petro-states' will baulk at nothing to remain in power, and thereby keep the oil rents flowing into their private bank accounts. This means that their competitors, after having been denied the opportunity to prevail at the ballot-box, perceive no option save armed revolt to secure their own place at the feeding trough. The result, more often than not, is a continuous cycle of coups, palace revolts and counter-coups – often supported by an impoverished and resentful population ready to rebel at the first sign of central government vulnerability (see Karl 1997).

Oil facilities as a target of attack

The problem of energy security is further compounded by the fact that oil facilities have *themselves* become a target of attack by insurgents and terrorists, who often view them as a concrete expression of America's (or the West's) reassertion of an imperialist agenda in the global South. This is especially true in the Islamic world, where many Muslim activists interpret the assertive US military presence as, essentially, an expression of America's insatiable thirst for Middle Eastern oil. Needless to say, those who oppose the American presence in the Middle East have other motives for doing so; but there is no escaping the fact that the pursuit of oil has been a driving force in the West's desire to establish a significant presence in the Middle East, and that this has transformed the region in ways that are often resented by many of its Muslim inhabitants. In particular, there is widespread resentment of the close association between Western governments and (what are often perceived as corrupt, authoritarian) pro-Western regimes in the region, such as the Mubarak government in Egypt and the House of Saud. The increasingly conspicuous presence of American military forces to protect these regimes and the vital oil installations only adds to this resentment (Klare 2006).

Aside from constituting a central feature of Muslim extremists' indictment of the major Western powers, oil is also seen by many terrorist groups as an *attractive* target in the struggle between militant Islam and its enemies. This is so in part due to its symbolic importance – as *the* major expression of Western intervention in the Middle East – and in part due to its critical role in sustaining the West's energy-intensive economies. Attack the oilfields and pipelines, the reasoning goes, and you not only focus attention on the imperial presence of the Western powers but also deliver a blow at their most vulnerable point – their excessive dependence on cheap Middle Eastern petroleum. 'Pipelines are very soft targets,' Robert Ebel of the Center for Strategic and International Studies (CSIS) observed in 2003. 'They're easy to go after. It doesn't take a rocket scientist to figure out where you can do the most damage, both physical and psychological, with the minimum amount of effort' (cited in Vieth and Rubin 2003).

An early expression of this strategy was the October 2002 terrorist attack on a French oil-tanker, the *Limburg*, while sailing off the coast of Yemen. This attack – widely attributed to al-Qa'ida – was seen as the opening salvo in a new campaign to punish and weaken the West by assaulting the exposed conduits of the global oil-supply system. The strategic nature of oil terrorism is also evident in Saudi Arabia, where al-Qa'ida and allied groups have targeted foreign firms and technicians employed by Saudi Arabia's oil industry, presumably to damage its operating capacity. The first such assault occurred on 1 May 2004, when gunmen killed five Western oil industry workers in Yanbu, the site of a major petrochemical complex. A second attack occurred four weeks later, on 29 May, when a group of armed militants said to be allied with al-Qa'ida stormed a residential compound occupied by Western oil workers in Khobar, near the oil centre of Dhahran. An even more ominous assault occurred on 23 February 2006, when suicide attackers attempted to break through the outer defence perimeter of the Abqaiq oil-processing facility and detonate explosive-laden vehicles in the Kingdom's most important energy installation, potentially jeopardizing 6.8 million barrels of daily output; although the attack was foiled before the bombers could get close to the facility itself, the determination with which they carried out the assault hints at the extent to which such facilities have come to be viewed as prime targets for attack.

For all of these reasons – an expected slowdown in the global output of oil, the shift in the locus of oil production from North to South, and the targeting of oil facilities by terrorists, insurgents and extremists – policy-makers have become increasingly alarmed about the future sufficiency of energy supplies and the safety of global energy flows. It is this anxiety, more than anything else, that explains the upsurge of interest in problems of energy security. 'As the years roll by, the entire world will face a prospectively growing problem of energy supply,' former US Secretary of Defense (and Energy) James R. Schlesinger told the Senate Foreign Relations Committee in November 2005. 'We shall have to learn to live with degrees of insecurity – rather than the elusive security we have long sought' (Schlesinger 2005).

Addressing energy (in)security

As concern over the various aspects of energy security – or energy *insecurity*, to use Schlesinger's term – has grown, policy-makers have developed a wide array of strategies to address these problems. These run the gamut from greater reliance on military force to protect the flow of oil to increased emphasis on the development of renewable sources of energy, especially wind and solar power. Although there is considerable debate as to which of these approaches is likely to prove most effective, there is general agreement that increased effort is needed to address the threats to energy security.

If there is anything that policy-makers agree on when it comes to addressing the problem of energy security, it is that more options are better than less. In terms of securing overseas sources of petroleum, for example, US policy favours maximizing the number of providers from which oil supplies are derived. 'Concentration of world oil production in any one region of the world is a potential contributor to market instability,' the 2001 *National Energy Policy* affirmed. 'Encouraging greater diversity of oil production . . . has obvious benefits to all market participants' (NEPDG 2001: ch.8, p. 6). Similarly, US policy, like that of many other states, favours reliance on many *types* of fuel so as to avoid overdependence on any single type, lest a future scarcity of that fuel leads to a severe energy crisis. Recognizing that growing public concern over global warming is likely to lead to curbs on the use of fossil fuels, moreover, policy-makers in many countries are coming to favour increased investment in energy alternatives, such as wind power and biofuels. Besides these generalizations, however, there is considerable debate over particular aspects of energy security, and over the degree of emphasis that should be placed on particular fuel types and energy alternatives.

One of the most contentious issues in this debate concerns the degree to which the protection of foreign energy supplies should be entrusted to military forces. For some policy-makers, especially in the USA, the growing risk to global petroleum flows has led to a greater emphasis on the use of military force to protect overseas oil suppliers and the maritime trade routes used to transport oil. 'As the world market for oil relies on increasingly distant sources of supply, often in insecure places, the need to protect the production and transportation infrastructure will grow', a Council on Foreign Relations task force observed in 2006. For this reason, the presence of American military forces is said to play a vital role in stabilizing key oil-producing regions and will be even more essential in the future. In addition, 'U.S. naval protection of the sea-lanes that transport oil is of paramount importance' (Deutch and Schlesinger 2006: 23, 30).

Some Western analysts believe that the Chinese authorities are also inclined to place greater reliance on the use of military force to protect vulnerable energy supply lines. For example, the 2006 edition of the US Department of Defense's annual report on the *Military Power of the People's Republic of China* reported,

> Securing adequate supplies of resources and materials has become a major driver of Chinese foreign policy. . . . PRC strategists have discussed the vulnerability of China's access to international waterways. Evidence suggests that China is investing in maritime surface and sub-surface weapons systems that could serve as the basis for a force capable of power projection to secure vital sea lines of communication and/or key geostrategic terrain.
>
> (US DoD 2006: 1)

Although still relatively modest by comparison with comparable US efforts, these initiatives – if confirmed by further investigation – suggest that Chinese officials, too, are prepared to employ military means in safeguarding the flow of vital energy supplies (Andrews-Speed *et al.* 2002).

However, if some policy-makers in Washington and elsewhere favour the expanded use of military forces to protect the global flow of oil, others see in this approach greater risk rather than greater safety, and so seek to enhance energy security by sharply reducing the country's dependence on imported fuels. America's reliance on imported petroleum 'is the albatross of U.S. national security', Senator Lugar declared in March 2006. The USA, he argued, is dependent on increasingly vulnerable energy supply lines at a time when 'Al Qaeda and other terrorist organizations have openly declared their intent to attack oil facilities to inflict pain on Western economies'. To protect these facilities, he continued, the USA is spending as much as $50 billion on 'oil-dedicated military expenditures in the Middle East' – with no guarantee that these massive outlays will prove effective. Rather than persist in its adherence to this risky and futile approach, Lugar affirmed, the USA should 'speed up the transition to alternative renewable energy sources' and sharply diminish its reliance on imported petroleum (Lugar 2006).

Lugar, like many other American politicians, favours the accelerated development of biofuels as an alternative to imported petroleum. 'Our policies should be targeted to replace hydrocarbons with carbohydrates', he declared (Lugar 2006). Because the USA has ample farmland, and the technology for converting corn and other crops into ethanol for transportation fuel is well developed, great emphasis is being placed on the substitution of ethanol for a significant proportion of America's imported petroleum. This was an important aspect of the 'Twenty in Ten' energy security initiative announced by President Bush in his State of the Union address of 23 January 2007, aimed at reducing US gasoline consumption by 20 per cent between 2007 and 2017 (White House 2007). In this respect, the USA is following in the footsteps of Brazil, which undertook several decades ago to reduce its reliance on imported oil (mainly to reduce its outflow of petrodollars) by converting sugarcane into ethanol on a very large scale (Luhnow and Samor 2006). In recognition of its success in this endeavour, the USA will cooperate with Brazil in the development of ethanol technology and commerce, under an agreement signed by President Bush and President Luiz Inácio Lula da Silva of Brazil in Sao Paulo on 9 March 2007. The USA is also exploring technologies for converting corn stalks and other waste biomass into liquid fuel, called cellulosic ethanol (Wald 2005). All of these measures, and others like them, are claimed by their proponents to fall under the rubric of energy security.

For the most part, the struggle to devise an effective response to the challenge of energy insecurity is likely to focus on efforts to expand the menu of energy options available to consumers – both in terms of the increased diversity of domestic and foreign suppliers and in the *types* of fuels available, including alternative fuels. Increasingly, however, we can expect this discussion to shift in the direction of environmental sensitivity and a need to *reduce consumption*, rather than increase supply through heroic, costly measures.

As awareness of humanity's impact on the global climate grows, policy-makers will come under increasing pressure to limit the consumption of fossil fuels, to increase reliance on climate-friendly alternatives, or to require the introduction of costly filtering technologies – such as 'carbon capture and sequestration' (CCS) – that prevent the release of carbon dioxide into the atmosphere (see Friedman and Homer-Dixon 2004). As this occurs, energy security will acquire a new meaning – the transition from energy practices that cause irreparable climate damage to those that minimize such damage.

Finally, energy security may come to mean using energy in a far more frugal and self-aware manner than we – at least those of us in the more advanced industrial states – tend to do so today. As supplies of certain primary fuels (especially oil and natural gas) become more scarce, as the geopolitical risks of relying on these fuels become more severe, and as the environmental hazards of consuming fossil fuels more apparent, citizens around the world will naturally choose to be more deliberate in their selection and use of primary energy, and more inclined to avoid unnecessary or wasteful expenditures of fuel. Indeed, one can already see many signs of such voluntary restraint: the growing popularity of hybrid-electric automobiles in the USA; a preference for smaller cars and fuel-efficient diesels in Europe; the renewed popularity of bicycles in many European cities; and so on. As times goes by, such behaviour is likely to play an ever increasing role in determining what is meant by energy security.

Further reading

Kenneth S. Deffeyes, *Hubbert's Peak: The Impending World Oil Shortage* (Princeton, NJ: Princeton University Press, 2001). An introduction to the problem of world oil production and its imminent decline.

Jan H. Kalicki and David L. Goldwyn (eds), *Energy Security* (Washington, DC: Woodrow Wilson Center Press, 2005). A valuable collection of essays that examine energy security region by region and from a variety of perspectives.

Michael T. Klare, *Blood and Oil: The Dangers and Consequences of America's Growing Dependency on Imported Petroleum* (New York: Metropolitan Books, 2004). An in-depth study of the close relationship between oil dependency and US foreign policy.

International Energy Agency (IEA), *World Energy Outlook* (Paris: IEA, annual). An annual survey of the international energy environment, with in-depth studies of particular current problems and extensive statistical data.

US Department of Energy, Energy Information Administration (USDoE), *International Energy Outlook* (Washington, DC: USDoE, annual). An annual survey of the world's energy demand and supply, with extensive statistical data.

CONCLUSION

WHAT FUTURE FOR SECURITY STUDIES?

CHAPTER 33

What Future for Security Studies?

Stuart Croft

CONTENTS

▊ Abstract

Security studies has been constructed as a subdiscipline of International Relations (IR), but also exists as a transdisciplinary subfield in which disparate research can connect over some common epistemological, methodological and empirical commitments. In this chapter I seek to identify the porous boundaries of both the subdiscipline – with its multiple mainstreams and character – and of the subfield. In so doing, I seek to identify how particular structures that we use to construct our work have themselves been constructed and the underlying patterns of power they reveal; and to examine some of the many locations of work that could and should be of relevance to the future development of security studies.

▊ Introduction: context and scope

Following so many chapters outlining the state of the art of contemporary security studies, a final chapter can take one of a variety of directions. It can look to summarize that which has gone before; it can look to synthesize those arguments into a new whole, or series of wholes; it can develop new and innovative strands of thought; it can review, endorse and reject aspects of the preceding analysis. There are some elements of most of those approaches in that which follows. However, the key focus is in a different area; in thinking through intellectually where we find security studies in the panoply of academic enquiry; and consequently in examining its place in both 'disciplinary' and 'transdisciplinary' locations. Since such locations do not just form 'naturally', I seek to examine some of the power structures that underlie those locations; and then seek to identify some of the key intellectual opportunities that currently exist to develop work in security studies now and in the immediate future. In particular, not only are there issues within the various theories of security studies in motion and under development, but there are also opportunities to engage across the disciplines in looking at new geographical concepts of space and time in relation to security, and in examining the role of memory in the construction of security, insecurity and post-security structures and discourses. I am not seeking here to be comprehensive in this commission; rather to engage the interest in particular directions.

Locating security studies

This volume has demonstrated the breadth and variety of issues and approaches to contemporary security studies. It is and has been a subdiscipline of IR that is and has been constantly contested, and one that repeatedly re-invents itself. Security studies is a subdiscipline that is both embedded within the main discipline of IR, and increasingly also a subfield that is multidisciplinary, in the sense of being driven by the intellectual agendas of disciplines other than IR. It

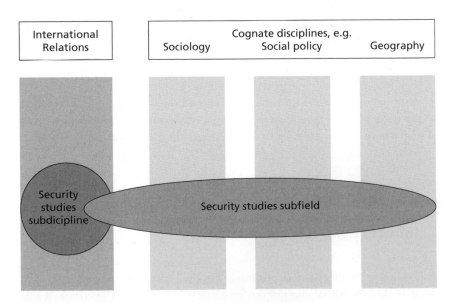

Figure 33.1 Security studies as a subfield and subdiscipline

is also a subdiscipline that ranges in focus from detailed policy prescription for governments, to philosophical statements on the nature of 'reality'.

Security studies has been, overwhelmingly, an American subdiscipline, dominated by a series of major debates (in the sense that they have been frequently cited) between key figures. True, not all of those figures have been American by birth or even by citizenship; there has been a significant European strand. But the size of the American intellectual market has been such that the subdiscipline has been largely one in which North American concerns have been in the ascendancy. One of the stories those in security studies (that is, those who are connected to the discipline of IR) tell about themselves is that it has been a subdiscipline that has 'evolved' in a fairly linear way (for a critique, see Smith 1999). Three steps can be identified in that contemporary narration of the subdiscipline.

The first step is in seeing security studies as having evolved from strategic studies, in which security was defined in a 'narrow' fashion: it was in essence about states, and about the military nature of insecurity. Thus, the myth has developed that security during the Cold War was 'simpler', as something approaching nostalgia for those times has come to be the conventional wisdom in media and other circles, being regularly deployed as a straightforward rhetorical device. Charles Norchi, for instance, wrote in the *New York Times* that 'When the cold war was hot, life seemed simpler', and Ian Thomsen wrote in the *International Herald Tribune* that 'Everything was simpler in the cold war for Americans' (Norchi 1998, Thomsen 1996). Contemporary complexity is defined and legitimized by an evolutionary metaphor: the present must be more complex than the past. Yet the flood of recent re-examinations of the Cold War period by historians would not support such a recasting of it as a period of simplicity (Ambrose 2006, Gaddis 2006, LaFeber 2006, Levering 2005).

The second step in the conventional telling of the security studies story is a period at the end of the Cold War when simplicity gave way to complexity. That complexity abroad – wars in the former Yugoslavia, genocide in Rwanda, stand-off in the Gulf, nuclear weapons development in South Asia – was matched by a debate over the broadening and widening of security studies as a subdiscipline. After a period of contestation, in which realists sought to maintain the 'narrow' definition, now there were to be a variety of referents for security – society, humanity, the individual – as well as the state, and a variety of sectors of security – economic, political, societal, environmental – to go alongside the military (above all see Buzan *et al.* 1998). In addition, scholars fought their own 'Cold War' as first neorealists and neoliberals fought over the meaning of security (largely in the pages of the journal *International Security* – see e.g. Jervis 1999, Waltz 2000), and then constructivists successfully struggled to become part of the (American) scholarly security studies mainstream (see the debate between Mearsheimer (1994/95) and Wendt (1995); see also Copeland 2006).

In the third and current phase of developments in security studies, scholars have sought to come to terms with the terrorist attacks on New York and Washington, DC in September 2001. This has been constructed as marking the new phase of International Relations and international security. Reflecting this new turn, Chris Seiple (2002: 261) argued that 'As in the early Cold War, the next five years are likely to establish patterns of global engagement and international relations that will define the next *fifty* years'. This phase emphasizes the 'newness' of issues in security studies – the novelty of mass/global terrorism, or of religion as a factor in international security. Whereas in the 1990s, the focus was on increasing the numbers of issues that could be considered under the rubric of 'security', those issues had been largely agreed upon from 2001, and in this more recent period there has been an additional and new focus towards terrorism/counter terrorism.

This 'evolution' of the subfield appears relatively natural; but it is of course based on a construction of meanings rather than some form of independent process, in which the power to label issues and approaches as significant has been key to those developments. There has not been an 'evolution' in the sense that theories have become more sophisticated and robust. These self-images of the subdiscipline receive their authority from their repetition and reproduction in texts and in class. Yet, as familiar as this might be as a way of understanding the 'evolution' of the subfield to those who see IR as their main discipline, it does not speak to many others who now consider themselves to be working in that subfield of security studies. It is the case that security studies may now be found in a variety of disciplines. In sociology, where scholars examine the nature of othering and the responsibilities of cosmopolitan commitments; and in the sociology of science, the beliefs and patterns in various elite communities, such as weapons scientists. In social policy and development studies, research is conducted into relations of violence between groups, focusing on giving voice to the silenced. Such anthropological methodology – living with communities, as well as focus groups and other means of gaining insight from those beyond the governing state elite – may also be found in geography and area studies, where scholars investigate local patterns of relations throughout the world. In economics, research into arms trade patterns and probabilities of societies repeating patterns of civil violence may be found; in architecture and urban studies, work has been undertaken into how the physical environment communicates messages and affects patterns of (violent) behaviour among urban communities in specific places, such as Jerusalem. And of course in political science and philosophy, problems of security studies are subjected to normative theorizing, to understand the ethical commitments of various participants.

Security studies is thus now located across a variety of disciplines, although certainly the work emanating from IR still tends to predominate. It represents a vital and fluid series of areas of research, informed by a variety of theoretical and epistemological positions, but one also deeply rooted in contemporary debates about physical and structural (or symbolic) violence. In this context, two particular themes stand out. First, in terms of 'security studies – the subfield', one of the most dynamic areas of multidisciplinary research concerns the relationships of security, culture, images and identity. Second, in terms of 'security studies – the subdiscipline', one of the most significant features of contemporary debate is the split between two forms of theorizing: that contained in the realism/liberalism/constructivism triangle, and the other based in various forms of critical engagement. They are reproduced in two different 'mainstreams' that seem to have few points of contact in the contemporary research debate.

Future directions in the subfield

Security studies has opened up to insights from cognate disciplines in the social sciences, humanities and arts in significant ways. Beginning in the late 1990s, cultural factors became worthy of discussion in the subdiscipline (Katzenstein 1996b, Duffield *et al.* 1999). This 'cultural turn' was initially a relatively 'thin' one, focusing on issues such as strategic culture and organizational culture, and in particular trying from within the discipline of IR to explain key disciplinary problems (if all units are alike, why do behaviours differ markedly?). From there, however, it was a relatively small step to introduce insights from cultural studies, anthropology, literary studies, film studies as well as gender into a 'thicker' cultural conception of security. Or, rather, security issues examined in those and other disciplines were suddenly read as relevant by some scholars who identified with the study of IR. A great deal of such development took place outside the USA, facilitated in particular by the moves to common under-standings across many disciplines facilitated by shared readings of authors that spoke across traditional disciplinary boundaries: Habermas, Adorno, Horkheimer, Foucault, Derrida, Lyotard, Bourdieu. However, as constructivist research centred on the construction of norms, identities and history, the subdiscipline witnessed greater levels of interest in cultural and other factors.

This focus on discourses is of course contested within the discipline of IR. However, it allows analysts to understand how particular policy directions can become the norm at certain times and in certain places; the ways in which cultural practices play central roles in contemporary security studies (see Williams, M. 2007). Issues in international security are not only dealt with by governments. Common understandings are created in, with and through wider society. Popular understandings of policy positions are constructed not only by the statements of leaders and media coverage. Debates about security may be found more widely in the media and popular culture. For example, Eric Lurio wrote a review of *The Last Samurai*, arguing that the film

> is evil. Why? Ideology. The villains are the heroes and the heroes villains. Screenwriters . . . have created a profoundly reactionary and anti-American tale where ancient oppressors are seen as saintly, and those who favor democracy and liberation awful fiends. . . . The sad part is that the film is sooooooo well done that it'll hurt America's international situation by giving aid and comfort to those who long to go back to the days of 1970s Bulgaria.
>
> (Lurio 2006)

Such statements are important in the reproduction of shared understandings of the world across society, legitimizing the commitments of political elites. Not only do cultural representations form a context for political communication within countries, they also do so between states. For example, when the film *300* was released in the USA, it sparked popular fury in Iran. *300* narrates a (largely fictional) version of the Battle of Thermopylae between the Spartans and Persians in 480 BC. Its contemporary relevance was the reading that Persia is Iran; that the historically inaccurate construction of the two enemy societies (the film shows Spartans as free rather than slave-owning, the Persians as slave-owning rather than free . . .) is a means of dehumanizing the new (Iranian) American enemy; that *300* is part of a social campaign, preparing Americans and the West for a real war (Mendelsohn 2007, Moaveni 2007).

Examining cultural representations of security studies is particularly prominent in contemporary research on the 'War on Terror' (see Croft 2006, Martin and Petro 2006). This is part of a new focus on the 'lived' or 'everyday' experience where reflection upon an experience that individuals have undergone constitutes a core element of their understanding of the world. Some lived experience may reveal a great sense of security; arguably it was the sense that everyday security had been breached that co-constituted the powerful social shock of 9/11 in the USA and in other developed countries. As John Lewis Gaddis (2004: 80) put it, 'It was not just the Twin Towers that collapsed on that morning of September 11, 2001: so too did some of our most fundamental assumptions about international, national, and personal security.' The shock to the lived experience of Americans – and not only those in New York and Washington, DC – dramatically inscribed socially a new security reality. Or as M. Shahid Alam put it, 9/11 was like 'an eruption, a volcanic eruption that has thrust lava and ashes from our netherworld, the dark netherworld of the Periphery, into the rich and tranquil landscape of America' (Alam 2004). This is not to argue that the developed world is a Kantian one, and the developing world a Hobbesian one (or that there are variations based on 'Mars' and 'Venus': see Elden and Bialasiewicz 2006). The developed world has its own range of insecurities based on gender, ethnicity and class; processes of actual and of symbolic violence. Rather it is to suggest that shocks to lived experience can in security terms be powerful in reconstituting expectations.

Research that focuses on the lived experience includes that on war crimes tribunals, which rely on the eyewitness testimony of those whose lived experience has involved them in crimes against humanity as victims or as perpetrators (Gow 2003). In a similar vein, important work has been conducted on understanding, for example, how those on the receiving end of peacekeeping missions interact with their 'protectors'. That involves an anthropological commitment to working and living with those communities, both those who live in the country and with the peacekeepers themselves in that country, and to a methodology of conducting fieldwork that allows individuals to speak in their own voice (Higate 2004, Pouligny 2006). The same commitment may be seen by those working with women in political post-conflict communities, allowing groups to speak to security in their own words (Hamber *et al.* 2006). In terms of seeking to mobilize support for a particular cause, organizations seek to include their donors, to inscribe in them an experience (*Live Earth*, for example) that will shape their commitments for the future. It is possible to extend this sense of the lived experience. *Eyes on Darfur*, for example, is an Amnesty International project that uses satellite imagery to show the impact of violence in Sudan on the lives of the people in particular villages under threat (see www.eyesondarfur.org/villages.html). The method is to extend the lived experience from villager to internet user, to bring in more involvement from those not immediately involved in the conflict, but whose involvement can be developed virtually.

These considerations raise in significance the geographical dimension of security studies. At one time, geography and international security were intimately connected, with the study of geopolitics made most famous by Halford Mackinder, who argued in 1904 that the Eurasian 'heartland' could only be offset by a combination of the maritime powers, a theory that connected with the work on seapower by Alfred Mahan. Such traditional geopolitics still has its advocates in contemporary strategic studies, but in parallel, a new focus in geography has developed in critical geopolitics (Ó Tuathail 1996). In this light, acts of representation and modes of narration, based on and mutually constituted by geopolitical cultures, becomes central. Here, geographical knowledge is deployed and reformulated in the interests of furthering particular political projects (Bialasiewicz *et al.* 2007). Gearóid Ó Tuathail (2000) has written of the 'Postmodern Geopolitical Condition' and here the work on critical geopolitics intersects with a wider subfield in geography, that which is known as postmodern geography. In that wider subfield, subjectivity, identity, representation and practice are key. Nigel Thrift gives full expression to this in a discussion of 'Space' which is seen to have four characteristics: that everything is spatially distributed, everything has 'its own geography'; that there are no boundaries, that all spaces are porous; all spaces are in constant motion; and that 'there is no one kind of space' (Thrift 2006: 140–141). If spatiality is not fixed (and as a consequence, Thrift argues against the view 'space [is] somehow separated from time'), the implications for thinking about the nature of security studies are profound.

Security studies, at its core, is concerned with a level of reality about which there is no epistemological argument. The collapse of security leads to real violence against real people, to acts of brutality that lie without any discussions of relativism. Powerful stories of loss are global in their reach. Of the numerous potent tales, the Kigali Memorial Centre, which commemorates those lost in the Rwandan genocide, holds many.[1] These histories, perhaps particularly those of whom we learn in the children's room, are unbearable. We see photographs of the murdered, and in so doing learn of Uwase, a 2-year-old whose favourite toy was her doll, who loved rice and chips, and whose best friend was her daddy. She was killed by being smashed against a wall. And then there was David Mugiraneza, a 10-year-old boy who loved football and wanted to be a doctor. He was killed by being tortured to death. When we debate security studies we should remember Uwase; we should remember David.

Questions of political violence have never been the monopoly of IR, or indeed of the discipline/combined disciplines of political science and IR. The 'construction of the Holocaust as the central event of the twentieth century' (Kansteiner 2004: 193) has had many political and ethical consequences. One is that it is hard to find any self-defined discipline in the social sciences, arts and humanities that has not at some level engaged with the Holocaust and, therefore, with that and other issues of political violence. Perhaps, as discourses of justice, ethics, responsibility, revulsion and indeed revenge have developed following events such as the Rwandan genocide, the Yugoslav wars, the 'War on Terror' and the violence in Darfur (to name but a few), issues of war and violence have become increasingly and more deeply examined by other disciplines. As IR becomes more open to other disciplines, it is clear that important new avenues of research are opening up. For example, the growth in memory studies provides opportunities for developing studies looking at the means by which memory issues affect security (from within the subdiscipline, a key text of this is Edkins 2003). Indeed, it could be argued that memory is crucial in the construction of a sense of belonging, of where we come from and where we are going, that it is at the heart of all identity debates and, as such, that it should be at the heart of security studies.[2] (This is not to argue that memory is objectively created; there are processes of the social construction of memory.) There has been a 'memory boom' in so many disciplines across the social sciences and the humanities (Huyssen 1994); it will inevitably interconnect with work on security studies. The role of memory in questions of political violence can connect those in IR with colleagues in literary studies, psychology, sociology, media studies, and a range of other disciplines. But in so doing, scholars need to take care with regard to deeply engrained arguments that exist in and between different disciplines over core concepts. For example, is trauma and its consequences – victimhood and entitlement – part of the everyday experience of human communication? Or does trauma imply 'the occurrence of some serious real or imagined injury with long-term psychological, political and moral consequences' (Kansteiner 2004)? These issues may seem some distance from international security; but given that the key 'case' surrounding such debates is the Holocaust, it is clear that they are not.

There is, then, an ongoing process of developing security studies as a subfield, in a multidisciplinary fashion. Of course, for many years that has already been the case, in particular under the rubric of area studies. In the future, many sites of such transdisciplinary cooperation seem possible; with perhaps the organizing devices of spatiality and memory providing the most immediate, and the commitment to researching the lived experience of those affected by (in)securities.

Future directions in the subdiscipline

There will be many in the IR subdiscipline of security studies who will simply see much of the above discussion as being irrelevant to them; that issues of space (including time) and memory are simply not matters of international security. For such colleagues, disciplinary power is the key, and that disciplinary power resides in the academic mainstream. Much of that mainstream is defined in, through and by the American intellectual market; what can be published in the mainstream US journals and academic publishing houses, and therefore what is likely to sell to the mass audience courses in American universities. Thus, a scholar outside North America is likely to be asked by a possible book publisher to consider how his or her volume might be seen to be attractive in that US marketplace. It is an economic (but also socially constructed) 'reality'. And so a mainstream is constructed towards which scholarship must be oriented to count as being at the heart of a discipline. A discipline, subdiscipline or subfield is, of course, itself socially constructed, as are the main components of each, and as are those texts that are seen to be central to the definition of that intellectual terrain. In this way, that which is seen to be 'core' or 'mainstream' security studies is driven by social factors.

In terms of the subdisciplinary mainstream, then, it is clear that one future avenue lies with the development of particular projects. That mainstream is not and never has been static; it is always in motion. Thus, contemporary research considers the International Relations of neoconservatism (Nuruzzaman 2006); or develops particular nuances on existing theoretical frames, for example, the development of 'offensive realism' (Mearsheimer 2001). As well as developing nuances and incremental alterations in particular theoretical veins, the mainstream has and is likely to continue to be shaped by 'great debates'. There is a long history of how many 'great debates' there have been in IR scholarship – it is one of the self-images of the discipline. In terms of the security studies mainstream, we have seen a great debate in the 1990s between realism and liberalism; and then a great debate in which realism and liberalism (the 'neo-neo' synthesis) debated whether constructivism could be part of that mainstream (or, rather, what form of constructivism could be seen to be recognized as such). Famously, the Fiftieth Anniversary edition of *International Organization* contained an editorial in which constructivism was legitimized as a part of IR (even in its 'critical' guise), but postmodernism was not. As Katzenstein *et al.* (1998: 678) asserted, in 'contrast to conventional and critical constructivism, postmodernism falls clearly outside of the social science enterprise, and in international relations research it risks becoming self-referential and disengaged from the world, protests to the contrary notwithstanding'. One of the functions of the widely cited 'Seizing the middle ground: constructivism in world politics' (Adler 1997) was to distinguish constructivism from the (unacceptable) postmodernist turn in IR, thus making constructivism's entry into the (American) mainstream easier. One of the functions of Wendt's *Social Theory of International Politics* was to consolidate a methodological legitimacy (in the eyes of the US mainstream) for constructivism (Wendt 1999). Realist acceptance came with Stephen Walt's 'International

Relations: one world, many theories' article, which included a graphic showing the three pillars of the International Relations/international security house to be realism, liberalism and constructivism (Walt 1998: 38). That, then, creates a new 'neo/neo/neo' synthesis in some ways, in terms of a mainstream that is self-referential and acts to exclude other modes of thought. Perhaps the nuances of those positions will be battled out in the future over which theory can most adequately explain the importance of religion/religious forces in world politics and security studies.

The mainstream is always in motion both in terms of the developments of individual theoretical streams and in terms of the patterns of contestation between different theories. However, in constituting a mainstream, it creates boundaries between it and the 'non-mainstream'. Following Thrift, we should not overemphasize the solidity of these boundaries; there is a porosity which allows for interaction. But this distinction between the mainstream and that outside is constituted in a variety of ways; an article may be written for *International Security* or for *Security Dialogue*; it is unlikely that there is a piece that could without amendment straddle both. The nature of security studies panels is very different at the *American Political Science Association* conference in relation to the *Standing Group on International Relations of the European Consortium on Political Research* conference. And so on. Security studies continues to operate in different ways inside and outside American circles (see most famously on this Wæver 1998).

One way in which there is some porosity between the mainstream and that outside is where particular ideas/schools/writers are taken up outside their defined territory. Thus it would be quite normal for American scholars, or American journals, to refer to securitization theory/the Copenhagen School/ Ole Wæver. Awareness, however, does not constitute acceptance in the mainstream. However, if we are to consider another 'mainstream' – that outside the USA – it is very clear that securitization theory/the Copenhagen School/ Ole Wæver is about as mainstream as it is possible to get. Thus, the sub-discipline of security studies is overlaid with many mainstreams: differently global, differently regional and sometimes differently national, with porosity between all.

The non-American English-language subdiscipline of security studies comprises a mainstream of four distinctive theoretical constructs. (I am here resisting the temptation to describe this as the 'European mainstream', but will shortly give ground to that.) Each seeks to be 'critical' in some form. Thus, we have a 'critical quadrangle' of the Copenhagen School; the Welsh School; the Paris School; and the human security school. Intriguingly from a critical geopolitics perspective, most seek to attach a geographical label except for 'human security'. On the one hand, this labelling refers simply to where sets of ideas were generated: in debates in Copenhagen, Aberystwyth and Paris respectively. It also covers each with some of the reflected legitimacy of the labelling of the 'English School' of IR (recalling that many in that school were not English). It also marks each as being critical in the sense of being non-American in origin and nature (see Van Munster 2007).

The 'critical quadrangle' comprises four theoretical perspectives each with one key 'brand' in terms of the intellectual debate. For the Copenhagen School, the brand is securitization (see Chapter 5, this volume).[3] This focuses on a specific rhetorical structure, in which an issue is identified as threatening survival, requiring a response to be urgent, outside of the norm, and that the 'audience' has to be convinced. In such an approach, existential threats, and thus securitizing moves, may be found in sectors other than the military. Hence the Copenhagen School focuses on the politics of the exception. The Paris School in contrast focuses on the politics of unease, on the ordinary rather than the exceptional in policy practice (see Chapter 9, this volume). Here the brand is insecuritization (insécurisation), a process by which elites and government authority lower the threshold of acceptability of others; a means by which external threat and internal life are connected through policies over terror and migration, enacted by the police, border officials and judiciary; where a variety of discourses are connected into a patchwork of insecurities allowing the transfer of practices from one policy frame to another (Bigo 1995, 2005). For the Welsh School, as Ken Booth first stated powerfully 15 years ago, the leitmotif is emancipation; indeed, security is emancipation (Booth 1991a, Chapter 7, this volume). Emancipation is therefore the goal of security practice (Booth 2005c). Rather than stressing the role of speech acts or the role of state agencies, securitization or insecuritization, the Welsh School would place individuals at the centre of security studies. Finally, there is a fragmented body of literature committed to achieving 'human security' (Newman 2001, Chapter 16, this volume). Perhaps the very fragmentation of that work has been a result of the lack of a geographical signifier, allowing greater access to the use of the term than is the case with 'Copenhagen', 'Welsh' or 'Paris'. Rather like the Welsh School, though, the commitment is to the individual level of security, and so perhaps the term that best sums up the 'brand' of the human security school is 'humanization'.

So here are the four brand concepts of the 'critical quadrangle': securitization; insecuritization; emancipation; and humanization.[4] There is often a determination to identify this 'critical quadrangle' in contradistinction to American thought, and in some ways as a contribution to the construction of a European mode of thinking (CASE Collective 2006). But of course such ideas as those discussed here may be found in other parts of the non-European but English-speaking world, notably in Australia and, in terms of human security, Canada. Rather like the 'other' 'American' mainstream, the 'critical quadrangle' mainstream is also dominated by two different forms of theoretical development. Each of the four theories has scholars engaged in the development of the particular theoretical perspectives themselves. In addition, a new literature is emerging in which 'bridges' between the four are identified and explored (e.g. Browning and McDonald 2007, Floyd 2007).

Perhaps one of the key distinguishing features, however, of the 'critical quadrangle' in relation to the 'American' mainstream is scale. There are enormous numbers of scholars who would see themselves as contributing to the US mainstream; many in terms of theoretical development, many more as 'technicians', implementing a template from one of the theoretical perspectives in relation to a particular case study. In contrast, the number of scholars in the Copenhagen, Welsh or Paris schools is far fewer. In part this reflects the size of the 'IR industry' in North America in relation to others; in part it reflects the exclusionary dimension of a geographical label (if I am not based in department x in city/town y, can I really be a part of the school? What is the mechanism of being included?). And perhaps partly it reflects the relative unwillingness of scholars in Europe to site themselves in particular intellectual spaces. In addition, one of the key distinctions between these two particular mainstreams is that the one labelled 'American' tends to emphasize methodology, while that which sometimes labels itself 'European' demonstrates a greater interest in epistemology.

Security studies, porous boundaries, and the struggle for coherence

There are many directions to the future of security studies. Some will be within the subdiscipline, within particular theories, and as scholars seek to understand and construct intellectual linkages between theories. As well as development within the subdiscipline, there will undoubtedly continue to be linkages between the subdiscipline and other disciplines, as the subfield of security studies continues with processes of connection. These boundaries are of course all constructs, and as such can and will be reconstituted. We seek to encapsulate sets of ideas through labels and categories – as I have in this chapter – when there is so much porosity, so much fluidity, and so much contestation between those ideas and their advocates. The desire to impose order on this is evident in this volume. Indeed, this is a recurrent theme in security studies – the production of volumes that seek to encapsulate the intellectual range of work that may be described as 'security studies'. This book stands as one contribution. The *International Studies Association*'s 'Compendium' project seeks to impose some form of order on all the subfields of IR, with a series of volumes – including one on security studies – to be produced from 2008 onward. There have been a variety of other examples over the years (e.g. Collins 2007, Terriff *et al.* 1999). This desire for codification is in part driven by teaching needs: if we are not able to set some boundaries around security studies, how might we teach it? And yet, again following Thrift, this is a process that can at best only provide a snapshot of thinking and research at a particular point in space and time. That which comprises security studies is always in motion in space – within the 'American' and 'European' mainstreams, and between those and other 'places' of research – and time, as issues rise and fall in importance in academic, policy and public discourses, demanding or resisting attention. And the boundaries between security studies and other areas are always porous, thus allowing the construction of new forms of thinking about these issues; or at least in allowing that sense of 'newness' to be shared by a number of like-minded researchers. Security – as with so many social concepts – is an essentially contested concept (Buzan 1991: 7). Perhaps, then, we should embrace the fluidity of debate, and worry less about the importance of encapsulating the social reality of security studies.

Notes

1   Thanks to Paul Jackson for drawing this museum to my attention; see www.kigalimemorialcentre.org/.
2   I am grateful to Matt McDonald and Chris Browning for this point.
3   It is true to say that the Copenhagen School has three main theoretical ideas: securitization, sectors, and regional security complexes – but securitization is the one with the highest profile.
4   I have greatly benefited from conversations with Rita Floyd in thinking about this section.

BIBLIOGRAPHY

Abraham, Itty (1998), *The Making of the Indian Atomic Bomb: Science, Secrecy and the Postcolonial State* (London: Zed Books).

Abraham, Itty (1999), 'Nuclear power and human security', *Bulletin of Concerned Asian Scholars*, 31(2): 10–13.

Abramovitz, Janet N. (2001), *Unnatural Disasters* (Washington, DC: Worldwatch Institute: Worldwatch Paper No. 169).

Acharya, Amitav (2000), *The Quest for Identity. International Relations of Southeast Asia* (Oxford: Oxford University Press).

Acharya, Amitav (2001), 'Human security: East versus West', *International Journal*, LVI(3): 442–460.

Adelman, Howard (2001), 'From refugees to forced migration: the UNHCR and human security', *International Migration Review*, 35(1): 7–32.

Adler, Emanuel (1997), 'Seizing the middle ground: constructivism in world politics', *European Journal of International Relations*, 3(3): 319–363.

Adler, Emanuel and Michael Barnett (eds) (1998), *Security Communities* (Cambridge: Cambridge University Press).

African Union (AU) (2005), 'Common African position on the proposed reform of the United Nations', AU Executive Council, Ext/EX.CL/2(VII), 7–8 March.

Alam, M. Shahid (2004), 'Making sense of our times: is there an Islamic problem?', *The Electronic Intifada*, 14 October: http://electronicintifada.net/cgi-bin/artman/exec/view.cgi/10/3231.

Albright, David and Corey Hinderstein (2005), 'Unravelling the A. Q. Khan and future proliferation networks', *The Washington Quarterly*, 28(2): 111–128.

Alexander, Martin S. and J.F.V. Keiger (2002), 'France and the Algerian War: strategy, operations and diplomacy', *Journal of Strategic Studies*, 25(2): 1–33.

Alker, Hayward (2005), 'Emancipation in the critical security studies project' in Booth (ed.) (2005c), pp. 189–213.

Alkire, Sabina (2002), 'Conceptual framework for the Commission on Human Security': www.humansecurity-chs.org/doc/frame.html.

Allison, Graham (2000), 'The impact of globalization on national and international security' in J.S. Nye and J.D. Donahue (eds), *Governance in a Globalizing World* (Washington, DC: Brookings Institution Press), pp. 72–85.

Allison, Graham (2006), 'Nuclear 9/11: the ongoing failure of imagination', *Bulletin of Atomic Scientists*, 62(5): 34–41.

Allison, Roy (ed.) (2004), 'Regionalism and the changing international order in Central Eurasia', Special Issue, *International Affairs*, 80(3).

Almqvist, Jessica (2005), 'A peacebuilding commission for the United Nations', *Fundacion par alas Relaciones Internacionales y el Dialogo Exterior* (Policy Paper no. 4).

Alston, Philip (ed.) (1992), *The United Nations and Human Rights: A Critical Appraisal* (Oxford: Oxford University Press).

Ambrose, Stephen E. *et al.* (2006), *The Cold War: A Military History* (New York: Random House).

Anand, Chaiwat S. (1990), 'The nonviolent crescent: eight theses on Muslim nonviolent action' in Ralph E. Crow, Philip Grant and Saad E. Ibrahim (eds), *Arab Nonviolent Political Struggle in the Middle East* (Boulder, CO: Lynne Rienner), pp. 25–40.

Andreas, Peter (2003), 'Redrawing borders and security in the 21st century', *International Security*, 28(2): 78–111.

Andrews-Speed, Philip, Xuanli Liao and Roland Dannreuther (2002), *The Strategic Implications of China's Energy Needs* (Oxford: Oxford University Press for the IISS, Adelphi Paper No. 346).

Annan, Kofi (1997), *Renewing the United Nations: A Programme for Reform* (New York: United Nations).

Annan, Kofi (1999a), 'The relevance of the U.N. Security Council', in *Vital Speeches of the Day*, 15 June 1999, Vol. 65, Issue 17.

Annan, Kofi (1999b), *Annual Report of the Secretary-General to the United Nations General Assembly* (UN doc. A/54/429).

Annan, Kofi (1999c), *The Question of Intervention: Statements by the Secretary-General* (New York: UN).

Annan, Kofi (2001), *Prevention of Armed Conflict: Report of the Secretary-General* (UN doc. A/55/985-S/2001/574).

Annan, Kofi (2005), *In Larger Freedom: Towards Development, Security and Human Rights for All* (New York: UN General Assembly paper A/59/2005/0527078).

Anthony, Ian (1989), 'The trade in major conventional weapons', in *SIPRI Yearbook 1989: World Armaments and Disarmament* (Oxford: SIPRI/Oxford University Press), pp. 195–210.

Aron, Raymond (1978), 'War and industrial society: a reappraisal', *Millennium*, 7(3): 195–210.

Ashdown, Lord Paddy (2007), 'Interview: The European Union and statebuilding in the Western Balkans', *Journal of Intervention and Statebuilding*, 1(1): 107–118.

Ashley, Richard K. and R.B.J. Walker (1991), 'Reading dissidence/writing the discipline: crisis and the question of sovereignty in international studies', *International Studies Quarterly*, 34(3): 367–416.

Austin, J.L. (1975), *How to Do Things with Words* (Oxford: Clarendon Press, 2nd edn).

Avant, Deborah (2005), *The Market for Force: The Consequences of Privatizing Security* (Cambridge: Cambridge University Press).

Axelrod, Robert (1984), *The Evolution of Cooperation* (New York: Basic Books).

Axworthy, Lloyd (2001), 'Human security and global governance: putting people first', *Global Governance*, 7(1): 19–23.

Aylwin-Foster, Brigadier Nigel (2005), 'Changing the army for counterinsurgency', *Military Review*, November–December: 2–15.

Ayoob, Mohammed (1995), *The Third World Security Predicament* (Boulder, CO: Lynne Rienner).

Bailey, Syndey and Sam Daws (1998), *The Procedure of the UN Security Council* (Oxford: Clarendon Press, 3rd edn).

Baldwin, David A. (ed.) (1993), *Neorealism and Neoliberalism: The Contemporary Debate* (New York: Columbia University Press).

Ball, Nicole (2001), 'Human security and human development: linkages and opportunities'. Report of a conference organized by the Programme for Strategic and International Studies, Graduate Institute of International Studies, Geneva, 8–9 March.

Balzacq, Thierry (2005), 'The three faces of securitization', *European Journal of International Relations*, 11(2): 171–201.

Banks, Jeffrey S. (1990), 'Equilibrium behavior in crisis bargaining games', *American Journal of Political Science*, 34(3): 599–614.

Barash, David P. (ed.) (2000), *Approaches to Peace: A Reader in Peace Studies* (Oxford: Oxford University Press).

Barash, David P. and Charles P. Webel (2002), *Peace and Conflict Studies* (Thousand Oaks, CA: Sage).

Barkawi, Tarak (2004), 'On the pedagogy of "small wars"', *International Affairs*, 80(1): 19–38.

Barkawi, Tarak (2006), *Globalization and War* (Lanham, MD: Rowman & Littlefield).

Barkawi, Tarak and Mark Laffey (eds) (2001), *Democracy, Liberalism and War: Rethinking the Democratic Peace Debate* (Boulder CO: Lynne Rienner).

Barkawi, Tarak and Mark Laffey (2006), 'The post-colonial moment in security studies', *Review of International Studies*, 32(2): 329–352.

Barnaby, Frank (2004), *How to Build A Nuclear Bomb: And Other Weapons of Mass Destruction* (New York: Nation Books).

Barnett, Michael (1998), *Dialogues in Arab Politics. Negotiations in Regional Order* (New York: Columbia University Press).

Barnett, Michael (1999), 'Culture, strategy and foreign policy change', *European Journal of International Relations*, 5(1): 5–36.

Barnett, Michael (2006), 'Building a republican peace', *International Security*, 30(4): 57–112.

Barnett, Michael and Jack Levy (1991), 'Domestic sources of alliances and alignments', *International Organization*, 45(3): 369–395.

Barnett, Michael and Martha Finnemore (1999), 'The politics, power, and pathologies of international organizations', *International Organization*, 53(4): 699–732.

Barnett, Michael and Martha Finnemore (2004), *Rules for the World: International Organizations in Global Politics* (Ithaca, NY: Cornell University Press).

Barnett, Michael and Robert Duvall (eds) (2005), *Power in Global Governance* (Cambridge: Cambridge University Press).

Barnett, Tony and Gwyn Prins (2006), 'HIV/AIDS and security', *International Affairs*, 82(2): 359–368.

Bayart, Jean-François (2005), *The Illusion of Cultural Identity* (Chicago, IL: Chicago University Press).

BBC (2006), 'Muslim convert who plotted terror', 7 November: http://news.bbc.co.uk/go/pr/fr/-/1/hi/uk/6121084.stm.

BBC (2007), 'Trident plan wins Commons support', 15 March: http://news.bbc.co.uk/2/hi/uk_news/politics/6448173.stm.

Beaulac, Stephane (2004), *The Power of Language in the Making of International Law: The Word Sovereignty in Bodin and Vattel and the Myth of Westphalia* (Boston, MA: Martinus Nijhoff).

Bellamy, Alex J. (2006), 'Whither the responsibility to protect? Humanitarian intervention and the 2005 World Summit', *Ethics and International Affairs*, 20(2): 143–169.

Bellamy, Alex J. and Paul D. Williams (2005), 'Who's keeping the peace? Regionalization and contemporary peace operations', *International Security*, 29(4): 157–195.

Bellamy, Alex J. and Nicholas J. Wheeler (2007), 'Humanitarian intervention in world politics' in John Baylis and Steve Smith (eds), *The Globalization of World Politics* (Oxford: Oxford University Press, 4th edn), pp. 522–539.

Bellamy, Alex J. and Paul D. Williams (2007), 'Peace operations' in Sandra Cheldelin, Daniel Druckman and Larissa Fast (eds), *Conflict* (New York: Continuum, 2nd edn), pp. 330–354.

Bellamy, Alex J., Paul D. Williams and Stuart Griffin (2004), *Understanding Peacekeeping* (Cambridge: Polity Press).

Bennett, D.S. (1996), 'Testing alternative models of alliance duration, 1816–1984', *American Journal of Political Science*, 41(3): 846–878.

Bennett, John T. (2007), 'A procurement "time bomb": building U.S. end strength leaves less money for arms', *Defense News*, 12 February, pp. 1 and 8.

Berdal, Mats (2001), 'Lessons not learned: the use of force in "peace operations" in the 1990s', in Adekeye Adebajo and Chandra Lekha Sriram (eds), *Managing Armed Conflicts in the 21st Century* (London: Frank Cass), pp. 55–74.

Berdal, Mats (2003), 'How "new" are "new wars"? Global economic change and the study of civil war', *Global Governance*, 9(4): 477–502.

Bialasiewicz, Luiza, David Campbell, Stuart Elden, Stephen Graham, Alex Jeffrey and Alison J. Williams (2007), 'Performing security: the imaginative geographies of current US strategy', *Political Geography*, 26(4): 405–422.

Bienefeld, Manfred (1995), 'Assessing current development trends: reflections on Keith Griffin's "Global prospects for development and human society [sic]"', *Canadian Journal of Development Studies*, XVI(3): 371–384.

Bigo, Didier (1995), 'Grands Débats dans un Petit Monde: les débats en relations internationales et leur lien avec le monde de la sécurité', *Cultures et Conflits*, 19–20: www.conflits.org/document872.html.

Bigo, Didier (1996), *Polices en réseaux: l'expérience européenne* (Paris: Presses de la Fondation nationale des sciences politiques).

Bigo, Didier (1998), 'L'Europe de la sécurité intérieure' in Anne Marie Le Gloannec (ed.), *Entre Union et Nations: L'Etat en Europe* (Paris: Presse de Sciences Po), pp. 55–90.

Bigo, Didier (2002), 'Security and immigration: toward a critique of the governmentality of unease', *Alternatives*, 27(Supplement): 63–92.

Bigo, Didier (2005), 'La mondialisation de l'(in)sécurité? Réflexions sur le champ des professionnels de la gestion des inquiétudes et analytique de la transnationalisation des processus d'(in)sécurisation', *Cultures et Conflits*, 58: www.conflits.org/document 1813.html.

Bigo, Didier (2006), 'Liberty, whose liberty? The Hague Programme and the conception of freedom' in Thierry Balzacq and Sergio Carrera (eds), *Security versus Freedom? A Challenge for Europe's Future* (London: Ashgate), pp. 35–45.

Bigo, Didier and R.B.J. Walker (2007a), 'Political sociology and the problem of the international', *Millennium*, 35(3): 725–739.

Bigo, Didier and R.B.J. Walker (2007b), 'International, political, sociology', *International Political Sociology*, 1(1): 1–5.

Bigo, Didier, Sergio Carrera, Elspeth Guild and R.B.J. Walker (2007a), *The Changing Landscape of European Liberty and Security: Mid-term Report on the Results of the CHALLENGE Project* (Research Paper No.4).

Bigo, Didier, Laurent Bonelli, Emmanuel Guittet, Christian Olsson and Anastassia Tsoukala (2007b), *Illiberal Practices of Liberal Regimes: The (In)security Games* (London: Routledge, Challenge Series).

Bilgin, Pinar (2002), 'Beyond statism in security studies? Human agency and security in the Middle East', *Review of International Affairs*, 2(1): 100–118.

Bilgin, Pinar (2004), 'Whose Middle East? Geopolitical inventions and practices of security', *International Relations*, 18(1): 17–33.

Bilgin, Pinar (2005), *Regional Security in the Middle East: A Critical Perspective* (New York: Routledge).

Bilgin, Pinar and Adam David Morton (2002), 'Historicising representations of "failed states": beyond the Cold War annexation of the social sciences?', *Third World Quarterly*, 23(1): 55–80.

Bilgin, Pinar and Adam David Morton (2004), 'From "rogue" to "failed" states? The fallacy of short-termism', *Politics*, 24(3): 169–180.

Bilgin, Pinar, Ken Booth and Richard Wyn Jones (1998), 'Security studies: the next stage?', *Naçao e Defesa*, 84(2): 129–157.

Blair, Bruce and Chen Yali (2006), 'The fallacy of nuclear primacy', *China Security*, Washington, DC: World Security Institute.

Blair, Tony (2006) 'Trident', *Hansard* [21], 4 December: www.publications.parliament.uk.

Blechman, Barry M. and Janne E. Nolan (1987), *The U.S.–Soviet Arms Transfer Negotiations* (Washington, DC: FPI Case Study No. 3, Foreign Policy Institute, SAIS, Johns Hopkins University).

Blyth, Mark (2002), *Great Transformations: Economic Ideas and Institutional Change in the Twentieth Century* (Cambridge: Cambridge University Press).

Booth, Ken (1979), *Strategy and Ethnocentrism* (London: Croom Helm).

Booth, Ken (1991a), 'Security and emancipation', *Review of International Studies*, 17(4): 313–326.

Booth, Ken (1991b), 'Security in anarchy: utopian realism in theory and practice', *International Affairs*, 67(3): 527–545.

Booth, Ken (1995), 'Human wrongs and International Relations', *International Affairs*, 71(1): 103–126.

Booth, Ken (1997), 'Security and self: reflections of a fallen realist' in Keith Krause and Michael C. Williams (eds), *Critical Security Studies: Concepts and Cases* (London: UCL Press), pp. 83–119.

Booth, Ken (1999a), 'Nuclearism, human rights and constructions of security (Part 1)', *International Journal of Human Rights*, 3(2): 1–24.

Booth, Ken (1999b), 'Nuclearism, human rights and constructions of security (Part 2)', *International Journal of Human Rights*, 3(3): 44–61.

Booth, Ken (ed.) (2000), *The Kosovo Tragedy: The Human Rights Dimensions* (London: Routledge).

Booth, Ken (2005a), 'Critical explorations' in Ken Booth (ed.), *Critical Security Studies and World Politics* (Boulder, CO: Lynne Rienner), pp. 1–25.

Booth, Ken (2005b), 'Offensive realists, tolerant realists and real realists', *International Relations*, 19(3): 350–354.

Booth, Ken (2005c), 'Morgenthau's realisms and transatlantic truth' in C. Hacke, G.K. Kindermann and K.M. Schellhorn (eds), *The Heritage, Challenge, and Future of Realism* (Göttingen: Bonn University Press), pp. 99–129.

Booth, Ken (ed.) (2005d), *Critical Security Studies and World Politics* (Boulder, CO: Lynne Rienner).

Booth, Ken (2007), *Theory of World Security* (Cambridge: Cambridge University Press).

Booth, Ken and Peter Vale (1995), 'Security in Southern Africa: after apartheid, beyond realism', *International Affairs*, 71(2): 285–304.

Booth, Ken and Peter Vale (1997), 'Critical security studies and regional insecurity: the case of Southern Africa' in Keith Krause and Michael C. Williams (eds), *Critical Security Studies: Concepts and Cases* (London: UCL Press), pp. 329–358.

Booth, Ken and Nicholas J. Wheeler (2008), *The Security Dilemma: Fear, Cooperation and Trust in World Politics* (London: Palgrave Macmillan).

Boulden, Jane and Thomas G. Weiss (eds) (2004), *Terrorism and the UN: Before and After September 11* (Bloomington: Indiana University Press).

Boulding, Kenneth (1970), 'Limits or boundaries of peace research', *International Peace Research Association Proceedings, 3rd General Conference Volume 1* (Assen: Van Gorcum), pp. 5–19.

Boulding, Kenneth (1979), *Stable Peace* (Austin, TX: University of Texas Press).

Bourdieu, Pierre and John B. Thompson (1991), *Language and Symbolic Power* (Cambridge, MA: Harvard University Press).

Bourne, John (2005), 'Total War 1: The Great War' in Townshend (ed.) (2005), pp. 117–137.

Boutros-Ghali, Boutros (1992), *An Agenda for Peace – Preventive Diplomacy, Peacemaking and Peacekeeping* (New York: United Nations).

Boutwell, Jeffrey, Michael T. Klare and Laura Reed (eds) (1995), *Lethal Commerce: The Global Trade in Small Arms and Light Weapons* (Cambridge, MA: American Academy of Arts and Sciences).

Bowman, Marion E. "Spike" (2007), 'Privatizing while transforming', *Defense Horizons*, 57 (July): www.ndu.edu/ctnsp/defense_horizons.htm.

BP (2006), *BP Statistical Review of World Energy 2006* (London: BP).

Brahimi Report (2000), *Report of the Panel on United Nations Peace Operations* (New York: UN Document A/55/305 S/2000/809, 21 August).

Brams, Steven J. (2002), 'Game theory in practice: problems and prospects in applying it to International Relations' in Frank P. Harvey and Michael Brecher (eds), *Evaluating Methodology in International Studies* (Ann Arbor, MI: University of Michigan Press), pp. 81–96.

Brams, Steven J. and D. Marc Kilgour (1988), *Game Theory and National Security* (New York: Blackwell).

Brass, Paul R. (1997), *Theft of an Idol: Text and Context in the Representation of Collective Violence* (Princeton, NJ: Princeton University Press).

Broad, William J. and David E. Sanger (2004), 'Pakistani's nuclear earnings: $100 million', *New York Times*, 16 March.

Broad, William J., David E. Sanger and Raymond Bonner (2004), 'How Pakistani's network offered the whole kit', *International Herald Tribune*, 13 February.

Brooks, Doug (2000), 'Write a cheque, end a war', *Conflict Trends*, 6.

Brooks, Doug (2003), 'Help for beleaguered peacekeepers', *Washington Post*, 2 June, p. A17.

Brown, Ben (2004), 'Reporting from Camp Dogwood', *BBC World Service News*, 11 March.

Brown, Chris (1992), 'Really existing liberalism and international order', *Millennium*, 21(3): 313–328.

Brown, M. E. (2007), 'New global dangers' in Chester Crocker, Fen Osler Hampson and Pamela Aall (eds), *Leashing the Dogs of War* (Washington, DC: USIP Press), pp. 39–51.

Brown, M.E., S. Lynn-Jones and S. Miller (eds) (1996), *Debating the Democratic Peace* (Cambridge, MA: MIT Press).

Brown, Seyom (1996), *International Relations in a Changing Global System* (Boulder, CO: Westview Press).

Browning, Chris and Matt McDonald (2007), 'Securitisation and emancipation', paper presented at the 48th ISA Annual Convention, Chicago, February/March.

Brundtland, Gro Harlem (1999), 'Why investing in global health is good politics', speech to the Council on Foreign Relations, 6 December: www.who.int/director-general/speeches/1999/english/19991206_new_york.html.

Buckley, Neil (2005), 'Moscow seeks to wield petropower as political tool', *Financial Times*, 23 December.

Bueno de Mesquita, Bruce (2002), 'Accomplishments and limitations of a game-theoretic approach to International Relations' in Frank P. Harvey and Michael Brecher (eds), *Evaluating Methodology in International Studies* (Ann Arbor, MI: University of Michigan Press), pp. 59–80.

Bueno de Mesquita, Bruce and David Lalman (1992), *War and Reason: A Confrontation Between Domestic and International Imperatives* (New Haven, CT: Yale University Press).

Bueno de Mesquita, Ethan (2005), 'The terrorist endgame: a model with moral hazard and learning', *Journal of Conflict Resolution*, 49(2): 237–258.

Bukovansky, Mlada (2002) *Legitimacy and Power Politics: The American and French Revolutions in International Political Culture* (Princeton, NJ: Princeton University Press).

Bull, Hedley (1977), *The Anarchical Society: A Study of Order in World Politics* (London: Macmillan).

Bush, George (1992), Address to McDonnell Douglas employees, Lambert Field, St Louis, Missouri, 11 September.

Bush, George W. (2001), 'Energy security', 2 March, www.whitehouse.gov.

Bush, George W. (2002), 'President Signs Public Health Security and Bioterrorism Bill', Remarks by the US President at Signing of H.R. 3448, the Public Health Security and Bioterrorism Response Act of 2002, Washington, DC, June.

Butterfield, Herbert (1951), *History and Human Relations* (London: Collins).

Butterfield, Herbert (1953), *Christianity, Diplomacy and War* (London: Epworth Press).

Buzan, Barry (1983), *People, States and Fear: The National Security Problem in International Relations* (Brighton: Wheatsheaf).

Buzan, Barry (1987), *An Introduction to Strategic Studies: Military Technology and International Relations* (London: Macmillan).

Buzan, Barry (1991), *People, States and Fear: An Agenda for International Security Studies in the Post-Cold War Era* (London: Harvester Wheatsheaf, 2nd edn).

Buzan, Barry (1995), 'The level of analysis problem in International Relations reconsidered' in Ken Booth and Steve Smith (eds), *International Relations Theory Today* (Cambridge: Polity Press), pp. 198–216.

Buzan, Barry and Ole Wæver (2003), *Regions and Powers: The Structure of International Security* (Cambridge: Cambridge University Press).

Buzan, Barry *et al.* (1990), *The European Security Order Recast* (London: Pinter).

Buzan, Barry, Ole Wæver and Jaap de Wilde (1998), *Security: A New Framework for Analysis* (Boulder, CO: Lynne Rienner).

Byman, Daniel (2006), 'Do targeted killings work?', *Foreign Affairs*, 85(2): 95–111.

Campbell, David (1992), *Writing Security* (Minneapolis: University of Minnesota Press).

Carlson, Lisa J. (1995), 'A theory of escalation and international conflict', *Journal of Conflict Resolution*, 39(3): 511–534.

Carpenter, R.C. (2005), '"Women, children and other vulnerable groups": gender, strategic frames, and the protection of civilians as a transnational issue', *International Studies Quarterly*, 49(2): 295–334.

Carr, Edward Hallett (1939/1946), *The Twenty Years' Crisis: An Introduction to the Study of International Relations* (New York: St Martin's Press).

Carter, Jimmy (1980), 'State of the Union Address', 23 January: www.jimmycarterlibrary.org.

CASE Collective (2006), 'Critical approaches to security in Europe: a networked manifesto', *Security Dialogue*, 37(4): 443–487.

Castles, S. and A. Davidson (2000), *Citizenship and Migration* (London: Macmillan).

Castles, S. and G. Kosack (1985), *Immigrant Workers and the Class Structure in Western Europe* (Oxford: Oxford University Press, 2nd edn).

Center on International Cooperation (CIC) (2006), *Annual Review of Global Peace Operations* (Boulder, CO: Lynne Rienner).

Center on International Cooperation (CIC) (2007) *Global Peace Operations 2007* (Boulder CO: Lynne Rienner).

Central Intelligence Agency (CIA) (2000), *The Global Infectious Disease Threat and Its Implications for the United States* (National Intelligence Estimate NIE99-17D): www.cia.gov/cia/publications/nie/report/nie99-17d.html.

Central Intelligence Agency (CIA) (2005), *Mapping the Global Future* (Washington, DC: Central Intelligence Agency).

Centre for International Cooperation and Security (CICS) (2005), *The Impact of Armed Violence on Poverty and Development* (Bradford University: CICS, www.bradford.ac.uk/cics), pp.1–98.

Cerny, Philip (1998), 'Neomedievalism, civil war and the new security dilemma: globalization as durable disorder', *Civil Wars*, 1(1): 36–64.

Cesarani, David (1996), *Citizenship, Nationality and Migration in Europe* (London: Routledge).

Ceyhan, Ayse (1998), 'Analyser la sécurité: Dillon, Wæver, Williams at les autres', *Cultures & Conflits*, 31/32: 35–56.

Cha, Victor D. and David C. Kang (2003), *Nuclear North Korea: A Debate on Engagement Strategies* (New York: Columbia University Press).

Chalk, F. and K. Jonassohn (1990), *The History and Sociology of Genocide* (New Haven, CT: Yale University Press).

Chandler, David (2006), *Empire in Denial: The Politics of State-building* (London: Pluto Press).

Charny, I.W. (1999), 'An international peace army: a proposal for the long-range future', in I.W. Charny (ed.), *The Encyclopedia of Genocide* (Santa Barbara, CA: ABC-CLIO), pp. 649–653.

Chase, Robert, Emily Hill and Paul Kennedy (1996), 'Pivotal states and U.S. strategy', *Foreign Affairs*, 75(1): 33–51.

Chatterjee, Partha and Matthias Finger (1994), *The Earth Brokers: Power, Politics, and World Development* (London: Routledge).

Checkel, J.T. (2005), 'International institutions and socialization in Europe: introduction and framework', *International Organization*, 59(4): 801–826.

Chesterman, Simon (2004), *You, The People: the United Nations, Transitional Administration, and State-building* (Oxford: Oxford University Press).

Chickering, Roger, Stig Förster and Bernd Grenier (eds) (2005), *A World at Total War: Global Conflict and the Politics of Destruction, 1937–1945* (Cambridge: Cambridge University Press).

China, People's Republic of (2005), 'Position Paper of the People's Republic of China on United Nations Reforms', 7 June.

Chowdhry, Geeta and Sheila Nair (eds) (2002), *Power, Postcolonialism and International Relations: Reading Race, Gender, and Class* (London: Routledge).

Christensen, Thomas J. (1996), *Useful Adversaries: Grand Strategy, Domestic Mobilization, and Sino-American Conflict, 1947–1958* (Princeton, NJ: Princeton University Press).

Christensen, Thomas J. and Jack Snyder (1990), 'Chain gangs and passed bucks: predicting alliance patterns in multipolarity', *International Organization*, 44(2): 137–168.

Chubin, Shahram (2006), *Iran's Nuclear Ambitions* (Washington, DC: Carnegie Endowment for International Peace).

Citizenship Rights in Africa Initiative (CRAI) (2007), 'African governments must guarantee effective citizenship and stop foreignizing Africans', *AfricaFocus Bulletin*, 31 March: 1–4.

Clark, Ian (1997), *Globalization and Fragmentation. International Relations in the Twentieth Century* (Oxford: Oxford University Press).

Clary, Christopher (2004), 'Dr. Khan's nuclear WalMart', *Disarmament Diplomacy*, 76 (March/April).

Clausewitz, Carl von (1976), *On War*, ed. and trans. Michael Howard and Peter Paret (Princeton, NJ: Princeton University Press).

Cleves, Patricia, Nat Colletta and Nicholas Sambanis (2002), 'Addressing conflict: emerging policy at the World Bank' in Fen Osler Hampson and David M. Malone (eds), *From Reaction to Conflict Prevention: Opportunities for the UN System* (Boulder, CO: Lynne Rienner), pp. 321–356.

Cocklin, Chris and Meg Keen (2000), 'Urbanization in the Pacific: environmental change, vulnerability and human security', *Environmental Conservation*, 27(4): 392–403.

Cohen, Avner (1998), *Israel and the Bomb* (New York: Columbia University Press).

Cohen, Lenard J. (1995), *Broken Bonds: Yugoslavia's Disintegration and Balkan Politics in Transition* (Boulder, CO: Westview Press).

Cohen, R. and Z. Layton-Henry (1997), *The Politics of Migration* (London: Edward Elgar).

Cohn, Carol (1987), 'Sex and death in the rational world of defense intellectuals', *Signs: Journal of Women in Culture and Society*, 12(4): 687–718.

Cohn, Carol (1993), 'Wars, wimps, and women: talking gender and thinking war' in Miriam Cooke and Angela Woollacott (eds), *Gendering War Talk* (Princeton, NJ: Princeton University Press), pp. 227–246.

Cohn, Carol, with Felicity Hill and Sara Ruddick (2005), 'The relevance of gender for eliminating weapons of mass destruction', The Weapons of Mass Destruction Commission Papers No. 38: www.wmdcommission.org/files/No38.pdf.

Collier, Paul (2007), 'Economic causes of civil conflict and their implications for policy' in Chester A. Crocker, Fen Osler Hampson and Pamela Aall (eds), *Leashing the Dogs of War* (Washington, DC: US Institute of Peace), pp. 197–218.

Collier, Paul *et al.* (2003), *Breaking the Conflict Trap: Civil War and Development Policy* (Oxford: Oxford University Press, for the World Bank).

Collins, Alan (ed.) (2007), *Contemporary Security Studies* (Oxford: Oxford University Press).

Collinson, Sarah (1993), *Beyond Borders; Western European Migration Policy Towards the 21st Century* (London: RIIA and Wyndham Place Trust).

Collinson, Sarah (1995), *Migration, Visa and Asylum Policies in Europe* (London: Wilton Park Paper No. 107, HMSO).

Connell, R.W. (1995), *Masculinities* (Berkeley, CA: University of California Press).

Control Arms Campaign (Amnesty International, International Action Network on Small Arms, Oxfam International) (2006), *Arms without Borders: Why a Globalised Trade needs Global Controls*: http://web.amnesty.org/library/Index/ENGPOL34 0062006?open&of=ENG-390.

Copeland, Dale (2000), 'The constructivist challenge to structural realism: a review essay', *International Security*, 25(2): 187–212.

Copeland, Dale (2001), *The Origins of Major War* (Ithaca, NY: Cornell University Press).

Copeland, Dale (2003), 'A realist critique of the English School', *Review of International Studies*, 29(3): 427–441.

Corera, Gordon (2006), *Shopping for Bombs: Nuclear Proliferation, Global Insecurity, and the Rise and Fall of the A.Q. Khan Network* (Oxford: Oxford University Press).

Cortright, David and George A. Lopez (2000), *The Sanctions Decade: Assessing UN Strategies in the 1990s* (Boulder, CO: Lynne Rienner).

Cox, Robert W. (1981), 'Social forces, states and world orders: beyond International Relations theory', *Millennium*, 10(2): 126–155.

Cox, Robert W. (1983), 'Gramsci, hegemony and International Relations', *Millennium: Journal of International Studies*, 12(2): 162–175.

Crawford, Neta C. (2003), *Argument and Change in World Politics* (Cambridge: Cambridge University Press).

Croft, Stuart (2006), *Culture, Crisis and America's War on Terror* (Cambridge: Cambridge University Press).

Cronin, Audrey Kurth and James M. Ludes (eds) (2004), *Attacking Terrorism: Elements of a Grand Strategy* (Washington, DC: Georgetown University Press).

Cronin, Richard P. *et al.* (2005), *Pakistan's Nuclear Proliferation Activities and the Recommendations of the 9/11 Commission: U.S. Policy Constraints and Options* (US Congressional Research Service, 24 May).

Cusimano, M. (ed.) (2000), *Beyond Sovereignty: Issues for a Global Agenda* (Boston, MA: Bedford Press).

Daalder, I.H. (1991), *The Nature and Practice of Flexible Response: NATO Strategy and Theater Nuclear Forces Since 1967* (New York: Columbia University Press).

Dalby, Simon (1999), 'Threats from the South: geopolitics, equity and environmental security' in Deudney and Matthew (eds) (1999), pp. 155–185.

Dalby, Simon (2002), *Environmental Security* (Minneapolis: University of Minnesota Press).

Dallaire, Roméo (2004), *Shake Hands with the Devil: The Failure of Humanity in Rwanda* (London: Arrow).

Dando, Malcolm (2005), *Bioterrorism: What is the Real Threat?* (London: The Nuffield Trust).

Davies, Simon J. (2004), 'Community versus deterrence: managing security and nuclear proliferation in Latin America and South Asia', *International Relations*, 18(1): 55–72.

de Nevers, R. (2007), 'NATO's international security role in the terrorist era', *International Security*, 31(4): 34–66.

de Soysa, Indra (2002), 'Ecoviolence: shrinking pie or honey pot?', *Global Environmental Politics*, 2(4): 1–34.

de Waal, Alex (2005), 'HIV/AIDS and the military', background paper to expert seminar and policy conference *AIDS, Security and Democracy*, Clingendael Institute, The Hague, 2–4 May.

Debrix, François (1997), *(Re-)envisioning Peacekeeping: The United Nations and the Mobilization of Ideology* (Minneapolis: University of Minnesota Press).

Declaration on the Inadmissibility of Intervention in the Domestic Affairs of States and their Independence and Sovereignty (1965), GA Res. 2131, 20th Session, Supplement No. 14, UN Doc. A/6014 (5).

Deffeyes, Kenneth S. (2001), *Hubbert's Peak: The Impending World Oil Shortage* (Princeton, NJ: Princeton University Press).

Deffeyes, Kenneth S. (2003), *Beyond Oil* (New York: Hill and Wang).

Dencik, Lars (1970), 'Peace research: pacification or revolution?', *International Peace Research Association Proceedings, 3rd General Conference Volume 1* (Assen: Van Gorcum), pp. 74–91.

Deng, Francis M. *et al.* (1996), *Sovereignty as Responsibility: Conflict Management in Africa* (Washington, DC: The Brookings Institution).

Deudney, Daniel (1999), 'Environmental security: a critique', in Deudney and Matthew (eds) (1999), pp. 187–219.

Deudney, Daniel and Richard Matthew (eds) (1999), *Contested Grounds: Security and Conflict in the New*

Environmental Politics (Albany: State University of New York Press).

Deutch, John and James R. Schlesinger (2006), *National Security Consequences of U.S. Oil Dependency* (New York: Council on Foreign Relations, Independent Task Force Report No. 58).

Deutsch, Karl W. (1957), *Political Community in the North Atlantic Area* (Princeton, NJ: Princeton University Press).

Deutsch, Karl W. and J. David Singer (1964), 'Multipolar power systems and international stability', *World Politics*, 16(3): 390–406.

DiCicco, Jonathan M. and Jack S. Levy (1999), 'Power shifts and problem shifts: the evolution of the Power Transition Research Program', *Journal of Conflict Resolution*, 43(6): 675–704.

DiCicco, Jonathan M. and Jack S. Levy (2003), 'The Power Transition Research Program: a Lakatosian analysis' in Colin Elman and Miriam Fendius Elman (eds), *Progress in International Relations Theory: Appraising the Field* (Cambridge, MA: MIT Press), pp. 109–157.

Diehl, Paul F. (2005), *The Politics of Global Governance* (Boulder, CO: Lynne Rienner, 3rd edn).

Dinan, Desmond (2005), *Ever Closer Union* (Basingstoke: Palgrave, 3rd edn).

Dittgen, Herbert and Dirk Peters (2001), 'EU and NATO: competing visions of security in Europe', Paper presented at the 4th Pan European International Relations Conference of the ECPR Standing Group on International Relations, 8–10 September, University of Kent, Canterbury.

Dodds, Felix and Tim Pippard (eds) (2005), *Human and Environmental Security: An Agenda for Change* (London: Earthscan).

Donnelly, Jack (1995), 'Realism and International Relations' in James Farr, John S. Dryzek and Stephen T. Leonard (eds), *Political Science in History* (New York: Cambridge University Press), pp. 175–197.

Donnelly, Jack (2000), *Realism and International Relations* (Cambridge: Cambridge University Press).

Doran, Charles F. (1989), 'Systemic disequilibrium, foreign policy role, and the power cycle: challenges for research design', *Journal of Conflict Resolution*, 33(3): 371–401.

Doran, Charles F. (2000), 'Confronting the principles of the power cycle: changing systems structure, expectations, and war' in Manus I. Midlarsky (ed.), *Handbook of War Studies II* (Ann Arbor, MI: University of Michigan Press), pp. 332–368.

Doran, Charles F. and Wes Parsons (1980), 'War and the cycle of relative power', *The American Political Science Review*, 74(4): 947–965.

Dorn, Walter (1998), 'Regional peacekeeping is not the way', *Peacekeeping and International Relations*, 27(2): 1–4.

Doty, Roxanne Lynn (1993) 'Foreign policy as social construction', *International Studies Quarterly*, 37(3): 297–320.

Doty, Roxanne Lynn (1998/99) 'Immigration and the politics of security', *Security Studies*, 8(2): 71–93.

Douglas, Mary and Aaron Wildavsky (1982), *Risk and Culture: An Essay on the Selection of Technological and Environmental Dangers* (Berkeley: University of California Press).

Downs, George and David Rocke (1990), *Tacit Bargaining, Arms Races, and Arms Control* (Ann Arbor, MI: University of Michigan Press).

Dowty, Alan (1987), *Closed Borders* (New Haven, CT: Yale University Press).

Doyle, Michael W. (1983), 'Kant, liberal legacies, and foreign affairs', *Philosophy and Public Affairs*, 12(3): 205–235.

Doyle, Michael W. (1998), *Ways of War and Peace* (New York: Norton).

Draper, Theodore (1987), *A Very Thin Line: The Iran–Contra Affairs* (New York: Hill and Wang).

Duffield, J.S. (1994/95), 'NATO's functions after the cold war', *Political Science Quarterly*, 109(5): 763–787.

Duffield, J.S. (1995), *Power Rules: The Evolution of NATO's Conventional Force Posture* (Stanford, CA: Stanford University Press).

Duffield, J.S. (1998), *World Power Forsaken: Political Culture, International Institutions, and German Security Policy After Unification* (Stanford, CA: Stanford University Press).

Duffield, J.S. (2006), 'International security institutions' in R. Rhodes *et al.* (eds), *The Oxford Handbook of Political Institutions* (Oxford: Oxford University Press), pp. 635–655.

Duffield, J., Theo Farrell and Richard Price (1999), 'Correspondence: isms and schisms: culturalism versus realism in security studies', *International Security*, 24(1): 156–180.

Duffield, Mark (2001a), 'Decoding the power of aid', *Disasters*, 25(4): 308–320.

Duffield, Mark (2001b), *Global Governance and the New Wars* (London: Zed Books).

Dumbrell, John and David Ryan (eds) (2007), *Vietnam in Iraq: Tactics, Lessons, Legacies and Ghosts* (London: Routledge).

Dunleavy, Steve (2001), 'Simply kill the bastards', *New York Post*, 12 September.

Ebeling, Richard (1991), 'A new world order: economic liberalism or the new mercantilism', *Freedom Daily*: www.fff.org/freedom/0791b.asp.

Ebeling, Richard (2000), 'Market liberalism, international order, and world peace: Part 2', *Freedom Daily*: www.fff.org/freedom/1200b.asp

Eckhardt, William (1981a), 'Pioneers of Peace Research I – Lewis Fry Richardson: Apostle of math', *International Interactions*, 8(3): 247–273.

Eckhardt, William (1981b), 'Pioneers of Peace Research II – Quincy Wright – Apostle of law', *International Interactions*, 8(4): 297–317.

Edidin, Peter (2004), 'Pakistan's hero: Dr. Khan got what he wanted, and he explains how', *New York Times*, 15 February.

Edkins, Jenny (2003), *Trauma and the Memory of Politics* (Cambridge: Cambridge University Press).

Egmond, F. (2004), 'Multiple underworlds in the Dutch Republic of the 17th and 18th centuries' in C. Fijnaut and L. Paoli (eds), *Organized Crime in Europe* (Dordrecht: Springer), pp. 77–106.

Eisenstein, Zillah (2004), 'Sexual humiliation, gender confusion and the horrors at Abu Ghraib', June. At *PeaceWomen*: www.peacewomen.org/news/Iraq/June 04/abughraib.

Ekins, Paul (1992), *A New World Order: Grassroots Movements for Global Change* (London: Routledge).

ElBaradei, Mohamed (2004), 'Nuclear non-proliferation: global security in a rapidly changing world', Carnegie International Non-proliferation Conference, 21 June.

Elbe, Stefan (2002), 'HIV/AIDS and the changing landscape of war in Africa', *International Security*, 27(2): 159–177.

Elbe, Stefan (2003), *The Strategic Implications of HIV/AIDS* (Adelphi Paper No. 357. Oxford: Oxford University Press for IISS).

Elbe, Stefan (2006), 'Should HIV/AIDS be securitized? The ethical dilemmas of linking HIV/AIDS and security', *International Studies Quarterly*, 50(1): 119–144.

Elden, Stuart and Luiza Bialasiewicz (2006), 'The new geopolitics of division and the problem of a Kantian Europe', *Review of International Studies*, 32(4): 623–644.

Elman, Colin (1996a), 'Horses for courses: Why *not* neorealist theories of foreign policy?', *Security Studies*, 6(1): 7–53.

Elman, Colin (1996b), 'Cause, effect, and consistency: a response to Kenneth Waltz', *Security Studies*, 6(1): 58–61.

Elman, Colin (2001), 'History, theory and the democratic peace', *The International History Review*, 23(4): 757–766.

Elman, Colin (2003), 'Introduction: Appraising balance of power theory' in John A. Vasquez and Colin Elman (eds), *Realism and the Balancing of Power: A New Debate* (Upper Saddle River, NJ: Prentice Hall), pp. 1–22.

Elman, Colin (2004), 'Extending offensive realism: the Louisiana Purchase and America's rise to regional hegemony', *American Political Science Review*, 98(4): 563–576.

Elman, Colin (2005a), 'Explanatory typologies in qualitative studies of international politics', *International Organization*, 59(2): 293–326.

Elman, Colin (2005b), 'Realism' in Martin Griffiths (ed.), *Routledge Encyclopedia of International Relations and Global Politics* (London: Routledge), pp. 707–713.

Elman, Colin (2007), 'Realism' in Martin Griffiths (ed.), *International Relations Theory for the Twenty-First Century* (London: Routledge), pp. 11–20.

Elman, Colin and Miriam Fendius Elman (1995), 'Correspondence: history vs. neo-realism: a second look', *International Security*, 20(1): 182–193.

Elman, Colin and Miriam Fendius Elman (2002), 'How not to be Lakatos intolerant: appraising progress in IR research', *International Studies Quarterly*, 46(2): 231–262.

Elman, Colin and Miriam Fendius Elman (eds) (2003), *Progress in International Relations Theory: Appraising the Field* (Cambridge, MA: MIT Press).

Enloe, Cynthia (1983), *Does Khaki Become You? The Militarization of Women's Lives* (London: South End Press).

Enloe, Cynthia (1996), 'Margins, silences and bottom rungs' in Smith *et al.* (eds) (1996), pp. 186–202.

Enloe, Cynthia (2000a), *Maneuvers: The International Politics of Militarizing Women's Lives* (Berkeley: University of Southern California Press).

Enloe, Cynthia (2000b), 'Masculinity as a foreign policy issue', *Foreign Policy in Focus*, 5(36), October.

Enloe, Cynthia (2007), 'Feminist readings on Abu Ghraib: Introduction', *International Feminist Journal of Politics*, 9(1): 35–37.

Eriksson, Mikael and Peter Wallensteen (2004), 'Armed conflict, 1989–2003', *Journal of Peace Research*, 41(5): 625–636.

European Security Strategy (2003), *A Secure Europe in a Better World* (Brussels: EU).

Evangelista, Matthew (1999), *Unarmed Forces: The Transnational Movement to End the Cold War* (Ithaca, NY: Cornell University Press).

Falk, Richard and Samuel Kim (eds) (1980), *The War System: An Interdisciplinary Approach* (Boulder, CO: Westview Press).

Farrell, Theo (2002), 'Constructivist security studies: portrait of a research paradigm', *International Studies Review*, 4(1): 71–92.

Fearon, James D. (1994), 'Domestic political audiences and the escalation of international disputes', *American Political Science Review*, 88: 577–592.

Fearon, James D. (1998), 'Domestic politics, foreign policy, and theories of International Relations', *Annual Review of Political Science*, 1: 289–313.

Fearon, James D. and David D. Laitin (1996), 'Explaining interethnic cooperation', *American Political Science Review*, 90(4): 715–735.

Fearon, James D. and David D. Laitin (2003), 'Ethnicity, insurgency, and civil war', *American Political Science Review*, 97(1): 75–90.

Feaver, Peter D., Gunther Hellmann, Randall L. Schweller, Jeffrey W. Taliaferro, William C. Wohlforth, Jeffrey W. Legro and Andrew Moravcsik (2000), 'Correspondence: Brother, can you spare a paradigm? (or was anybody ever a realist?)', *International Security*, 25(1): 165–169.

Fierke, Karin M. (1998), *Changing Games, Changing Strategies: Critical Investigations in Security* (Manchester: Manchester University Press).

Fierke, Karin M. (2007), *Critical Approaches to International Security* (Oxford: Polity Press).

Findlay, Trevor (2002), *The Use of Force in UN Peace Operations* (Oxford: Oxford University Press/ Stockholm International Peace Research Institute).

Finkenauer, J. and E. Waring (1998), *Russian Mafia in America: Immigration, Culture and Crime* (Boston, MA: Northeastern University Press).

Finn, Peter (2003), 'Al Qaeda arms traced to Saudi National Guard; 3 attackers identified in Riyadh bombing', *Washington Post*, 19 May.

Finnemore, Martha (1996), *National Interests in International Society* (Ithaca, NY: Cornell University Press).

Finnemore, Martha and Kathryn Sikkink (1998), 'International norm dynamics and political change', *International Organization*, 52(4): 887–917.

Flannery, Tim (2006), *The Weather Makers: How We are Changing the Climate and What it Means for Life on Earth* (Toronto: HarperCollins).

Floyd, Rita (2007), 'Towards a consequentialist evaluation of security: bringing together the Copenhagen and the Welsh schools of security studies', *Review of International Studies*, 33(2): 327–350.

Foreign Policy and Fund for Peace (2006), 'The failed State Index', *Foreign Policy*, (May/June): www.foreignpolicy.com/story/cms.php?story_id=3420.

Fournier, Donald F. and Eileen T. Westervelt (2005), *Energy Trends and Their Implications for U.S. Army Installation* (Washington, DC: US Army Corps of Engineers, Engineer Research and Development Center, Construction Engineering Research Laboratory, ERDC/CERL TR-05-21, September).

Freedman, Lawrence (1989), *The Evolution of Nuclear Strategy* (New York: St Martin's Press, 2nd edn).

Freedman, Lawrence (1998), 'International security: changing targets', *Foreign Policy*, 110: 48–63.

Freedman, Lawrence (2001/02), 'The Third World War?', *Survival*, 43(4): 61–88.

Friedman, S. Julio and Thomas Homer-Dixon (2004), 'Out of the energy box', *Foreign Affairs*, 83(6): 71–82.

Friedman, Thomas (2000), *The Lexus and the Olive Tree* (London: HarperCollins).

Frost, Robin M. (2005), *Nuclear Terrorism after 9/11* (London: IISS, Adelphi Paper No. 378).

Furtado, Xavier (2000), 'Human security and Asia's financial crisis', *International Journal*, LV(3): 335–375.

Gaddis, John L. (1987), *The Long Peace: Inquiries into the History of the Cold War* (Oxford: Oxford University Press).

Gaddis, John L. (2004), *Surprise, Security and the American Experience* (Cambridge, MA: Harvard University Press).

Gaddis, John L. (2006), *The Cold War – A New History* (New York: Penguin).

Gagnon, V. P. (1995), 'Ethnic nationalism and international conflict: the case of Serbia,' *International Security*, 19(3): 130–166.

Gallie, W.B. (1956), 'Essentially contested concepts', *Proceedings of the Aristotelian Society*, 56: 167–198.

Galtung, Johan (1964), 'An editorial', *Journal of Peace Research*, 1(1): 1–4.

Galtung, Johan (1969), 'Violence, peace and peace research', *Journal of Peace Research*, 6(3): 167–191.

Galtung, Johan (1971), 'A structural theory of imperialism', *Journal of Peace Research*, 8(2): 81–117.

Galtung, Johan (1975a), 'Dedication', in Johan Galtung, *Peace, Research, Education, Action* [Essays in Peace Research Volume I] (Copenhagen: Christian Ejlers), pp. 17–18.

Galtung, Johan (1975b), 'International programmes of behavioural science: research in human survival' in Johan Galtung, *Peace, Research, Education, Action* [Essays in Peace Research Volume I] (Copenhagen: Christian Ejlers), pp. 167–187.

Galtung, Johan (1975c), 'Peace Research', in Johan Galtung, *Peace, Research, Education, Action* [Essays in Peace Research Volume I] (Copenhagen: Christian Ejlers), pp. 150–166.

Galtung, Johan (1980), *The True Worlds: A Transnational Perspective* (New York: The Free Press/Institute for World Order).

Galtung, Johan (1981), 'Western civilisation: anatomy and pathology', *Alternatives*, 7: 145–169.

Galtung, Johan (1988), 'Dialogues as development' in Johan Galtung, *Methodology and Development* [Essays in Methodology Volume 3], (Copenhagen: Christian Ejlers), pp. 68–89.

Galtung, Johan (1990), 'Cultural violence', *Journal of Peace Research*, 27(3): 291–305.

Galtung, Johan (1996), *Peace by Peaceful Means: Peace, Conflict, Development and Civilisation* (London: Sage and PRIO).

Galula, David (1964), *Counterinsurgency Warfare: Theory and Practice* (London: Pall Mall).

Gardam, Judith G. and Michelle J. Jarvis (2001), *Women, Armed Conflict and International Law* (The Hague: Kluwer Law International).

Garnett, John C. (ed.) (1970), *Theories of Peace and Security* (London: Macmillan).

Garrett, Laurie (2005), *HIV and National Security: Where are the Links?* (New York: Council on Foreign Relations).

Garrett, Laurie (2007), 'The challenge of global health', *Foreign Affairs*, 86(1): 14–38.

Garst, Daniel (1989), 'Thucydides and neorealism', *International Studies Quarterly*, 33(1): 3–27.

Gartzke, Erik (2005), 'Economic freedom and peace' in *Economic Freedom of the World, Annual Report*, pp. 29–44.

Gaubatz, K.T. (1996), 'Democratic states and commitment in international relations', *International Organization*, 50(1): 109–150.

Gavrilis, James A. (2005), 'The Mayor of Ar Rutbah', *Foreign Policy*, 151: 28–35.

Geis, Anna, Lothar Brock and Harald Muller (2006), *Democratic Wars: Looking at the Dark Side of Democratic Peace* (Basingstoke: Palgrave Macmillan)

Geisler, Charles and Ragendra de Sousa (2001), 'From refuge to refugee: the African case', *Public Administration and Development*, 21(2): 159–170.

George, Alexander L. (ed.) (1991), *Western State Terrorism* (Cambridge: Polity Press).

George, Alexander L. and William E. Simons (eds) (1994), *The Limits of Coercive Diplomacy* (Boulder, CO: Westview Press, 2nd edn).

Ghobarah, Hazem, Paul Huth and Bruce Russett (2001), 'Civil wars kill and maim people – long after the shooting stops'. Paper presented to the Kennedy School of Government, Harvard University, 1–2 December.

Gibbons, Robert (1992), *Game Theory for Applied Economists* (Princeton, NJ. Princeton University Press).

Giles, Wenona and Jennifer Hyndman (eds) (2004), *Sites of Violence: Gender and Conflict Zones* (Berkeley: University of Southern California Press).

Giles, Wenona, Malathi de Alwis, Edith Klein and Neluka Silva (eds) (2003), *Feminists Under Fire: Exchanges Across War Zones* (Toronto: Between the Lines).

Gilpin, Robert (1981), *War and Change in World Politics* (New York: Cambridge University Press).

Gilpin, Robert (1988), 'The theory of hegemonic war', *Journal of Interdisciplinary History*, 18(4): 591–613.

Glaser, Charles L. (1992), 'Political consequences of military strategy: expanding and refining the spiral and deterrence models', *World Politics*, 44(4): 497–538.

Glaser, Charles L. (1994/95), 'Realists as optimists: cooperation as self-help', *International Security*, 19(3): 50–90.

Glaser, Charles L. (1997), 'The security dilemma revisited', *World Politics*, 50(1): 171–201.

Glaser, Charles L. (2003), 'The necessary and natural evolution of structural realism' in John A. Vasquez and Colin Elman (eds), *Realism and the Balancing of Power: A New Debate* (Upper Saddle River, NJ: Prentice Hall), pp. 266–279.

Gleditsch, N.P. (1998), 'Armed conflict and the environment: a critique of the literature', *Journal of Peace Research*, 35(3): 381–400.

Goodstein, David (2004), *Out of Gas* (New York: Norton).

Goodwin-Gill, Guy (1983), *The Refugee in International Law* (Oxford: Clarendon Press).

Gordenker, Leon (1987), *Refugees in International Politics* (New York: Columbia University Press).

Gordenker, Leon (2005), *The UN Secretary-General and Secretariat* (London: Routledge).

Gore, Al (2006), *An Inconvenient Truth* (New York: Rodale Books).

Goulding, Marrack (2002), *Peacemonger* (London: John Murray).

Gow, James (2003), *The Serbian Project and its Adversaries* (London: Hurst).

Grewal, Shabnam (2007), 'All female UN squad a success', BBC 21 June: http://news.bbc.co.uk/1/hi/programmes/this_world/6223246.stm.

Grieco, Joseph M. (1988), 'Anarchy and the limits of cooperation: a realist critique of the newest liberal institutionalism', *International Organization*, 42(3): 485–508.

Grieco, Joseph M. (1993), 'Anarchy and the limits of cooperation: a realist critique of the newest liberal internationalism' in Baldwin (ed.) (1993), pp. 116–140.

Grieco, Joseph M., Robert Powell and Duncan Snidal (1993), 'The relative-gains problem for international cooperation', *American Political Science Review*, 87(3): 729–743.

Griffin, Keith (1995), 'Global prospects for development and human security', *Canadian Journal of Development Studies*, XVI(3): 359–370.

Grimmett, Richard F. (2003), *Conventional Arms Sales to Developing Nations* (Washington, DC: Congressional Research Service, 26 August).

Grimmett, Richard F. (2006), *Conventional Arms Sales to Developing Nations* (Washington, DC: Congressional Research Service, 23 October).

Gross, Leo (1948), 'The Peace of Westphalia, 1648–1948', *American Journal of International Law*, 42(1): 20–41.

Gruber, Lloyd (2000), *Ruling the World: Power Politics and the Rise of Supranational Institutions* (Princeton, NJ: Princeton University Press).

Guéhenno, Jean-Marie (2003), 'Everybody's doing it', *World Today*, 59(8/9): 35–36.

Guéhenno, Jean-Marie (2005), 'Peace Operations 2010', letter to all DPKO and mission staff, New York, 30 November.

Guevara, Che (1963), 'Guerilla warfare: a method', *Cuba Socialista*, Havana (September 1963), pp. 1–17. Reproduced in Che Guevara, *Guerrilla Warfare* (London: Souvenir Press, 2003).

Guild, Elspeth (2003), 'Exceptionalism and transnationalism: UK judicial control of the detention of foreign "international terrorists"', *Alternatives*, 28(4): 491–515.

Gurr, Ted Robert (2000), *Peoples Versus States* (Washington, DC: United States Institute of Peace).

Haas, Ernst (1958), *The Uniting of Europe* (Stanford, CA: Stanford University Press).

Haas, Ernst (1993), 'Collective conflict management. evidence for a new world order?' in Thomas G. Weiss (ed.), *Collective Security in a Changing World* (Boulder, CO: Lynne Rienner), pp. 63–117.

Haftendorn, Helga, Robert O. Keohane and Celeste A. Wallander (eds) (1999), *Imperfect Unions: Security Institutions over Space and Time* (Oxford: Oxford University Press).

Hamber, Brandon, Paddy Hillyard, Amy Maguire, Monica McWilliams, Gillian Robinson, David Russell and Margaret Ward (2006), 'Discourses in transition: re-imagining women's security', *International Relations*, 20(4): 487–502.

Hammar, Thomas (ed.) (1985), *European Immigration Policy: a Comparative Study* (Cambridge: Cambridge University Press).

Hampson, Fen Osler (2004), 'Can the UN still mediate?' in Price and Zacher (eds) (2004), pp. 75–92.

Hampson, Fen Osler *et al.* (2002), *Madness in the Multitude* (Toronto: Oxford University Press).

Hansen, Lene (2000), 'The Little Mermaid's silent security dilemma and the absence of gender in the Copenhagen School', *Millennium*, 29(2): 289–306.

Haq, Mahbub (1995), *Reflections on Human Development* (Oxford: Oxford University Press).

Harbom, Lotta and Peter Wallensteen (2007), 'Armed conflict, 1989–2006', *Journal of Peace Research*, 44(5): 623–634.

Hardin, Russell (1995), *One for All: The Logic of Group Conflict* (Princeton, NJ: Princeton University Press).

Harsanyi, John C. (1977), 'Advances in understanding rational behavior' in Robert E. Butts and Jaakko Hintikka (eds), *Foundational Problems in the Special Sciences* (Dordrecht: D. Reidel), pp. 315–343.

Hartung, William D. (1995), *And Weapons for All* (New York: HarperCollins).

Hartung, William D. (2000), 'A tale of three arms trades: the changing dynamics of conventional weapons proliferation 1991–2000' in Ann Markusen (ed.), *America's Peace Dividend* (New York: Columbia International Affairs Online), ch. 5.

Hartung, William D. and Frida Berrigan (2005), *U.S. Weapons at War: Promoting Democracy or Fueling Conflict?* (New York: World Policy Institute, June).

Haslam, Jonathan (2002), *No Virtue Like Necessity: Realist Thought in International Relations since Machiavelli* (New Haven, CT: Yale University Press).

Haywood, O.J., Jr. (1954), 'Military decision and game theory', *Operations Research*, 2: 365–385.

Heinecken, Lindy (2003), 'Facing a merciless enemy: HIV/AIDS and the South African armed forces', *Armed Forces and Society*, 29(2): 281–300.

Held, David (1995) *Democracy and the Global Order* (Cambridge: Polity Press).

Held, David (ed.) (2007), *Understanding Globalization: Approaches and Controversies* (Oxford: Oxford University Press).

Held, David *et al.* (1999), *Global Transformations* (Cambridge: Polity Press).

Helsinki Process on Globalization and Democracy (2005), *Empowering People At Risk: Human Security Priorities for the 21st Century. Report of the Human Security Track* (Helsinki, Finland): www.cmi.fi/files/HP_report_track3.pdf.

Hendrickson, Dylan and Nicole Ball (2002), *Off-budget Military Expenditure and Revenue* (London: Conflict, Security and Development Group Occasional Paper No. 1 (January), Kings College): http://csdg.kcl.ac.uk/Publications/assets/PDF%20files/OP1_Off-Budget%20Military%20Expenditure.pdf.

Hendrickson, R.C. (2006), *Diplomacy and War at NATO* (Columbia: University of Missouri Press).

Herz, John (1950), 'Idealist internationalism and the security dilemma', *World Politics*, 2(2): 157–180.

Herz, John (1951), *Political Realism and Political Idealism: A Study in Theories and Realities* (Chicago, IL: Chicago University Press).

Herz, John (1959), *International Politics in the Atomic Age* (New York: Columbia University Press).

Hettne, Bjorn (2004), 'The new regionalism revisited' in Frederick Soderbaum and Timothy Shaw (eds), *Theories of New Regionalism* (London: Palgrave), pp. 22–42.

Heymann, Philip B. and Juliette N. Kayyem (2005), *Protecting Liberty in an Age of Terror* (Cambridge, MA: MIT Press).

Higate, Paul (2004), *Peacekeepers and Gender: DRC and Sierra Leone* (Pretoria: Institute for Security Studies, Monograph No. 91): www.iss.org.za/pubs/Monographs/No91/Contents.html.

Higgott, Richard (2006), 'International political institutions' in R. Rhodes *et al.* (eds), *The Oxford Handbook of Political Institutions* (Oxford: Oxford University Press), pp. 611–632.

Highman, S. and J. Stephens (2004), 'New details of prison abuse emerge: Abu Ghraib detainees' statements describe sexual humiliation and savage beatings', *The Washington Post*, 21 May: A01.

Hilberg, R. (2003), *The Destruction of the European Jews* (3 vols) (New Haven, CT: Yale University Press, 3rd edn).

Hills, Alice (2004), *Future War in Cities* (London: Frank Cass).

Hirst, Paul (2002), 'Another century of conflict? War and the international system in the 21st century', *International Relations*, 16(3): 327–342.

Hobsbawm, Eric and Terence Ranger (eds) (1992), *The Invention of Tradition* (Cambridge: Cambridge University Press).

Hoffman, Bruce (2004), *Insurgency and Counterinsurgency in Iraq* (The Rand Corporation: RAND Occasional Paper, June).

Hoffmann, Stanley (1965), *The State of War. Essays on the Theory and Practice of International Politics* (London: Pall Mall Press).

Hoffman, Stanley (1977), 'An American social science: International Relations', *Daedalus*, 106(3): 41–60.

Holt, Victoria and Tobias Berkman (2006), *The Impossible Mandate? Military Preparedness, the Responsibility to Protect and Modern Peace Operations* (Washington, DC: The Stimson Center).

Holzgrefe, J.L. and Robert O. Keohane (eds) (2003), *Humanitarian Intervention; Ethical, Legal, and Political Dilemmas* (Cambridge: Cambridge University Press).

Homer-Dixon, Thomas (1994), 'Environmental scarcities and violent conflict: evidence from cases', *International Security*, 19(1): 5–40.

Homer-Dixon, Thomas (1999), *Environment, Scarcity, and Violence* (Princeton, NJ: Princeton University Press).

Hooper, Charlotte (2001), *Manly States: Masculinities, International Relations and Gender Politics* (New York: Columbia University Press).

Hopf, Ted (1991), 'Polarity, the offense–defense balance, and war', *American Political Science Review*, 85(2): 475–493.

Hopf, Ted (1998), 'The promise of constructivism in International Relations theory', *International Security*, 23(1): 171–200.

Horkheimer, Max (1982), 'Traditional and critical theory', in *Critical Theory: Selected Essays*, trans. Matthew J. O'Connell *et al.* (New York: Continuum), pp. 188–243.

Horowitz, Donald L. (1985), *Ethnic Groups in Conflict* (Berkeley: University of California Press).

Horowitz, Donald L. (2000), *The Deadly Ethnic Riot* (Berkeley: University of California Press).

Howard, John W. III and Laura C. Prividera (2004), 'Rescuing patriarchy or saving "Jessica Lynch": the rhetorical construction of the American woman soldier', *Women and Language*, 27(2): 89–97.

Howard, Michael (2000), *The Invention of Peace* (London: Profile Books).

Hughes, J. Donald (2006), *What is Environmental History?* (Cambridge: Polity Press).

Human Rights Watch (HRW) (1994), *India: Arms and Abuses in Indian Punjab and Kashmir* (Washington, DC: Arms Project, September).

Human Security Centre (2005), *Human Security Report, 2005: War and Peace in the 21st Century* (Oxford: Oxford University Press).

Hunt, Krista (2002), 'The strategic co-optation of women's rights: discourse in the "War on Terrorism"',

International Feminist Journal of Politics, 4(1): 116–121.

Huntington, Samuel P. (1993), 'The clash of civilisations', *Foreign Affairs*, 72(3): 22–49.

Huntington, Samuel P. (1996), *The Clash of Civilisations and the Remaking of World Order* (New York: Simon & Schuster).

Huth, Paul (1988), *Extended Deterrence and the Prevention of War* (New Haven, CT: Yale University Press).

Huysmans, Jef (1995), 'Migrants as a security problem' in R. Miles and D. Thränhardt (eds), *Migration and European Integration* (London: Pinter), pp. 53–72.

Huysmans, Jef (1998), 'Security? What do you mean? From concept to thick signifier', *European Journal of International Relations*, 4(2): 226–255.

Huysmans, Jef (2006), *The Politics of Insecurity: Fear, Migration and Asylum in the EU* (London: Routledge).

Huyssen, Andreas (1994), *Twilight Memories: Marking Time in a Culture of Amnesia* (London: Routledge).

Hyndman, Jennifer (2001), 'Towards a feminist geopolitics', *The Canadian Geographer*, 45(2): 210–222.

Ikenberry, G. John and Anne-Marie Slaughter (dir.) (2006), *Forging A World Of Liberty Under Law: U.S. National Security in the 21st Century*, Final Report of the Princeton Project on National Security, 27 September.

Imlay, Talbot (2007), 'Total war', *Journal of Strategic Studies*, 30(3): 547–570.

International Alert (1999), *Women, Violent Conflict and Peacebuilding: Global Perspectives*. Proceedings from an International Conference, London, 5–7 May.

International Commission on Intervention and State Sovereignty (ICISS) (2001), *The Responsibility to Protect* (Ottawa: International Development Research Centre).

International Committee of the Red Cross (2001), *Women Facing War* (Geneva: International Committee of the Red Cross).

International Consortium of Investigative Journalists (ICIJ) (2002a), *Making a Killing: The Business of War* (Washington, DC: Public Integrity Books).

International Consortium of Investigative Journalists (ICIJ) (2002b), *The Business of War: Privatizing Combat, the New World Order* (Washington, DC: The Center for Public Integrity).

International Crisis Group (ICG) (2001), *HIV/AIDS as a Security Issue* (Brussels: ICG).

International Crisis Group (ICG) (2006), *In Their Own Words: Reading the Iraqi Insurgency* (ICG, Middle East Report No. 50, 15 February).

International Herald Tribune (2004), 'Non-proliferation and disarmament go hand in hand', 2 September.

International Institute for Strategic Studies (IISS) (2005), *The Military Balance, 2004–2005* (London: Taylor & Francis).

International Organization for Migration (IOM) (2005), *World Migration 2005: Costs and Benefits of International Migration* (IOM).

International Peace Operations Association (IPOA) (2007): http://ipoaonline.org/php/

International Security, 19(3): 5–49.

Iraq Study Group (ISG) (2006), *The Iraq Study Group Report: The Way Forward – A New Approach* (New York: Vintage Books).

Isaacs, Harold R. (1975), *The Idols of the Tribe: Group Identity and Political Change* (New York: Harper & Row).

Isikoff, Michael (1989a), 'Colombia urges U.S. to curb flow of semi-automatic guns; drug cartels said to be hoarding weapons', *Washington Post*, 8 September.

Isikoff, Michael (1989b), 'Cartels turn to U.S. for weapons; Colombians said to rely on "easy availability" for War of Terror', *Washington Post*, 2 November.

Jacobs, Susie, Ruth Jacobson and Jennifer Marchbank (eds) (2000), *States of Conflict: Gender, Violence and Resistance* (London: Zed Books).

Jacoby, Tim (2007), 'Hegemony, modernisation and postwar reconstruction', *Global Society*, 21(4): 521–537.

Jahn, Beate (2007), 'The tragedy of liberal diplomacy, democratisation, intervention, statebuilding', *Journal of Intervention and Statebuilding*, Part 1, 1(1): 87–106; Part 2, 1(2): 211–229.

Jenkins, Philip (2003), *Images of Terror: What We Can and Can't Know About Terrorism* (New York: Aldine de Gruyter).

Jeong, Ho-Won (ed.) (1999), *The New Agenda for Peace Research* (Aldershot: Ashgate).

Jervis, Robert (1976), *Perception and Misperception in International Politics* (Princeton, NJ: Princeton University Press).

Jervis, Robert (1982), 'Security regimes', *International Organization*, 36(2): 357–378.

Jervis, Robert (1988), 'Realism, game theory, and cooperation', *World Politics*, 40(3): 317–349.

Jervis, Robert (1997), *Systems Effects: Complexity in Political and Social Life* (Princeton, NJ: Princeton University Press).

Jervis, Robert (1999), 'Realism, neoliberalism, and cooperation: understanding the debate', *International Security*, 24(1): 42–63.

Jervis, Robert (2002), 'Theories of war in an era of leading-power peace: Presidential Address, American Political Science Association', *American Political Science Review*, 96(1): 1–14.

Jervis, Robert and Jack Snyder (eds) (1991), *Dominoes and Bandwagons* (New York: Oxford University Press).

Job, Brian (2004), 'The UN, regional organizations, and regional conflict' in Price and Zacher (eds) (2004), pp. 227–243.

Johnson, Rebecca (2005), 'Politics and protection: why the 2005 NPT Review Conference failed',

Disarmament Diplomacy, No. 80: www.acronym. org.uk/dd/dd80/80npt.htm.

Johnston, A.I. (2001), 'Treating international institutions as social environments', *International Studies Quarterly*, 45(4): 487–515.

Johnstone, Ian (2006), 'Dilemmas of robust peace operations' in *Annual Review of Global Peace Operations, 2006* (Boulder, CO: Lynne Rienner), pp. 2–14.

Jupille, Joseph and James A. Caporaso (1999), 'Institutionalism and the European Union: beyond International Relations and comparative politics', *Annual Review of Political Science*, 2: 429–444.

Justice Africa (2004), *HIV/AIDS and the Threat to Security in Africa*, submission to the UN Secretary General's High-level Panel on Threats, Challenges and Change, 2 May: www.justiceafrica.org/aids_mainpapers.htm.

Kahl, Colin (2006), *States, Scarcity, and Civil Strife in the Developing World* (Princeton, NJ: Princeton University Press).

Kahler, Miles (1997), 'Inventing International Relations: International Relations theory after 1945' in Michael W. Doyle and G. John Ikenberry (eds), *New Thinking in International Relations Theory* (Boulder, CO: Westview Press), pp. 20–53.

Kaldor, Mary (1997), 'Introduction' in M. Kaldor and B. Vashee (eds), *Restructuring the Global Military Sector: Volume I: New Wars* (London: Pinter), pp. 3–33.

Kaldor, Mary (1999), *New and Old Wars: Organized Violence in a Global Era* (Cambridge: Polity Press [and 2nd edn, 2006]).

Kalicki, Jan H. and David L. Goldwyn (2005), 'Introduction: The need to integrate energy and foreign policy' in Jan H. Kalicki and David L. Goldwyn (eds), *Energy Security* (Washington, DC: Woodrow Wilson Center Press), pp.1–16.

Kalyvas, S.N. (2001), '"New" and "old" civil wars: a valid distinction?', *World Politics*, 54(1): 99–118.

Kansteiner, Wulf (2004), 'Genealogy of a category mistake: a critical intellectual history of the cultural trauma metaphor', *Rethinking History*, 8(2): 193–221.

Kant, I. (1991a) 'Perpetual peace: a philosophical sketch' in *Kant: Political Writings*, ed. H. Reiss (Cambridge: Cambridge University Press, 2nd edn).

Kant, I. (1991b) 'On the relationship of theory to practice in political right' in *Kant: Political Writings*, ed. H. Reiss (Cambridge: Cambridge University Press, 2nd edn).

Kaplan, Robert D. (1994), 'The coming anarchy', *The Atlantic Monthly*, 273(2): 44–76.

Kaplan, Robert D. (2005), *Imperial Grunts: On the Ground With The American Military* (New York: Vintage Books).

Karl, Terry Lynn (1997), *The Paradox of Plenty* (Berkeley: University of California Press).

Katz, S.T. (1994), *The Holocaust in Historical Context, Vol. 1: The Holocaust and Mass Death before the Modern Age* (Oxford: Oxford University Press).

Katzenstein, Peter J. (1996a), *Cultural Norms and National Security* (Ithaca, NY: Cornell University Press).

Katzenstein, Peter J. (ed.) (1996b), *The Culture of National Security* (New York: Columbia University Press).

Katzenstein, Peter J., Robert O. Keohane and Stephen D. Krasner (1998), '*International Organization* and the study of world politics', *International Organization*, 52(4): 645–685.

Katzman, Kenneth (1993), *Afghanistan: U.S. Policy Options* (Washington, DC: Congressional Research Service Issue Brief, 29 November).

Kaufman, Stuart J. (2001), *Modern Hatreds: The Symbolic Politics of Ethnic War* (Ithaca, NY: Cornell University Press).

Kaufman, Stuart J. (2006), 'symbolic politics or rational choice? Testing theories of extreme ethnic violence', *International Security*, 30(4): 45–86.

Kaufmann, Chaim (1996), 'Possible and impossible solutions to ethnic civil wars', *International Security*, 20(4): 136–175.

Kay, Cristóbal (1997), 'Introduction: globalisation, competitiveness and human security', *European Journal of Development Research*, 9(1): 1–5.

Keck, Margaret E. and Kathryn Sikkink (1998), *Activists Beyond Borders: Advocacy Networks in International Politics* (Ithaca, NY: Cornell University Press).

Keegan, John (1994), *A History of Warfare* (London: Vintage Books).

Keen, David (1998), *The Economic Functions of Violence in Civil Wars* (Oxford: Oxford University Press for the IISS, Adelphi Paper No. 320).

Kemp, Geoffrey (2001), 'Military technology and conflict' in Chester A. Crocker, Fen Osler Hampson and Pamela Aall (eds), *Turbulent Peace: The Challenges of Managing International Conflict* (Washington, DC: US Institute of Peace Press), pp. 69–82.

Kennan, George F. (1951), *American Diplomacy, 1900–1950* (Chicago, IL: University of Chicago Press).

Kennedy, Paul (2006), *The Parliament of Man: The Past, Present, and Future of the United Nations* (New York: Random House).

Kennedy-Pipe, Caroline (2004), 'Whose security? State-building and the "emancipation" of women in Central Asia', *International Relations*, 18(1): 91–107.

Kennedy-Pipe, Caroline and Penny Stanley (2000), 'Rape in war: lessons of the Balkans conflicts in the 1990s' in Booth (ed.) (2000), pp. 67–84.

Keohane, Robert O. (1984), *After Hegemony: Cooperation and Discord in the World Political Economy* (Princeton, NJ: Princeton University Press).

Keohane, Robert O. (ed.) (1986), *Neorealism and its Critics* (New York: Columbia University Press).

Keohane, Robert O. (1988), 'International institutions: two approaches', *International Studies Quarterly*, 32(4): 379–396.

Keohane, Robert O. (1989), *International Institutions and State Power* (Boulder, CO: Westview Press).

Keohane, Robert O. and Joseph S. Nye (1977), *Power and Interdependence: World Politics in Transition* (Boston, MA: Little, Brown).

Keohane, Robert O. and Lisa Martin (2003), 'Institutional theory as a research program' in Elman and Elman (eds) (2003), pp. 71–107.

Khong, Yuen Foong (2001), 'Human security: a shotgun approach to alleviating human misery?', *Global Governance*, 7(3): 231–236.

Kiernan, B. (2004), 'The first genocide: Carthage, 146 BC', *Diogenes*, 203: 27–39.

Kiernan, B. (2007), *Blood and Soil: Genocide and Extermination from Carthage to Darfur* (New Haven, CT: Yale University Press).

Kilcullen, David (2006–07), 'Counter-insurgency Redux', *Survival*, 48(4): 111–130.

Kim, Woosang (1991), 'Alliance transitions and Great Power war', *American Journal of Political Science*, 35(4): 833–850.

Kim, Woosang (1992), 'Power transitions and Great Power war from Westphalia to Waterloo', *World Politics*, 45(1): 153–172.

Kim, Woosang (1996), 'Power parity, alliances, and war from 1648 to 1975' in Jacek Kugler and Douglas Lemke (eds), *Parity and War* (Ann Arbor, MI: University of Michigan Press), pp. 93–105.

Kim, Woosang (2002), 'Power parity, alliance, dissatisfaction, and wars in East Asia, 1860–1993', *The Journal of Conflict Resolution*, 46(5): 654–671.

King, Gary and Christopher Murray (2001/02), 'Rethinking human security', *Political Science Quarterly*, 116(4): 585–610.

Klare, Michael T. (1984), *American Arms Supermarket* (Austin: University of Texas Press).

Klare, Michael T. (1995), 'Stemming the trade in small arms and light weapons', *Issues in Science and Technology* (Fall).

Klare, Michael T. (2004), *Blood and Oil: The Dangers and Consequences of America's Growing Dependence on Imported Petroleum* (New York: Metropolitan Books).

Klare, Michael T. (2006), 'Fueling the fires: the oil factor in Middle Eastern terrorism' in James J.F. Forest (ed.), *The Making of a Terrorist*, Vol. 3 (Westport, CT: Praeger Security International), pp. 140–159.

Klein, Naomi (2005), *No War: America's Real Business in Iraq* (London: Gibson Sq).

Koremos, Barbara, Charles Lipson and Duncan Snidal (2004), *The Rational Design of International Institutions* (Cambridge: Cambridge University Press).

Kraig, Michael R. (1999), 'Nuclear deterrence in the developing world: a game-theoretic treatment', *Journal of Peace Research*, 36(2): 141–167.

Kramer, Andrew E. (2006), 'Gazprom threatens to cut off gas if Belarus rejects higher price', *New York Times*, 27 December.

Krasner, Stephen D. (2005), 'The case for shared sovereignty', *Journal of Democracy*, 16(1): 69–83.

Kratochwil, Friedrich (1993), 'The embarrassment of changes: neo-realism as the science of realpolitik without politics', *Review of International Studies*, 19(1): 63–80.

Krause, Keith and Michael C. Williams (eds) (1997), *Critical Security Studies: Concepts and Cases* (London: UCL Press).

Krauthammer, Charles (2001), 'The Bush Doctrine: ABM, Kyoto and the New American unilateralism', *The Weekly Standard* (Washington, DC), 6(36), 4 June.

Krepinevich, Andrew (2005), 'How to win in Iraq', *Foreign Affairs*, 84(5): 87–104.

Kritz, M., C. Keely and S. Tomasci (eds) (1981), *Global Trends in Migration: Theory and Research on International Population Movements* (New York: The Center for Migration Studies).

Krulak, Charles C. (1999), 'The strategic corporal: leadership in the Three Block War', *Marine Corps Gazette*, 83(1): 18–22.

Kubursi, Atif (2006), 'Oil and the global economy' in Rick Fawn and Raymond Hinnebusch (eds), *The Iraq War: Causes and Consequences* (Boulder, CO: Lynne Rienner), pp. 247–256.

Kugler, Jacek and A.F.K. Organski (1989), 'The power transition: a retrospective and prospective evaluation' in Manus I. Midlarsky (ed.), *Handbook of War Studies* (Boston, MA: Unwin Hyman), pp. 171–194.

Kugler, Jacek and Douglas Lemke (2000), 'The power transition research program: assessing theoretical and empirical advances' in Manus Midlarsky (ed.), *The Handbook of War Studies II* (Ann Arbor, MI: Michigan University Press), pp. 129–163.

Kumar, Krishna (ed.) (2001), *Women and Civil War: Impact, Organizations, and Action* (Boulder, CO: Lynne Rienner).

Kuper, L. (1981), *Genocide: Its Political Use in the Twentieth Century* (New Haven, CT: Yale University Press).

Kydd, Andrew H. (1997a), 'Game theory and the spiral model', *World Politics*, 49(3): 371–400.

Kydd, Andrew H. (1997b), 'Sheep in sheep's clothing: why security seekers do not fight each other', *Security Studies*, 7(1): 114–154.

Kydd, Andrew H. (2000), 'Trust, reassurance and cooperation', *International Organization*, 54(2): 325–359.

Kydd, Andrew H. (2001), 'Trust building, trust breaking: the dilemma of NATO enlargement', *International Organization*, 55(4): 801–829.

Kydd, Andrew H. (2005), *Trust and Mistrust in International Relations* (Princeton, NJ: Princeton University Press).

Labs, Eric J. (1997), 'Beyond victory: offensive realism and the expansion of war aims', *Security Studies*, 6(4): 1–49.

LaFeber, Walter (2006), *America, Russia and the Cold War 1945–2006* (New York: McGraw Hill).

Laïdi, Zaki (1998), *A World Without Meaning: The Crisis of Meaning in International Politics* (London: Routledge, orig. 1994).

Lakatos, Imre (1970), 'Falsification and the methodology of scientific research programmes' in Imre Lakatos and Alan Musgrave (eds), *Criticism and the Growth of Knowledge* (New York: Cambridge University Press), pp. 91–196.

Lake, David (2001), 'Beyond anarchy: the importance of security institutions', *International Security*, 26(1): 129–160.

Lake, David and Patrick Morgan (1997), *Regional Orders. Building Security in a New World* (Pennsylvania: Pennsylvania State University Press).

Lapid, Yosef and Friedrich Kratochwil (1996), *The Return of Culture and Identity in IR Theory* (Boulder, CO: Lynne Rienner).

Lasswell, Harold D. (1936), *Politics: Who Gets What, When and How* (New York: McGraw-Hill).

Lauren, Paul Gordon (1998), *The Evolution of Human International Rights: Visions Seen* (University Park: Pennsylvania State University Press).

Lawler, Peter (1995), *A Question of Values: Johan Galtung's Peace Research* (Boulder, CO: Lynne Rienner).

Lawler, Peter (2002), 'Peace research, war, and the problem of focus', *Peace Review*, 14(1): 7–14.

Le Billon, Philippe (2005), *Fuelling War: Natural Resources and Armed Conflict* (London: Routledge for the International Institute of Strategic Studies, Adelphi Paper No. 373).

Lee, Kelley (2003), *Globalization and Health* (Basingstoke: Palgrave Macmillan).

Leeds, B.A. *et al.* (2002), 'Alliance treaty obligations and provisions, 1815–1944', *International Interactions*, 28(3): 237–260.

Legro, Jeffrey W. and Andrew Moravcsik (1999), 'Is anybody still a realist?', *International Security*, 24(2): 5–55.

Lemke, Douglas (1995), 'Toward a general understanding of: parity and war', *Conflict Management and Peace Science*, 14: 143–162.

Lemke, Douglas (1996), 'Small states and war: an expansion of power transition theory' in Jacek Kugler and Douglas Lemke (eds), *Parity and War* (Ann Arbor, MI: University of Michigan Press), pp. 77–91.

Lemkin, R. (1944), *Axis Rule in Occupied Europe* (Washington, DC: Carnegie Institute for International Peace).

Lentz, Theodore F. (1955), *Towards a Science of Peace: Turning Point in Human Destiny* (London: Halycon Press).

Leon, David A. and Gill Walt (2001), *Poverty, Inequality, and Health: An International Perspective* (New York: Oxford University Press).

Levering, Ralph B. (2005), *The Cold War: A Post Cold War History* (Wheeling, IL: Harlan Davidson).

Liberman, Peter (1993), 'The spoils of conquest', *International Security*, 18(2): 125–153.

Lieber, Karl A. and Darryl G. Press (2006), 'The end of MAD? The nuclear dimension of US primacy', *International Security*, 30(4): 7–44.

Lieberman, Elli (1995), 'What makes deterrence work', *Security Studies*, 4(4): 833–892.

Lijphart, Arend (1985), *Power-sharing in South Africa*, Policy Papers in International Affairs No. 24 (Berkeley: Institute of International Studies, University of California).

Lin, Shi-chin (2004), *The A.Q. Khan Revelations and Subsequent Changes to Pakistani Export Controls* (Center for Nonproliferation Studies (CNS), Monterey Institute of International Studies).

Linklater, Andrew (2005), 'Political community and human security' in Booth (ed.) (2005c), pp. 113–131.

Liotta, P.H. (2002), 'Boomerang effect: the convergence of national and human security', *Security Dialogue*, 33(4): 473–488.

Looney, R. (2005), 'The business of insurgency', *The National Interest*, 81: 67–72.

Luck, Edward C. (1999), *Mixed Messages: American Politics and International Organization 1919–1999* (Washington, DC: Brookings).

Luck, Edward C. (2006), *UN Security Council: Promise and Practice* (London: Routledge).

Lugar, Richard G. (2005), 'Opening statement, Hearing on the high costs of oil dependency', Senate Committee on Foreign Relations, 16 November: http://foreign.senate.gov.

Lugar, Richard G. (2006), 'Address to the Brookings Institution, Washington, D.C., 13 March': http://lugar.senate.gov.

Luhnow, David and Geraldo Samor (2006), 'As Brazil fills up on ethanol, it weans off energy imports', *Wall Street Journal*, 9 January.

Lukes, Steven (1986), *Power* (New York: New York University Press).

Lumpe, Lora (ed.) (2000), *Running Guns: The Global Black Market in Small Arms* (London: Zed Books).

Lurio, Eric (2006), 'The Last Samurai', *Greenwich Village Gazette*, 6(26): www.nycny.com/movies/last_samurai/index.html.

Lynn-Jones, Sean M. (1995), 'Offense–defense theory and its critics', *Security Studies*, 4(4): 660–691.

Lynn-Jones, Sean M. (2001), *Does Offense–Defense Theory Have a Future?* (Working Paper, Research Group in International Security, Université de Montréal).

Maass, Peter (2004), 'Professor Nagl's War', *New York Times Magazine*, 11 January.

McAdam, Doug, Sidney Tarrow and Charles Tilly (2001), *Dynamics of Contention* (Cambridge: Cambridge University Press).

McCalla, R.B. (1996), 'NATO's persistence after the cold war', *International Organization*, 50(3): 445–475.

McDonald, John and John W. Tukey (1949), 'Colonel Blotto: a problem of military strategy', *Fortune*, June.

McDonald, Matt (2002), 'Human security and the construction of security', *Global Society*, 16(3): 277–295.

McDonald, Matt (2005), 'Constructing insecurity: Australian security discourse and policy post-2000', *International Relations*, 19(3): 297–320.

MacFarlane, S. Neil and Yuen Foong Khong (2006), *Human Security and the UN: A Critical History* (Bloomington: Indiana University Press).

McFate, Montgomery and Andrea V. Jackson (2006), 'The object beyond war: counterinsurgency and the four tools of political competition', *Military Review*, 86(1): 13–26.

McInnes, Colin (2001), 'Fatal attraction: airpower and the West', *Contemporary Security Policy*, 22(3): 28–51.

McInnes, Colin (2002), *Spectator–Sport War: The West and Contemporary Conflict* (Boulder, CO.: Lynne Rienner).

McInnes, Colin (2006), 'HIV/AIDS and security', *International Affairs*, 82(2): 315–326.

Mack, Andrew (2001), 'Notes on the creation of a Human Security Report'. Paper presented to the Kennedy School of Government, Harvard University, 1–2 December.

Mack, Andrew (2005), *Human Security Report 2005: War and Peace in the 21st Century* (New York: Oxford University Press).

Mack, Andrew (2007), *Global Political Violence: Explaining the Post-Cold War Decline* (New York: International Peace Academy Coping with Crisis Working Paper, March).

McKenna, Thomas M. (1998), *Muslim Rulers and Rebels: Everyday Politics and Armed Separatism in the Southern Philippines* (Berkeley: University of California).

McNeill, J.R. (2000), *Something New Under the Sun: An Environmental History of the Twentieth-century World* (New York: Norton).

McRae, Robert G. and Donald Hubert (2001), *Human Security and the New Diplomacy: Protecting People, Promoting Peace* (Kingston and Montreal: McGill-Queen's University Press).

McSweeney, Bill (1999), *Security, Identity and Interests: A Sociology of International Relations* (Cambridge: Cambridge University Press).

Malone, David M. (ed.) (2004), *The UN Security Council: From the Cold War to the 21st Century* (Boulder, CO: Lynne Rienner).

Mann, Michael (1988), *States, War and Capitalism* (Oxford: Blackwell).

Mansaray, Binta (2000), 'Women against weapons: a leading role for women in disarmament' in Anatole Ayissi and Robin-Edward Poulton (eds), *Bound to Cooperate: Conflict, Peace and People in Sierra Leone* (Geneva: United Nations Institute for Disarmament Research), pp. 139–162.

Mansfield, Edward D. (1993), 'Concentration, polarity, and the distribution of power', *International Studies Quarterly*, 37(1): 105–128.

Mansfield, Edward D. and Brian M. Pollins (2001), 'The study of interdependence and conflict', *Journal of Conflict Resolution*, 45(6): 834–859.

March, James G. and Johan P. Olsen (1989), *Rediscovering Institutions: The Organizational Basis of Politics* (New York: Free Press).

Marshall, Monty G. (2007), 'Caveats to the "pacification" of the global system: Global Report on Governance, Conflict, and Systemic Development'. Paper presented to the International Studies Association 2007 Annual Meeting, Chicago, 1 March.

Martin, Andrew and Patrice Petro (2006), *Rethinking Global Security: Media, Popular Culture, and the 'War on Terror'* (New York: Rutgers University Press).

Martin, James (2006), *The Meaning of the 21st Century. A Vital Blueprint for Ensuring Survival* (London: Eden Project Books).

Martin, Lisa (1999), 'The contributions of rational choice: a defense of pluralism', *International Security*, 24(2): 74–83.

Mearsheimer, John J. (1983), *Conventional Deterrence* (Ithaca, NY: Cornell University Press).

Mearsheimer, John J. (1990), 'Back to the future: instability in Europe after the Cold War', *International Security*, 15(1): 5–56.

Mearsheimer, John J. (1994/95), 'The false promise of international institutions', *International Security*, 19(3): 5–49.

Mearsheimer, John J. (2001), *The Tragedy of Great Power Politics* (New York: W.W. Norton).

Meldrum, A. (2004), 'German Minister says sorry for genocide in Namibia', *Guardian*, 16 August: www.guardian.co.uk/print/0,3858,4993918-103532,00.html.

Melvern, L. (2000), *A People Betrayed: The Role of the West in Rwanda's Genocide* (London: Zed Books).

Melvern, L. (2006), *Conspiracy to Murder: The Rwandan Genocide.* (London: Verso, 2nd edn).

Mendelsohn, Daniel (2007), 'Duty', *New York Review of Books*, 54(9), 31 May: www.nybooks.com/articles/article-preview?article_id=20231.

Merle, Renae (2006), 'Census counts 100,000 contractors in Iraq', *Washington Post*, 5 December: D1.

Mernissi, Fatima (1989), *Doing Daily Battle: Interviews with Moroccan Women*, trans. Mary Jo Lakeland (New Brunswick, NJ: Rutgers University Press).

Miguel, E. (2006), 'Global poverty, conflict and insecurity', *The Brookings Blum Roundtable*, 2 August.

Milliken, Jennifer and Keith Krause (2002), 'State failure, state collapse, and state reconstruction', *Development and Change*, 33(5): 753–774.

Mills, Greg (2004), 'Relearning the lessons of Vietnam and Malaya', *Straits Times* (Singapore), 29 January.

Mises, Ludwig von (1949), *Human Action: A Treatise on Economics* (Inning-on-Hudson, NY: The Foundation for Economic Education).

Mitchell, Ronald B. (2006), 'Institutional design and the relative effectiveness of international environmental agreements', *Global Environmental Politics*, 6(3): 72–89.

Mittelman, James (2000), *The Globalization Syndrome* (Princeton, NJ: Princeton University Press).

Mitzen, Jennifer (2006), 'Ontological security in world politics: state identity and the security dilemma', *European Journal of International Relations*, 12(3): 341–370.

Moaveni, Azadeh (2007), '300 sparks an outcry in Iran', *Time Magazine*, 13 March: www.time.com/time/world/article/0,8599,1598886,00.html.

Modelski, G. (1963), 'The study of alliances: a review', *Journal of Conflict Resolution*, 7(4): 769–776.

Moore, Jonathan (1996), *The UN and Complex Emergencies: Rehabilitation in Third World Transitions* (Geneva: UNRISD).

Moravcsik, Andrew (2001), *Liberal International Relations Theory: A Social Scientific Assessment* (Cambridge, MA: Harvard University Press).

Morgenthau, Hans (1948), *Politics Among Nations: The Struggle for Power and Peace* (New York: A.A. Knopf, 1st edn).

Morgenthau, Hans (1985), *Politics Among Nations: The Struggle for Power and Peace* (New York: McGraw-Hill, 6th edn).

Morrow, James D. (1994), *Game Theory for Political Scientists* (Princeton, NJ: Princeton University Press).

Morsink, Johannes (1998), *The Universal Declaration of Human Rights* (University Park: University of Pennsylvania Press).

Moser, Caroline O.N. and Fiona C. Clark (eds) (2001), *Victims, Perpetrators or Actors? Gender, Armed Conflict and Political Violence* (London: Zed Books).

Motta, Mary (2006), 'Reporters get first-hand look at Libyan WMD', *VOA News*, 14 March.

Mowle, Thomas S. and David H. Sacko (2007), *The Unipolar World* (New York: Palgrave).

Mueller, John (1989), *Retreat From Doomsday: The Obsolescence of Major War* (New York: Basic Books).

Mueller, John (2000), 'The banality of ethnic war', *International Security*, 25(1): 42–70.

Mueller, John (2004), *The Remnants of War* (Ithaca, NY: Cornell University Press).

Mueller, John (2005), 'Simplicity and spook: terrorism and the dynamics of threat exaggeration', *International Studies Perspectives*, 6(2): 208–234.

Mueller, John (2006a), 'Is there still a terrorist threat? The myth of the omnipresent enemy', *Foreign Affairs*, 85(5): 2–8.

Mueller, John (2006b), *Overblown* (New York: Free Press).

Muggah, Robert (2001), 'A question of data: criminal violence as a measure of human insecurity'. Paper presented to the Kennedy School of Government, Harvard University, 1–2 December.

Munkler, Herfried (2004), *The New Wars* (Cambridge: Polity Press).

Musah, A-F. and K. Fayemi (2000), 'Africa: in search of security' in A-F. Musah and K. Fayemi (eds), *Mercenaries: An African Security Dilemma* (London: Pluto Press), pp. 13–42.

Myint-U, Thant and Amy Scott (2007), *The UN Secretariat: A Brief History (1945–2006)* (New York: International Peace Academy).

Nadelmann, E. (1990), 'Global prohibition regimes: the evolution of norms in international society', *International Organization*, 44(4): 479–526.

Nafziger, E.W. and J. Auvinen (2002), 'Economic development, inequality, war and state violence', *World Development*, 30(2): 153–163.

Nagl, John A. (2005), *Learning to Eat Soup With A Knife: Counterinsurgency Lessons from Malaya and Vietnam* (Chicago, IL: University of Chicago Press).

Nantais, Cynthia and Martha F. Lee (1999), 'Women in the United States Military: protectors or protected? The case of prisoner of war Melissa Rathbun-Nealy', *Journal of Gender Studies*, 8(2): 181–191.

Nash, John (1951), 'Non-cooperative games', *Annals of Mathematics*, 54(2): 286–295.

National Advisory Committee on Criminal Justice Standards and Goals (NACCJSG) (1976), *Report of the Task Force on Disorders and Terrorism* (Washington, DC: US Government Printing Office).

National Energy Policy Development Group (NEPDG) (2001), *National Energy Policy* (Washington, DC: The White House, 17 May).

National Film Board (1997), *Chronicle of a Genocide Foretold, Part 2: 'We Were Cowards'* (Ottawa: National Film Board).

National Nuclear Security Administration (NNSA) (2005), *Future of the Nuclear Weapons Complex*: www.nnsa.doe.gov/docs/Future_of_the_Nuclear_Weapons_Complex.pdf.

National Nuclear Security Administration (NNSA) (2007), 'NNSA releases report on plans for future of the nuclear weapons complex': www.nnsa.doe.gov/docs/newsreleases/2007/PR_2007-2-2_NA-07-03.htm.

Navari, Cornelia (2006), 'Globalization and security: much ado about nothing?' in William Bain (ed.), *The Empire of Security and the Safety of the People* (Abingdon: Routledge), pp. 116–138.

Nef, Jorge (2002), *Human Security and Mutual Vulnerability* (Ottawa: International Development Research Centre).

Neufeld, Mark (2004), 'Pitfalls of emancipation and discourses of security: reflections on Canada's "Security with a human face"', *International Relations*, 18(1): 109–123.

Newman, Edward (1998), *The UN Secretary-General From The Cold War To The New Era* (Basingstoke: Macmillan).

Newman, Edward (2001), 'Human security and constructivism', *International Studies Perspectives*, 2(3): 239–251.

Newman, Edward (2004), 'The "New Wars" debate: a historical perspective is needed', *Security Dialogue*, 35(2): 173–189.

Nicolson, Harold (1939), *Diplomacy* (London: Oxford University Press).

Niebuhr, Reinhold (1940), *Christianity and Power Politics* (New York: Scribner's).

Niou, Emerson, Peter Ordeshook and Gregory F. Rose (1989), *The Balance of Power: Stability in International Systems* (Cambridge: Cambridge University Press).

Nixon, Richard (1971), 'Informal remarks by Richard Nixon in Guam with newsmen', 25 July 1969 in *Public Papers of the Presidents of the United States – Richard Nixon, 1969* (Washington, DC: US Government Printing Office).

Non-aligned Movement (NAM) (2005), 'Statement By Chairman of the Non-aligned Movement concerning the draft outcome document of the High-level Plenary Meeting of the General Assembly', 21 June.

Norchi, Charles (1998), 'Cold War reheated', *New York Times*, 20 September: www.nytimes.com/books/98/09/20/reviews/980920.20norchit.html.

Norris, Robert J. and Hans M. Kristensen (2006), 'Nuclear notebook: global nuclear stockpiles, 1945–2006', *Bulletin of Atomic Scientists*, 62(4): 64–66.

North, Douglass, C. (1990), *Institutions, Institutional Change and Economic Performance* (Cambridge: Cambridge University Press).

NPT Review Conference (2000), *Final Document: 2000 Review Conference of the Parties to the Treaty on the Non-proliferation of Nuclear Weapons* (New York: NPT/CONF 2000/28, Parts I and II).

Nuruzzaman, Mohammed (2006), 'Beyond the realist theories: "neo-conservative realism" and the American invasion of Iraq', *International Studies Perspectives*, 7(3): 239–253.

Nye, Joseph (1968), *International Regionalism* (Boston, MA: Little Brown).

Nye, Joseph (1971), *Peace in Parts: Integration and Conflict in Regional Organization* (Boston, MA: Little Brown).

Ó Tuathail, Gearóid (1996), *Critical Geopolitics: The Politics of Writing Global Space* (London: Routledge).

Ó Tuathail, Gearóid (2000), 'The postmodern geopolitical condition: states, statecraft, and security at the millennium', *Annals of the Association of American Geographers*, 90(1): 166–178.

O'Brien, Kevin (1998), 'Freelance forces: exploiters of old or new-age peacebrokers?', *Janes Intelligence Review*, 10(8): 42–46.

O'Brien, Kevin (2000), 'PMCs, myths, and mercenaries', *Royal United Service Institute Journal* (February): 59–64.

O'Neill, Barry (1994a), 'Sources in game theory for International Relations specialists' in Michael D. Intriligator and Urs Luterbacher (eds), *Cooperative Models in International Relations Research* (Boston, MA: Kluwer), pp. 9–30.

O'Neill, Barry (1994b), 'Game theory models of peace and war' in Robert J. Aumann and Sergiu Hart (eds), *Handbook of Game Theory*. Vol. 2 (Amsterdam: Elsevier), pp. 995–1090.

O'Neill, Helen (1997), 'Globalisation, competitiveness and human security: challenges for development policy and institutional change', *European Journal of Development Research*, 9(1): 7–37.

Oakley, Robert, B., Michael J. Dziedzic and Eliot M. Goldberg (1997), *Policing the New World Disorder: Peace Operations and Public Security* (Washington, DC: National Defense University).

Oberdorfer, Don (1992), '1982 arms policy with China victim of Bush Campaign, Texas lobbying', *Washington Post*, 4 September.

Office of the Special Advisor on Gender Issues and Advancement of Women (2006), 'The status of women in the United Nations System (OHRM data from 31 December 2003 to 31 December 2004) and in the Secretariat (OHRM data from 1 July 2004 to 30 June 2006)': www.un.org/womenwatch/osagi/pdf/Fact%20sheet%2028%20september.pdf.

Olsson, Louise and Torunn L. Tryggestad (eds) (2001), *Women and International Peacekeeping* (London: Frank Cass).

Oneal, John and Bruce Russett (1997), 'The Classical Liberals were right: democracy, interdependence, and conflict 1950–85', *International Studies Quarterly*, 41(2): 267–293.

Onuf, Nicholas (1989), *World of Our Making* (South Carolina: University of Southern California Press).

Onuf, Nicholas (1991), 'Sovereignty: outline of a conceptual history', *Alternatives*, 16(4): 425–446.

Organski, A.F.K. (1968), *World Politics* (New York: Knopf, 2nd edn).

Organski, A.F.K. and Jacek Kugler (1980), *The War Ledger* (Chicago, IL: University of Chicago Press).

Osgood, R.E. (1962), *NATO, the Entangling Alliance* (Chicago, IL: University of Chicago Press).

Osgood, R.E. (1968), *Alliances and American Foreign Policy* (Baltimore, MD: The Johns Hopkins University Press).

Osiander, Andreas (1998), 'Rereading early twentieth century IR theory: idealism revisited', *International Studies Quarterly*, 42(3): 409–432.

Overy, Richard (2005), 'Total War 2: the Second World War' in Townshend (ed.) (2005), pp. 138–157.

Owen, John M. (1996), 'How liberalism produces democratic peace' in Brown *et al.* (eds) (1996), pp. 116–156.

Oye, Kenneth A. (1986), *Cooperation Under Anarchy* (Princeton, NJ: Princeton University Press).

Ozerdem, A. (2007), 'Learning from the "mountain tsunami" – Kashmir's earthquake': www.id21.org/society/s10bao1g1.html.

Packer, George (2005), *The Assassin's Gate: America in Iraq* (New York: Farrar, Straus & Giroux).

Palme, Olaf (1982) 'Introduction', in The Report of the Independent Commission on Disarmament and Security Issues, *Common Security: A Blueprint for Survival* (London: Pan).

Palmer, Michael A. (1992), *Guardians of the Gulf* (New York: Free Press).

Pape, Robert A. (1996), *Bombing to Win: Air Power and Coercion in War* (Ithaca, NY: Cornell University Press).

Paris, Roland (1997), 'Peacebuilding and the limits of liberal internationalism', *International Security*, 22(2): 54–89.

Paris, Roland (2001), 'Human security: paradigm shift or hot air?', *International Security*, 26(2): 87–102.

Paris, Roland (2004), *At War's End* (Cambridge: Cambridge University Press).

Pasha, Mustapha Kamal (1996), 'Security as hegemony', *Alternatives*, 21(3): 283–302.

Passas, N. (1999), 'Globalization, criminogenic asymmetries, and economic crime', *European Journal of Law Reform*, 1(4): 399–423.

Pastzor, Andy (1991), 'Investigators say Chilean dealer smuggled U.S. weapons to Iraq', *Wall Street Journal*, 20 November.

Perito, Robert (2002), *The American Experience with Police in Peacekeeping Operations* (Clementsport, NS: Canadian Peacekeeping Press).

Perkovich, George (1999), *India's Nuclear Bomb: The Impact on Nuclear Proliferation* (Berkeley, CA: University of California Press).

Peterson, M.J. (2005), *The UN General Assembly* (London: Routledge).

Peterson, V. Spike and Anne Sisson Runyan (1999), *Global Gender Issues* (Boulder, CO: Westview Press, 2nd edn).

Philipose, L. (2007), 'The politics of pain and the end of empire', *International Feminist Journal of Politics*, 9(1): 60–81.

Phillips, Kevin (2006), *American Theocracy* (New York: Viking Press).

Pierre, Andrew J. (1982), *The Global Politics of Arms Sales* (Princeton, NJ: Princeton University Press).

Pillar, Paul R. (ed.) (2003), *Terrorism and U.S. Foreign Policy* (Washington, DC: Brookings Institution Press).

Pippard, T. and V. Lie (2004), 'Enhancing the rapid reaction capability of the United Nations: exploring the options' (United Nations Association–UK, July): www.una-uk.org/UNandC/rapidreaction.html.

Pirages, D.C. and T.M. DeGeest (2004), *Ecological Security: An Evolutionary Perspective on Globalization* (Lanham, MD: Rowman & Littlefield).

Policy Post (2001), *International Relations*, 19(3): 297–320.

Pollitt, Katha (2001), 'Where are the women?', *The Nation*, 22 October.

Posen, Barry (1993), 'The security dilemma and ethnic conflict', *Survival*, 35(1): 27–47.

Posner, Richard A. (2005), *Preventing Surprise Attacks: Intelligence Reform in the Wake of 9/11* (Lanham, MD: Rowman & Littlefield).

Pouligny, Béatrice (2006), *Peace Operations Seen From Below* (London: Hurst).

Powell, Robert (1991), 'Absolute and relative gains in International Relations theory', *American Political Science Review*, 85(4): 1303–1320.

Powell, Robert (2003), 'Nuclear deterrence theory, nuclear proliferation, and national missile defense', *International Security*, 27(4): 86–118.

Price, Richard (1997), *The Chemical Weapons Taboo* (Ithaca, NY: Cornell University Press).

Price, Richard and Christian Reus-Smit (1998), 'Dangerous liaisons? Critical international theory and constructivism', *European Journal of International Relations*, 4(3): 259–294.

Price, Richard and Mark Zacher (eds) (2004), *The United Nations and Global Security* (New York: Palgrave).

Priest, Dana (2004), 'Private guards repel attack on US headquarters', *Washington Post*, 6 April, p. A1.

Prins, Gwyn and Robbie Stamp (1991), *Top Guns and Toxic Whales: The Environment and Global Security* (London: Earthscan).

Prunier, Gerard (1995), *The Rwanda Crisis: History of a Genocide* (London: Hurst).

Pugh, Michael and W.P.S. Sidhu (eds) (2003), *The United Nations and Regional Security* (Boulder, CO: Lynne Rienner).

Quackenbush, Stephen L. (2006), 'National missile defense and deterrence', *Political Research Quarterly*, 59(4): 533–541.

Quigley, J. (2006), *The Genocide Convention: An International Law Analysis* (London: Ashgate).

Ramcharan, Bertrand G. (2008), *The UN and Preventive Diplomacy* (Bloomington: Indiana University Press).

Rapoport, Anatol (1968), 'Introduction' in Carl von Clausewitz, *On War* ed. Anatol Rapoport (London: Penguin), pp. 11–80.

Rasler, Karen and William R. Thompson (2001), 'Malign autocracies and major power warfare: evil, tragedy, and International Relations theory', *Security Studies*, 10(3): 46–79.

Ray, James Lee (2003), 'A Lakatosian view of the Democratic Peace Research Program', in Colin Elman and Miriam Fendius Elman (eds), *Progress in International Relations Theory* (Cambridge, MA: MIT Press), pp. 205–243.

Rees, Martin (2003), *Our Final Century* (London: Heinemann).

Reform the UN (2005), 'State-by-state positions on the responsibility to protect', 15 August: www.reform theun.org/index.php/issues/100?theme=alt42005.

Report of the Commission on Human Security (2003), *Human Security Now: Protecting and Empowering People* (New York: United Nations).

Reus-Smit, Chris (2002), 'Imagining society: constructivism and the English School', *British Journal of Politics and International Relations*, 4(3): 487–509.

Review Conference of the Parties to the Treaty on the Non-proliferation of Nuclear Weapons (NPT RevCon) (2000), *Final Document*: www.un.org/spanish/Depts/dda/2000FD.pdf.

Richmond, Oliver (2005), *The Transformation of Peace* (Basingstoke: Palgrave).

Richter-Montpetit, M. (2007), 'Empire, desire and violence: a queer transnational feminist reading of the prisoner "abuse" in Abu Ghraib and the question of "gender equality"', *International Feminist Journal of Politics*, 9(1): 38–59.

Rieff, David (1996), *Slaughterhouse: Bosnia and the Failure of the West* (New York: Simon & Schuster).

Rivlin, Benjamin, and Leon Gordenker (1993), *The Challenging Role of the UN Secretary-General* (Westport, CT: Praeger).

Roberts, Adam (2005), 'Against war' in Townshend (ed.) (2005), pp. 317–340.

Roberts, Paul (2004), *The End of Oil* (Boston, MA: Houghton Mifflin).

Rocca, Ambassador Christina (2007), 'Creating the environment necessary for nuclear disarmament', Statement to the Conference on Disarmament, 6 February: www.usmission.ch/Press2007/0206 Rocca.html.

Rose, Gideon (1998), 'Review: Neoclassical realism and theories of foreign policy', *World Politics*, 51(1): 144–172.

Rosenau, James (1990), *Turbulence in World Politics* (Princeton, NJ: Princeton University Press).

Rosenthal, Joel H. (1991), *Righteous Realists: Political Realism, Responsible Power, and American Culture in the Nuclear Age* (Baton Rouge, LA: Lousiana State University Press).

Rothschild, Emma (1995), 'What is security?', *Daedalus*, 124(3): 53–98.

Rothstein, Robert (1977), *The Weak in the World of the Strong: Developing Countries in the International System* (New York: Columbia University Press).

Rousseau, David L. (2002), 'Motivations for choice: the salience of relative gains in international politics', *Journal of Conflict Resolution*, 46(3): 394–426.

Rousseau, Jean Jacques (1917), *A Lasting Peace Through the Federation of Europe and The State of War*, trans. C.E.Vaughn (London: Constable).

Ruane, Joseph and Jennifer Todd (1996), *The Dynamics of Conflict in Northern Ireland* (Cambridge: Cambridge University Press).

Ruggie, John (1999), *Constructing the World Polity* (London: Routledge).

Rummel, R.J. (1994), *Death by Government* (New Brunswick, NJ: Transaction Publishers).

Russett, Bruce (1967), *International Regions and the International System* (Chicago, IL: Rand McNally).

Russett, Bruce (1993), *Grasping the Democratic Peace* (Princeton, NJ: Princeton University Press).

Russett, Bruce (1996), 'Why liberal peace?' in Brown *et al.* (eds) (1996), pp. 82–115.

Russett, Bruce and John Oneal (2001), *Triangulating Peace* (New York: Norton).

Sabrosky, Alan (ed.) (1985), *Polarity and War: The Changing Structure of International Conflict* (Boulder, CO: Westview Press).

Sachs, Wolfgang, Reinhard Loske and Manfred Linz (1998), *Greening the North: A Post-industrial Blueprint for Ecology and Equity* (London: Zed Books).

Sagan, Scott and Kenneth Waltz (2003), *The Spread of Nuclear Weapons: A Debate Renewed* (New York: W.W. Norton, 2 edn).

Said, Edward W. (1994), *Representations of the Intellectual* (New York: Pantheon Books).

Saideman, Stephen M. (2001), *The Ties That Divide: Ethnic Politics, Foreign Policy and International Conflict* (New York: Columbia University Press).

Sampson, Anthony (1977), *The Arms Bazaar* (New York: Viking Press).

Samuel, Kumudini (2001), 'Gender difference in conflict resolution: the case of Sri Lanka' in Inger Skjelsbæk and Dan Smith (eds), *Gender, Peace and Conflict* (London: Sage), pp. 184–204.

Sarkees, Meredith Reid (2000). 'The correlates of war data on war: an update to 1997', *Conflict Management and Peace Science*, 18(1): 123–144.

Sarooshi, Danesh (1998), *The United Nations and the Development of Collective Security* (Oxford: Oxford University Press).

Satha-Anand, Chaiwat (1990), 'The non-violent crescent: eight theses on Muslim non-violent action' in Ralph E. Crow, Philip Grant and Saad E. Ibrahim (eds), *Arab Nonviolent Struggle in the Middle East* (London: Lynne Rienner), pp. 25–40.

Savranskaya, Svetlana (ed.) (2001), *September 11th Sourcebooks Volume II: Afghanistan: Lessons from the Last War The Soviet Experience in Afghanistan: Russian Documents* (9 October). The National Security Archive at the George Washington University:

www.gwu.edu/~nsarchiv/NSAEBB/NSAEBB57/soviet.html.

Schelling, Thomas C. (1960). *The Strategy of Conflict* (Cambridge, MA: Harvard University Press).

Schelling, Thomas C. (1966), *Arms and Influence* (New Haven, CT: Yale University Press).

Schlesinger, James R. (2005), 'Statement before the Senate Foreign Relations Committee', 16 November: http://foreign.senate.gov.

Schmeidl, Susanne (2002), '(Human) security dilemmas: long-term implications of the Afghan refugee crisis', *Third World Quarterly*, 23(1): 7–29.

Schmid, Herman (1968), 'Peace research and politics', *Journal of Peace Research*, 5(3): 217–232.

Schreuer, Christoph (1995), 'Regionalism v. universalism', *European Journal of International Law*, 6(3): 1–23.

Schroeder, P. (1976), 'Alliances, 1815–1945: weapons of power and tools of management' in K. Knorr (ed.), *Historical Dimensions of National Security* (Lawrence: University Press of Kansas), pp. 227–262.

Schultz, George P., William J. Perry, Henry A. Kissinger and Sam Nunn (2007), 'A world free of nuclear weapons', *Wall Street Journal*, 4 January.

Schwartz, Peter and Doug Randall (2003), 'An abrupt climate change scenario and its implications for United States national security', October: www.ems.org/climate/pentagon_climatechange.pdf.

Schwarzenberger, Georg (1941), *Power Politics* (New York: Praeger).

Schweller, Randall L. (1992), 'Domestic structure and preventive war: are democracies more pacific?', *World Politics*, 44(2): 235–269.

Schweller, Randall L. (1993), 'Tripolarity and the Second World War', *International Studies Quarterly*, 37(1): 73–103.

Schweller, Randall L. (1994), 'Bandwagoning for profit: bringing the revisionist state back in', *International Security*, 19(1): 72–107.

Schweller, Randall L. (1996), 'Neorealism's status-quo bias: what security dilemma?', *Security Studies*, 5(3): 90–121.

Schweller, Randall L. (1998), *Deadly Imbalances: Tripolarity and Hitler's Strategy of World Conquest* (New York: Columbia University Press).

Schweller, Randall L. (2003), 'The progressiveness of neoclassical realism' in Colin Elman and Miriam Fendius Elman (eds), *Progress in International Relations Theory: Appraising the Field* (Cambridge, MA: MIT Press), pp. 311–347.

Schweller, Randall L. (2006), *Unanswered Threats: Political Constraints on the Balance of Power* (Princeton, NJ: Princeton University Press).

Seiple, Chris (2002), 'Homeland security concepts and strategies', *Orbis*, 46(2): 259–273.

Selten, Reinhard (1975), 'A re-examination of the perfectness concept for equilibrium points in extensive games', *International Journal of Game Theory*, 4: 25–55.

Shane III, Leo (2005), 'Military issues content warning to combat-zone bloggers', *Stars and Stripes*, 1 October: http://stripes.com.

Sharoni, Simona (1996), 'Gender and the Israeli-Palestinian accord: feminist approaches to international politics' in Deniz Kandiyoti (ed.), *Gendering the Middle East: Emerging Perspectives* (Syracuse, NY: Syracuse University Press), pp. 107–126.

Shaw, Martin (1994), '"There is no such thing as society": beyond individualism and statism in international security studies', *Review of International Studies*, 19(2): 159–176.

Shaw, Martin (2000), 'The contemporary mode of warfare? Mary Kaldor's theory of new wars', *Review of International Political Economy*, 7(1): 171–192.

Shaw, Martin (2003), *War and Genocide* (Cambridge: Polity Press).

Shearer, David (1998), *Private Armies and Military Intervention* (Oxford: Oxford University Press, Adelphi Paper No. 316).

Sheffer, Gabriel (ed.) (1986), *Modern Diasporas in International Politics* (London: Croom-Helm).

Shimshoni, Jonathan (1988), *Israel and Conventional Deterrence: Border Warfare from 1953 to 1970* (Ithaca, NY: Cornell University Press).

Shultz, Kenneth A. (2001), *Democracy and Coercive Diplomacy* (Cambridge: Cambridge University Press).

Shuman, Frederick (1933), *International Politics* (New York: McGraw-Hill).

Sick, Gary (1985), *All Fall Down* (New York: Random House).

Silverston, Ken (1998), 'Privatizing war', *The Nation*, 7 July.

Simma, Bruno (ed.) (2002), *The Charter of the United Nations*, 2 vols (Oxford: Oxford University Press, 2nd edn).

Simmons, Matthew R. (2005), *Twilight in the Desert* (New York: John Wiley).

Simon, J. (1997), 'Biological terrorism: preparing to meet the threat', *Journal of the American Medical Association*, 278(5): 428–430.

Singer, P.W. (2001/02), 'Corporate warriors: the rise of the privatized military industry and its ramifications for international security', *International Security*, 26(3): 186–220.

Singer, P.W. (2003a), *Corporate Warriors: The Rise of the Privatized Military Industry* (Ithaca, NY: Cornell University Press).

Singer, P.W. (2003b), 'Peacekeepers, Inc.', *Policy Review* (June).

Singer, P.W. (2005), *Children At War* (London: Pantheon).

SIPRI (2006), *SIPRI Yearbook 2006* (Oxford: Oxford University Press).

Sjoberg, L. (2007), 'Agency, militarized femininity and enemy others: observations from the war in Iraq', *International Feminist Journal of Politics*, 9(1): 82–101.

Small Arms Survey (2002), *Small Arms Survey 2002: Counting the Human Cost* (Oxford: Oxford University Press).

Small Arms Survey (2004), *Small Arms Survey 2004: Rights at Risk* (New York: Oxford University Press).

Small, Melvin and J. David Singer (1982), *Resort to Arms: International and Civil War, 1816–1980* (Beverly Hills, CA: Sage).

Smith, Alastair (1995), 'Alliance formation and war', *International Studies Quarterly*, 39(4): 405–425.

Smith, Anthony D. (1986), *The Ethnic Origins of Nations* (New York: Blackwell).

Smith, Chris (1995), 'Light weapons and ethnic conflict in South Asia' in Boutwell *et al.* (1995), pp. 61–80.

Smith, Michael J. (1986), *Realist Thought From Weber to Kissinger* (Baton Rouge: Louisiana State University Press).

Smith, Rupert (2005), *The Utility of Force* (London: Allen Lane).

Smith, Steve (1996), 'Positivism and beyond' in Smith *et al.* (eds) (1996), pp. 11–44.

Smith, Steve (1999), 'The increasing insecurity of security studies: conceptualizing security in the last twenty years', *Contemporary Security Policy*, 20(3): 72–101.

Smith, Steve (2000), 'The discipline of International Relations: still an American social science?', *British Journal of Politics and International Relations*, 2(3): 374–402.

Smith, Steve (2005), 'The contested concept of security' in Booth (ed.) (2005c), pp. 27–62.

Smith, Steve, Ken Booth and Marysia Zalewski (eds) (1996), *International Theory: Positivism and Beyond* (Cambridge: Cambridge University Press).

Snidal, Duncan (1991a), 'International cooperation among relative gains maximizers', *International Studies Quarterly*, 35(4): 387–402.

Snidal, Duncan (1991b), 'Relative gains and the pattern of international cooperation', *American Political Science Review*, 85(3): 701–726.

Snidal, Duncan (2002), 'Rational choice and International Relations' in Walter Carlsnaes, Thomas Risse and Beth A. Simmons (eds), *Handbook of International Relations* (London: Sage), pp. 73–94.

Snyder, Glenn H. (1958), *Deterrence by Denial and Punishment* (Princeton, NJ: Center of International Studies).

Snyder, Glenn H. (1997), *Alliance Politics* (Ithaca, NY: Cornell University Press).

Snyder, Glenn H. and Paul Diesing (1977), *Conflict Among Nations* (Princeton, NJ: Princeton University Press).

Snyder, Jack (1991), *Myths of Empire: Domestic Politics and International Ambition* (Ithaca, NY: Cornell University Press).

Snyder, Jack (2000), *From Voting to Violence: Democratization and Nationalist Conflict* (New York: W.W. Norton).

Söderbaum, Fredrik and Timothy Shaw (eds) (2003), *Theories of New Regionalism* (Basingstoke: Palgrave).

Solomon, Norman (2001), 'The "wimp" factor: goading to shed blood', *Media Beat* 28: www.fair.org/mediabeat/010928.html.

Special Inspector General for Iraq Reconstruction: www.sigir.mil/.

Spiro, David E. (1996), 'The insignificance of the liberal peace' in Brown *et al.* (eds) (1996), pp. 202–238.

Spirtas, Michael (1996), 'A house divided: tragedy and evil in realist theory', *Security Studies*, 5(3): 385–423.

Stamnes, Eli (2004), 'Critical security studies and the United Nations preventive deployment in Macedonia', *International Peacekeeping*, 11(1): 161–181.

Stamnes, Eli and Richard Wyn Jones (2000), 'Burundi: a critical security perspective', *Peace and Conflict Studies*, 7(2): 37–55.

Steans, Jill (1998), *Gender and International Relations: An Introduction* (New Jersey: Rutgers University Press).

Stewart, Frances (2003), 'Conflict and the millennium development goals', *Journal of Human Development*, 4(3): 325–351.

Stewart, Frances (2004), 'Development and security', *Conflict, Security and Development*, 4(3): 261–287.

Stewart, Frances and Valpy Fitzgerald (2001), *War and Underdevelopment*, Vols 1 and 2 (Oxford: Oxford University Press).

Stewart, Frances and Graham Brown (2007), 'Motivations for conflict: groups and individuals' in Chester A. Crocker, Fen Osler Hampson and Pamela Aall (eds), *Leashing the Dogs of War* (Washington, DC: US Institute of Peace), pp. 197–219.

Stoddard, Abby, Adele Harmer and Katherine Haver (2006), *Providing Aid in Insecure Environments: Trends in Policy and Operations* (London: Humanitarian Policy Group, HPG Report No. 23).

Strange, Susan (1996), *Retreat of the State* (Cambridge: Cambridge University Press).

Swatuk, Larry A. and Peter Vale (1999), 'Why democracy is not enough: Southern Africa and human security in the twenty-first century', *Alternatives*, 24: 361–389.

Taliaferro, Jeffrey W. (2001), 'Security seeking under anarchy: defensive realism revisited', *International Security*, 25(3): 128–161.

Tannenwald, Nina (2007), *The Nuclear Taboo* (Cambridge: Cambridge University Press).

Taylor, Anita, and M.J. Hardman (2004), 'War, language and gender, what new can be said? Framing the issues', *Women and Language*, 27(2): 3–19.

Teitelbaum, M.S. (1980), 'Right vs. right: immigration and refugee policy in the United States', *Foreign Affairs*, 59(1): 21–59.

Terriff, Terry, Stuart Croft, Lucy James and Patrick Morgan (1999), *Security Studies Today* (Cambridge: Polity Press).

The Star (2004), 'Are we fighting foreign wars?', 10 February.

Thomas, Caroline (1987), *In Search of Security: The Third World in International Relations* (Boulder, CO: Lynne Rienner).

Thomas, Caroline (2000), *Global Governance, Development and Human Security* (London: Pluto Press).

Thomas, Caroline (2001), 'Global governance, development and human security: exploring the links', *Third World Quarterly*, 22(2): 159–175.

Thomsen, Ian (1996), 'After the Cold War, who's the "enemy"?', *International Herald Tribune*, 24 July: www.iht.com/articles/1996/07/24/oswimny.t_0.php.

Thomson, Janice (1994), *Mercenaries, Pirates and Sovereigns* (Princeton, NJ: Princeton University Press).

Thornton, Rob (2000), 'The role of peace support operations doctrine in the British Army', *International Peacekeeping*, 7(2): 41–62.

Thoumi, F. (2003), *The Numbers' Game: Let's All Guess the Size of the Illegal Drugs Industry!* (Amsterdam: The Transnational Institute).

Thrift, Nigel (2006), 'Space', *Theory, Culture and Society*, 23(2–3): 139–146.

Thucydides (1972), *History of the Peloponnesian War* (London: Penguin Books). Translated by Rex Warner with an Introduction and Notes by M.I. Finley

Tilly, Charles (1978), *From Mobilization to Revolution* (Reading, MA: Addison-Wesley).

Tirman, John (1997), *Spoils of War: The Human Costs of America's Arms Trade* (New York: Free Press).

Tomes, Robert R. (2004), 'Relearning counterinsurgency warfare', *Parameters, US Army War College Quarterly*, 34(1): 16–28.

Tooze, Roger (2005), 'The missing link: security, critical international political economy, and community' in Booth (ed.) (2005c), pp. 133–158.

Tow, William T., Ramesh Thakur and In-Tayek Hyun (eds), (2000), *Asia's Emerging Regional Order: Reconciling Traditional and Human Security* (Tokyo: UN University Press).

Townshend, Charles (ed.) (2005), *The Oxford History of Modern War* (Oxford: Oxford University Press, new edn).

Treaty on the Non-proliferation of Nuclear Weapons (NPT) (1968), 1 July: http://disarmament.un.org/wmd/npt/npttext.html.

Turshen, Meredeth and Clotilde Twagiramariya (eds) (1998), *What Women Do in Wartime: Gender and Conflict in Africa* (London: Zed Books).

Tuschhoff, C. (1999), 'Alliance cohesion and peaceful change in NATO' in Haftendorn *et al.* (eds) (1999), pp. 140–161.

Tversky, Amos and Daniel Kahneman (eds) (2000), *Choices, Values, and Frames* (Cambridge: Cambridge University Press).

Tversky, Amos, Paul Slovic and Daniel Kahneman (eds) (1982), *Judgment Under Uncertainty* (Cambridge: Cambridge University Press).

UK Ministry of Defence (2004), *The Military Contribution to Peace Support Operations*. Joint Warfare Publication 3–50 (London: HMSO, June, 2nd edn).

Ullman, Richard (1983), 'Redefining security', *International Security*, 8(1): 129–153.

UN (1995), *The Copenhagen Declaration and Programme of Action* (World Summit for Social Development, 6–12 March. New York: Oxford University Press).

UN (1999), *Report of the Group of Governmental Experts on Small Arms in Pursuance of General Assembly Resolution 52/38 J* (UN doc. A/54/258, 19 August): www.iansa.org/documents/un/un_pub/reports/rep54258e.pdf.

UN Department of Peacekeeping Operations (DPKO) (2007): www.un.org/Depts/dpko/dpko.

UN Development Programme (UNDP) (1994), *Human Development Report* (New York: Oxford University Press).

UN Development Programme (UNDP) (1997), *Human Development Report* (New York: Oxford University Press).

UN Development Programme (UNDP) (2003), *Making Global Trade Work for People* (London: Earthscan): www.undp.org/mainundp/propoor/docs.trade-jan2003.pdf.

UN Development Programme (UNDP) (2005), *Human Development Report 2005* (New York: UN).

UN General Assembly (1997), *Report of the Panel of Governmental Experts on Small Arms* (New York: UN doc. A/52/298, 27 August).

UN General Assembly (2004), UN document A/59/565 (New York: UN).

UN General Assembly (2005), *World Summit Outcome* (UN: New York A/RES/60/1).

UN High Commission for Refugees (UNHCR) (2005), *Statistical Yearbook 2005: Trends in Displacement, Protection and Solutions* (New York: UN).

UN Mission in Sudan (UNMIS) (2006), 'Military component': www.unmis.org/english/military.htm.

UN Report (2002), *The Issue of Missiles in All Its Aspects: Report of the Secretary-General* (General Assembly document A/57/229, 23 July).

UN Secretariat (2003), *The Impact of AIDS* (Report by the Population Division, Department of Economic and Social Affairs, 2 September. New York: United Nations).

UN Secretary-General Study (2002), *Women, Peace, and Security* (New York: UN).

UN Secretary-General's High-level Panel on Threats, Challenges, and Change (2004), *A More Secure World: Our Shared Responsibility* (New York: UN).

UN Security Council (2000), *Final Report of the Monitoring Mechanism on Angola Sanctions* (UN: S/2000/1225, 21 December).

UN Security Council (2001), *Report of the Panel of Experts Pursuant to Security Council Resolution 1343 (2001), Paragraph 19, Concerning Liberia* (UN: S/2001/1015, 21 October).

UN Security Council Resolution 1325 (2000), *Women, Peace and Security* (UN doc. S/Res/1325, 2000).

UNAIDS (2003), *On the Front Line: A Review of Policies and Programmes to Address HIV/AIDS Among Peacekeepers and Uniformed Services* (Geneva: UNAIDS).

UNCTAD (2006), *Trade and Development Report* (Geneva: UNCTAD).

Ungar, Sanford J. and Peter Vale (1985/86), 'South Africa: why constructive engagement failed', *Foreign Affairs*, 64(2): 234–258.

United States (1978), *The Presidential Campaign 1976 Part 1: Jimmy Carter* (Washington, DC: US Government Printing Office).

United States (1998), *A National Security Strategy for a New Century* (Washington, DC: The White House, October).

Urdal, Henrik (2005), 'People vs. Malthus: population pressure, environmental degradation, and armed conflict revisited', *Journal of Peace Research*, 42(4): 417–434.

Urquhart, Brian (1987), *A Life in Peace and War* (New York: Harper & Row).

US Arms Control and Disarmament Agency (ACDA) (2004), *World Military Expenditures and Arms Transfers 1972–1982* (Washington, DC: ACDA).

US Army (1990), *FM 100-20/AFP 3-20: Military Operations in Low Intensity Conflicts* (Washington, DC: Departments of the Army and Air Force, 5 December).

US Army (2007), *The U.S. Army and Marine Corps Counterinsurgency Field Manual* with Forewords by General David H. Petraeus, Lt. General James F. Amos and Lt. Colonel John A. Nagl, and by Sarah Sewall (Chicago, IL: University of Chicago Press).

US Department of Defense (DoD) (2003), *Foreign Military Sales, Foreign Military Construction Sales, and Military Assistance Facts as of September 30, 2003* (Washington, DC: Defense Security Cooperation Agency).

US Department of Defense (DoD) (2006), *Military Power of the People's Republic of China 2006*, Annual Report to Congress (Washington, DC: DoD).

US Department of Defense (2007), *US Doctrine, Department of Defense Dictionary of Military Terms*: www.dtic.mil/doctrine/jel/doddict/.

US Department of Energy, Energy Information Administration (USDoE) (2006), *International Energy Outlook 2006* (Washington, DC: DoE/EIA).

US Department of State (2001) *Annual Country Reports on Terrorism* (Washington, DC: US Government Printing Office).

US Government Accountability Office (2007), 'Observations on costs, strengths, and limitations of U.S. and UN operations', testimony by Joseph A. Christoff before the Subcommittee of International Organizations, Human Rights, and Oversight, Committee on Foreign Affairs, House of Representatives, 13 June, GAO-07-998T.

Vale, Peter (2003), *Security and Politics in South Africa: The Regional Dimension* (Boulder, CO: Lynne Rienner).

Valenius, Johanna (2007), 'A few kind women: gender essentialism and Nordic peacekeeping operations', *International Peacekeeping*, 14(4): 510–523.

Van Creveld, Martin (1991), *On Future War* (London: Brassey's).

Van Evera, Stephen (1994), 'Hypothesis on nationalism and war', *International Security*, 19(1): 5–39.

Van Evera, Stephen (1999), *Causes of War: Vol. I: The Structure of Power and the Roots of War* (Ithaca, NY: Cornell University Press).

Van Munster, Rens (2007), 'Review essay: Security on a shoestring: a hitchhiker's guide to critical schools of security in Europe', *Cooperation and Conflict*, 42(2): 235–243.

Varshney, Ashutosh (2002), *Ethnic Conflict and Civic Life: Hindus and Muslims in India* (New Haven, CT: Yale University Press).

Vasquez, John A. (1997), 'The realist paradigm and degenerative versus progressive research programs: an appraisal of neotraditional research on Waltz's balancing proposition', *American Political Science Review*, 91(4): 899–912.

Vasquez, John A. and Colin Elman (eds) (2003), *Realism and the Balancing of Power: A New Debate* (Upper Saddle River, NJ: Prentice Hall).

Vieth, Warren and Alissa J. Rubin (2003), 'Iraq pipelines easy targets for a saboteur', *Los Angeles Times*, 26 June.

Vines, Alex (1999), 'Mercenaries and the privatization of security in Africa in the 1990s' in Greg Mills and John Stremlau (eds), *The Privatization of Security in Africa* (Johannesburg: SAIIA), pp. 47–80.

Volkan, Vamik (1997), *Bloodlines: From Ethnic Pride to Ethnic Terrorism* (New York: Farrar, Straus & Giroux).

Von Neumann, John and Oskar Morgenstern (1944), *Theory of Games and Economic Behavior* (Princeton, NJ: Princeton University Press).

Wæver, Ole (1994), 'Insecurity and identity unlimited' in Anne-Marie Le Gloannec and Kerry McNamara (eds), *Entre Union et Nations, L'Etat en Europe* (Paris: CERI FNSP), pp. 91–127.

Wæver, Ole (1995), 'Securitization and desecuritization' in Ronnie D. Lipschutz (ed.), *On Security* (New York: Columbia University Press), pp. 46–86.

Wæver, Ole (1997), *Concepts of Security* (Copenhagen: Copenhagen Institute for Political Science, University of Copenhagen).

Wæver, Ole (1998), 'The sociology of a not so international discipline: American and European developments in International Relations', *International Organization*, 52(4): 687–727.

Wæver, Ole (2000), 'The EU as a security actor' in Morten Kelstrup and Michael C. Williams (eds), *International Relations Theory and the Politics of European Integration* (London: Routledge), pp. 250–294.

Wæver, Ole (2004), 'Aberystwyth, Paris, Copenhagen: new schools in security theory and their origins between core and periphery'. Paper presented at *International Studies Association* Conference, Montreal, 17–20 March.

Wæver, Ole, Barry Buzan, Morten Kelstrup and Pierra Lemaitre (1993), *Identity, Migration and the New Security Agenda in Europe* (London: Pinter).

Wald, Matthew L. (2005), 'Both promise and problems for new tigers in your tank', *New York Times*, 26 October.

Walker, R.B.J. (1993), *Inside/Outside: International Relations as Political Theory* (Cambridge: Cambridge University Press).

Walker, R.B.J. (1997), 'The subject of security' in Keith Krause and Michael C. Williams (eds), *Critical Security Studies* (London: UCL Press), pp. 61–81.

Wallander, Celeste A. (2000), 'Institutional assets and adaptability: NATO after the cold war', *International Organization*, 54(4): 705–735.

Wallander, Celeste A. and Robert O. Keohane (1999), 'Risk, threat and security institutions' in Haftendorn *et al.* (eds) (1999), pp. 21–47.

Wallensteen, Peter (2002), *Understanding Conflict Resolution* (London: Sage).

Wallensteen, Peter and M. Sollenberg (1999), 'Armed conflict, 1989–98', *Journal of Peace Research*, 36(5): 593–606.

Walt, Stephen M. (1985), 'Alliance formation and the balance of world power', *International Security*, 9(4): 1–43.

Walt, Stephen M. (1987), *The Origins of Alliances* (Ithaca, NY: Cornell University Press).

Walt, Stephen M. (1988), 'Testing theories of alliance formation: the case of Southwest Asia', *International Organization*, 42(2): 275–316.

Walt, Stephen M. (1991a), 'Alliance formation in Southwest Asia: balancing and bandwagoning in Cold War competition' in Robert Jervis and Jack Snyder (eds), *Dominoes and Bandwagons* (New York: Oxford University Press), pp. 51–84.

Walt, Stephen M. (1991b), 'The renaissance of security studies', *International Studies Quarterly*, 35(2): 211–239.

Walt, Stephen M. (1992a), 'Revolution and war', *World Politics*, 44(3): 321–368.

Walt, Stephen M. (1992b), 'Alliances, threats, and U.S. grand strategy: a reply to Kaufman and Labs', *Security Studies*, 1(3): 448–482.

Walt, Stephen M. (1996), *Revolution and War* (Ithaca, NY: Cornell University Press).

Walt, Stephen M. (1997), 'Why alliances endure or collapse', *Survival*, 39(1): 156–179.

Walt, Stephen M. (1998), 'International Relations: one world, many theories', *Foreign Policy*, 110: 29–46.

Walt, Stephen M. (1999), 'Rigor or rigor mortis? Rational choice and security studies', *International Security*, 23(4): 5–48.

Walt, Stephen M. (2000), 'Containing rogues and renegades: coalition strategies and counterproliferation' in Victor A. Utgoff (ed.), *The Coming Crisis: Nuclear Proliferation, U.S. Interests and World Order* (Cambridge, MA: MIT Press), pp. 191–226.

Walt, Stephen M. (2002), 'The enduring relevance of the realist tradition' in Ira Katznelson and Helen V. Milner (eds), *Political Science: State of the Discipline* (New York: W.W. Norton), pp. 197–230.

Waltz, Kenneth N. (1979), *Theory of International Politics* (Reading, MA: Addison Wesley).

Waltz, Kenneth N. (1981), *The Spread of Nuclear Weapons: More May Be Better* (London: IISS, Adelphi Paper No. 171).

Waltz, Kenneth N. (1993), 'The emerging structure of international politics', *International Security*, 18(2): 44–79.

Waltz, Kenneth N. (1996), 'International politics is not foreign policy', *Security Studies*, 6(1): 54–57.

Waltz, Kenneth N. (2000), 'Structural realism after the Cold War', *International Security*, 25(1): 5–41.

Wardlaw, Grant (1982), *Political Terrorism: Theory, Tactics and Counter-measures* (Cambridge: Cambridge University Press).

Waterman, Shaun (2006), 'Thai militants learn from Iraq insurgency', *United Press International*, 15 February.

Wayman, Frank (1984), 'Bipolarity and war: the role of capability concentration and alliance patterns among major powers, 1816–1965', *Journal of Peace Research*, 21(1): 25–42.

Wayne, Leslie (2006), 'Foreign sales by U.S. arms makers doubled in a year', *New York Times*, 11 November.

WBEZ Chicago (2007), '"This American life" show on the Center for Lessons Learned', 25 May. Podcast: www.thislife.org/Radio_Archive.aspx#5.

Weber, Max (1964), *The Theory of Social and Economic Organization* (New York: Free Press).

Weiner, Myron (1995) *The Global Migration Crisis* (New York: HarperCollins).

Weiss, Thomas G. (ed.) (1998), *Beyond UN Subcontracting: Task Sharing with Regional Security Arrangements and Service Providing NGOs* (London: Macmillan).

Weiss, Thomas G. (2005), *Overcoming the Security Council Impasse* (Berlin: Friedrich Ebert Stiftung Foundation, Occasional Paper No. 25).

Weiss, Thomas G. and Sam Daws (eds) (2007), *The Oxford Handbook on the United Nations* (Oxford: Oxford University Press).

Weiss, Thomas G. (2005), *Overcoming the Security Council Impasse* (Berlin: Friedrich Ebert Stiftung Foundation, Occasional Paper No. 25).

Weiss, Thomas G., David Forsythe, Roger Cote and Kelly-Kate Pease (2007), *The UN and Changing World Politics* (Boulder, CO: Westview Press, 5th edn).

Weissman, Steve and Herbert Krosney (1981), *The Islamic Bomb* (New York: The New York Times Book Co).

Weitsman, P.A. (2004). *Dangerous Alliances: Proponents of Peace, Weapons of War* (Stanford, CA: Stanford University Press).

Weldes, Jutta (1996), 'Constructing national interests', *European Journal of International Relations*, 2(3): 275–318.

Weldes, Jutta, Mark Laffey, Hugh Gusterson and Raymond Duvall (1999), 'Introduction' in Jutta Weldes *et al.* (eds), *Cultures of Insecurity* (Minneapolis: University of Minnesota Press), pp. 1–33.

Welsh, Jennifer (2004), 'Conclusion' in Jennifer Welsh (ed.), *Humanitarian Intervention and International Relations* (Oxford: Oxford University Press), pp. 176–183.

Wendt, Alexander (1992), 'Anarchy is what states make of it', *International Organization*, 46(2): 391–425.

Wendt, Alexander (1995), 'Constructing international politics', *International Security*, 20(1): 71–81.

Wendt, Alexander (1999), *Social Theory of International Politics* (Cambridge: Cambridge University Press).

Wendt, Alexander (2000), 'On the via media: a response to the critics', *Review of International Studies*, 26(1): 165–180.

Wheeler, Nicholas J. (2000), *Saving Strangers: Humanitarian Intervention in International Society* (Oxford: Oxford University Press).

Whitaker, B. (1985), *Revised and Updated Report on the Question of the Prevention and Punishment of the Crime of Genocide. United Nations Economic and Social Council* (UN Commission on Human Rights, 2 July): www.abarundi.org/documents/Whitaker_Report_July_1985.html.

White House (2002), *The National Security Strategy of the United States*.

White House (2007), 'Twenty in ten: strengthening America's energy security', 23 January: www.whitehouse.gov.

White, Josh (2007), 'U.S. falters in bid to boost Iraqi business: few products sold to American firms', *Washington Post*, 24 August, pp. A1 and A11.

Whitworth, Sandra (1994), *Feminism and International Relations* (Basingstoke: Palgrave).

Whitworth, Sandra (2002), '11 September and the aftermath', *Studies in Political Economy*, 67: 33–38.

Whitworth, Sandra (2004), *Men, Militarism and UN Peacekeeping* (Boulder, CO: Lynne Rienner).

Whitworth, Sandra (2008), 'Feminism' in Christian Reus-Smit and Duncan Snidal (eds), *Oxford Handbook of International Relations* (Oxford: Oxford University Press).

WHO (2003), *Severe Acute Respiratory Syndrome (SARS): Report by the Secretariat* EB113/33, 27 November 2003 (Geneva: WHO).

Wight, Martin (1946), *Power Politics* (Looking Forward Pamphlet No. 8. London: Royal Institute of International Affairs).

Wilkin, Peter (2002), 'Global poverty and orthodox security', *Third World Quarterly*, 23(4): 633–645.

Willett, Susan (2001), 'Insecurity, conflict and the new global disorder', *IDS Bulletin*, 32(2): 35–47.

Williams, Michael C. (1998), 'Modernity, identity and security: a comment on the Copenhagen controversy', *Review of International Studies*, 23(3): 435–440.

Williams, Michael C. (2003), 'Words, images, enemies: securitization and international politics', *International Studies Quarterly*, 47(4): 511–531.

Williams, Michael C. (2007), *Culture and Security: Symbolic Power and the Politics of International Security* (London: Routledge).

Williams, Paul D. (2000), 'South African foreign policy: getting critical?', *Politikon: South African Journal of Political Studies*, 27(1): 73–91.

Williams, Paul D. (2007), 'Thinking about security in Africa', *International Affairs*, 83(6): 1021–1038.

Williams, Paul D. and Alex J. Bellamy (2007), 'Contemporary peace operations: four challenges for the Brahimi paradigm' in H. Langholtz, B. Kondoch and A. Wells (eds), *International Peacekeeping: The Yearbook of International Peace Operations*, Vol.11 (Leiden: Martinus Nijhoff), pp. 1–28.

Wines, Michael (1991), 'U.S. tells of prewar technology sales to Iraq worth $500 million', *New York Times*, 12 March.

Wines, Michael (1992), '$8 billion directed to wheat farmers and arms workers', *New York Times*, 3 September.

Wiseman, Geoff (2002), *Concepts of Non-provocative Defence: Ideas and Practices in International Security* (London: Palgrave Macmillan).

Wivel, Anders (2005), 'Explaining why State X made a certain move last Tuesday: the promise and limitations of realist foreign policy analysis', *Journal of International Relations and Development*, 8(4): 355–380.

Wohlforth, William C. (1993), *The Elusive Balance: Power and Perceptions during the Cold War* (Ithaca, NY: Cornell University Press).

Wolfers, Arnold (1962), *Discord and Collaboration: Essays on International Politics* (Baltimore, MD: Johns Hopkins University Press).

Women Against Fundamentalisms (2007): www.gn.apc. org/waf/.

Woodrow, Thomas (2001), 'Time to use the nuclear option', *Washington Times*, 14 September.

Woodward, Bob (1991), *The Commanders* (New York: Simon & Schuster).

World Bank (2006), *Development and the Next Generation: World Development Report 2007* (Washington, DC: World Bank).

World Bank (2007a), *Global Economic Prospects 2007: Managing the Next Wave of Globalization* (Washington, DC: World Bank).

World Bank (2007b), 'Fact sheet: Halving global poverty by 2015 – a stocktaking': http://web.worlbank. org/external/default/main?print=Y&contentMDK= 21256704&men.

World Bank (2007c), *Global Monitoring Report 2007*: http://web.worldbank.org/WBSITE/EXTERNAL/ EXTDEC/EXTGLOBALMONITOR/EXTGLO MONREP2007/0,,menuPK:3413296~pagePK:642 18926~piPK:64218953~theSitePK:3413261,00. html.

World Commission on Environment and Develop-ment (1987), *Our Common Future* (Oxford: Oxford University Press).

World Economic Forum (2007), *Global Risks 2007: A Global Risk Network Report*: www.weforum.org/pdf/ CSI/Global_Risks_2007.pdf.

World Wildlife Fund (WWF) (2006), *Living Planet Report 2006* (Gland, Switzerland: World Wildlife Fund): www.panda.org.

Wright, Quincy (1983), *A Study of War* (Chicago, IL: University of Chicago Press, 2nd edn. First published 1942).

Wright, R. (2004), *A Short History of Progress* (Toronto: Anansi Press).

Wyn Jones, Richard (1999), *Security, Strategy and Critical Theory* (Boulder, CO: Lynne Rienner).

Wyn Jones, Richard (2005), 'On emancipation: necessity, capacity and concrete utopias', in Booth (ed.) (2005c), pp. 215–235.

Yergin, Daniel (2002), 'A crude view of the crisis in Iraq', *Washington Post*, 6 December.

Zacher, Mark and Richard Matthews (1995), 'Liberal international theory: common threads, divergent strands' in Charles Negley (ed.), *Controversies in International Relations Theory* (New York: St Martin's Press), pp. 107–150.

Zagare, Frank C. (1984), *Game Theory: Concepts and Applications* (Beverly Hills, CA: Sage University Paper Series on Quantitative Applications in the Social Sciences).

Zagare, Frank C. (1990), 'Rationality and Deterrence', *World Politics*, 42(2): 238–260.

Zagare, Frank C. (1996), 'Classical deterrence theory: a critical assessment', *International Interactions*, 21(4): 365–387.

Zagare, Frank C. (2004), 'Reconciling rationality with deterrence: a re-examination of the logical founda-tions of deterrence theory', *Journal of Theoretical Politics*, 16(2): 107–141.

Zagare, Frank C. and D. Marc Kilgour (2000), *Perfect Deterrence* (Cambridge: Cambridge University Press).

Zagare, Frank C. and D. Marc Kilgour (2003), 'Alignment patterns, crisis bargaining, and extended deterrence: a game-theoretic analysis', *International Studies Quarterly*, 47(4): 587–615.

Zakaria, Fareed (1998), *From Wealth to Power: The Unusual Origins of America's World Role* (Princeton, NJ: Princeton University Press).

Zakaria, Fareed (2001), 'Don't oversell missile defense: the old theory of nuclear deterrence still makes sense. Just ask the man who invented it', *Newsweek*, 14 May.

Zalewski, Marysia (2000), *Feminism After Post-modernism: Theorising Through Practice* (London: Routledge).

Zaman, Rashed Uz (2002), 'WMD terrorism in South Asia: trends and implications', *Journal of International Affairs*, 7(3): www.sam.gov.tr/perceptions/Volume7/ September-November2002/Perception_Rashed UzZaman.pdf.

Zartman, William I. (1985), *Ripe for Resolution: Conflict and Intervention in Africa* (New York: Oxford University Press).

Zeid, Prince Ra'ad (2005), 'A comprehensive strategy to eliminate future sexual exploitation and abuse in UN peacekeeping operations' (UN doc. A/59/710, 24 March).

Zimmern, Ralph (1945), *The League of Nations and the Rule of Law* (London: Macmillan).

Zolberg, A. (1981), 'International migrations in politi-cal perspective' in M. Kritz *et al.* (eds), *Global Trends in Migration* (New York: The Center for Migration Studies), pp. 3–27.

Zolberg, A., A. Suhrke and S. Aguayo (1989), *Escape from Violence* (Oxford: Oxford University Press).

INDEX